The Opera Lover's Companion

The Opera Lover's Companion

CHARLES OSBORNE

Yale University Press
New Haven and London

For information about this and other Yale University Press
publications, please contact:
U.S. Office: sales.press@yale.edu   yalebooks.com
Europe Office: sales@yaleup.co.uk   www.yaleup.co.uk

Set in Minion by Alliance Interactive Technology, Pondicherry, India
Printed in the United States of America

ISBN 978-0-300-12373-9 (pbk. : alk. paper)

Library of Congress Control Number 20041074452004107445

A catalogue record for this book is available from the British Library

The paper in this book meets the guidelines for permanence and durablility of the
Committee on Production Guidelines for Book Longevity of the Council on
Library Resources.

2 4 6 8 10 9 7 5 3 1

For Ken Thomson

Contents

Preface

Dr Johnson, in the eighteenth century, took the idiosyncratic view that opera was 'an exotic and irrational entertainment'. Opera was certainly that at its inception more than a hundred years before Samuel Johnson's birth, when a group of noblemen in Florence, intent on reviving the drama of ancient Greece, encouraged into existence a new theatrical art form which combined words and music. In the very first opera, *Dafne*, composed by Jacopo Peri in 1597, although the entire text was sung the words took precedence over the music, not by intention but because the music for the most part followed the inflections of speech, only occasionally broadening into something approaching melody.

With the stage works of Claudio Monteverdi, the first great composer of opera, the division between this heightened speech (recitative) and the quasi-melodic sections of the drama (arioso) became more pronounced. Italian opera developed quickly and was soon being staged by the imperial court in Vienna as well as at smaller princely courts throughout the German-speaking countries. In due course it spread to France and eventually, after the Restoration, to London, where the first real English opera, Purcell's *Dido and Aeneas*, was staged in 1689. Early in the eighteenth century, Italian opera established itself in London, and what had begun as an entertainment for aristocratic intellectuals gradually became popular with a wider public.

In Italy opera soon became the most popular form of theatre, remaining so throughout the nineteenth century and well into the twentieth. In other European countries, especially Germany and Austria, it often shared the stages of civic theatres with straight plays. Now, at the beginning of the twenty-first century, there are in the United States of America and Canada more than 140 professional companies staging regular (although, outside the principal cities, not necessarily lengthy) annual seasons of opera, while in Britain there are several well-established companies, ranging from the Royal Opera, English National Opera, Glyndebourne Festival Opera, Opera North, Scottish Opera and Welsh National Opera to such smaller-scale companies as English Touring Opera, City of Birmingham Touring Opera and British Youth Opera.

The staples of the operatic diet today are the major works of five great composers – Mozart, Verdi, Wagner, Puccini and Strauss (and one could add Beethoven here for his only opera, *Fidelio*, a masterpiece that I consider *hors concours*) – as well as operas by Handel, Rossini, Donizetti, Bellini, Bizet, Massenet,

Tchaikovsky, Mussorgsky and Britten, and selected works of a large number of other composers, among them Berlioz, Gluck, Gounod, Humperdinck, Janáček, Leoncavallo, Mascagni, Offenbach, Saint-Saëns, Smetana and Weber (in tactful alphabetical order).

I have included nearly two hundred operas in this guide – all of those that are regularly performed today, as well as a good many that one encounters in the opera house less frequently. I have placed each opera in context in its composer's development, and have also discussed the circumstances surrounding its composition and first production. I have followed this with a brief synopsis of the plot, and also my personal assessment of the music, paying particular attention to the most important and significant arias, duets and ensembles.

C.O.

DANIEL-FRANÇOIS-ESPRIT AUBER

(b. Caen, 1782 – d. Paris, 1871)

Fra Diavolo, ou L'hôtellerie de Terracine

(Fra Diavolo, or The Inn of Terracina)

opéra comique in three acts (approximate length: 3 hours)

Fra Diavolo, a bandit chief   *tenor*
Lord Cockburn, an English traveller   *tenor*
Lady Pamela, his wife   *mezzo-soprano*
Lorenzo, an officer   *tenor*
Matheo, an innkeeper   *bass*
Zerline, his daughter   *soprano*
Giacomo, a bandit   *bass*
Beppo, a bandit   *tenor*

LIBRETTO BY EUGÈNE SCRIBE; TIME: 1830; PLACE: THE COUNTRYSIDE NEAR ROME;
FIRST PERFORMED AT THE OPÉRA-COMIQUE, PARIS, 28 JANUARY 1830

The composer of forty-eight operas, most of them in a light vein and written in collaboration with the librettist Eugène Scribe, Auber was one of the leading figures in the development of nineteenth-century French opera. His *Gustav III* (1833) is the work whose libretto Verdi made use of for *Un ballo in maschera* twenty-six years later. *Le Domino noir* (The Black Domino, 1837) has one of Auber's most elegant scores, and a performance in Brussels in 1830 of *La Muette de Portici* (The Mute Girl of Portici) is said to have sparked off the Belgian revolution.

Fra Diavolo, the most successful of Auber's operas when it was first staged in 1830, had by 1907 been performed more than nine hundred times at the Opéra-Comique in Paris. Alessandro Bonci and, later, Tito Schipa were famous Diavolos. The opera is still to be encountered, especially in France, Germany and Italy, and in 1969, making his San Francisco debut, the Swedish tenor Nicolai Gedda was a greatly admired Diavolo. In 1933 those great comedians Stan Laurel and Oliver Hardy starred in *Fra Diavolo*, a highly amusing movie burlesque of the opera, with its principal numbers retained. Laurel and Hardy played Stanlio and Olio, two wandering vagrants who become accomplices of Diavolo (performed by Dennis King, a popular American operetta tenor of the day). The film turns up occasionally on TV and still retains its ability to entertain.

Act I. A tavern. The bandit Fra Diavolo, calling himself the Marquis of San Marco, is involved in a plan to steal money and jewels from two English travellers, Lord and Lady Cockburn. (Diavolo was based by Scribe on a real-life bandit, Michele Pezze, who flourished in southern Italy around 1810.) At the inn where the English couple are staying, in the vicinity of Terracina, Diavolo contrives to remove Lady Pamela's diamond necklace while she is wearing it. A sub-plot involves Zerline, the innkeeper's daughter. She is in love with Lorenzo, a poor officer in the Roman dragoons, but is being forced by her father to marry Francesco, a rich farmer.

Act II. Zerline's bedroom. Diavolo, still posing as the Marquis, enters Zerline's room, hoping to gain access from it to the rooms occupied by the English couple, and is joined by his fellow bandits, Beppo and Giacomo. When his presence is discovered he pretends to have been summoned by Zerline to a rendezvous, thus arousing Lorenzo's jealousy.

Act III. The mountains nearby. Fra Diavolo conceals his instructions to Beppo and Giacomo in a hollow tree. The wedding procession of Zerline and Francesco appears, and Diavolo's two followers find their instructions and mingle with the guests, among them Lorenzo who is in despair at having lost his Zerline. Betraying themselves by talking carelessly, the two bandits are arrested and forced to give their chief the signal to appear. When Diavolo suddenly emerges on the rocky hillside he is shot by Lorenzo's dragoons and falls to his death. (In Auber's original ending Diavolo is merely taken prisoner.) But the opera ends satisfactorily for Lorenzo and Zerline, who are allowed to marry.

The most attractive numbers in Auber's light, tuneful and, in places, Rossinian score include a rousing drinking song at the beginning of the opera and, later in Act I, a charming aria, 'Voyez sur cette roche', in which Zerline describes to the supposed Marquis the exploits of the bandits. An Act I duet for the aristocratic English couple is amusing, and so is the quintet that follows it. Diavolo's aria at the beginning of Act III is a real *tour de force*, giving the tenor fine opportunities for vocal display. Throughout this comic opera Auber's delightful melodic facility is well in evidence.

Recommended recording: Nicolai Gedda (Diavolo), Mady Mesplé (Zerline), Jane Berbie (Lady Pamela), Thierry Dran (Lorenzo), Remi Corazza (Lord Cockburn), Jules Bastin (Matheo), Michel Hamel (Beppo), Michel Marimpouy (Giacomo), with the Jean Laforge Chorale Ensemble, and the Monte Carlo Philharmonic Orchestra, conducted by Marc Soustrot. EMI CDS7 54810–2. Nicolai Gedda brings his lyrical charm and high-ranging tenor to Diavolo, Mady Mesplé is a faultless Zerline, and Remi Corazza a delightful Lord Cockburn, though his English accent comes and goes.

SAMUEL BARBER

(b. West Chester, PA, 1910 – d. New York, 1981)

Vanessa

opera in four acts (approximate length: 2 hours)

Vanessa *soprano*
Erika, her niece *mezzo-soprano*
The Old Baroness, her mother *contralto*
Anatol *tenor*
The Doctor *baritone*
Nicholas *bass*
Footman *bass*

LIBRETTO BY GIAN CARLO MENOTTI, BASED ON A STORY BY ISAK DINESEN; TIME: AROUND 1905; PLACE: AN UNSPECIFIED NORTHERN COUNTRY; FIRST PERFORMED AT THE METROPOLITAN OPERA HOUSE, NEW YORK, 15 JANUARY 1958

A nephew of the famous contralto Louise Homer, and himself a baritone (taught by his aunt), Barber began composing while still a child, and later studied at the Curtis Institute in Philadelphia. He showed a particular interest in vocal music throughout his career, and an early work, his setting for voice and string quartet of Matthew Arnold's *Dover Beach* in 1931, made his name known outside the United States. It was, however, not until the 1950s that he composed his first opera. He was a friend of the opera composer Gian Carlo Menotti, and it was to a large extent at the instigation of Menotti that he composed *Vanessa*, for which Menotti wrote the libretto, based on a story in *Seven Gothic Tales* by the Danish short-story writer Isak Dinesen (published in 1934). *Vanessa* was staged at the old Metropolitan Opera House, New York, in 1958, and later in the same year at the Salzburg Festival. A revised version in three acts had its premiere at the old Met in 1964, but it is the original four-act opera that is now usually performed. When the Metropolitan Opera moved to its new home at Lincoln Center in 1966,

Barber was commissioned to compose the opening opera, *Anthony and Cleopatra*. Unfortunately, it was generally considered a failure.

The entire action takes place at Vanessa's country manor house.

Act I. Vanessa, her mother the Baroness and her niece Erika are awaiting the return of Anatol, Vanessa's lover who left her twenty years ago. The Anatol who arrives, however, is the son of Vanessa's lover who is no longer alive. Mistaking the young man for his father, Vanessa asks if he still loves her and is devastated when she realizes her mistake. Her niece Erika entreats Anatol to leave, but he refuses.

Act II. A month later. Erika confesses to the Baroness that Anatol seduced her on the night of his arrival, and that she refused his offer of marriage. Vanessa and Anatol return from ice-skating, and announce plans for a splendid ball on New Year's Eve. Erika realizes that her aunt is in love with Anatol.

Act III. New Year's Eve. At the ball, Anatol and Vanessa pledge their love in public. Erika, carrying Anatol's child, stumbles out into the cold towards the lake.

Act IV. Erika is recovering after having attempted suicide. Anatol and Vanessa, now married, are about to depart for Paris, while Erika prepares to withdraw from the world.

Barber's late Romantic style is agreeable and assured, and the score of *Vanessa* is rich in harmony and melodically generous, though not strongly individual. The opera is composed as individual numbers linked by arioso or recitative, and the finest number is a dramatic quintet in Act IV ('To leave, to break, to find, to keep').

BÉLA BARTÓK
(b. Nagyszentmiklós, Hungary, 1881 – d. New York, 1945)

Duke Bluebeard's Castle
(A kékszákállú herceg vára)
opera in one act (approximate length: 1 hour)

Duke Bluebeard   *bass*
Judith, his wife   *mezzo-soprano*
Prologue   *spoken role*

LIBRETTO BY BÉLA BALAZS; TIME: THE LEGENDARY PAST; PLACE: A ROOM IN DUKE BLUEBEARD'S CASTLE; FIRST PERFORMED AT THE OPERA HOUSE, BUDAPEST, 24 MAY 1918 (IN A DOUBLE BILL WITH BARTÓK'S 1917 BALLET *The Wooden Prince*)

Most of the major works of Bartók, the foremost Hungarian composer of the twentieth century, are orchestral or instrumental. Of his three pieces for the stage, all of which date from the early part of his career, two – *The Wooden Prince* and *The Miraculous Mandarin* – are ballet scores. The one-act *Duke Bluebeard's Castle*, composed to a libretto in Hungarian, is his only opera.

The character of Bluebeard is taken from the fairy tale 'La Barbe-bleue' in Charles Perrault's 1697 collection *Les Contes de ma Mère l'Oye* (Tales of Mother Goose). The symbolism of Balazs's text is open to more than one interpretation, but the work is generally understood as an allegory on the essential loneliness of the human condition. This short opera, lasting less than an hour, was composed in 1911. However, it had to wait until 1918 for its first production, after which it was not performed again in Hungary for nearly twenty years, because the country's reactionary regime would not allow the librettist's name to be credited since he was a socialist, and Bartók would not allow performances if it were not.

A speaker introduces the action, which takes place in the vast windowless hall of a Gothic castle with seven huge doors leading from it. Through a smaller door, Duke Bluebeard enters with his new wife Judith, whom he leads by the hand. She seems nervous of him, but when he gives her a chance to reconsider her decision to share his life she insists that she will stay with him for ever. As she begins to regain her courage, she asks that the seven doors be opened to allow light and air into the hall.

Bluebeard refuses, but Judith persuades him to give her the key to the first door. The castle seems to emit a sigh as she opens the door to reveal a torture chamber, graphically conjured up by a beam of red light from beyond the door and, in the orchestra, harsh scale passages from the woodwind and xylophone. On the walls of the chamber there is blood, but Judith, undeterred, interprets the red as being the colour not of blood but of dawn. She reaffirms her love for Bluebeard and demands the remaining keys.

The second key unlocks the door to Bluebeard's bronze-coloured armoury, its weapons bloodstained. When Judith opens the third room, a golden treasury, she enters it and emerges with a jewelled robe and a crown. The fourth door opens to reveal the bluish light of a garden on whose flowers there is blood, and the fifth opens on the dazzling white light of Bluebeard's kingdom. But there is blood even here, in the clouds hanging over the kingdom.

Although warned by Bluebeard not to continue, Judith next opens the sixth door, to the accompaniment of harp and clarinet arpeggios, revealing a lake which Bluebeard tells her contains the water of tears. He takes her in his arms and attempts to dissuade her from opening the seventh and last door. Judith asks him if he has loved other women before her. When he evades her question, she demands the key. As she opens the seventh door, the light in the hall becomes dimmer, and three beautiful women, Bluebeard's former wives, step forth. Bluebeard addresses them as his loves of the morning, noon and evening of his life, and assures Judith that she, the most beautiful of them all, is his last love, the love of his night-time. Judith follows the other wives back through the seventh door, which closes behind them leaving Bluebeard finally alone to face eternal darkness.

Bartók's powerful score, with its wide range of colour and its voice parts written in an expressive arioso, is intensely dramatic – the magnificent C-major blaze of sound from the orchestra when the fifth door is opened is a superb moment.

Recommended recording: Dietrich Fischer-Dieskau (Bluebeard), Julia Varady (Judith), with the Bavarian State Orchestra, conducted by Wolfgang Sawallisch. DG 2531 172. 'The passionately insistent voice of Varady and the sad, foredoomed tones of Fischer-Dieskau carry the drama', wrote Arthur Jacobs in Opera. *Wolfgang Sawallisch brings out superbly the inner richness of the score.*

LUDWIG VAN BEETHOVEN
(b. Bonn, 1770 – d. Vienna, 1827)

Fidelio
opera in two acts (approximate length: 2 hours, 15 minutes)

Florestan, a prisoner   *tenor*
Leonore, his wife, alias Fidelio   *soprano*
Rocco, a gaoler   *bass*
Marzelline, his daughter   *soprano*
Jacquino, assistant to Rocco   *tenor*
Don Pizarro, governor of the prison   *baritone*
Don Fernando, minister of state   *bass*

LIBRETTO BY JOSEPH VON SONNLEITHNER AND GEORG FRIEDRICH TREITSCHKE, BASED ON JEAN-NICOLAS BOUILLY'S *LÉONORE, OU L'AMOUR CONJUGAL*; TIME: THE LATE EIGHTEENTH CENTURY; PLACE: A PRISON NEAR SEVILLE; FIRST PERFORMED IN ITS FINAL FORM, AS *FIDELIO*, AT THE KÄRNTNERTORTHEATER, VIENNA, 23 MAY 1814 (TWO EARLIER VERSIONS, BOTH ENTITLED *LEONORE*, FIRST PERFORMED AT THE THEATER AN DER WIEN, VIENNA, 20 NOVEMBER 1805 AND 29 MARCH 1806)

Beethoven, generally regarded as one of the greatest composers, concentrated on symphonic, orchestral and chamber music, producing nine symphonies, sixteen string quartets, thirty-two piano sonatas, five piano concertos and a violin concerto which are central to the experience of most music lovers. Less at ease with vocal music, in which it seems his imagination was hampered by the physical limitations of the human voice, he completed only one opera, *Fidelio*, at a period in his life when he had already composed his third symphony and his first group of six string quartets.

When, during the winter of 1803–4, his attention was drawn to a libretto, *Léonore, ou L'Amour conjugal*, by Jean-Nicolas Bouilly, which had been set by French composer Pierre Gaveaux and performed with great success in Paris in 1798, Beethoven abandoned his opera *Vestas Feuer*, of which he had written no more than the first scene. He had Bouilly's libretto translated into German and revised by the Viennese court secretary Joseph von Sonnleithner, and by the end of January 1804 he was at work on his *Leonore*.

On 20 November 1805, when Vienna was under the occupation of Napoleon's troops, the opera was given its premiere at the Theater an der Wien. (Not the Theater auf der Wieden. These two Viennese theatres are frequently mistaken for each other by writers.) *Leonore* achieved only three performances. After Beethoven had revised it, reducing its three acts to two, the opera was staged again at the Theater an der Wien on 29 March 1806, with only one further performance several days later. By the time it was next seen, at the Kärntnertortheater on 23 May 1814, it had progressed to its third and final version, with its libretto revised by Georg Friedrich Treitschke, the theatre's resident poet, and it was now called *Fidelio* (though Beethoven continued to prefer its earlier title). Three overtures composed for the earlier Vienna performances and for a planned production in Prague are now known as the *Leonore* overtures nos 1, 2, and 3. The overture to *Fidelio* dates from 1814.

Florestan has been unjustly imprisoned by his enemy the prison governor Don Pizarro. Florestan's wife Leonore, determined to find him and secure his release, disguises herself as a young man, Fidelio, and takes employment at the prison as assistant to the gaoler Rocco, whose daughter Marzelline falls in love with the supposed youth.

Act I, scene i. A room in Rocco's quarters. The gaoler's young assistant, Jacquino, who is in love with Marzelline and has until now had reason to think his affection was reciprocated, is attempting to persuade her to name a date for their wedding ('Jetzt, Schätzchen, jezt sind wir allein'). Interrupted by a knocking at the door, he goes off to investigate, leaving Marzelline to reflect that, although she was once in love with him, since the arrival of Fidelio she has been able to think only of her father's new young assistant ('O wär ich schon mit dir vereint').

Rocco and Fidelio enter with Jacquino, and Rocco makes it clear that he would be more than willing to accept his new young helper as a son-in-law. All express their feelings inwardly ('Mir ist so wunderbar'), and Rocco then offers Fidelio and Marzelline practical advice on the need for money as well as love ('Hat man nicht auch Gold beineben'). Fidelio asks to be allowed to help Rocco look after all of the prisoners, but he tells him there is one, incarcerated in a dungeon, whom he cannot let him see. The poor man, he says, will in any case not survive for long, as he is being starved on the orders of the governor. Leonore fears that the prisoner may be her husband, Florestan.

Act I, scene ii. The courtyard of the prison. A platoon of guards marches in, followed by Don Pizarro, the prison governor, who calls for his despatches. He reads one that warns him that the minister of state has been apprised that some of the prisons under Pizarro's jurisdiction contain victims of injustice, and that he intends to surprise Pizarro with an inspection. Pizarro decides to have Florestan killed immediately, to prevent his being found ('Ha! Welch' ein Augenblick'). Ordering a trumpeter to mount the tower, keep a close watch on the road to Seville, and give a signal as soon as a coach with outriders appears, Pizarro then tries to bribe Rocco into murdering the prisoner in the dungeon. Failing in this, he resolves to kill his enemy himself. He orders Rocco to precede him into the dungeon and dig a grave. Leonore, who has overheard them, is strengthened in her resolve to save Florestan ('Komm, Hoffnung').

Fidelio persuades Rocco to allow the prisoners out into the courtyard, since the weather is so beautiful. Rocco reluctantly agrees but, when the prisoners emerge into the sunlight ('O welche Lust'), Leonore is disappointed not to find Florestan among them. Rocco promises to allow Fidelio to help him dig the grave of the unfortunate wretch in the dungeon, and Leonore now feels certain that this must be Florestan. As they are about to descend to the dungeon, Pizarro returns.

Furious at finding the prisoners allowed out into the courtyard, he orders them to be herded back into their cells.

Act II, scene i. A dungeon cell. Florestan, fettered to the wall by a long chain, muses on his fate and imagines he is visited by an angel in the form of his wife, who has come to lead him to heaven ('In des Lebens Frühlingstagen'). As he sinks exhausted into sleep, Rocco and Fidelio enter, carrying a jug of wine, tools for digging, and a lamp. They begin to clear out an old cistern as a grave for the prisoner, but Leonore, who cannot see his face, expresses her determination to save the poor man, whoever he might be. When Florestan awakens, Leonore recognizes her husband. Florestan asks Rocco the name of the governor of the prison. When told it is Pizarro, whose crimes he has dared to reveal, he begs Rocco to send a message to his wife in Seville. Rocco answers that he dare not, and that it would in any case be to no avail. Florestan asks for water, and Rocco lets him have the dregs of the wine in his jug and allows Fidelio to give the prisoner a piece of stale bread ('Euch werde Lohn').

At a signal from Rocco, Pizarro descends into the dungeon. He draws a dagger and is about to kill Florestan when Leonore springs forward to shield him. She draws a pistol, aiming it at Pizarro with a cry of 'First kill his wife!' A trumpet sounds from the tower, heralding the arrival of the minister of state. When it sounds a second time, Jacquino appears at the top of the stairs, announcing that the minister and his retinue are already in the prison yard. Pizarro hurries out, followed by Rocco, while a joyous Leonore and Florestan embrace ('O namenlose Freude').

Act II, scene ii. The parade ground of the prison. The minister, Don Fernando, addresses a crowd of citizens who have rushed in to petition him, and assures them that he has come to free them from tyranny. Rocco leads Leonore and Florestan forward, and the minister, shocked to see his old friend in chains, orders Pizarro to be led away by guards and allows Leonore to remove her husband's chains ('O Gott! O welch' ein Augenblick!'). Marzelline is disconcerted to find her beloved Fidelio revealed to be the wife of Florestan, but all join in singing a hymn of praise to the woman who has saved her husband's life ('Wer ein holdes Weib errungen').

The form of Beethoven's opera, which is that of a French *opéra comique* with spoken dialogue separating the musical numbers, is thought by some to be inappropriate to its subject matter, and indeed it has to be admitted that, formally, *Fidelio* is unsatisfactory. But Beethoven, moved by the story of a woman's heroism in rescuing her husband, has composed a work that can be said to transcend opera and its forms; a work that is a magnificent hymn to the human spirit, to love and to the concept of freedom.

Fidelio begins conventionally enough with the music of Marzelline and Jacquino, but as early as the deeply moving quartet 'Mir ist so wunderbar', in canon form, the drama moves on to a higher plane. This is one of the most beautiful numbers in the score. Rocco's cynical little song 'Hat man nicht auch Gold beineben' is a return to a more mundane level (and could be omitted with impunity), but from that point onward the music represents Beethoven at his greatest. The final chorus, in a triumphant C major, is a glorious expression of universal love, while the hushed prisoners' chorus ('O welche Lust') and the ecstatic duet for Leonore and Florestan ('O namenlose Freude') are other highlights of Beethoven's divine score. Leonore and Florestan are each given an imposing aria preceded by expressive recitative. Leonore's profoundly moving 'Komm, Hoffnung' beautifully conveys the power of love and hope, while the mood of Florestan's 'In des Lebens Frühlingstagen' moves from resignation to joyous anticipation.

Great interpreters of the leading roles, within living memory, have included Birgit Nilsson, Christa Ludwig, the incomparable Lotte Lehmann (whose recording of Leonore's aria on a 78 rpm disc can be found on CD) and Julius Patzak, the Viennese tenor whose Florestan in the years following World War II has surely remained in the memory of all who saw him in the role. His opening cry of 'Gott! Welch' Dunkel hier' must still be ringing in the rafters of the opera houses of Vienna and London.

Recommended recording: Christa Ludwig (Leonore), Jon Vickers (Florestan), Gottlob Frick (Rocco), Walter Berry (Don Pizarro), Gerhard Unger (Jacquino), Ingeborg Hallstein (Marzelline), Franz Crass (Don Fernando) and the Philharmonia Chorus and Orchestra, conducted by Otto Klemperer. EMI CDS 5 55170–2. By common consent, Klemperer was regarded as the greatest of Beethoven conductors in the second half of the twentieth century. He conducts a most moving performance of Beethoven's marvellous score, and has the advantage of a superb cast, all of whose members are fully in accord with his authoritative approach to the work. Christa Ludwig brings Leonore vividly to life, Jon Vickers is an eloquent Florestan, and Gottlob Frick successfully conveys Rocco's ambiguous personality.

VINCENZO BELLINI
(b. Catania, Sicily, 1801 – d. Puteaux, near Paris, 1835)

I Capuleti e i Montecchi
(The Capulets and the Montagues)
lyrical tragedy in two acts (approximate length: 2 hours, 20 minutes)

> Giulietta (Juliet), a Capulet　*soprano*
> Romeo, a Montague　*mezzo-soprano*
> Tebaldo (Tybalt), a Capulet　*tenor*
> Capellio (Capulet), Giulietta's father　*bass*
> Lorenzo (Friar Laurence), a physician　*baritone*

LIBRETTO BY FELICE ROMANI; TIME: THE THIRTEENTH CENTURY; PLACE: VERONA;
FIRST PERFORMED AT THE TEATRO LA FENICE, VENICE, 11 MARCH 1830

Bellini's first opera, *Adelson e Salvini*, was produced in 1825 at the Naples Conservatorium while the composer was still a student there. Its success led to his being commissioned to write an opera for the Teatro San Carlo in Naples, where *Bianca e Gernando* (its title later changed to *Bianca e Fernando*) was successfully premiered the following year. After this, the young composer's future was assured.

The libretto of his next opera, *Il pirata* (The Pirate; 1827), was provided by Felice Romani, the most famous librettist of his day, who went on to collaborate with Bellini on all but one of his subsequent operas. The first of these, *La straniera* (The Stranger; 1829), was enthusiastically received, but *Zaira* (also 1829) was a failure, so Bellini withdrew his score and used nearly half of it again in his next opera, *I Capuleti e i Montecchi*, composed for the Teatro La Fenice in Venice, where it was staged in 1830.

Romani's libretto, a version of the Romeo and Juliet story, was an adaptation of the libretto he had written five years earlier for Nicola Vaccai's *Giulietta e Romeo*. It is based not on Shakespeare but on Giuseppe Maria Foppa's libretto for another operatic version of the story, Niccolo Zingarelli's *Giulietta e Romeo* (1796), whose ultimate derivation was a fifteenth-century novella by Masuccio Salernitano. (The immediate source of Shakespeare's *Romeo and Juliet* in 1594 was a narrative poem published thirty years earlier, *The Tragical History of Romeus and Juliet* by Arthur Brooke, which in turn was based on a sixteenth-century French version of the story.)

Bellini's opera was enthusiastically received at its premiere and was performed eight times within the ten days remaining before the end of the opera season. After the third performance, the composer was accompanied to his lodgings by a huge crowd of admirers and a military band playing excerpts from his other operas. (Bellini later said '*Zaira* got its revenge with *I Capuleti e i Montecchi*.') The new opera remained popular in Italy and abroad until the end of the nineteenth century, and Wagner acknowledged its influence on Act II of *Tristan und Isolde*.

In recent years *I Capuleti e i Montecchi* has been frequently revived, though not always authentically. In the nineteenth century a practice arose, begun by the singer Maria Malibran in 1832, of substituting the final scene from Vaccai's *Giulietta e Romeo* for Bellini's final scene. This no longer happens, but in 1966 Claudio Abbado conducted at La Scala, Milan, his own adaptation of Bellini's score, with the mezzo-soprano *travesti* role of Romeo rewritten for the tenor voice and sung by Giacomo Aragall.

Act I, scene i. A gallery in Capellio's palace. In the warfare between the Guelphs and Ghibellines, the Capulet family are supporters of the Guelphs, while the Montagues are on the side of the Ghibellines. Tebaldo, who is in love with his cousin Giulietta, tells his fellow Capulets that an attack led by Romeo, a Montague who has already slain Capellio's son in battle, is shortly to be expected ('E serbata a questo acciaro'). Capellio, the head of the Capulet family, announces that an offer of peace has been received from Romeo, but he rejects it and agrees to the immediate marriage of his daughter Giulietta to Tebaldo.

Romeo arrives, pretending to be his own envoy, and asks that peace between the two families be sealed by the marriage of Giulietta to Romeo, who, he says, still weeps over having killed Capellio's son ('Se Romeo t'uccise un figlio'). When he is told that Giulietta is to be married to Tebaldo, Romeo reveals his identity and swears vengeance upon the Capulets.

Act I, scene ii. A room in Giulietta's apartment. Arrayed in her wedding dress, an unhappy Giulietta longs to see Romeo, whom she loves ('Oh! Quante volte'). The physician Lorenzo brings Romeo to her, and the two lovers greet each other rapturously. But when Romeo asks Giulietta to escape with him, her sense of duty to her father leads her to refuse. Distraught, Romeo leaves by the secret door through which he had entered.

Act I, scene iii. A courtyard in Capellio's palace where the wedding festivities have begun. Romeo, disguised as a Guelph, confides to Lorenzo that an army of a thousand Ghibellines in disguise is already in Verona, poised to interrupt Giulietta's wedding. The two men rush off as the noise of battle is heard. Giulietta enters in distress, and Romeo returns to ask her once again to flee with him. They are interrupted by the arrival of Tebaldo, to whom Romeo reveals his identity. Act I ends with the Guelphs and Ghibellines threatening one another, and with the young lovers in despair.

Act II, scene i. An apartment in Capellio's palace. Lorenzo tells Giulietta that Romeo has escaped, but that she can avoid her imminent marriage to Tebaldo by swallowing a potion that will give her sleep the semblance of death. She will be laid to rest in the family tomb, and will awaken in the arms of her beloved Romeo. Despite her forebodings, Giulietta drinks the potion. When her father arrives to find her too unwell to proceed with the wedding, he begins to suspect treachery on the part of Lorenzo, and orders a close watch to be kept on him.

Act II, scene ii. A deserted spot near Capellio's palace. Romeo waits in vain for Lorenzo, who was to have explained about the potion and taken him to Giulietta. Tebaldo arrives, and the two men are about to fight when the sound of a dirge is heard, and Giulietta's funeral procession appears. Horrified, Romeo and Tebaldo express their despair.

Act II, scene iii. The funeral vaults of the Capulets. Romeo enters with his followers and prises open the lid of Giulietta's coffin. The other Montagues leave, but Romeo, grief-stricken, begs Giulietta's soul to take him to heaven with her ('Deh! Tu bell' anima'), and he swallows some poison. As he loses consciousness, Giulietta rises from her coffin. Romeo dies in her arms, and Giulietta expires from grief as her father and Lorenzo arrive.

Despite the disconcerting fact that eight of its ten numbers contain music initially composed for earlier Bellini operas, notably *Zaira*, Bellini's Romeo and Juliet opera, with its blend of elegiac melancholy and martial ardour, succeeds in capturing the essence of the story, and his decision to write the role of the adolescent Romeo for a female mezzo-soprano can be made to work perfectly well with careful and suitable casting. The highlights of the opera include Romeo's moving larghetto aria, 'Se Romeo t'uccise un figlio', one of Bellini's typically long-breathed melodies; Giulietta's touching romanza with harp accompaniment, 'Oh! Quante volte'; the dramatic and fervent love duet, 'Si, fuggire'; and, in the final scene, Romeo's andante aria, 'Deh! Tu bell' anima'.

Unlike many bel canto operas, Bellini's *I Capuleti e i Montecchi* never completely disappeared from the repertoire. In 1935 it was staged in the composer's home town, Catania, to commemorate the hundredth anniversary of his death, and in 1954 it was performed in Palermo with the great Italian mezzo-soprano Giulietta Simionato as Romeo. Other notable performers of the roles of the young lovers have included Tatiana Troyanos (Romeo) and Beverly Sills (Giulietta) in Boston (1975), Agnes Baltsa (Romeo) and Celia Gasdia (Giulietta) in Florence (1981), Baltsa and Edita Gruberova (London, 1984) and Anne Sofie von Otter and Amanda Roocroft (London, 1992).

Recommended recording: Eva Mei (Giulietta), Vesselina Kasarova (Romeo), Ramon Vargas (Tebaldo), Umberto Chiummo (Capellio), Simone Alberghini (Lorenzo), with the Bavarian Radio Chorus and Munich Radio Orchestra, conducted by Roberto Abbado. RCA 09026 68899. Vesselina Kasarova is superb as the impulsive lover, and Eva Mei immensely appealing as his beloved. The other roles are strongly sung and characterized, and Abbado secures a fine, stylistically perfect performance from the orchestra.

La sonnambula
(The Sleepwalker)
opera semiseria in two acts (approximate length: 3 hours)

Amina, an orphan raised by Teresa   *soprano*
Lisa, an innkeeper   *soprano*
Teresa, owner of the village mill   *mezzo-soprano*
Elvino, a wealthy farmer   *tenor*
Count Rodolfo, lord of the village   *bass*
Alessio, a villager   *bass*

LIBRETTO BY FELICE ROMANI; TIME: THE EARLY NINETEENTH CENTURY; PLACE: A VILLAGE IN SWITZERLAND; FIRST PERFORMED AT THE TEATRO CARCANO, MILAN, 6 MARCH 1831

After the success of *I Capuleti e i Montecchi* in Venice in the spring of 1830, Bellini's next commission was to compose an opera for Milan – not for the most prestigious Milanese theatre, La Scala, but for the Teatro Carcano, one of several other theatres in the city. Bellini and his librettist Felice Romani at first intended to base their opera on Victor Hugo's play *Hernani*, and indeed they completed four musical numbers before abandoning the project, probably because they feared that the opera's revolutionary subject might run into difficulties with the censorship authorities. By early January 1831 they were at work on the politically innocuous *La sonnambula*, which they wrote very quickly.

The plot was taken from the scenario of a ballet, *La Sonnambule*, by the French playwright and librettist Eugène Scribe which had been staged in Paris three years previously, and which had in turn derived from a two-act comedy by Scribe and Casimir Delavigne, first performed in Paris in 1819. At its premiere in Milan, when it shared a double bill with a ballet, the success of Bellini's *La sonnambula* was immense, with its leading roles of Amina and Elvino performed by two of the greatest singers of the time, the soprano Giuditta Pasta and the tenor Giovanni Battista Rubini. The following day Bellini wrote to a friend:

> Here you have the happy news of the uproarious success of my opera last night at the Carcano. I will say nothing about the music, for you will read of that in the press. I can only assure you that Rubini and Pasta are two angels who enraptured the entire audience to the point of madness.

The Russian composer Mikhail Glinka had been in the audience. In his *Memoirs* he wrote:

> Pasta and Rubini sang with the most evident enthusiasm to support their favourite conductor. In the second act the singers themselves wept and carried their audience along with them so that, in that happy season of carnival, tears were continually being wiped away in boxes and stalls alike. Embracing Shterich [Glinka's travelling companion, an amateur composer] in the Ambassador's box, I too shed tears of emotion and ecstasy.

Act I, scene i. A square in the village, outside the mill. The villagers have assembled to celebrate the imminent marriage of Amina, an orphan brought up by Teresa, the owner of the village mill, to Elvino, a wealthy young farmer. Lisa, the proprietress of the local inn, does not take part in the general air of rejoicing, for she is in love with Elvino ('Tutto è gioia, tutto è festa') and is not interested in the attentions of Alessio, a young villager who loves her. Amina and Teresa arrive, and Amina thanks her friends, especially Teresa, who has always behaved like a mother to her ('Come per me sereno'). Elvino appears, having been praying at his mother's tomb, and the marriage contract is signed and witnessed, the wedding itself to take place next day in the church. Elvino tenderly places a ring on Amina's finger ('Prendi, l'anel ti dono').

A carriage draws up, from which there emerges a handsome stranger who seeks directions to the castle. On being told it is some distance away, he decides to stay overnight at the inn in this village which seems to have fond associations for him ('Vi ravviso, o luoghi ameni'). Although the villagers do not realize it, the stranger is in fact their feudal lord, Count Rodolfo, returning after a long absence to take up residence in the castle on the death of his father. To the annoyance of Elvino, the Count pays compliments to Amina, who, he says, reminds him of his own lost love ('Tu non sai con quei begli occhi'). As evening falls, the villagers warn the stranger of a phantom which they claim has been haunting their village, a warning that Rodolfo accepts with scepticism. He is conducted by a flirtatious Lisa to her inn, while Elvino, left alone with Amina, gently chides her for having allowed the stranger to pay compliments to her. However, Amina easily reassures the jealous Elvino of her love for him ('Son geloso del zeffiro errante').

Act I, scene ii. Count Rodolfo's room at the inn. Lisa flirts with the Count, whose identity the villagers have by now discovered. Hearing a noise outside, she escapes to an adjoining room, inadvertently dropping a handkerchief which Rodolfo retrieves and hangs over a bedpost. Amina, wearing a white nightgown, now enters through a window, and Rodolfo realizes that she is walking in her sleep and that it is no doubt her somnambulism that has given rise to the rumour of a phantom haunting the village at night. Lisa, who has glimpsed Amina entering Rodolfo's room, assumes that she has an assignation with him, and quietly goes off to inform Elvino. Meanwhile, Amina has begun to talk in her sleep about her marriage and Elvino's jealousy. Rodolfo is touched by her words, and in order to avoid embarrassing her he leaves as Amina, still asleep, lies on the bed.

The villagers arrive to pay homage to the Count. Entering his room, they espy the figure of a sleeping woman on his bed, and are about to withdraw when Lisa returns with Elvino and reveals to him that the woman on the bed is his betrothed, Amina. Awakened by the noise, Amina is unable to explain her presence in the Count's room. Although she protests her innocence ('D'un pensiero e d'un accento'), she is denounced by Elvino and by all the assembled villagers except her foster-mother, Teresa, who takes the handkerchief that is hanging over the bedpost, places it around Amina's neck and catches her as she swoons.

Act II, scene i. A forest between the village and the castle. The villagers are on their way to the castle to ask the Count to help establish the truth. As they leave, Amina and Teresa appear. They encounter Elvino, who confirms his rejection of Amina. The villagers return with the news that the Count has declared Amina innocent, but Elvino, furious at the very mention of Rodolfo's name, snatches the wedding ring from Amina's finger, though he admits to himself that he still cannot hate her ('Ah, perchè non posso odiarti?').

Act II, scene ii. The village square. Lisa's unhappy suitor Alessio learns from her that Elvino now intends to marry her instead of Amina. Lisa rejoices in this change of circumstances ('De' lieti auguri a voi son grata'). Rodolfo attempts to explain the events of the previous evening to Elvino but, like everyone else in the village, Elvino has never heard of somnambulism and does not believe him. Teresa arrives, asking the villagers to make less noise as Amina is asleep in the millhouse. When she hears that Elvino is to marry Lisa, Teresa produces, to Lisa's evident confusion, the handkerchief that she had discovered in the Count's room. Elvino wonders if there are any honest women in the world, and Count Rodolfo repeats that Amina is innocent. When Elvino asks who can prove it, Rodolfo is able to reply that Amina herself can do so, for at that moment she is seen to emerge, obviously asleep, from an upper window in the millhouse, and to walk across a dangerous ledge on the roof. After she has reached safety, she enters the square still asleep, dreaming of Elvino and the loss of his love ('Ah! non credea mirarti'). At Rodolfo's urging, Elvino replaces on her finger the ring he had taken from her. A cry of 'Viva Amina!' from the villagers awakens Amina, who is over-joyed to find Elvino kneeling at her feet and seeking her forgiveness ('Ah! Non giunge uman pensiero').

La sonnambula, the earliest of his mature masterpieces, has a fair claim to be regarded as the quintessential Bellini opera, with its long-breathed elegiac melodies, its radiant coloratura and its expressive lyricism. Amina's aria and cabaletta in Act I represent the composer at his most individual, the aria ('Come per me sereno') a beguiling expression of the innocence of young love, and the cabaletta ('Sovra il sen la man mi posa') an exhilarating outburst of sheer happiness. The Count's smoothly flowing, nostalgic cavatina ('Vi ravviso, o luoghi ameni') is one of the most attractive arias written for the bass voice, while Elvino is given splendid opportunities for display in the cabaletta to his Act I duet with Amina ('Ah! Vorrei trovar parola'), in which he is required to produce his top C four times. The ensemble finale to Act I ('D'un pensiero e d'un accento') was surely in Sir Arthur Sullivan's mind when he wrote his parody of an operatic ensemble, 'A nice dilemma we have here', in Trial by Jury; and Amina's 'Ah! Non credea mirarti', one of the great peaks of the bel canto soprano's repertoire, is very likely the aria that Verdi had in mind when he wrote admiringly of Bellini's 'long, long, melodies'. Its opening notes are inscribed on Bellini's tomb in his home town of Catania.

La sonnambula is a work of immense charm, but a successful performance requires virtuoso singers of the quality of its first interpreters, Pasta and Rubini, or in more recent times sopranos such as Maria Callas, Joan Sutherland or June Anderson and tenors of the calibre of Nicolai Gedda or Alfredo Kraus. When the great Swedish soprano Jenny Lind, nicknamed 'the Swedish Nightingale', sang

Amina at Her Majesty's Theatre, London, in 1847, Queen Victoria wrote in her diary of her performance of 'Ah! Non credea mirarti':

> It was all *piano* and clear and sweet, and like the sighing of a zephyr; yet all heard. Who could describe those long notes, drawn out until they quite melt away; that shake which becomes softer and softer; those very piano- and flute-like notes, and those round, fresh tones that are so youthful?

More than a hundred years later the Australian Joan Sutherland sang many performances of *La sonnambula* all over the world. Harold Schonberg wrote in the *New York Times*:

> [The second act] has the two great arias, 'Ah! non credea' and 'Ah, non giunge'. The first is a long, unembellished melody that cannot be sung without a flawless technique. The second is one of the all-time coloratura showpieces. In both, Miss Sutherland was as perfect as one could desire . . . when she finished an explosive roar went up from the audience. It was fully deserved. For this was not merely coloratura singing, it was singing in the grand line, and it was the stuff of which legends are made.

Of her Elvino, Nicolai Gedda, the critic of *Opera* wrote: 'The role of Elvino should (and probably does) strike terror into the hearts of our modern tenors, but Mr Gedda sang it with remarkable command of its shadings of volume, its florid decoration, and its terrifying demands on breath control.'

Recommended recording: Joan Sutherland (Amina), Luciano Pavarotti (Elvino), Della Jones (Teresa), Nicolai Ghiaurov (Rodolfo), Isabel Buchanan (Lisa), with the London Opera Chorus and National Philharmonic Orchestra, conducted by Richard Bonynge. Decca 417 424–2. Joan Sutherland is in her finest voice, spinning out Bellini's languorous melodies with a fine legato and sailing through the cabalettas with apparently the greatest of ease. Pavarotti, too, is in rich voice, and gives one of his most engaging performances on disc, while Richard Bonynge, completely at home in the bel canto repertoire, conducts most stylishly.

Norma
opera seria in two acts (approximate length: 3 hours)

Norma, high priestess of the Druid temple   *soprano*
Adalgisa, a virgin of the temple   *mezzo-soprano*

Pollione, Roman proconsul in Gaul   *tenor*
Oroveso, Archdruid, Norma's father   *bass*
Clotilde, Norma's confidante   *soprano*
Flavio, a Roman centurion   *tenor*

LIBRETTO BY FELICE ROMANI, BASED ON ALEXANDRE SOUMET'S PLAY *NORMA, OU L'INFANTICIDE*; TIME: AROUND 50 BC; PLACE: GAUL; FIRST PERFORMED AT THE TEATRO ALLA SCALA, MILAN, 26 DECEMBER 1831

By the time of *La sonnambula*'s successful premiere at the Teatro Carcano, Milan, in March 1831, Bellini had already agreed to write his next opera, for La Scala. By the end of July he and his librettist Felice Romani had decided on the opera's subject: it was to be based on *Norma*, the French dramatist Alexandre Soumet's new play, which had opened in Paris in April to great acclaim. The usually dilatory Romani produced his libretto very quickly, and Bellini began to compose the opera early in September. *Norma* was given its premiere at La Scala on 26 December, the traditional date for the opening of the carnival season.

To the surprise of everyone connected with the production, the audience at the first performance seemed not to enjoy the opera. Writing to his closest friend, the music historian Franco Florimo, whom he had known since their student days together in Naples, Bellini complained of his great disappointment:

> I am writing to you in a state of bitter grief which I cannot express, but which you alone will understand. I have just come from La Scala where the first performance of *Norma* was, would you believe it, a dismal fiasco!!! I tell you truly, the audience was very severe, and seemed to me to want my poor *Norma* to suffer the same fate as the Druid priestess. I no longer recognized those dear Milanese, who had greeted *Il Pirata*, *La Straniera* and *La Sonnambula* with joy on their faces and warmth in their hearts, although I had hoped that with *Norma* I had given them something just as worthy.

The reaction of the first-night audience may to some extent have been organized by a faction supported by the mistress of the composer Giovanni Pacini, whose opera *Il corsaro* was about to be given its premiere at La Scala. Bellini certainly suspected this to be the case. After its first night *Norma* was greeted by its audiences with enormous enthusiasm, and it was performed thirty-nine times during the season. It went on to become the most popular of Bellini's works in Italy and abroad, has retained its popularity to the present day and is regarded as his masterpiece.

Three years after Bellini's death at the early age of thirty-four, the young Richard
Wagner wrote an essay on *Norma*, calling it 'indisputably Bellini's most successful composition'. The title role was conceived for the Italian soprano Giuditta
Pasta, who some months earlier had created the role of Amina in Bellini's *La sonnambula*. Pasta made comments to the composer on her music as it was being
written. At first she disliked her aria, 'Casta diva', but Bellini asked her to practise
it every day for a week, promising to rewrite it if after that she still thought it ill-
suited to her voice. In the event, he did not have to make any changes to it, and
Pasta's performance of 'Casta diva' became famous throughout Europe. (Bellini's
original key of G major was too high for her, so she transposed both the aria and
its cabaletta down to F, the key in which they are now usually performed.)

Act I, scene i. The sacred forest of the Druids. Oroveso, the Archdruid, arrives
with priests and Gallic soldiers to await the rising of the new moon, at which
moment his daughter Norma, the high priestess, will perform the ceremony of
cutting the sacred mistletoe ('Ite sul colle, o Druidi'). The Druids beg their god,
Irminsul, to arouse in Norma feelings of hatred and rebellion against the
Romans, who have invaded their country. As the Gauls all move off into the forest, two Romans arrive. They are Pollione, the Roman proconsul, and his friend
Flavio, a centurion. Pollione has been Norma's lover and they have had two children, but he confides to Flavio that he now loves Adalgisa, a virgin priestess of the
Druid temple, who returns his love ('Meco all' altar di Venere'). However, he fears
the wrath of Norma. As the sound of a gong heralds the return of the Druids,
Pollione and Flavio depart.

The Druids return with their high priestess, Norma, who approaches the altar
stone with a golden sickle in her hand. Expected to incite the Gauls to rise against
their Roman oppressors, Norma instead counsels peace, asserting that Rome one
day will fall, not through any action on the part of the Gauls but because of its
own vices. She cuts a branch from the sacred mistletoe, and all kneel as she raises
her arms to the moon and appeals to that chaste goddess to temper the ardent
spirits of the Gauls ('Casta diva'). Although Norma promises that, should the god
Irminsul ever demand the blood of the Romans, her voice will thunder forth
from the Druids' temple, she tells herself that her heart would never allow her to
punish Pollione. She longs for him to return to her.

All the Druids depart, except the young novice Adalgisa, who prays to Irminsul
for help and protection as she awaits her lover, Pollione. When Pollione arrives, he
tells her that he has been recalled to Rome, and begs her not to devote her life to
the service of her cruel god but to flee with him ('Vieni in Roma, ah vieni, o cara').

Adalgisa agrees to meet him the following day in the sacred grove and accompany him to Rome.

Act I, scene ii. Norma's secret dwelling in the forest. Torn between her love for the two children she has borne to Pollione and shame at their situation, Norma asks her confidante, Clotilde, to remove the children from her sight. She knows that Pollione has been recalled to Rome, and fears that he may intend to leave her and her children behind. At the sound of someone approaching, Clotilde takes the children away.

Adalgisa enters to confess to her superior, Norma, that she has broken her vow of chastity and with a Roman. Since Norma has done the same, she forgives Adalgisa and is about to free her from her vow when Pollione enters. Realizing that he is the Roman whom Adalgisa loves, Norma reveals to Adalgisa that she too has been Pollione's lover, and she proceeds to revile him ('Oh! Di qual sei tu vittima'). Adalgisa spurns him and, as the hapless Roman attempts to justify himself, the sacred gong sounds, summoning Norma to the temple.

Act II, scene i. Norma's dwelling. Norma enters the room in which her two children are sleeping. She is carrying a knife, for she intends to kill the children rather than allow them to live in shame. Approaching the bed, she raises the dagger but finds that she is unable to strike. She sends Clotilde to fetch Adalgisa, having now decided to entrust the children to the care of Adalgisa and Pollione and then kill herself. Adalgisa, however, says that she will go to Pollione only to remind him of his duty to Norma ('Mira, o Norma'). She and Norma swear eternal friendship ('Si, fino all' ore estreme').

Act II, scene ii. The Druids' sacred grove in the forest. The Gallic warriors await Oroveso, who arrives to declare that the time is not yet ripe for them to rise against the Romans ('Ah! Del tebro'). After Oroveso and the warriors have departed, Norma enters to await the result of Adalgisa's plea to Pollione on her behalf. Clotilde arrives with the news that Adalgisa's approach to Pollione was unsuccessful, and that Adalgisa has returned, weeping, to the temple. In a fury, Norma rushes to the altar and strikes three times upon the sacred shield, summoning Oroveso and the Druids, whom she now incites to war, carnage and destruction.

A noise is heard in the distance, and Clotilde rushes in to announce that a Roman has been captured in the quarters of the virgin novices. Pollione is now led in by soldiers, ready to face the penalty of death rather than reveal that he had been attempting to carry off Adalgisa. Norma is about to strike the fatal blow, when she feels a sudden pity for Pollione. On the pretext of wishing to question him to discover whom he was planning to abduct, she persuades the Druids to withdraw.

Norma offers to spare Pollione's life if he will swear never to see Adalgisa again ('In mia man alfin tu sei'). When he refuses, she summons the Druids, confesses that she herself is the priestess who has broken her sacred vows, and orders her funeral pyre to be prepared. Entrusting her children to the care of her father, Oroveso, whose forgiveness she begs, she mounts the pyre accompanied by Pollione, whose love for her has been reawakened by her greatness of spirit.

Norma is generally regarded as Bellini's masterpiece, a work in which his sensuous, long-breathed melodies are placed in the service of immensely strong dramatic situations. Its overture is somewhat melodramatic – Bellini's genius was for arias and duets rather than orchestral music. Nevertheless, referring to a theme first heard in the orchestral introduction to Oroveso's Act I cavatina, Verdi wrote that no other composer had created a phrase 'more beautiful and heavenly'. Throughout the opera, the confidence, variety and sheer beauty of Bellini's melody are amazing. Norma's aria 'Casta diva', the wonderfully flowing vocal line of which has been likened to a Chopin nocturne, is one of the peaks of the dramatic soprano repertoire, and the Act II duet, 'Mira, o Norma', for Norma and Adalgisa, their soprano and mezzo-soprano voices blending sympathetically in thirds, is both forceful and moving. The duet 'In mia man alfin tu sei', at the opera's climax, is positively Verdian in its dramatic impetus.

The score of *Norma* seems so perfectly wedded to its libretto that it is difficult to believe that some of it had originally been composed by Bellini for other operas, among them *Bianca e Fernando*, *Adelson e Salvini* and *Zaira*. His orchestration is hardly complex, but it is always appropriate. Asked by a French publisher to reorchestrate the score of *Norma*, Bizet discovered that the task was neither possible nor necessary. Let the final word be Bellini's: 'If I were shipwrecked,' he wrote, 'I would leave all of my other operas and try to save *Norma*.'

When the great Wagnerian soprano Lilli Lehmann sang Norma (in German) at the Metropolitan Opera House, New York, in 1890, she said that she found it easier to sing all three Brünnhildes than one Norma. 'In Wagner,' she explained, 'you are so carried away by the dramatic emotion, the action and the scene that you do not have to think how to sing the words. That comes of itself. But in Bellini you must always have a care for beauty of tone and correct emission.' Great twentieth-century interpreters of the title role have included Rosa Ponselle, Maria Callas (for whom Norma was surely her greatest role), Leyla Gencer, Joan Sutherland and Montserrat Caballé. The mezzo-soprano role of Adalgisa, Norma's rival in love, has had such distinguished performers as Fedora Barbieri, Ebe Stignani, Giulietta Simionato, Marilyn Horne and Grace Bumbry (who also sang Norma).

Recommended recording: Maria Callas (Norma), Ebe Stignani (Adalgisa), Mario Filippeschi (Pollione), with the Chorus and orchestra of La Scala, Milan, conducted by Tullio Serafin. EMI CDS5 56271–2. Norma was surely Callas's greatest role, one in which her occasional vocal imperfections on this recording are spectacularly outweighed by the dramatic fervour of her portrayal of the wronged Druid priestess. Ebe Stignani is a most sympathetic Adalgisa, her duet scenes with Callas both moving and exciting, and Mario Filippeschi is a suitably stentorian Pollione. Callas's great mentor Tullio Serafin keeps the opera moving at a brisk pace while sacrificing none of its drama.

I puritani
(The Puritans)
opera seria in three acts (approximate length: 2 hours, 50 minutes)

Arturo (Lord Arthur Talbot), a royalist   *tenor*
Gualtiero (Lord Walton), governor of a Puritan fortress   *bass*
Giorgio (Sir George Walton), his brother   *bass*
Riccardo (Sir Richard Forth), a Puritan   *baritone*
Sir Bruno Roberton, a Puritan   *tenor*
Elvira, daughter of Gualtiero   *soprano*
Enrichetta (Henrietta, widow of Charles I)   *soprano*

LIBRETTO BY COUNT CARLO PEPOLI, BASED ON THE PLAY *TÊTES RONDES ET CAVA-LIERS*, BY JACQUES-ARSÈNE ANCELOT AND JOSEPH-XAVIER-BONIFACE SAINTINE; TIME: 1649; PLACE: IN AND AROUND PLYMOUTH; FIRST PERFORMED AT THE THÉÂTRE ITALIEN, PARIS, 24 JANUARY 1835

Bellini's next opera after *Norma* was *Beatrice di Tenda*, which he composed for the Teatro La Fenice in Venice, where it had its premiere in March 1833. Although it was accorded a cool reception at its first performance, *Beatrice di Tenda* was staged in several other Italian cities and abroad before the end of the decade, and is occasionally revived today. It was the last opera on which Bellini and Felice Romani collaborated, for the librettist had not only been dilatory in producing his text for Bellini to set, thus causing the premiere to be postponed, but he had also published a letter in a Venice newspaper blaming the composer for the postponement. Bellini and Romani were never to meet again.

When, early in 1834, the composer was asked to provide a new opera for the Théâtre Italien in Paris, he turned to Count Carlo Pepoli, an Italian poet and patriot living in exile in Paris, to write the libretto. The subject they eventually chose was a play, *Têtes rondes et cavaliers* (Roundheads and Cavaliers) by Jacques-Arsène Ancelot and Joseph-Xavier-Boniface Saintine, that had been produced in Paris the previous year. (Though one sometimes reads that the play was based on Sir Walter Scott's novel *Old Mortality*, this is incorrect. The plots and characters of the two works are completely dissimilar.) The opera's full title, rarely used today, is *I puritani di Scozia* (The Puritans of Scotland) – although the action takes place in Plymouth, which is in the south of England, the librettist had thought that Plymouth was in Scotland!

When it was staged in Paris on 24 January 1835, *I puritani* had in its leading roles four of the most famous singers of the time: Giulia Grisi (Elvira), Giovanni Battista Rubini (Arturo), Antonio Tamburini (Riccardo) and Luigi Lablache (Giorgio). It was an immense success at its premiere and was soon being staged all over Europe, frequently with the original singers, who became known as 'the *Puritani* quartet'.

Act I, scene i. The courtyard of a fortress near Plymouth, at dawn. Sir Bruno and the Puritan guards welcome the approach of day, prepare themselves for victory over the Stuarts, and then, as the sound of a morning hymn is heard from the nearby chapel, kneel in prayer. The women of the fortress enter, excitedly discussing preparations for the wedding of Elvira, daughter of Gualtiero, the governor of the fortress. When they leave, Riccardo, a Puritan officer, confides to Bruno his great sorrow at the approaching marriage ('Ah, per sempre io ti perdei'). In love with Elvira, Riccardo was promised her hand in marriage by her father, who subsequently informed him that Elvira had confessed her love for Arturo, a Stuart partisan, and that, although he was distressed that she should have chosen a political enemy, he was not prepared to stand in the way of his daughter's happiness and had agreed to allow her marriage to Arturo. Bruno now attempts to comfort Riccardo by reminding him that he has been chosen to lead the Puritan troops, but Riccardo can think only of his love for Elvira ('Bel sogno beato').

Act I, scene ii. Elvira's apartment in the castle. Elvira tells her uncle, Giorgio, whom she loves as a second father, that she will die of grief if she is dragged to the altar to marry Riccardo ('Sai com' arde in petto mio'). When Giorgio assures her that he has persuaded her father to allow her to marry the Cavalier, Arturo, whom she loves, Elvira is overjoyed. She and Giorgio leave to greet Arturo, whose arrival they hear announced by the castle's retainers and soldiers.

Act I, scene iii. The great hall of the castle. Arturo and his attendants enter laden with bridal gifts, including a long white veil, and Arturo addresses words of love to Elvira ('A te, o cara'). Gualtiero announces that he will have to absent himself from his daughter's wedding, as he must escort a female prisoner to Parliament, in London. After Elvira has left to dress for the wedding, the prisoner seizes an opportunity to approach Arturo, identifying herself as Enrichetta, widow of the recently executed Charles I. Arturo resolves to help her escape. Elvira now returns, dressed for her wedding and carrying her veil. Singing light-heartedly ('Son vergin vezzosa'), she places the veil on Enrichetta's head to see how it will look, and then rushes off to finish her preparations for the wedding. Enrichetta begins to remove the veil but Arturo prevents her, realizing that it makes an excellent disguise. He is about to leave the castle with her when Riccardo rushes in. Thinking that he has found Arturo with his bride, Riccardo exclaims that he cannot allow her to marry a royalist, an enemy of the Puritan cause. The two men draw swords, and when Enrichetta attempts to stop them from fighting she inadvertently loses her veil. Recognizing the prisoner, Riccardo coldly permits her and Arturo to leave.

When Elvira and the others return to begin the wedding procession to the chapel, they discover that the bridegroom has left the castle with the female prisoner. Elvira is so distressed that her mind immediately begins to give way and she imagines herself in the chapel being married to Arturo ('O vieni al tempio').

Act II. A hall in the castle, with a view of the fortifications and, in the distance, the camp of the opposing Stuart army. The Puritan retainers are discussing Elvira's pitiful condition. When Giorgio enters he is asked for news of her, and he describes how Elvira wanders about the castle and its grounds, garlanded with flowers, her hair in disarray, at times imagining that she is being married to Arturo and at other times weeping and longing for death ('Cinta di fiori'). Riccardo arrives to announce that Parliament has condemned Arturo to death, and Elvira enters, unable to recognize her friends, and imagines that she sees Arturo ('Qui la voce sua soave'). After she has left, Giorgio tells Riccardo that, for the sake of Elvira, he must save his rival Arturo from execution ('Il rival salvar tu dei'). Riccardo is moved by Giorgio's words, but both men agree that if, on the morrow, Arturo should fight against them with the Stuart forces, he must be defeated ('Suoni la tromba').

Act III. The countryside near the fortress. As a violent storm gradually subsides, Arturo enters, congratulating himself on having eluded his enemies and made his way back to the castle where he hopes to find Elvira. Hearing her voice singing plaintively in the distance, he takes up her song ('A una fonte'), but conceals himself when he hears soldiers searching for him. Elvira enters, and she and Arturo greet each other ecstatically. He explains to her that the woman with whom he had fled the castle was the Queen.

Elvira and Arturo swear their love for each other ('Vieni fra queste braccie'), but when military music is heard Elvira's mind begins to wander again. She imagines she is losing Arturo, and her cries bring soldiers rushing to the scene, among them Riccardo and Giorgio. Arturo is seized, and Riccardo informs him that he has been sentenced to death. The word death ('morte') shocks Elvira back to her senses, and the situation of the lovers is pitied by all ('Credeasi, misera'). Suddenly a fanfare is heard, followed by the arrival of a messenger who announces that the Stuarts have been defeated and that a victorious Cromwell has granted amnesty to all prisoners. Everyone rejoices at this unexpected happy outcome.

Although it may lack the dramatic cohesion of *Norma*, Bellini's final opera contains some of his most beautiful and most characteristic music. The soprano and tenor roles of Elvira and Arturo abound in soulful and affecting melodies. Elvira's 'mad scene' consists of the elegantly melancholy 'Qui la voce sua soave', one of the most beautiful arias ever composed, with its magnificent and feverishly brilliant cabaletta ('Vien, diletto'). The stirring duet 'Suoni la tromba' brought the entire audience to its feet at the premiere, and the performance could not continue until Bellini had appeared on stage to acknowledge the applause.

The tessitura of Arturo's music is dauntingly high, rising to the tenor's C sharp in the reprise of the long, gracefully beguiling melody of his elegant entrance aria, 'A te, o cara'. He produces a D natural (twice) in his Act III duet with Elvira, the impassioned 'Vieni fra queste braccie', and in the final ensemble ('Credeasi, misera') a high F sung in the *voix mixte* or supported falsetto which most tenors of Bellini's day used even for less stratospheric notes, but which held no terrors for Rubini. (On one recording of the opera Nicolai Gedda demonstrates how to produce a high F à la Rubini, while on another Luciano Pavarotti demonstrates how not to, by employing a poorly supported falsetto.) Vocally the most dazzling of Bellini's operas, *I puritani* is a work which has a special place in the affections of enthusiasts for the bel canto style of early nineteenth-century Italian opera. Rossini considered that, along with *Norma*, it offered the most unmistakable proof of Bellini's greatness.

Famous modern interpreters of the role of Elvira have included Joan Sutherland, Maria Callas, Beverly Sills and June Anderson. The high-lying tenor role of Arturo has been sung to great acclaim by Nicolai Gedda and Alfredo Kraus. Of a 1963 concert performance at Carnegie Hall in New York with Sutherland and Gedda, a critic in *Opera* wrote:

> For sheer bravura and unbelievable perfection Joan Sutherland's performance as Elvira was the highlight of the season. She has never been so free, so

radiant, so transcendent; and when Nicolai Gedda soared to a high D in their duet in the last act and Miss Sutherland disappeared into the tonal stratosphere, the audience could scarcely be blamed for becoming hysterical.

An equally magnificent performance in Philadelphia two nights later, with the same cast, was recorded live.

Recommended recordings: Beverly Sills (Elvira), Nicolai Gedda (Arturo), Louis Quilico (Riccardo), Paul Plishka (Giorgio), Richard Van Allan (Gualtiero), with the Ambrosian Opera Chorus and London Philharmonic Orchestra, conducted by Julius Rudel. Opera Edition, MCD 80356 (this is the one with Gedda's spectacular high F); Joan Sutherland (Elvira), Luciano Pavarotti (Arturo), Nicolai Ghiaurov (Giorgio), Piero Cappuccilli (Riccardo), with the Welsh National Opera Chorus & Orchestra, conducted by Richard Bonynge. Decca 414 476–2.

ALBAN BERG
(b. Vienna, 1885 – d. Vienna, 1935)

Wozzeck
opera in three acts (approximate length: 1 hour, 35 minutes)

Wozzeck, a soldier   *baritone*
The Drum-Major   *tenor*
Andres, a soldier   *tenor*
The Captain   *tenor*
The Doctor   *bass*
An Idiot   *tenor*
Marie   *soprano*
Margret, Marie's neighbour   *contralto*
Marie's Child   *treble*

LIBRETTO BY THE COMPOSER, BASED ON GEORG BÜCHNER'S PLAY *WOZZECK*; TIME: THE EARLY NINETEENTH CENTURY; PLACE: A TOWN IN GERMANY; FIRST PERFORMED AT THE STAATSOPER, BERLIN, 14 DECEMBER 1925

It was after he had attended the Viennese premiere in 1914 of Büchner's play *Woyzeck* (at the time spelt *Wozzeck*, due to someone's misreading of the playwright's handwriting) that Alban Berg began to construct a libretto from Büchner's text and to make some musical sketches for the opera he felt immediately inspired to write. But World War I intervened, and it was not until the middle of 1919 that he managed to finish the first of the opera's three acts. By 1922 Berg's *Wozzeck* was completed and orchestrated; a concert performance of excerpts was conducted by Hermann Scherchen in Frankfurt in 1924. The opera's premiere in Berlin, conducted by Erich Kleiber, required thirty-four orchestral rehearsals and fourteen full rehearsals with the singers, for Berg's complex score was found exceedingly difficult to perform. Despite some interruptions from the audience during the first performance, the opera was produced in a number of other German and Austrian towns until, after the Nazis came to power in 1933, it was labelled decadent and was suppressed.

During his brief life, the German playwright Georg Büchner (1813–1837), whose socialist sympathies were aroused in his student days by the ideals of the French Revolution, wrote two starkly realistic plays, *Woyzeck* and *Danton's Tod* (Danton's Death), and a satirical comedy, *Leonce and Lena*, none of which were staged until several decades after his death. *Woyzeck* is a terse expression of Büchner's sympathy for the brutalized lower echelons of society in nineteenth-century Germany.

Act I, scene i. The Captain's room. It is morning. The Captain is being shaved by his batman, the illiterate, simple-minded, highly nervous Wozzeck. He teases Wozzeck for having produced a child out of wedlock, and is disconcerted when Wozzeck is provoked to assert that 'we poor folk' cannot afford the morality of the rich.

Act I, scene ii. A field outside the town, in late afternoon. Wozzeck and his friend Andres, a fellow soldier, are cutting wood. Andres sings a cheerful folk song, while Wozzeck, who feels the place to be haunted, imagines the sunset to be a great fire consuming the world.

Act I, scene iii. Marie's house, in the evening. Marie, the mother of Wozzeck's Child, is talking to her neighbour Margret, when a military band passes her window and she acknowledges a wave from the Drum-Major. Margret comments on Marie's interest in soldiers, and the two women quarrel. Marie sings her Child to sleep with a lullaby, and Wozzeck appears at the window, babbling confusedly of the terror he experienced in the field that afternoon. After he has run off, the distraught Marie also rushes out.

Act I, scene iv. The Doctor's study, on the afternoon of the following day. In return for a small amount of money, Wozzeck has agreed to act as a guinea pig for the Doctor's experiments concerning diet. The Doctor complains of Wozzeck's behaviour, listens to him raving about his visions in the field, and then contemplates the fame he expects to achieve through the medical discoveries that will result from his study of Wozzeck.

Act I, scene v. Outside Marie's house. Twilight. Marie is talking to the boastful Drum-Major. When he embraces her she at first resists, but soon she changes her mind and leads him into the house.

Act II, scene i. Marie's room. Marie admires herself and her new earrings in a broken mirror, while simultaneously trying to get her Child to sleep. Wozzeck arrives and is suspicious of the earrings, which she tells him she has found. He contemplates the now sleeping Child, then gives Marie some money he has received from the Captain and the Doctor. After he has left, Marie expresses remorse at her infidelity to Wozzeck.

Act II, scene ii. A street. The Doctor, hurrying along, is overtaken by the Captain, whom he upsets with his talk of disease and death. The two men stop Wozzeck as he passes and taunt him with innuendoes about Marie and the Drum-Major. They follow the distraught Wozzeck as he rushes off.

Act II, scene iii. Outside Marie's house. Wozzeck confronts Marie with his suspicions. When he seems about to strike her, she warns him, 'Rather a knife in my heart than lay a hand on me.' Wozzeck repeats her words in a daze as she enters the house.

Act II, scene iv. The garden of a tavern, in the evening. Soldiers and their women are drinking and dancing to the tune of a slow ländler. Wozzeck enters to find Marie dancing with the Drum-Major. The soldiers, led by Andres, sing a hunting song, an apprentice climbs on a table to deliver a drunken discourse, and an Idiot appears, talking incoherently to Wozzeck of blood. As the dancing is resumed, Wozzeck can think of nothing but blood.

Act II, scene v. The barracks, at night. The soldiers are asleep, except for Wozzeck, who tells a somnolent Andres that thinking of the tavern is keeping him awake. The Drum-Major staggers into the room, boasting of his sexual conquest that evening and hinting at the woman's identity. When Wozzeck refuses to drink with him the Drum-Major attacks him, beats him viciously and leaves. Wozzeck sits on his bed, staring vacantly in front of him.

Act III, scene i. Marie's room, at night. Alone with her Child, Marie reads in her Bible, by candlelight, the story of the woman taken in adultery. She prays for mercy.

Act III, scene ii. A path by a pond in the wood, at night. Marie and Wozzeck are walking by the pond. She wants to go home, but he prevents her. He recalls their first meeting, kisses her, and then, as a blood-red moon rises, takes out a knife and cuts her throat.

Act III, scene iii. The tavern, later that night. Youths and girls are dancing a polka. Wozzeck watches, and then he calls Margret over and begins to make love to her. When she notices blood on his hand he tells her he has cut himself and then rushes off, pushing his way through the crowd that has gathered around them.

Act III, scene iv. The path by the pond. Wozzeck has returned to search for the knife, which he had dropped. Finding it, he throws it into the water and watches it sink then walks into the pond to wash away the blood which seems to him now to have spread all over him. He drowns. The Doctor and the Captain arrive in time to hear a sound which the Doctor thinks may be that of a man drowning, but the Captain, made uneasy by the atmosphere of the place, drags the Doctor away.

A dramatic orchestral interlude, recapitulating the opera's main themes, precedes the final scene.

Act III, scene v. The street outside Marie's house, the next morning. Children are playing, among them Marie's Child. Other children arrive, one of whom tells Marie's Child that its mother is dead. The Child, who does not understand, at first continues to play on an imaginary hobby-horse, but then runs off after the others.

Berg studied composition with Arnold Schoenberg, whom he eventually followed down the path of atonalism, a method of composing without using a key system which stayed in vogue for two or three decades in the first half of the twentieth century. However, it was only after the composition of *Wozzeck* that Berg completely embraced Schoenberg's twelve-note method of composition. The structure of *Wozzeck*'s musical language is complex, but its dramatic effect is immediate and overwhelming, even though Berg makes frequent use of the unsatisfactory device, borrowed from Schoenberg, of *Sprechgesang* (speech-song), a compromise between speech and song in which the singer's voice hits the pitch of each note but does not sustain it, dropping instead into the cadences of speech. The problem with *Sprechgesang* is that, as the critic Ernest Newman expressed in an essay published eight years after Berg's death, 'it fails to carry conviction either as song, as speech, or as a fusion of the two; it is neither speech achieving melody nor song biting like speech, but a bastard by-product of speech and song, which neither captivates the ear nor commands the assent of the intellect.'

Berg himself described his three-act opera, somewhat dauntingly, as an A–B–A structure of which the central act, a 'symphony in five movements', is preceded by an act the five scenes of which are 'five character pieces', and is followed by one of which the orchestral interlude and five scenes are 'Inventions'. Fortunately, in an article published three years after the premiere of *Wozzeck*, he wrote that 'from the moment the curtain rises until it falls for the last time, no-one in the audience ought to notice anything of these various fugues and inventions, suites and sonata movements, variations and passacaglias.' Berg makes extensive use of the *Sprechgesang* technique, but his music also moves towards a simpler language to express less complex emotions or feelings; for instance, in Marie's lullaby or in Andres's hunting song. The influence of Mahler, too, is evident in *Wozzeck*, especially in the tavern scene in Act II, which begins with soldiers and their girls dancing a slow ländler, which is soon followed by a waltz. The orchestral interlude preceding the opera's final scene is one of the most impressive sections of the entire work. It quotes music from earlier scenes, but begins with an adagio for strings, which is thought to derive from a symphony that Berg began composing in 1913 but soon abandoned.

Despite its frequent use of *Sprechgesang*, Berg's wonderfully evocative and expressive *Wozzeck* is one of the masterpieces of twentieth-century opera. A number of famous baritones have been attracted to its title role, among them Tito Gobbi, Geraint Evans, Hermann Uhde and Eberhard Waechter. At the Metropolitan Opera House, New York, in 1931 the tenor role of the Drum-Major was sung by the then thirty-year-old high baritone Nelson Eddy, who later had a successful career in Hollywood films.

Recommended recording: Franz Grundheber (Wozzeck), Hildegard Behrens (Marie), Heinz Zednik (Captain), Aage Haugland (Doctor), Philip Langridge (Andres), Walter Raffeiner (Drum-major), Anna Gonda (Margret), Peter Jelosits (Idiot), with the Vienna Boys' Choir, Vienna State Opera Chorus, Vienna Philharmonic Orchestra, conducted by Claudio Abbado. DGG 423 587–2. A first-rate cast offers vivid characterizations, and the great Vienna Philharmonic Orchestra responds superbly to Abbado's highly dramatic direction.

Lulu
opera in a prologue and three acts (approximate length: 2 hours, 50 minutes)

Lulu   *high soprano*
Countess Geschwitz   *dramatic mezzo-soprano*

A Wardrobe-Mistress   *contralto*
A Schoolboy   *contralto*
The Doctor   *spoken role*
The Painter   *lyric tenor*
Dr Schoen   *heroic baritone*
Alwa Schoen, his son   *heroic tenor*
An Animal-Tamer   *bass*
Rodrigo, an athlete   *bass*
Schigolch, an old man   *high character bass*
The Prince   *tenor*
The Theatre Director   *buffo bass*
The Marquis   *tenor*
The Professor   *tenor*
Jack the Ripper   *baritone*

LIBRETTO BY THE COMPOSER, BASED ON FRANK WEDEKIND'S PLAYS *ERDGEIST* AND *DIE BÜCHSE DER PANDORA*; TIME: THE END OF THE NINETEENTH CENTURY; PLACE: A GERMAN TOWN, PARIS AND LONDON; FIRST PERFORMED, IN INCOMPLETE TWO-ACT FORM, AT THE STADTTHEATER, ZURICH, 2 JUNE 1937; FIRST PERFORMANCE OF THE THREE-ACT VERSION, COMPLETED BY FRIEDRICH CERHA, AT THE PARIS OPÉRA, 24 FEBRUARY 1979

After the premiere in 1925 of his first opera, *Wozzeck*, Berg decided to write another, and he began to look for a subject. He soon found what he wanted in two plays by the German playwright Frank Wedekind, *Erdgeist* (Earth Spirit) and *Die Büchse der Pandora* (Pandora's Box). Their central character is Lulu, a beautiful, sensuous creature who drifts from promiscuity to prostitution. Fashioning a libretto from both plays, Berg began work on the opera that was to occupy him for several years and that was still not complete when he died on Christmas Eve in 1935, at the age of fifty. He had almost finished the work in short score and had orchestrated the first two acts but very little of the third.

Berg's widow, Helene, asked first Arnold Schoenberg and then Anton von Webern to complete *Lulu* so that it could be performed, but both composers declined, and when the opera was given its premiere in Zurich in 1937 it was in the unfinished state in which Berg had left it. Helene Berg subsequently refused to allow the orchestration of Act III to be completed by others, and it was only after her death in 1976 that *Lulu* was performed complete, the orchestration of Act III having been finished by another Viennese composer, Friedrich Cerha.

The German playwright and actor Frank Wedekind (1864–1918), though influenced by the naturalism of August Strindberg, is generally considered a forerunner of the expressionists. His first plays, *Die junge Welt* (The Young World) and *Frühlings Erwachen* (Spring's Awakening), deal with the problems created by adolescent ignorance of sex, while *Erdgeist* (1895) and *Die Büchse der Pandora* (1904) portray sexual licence with a frankness that many in Wedekind's audience found shocking. The loose and shambling structure of the 'Lulu' plays is reflected in the rather shapeless libretto that Berg assembled from them.

Prologue. The Animal-Tamer, whip in hand, appears before the curtain to introduce his beasts, among them Lulu.

Act I, scene i. The Painter's studio. Lulu is having her portrait painted, watched by her ex-lover Dr Schoen, whose son Alwa, a writer, arrives to take his father to a performance of his play. When the two men have left, the Painter attempts to make love to Lulu, but is interrupted by the sudden arrival of Lulu's elderly husband, who immediately collapses in a state of shock and dies. Apparently unmoved, Lulu realizes that she is now both free and rich.

Act I, scene ii. An elegantly furnished room in Lulu's house. She is now married to the Painter, and his finished portrait of her is hanging on a wall. Lulu reads a letter from Dr Schoen which, to her annoyance, announces his engagement. Schigolch, an old beggar who considers himself Lulu's adoptive father, enters. He is delighted to find Lulu living in such luxury, but leaves when Dr Schoen arrives to say farewell to Lulu. She tells Schoen that her husband seems not to notice anything she does. When the Painter enters, Lulu leaves, and Schoen reveals to her husband that he was Lulu's lover for years, and has bought every picture the Painter has sold in order to provide Lulu with riches. The Painter's immediate response to this revelation is to rush out and slit his throat in the bathroom. Alwa Schoen enters, announcing that revolution has broken out in Paris. His father is worried that the suicide of Lulu's husband may affect his own marriage plans, and Lulu expresses her confidence that Dr Schoen will, in due course, change those plans and marry her.

Act I, scene iii. A theatre dressing-room. Lulu, now a famous dancer, is visited by Alwa Schoen, who is in love with her. She leaves to go on stage, while Alwa considers writing an opera about her. Lulu returns, claiming that the sight of Dr Schoen's fiancée in the audience has made her too ill to dance. A Prince, who wants to take Lulu to Africa, enters and sings her praises. When Dr Schoen arrives, Lulu threatens to run off to Africa with the Prince, at which Schoen agrees to break off his engagement to his fiancée.

Act II, scene i. A magnificent room in Dr Schoen's house. Lulu is now married to Schoen, whom she makes wildly jealous by flirting with the lesbian Countess Geschwitz, the athlete Rodrigo, and a Schoolboy whose meeting with her has been arranged by Schigolch. When Alwa Schoen arrives, the others hide. Dr Schoen overhears Lulu telling Alwa that she was responsible for his mother's death. Getting rid of the others, Dr Schoen brandishes a gun at Lulu and suggests that she should kill herself. Instead, she fires at Schoen, who dies calling on his son to avenge him. Despite Lulu's pleas Alwa calls the police, who arrest her. A silent film sequence (anticipating the next scene) shows Lulu's trial, her imprisonment and her eventual escape from a cholera ward with the aid of Countess Geschwitz.

Act II, scene ii. The same room, in a state of neglect. Countess Geschwitz, Alwa and Rodrigo the athlete await Schigolch, who is to take the Countess to the hospital to change places with Lulu. Schigolch arrives, and he and the Countess Geschwitz leave together. Soon, Schigolch returns with Lulu, whose sickly appearance causes the athlete to abandon his plan to marry her and take her to Paris as his performing partner. Lulu and Alwa Schoen leave for Paris together.

Act III, scene i. A salon in a Paris casino. The Marquis, a white-slave trafficker, threatens to expose Lulu to the police unless she agrees to be sold to a brothel in Cairo. The athlete and Schigolch attempt to get money from Lulu, the Marquis calls the police, and Lulu, dressed as a boy, escapes with Alwa.

Act III, scene ii. A garret in London. Alwa and Schigolch await the return of Lulu, who is now a prostitute and supporting them both. Lulu arrives with a client, a Professor whose pockets are picked by Schigolch. Her next client is a negro who has an altercation with Alwa and kills him. Lulu's final client turns out to be Jack the Ripper, who kills both her and Countess Geschwitz who has attempted to come to her aid.

The score of *Lulu*, in which Berg utilized Schoenberg's twelve-note system much more consistently than in *Wozzeck*, is a treasure-trove for musical analysts, for it was put together by Berg in an almost clinically intellectual manner, with the music of individual scenes fashioned to fit the requirements of various forms of absolute music. One scene is a rondo, another a movement in sonata form, a third a set of variations, and so on. In Act II, the music accompanying a silent film sequence is a palindrome, with the notes reading the same backwards as forwards.

Due to a large extent to its provenance in Wedekind's disjunct plays, *Lulu* is aesthetically less satisfying than Berg's earlier opera, *Wozzeck*, and it has to be admitted that its eponymous heroine is an absolutely repulsive creature. Remarkably, however, although it is an uneven work, *Lulu* contains passages of great emotional impact, and its dramatic climaxes are shattering.

Recommended recording: Teresa Stratas (Lulu), Yvonne Minton (Countess Geschwitz), Franz Mazura (Dr Schoen), Kenneth Riegel (Alwa Schoen), Paris Opera Orchestra, conducted by Pierre Boulez. DGG 415 489–2. These are the singers and conductor of the 1979 Paris premiere of the complete work. An intensely exciting performance.

HECTOR BERLIOZ
(b. La Côte-Saint-André, Isère, 1803 – d. Paris, 1869)

Benvenuto Cellini
opera semiseria in two acts (approximate length: 2 hours, 40 minutes)

Benvenuto Cellini   *tenor*
Balducci, Papal treasurer   *bass*
Teresa, his daughter   *soprano*
Ascanio, Cellini's apprentice   *mezzo-soprano*
Fieramosca, a sculptor   *baritone*
Pope Clement VII   *bass*
Francesco, an artisan   *tenor*
Bernardino, an artisan   *baritone*
Pompeo, a ruffian   *baritone*

LIBRETTO BY LÉON DE WAILLY AND AUGUSTE BARBIER; TIME: 1532; PLACE: ROME; FIRST PERFORMED AT THE PARIS OPÉRA, 10 SEPTEMBER 1838

Although Berlioz's talents were usually more impressively deployed in the concert hall than in the opera house, his great ambition was to succeed as a composer of opera. The enormous sucess of Meyerbeer's *Les Huguenots* at the Paris Opéra in 1836 encouraged Berlioz to revise his first opera, *Benvenuto Cellini*, which, in its original form as an opera whose musical numbers were separated by spoken dialogue, had been rejected by the Opéra-Comique. Its libretto was very loosely adapted from the memoirs of the fifteenth-century Florentine sculptor

Benvenuto Cellini, which Berlioz had read shortly after his return from a year spent in Rome. (He called Cellini 'that bandit of genius'.) With its dialogue replaced by recitatives, *Benvenuto Cellini* was accepted by the Paris Opéra.

The work was a failure at its premiere in 1838, probably not so much due to its poor libretto – which uneasily attempts to juxtapose heroic and farcical genres – as to its unwieldy structure and the uneven quality of Berlioz's music. Also, the tenor Gilbert-Louis Duprez apparently sang badly in the title role. After four performances the opera disappeared from the stage until 1852, when Liszt staged it at Weimar, on which occasion Berlioz took the opportunity to revise his score, simplifying some of its technical difficulties and toning down the light-hearted elements that had been written with the Opéra-Comique in mind. At Liszt's suggestion, he also shortened the opera somewhat. For many years it continued to be performed in this Weimar version, but in recent times the Paris 1838 score has been preferred, though occasionally with the recitatives replaced by dialogue from the original Opéra-Comique version.

Act I, scene i. The house of Balducci, the papal treasurer. Shrove Monday, at night. Balducci is annoyed because the Pope has summoned the Florentine goldsmith Cellini to Rome to make a statue of Perseus, a commission that Balducci had hoped would be won by Fieramosca, the official Papal sculptor, whom Balducci intends to become his son-in-law. His daughter Teresa, however, has other plans. She is delighted to receive a note thrown in from the street by a masked reveller, Cellini, who enters after Balducci has left angrily, and who arranges with Teresa that they will elope on the following evening. Cellini and Teresa are overheard by Fieramosca (in the trio 'Demain soir, mardi gras'). When Balducci returns, suspicious at finding his daughter still awake so late, Cellini manages to make his escape from the house unobserved, but Fieramosca is discovered and dragged off by women neighbours to be given a ducking in the public bath house.

Act I, scene ii. The courtyard of a tavern in the Piazza Colonna, on Shrove Tuesday evening. Cellini and his fellow metalworkers plan their revenge on Balducci, who has sent only a meagre sum as advance payment for the statue of Perseus that Cellini must complete by the following morning. Fieramosca and his accomplice Pompeo make plans to frustrate Cellini's intended elopement with Teresa. At an open-air theatre on the other side of the piazza a play is performed, satirizing Balducci. Among the spectators are Cellini, his apprentice Ascanio, Fieramosca and Pompeo, all attired as monks, the guise in which Cellini has arranged to meet Teresa. A fight breaks out between the opposing factions, in the course of which Cellini stabs Pompeo, mortally wounding him. Cellini is seized by the crowd but, in the confusion following the boom of a cannon to signal the end of the carnival, he escapes, and another 'monk', Fieramosca, is apprehended in his place.

Act II, scene i. Cellini's studio, at dawn on Ash Wednesday. Ascanio comforts Teresa, who is concerned for Cellini's safety. Cellini arrives, describes how he made his escape, and urges Teresa to flee with him immediately to Florence. Their departure is frustrated by the arrival of Balducci and Fieramosca, who denounce Cellini. The subsequent quarrel is interrupted by the arrival of Pope Clement VII. (At the opera's premiere in 1838 it was a Cardinal Salviati who appeared, the censor having forbidden the theatrical impersonation of a pope.) Annoyed at finding his statue not yet cast, the Pope issues an ultimatum. If Perseus is finished by the end of the day, Cellini will be pardoned and allowed to marry Teresa. If not, he will be hanged for the murder of Pompeo.

Act II, scene ii. Cellini's foundry, that evening. Ascanio sings a lively aria recounting the events of the day ('Tra la la, mais quai-je donc?'). In his aria, 'Sur les monts les plus sauvages', Cellini expresses his longing to exchange the cares of the artist for the simple life of a shepherd tending his flock on a remote mountainside. Fieramosca enters, challenging Cellini to a duel, and the two men go off to fight, leaving the foundry workers furious at their master's absence and in no mood to continue with their task. However, when Fieramosca returns and attempts to bribe them to leave Cellini and come to work for him instead, they turn on him in anger. Cellini reappears and berates Fieramosca for not having kept their rendezvous for the duel, and Fieramosca is now forced to help in the foundry.

The Pope arrives, and the casting of the statue begins. When Fieramosca announces that there is not enough metal to complete the work, Cellini orders all of his other precious statues to be melted down to replenish the furnace. The metal fills the mould, and the statue is cast. The Pope pardons Cellini, grants him Teresa's hand in marriage, and leaves a scene of general rejoicing.

Though its score may lack cohesion, some of *Benvenuto Cellini*'s individual numbers represent Berlioz at his most resourceful in terms of rhythmic complexity and orchestral colouring; for example the charming, lyrically expansive trio, 'Demain soir, mardi gras', in Act I, and the scintillating carnival scene, some of the music of which Berlioz used for his *Carnaval romain* concert overture (1844). This scene also contains the goldsmiths' chorus, 'Honneurs aux maîtres ciseleurs', one of the musical highlights of the opera. There is also the beautiful duet, 'Sainte Vierge Marie', in which Teresa and Ascanio pray for Cellini's safety, with the monks chanting in the background. And Cellini's superb andante aria 'Sur les monts les plus sauvages', in which he yearns for the simple life, provides the opera's most lyrical moment of repose, a complete contrast to the evocative rhythms of the forging scene. 'A variety of ideas, a vitality and zest and a brilliance of musical colour such as I shall perhaps never find again': this was Berlioz's own judgment on his opera. A fair verdict, but he should perhaps have added that the work's musical complexity makes it difficult to perform, and that some of the finest musical numbers present the most difficulties.

Recommended recording: Nicolai Gedda (Benvenuto Cellini), Christiane Eda-Pierre (Teresa), Jane Berbie (Ascanio), Robert Massard (Fieramosca), Jules Bastin (Balducci), Roger Soyer (Pope Clement VII), Derek Blackwell (Francesco), Robert Lloyd (Bernardino), Raimund Herincx (Pompeo), with the Royal Opera House Chorus and the BBC Symphony Orchestra, conducted by Colin Davis. Philips 416 955–2.

For many years Nicolai Gedda was the leading exponent of the role of Cellini, and Colin Davis remains the finest Berlioz conductor. An exemplary performance and recording.

Béatrice et Bénédict
opéra comique in two acts (approximate length: 1 hour, 30 minutes)

Béatrice, niece of Leonato *soprano*
Bénédict, an officer *tenor*
Hero, daughter of Leonato *soprano*
Claudio, an officer *baritone*
Don Pedro, a general in the army *bass*
Leonato, governor of Messina *spoken role*
Ursula, Hero's companion *mezzo-soprano*
Somarone, a music master *bass*

LIBRETTO BY THE COMPOSER, BASED ON SHAKESPEARE'S PLAY *MUCH ADO ABOUT NOTHING*; TIME: THE PAST; PLACE: MESSINA, SICILY; FIRST PERFORMED AT THE NEUES THEATER, BADEN-BADEN, 9 AUGUST 1862

Commissioned in 1858 by the theatre attached to the casino in the German spa town of Baden-Baden to write an opera about the Thirty Years War, Berlioz persuaded the management to allow him instead to produce an operatic version of Shakespeare's comedy *Much Ado About Nothing*, under the title of *Béatrice et Bénédict*. (Shakespeare's spelling of his hero's name is Benedick.) Berlioz himself wrote the libretto, dispensing with Don John and the sub-plot involving the attempted discrediting of Hero, and substituting a tedious new character, the musician Somarone, for Shakespeare's engaging Dogberry.

Act I. The garden of Leonato's palace. The citizens of Messina rejoice because a threatened Moorish invasion has been averted and await the return of their victorious army. Leonato's daughter Hero learns that her fiancé, Claudio, has distinguished himself in battle, and her cousin Béatrice enquires disdainfully after Bénédict, with whom she has long enjoyed a relationship based on supposedly witty bickering.

The citizens dance a *sicilienne* and then disperse. Hero joyously anticipates her reunion with Claudio in an attractive two-part aria, its calm opening larghetto ('Je vais le voir') followed by an exhilarating allegro ('Il me revient fidele'). When Bénédict, Claudio and their general, Don Pedro, arrive, the light-hearted banter between Béatrice and Bénédict ('Comment le dedain pourrait-il mourir?') amuses Bénédict's two comrades, who hatch a plot to make Béatrice and Bénédict fall in love with each other.

After the music master Somarone has rehearsed his chorus and orchestra in their contribution to the forthcoming wedding of Claudio and Hero, Bénédict overhears his colleagues and Leonato discussing, in apparent seriousness, Béatrice's love for him. He resolves to requite her love ('Ah, je vais l'aimer'). As night falls, Hero and her companion Ursula, who have practised a similar deception upon Béatrice, extol the beauty of the evening in a lyrical duet ('Nuit paisible et sereine').

Act II. A room in Leonato's palace. After an entr'acte which makes use of the *sicilienne* from the previous scene, the act begins with dialogue, followed by Somarone leading a drinking song ('Le vin de Syracuse'). Béatrice enters, reflecting on the true nature of her feeling for Bénédict in an aria ('Il m'en souvient') in whose concluding section ('Je l'aime donc?') she discovers that feeling to be one of love. She confesses that this is so, in an exquisite trio with Hero and Ursula ('Je vais d'un coeur aimant').

Béatrice and Bénédict are still reluctant to admit to each other their changed feelings, but after a Wedding March and the exchange of contracts between Hero and Claudio they are finally persuaded to confess that they love each other, and to sign their own wedding contract. The opera ends with a sparkling duet for Béatrice and Bénédict ('L'Amour est un flambeau').

Béatrice et Bénédict, its fifteen numbers separated by spoken dialogue, can hardly be regarded as a satisfactory musical adaptation of Shakespeare's play. A less complex work than *Much Ado About Nothing*, it is, however, a pleasant romantic comedy whose lively and brilliantly scored overture (utilizing tunes to be heard later in the opera) became a highly popular concert item. The pace of Berlioz's score throughout the opera is, in general, leisurely.

Recommended recording: Susan Graham (Béatrice), Jean-Luc Viala (Bénédict), Sylvia McNair (Hero), Gilles Cachemaille (Claudio), Gabriel Bacquier (Somarone), with the chorus and orchestra of the Opéra de Lyon, conducted by John Nelson. Erato Musifrance 2292–45773–2. A fine cast, with Viala a superb Bénédict, a stylish French orchestra and chorus, an American conductor well-known for his Berlioz performances, and the dialogue in full delivered by French actors.

Les Troyens
(The Trojans)
grand opéra in five acts (approximate length: 3 hours, 45 minutes)

Cassandra, daughter of Priam   *soprano*
Ascanius, son of Aeneas   *soprano*
Hecuba, wife of Priam   *mezzo-soprano*
Polyxenes, daughter of Priam   *soprano*
Aeneas, a Trojan warrior   *tenor*
Choroebus, betrothed to Cassandra   *baritone*
Pantheus, a Trojan priest   *bass*
Ghost of Hector   *bass*
Priam, King of Troy   *bass*
Helenus, son of Priam   *tenor*
Andromache, widow of Hector   *mime*
Astyanax, her son   *mime*
A Greek Captain   *bass*
Dido, Queen of Carthage   *mezzo-soprano*
Anna, her sister   *contralto*
Iopas, a Carthaginian poet   *tenor*
Narbal, minister of Dido   *bass*
Hylas, a young Phrygian sailor   *tenor*
The god Mercury   *bass*

LIBRETTO BY THE COMPOSER, BASED ON BOOKS 1, 2 AND 4 OF VIRGIL'S *AENEID*;
TIME: CLASSICAL ANTIQUITY; PLACE: TROY AND CARTHAGE; PART TWO, COMPRIS-
ING ACTS III, IV AND V, FIRST PERFORMED AT THE THÉÂTRE-LYRIQUE, PARIS, 4
NOVEMBER 1863. FIRST PERFORMED COMPLETE AT THE HOFTHEATER, KARLSRUHE,
5 DECEMBER 1890

From his boyhood, when he first made the acquaintance of Virgil's *Aeneid*, Berlioz was fascinated by the ancient world of Greece and Rome. However, it was not until he reached middle age that he felt ready to compose an opera about events in classical antiquity. Writing his own libretto based on Virgil, he proceeded to create *Les Troyens*, a grand opera in two parts. It used to be thought far too long to be staged complete in one evening, although it actually takes less than four hours to perform (excluding intervals). The work was not staged in its entirety until twenty-one years after its composer's death. Part Two alone, 'Les Troyens à Carthage' (The Trojans at Carthage), had its premiere in 1863, but it disappeared from the repertoire of the Théâtre-Lyrique after twenty-one performances – some with extensive cuts – given over a period of six weeks. Part One, 'La Prise de Troie' (The Capture of Troy), had to wait until 1890, when finally a complete performance of *Les Troyens* was given in Karlsruhe on two consecutive nights. Although some stagings in the first half of the twentieth century were of all five acts, they were never entirely complete. At the Royal Opera House, Covent Garden, in 1957 the opera was performed virtually complete, and a Scottish Opera production in 1969 claimed to have subjected the work to no cuts at all.

Part One: 'La Prise de Troie' (The Capture of Troy)

Act I. The abandoned camp of the Greek army outside the walls of Troy. The Greeks have apparently departed, leaving behind them only a huge wooden horse. The Trojans emerge from the city to examine it. When Cassandra, prophetess and daughter of the Trojan King Priam, tells her betrothed, Choroebus, that she has dreamed of the downfall of Troy, and urges him to flee, Choroebus dismisses her fears ('Quitte-nous des ce soir'). King Priam and his wife, Hecuba, lead their people in a hymn of thanks for deliverance from the Greeks, while Andromache, widow of the slain hero Hector, enters with her infant son, in silent mourning for her husband.

Aeneas, a Trojan warrior, enters with the shocking announcement that the high priest Laocoon was devoured by sea serpents when he attempted to incite the populace to destroy the wooden horse which he suspected of being some kind of Greek ambush. The citizens react in horror ('Châtiment effroyable'). King

Priam orders the horse to be brought into the city. Cassandra utters a warning, but even the ominous sound of clashing arms from within the horse fails to deter the citizens of Troy from dragging it into their city.

Act II, scene i. A room in Aeneas's palace. The Ghost of Hector appears to Aeneas, telling him to flee from Troy and to found a new empire in Italy ('Ah! fuis, fils de Vénus'). The Greeks who were hidden in the horse have captured Troy, and King Priam is dead. Choroebus enters with a band of followers, and Aeneas joins them as they rush off to fight.

Act II, scene ii. The temple of Vesta. The Trojan women are praying at the altar of the goddess ('Ha! puissante Cybèle') when Cassandra rushes in. She tells them that Aeneas and his followers will escape to build a new Troy in Italy, but that they, the women of Troy, should kill themselves rather than become slaves of the Greeks. Those few women who are afraid to do so are driven out by the others, and as the first of the Greek soldiers enter Cassandra stabs herself. Her example is followed by the other women, some of whom leap from the colonnade, meeting death with a cry of 'Italy' on their lips.

Part Two: 'Les Troyens a Carthage' (The Trojans at Carthage)

Act III. Dido's palace in Carthage. In the city founded by Dido after she and her followers had fled from Troy, the people are celebrating their new-found prosperity. They greet their Queen, Dido ('Gloire à Didon'), who, when left alone with her sister Anna, confesses to her that she feels a strange sadness. Anna advises her to remarry and thus provide Carthage with the security of a king, but Dido resists, swearing to be faithful to the memory of her dead husband, although to herself she confesses that Anna's suggestion has its attractions ('Sa voix fait naître dans mon sein').

Iopas, the court poet, enters to announce that a fleet of foreign ships has been driven ashore by storms. The shipwrecked sailors appear. They are the Trojans, among them a disguised Aeneas. Aeneas's son, Ascanius, presents Dido with ceremonial trophies from Troy, and one of the Trojans, the priest Pantheus, explains that they were on their way to Italy to found the new Troy.

Narbal, Dido's minister, arrives with the news that a threatened invasion by the Numidians has now begun. Aeneas reveals his identity and offers to defend Carthage. Dido gratefully accepts his offer, and after leaving Ascanius in her care Aeneas departs to lead the combined Carthaginians and Trojans into battle against the Numidians.

Act IV, scene i. A forest near Carthage. Naiads, bathing in a stream, are frightened off by the arrival of a hunting party. A storm breaks out. Separated from the other hunters, Dido and Aeneas take refuge in a cave. The intensity of their passionate love for each other is symbolized by flashes of lightning, as dancing fauns and nymphs utter cries of 'Italy!' (The music of this scene is the orchestral sequence known in concert performances as the Royal Hunt and Storm.)

Act IV, scene ii. A garden of Dido's palace by the sea. Aeneas has defeated the Numidians, but Anna and Narbal, conversing, disagree as to whether the love of Dido and Aeneas will prove advantageous to Carthage. The lovers enter, with Ascanius and attendants, and celebratory dances are performed before them. At Dido's command Iopas sings ('O blonde Cérès'). Aeneas informs Dido that Andromache, Hector's widow, has now married the son of her husband's slayer, and this leads Dido to ponder the possibility of remarrying.

All marvel at the beauty of the evening ('Tout n'est que paix et charme') and, when finally they are alone, Dido and Aeneas declare their love for each other in an exquisite duet ('Nuit d'ivresse et d'extase infinie'), some of its text charmingly modelled on the love scene between Lorenzo and Jessica in Act V of Shakespeare's *The Merchant of Venice*. As Dido and Aeneas wander off together, Mercury, the messenger of the gods, appears, uttering three times an admonitory cry to Aeneas of 'Italy!'

Act V, scene i. The harbour at Carthage, by night. Hylas, a young Phrygian sailor on one of the Trojan vessels, sings nostalgically of his homeland ('Vallon sonore'). Pantheus and the Trojan chiefs agree that they must set sail for Italy immediately, to the dismay of two Trojan sentries who are annoyed at having to leave their easy life in Carthage.

Aeneas enters and soliloquizes on the conflict between his love for Dido and his duty to obey the command of the gods and sail for Italy ('Inutiles regrets'). When the ghosts of Priam, Hector, Cassandra and Choroebus appear, urging him to do his duty, Aeneas rouses the sleeping Trojan soldiers, ordering them to prepare for departure. Dido enters hurriedly, begging him to stay, but Aeneas, as he hears the distant sound of the Trojan march, rushes on board his ship with a cry of 'Italy!'

Act V, scene ii. A room in Dido's palace. Told that the Trojan fleet has put out to sea, Dido at first expresses her fury, which when she is alone turns to bitter grief. She determines upon death ('Ah, je vais mourir'), wondering if Aeneas will see from his ship the flames of her funeral pyre. She then bids a farewell to the city of Carthage ('Adieu, fière cité').

Act V, scene iii. A terrace overlooking the sea. Narbal and Anna pronounce a solemn curse on Aeneas and the Trojans, and Dido mounts the steps of the pyre. Taking Aeneas's sword, she utters a prophecy that one day a warrior (Hannibal) will arise to avenge the shame brought on her by Aeneas. She then stabs herself. As she dies, Dido is vouchsafed a vision of Rome, the eternal city.

Admirers of Berlioz consider *Les Troyens* his masterpiece, but others have found it excessively long for the amount of really inspired music it contains. The English composer Ralph Vaughan Williams referred to the opera tantalizingly as 'the second most boring opera in the world', and more than one distinguished writer on opera has criticized the work not only for its unevenness of musical quality but also for its shortcomings as drama. It has to be admitted that Berlioz lacked the theatrical instincts of such dedicated composers of opera as Meyerbeer, Verdi or Wagner; he was not, in the sense that they were, a man of the theatre. Nevertheless, *Les Troyens*, though it may include stretches in which tedium is not always kept at bay, contains some of Berlioz's most beautiful music. The orchestral Royal Hunt and Storm, the exquisite love duet of Dido and Aeneas ('Nuit d'ivresse et d'extase infinie'), and Aeneas's stirring 'Inutiles regrets' are but a few of the opera's most effective numbers.

Les Troyens, requiring vast forces and many changes of scene, is a difficult opera to stage, and the role of Aeneas calls for a dramatic tenor of great range, vocal flexibility and stamina. Jon Vickers, one of the finest heroic tenors of his day, was a magnificent Aeneas at Covent Garden in 1957, a production, conducted by Rafael Kubelik, which led to a renaissance of interest in Berlioz's vast work. A definitive score was published in 1969, the composer's centennial year, and a new staging at Covent Garden conducted by Colin Davis in that year, with Jon Vickers repeating his acclaimed Aeneas, and the role of Dido shared by Josephine Veasey and Janet Baker, led to the release of a now famous recording. In 1974 the Metropolitan Opera, New York, staged the opera substantially complete, with Kubelik conducting, Vickers predictably superb as Aeneas and Christa Ludwig a Dido of great charm. In 2000 the Salzburg Festival oddly chose to present *Les Troyens*, one of the grandest epics ever composed, in a minimalist production, which was generally derided by critics and audiences.

Recommended recording: Jon Vickers (Aeneas), Josephine Veasey (Dido), Berit Lindholm (Cassandra), with the chorus and orchestra of the Royal Opera House, Covent Garden, conducted by Colin Davis. Philips 416 432–2. Davis gives a magisterial account of the work, Jon Vickers, predictably, is a splendidly heroic Aeneas, Josephne Veasey a commanding Dido, and Berit Lindholm an effective Cassandra. The large supporting cast includes some of the Royal Opera's most reliable performers of the time, and the quality of the recorded sound is superb.

GEORGES BIZET
(b. Paris, 1838 – d. Bougival, 1875)

Les Pêcheurs de perles
(The Pearl Fishers)
opera in three acts (approximate length: 1 hour, 45 minutes)

Leîla, priestess of Brahma *soprano*
Nadir, a fisherman *tenor*
Zurga, chief fisherman *baritone*
Nourabad, high priest of Brahma *bass*

LIBRETTO BY EUGÈNE CORMON AND MICHEL CARRÉ; TIME: THE ANCIENT PAST; PLACE: CEYLON; FIRST PERFORMED AT THE THÉÂTRE LYRIQUE, PARIS, 30 SEPTEMBER 1863

Throughout his brief life Bizet's main interest remained the composition of operas, several of which were never performed, among them his first, a one-act *opéra comique*, *La Maison du docteur* (The Doctor's House), written during his teenage student years, and the five-act *Don Rodrigue*, composed in 1873 immediately before he embarked upon *Carmen*. Bizet's earliest success came with a one-act comic opera, *Le Docteur Miracle*, which won a prize offered by Jacques Offenbach and was staged at Offenbach's theatre, the Bouffes-Parisiens, in 1857. Thereafter, although *Les Pêcheurs de perles* (1863), *La Jolie Fille de Perth* (The Fair Maid of Perth; 1866), *Djamileh* (1872) and Bizet's one undisputed masterpiece, *Carmen* (1875), were staged, only *Carmen* achieved a real and lasting success. *Les Pêcheurs de perles* was given no more than eighteen performances at its first appearance in 1863 and was not taken into the Théâtre Lyrique's repertoire. It was more than twenty years after Bizet's death that it began to be staged elsewhere, but it is now quite frequently revived.

Act I. A rocky beach in Ceylon. The pearl fishers are in celebratory mood, singing and dancing as they prepare their nets for the coming season. Reminded by one of their number, Zurga, that they must choose a leader, the other fishermen immediately select Zurga himself. A young fisherman, Nadir, now emerges from the forest, and Zurga greets him as a dear friend with whom he had lost contact. Nadir and Zurga had both fallen in love with a beautiful young woman whom they had encountered at the Brahmin temple in the town of Kandy, but they had vowed to renounce her so as not to disturb their friendship. The two men now reminisce ('Au fond du temple saint') and swear to remain friends ('Amitié sainte').

A boat arrives, carrying Nourabad, the high priest of Brahma, and a veiled young woman, the virgin priestess whose task it will be to pray for the fishermen's safety during the coming season. The young priestess is welcomed with flowers by the fishermen ('Sois la bienvenue') and takes the sacred oath of obedience administered by Zurga. As she does so, she and Nadir recognize each other, for she is Leîla, the young woman he and Zurga had fallen in love with in Kandy.

Leîla is conducted by Nourabad to the ruins of a temple on the cliff above the beach, where she is to keep her vigil. When the others have all departed, Nadir reflects on his love for her in a gently seductive aria ('Je crois entendre encore'), and then he falls asleep. Leîla emerges from the temple above, and sings an invocation to Brahma ('O dieu Brahma'), interrupted by the voice of Nadir who, awakened by her singing, ardently reaffirms his love.

Act II. The temple ruins, at night. Nourabad warns Leîla to be faithful to her religious vows. Before he leaves her to watch and pray throughout the night, Leîla tells him how, as a child, at the risk of her own life, she had saved the life of a stranger who, in return, gave her a necklace which she still wears. Left alone, she sings of her love for Nadir ('Comme autrefois dans la nuit sombre'). Nadir arrives, and a passionate love duet ensues ('Ton coeur n'a pas compris le mien').

Nadir and Leîla agree to meet again the next day. However, as Nadir leaves, he is seen by Nourabad, who calls upon guards to pursue him. Nadir is captured and, incited by Nourabad, who accuses the lovers of sacrilege, an angry crowd calls for him and Leîla to be put to death. In order to save his friend, Zurga claims the right, as chief of the fishermen, to spare their lives. When Nourabad tears the veil from Leîla's face, Zurga recognizes her and, consumed with jealous fury, orders the lovers to be executed. As Leîla and Nadir are led away, all pray to Brahma for guidance.

Act III, scene i. Zurga's tent. Zurga recalls the past, regrets the present and, in a tender, lyrical aria ('O Nadir, tendre ami de mon jeune age'), thinks fondly of his old friend whom he has condemned to death. Leîla, under guard, arrives to plead for Nadir's life. However, when Zurga realizes how greatly she loves his friend and rival his jealousy is aroused again, and he reaffirms the sentence of death upon them both. As Nourabad and the fishermen come to lead Leîla away, she removes her necklace and gives it to a young fisherman, asking him to see that her mother receives it. Zurga recognizes it as the necklace that he gave, years previously, to a young girl who saved his life.

Act III, scene ii. The place of execution: a funeral pyre beneath a statue of

Brahma. Preparations for the execution of Nadir and Leîla are under way when suddenly flames are seen in the sky, and Zurga enters to announce that the fishermen's camp is ablaze. The others rush off to save the camp, and Zurga tells the two captives that it was he who started the fire. He shows Leîla the necklace and urges her to escape with Nadir. As the lovers flee together, Zurga watches the villagers escaping through the forest and awaits the return of Nourabad, who will no doubt decide his fate.

Although Bizet was only twenty-four when he wrote it, *Les Pêcheurs de perles* is a mature and individual work with his melodic gift very much to the fore. There are naive touches of the exotic in its orchestration, to emphasize the fact that it is set in the East; in Ceylon, to be precise, although Mexico was the librettists' initial choice of locale. The opera's most popular numbers are the languid tenor aria 'Je crois entendre encore' and the duet for tenor and baritone, 'Au fond du temple saint', with its broad, sweeping melody.

Recommended recording: Barbara Hendricks (Leîla), John Aler (Nadir), Gino Quilico (Zurga), with the Toulouse Capitole Chorus and Orchestra conducted by Michel Plasson. EMI CDS 7 49837 2.

No one in recent years has sung the beautiful tenor aria, 'Je crois entendre encore' as enchantingly as Nicolai Gedda (who has recorded it on one of his recital discs). However, despite the superb performances of Gedda and Ernst Blanc as Nadir and Zurga in an earlier EMI recording conducted in masterly style by Pierre Dervaux, that version must yield pride of place to Michel Plasson's account of the opera. Plasson allows Bizet's sensuous melodies to speak for themselves in leisurely tempi which seem to have a natural sense of flow. Barbara Hendricks is a sweet-voiced Leîla, John Aler's high tenor is well suited to the role of Nadir, and Gino Quilico makes an ideal Zurga.

Carmen
opéra comique in four acts (approximate length: 2 hours, 45 minutes)

Carmen, a gypsy   *mezzo-soprano*
Don José, a corporal   *tenor*
Escamillo, a toreador   *baritone*
Micaëla, a peasant girl   *soprano*
Zuniga, a lieutenant   *bass*

> Morales, a corporal   *baritone*
> Frasquita, a gypsy   *soprano*
> Mercèdes, a gypsy   *soprano*
> Le Dancaire, a smuggler   *tenor or baritone*
> Le Remendado, a smuggler   *tenor*
> Lillas Pastia, an innkeeper   *spoken role*

LIBRETTO BY HENRI MEILHAC AND LUDOVIC HALÉVY, BASED ON THE NOVELLA *CARMEN*, BY PROSPER MÉRIMÉE; TIME: THE 1820S; PLACE: SEVILLE; FIRST PERFORMED AT THE OPÉRA-COMIQUE, PARIS, 3 MARCH 1875

In 1867 Bizet's four-act opera *La Jolie Fille de Perth* had its premiere in Paris at the Théâtre-Lyrique. Its libretto by Jules-Henri Vernoy de Saint-Georges and Jules Adenis, loosely based on Sir Walter Scott's novel *The Fair Maid of Perth*, tells of the love of Henry Smith, an armourer, for Catherine Glover, the daughter of Simon, a glovemaker in the Scottish town of Perth. The opera closed after only eighteen performances, and five years later his next work for the stage, *Djamileh*, a comic opera in one act, was even less successful. In 1873 Bizet was invited to compose a new work for the Opéra-Comique, despite the failure of his *Djamileh* at that theatre in the previous year. The composer himself decided upon Prosper Merimée's novella *Carmen* (first published in 1845) as his subject, and a libretto was commissioned from the experienced team of Meilhac and Halévy.

Prosper Mérimée (1803–70), a French novelist and playwright whose historical novels were highly regarded in his lifetime, was a civil servant whose interest in archaeology led to his being appointed Inspector of Ancient Monuments. His best-known work, *Carmen*, told the story of Don José, a simple country lad whose infatuation with the sultry gypsy temptress Carmen ends in tragedy, a story much of the details of which were somewhat altered by Bizet's librettists, not only to provide more opportunities for musical numbers but also to modify Mérimée's realism.

Bizet's opera was far from being an unqualified success at its first performances, many audiences and critics finding it too unusual in structure as well as shockingly immoral in content. It nevertheless achieved thirty-five performances in 1875 and was revived the following season. Gradually its popularity grew until in due course it became one of the best-loved of operas. Its composer, however, had died of a throat infection at the early age of thirty-six, three months after *Carmen*'s premiere.

As first performed in Paris, *Carmen* was an *opéra comique*, that is to say an opera with musical numbers separated by spoken dialogue. When it was staged in Vienna some months later in German translation, its dialogue was replaced by recitatives written by Bizet's friend and fellow composer Ernest Guiraud. For many years thereafter, *Carmen* continued to be heard with Guiraud's recitatives, but it is now almost invariably performed in its original version with dialogue. The 1964 edition by Fritz Oeser, a German musicologist, restored to the score music that had been discarded by Bizet before the opera's premiere; however, *Carmen*, which is now by far the most popular of French operas, works best on stage when performed in the original version that Paris audiences heard in 1875. Famous nineteenth-century composers such as Tchaikovsky, Brahms and Wagner expressed their admiration for *Carmen*, and Nietzsche declared it to be the perfect antidote to Wagnerian neurosis.

Act I. A square in Seville, with a tobacco factory on one side and a military guard-house on the other. Corporal Morales and the other soldiers on guard are idly observing the passers-by ('Sur la place, chacun passe') when Micaëla, a young woman with fair hair bound in plaits, enters and asks for a corporal called Don José. Morales tells her that José will arrive shortly with the changing of the guard. He and his fellow soldiers attempt to flirt with Micaëla, at which she shyly makes her escape.

Preceded by a gang of children imitating them, the new company of guards arrives, among them Don José and his superior officer, Lieutenant Zuniga. Before the guards they are replacing march off, Morales tells José that a pretty girl has been asking for him, and from his description of her José recognizes Micaëla. The factory bell now rings and the girls who work in the factory begin to saunter back after their break ('La cloche a sonné'), with the young men in the square making light-hearted attempts to intercept them. As the soldiers wonder where the most popular of the factory girls, the gypsy Carmen, can be, Carmen herself appears, expounding her fickle philosophy of love in the Habanera, 'L'amour est un oiseau rebelle', all the while keeping a provocative eye on José who appears to be paying no attention to her. As she finishes her song, Carmen flings a red flower in José's face and runs off into the factory with the other girls.

José retrieves Carmen's flower and places it in his tunic as Micaëla returns. She has brought from José's mother in the country a fond kiss, which she proceeds to deliver, and a letter in which his mother urges José to marry Micaëla, his childhood sweetheart ('Parle-moi de ma mère'). When Micaëla departs again, José tells himself that he will do as his mother asks – marry Micaëla, and forget the sorceress who threw him a flower. He is about to tear Carmen's flower from his tunic when an uproar begins in the factory and a number of factory girls emerge, some accusing Carmen of having stabbed another girl, while others side with Carmen. Zuniga sends José and two soldiers into the factory to investigate, and they return with Carmen, who refuses to answer any questions.

Ordering José to bind Carmen's hands, Zuniga goes off to write an order for her detention. Left alone with José, Carmen has little difficulty in persuading him to let her escape (Seguidilla: 'Près des remparts de Séville'). As José marches her away, she gives him a push, and he obligingly falls in the way of the other two soldiers accompanying them. Carmen escapes, and José is placed under arrest.

Act II. Lillas Pastia's tavern, by the ramparts of Seville. Carmen and two other gypsy girls, Mercèdes and Frasquita, have been dining with Lieutenant Zuniga, Corporal Morales and a third soldier. Carmen sings a lively gypsy song ('Les tringles des sistres tintaient'), with Mercèdes and Frasquita joining her in the refrain. Zuniga informs Carmen that the soldier who was sent to prison for allowing her to escape has now been released. Lillas Pastia is about to close the tavern for the night when a crowd is heard in the street outside, acclaiming the toreador Escamillo. When Escamillo and his admirers enter the tavern, the toreador is toasted by Zuniga and responds with a boastful song about his exploits in the bullring ('Votre toast, je peux vous le rendre').

When his approaches to Carmen are rebuffed, Escamillo leaves with his entourage. Zuniga also leaves, but tells Carmen he will return later. After the tavern's customers have all departed, Carmen and her friends are joined by Le Dancaire and Remendado, leaders of a gang of smugglers who use the inn as a base. In a quintet ('Nous avons en tête un affaire') the men describe their next expedition, for which they need the help of the girls to divert the attention of the customs officers. Carmen refuses to go with them, claiming that she is in love with the soldier who helped her and who has just been released after two months in prison. Le Dancaire suggests that Carmen should persuade her soldier to join them, and she agrees to try. The smugglers and the other two girls retire, leaving Carmen alone to await José, whose voice can now be heard raised in song as he approaches the tavern.

Carmen sets out to charm José by singing and dancing for him, but when he hears bugles in the distance sounding the retreat he tells her he must return to barracks immediately. However, when Carmen contemptuously orders him to rush back to his fellow soldiers if he is not interested in her, José takes from his tunic the flower she once threw at him, describes how it comforted him throughout his time in prison ('La fleur que tu m'avais jetée') and declares that he loves her. Carmen almost succeeds in persuading him to flee with her to the mountains

('Là-bas, là-bas, dans la montagne'), but he cannot bring himself to become a deserter. He is about to leave, when Zuniga returns for his hoped-for assignation with Carmen. The two men fight, but are separated by Le Dancaire and Remendado, who take Zuniga prisoner. Now hopelessly compromised, José departs for the mountains with Carmen and the smugglers.

Act III. A rocky gorge in the mountains. The smugglers and their companions are carrying contraband goods up to a hiding place, but decide to rest for an hour at the suggestion of Le Dancaire. Carmen and José are bickering. José reminds himself that down in the valley there lives a blameless old lady, his mother, who mistakenly believes him to be honest. But when Carmen tells him to go back to mother he reacts threateningly. Mercèdes, Frasquita and Carmen decide to tell their fortunes with a pack of cards. Lovers are predicted for the other two girls, but the cards turned up for Carmen all represent death ('Mêlons! Coupons!').

Le Dancaire orders the men to move the contraband goods while the women distract the attention of the customs officers. Left to stay on guard, José moves further up the mountain path, failing to see a guide entering from below with Micaëla, who has come at the behest of José's mother to attempt to rescue José from the clutches of the evil woman who has turned him into a criminal ('Je dis que rien ne m'épouvante'). Micaëla catches sight of José on his lookout above, just as he is raising his rifle to fire at someone further off. As he fires, Micaëla hides among the rocks in fear.

Escamillo, who had been José's target, now appears, examining the bullet-hole in his hat. Ordered by José to halt, he reveals his identity, and the two men chat amiably until Escamillo intimates that he has ventured into the smugglers' lair to visit Carmen, who he has been told is tired of her present lover, a deserter. In a jealous fury, José challenges Escamillo to a duel, and the two men fight with knives. Escamillo falls and is saved from being stabbed only by the intervention of Carmen, who arrives with the rest of the gang. Escamillo, as he leaves, invites the entire company to his next bullfight in Seville. José attempts to attack him again, but is restrained.

Micaëla, whose hiding place is now discovered, begs José to return with her to his mother. Carmen tells him to go, as he is clearly not cut out for the life of a smuggler, but José declares that he will never give her the opportunity to run off to a new lover. When Micaëla reveals that his mother is dying, José agrees to go with her, but assures Carmen that they will meet again. As he and Micaëla hurry away, the voice of Escamillo singing his toreador song can be heard in the distance. Carmen rushes off in the direction of the voice, while the others prepare to move.

Act IV. A square in Seville, in front of the bullring. Sellers of wine, fruit, water and fans circulate among the crowd of people entering the arena, among them Zuniga with Mercèdes and Frasquita. A procession of the participants in the bullfight marches past ('Les voici! Voici la quadrille'), and finally Escamillo appears, accompanied by a radiant and sumptuously attired Carmen. After the mayor has arrived to take his place at the head of the procession, Frasquita warns Carmen that José has been glimpsed lurking in the crowd. Catching sight of him, Carmen decides to stay in the square and confront him.

When the others have all entered the arena, José approaches. He implores Carmen to return to him, but she makes it clear that all is over between them. Although he continues to plead with her, she tells him flatly that she no longer loves him, that she was born free and that she will die free. Hearing the crowd inside acclaiming Escamillo, Carmen attempts to enter the arena, but José prevents her. Carmen admits that Escamillo is now her lover. When José again tries to persuade her to leave with him, she tears from her finger the ring he had once given her and flings it away. Mad with jealousy, José draws his knife. Carmen rushes towards the entrance to the bullring, but he blocks her way and stabs her in the heart. She falls lifeless to the ground and, as the crowd emerges from the arena, José confesses that he has killed her. He flings himself upon her body with a cry of 'Carmen, my adored Carmen!'.

Carmen has proved to be one of the most popular and immediately accessible of operas, full of tuneful solos and ensembles, and colourfully orchestrated in a style which, at least for the purpose of the opera, passes as authentically Spanish, and which also emphasizes brilliantly the work's most dramatic moments. The motifs representing Carmen and fate are appropriately and imaginatively re-scored as they reappear. Each of the opera's four acts is preceded by an orchestral movement – the prelude to Act I introducing, among other themes, the famous Toreador's Song; and each of the three entr'actes conveys the general mood of the act that follows.

In 1943 a Broadway musical, *Carmen Jones*, utilized and reorchestrated much of Bizet's score, with the opera's libretto updated and transferred by Oscar Hammerstein II to the American South during World War II and the characters turned into black Americans. Carmen is a worker in a parachute factory, José (renamed Joe) a corporal in the US army, and Escamillo (now Husky Miller) a boxer. *Carmen Jones* has often been revived, and a successful film version was made in 1954.

Recommended recording: Maria Callas (Carmen), Nicolai Gedda (Don José), Andrea Guiot (Micaëla), Robert Massard (Escamillo), with the Orchestre du Théâtre National de l'Opéra, Paris, conducted by Georges Prêtre. Maria Callas is a powerfully magnetic Carmen. Although she never performed the role on stage, she is completely convincing, and sings throughout with consummate ease. Intensely dramatic in the Card Scene of Act III, she is splendidly seductive in the Act I Habanera. Her impassioned José is Nicolai Gedda, whose fine vocal acting is matched by a superb assimilation of the French style. Andrea Guiot's individual French timbre helps to make Micaëla a very positive character, while Robert Massard brings Gallic flair, and again the right timbre, to the tricky role of Escamillo, successfully negotiating the awkward tessitura of the Toreador's Song which defeats so many baritones. The smaller roles are capably handled by experienced French performers, and Georges Prêtre conducts with style. The score used is that of the opera's 1875 premiere.

ALEXANDR BORODIN
(b. St Petersburg, 1833 – d. St Petersburg, 1887)

Prince Igor
(Knyaz' Igor')
opera in a prologue and four acts (approximate length: 3 hours, 30 minutes)

Igor Sviatoslavich, Prince of Seversk   *baritone*
Yaroslavna, his wife   *soprano*
Vladimir Igorevich, Igor's son   *tenor*
Vladimir Yaroslavich, Prince Galitzky, brother of Yaroslavna   *bass*
Konchak, a Polovtsian prince   *bass*
Gzak, a Polovtsian prince   *silent role*
Konchakovna, Konchak's daughter   *mezzo-soprano*
Ovlur, a Polovtsian   *tenor*
Skula, a gudoc player   *bass*
Eroshka, a gudoc player   *tenor*
Yaroslavna's Nurse   *soprano*
A Polovtsian Maiden   *soprano*

LIBRETTO BY THE COMPOSER, BASED ON A SCENARIO BY VLADIMIR STASOV; TIME: 1185; PLACE: THE CITY OF PUTIVL IN THE SEVERSK REGION, AND A POLOVTSIAN ENCAMPMENT; FIRST PERFORMED AT THE MARYINSKY THEATRE, ST PETERSBURG, 4 NOVEMBER 1890

Borodin's two great passions were music and chemistry. After graduating from the Academy of Physicians in St Petersburg, he adopted chemistry as his profession, although he had already begun to compose music. In due course he became a professor at the Academy of Physicians. His first work for the stage was a farce or parody, *The Heroic Warriors.* This was the only opera that Borodin actually completed, but it was by no means entirely original, much of its score being arranged from themes by other composers such as Rossini, Meyerbeer, Verdi and Offenbach. It was given only one performance at the Bolshoi Theatre, Moscow, in November 1867, after which it disappeared until the 1930s, when it was revived in Moscow only to be withdrawn again, this time due to government rather than public disapproval. A second opera, *The Tsar's Bride,* did not progress beyond a few sketches, which are now lost.

When the critic Vladimir Stasov sent Borodin the scenario for an opera, *Prince Igor,* which Stasov had based on what is supposed to be a twelfth-century Russian epic but which may be an eighteenth-century forgery, the composer turned his attention to it, at first enthusiastically. However, although he worked on it intermittently for some years, Borodin did not complete the opera. After his sudden death from heart disease it was completed and partly orchestrated by Rimsky-Korsakov and Glazunov. The opera now exists in several different performing editions, made at various times since its 1890 premiere, the most recent of which was put together in Russia and first performed in Vilnius in 1974.

Prologue. A square in Putivl. Igor, Prince of Seversk, is acclaimed as he prepares to lead his Christian army against the pagan Polovtsians who are threatening to attack the city. A sudden eclipse of the sun is regarded as a bad omen but, after saying farewell to his wife Yaroslavna, Igor departs, taking with him Vladimir, his son by his first wife. Two drunken musicians, Skula and Eroshka, desert from Igor's forces, preferring to serve under the irresponsible Prince Galitzky, Yaroslavna's brother.

Act I, scene i. Prince Galitzky's house. Galitzky's retainers, Skula and Eroshka among them, are carousing. The hedonistic Galitzky boasts of his light-hearted philosophy ('I hate a dreary life') and refuses to listen to a group of young women who enter to complain that one of their number has been abducted by his followers. Skula and Eroshka lead a drinking song in praise of Galitzky, whom his retainers would prefer as their ruler in place of Igor.

Act I, scene ii. A room in Yaroslavna's quarters. Yaroslavna, disturbed by evil dreams, pines for her husband. The young women whose companion has been abducted enter to seek Yaroslavna's aid. When Galitzky, her brother, arrives, Yaroslavna extracts from him a promise to release the girl. A group of boyars enters with the news that Igor's army has been defeated and that he and his son Vladimir have been captured by the Polovtsians, who are now marching on Putivl.

Act II. The Polovtsian camp. It is evening. Polovtsian maidens sing and dance for their mistress, Konchakovna, the daughter of Prince Konchak. During his captivity, Vladimir has fallen in love with Konchakovna. Her thoughts dwell on him ('Now the daylight dies'), and when he returns with the other prisoners from their forced labour, Vladimir makes his way to her. They embrace tenderly ('Is it you, my Vladimir?') but depart as Vladimir's father, Prince Igor, approaches.

Igor sings of his longing for freedom and of his love for Yaroslavna ('No sleep, no rest'). Ovlur, a Polovtsian who has secretly become a Christian convert, offers to help Igor escape, but the Prince rejects such dishonourable behaviour. When Prince Konchak himself offers him his freedom in return for a treaty of peace, Igor declines, insisting that if he were free he would immediately take arms against the Polovtsians. Konchak, appreciating Igor's frankness, orders his slaves to sing and dance for his guest's entertainment, offering Igor his choice of the dancing girls (the Polovtsian Dances).

Act III. The Polovtsian camp. Evening. Prince Gzak, a Polovtsian leader and Konchak's ally, arrives with his army, celebrating another victory. Word spreads in the camp that the town of Putivl has been captured, and Igor is urged by his followers to escape and continue the fight. After the carousing Polovtsian guards have fallen into a drunken stupor Ovlur enters, and this time Igor accepts his help for the sake of their cause. Torn between love and duty, Vladimir agrees to leave with his father, but Konchakovna raises the alarm and, although Igor escapes, Vladimir is recaptured. The guards are about to execute him when they are prevented by the entrance of Konchak, who magnanimously pardons Vladimir and allows him to marry Konchakovna.

Act IV. The city walls of Putivl. Yaroslavna laments the plight of her husband and her country ('Ah, bitterly I weep'), but is overjoyed to recognize Igor approaching the city on horseback, accompanied by Ovlur. Husband and wife embrace ecstatically, and hurry off to the citadel. Skula and Eroshka have been drunkenly playing their gudocs (old Russian three-stringed instruments), but when they see Igor they fear they may be punished for having deserted him. They decide to protect themselves by climbing the bell tower and ringing the bells to celebrate Prince Igor's return. The citizens assemble, joyfully acclaiming Igor as he and Yaroslavna emerge from the citadel. The two deserters are forgiven, and the entire populace confidently anticipates victory.

Prince Igor is a long and sprawling work whose third act (the one left most incomplete by Borodin) is often omitted from performance. Glazunov was responsible for finishing this act, and for writing out and orchestrating the opera's stirring overture, for Borodin had never written it down although Glazunov had often heard him play it on the piano. (Rimsky-Korsakov's major contribution to the completion of the opera was his orchestration of it.)

Although both he and his enemy, Konchak, are sympathetic characters, Igor himself is hardly the most exciting of heroes. If Borodin's opera continues to give pleasure, this is not only because of its beautifully lyrical and reflective arias but also, and especially, because of the savage, quasi-oriental splendour of the Polovtsian Dances, which have become widely popular outside the context of the opera.

Recommended recording: Mikhail Kit (Igor), Galina Gorchakova (Yaroslavna), Gegam Grigorian (Vladimir), Olga Borodina (Konchakovna), with the Kirov Opera chorus and orchestra, conducted by Valery Gergiev. Philips 442 537–2.

No one today conducts Russian opera more vividly and masterfully than Gergiev, and his Kirov company contains some of the finest of Eastern European singers. Gergiev's own performing edition of the opera is recorded here for the first time.

BENJAMIN BRITTEN
(b. Lowestoft, 1913 – d. Aldeburgh, 1976)

Peter Grimes
opera in a prologue and three acts (approximate length: 2 hours, 15 minutes)

Peter Grimes, a fisherman   *tenor*
A Boy Apprentice   *silent role*
Ellen Orford, a widow, schoolmistress   *soprano*
Captain Balstrode, retired merchant skipper   *baritone*
Auntie, landlady of The Boar   *contralto*

Her Two Nieces   *sopranos*
Bob Boles, fisherman and Methodist   *tenor*
Swallow, a lawyer   *bass*
Mrs Sedley, a widow   *mezzo-soprano*
Rev. Horace Adams, the rector   *tenor*
Ned Keene, apothecary   *baritone*
Dr Thorp   *silent role*
Hobson, the carrier   *bass*

LIBRETTO BY MONTAGU SLATER, BASED ON A POEM, *THE BOROUGH*, BY GEORGE
CRABBE; TIME: AROUND 1830; PLACE: THE BOROUGH, A FISHING VILLAGE ON THE
EAST COAST OF ENGLAND; FIRST PERFORMED AT SADLER'S WELLS THEATRE, LON-
DON, 7 JUNE 1945

The leading British composer of his time, Britten wrote music in a number of forms but was primarily interested in vocal music, and especially opera. His first work for the stage was an operetta, *Paul Bunyan*, written in collaboration with the poet W.H. Auden when Auden, Britten and Britten's lifelong companion, the tenor Peter Pears, were living in the United States in the early years of World War II. *Paul Bunyan* was staged at Columbia University, New York, in 1941. Britten's first opera was *Peter Grimes*, based on a poem by George Crabbe, an East Anglian poet of the late eighteenth and early nineteenth centuries, whose work the composer had first become acquainted with when Pears found a volume of Crabbe's poems in a second-hand bookshop in Los Angeles while he and Britten were visiting California in 1941.

George Crabbe is the author of a number of long poems that are really novels in verse. The best-known of them is *The Village*, written as a response to what Crabbe considered the artificialities of the pastoral convention as exemplified by Oliver Goldsmith's *The Deserted Village*. Another of Crabbe's long poems, *The Borough* (1810), is a description of life in a fishing village which is clearly Aldeburgh, the poet's birthplace. The poem is made up of twenty-four letters written in heroic couplets, one of which (Letter XXII) is about Peter Grimes, a character apparently based on an actual fisherman named Tom Brown who lived in Aldeburgh in the middle of the eighteenth century.

Back in England in 1942, after his American sojourn, Britten commissioned a libretto, based on the Peter Grimes episode in Crabbe's poem, from Montagu Slater, a poet and dramatist for some of whose plays Britten had provided incidental music. Britten and Pears had already begun to shape a libretto, using

Crabbe's poem as a starting point, and now, incorporating characters from other parts of the poem, for example Ellen Orford, the widowed schoolmistress (Letter XX), Slater updated the action of the drama from the latter part of the eighteenth century to around 1830, omitting Grimes's father, reducing the number of the fisherman's unfortunate apprentices from three to two, and promoting Ellen Orford to the position of Grimes's friend and confidante. The Peter Grimes of Britten and Slater is not really the sadistic, psychotic fisherman of Crabbe's poem, but an almost Byronic character at odds with the society of his time.

Britten began the composition of *Peter Grimes* in January 1944, completing it by February of the following year. The opera's premiere in June 1945 marked the return of the Sadler's Wells Opera Company to Sadler's Wells Theatre, which had been closed to the public during the war years and used as a rest-centre for evacuees. Peter Pears sang the role of Grimes, and Joan Cross, the company's director, appeared as Ellen Orford. The success of the opera was immediate and decisive. Within a comparatively short time Britten's fame as a composer of opera was worldwide, and he was encouraged to embark upon further operatic projects. *Peter Grimes* has a secure place in the international repertoire as one of the finest operas of the twentieth century.

Prologue. The interior of the Moot Hall, where an inquest is being held into the death of Peter Grimes's apprentice. Grimes explains that the boy died of exhaustion when the boat in which they were fishing in the North Sea was blown off course and they drifted for three days. The lawyer Swallow, acting as coroner, notes that Grimes had earlier saved the boy from drowning and brings in a verdict of death by accident, but Grimes observes angrily that the villagers will continue to blame him.

An orchestral interlude, depicting dawn, links the prologue and the first scene of Act I.

Act I, scene i. A street by the sea, with a view of the Moot Hall and the village's public house, The Boar. Grimes is finding it difficult to work his fishing boat single-handed. Ned Keene, the apothecary, says that he has found another workhouse orphan whom Grimes can purchase. When Hobson, the carrier, refuses to collect the Boy in his cart, Ellen Orford, the schoolmistress, offers to go with him and look after the lad on the journey ('Let her among you without fault cast the first stone'). Hobson and Ellen Orford depart, to the general disapproval of the villagers.

A storm begins, and the fishermen hasten to make their boats fast and bring in their nets. Balstrode, the retired captain of a merchant vessel, suggests to Grimes that he might be better off working on a ship at sea, away from the gossiping villagers, but Grimes's answer is that he feels rooted to his native landscape. He describes the dreadful occasion when his apprentice died at sea ('Picture what that day was like') and, when Balstrode has left, reflects on how his life could be transformed if he were to marry Ellen Orford ('What harbour shelters peace?').

An orchestral interlude portrays the storm.

Act I, scene ii. The interior of The Boar, that evening. The pub is full, with people continuing to arrive, seeking shelter from the storm. Mrs Sedley, a widow, nervously awaits the laudanum which, prescribed for her by Ned Keene, is to be delivered to her at the pub by Hobson. The two pretty Nieces of Auntie, the landlady, attract the drunken advances of Bob Boles, a fisherman and ardent Methodist. Balstrode intervenes and manages to avert a quarrel ('We live and let live and, look, we keep our hands to ourselves'). Grimes enters to await the arrival of his new Apprentice ('Now the Great Bear and Pleiades'). The mounting hostility of the other villagers to Grimes is defused by Ned Keene, who leads the company in a round ('Old Joe has gone fishing'). Despite the storm still raging when Hobson and Ellen Orford arrive with the Boy from the workhouse, Grimes insists on taking the Boy away immediately to the desolate hut in which he lives.

An orchestral interlude depicts Sunday morning in the village.

Act II, scene i. The street by the sea, as in Act I, scene i. Ellen Orford and the new Apprentice sit in the sun enjoying a view of the beach and the sea, while the Sunday morning service takes place in the parish church. Ellen notices that the Boy's clothes are torn and his neck bruised. When Grimes, who has caught sight of a shoal of fish not far out at sea, arrives to take the Boy fishing, Ellen protests that it is Sunday. Grimes reacts violently and drags the Boy away. His quarrel with Ellen has been overheard by some of the villagers, and when others emerge from the church the news is spread ('Grimes is at his exercise'). The men of the village decide to march to Grimes's hut to investigate, while Ellen, Auntie and her Two Nieces reflect on the sadness of their lives ('From the gutter, why should we trouble at their ribaldries?').

An orchestral interlude in the form of a passacaglia leads to the next scene.

Act II, scene ii. The interior of Grimes's hut, an old upturned boat on the edge of a cliff. Grimes is hastily getting his fishing gear together while attempting to soothe the frightened Boy. Hearing the sound of the villagers climbing the hill, he flings his nets out of the cliff-side door, roughly bundling the Boy out as well. Losing his footing, the Boy falls to his death. Grimes scrambles down the cliff after him, and when the men from the village burst into the hut they are surprised to find it neat and well-kept but with no sign of its occupants.

An orchestral interlude depicts moonlight.

Act III, scene i. The village street, a few nights later. A dance is being held at the Moot Hall, from which Auntie's Nieces emerge pursued by Swallow ('Assign your prettiness to me'). Neither Grimes nor his Apprentice has been seen for some days, but Mrs Sedley overhears Balstrode telling Ellen that Grimes's boat is back in its berth. Ellen has found, washed up on the beach, the jersey she embroidered for the Boy ('Embroidery in childhood'). Mrs Sedley communicates her suspicions to Swallow, who organizes a posse to hunt for Grimes.

An atmospheric orchestral interlude leads to the final scene.

Act III, scene ii. The street by the seashore, some hours later. A foghorn and the distant voices of the search party are heard, as a physically exhausted and mentally disturbed Grimes wanders onto the beach, where he is discovered by Ellen and Balstrode. Balstrode advises Grimes to take what seems the only course of action left to him, to take his boat out to sea, scuttle it, and sink with it. He helps Grimes to push the boat out, then leads Ellen away. As dawn breaks, people begin to emerge and a new working day commences. When the coastguard station reports a boat sinking out at sea Auntie dismisses it as a rumour, and the people of the fishing village go about their usual daily tasks.

The chorus plays a highly important role in *Peter Grimes*, a work whose strengths also include the impressive musical characterization of a number of individual roles, such as those of Bob Boles, Mrs Sedley, Swallow, Auntie and the Rev. Horace Adams. What makes *Peter Grimes* a great opera is Britten's creation of the complex, ambivalent character of Grimes himself, who gains the audience's understanding through the compassionate music the composer has lavished upon him. Peter Pears, the creator of the role, was the definitive Grimes for many years. In the 1960s and 70s the Canadian tenor Jon Vickers made the role his own, and more recent notable interpreters have included Robert Brubaker, Anthony Dean Griffey and Philip Langridge.

Recommended recording: Peter Pears (Peter Grimes), Claire Watson (Ellen Orford), James Pease (Captain Balstrode), with the chorus and orchestra of the Royal Opera House, Covent Garden, conducted by Benjamin Britten.

Of the several complete recordings of Peter Grimes, this one, conducted by its composer, is easily the best. Not all composers are their own best interpreters, but Britten was an exemplary conductor of other composers' music as well as his own, and the authoritative recordings of his operas featuring Peter Pears, for whom his leading tenor roles were conceived, are the versions to be preferred. Pears was an intensely moving Grimes on stage, and the essence of his interpretation is captured on these discs. The American soprano Claire Watson sings most beautifully the role of Ellen Orford, and James Pease, another American, makes a forthright and sympathetic Captain Balstrode. Other character roles are handled by such reliable British singers as Jean Watson, John Lanigan, Owen Brannigan, Geraint Evans, John Dobson and David Kelly, and the recording is marvellously atmospheric.

The Rape of Lucretia
opera in two acts (approximate length: 1 hour, 45 minutes)

Male Chorus   *tenor*
Female Chorus   *soprano*
Lucretia   *contralto*
Collatinus, her husband   *bass*
Tarquinius, Prince of Rome   *baritone*
Junius, a Roman general   *baritone*
Lucia, Lucretia's attendant   *soprano*
Bianca, Lucretia's nurse   *mezzo-soprano*

LIBRETTO BY RONALD DUNCAN, BASED ON THE PLAY *LE VIOL DE LUCRÈCE*, BY ANDRÉ OBEY; TIME: 500 BC; PLACE: ROME AND ITS ENVIRONS; FIRST PERFORMED AT GLYNDEBOURNE, 12 JULY 1946

Although the premiere of *Peter Grimes* by Sadler's Wells Opera in 1945 had been immensely successful, dissatisfaction with the management of the company and its artistic principles led Britten to compose his next opera for performance at Glyndebourne. *The Rape of Lucretia* was planned by Britten as a small-scale or chamber opera, scored for eight singers and an orchestra of no more than thirteen. Despite its description in the Glyndebourne programme as being based not only on André Obey's *Le Viol de Lucrèce* (a play first staged in 1931) but also on works by Livy, Shakespeare, Nathaniel Lee, Thomas Heywood and François Ponsard, Duncan's libretto stays fairly close to Obey's play.

The Rape of Lucretia was successful enough at its premiere to achieve seventy-five performances at Glyndebourne and on tour before the end of the year. On the opening night Peter Pears and Joan Cross, the two leading singers from the previous year's *Peter Grimes*, sang the roles of Male Chorus and Female Chorus, and Lucretia was the greatly admired contralto Kathleen Ferrier. Ernest Ansermet conducted.

Before the action begins, two solo singers, Male Chorus and Female Chorus, comment on the situation from a deliberately anachronistic Christian perspective ('Rome is now ruled by the Etruscan upstart').

Act I, scene i. A tent in an army camp outside Rome. Collatinus and his colleagues Tarquinius and Junius are drinking and discussing women. When six generals had ridden back to Rome the previous night after making bets on the fidelity of their wives, only Collatinus' wife Lucretia was found at home and alone. Junius' wife, the unmarried Tarquinius now reminds him, was discovered with a black lover. Tarquinius and Junius quarrel, but are separated by Collatinus. The three men drink a toast, proposed by Tarquinius, 'to the chaste Lucretia'. Tarquinius continues to taunt Junius, who is furious at hearing so much about the virtuous Lucretia. After Collatinus has retired to bed, Junius suggests to Tarquinius that not even he would dare attempt to put Lucretia's chastity to the test. Calling for his horse, Tarquinius immediately rushes off to do precisely that.

The Male Chorus describes Tarquinius's ride to Rome ('Tarquinius does not wait').

Act I, scene ii. Lucretia's house in Rome. Lucretia sits sewing in the company of Bianca and Lucia, who are seated at spinning wheels, while the Female Chorus comments with a spinning song. A loud knocking heralds the arrival of Tarquinius, who claims Lucretia's hospitality for the night. He is shown to a room.

Act II, scene i. Lucretia's bedroom. The Male Chorus and Female Chorus describe the political situation and revolutionary feeling in Rome. Lucretia is seen asleep in bed as the Female Chorus sings a lullaby. The Male Chorus now narrates the stealthy approach of Tarquinius to Lucretia's room ('When Tarquin desires, then Tarquin will dare'). Tarquinius awakens Lucretia with a kiss. In her sleep, dreaming of her husband Collatinus, she draws Tarquinius to her, but when she awakens she attempts to repulse him. However, he overcomes Lucretia and rapes her. The Male Chorus and Female Chorus comment on the scene in Christian terminology, invoking the compassion of Christ.

Act II, scene ii. Lucretia's house, next morning. While they arrange flowers, Lucia and Bianca sing of the beauty of the morning, and discuss whether it was Tarquinius whom they heard leaving on horseback before dawn. Lucretia enters in a trance-like condition, but becomes hysterical at the sight of the orchids she is given to arrange. She orders a servant to be despatched to Collatinus with an orchid and the message that it has been sent to him by a Roman harlot. She binds the remaining orchids into a wreath ('Flowers bring to every year the same perfection').

After Lucretia has left the room, Bianca asks Lucia to prevent the messenger from reaching Collatinus. It is too late, however, and soon afterwards Collatinus arrives with Junius, who alerted him after observing Tarquinius leave the camp at night and then return before dawn. Lucretia enters dressed in mourning ('Now there is no sea deep enough to drown my shame'), and tells Collatinus what has occurred. He attempts to comfort her, but she stabs herself and dies in his arms. The other characters, including the Male Chorus and Female Chorus, sing a threnody, and the Female Chorus then asks, 'Is this it all?' She is answered by the Male Chorus, who sings of man's redemption from sin through Christ ('It is not all').

Although it is not one of Britten's strongest or most colourful scores, there are a number of attractive lyrical passages in *The Rape of Lucretia*, a work whose libretto, with its stilted diction and solemnly dogmatic Christian commentary by the Male Chorus and the Female Chorus, has played a part in preventing it from becoming more widely popular.

Recommended recording: Janet Baker (Lucretia), Benjamin Luxon (Tarquinius), Peter Pears (Male Chorus), Heather Harper (Female Chorus), with the English Chamber Orchestra, conducted by Benjamin Britten. Decca 425 666–2. Janet Baker's Lucretia is both dramatically convincing and very beautifully sung. Benjamin Luxon brings Tarquinius vividly to life, and the comments on the action by the Male Chorus and Female Chorus are clearly articulated by Peter Pears and Heather Harper.

Albert Herring
opera in three acts (approximate length: 2 hours, 15 minutes)

Lady Billows, an elderly autocrat   *soprano*
Florence Pike, her housekeeper   *contralto*
Miss Wordsworth, head teacher   *soprano*
Mr Gedge, the vicar   *baritone*
Mr Upfold, the mayor   *tenor*
Superintendent Budd   *bass*
Sid, a butcher's assistant   *baritone*
Albert Herring   *tenor*
Nancy   *mezzo-soprano*
Mrs Herring, Albert's mother   *mezzo-soprano*

Emmie   *soprano*
Cis   *soprano*
Harry   *treble*

LIBRETTO BY ERIC CROZIER, BASED ON THE STORY *LE ROSIER DE MADAME HUSSON*, BY GUY DE MAUPASSANT; TIME: APRIL AND MAY 1900; PLACE: LOXFORD, A SMALL MARKET TOWN IN EAST SUFFOLK; FIRST PERFORMED AT GLYNDEBOURNE, 20 JUNE 1947

At the conclusion of the tour of *The Rape of Lucretia* in 1946, Britten and his colleagues decided to set up a permanent small-scale opera ensemble, to be called the English Opera Group. It was arranged that the group would perform at Glyndebourne the following year, so Britten set about composing a new opera, for the same size of ensemble as *The Rape of Lucretia*, but as different as possible in subject matter. He and his librettist Eric Crozier chose a subject whose basic idea they derived from a story, *Le Rosier de Madame Husson* (Madame Husson's Rose Bush), by the French novelist and short-story writer Guy de Maupassant (1850–93). They adapted the story very freely, transferring its action from Normandy to Suffolk, calling their opera *Albert Herring*, and making its leading character, Albert, much more innocuous than his French counterpart, Isidore, who indulges in a week of drunkenness and dissipation, after which 'he smelt of the sewer and the gutter and every haunt of vice'. Albert Herring does nothing worse than have a night on the town – a small market town.

At the Glyndebourne premiere of *Albert Herring*, Britten's two favourite singers were cast in leading roles for the third time. Peter Pears sang Albert, and Joan Cross was the formidable Lady Billows. The composer himself conducted, and the opera was well received.

Recommended recording: Christopher Gillett (Albert), Josephine Barstow (Lady Billows), Della Jones (Mrs Herring), Ann Taylor (Nancy), Gerald Finley (Sid), Robert Lloyd (Superintendant Budd), with the Northern Sinfonia conducted by Steuart Bedford. Collins Classics 70422. There is an earlier recording, conducted by the composer, but Peter Pears, although he was the creator of the role, was never believable as young Albert, and on disc he sounds too refined and middle-aged. Christopher Gillett's Albert is masterly, his youthful tenor perfect for the role. There is not a weak link in the cast, and Steuart Bedford conducts a witty account of the score, better even than Britten himself.

Billy Budd

opera in a prologue, two acts and an epilogue
(approximate length: 2 hours, 45 minutes)

Billy Budd, able seaman   *baritone*
Captain Vere, in command of HMS   *Indomitable tenor*
Claggart, master-at-arms   *bass*
Mr Redburn, first lieutenant   *baritone*
Mr Flint, sailing master   *bass-baritone*
Lieutenant Ratcliffe   *bass*
Red Whiskers, an impressed man   *tenor*
Donald, a sailor   *baritone*
Dansker, an old seaman   *bass*
A Novice   *tenor*
Squeak, ship's corporal   *tenor*
Bosun   *baritone*
First Mate   *baritone*
Second Mate   *baritone*
Maintop   *tenor*
The Novice's Friend   *baritone*
Arthur Jones, an impressed man   *baritone*
Four Midshipmen   *boys' voices*

LIBRETTO BY E.M. FORSTER AND ERIC CROZIER, BASED ON HERMAN MELVILLE'S
NOVELLA BILLY BUDD, FORETOPMAN; TIME: DURING THE ENGLISH–FRENCH WARS
OF 1797; PLACE: ON BOARD HMS INDOMITABLE; FIRST PERFORMED AT THE ROYAL
OPERA HOUSE, COVENT GARDEN, LONDON, 1 DECEMBER 1951

After *Albert Herring* in 1947, Britten's next work for the stage was a new version of John Gay's eighteenth-century ballad opera *The Beggar's Opera*, produced by the English Opera Group at the Arts Theatre, Cambridge, in May 1948. This was followed, in June 1949, by *Let's Make an Opera*, an entertainment for young people that incorporated a one-act opera, *The Little Sweep*. Later that year Britten received a commission from the Arts Council of Great Britain to compose a new opera for performance during the Festival of Britain year, 1951. He chose as his subject *Billy Budd, Foretopman*, a novella by Herman Melville (1819–91) which had been published posthumously in 1924, and engaged the novelist E.M. Forster and Eric Crozier, the librettist of *Albert Herring*, to write the libretto in collaboration.

Britten began to compose the opera in February 1950, and had completed it by the end of September 1951. He conducted the first performance of *Billy Budd* at the Royal Opera House, Covent Garden, on 1 December 1951, with a young American baritone, Theodor Uppman, in the title role, and Peter Pears as Captain Vere. Britten had composed the opera in four acts, and this was the form in which it was first staged. However, in 1960 he revised it, reducing its four acts to two. This definitive two-act version was first performed on BBC radio in November 1960.

Herman Melville, best known as the author of *Moby Dick*, completed *Billy Budd, Foretopman*, a parable of innocence destroyed by evil, only a few months before his death, expanding it from a short story, 'Baby Budd, Sailor', that he had written two or three years previously. The actual events that inspired him occurred not on an English vessel in 1797, where Melville places them, but on an American warship, the *Somers*, in 1842. Except for allowing Captain Vere to live to old age in order to appear in a prologue and epilogue in which he recalls the past, Forster and Crozier stayed close to Melville's novella in their adaptation which, unusually for an opera libretto, is for the most part written in prose, since Forster considered himself incapable of writing poetry. The opera is unusual also in that it contains no female roles.

Prologue. Captain Vere, an old man, meditates on his life and on what he has learned of good and evil. Even what is most good, he has found, has some flaw embedded in it. His thoughts go back to the year 1797 and to his ship, the *Indomitable*.

Act I, scene i. The main deck and quarterdeck of HMS *Indomitable*. Sailors are working on the main deck. When one of them, a young Novice, accidentally bumps into the Bosun and then slips on the deck, he is dragged away to be flogged. A boat returns from a press-ganging of some members of the crew of a passing merchant vessel. As the three new recruits are brought on board, Claggart, the *Indomitable*'s master-at-arms, steps forward to interrogate them. They are Red Whiskers, who protests at having been press-ganged, Arthur Jones, who responds meekly to Claggart's questioning, and Billy Budd, an extremely handsome young sailor who is enthusiastic about his transfer to the *Indomitable*, and whose only defect, a minor one, is that he occasionally stammers. When he calls out to his old ship, 'Farewell, Rights o' Man', the *Indomitable*'s officers assume that he is referring not to the ship he has just left, but to the liberal views expressed by Thomas Paine in his book *The Rights of Man*. He is marked out as a dissident and a potential troublemaker. Claggart orders Squeak, the ship's corporal, to keep an eye on Billy. The Novice who has been flogged is now brought back, unable to walk, and half-carried by other sailors. Dansker, an old seaman, befriends Billy Budd, warning him to beware of Claggart. The sailors sing enthusiastically of their captain, whom they call 'Starry' Vere, and Billy looks forward to serving under him.

Act I, scene ii. Captain Vere's cabin, a week later. Vere interrupts his reading of Plutarch to invite his officers to join him for a glass of wine. Mr Redburn and Mr Flint enter, drink the King's health, and begin to discuss the possibility of imminent action. The two officers express their opinions of the French ('Don't like the French'), and talk of the recent British naval mutinies at Spithead and the Nore. When the officers mention Billy Budd and his reference to the 'Rights o' Man', Vere assures them that Billy is not likely to cause trouble. The officers leave, and Vere resumes his reading as the sound of the crew singing a shanty drifts up from below decks.

Act I, scene iii. The berth-deck. Billy, Red Whiskers and another seaman, Donald, sing a shanty ('Blow her away'). When Dansker refuses to join in, claiming that he is too old and that all he wants is tobacco, Billy goes to his kitbag to get some, but finds Squeak in the act of rifling it. Squeak draws a knife, and they fight. In the ensuing commotion, Claggart appears. Told by Dansker what had caused the fight, Claggart has Squeak clapped in irons, and praises Billy.

When the seamen have retired to their hammocks, Claggart gives voice to his envy of Billy's handsomeness and goodness. He determines to destroy him, and persuades the Novice, who fears he will be flogged again if he disobeys, to tempt Billy, with money provided by Claggart, into leading a mutiny. The Novice goes to Billy's hammock to carry out this plan, but he succeeds only in making Billy angry and inducing his stammer. Dansker awakes, and Billy tries to explain to him what has happened. Dansker warns Billy that Claggart is his enemy, but Billy is convinced that Claggart thinks highly of him, and that he is likely to be promoted.

Act II, scene i. The main deck and quarterdeck, some days later. There is a heavy mist. Claggart begins to inform Vere of the imminent danger of mutiny, but he is interrupted by a shout from the maintop of 'Enemy sail on starboard bow', and the ship swings into action against a French vessel ('This is the moment'). A cannon is fired, but the French ship escapes in the mist. The crew disperses, and Claggart continues his story, claiming that Billy has offered gold to the Novice as an inducement to join a mutiny. An incredulous Vere angrily warns Claggart of the penalty for indulging in false testimony, but is forced to investigate his accusation and agrees to question Billy in Claggart's presence.

Act II, scene ii. Captain Vere's cabin. Vere is confident that Billy will be able to prove his innocence. Billy enters and, thinking that he has been summoned to hear of his promotion, talks enthusiastically and openly. Claggart is admitted and proceeds to charge Billy with incitement to mutiny. When Vere orders Billy to answer the charge, the lad's stammer prevents him from speaking. In frustration, he strikes Claggart, hitting him in the forehead and knocking him to the floor. Vere examines Claggart and discovers that he is dead. Sending Billy into the next room, he calls his two officers and convenes an immediate court-martial. Billy is brought in and has to admit that the facts, as stated by Vere, are true. He tries to explain that it was the only way he could answer Claggart's false charge, and he appeals to Captain Vere to save him, but Vere remains silent. Billy is sent out of the cabin again, and the officers have no option but to return a verdict of guilty. Billy is to be hanged the next morning. Vere, though he agonizes over having to destroy beauty and goodness, goes into the adjoining room to inform Billy of his fate.

Act II, scene iii. A bay of the gun deck, shortly before dawn the next day. Billy, in irons, calmly contemplates his fate ('Look, through the port comes the moonshine astray'). Dansker brings him grog and also the news that some of his shipmates are planning to rescue him, but Billy tells Dansker to stop them, for fate decreed that he strike Claggart, and fate has decreed, too, that Captain Vere should sentence him. When Dansker has left, Billy sings a farewell to life.

Act II, scene iv. The main deck and quarterdeck, at dawn. The ship's company assembles for the execution. As Billy is led out to be hanged, he turns to Captain Vere and cries, 'Starry Vere, God bless you!' At the moment of Billy's death, the seamen turn menacingly on Vere and his officers, but are forced by the marines to disperse.

Epilogue. The elderly Vere is seen, standing alone. He admits that he could have saved Billy, but tells himself that, in fact, Billy has saved him, and brought him peace and contentment.

Billy Budd has come to be recognized as one of Britten's finest operas, a work of psychological subtlety and immense compassion, with a richly orchestrated score of great power and lyrical beauty. Act I contains a most moving trio, after the flogging of the Novice, and in Act II Billy's ballad, the slow, melancholy tune with which he accepts his fate, is one of Britten's finest inventions.

Recommended recording: Peter Glossop (Billy), Peter Pears (Captain Vere), Michael Langdon (Claggart), Wandsworth School Boys Choir, Ambrosian Opera Chorus, with the London Symphony Orchestra, conducted by Benjamin Britten. Decca 417 428–2 Peter Glossop is an open and honest Billy, with Michael Langdon giving a masterly portrayal of the evil and repressed Claggart. Peter Pears, in the role he created on stage, is perfect as the equally repressed Captain Vere. The smaller roles are all well sung and firmly characterized, and the composer himself conducts impressively.

Gloriana

opera in three acts (approximate length: 2 hours, 30 minutes)

Queen Elizabeth I   *soprano*
Robert Devereux, Earl of Essex   *tenor*
Frances, Countess of Essex   *mezzo-soprano*
Charles Blount, Lord Mountjoy   *baritone*
Penelope, Lady Rich, sister of Essex   *soprano*
Sir Robert Cecil, secretary of the council   *baritone*
Sir Walter Raleigh, captain of the guard   *bass*
Henry Cuffe, a satellite of Essex   *baritone*
A Lady-in-Waiting   *soprano*
A Blind Ballad-Singer   *bass*
The Recorder of Norwich   *bass*
A Housewife   *mezzo-soprano*
The Spirit of the Masque   *tenor*
The Master of Ceremonies   *tenor*
The City Crier   *baritone*

LIBRETTO BY WILLIAM PLOMER; TIME: THE LATER YEARS OF ELIZABETH I'S REIGN; PLACE: ENGLAND; FIRST PERFORMED AT THE ROYAL OPERA HOUSE, COVENT GARDEN, LONDON, 8 JUNE 1953

The death of King George VI in February 1952 and the accession to the English throne of his daughter Elizabeth gave Britten the idea of writing an opera about Queen Elizabeth I and her relationship with the Earl of Essex. The Royal Opera commissioned the work, which Britten dedicated to Elizabeth II 'in honour of whose coronation it was composed', and *Gloriana* was given its premiere at the Royal Opera House, Covent Garden, on 8 June 1953, in the presence of the Queen and members of the royal family, with Britten's usual team of Joan Cross and Peter Pears in the leading roles of Elizabeth and Essex.

The audience on that glittering occasion, comprised largely of diplomats, civil servants and socialites, was hardly a musical one and, in the words of musicologist Eric Walter White, who was present, 'the atmosphere in the Royal Opera House, when compared with that of a normal opera or ballet performance [was] distinctly frigid.' Some people were of the opinion that the subject of the opera was not fitting for a coronation gala and, although subsequent performances were well attended, *Gloriana* came to be thought of as a failure. However, a concert performance at the Royal Festival Hall, London, on 23 November 1963 (the composer's fiftieth birthday), vindicated the work, and its stage revival in 1967 by the Sadler's Wells Opera Company, for which Britten made a few revisions to his score, was hugely successful.

Gloriana's libretto was written by the poet William Plomer, who took Lytton Strachey's volume of history *Elizabeth and Essex* as his starting point but soon moved away from it, becoming, as Plomer himself put it, 'less concerned than Strachey with the amatory motives of the two principal characters and more concerned with the Queen's pre-eminence as a Queen, a woman and a personality'.

Act I, scene i. Outside a tilting ground where a tournament is taking place. Cuffe watches the tournament and announces to the Earl of Essex that the winner is Lord Mountjoy. When Mountjoy emerges, having received his prize from the Queen herself, the envious Essex provokes him to a fight in which Essex is slightly wounded. Queen Elizabeth and her courtiers emerge from the tilting ground, and Elizabeth rebukes both men for fighting in her presence. She effects their reconciliation, urging them to attend her court as friends. The assembled courtiers and spectators acclaim the Queen.

Act I, scene ii. A private room of the Queen in Nonesuch Palace. Elizabeth is closeted with her adviser, Sir Robert Cecil, with whom she is discussing the rivalry between Essex and Mountjoy. She speaks of Penelope, Lady Rich, who is Essex's sister and Mountjoy's mistress, but when she expresses her admiration for Essex, Cecil warns her not to show too great an affection for the impulsive Earl. They turn to discussing affairs of state, and Cecil reports that a new armada may be on the way from Spain. Essex is announced. He enters and, when Cecil has left, the Queen asks him to sing to her. To his own lute accompaniment Essex sings two songs, the light-hearted 'Quick music's best when the heart is oppressed' and the more reflective 'Happy were he'. Essex asks the Queen to send him to Ireland to suppress a rebellion led by Tyrone, but Elizabeth resists, and dismisses him. Left alone, the Queen prays for the strength to rule her people wisely.

Act II, scene i. The Guildhall at Norwich. Attended by courtiers, among them Essex, Mountjoy, Cecil and Raleigh, Elizabeth is welcomed by the Recorder of Norwich. She thanks him for his greetings, and is acclaimed by the citizens. Asked if she will allow a masque to be performed in her honour, the Queen agrees, despite an expression of impatience from Essex, who still has Ireland on his mind. At the conclusion of the masque, which has consisted of six dances performed to a choral accompaniment, Elizabeth thanks the citizens of Norwich.

Act II, scene ii. The garden of Essex's house. Mountjoy awaits his lover, Penelope.

When she appears, a love duet ensues. In another part of the garden Essex and his wife, Frances, discuss the Queen's refusal to send Essex to Ireland. The two couples meet and, in a quartet, sing of their hope to gain greater power as the Queen ages. Although the Countess of Essex urges caution, they imagine themselves choosing the next ruler.

Act II, scene iii. The Palace of Whitehall, where a ball is in progress. The entire court dances a pavane. The splendour of the Countess of Essex's dress is commented upon, which makes her nervous as she fears it may incur the Queen's disapproval. After the next dance, a galliard, Elizabeth enters, makes a point of observing the Countess's attire and orders an energetic dance, 'La Volta', after which she commands the ladies to withdraw with her to change their linen. While they are out of the room a morris dance is performed for those who remain. When the ladies return, the Countess complains that while she was changing, her new dress was stolen. Suddenly the Queen enters wearing the dress, which is far too small for her. She strides about in it and then flounces out while Essex, Mountjoy and Penelope attempt to comfort the Countess. When the Queen returns, it is to announce that Essex is appointed Lord Deputy in Ireland, with a commission to put down Tyrone's rebellion. Everyone joins in dancing a celebratory coranto.

Act III, scene i. The Queen's private room in Nonesuch Palace. Ladies-in-waiting discuss Essex's failure to put down the rebellion in Ireland. Suddenly Essex appears, demanding to see the Queen. When he is told that she is not yet dressed, he sweeps a curtain aside and bursts into an inner chamber where Elizabeth is sitting at her dressing table without her wig. She dismisses her attendants and at first speaks sympathetically to Essex, but when he begins to complain of his enemies in England she accuses him of having failed in his duty to her. After he has left, the Queen finishes dressing, and Lord Cecil is admitted to her presence. He tells her that Essex has not only failed to subdue Tyrone, but has also returned to England with an unruly band of followers. The Queen orders that Essex be kept under guard.

Act III, scene ii. A street in the City of London. A Blind Ballad-Singer regales his audience with the story of Essex's attempt to lead a rebellion in England. His recital is interrupted, first by some of Essex's followers and then by the City Crier proclaiming Essex a traitor.

Act III, scene iii. A room in the Palace of Whitehall. Members of the council await the Queen, in order to inform her that Essex has been found guilty of treason. When Elizabeth arrives she refuses to sign Essex's death warrant. The Countess of Essex, Mountjoy and Penelope enter to plead for Essex's life, but Penelope's assertion that Essex deserves a pardon by virtue of his rank infuriates the Queen, and she hastily signs the warrant. The action now abandons realism. The Queen is seen standing alone, while various episodes that are to occur towards the end of her life pass before her eyes.

Although, because of its loose and almost pageant-like structure, *Gloriana* is less tautly dramatic than *Peter Grimes* or *Billy Budd*, it is one of Britten's most moving and richly melodic works. The hymn with which the Queen is acclaimed in the first scene is one of the composer's most delightful choruses, and throughout the opera there are a number of intimate lyrical ensembles. Elizabeth's soliloquy and prayer in the second scene are particularly impressive, as is her duet with Essex in the last act. Unfortunately the opera's final scene, abandoning music to resort to the spoken word, is something of an anticlimax. One wishes that Britten had composed a solo finale for Elizabeth.

Recommended recording: Josephine Barstow (Elizabeth), Philip Langridge (Essex), with the Welsh National Opera Chorus and Orchestra, conducted by Charles Mackerras. Argo 440 213–2.

The Turn of the Screw
opera in a prologue and two acts (approximate length: 2 hours, 30 minutes)

The Narrator/Peter Quint, a former manservant   *tenor*
The Governess   *soprano*
Miles   *treble*
Flora   *soprano*
Mrs Grose, the housekeeper   *soprano*
Miss Jessel, a former governess   *soprano*

LIBRETTO BY MYFANWY PIPER, AFTER A STORY, *THE TURN OF THE SCREW*, BY HENRY JAMES; TIME: THE MIDDLE OF THE NINETEENTH CENTURY; PLACE: BLY, AN ENGLISH COUNTRY HOUSE; FIRST PERFORMED AT THE TEATRO LA FENICE, VENICE, 14 SEPTEMBER 1954

After *Billy Budd* and *Gloriana*, Britten's two large-scale operas written for Covent Garden, it was time for the composer to consider the requirements of his English Opera Group and return for a time to writing operas on a smaller scale. While he was still at work on *Gloriana* he gave some thought to his next opera, which had been commissioned for the 1954 Venice Biennale. Britten chose as his subject Henry James's story *The Turn of the Screw* (1898), from which a libretto was fashioned by Myfanwy Piper. The first performance of the opera, given by the English Opera Group at the Teatro La Fenice in Venice on 14 September 1954, conducted by the composer, was a triumphant success. Peter Pears and Joan Cross, of course, played two of the leading roles. Some weeks later the opera was heard in Britain for the first time, during a two-week season given by the English Opera Group at Sadler's Wells Theatre, London.

Myfanwy Piper's libretto was extremely faithful to the spirit, and indeed the letter, of the Henry James story, with the exception that, as required by Britten, who intended to write music for the ghosts of Peter Quint and Miss Jessel to sing, and who had decreed that there would be 'no nice, anonymous supernatural humming or groaning', she provided words for the ghosts who in James's story remain chillingly silent. The opera consists of a prologue and sixteen scenes – eight scenes in each of its two acts – linked by orchestral interludes. Britten decided that these interludes should consist of a theme and fifteen variations. The theme is heard between the Prologue and the first scene of Act I, and each subsequent scene is preceded by one of the variations.

Prologue. A male Narrator begins to tell the story of the Governess who accepted a position looking after two orphaned children in a country house, a condition of her employment being that she should never communicate with their busy absentee guardian. (The Narrator is usually sung by the tenor who later in the opera performs the role of Peter Quint.)

Act I, scene i: 'The Journey'. The Governess, travelling by coach to the house in the country, wonders what she will find there.

Act I, scene ii: 'The Welcome'. The two children, Miles and Flora, practise bowing and curtseying as they and Mrs Grose, the housekeeper, await the Governess, who, when she arrives, finds the children charming.

Act I, scene iii: 'The Letter'. Mrs Grose gives the Governess a letter from Miles's school which states that he has been expelled. The two women watch the children singing an innocent nursery rhyme, and decide that the school has acted in error.

Act I, scene iv: 'The Tower'. As the Governess strolls in the grounds on a summer evening, thinking contentedly about the children, she suddenly observes the shape of a man on the tower of the house and is filled with dread.

Act I, scene v: 'The Window'. While the children are playing, the Governess sees the figure of the man again, in the window. She describes him to Mrs Grose, who recognizes him as Peter Quint, the master's valet who was dismissed for getting Miss Jessel, the children's former governess, pregnant, and who had also been very free with Miles. But Miss Jessel died before giving birth, and Quint was killed when he fell on an icy road. The Governess vows to protect the children, without bothering their guardian.

Act I, scene vi: 'The Lesson'. The Governess is giving the children a Latin lesson. Miles sings a strangely plaintive song about various meanings of the word 'malo'.

Act I, scene vii: 'The Lake'. The Governess sits by the lake with Flora. Asked to name all the seas she knows, the child ends with the Dead Sea. The Governess sees Miss Jessel on the other side of the lake and realizes that Flora must have seen her as well. She fears for the children's souls.

Act I, scene viii: 'At Night'. Miles is in the garden, when Quint's voice calls to him. Miss Jessel calls to Flora. When the Governess and Mrs Grose arrive, the ghosts disappear. Miles tells the Governess that he is bad.

Act II, scene i: 'Colloquy and Soliloquy'. The ghosts of Peter Quint and Miss Jessel sing of the power they exercise over Miles and Flora. They disappear, and the Governess enters, fearful that she will be unable to save the children ('Lost in my labyrinth').

Act II, scene ii: 'The Bells'. In the churchyard, Miles and Flora sing a religious duet, a benedicite, that never quite slips into outright mockery. Mrs Grose is reassured by their behaviour, but the Governess tells her that they are really 'with the others'. The Governess is still reluctant to contact the children's guardian, but after an odd exchange with Miles, ostensibly about the church bells, she thinks of leaving the house.

Act II, scene iii: 'Miss Jessel'. When the Governess enters the schoolroom she finds Miss Jessel sitting at a desk, lamenting her plight ('Here my tragedy began'). The Governess confronts her and she disappears. At last the Governess begins a letter to the children's guardian.

Act II, scene iv: 'The Bedroom'. Miles is singing his 'Malo' song to himself. The Governess enters and, unable to persuade him to confide in her, tells Miles she has written to his guardian. The boy hears the voice of Quint calling to him.

Act II, scene v: 'Quint'. At Quint's urging, Miles sneaks into the schoolroom, steals the letter the Governess has written, and takes it back to his bedroom.

Act II, scene vi: 'The Piano'. While Miles is playing the piano, to the admiration of the Governess and Mrs Grose, Flora slips away. When they become aware of her absence, the two women rush off in search of her, while Miles triumphantly plays on.

Act II, scene vii: 'Flora'. The two women discover Flora by the lake. Miss Jessel appears, but is not visible to Mrs Grose. Flora shouts abuse at the Governess, Mrs Grose takes the child away to comfort her, and the Governess is left in a state of despair.

Act II, scene viii: 'Miles'. Mrs Grose, shocked by what she has heard Flora utter in her sleep, takes the girl away to her guardian, though she and the Governess are now aware that he will not have received the Governess's letter. Miles confronts the Governess with great self-assurance. As she questions him about the letter, Quint hovers, warning the boy not to betray him. It is only when the Governess forces Miles to speak Quint's name that the ghost disappears. Miles, however, collapses and dies. The Governess sings the boy's 'Malo' song as a requiem.

Imaginatively scored for the thirteen instruments of its chamber orchestra, Britten's opera penetrates deeply and unerringly into the psychological world of Henry James's story. There is no doubt that it can prove immensely effective in the theatre.

Recommended recording: Helen Donath (Governess), Robert Tear (Peter Quint), Heather Harper (Miss Jessel), Ava June (Mrs Grose), Michael Ginn (Miles), Lilian Watson (Flora), with the Orchestra of the Royal Opera House, Covent Garden, conducted by Sir Colin Davis. Philips 446 325–2PH2

A Midsummer Night's Dream
opera in three acts (approximate length: 2 hours, 30 minutes)

Oberon, King of the Fairies   *counter-tenor or contralto*
Tytania, Queen of the Fairies   *coloratura soprano*
Puck   *spoken role*
Theseus, Duke of Athens   *bass*
Hippolyta, betrothed to Theseus   *contralto*
Lysander   *tenor*
Demetrius   *baritone*
Hermia, Lysander's lover   *mezzo-soprano*
Helena, Hermia's friend   *soprano*
Bottom, a weaver   *bass-baritone*
Peter Quince, a carpenter   *bass*
Flute, a bellows-mender   *tenor*

Snug, a joiner   *bass*

Snout, a tinker   *tenor*

Starveling, a tailor   *baritone*

Cobweb, a fairy   *treble*

Peaseblossom, a fairy   *treble*

Mustardseed, a fairy   *treble*

Moth, a fairy   *treble*

LIBRETTO BY BENJAMIN BRITTEN AND PETER PEARS, AFTER THE PLAY *A MIDSUM-MER NIGHT'S DREAM*, BY WILLIAM SHAKESPEARE; TIME: THE CLASSICAL PAST; PLACE: ATHENS AND A NEARBY WOOD; FIRST PERFORMED AT THE JUBILEE HALL, ALDEBURGH, 11 JUNE 1960

After *The Turn of the Screw* in 1954, Britten's next full-length work for the theatre was a score for *The Prince of the Pagodas*, a ballet that was first performed at Covent Garden in 1957. For his English Opera Group he composed *Noye's Fludde*, a one-act setting of the mediaeval Chester miracle play, performed in the church at Orford during the 1958 Aldeburgh Festival. After the 1959 festival, Aldeburgh's Jubilee Hall was renovated, its stage and orchestra pit enlarged and its seating capacity increased (to a modest 316). To celebrate these improvements, Britten decided to compose a new opera for the 1960 festival. *A Midsummer Night's Dream* was one of his favourite Shakespeare plays, and he set to work with Peter Pears to fashion a libretto from it, cutting Shakespeare's text by about half in order to reduce it to reasonable libretto-length, and beginning the action not at the court of the Duke of Athens as in the play, but in the forest (the play's Act II, scene i).

Britten began to compose the opera in October 1959, and had completed it by the following Easter. At its Aldeburgh premiere in June 1960, *A Midsummer Night's Dream* was an unqualified success, and when it entered the repertoire of the Royal Opera, Covent Garden, in the following year (with a larger complement of strings in the orchestra) it was enthusiastically received. It has remained one of the most popular of Britten's operas.

Act I. The wood, at twilight. Peaseblossom, Cobweb, Moth and Mustardseed, four attendants of Tytania, the Fairy Queen, encounter Puck, the messenger of Oberon, King of the Fairies. Oberon and Tytania are quarrelling because she refuses to give him one of her attendants, 'a lovely boy, stol'n from an Indian king'. When Oberon and Tytania meet in the wood, the quarrel breaks out anew ('Ill met by moonlight'). In order to be revenged on Tytania, Oberon orders Puck to fetch him a certain herb which has magical properties. Its juice, squeezed on Tytania's eyes as she sleeps, will cause her to fall in love with the first creature she looks upon when she awakes.

After Puck has departed on his errand, the lovers Lysander and Hermia enter, having fled from Athens in order to escape the cruel edict of Hermia's father that she should marry Demetrius. Alerted to their flight by Hermia's friend Helena, Demetrius follows them into the wood, himself pursued by Helena who loves him to distraction but whom he detests. When Puck returns with the magic herb, Oberon, who has overheard these young Athenians, tells him to take some of the juice and squeeze it on the eyes of 'the Athenian youth' (by whom he means Demetrius) when the next person he sees will be Helena. Oberon himself will deal with Tytania ('I know a bank where the wild thyme blows').

Six rustic artisans from Athens arrive to plan their rehearsals of a play, *Pyramus and Thisbe*, that they are hoping to present at the wedding festivities of Theseus, Duke of Athens, who is about to marry Hippolyta, Queen of the Amazons. After Peter Quince, the leader of the group, has allotted the parts and managed to dissuade Bottom, the weaver, from undertaking every role himself, they all leave, agreeing to return later to rehearse.

Lysander and Hermia reappear, lost, tired, and preparing to sleep on the ground. Thinking that he has found the young Athenian described by Oberon, Puck squeezes the magic juice on the sleeping Lysander's eyes. Demetrius now arrives, pursued closely by Helena. When he runs away from her, she awakens Lysander, only to be disconcerted by the ardent passion with which Hermia's lover addresses her. She flees, pursued by Lysander. Hermia awakes and, terrified at finding herself alone, rushes off in search of Lysander. Tytania enters with her attendants, who sing her to sleep with a lullaby. While she sleeps, Oberon enters and squeezes the magic juice on her eyes, bidding her awake 'when some vile thing is near'.

Act II. The wood, later that night. Tytania sleeps as the rustics rehearse their play. When Bottom (as Pyramus) makes an exit, the mischievous Puck, who has been observing the rehearsal, causes Bottom to return wearing an ass's head. Bottom's fellow actors scatter in terror, while to keep his spirits up Bottom sings loudly. His song ('The woosel-cock, so black of hue') awakens Tytania, who immediately falls in love with him, summons her fairies to attend on him ('Be kind and courteous'), and entreats him to stay with her. Soothed by the serenading of the fairies, Bottom eventually falls asleep in Tytania's arms.

Oberon is pleased with Puck's activities until Demetrius and Hermia appear and it becomes clear that Puck has anointed the wrong pair of eyes. As Demetrius sleeps, Oberon applies the magic juice to his eyes to ensure that he will love

Helena when he awakes. This indeed happens, but Helena, thinking that he is making fun of her, turns on him angrily, and quarrels also with her friend Hermia, whom she is convinced is part of the plot. Oberon is now furious with Puck, who makes amends by luring the four lovers to various parts of the forest, sending them to sleep, and ensuring that each will awake next to his true partner. Puck then squeezes a correcting dose of the magic juice onto Lysander's eyes.

Act III, scene i. The wood, early next morning. Oberon explains to Puck that he has now acquired the Indian boy, so Tytania is released from her spell and Bottom loses his ass's head. Oberon and Tytania celebrate their reconciliation with a courtly dance. The four lovers awake to discover with some bewilderment that they too are reconciled, Hermia with Lysander and Helena with Demetrius. They express their wonderment in a quartet, begun by Helena: 'And I have found Demetrius like a jewel'. Bottom awakes as his companions arrive in search of him. Their play, they tell him excitedly, is to be performed that evening before the Duke and his court.

Act III, scene ii. The Duke's palace, that evening. The rustics give a dreadful but spirited performance of *Pyramus and Thisbe* to an irreverent audience. At the stroke of midnight, after all have retired for the night, Oberon and Tytania arrive to bless the house and its inhabitants ('Now until the break of day'). Puck is allowed the last word.

A Midsummer Night's Dream is one of Britten's most entertaining operas, with an enchanting score written for a medium-sized orchestra and very imaginatively orchestrated. Oberon's counter-tenor voice gives him an ethereal, other-worldly quality, while the role of Puck, whose spoken lines are generally accompanied by trumpet arpeggios and drum, is a gift to an agile young actor. The rustics' play, as performed for the Duke of Athens and his guests, is a highly organized miniature *opera buffa*, the fourteen brief numbers of which delightfully parody the conventions and style of early nineteenth-century Italian opera; Pyramus's 'O grim-looked night', for example, offers an affectionate tongue-in-cheek homage to early Verdi. Britten differentiates superbly between the natural and the supernatural worlds in this lovable opera. In the words of the Britten authority Eric Walter White in 1948, 'Whereas formerly the only fully satisfactory Shakespeare operas could be said to be Verdi's *Macbeth*, *Otello* and *Falstaff*, now Britten's *Dream* must be added to that short but distinguished list.'

Recommended recording: Alfred Deller (Oberon), Elizabeth Harwood (Tytania), Peter Pears (Lysander), Thomas Hemsley (Demetrius), Josephine Veasey (Hermia),

Heather Harper (Helena), Owen Brannigan (Bottom), Stephen Terry (Puck), with the London Symphony Orchestra, conducted by Benjamin Britten. Decca London 425 663–2LH2

Death in Venice
opera in two acts (approximate length: 2 hours, 30 minutes)

Gustav von Aschenbach, a novelist   *tenor*
The Traveller/the Elderly Fop/the Old Gondolier/the Hotel Manager/the
   Hotel Barber/the Leader of the Players/the Voice of Dionysus   *baritone*
The Voice of Apollo   *counter-tenor*
The Polish Mother   *dancer*
Tadzio, her son   *dancer*
Jaschiu, Tadzio's friend   *dancer*

LIBRETTO BY MYFANWY PIPER, BASED ON THOMAS MANN'S NOVELLA *DER TOD IN VENEDIG*; TIME: 1911; PLACE: MUNICH AND VENICE; FIRST PERFORMED AT THE MALTINGS, SNAPE, 16 JUNE 1973

Britten's next operas after *A Midsummer Night's Dream* were three one-act pieces which the composer called parables, written to be performed in churches. These were *Curlew River* (1964), *The Burning Fiery Furnace* (1966) and *The Prodigal Son* (1968). *Owen Wingrave*, based on a short story by Henry James, was composed for television and first seen on BBC TV in 1971. Two years later it was adapted for the stage.

It was shortly after he had completed *Owen Wingrave* that Britten asked Myfanwy Piper to write the libretto of his next opera, a version of Thomas Mann's 1912 novella *Der Tod in Venedig* (Death in Venice). Britten began to compose the opera in December 1971, completing it by the end of 1972. At its first performances, in Snape as part of the 1973 Aldeburgh Festival, at Covent Garden later that year, and the following year at the Metropolitan Opera House, New York, in all of which Peter Pears, to whom the opera is dedicated, sang the role of Aschenbach, the work was received respectfully rather than enthusiastically. It was not until it was revived at Covent Garden in 1992, with Philip Langridge as Aschenbach, that *Death in Venice* came to be seriously reassessed and acclaimed as one of its composer's finest achievements.

In Thomas Mann's story, about a distinguished German author who is proud of his achievements and of his self-discipline, the author Gustav von Aschenbach leaves his home in Munich to travel to Venice, where he falls victim not only to sexual potentialities within himself of which he had previously been unaware, but also to a cholera epidemic. Mann's densely written novella is heavy with symbolism. Myfanwy Piper's libretto makes Aschenbach serve as narrator, and Britten's opera is almost an extended, interrupted monologue for Aschenbach, composed with the voice of Peter Pears in mind.

Act I, scene i: 'Munich'. The great writer Aschenbach, worried about his present inability to work, encounters a Traveller who talks of the marvels of distant places and urges him to 'Go, travel to the South'. Aschenbach decides that a holiday in the sun could well restore his flagging creativity.

Act I, scene ii: 'On the Boat to Venice'. Among the predominantly youthful passengers is an Elderly Fop with heavily rouged cheeks. Aschenbach thinks him disgusting and begins to wonder if he has made a mistake in deciding to go to Venice.

Act I, scene iii: 'The Journey to the Lido'. In a gondola, Aschenbach sings the praises of Venice, the 'Serenissima'. On their arrival at the hotel, the Old Gondolier, who has displeased him, does not wait to be paid. Aschenbach muses on the idea of a black gondola as a vision of death.

Act I, scene iv: 'The First Evening at the Hotel'. The obsequious Hotel Manager escorts Aschenbach to his room, which has a marvellous view of the beach. Among the hotel guests Aschenbach notices a Polish family, consisting of Mother, two daughters and a beautiful boy. Aschenbach meditates on the relationship of form and content, and the artist's sense of beauty.

Act I, scene v: 'On the Beach'. Aschenbach finds the atmosphere disagreeable. He watches the Polish boy playing with other youngsters on the beach and hears the boy's name, Tadzio.

Act I, scene vi: 'The Foiled Departure'. On a visit to the city proper, which he finds crowded and stifling, Aschenbach decides to leave Venice. He informs the Hotel Manager accordingly, but when he discovers that his luggage has been sent on to the wrong destination he changes his mind. He sees Tadzio playing on the beach and realizes it is the boy's presence that has made him reluctant to depart.

Act I, scene vii: 'The Games of Apollo'. Aschenbach watches Tadzio's participation in beach sports, and thinks that, through Tadzio, he might find the inspiration to resume writing ('The power of beauty sets me free'). When Tadzio, passing him on his way back to the hotel, smiles at Aschenbach, the writer exclaims, after the lad has gone, 'I love you!'

Act II, scene i: 'The Hotel Barber's Shop'. While having his hair cut, Aschenbach hears the first mention of a mysterious sickness that is causing people to leave Venice. His Barber refuses to be drawn on the matter.

Act II, scene ii: 'The Pursuit'. Aschenbach crosses from the Lido to the city, where he finds notices advising the citizens to take precautions against infection, but reads in a newspaper a denial that there is an outbreak of cholera. He follows the Polish family around the city and back to the hotel, without making any contact with Tadzio.

Act II, scene iii: 'The Strolling Players'. At the hotel, he watches a performance by a troupe of strolling players. When he questions the Leader of the Players about the plague, he receives an unsatisfactory reply.

Act II, scene iv: 'The Travel Bureau'. People are seeking information, and at first the Travel Clerk is evasive. However, he reveals to Aschenbach that 'the plague is with us', and advises him to leave.

Act II, scene v: 'The Lady of the Pearls'. Aschenbach wants to warn Tadzio's Mother of the danger, but when he sees her at the hotel he finds himself unable to speak to her.

Act II, scene vi: 'The Dream'. In his sleep he hears a debate between Apollo and Dionysus, which ends with a Dionysian dance of triumph. On waking, he recognizes the dream as symbolizing the struggle that is going on in his own mind.

Act II, scene vii: 'The Empty Beach'. Aschenbach watches Tadzio and his friends playing on the almost deserted beach.

Act II, scene viii: 'The Hotel Barber's Shop'. Aschenbach has his hair dyed and his cheeks rouged, in the style of the Elderly Fop who had so disgusted him on the boat to Venice.

Act II, scene ix: 'The Last Visit to Venice'. A rejuvenated Aschenbach takes a gondola to the city. Again he attempts to follow the Polish family around Venice. He buys some strawberries, but finds them musty and overripe. He soliloquizes about a debate between Socrates and Phaedrus on the subject of the poet's response to beauty.

Act II, scene x: 'The Departure'. Guests are leaving the hotel. Aschenbach goes to the deserted beach where Tadzio and his friends are playing. When Tadzio is knocked down by one of his friends, Aschenbach calls out. Tadzio beckons to him, but Aschenbach slumps dead in his chair. The boy walks away towards the sea.

Although it may look as if *Death in Venice* has a large cast, in fact it is virtually an opera for two solo voices and orchestra. The action – or rather the situation, for there is not a great deal of action – is dominated by the tenor voice of Aschenbach. The seven baritone roles are all intended to be performed by the same singer;

these cameo roles act as foils for Aschenbach or, more accurately, as one critic expressed it in reviewing the opera's 1973 premiere, 'they play Mephistopheles to Aschenbach's Faust, Lindorf to his Hoffmann.' Britten's richly coloured score is one of his most intriguing and, while *Death in Venice* may be too introspective a work to surpass *Peter Grimes* or *A Midsummer Night's Dream* in popularity, it is, in its uniqueness and complexity, undoubtedly a masterpiece.

Recommended recording: Peter Pears (Aschenbach), John Shirley-Quirk (the other roles), with the English Chamber Orchestra, conducted by Steuart Bedford. Decca London 425 669–2

This is conducted by Steuart Bedford, who took over the work's premiere when its composer was too ill to conduct. But Britten attended the subsequent recording sessions, and his guiding hand is evident throughout. Peter Pears is in remarkable voice for a tenor then in his mid-sixties, and brings consummate artistry and penetrating intelligence to his portrayal of an extremely taxing role. The cameo roles are all brought convincingly to life by John Shirley-Quirk.

FERRUCCIO BUSONI
(b. Empoli, 1866 – d. Berlin, 1924)

Doktor Faust
opera in two prologues, an interlude and three scenes
(approximate length: 2 hours, 30 minutes)

Doctor Faust   *baritone*
Wagner, his attendant   *bass*
Mephistopheles   *tenor*
The Duke of Parma   *tenor*
The Duchess of Parma   *soprano*
The Master of Ceremonies   *bass*
Gretchen's brother, a soldier   *baritone*
A Lieutenant   *tenor*
A Theologian   *baritone*
A Jurist   *baritone*
A Scientist   *baritone*

LIBRETTO BY THE COMPOSER; TIME: THE SIXTEENTH CENTURY; PLACE: WITTEN-
BERG AND PARMA; FIRST PERFORMED AT THE SÄCHSISCHES STAATSTHEATER,
DRESDEN, 21 MAY 1925

Primarily a composer of orchestral and piano music, the German–Italian Ferruccio Busoni, who was both composer and pianist, wrote four operas which, though they have not achieved great popularity, nevertheless have their admirers. (A fifth opera, the early *Sigune*, has remained unperformed and unpublished.) *Die Brautwahl* (The Bridal Choice; based on a story by E.T.A. Hoffmann) was first performed in Hamburg in 1912, and *Turandot* (taken from the play by Gozzi which Puccini was to use some years later) and *Arlecchino* were given their premieres on the same evening in 1917 in Zurich. Busoni had by this time already begun to compose his next and last opera, on the subject of the Faust legend. He had written his own libretto, based not on Goethe's great dramatic poem (used by Gounod for his *Faust*) but on sixteenth-century puppet plays and, to some extent, on Christopher Marlowe's play, *Doctor Faustus* (1588).

Busoni had been at work on *Doktor Faust* for more than eight years when he died in 1924, leaving the opera unfinished. Much of its penultimate scene and the whole of the final scene were composed by Philipp Jarnach, a young friend and colleague (but not, as some writers have asserted, a pupil) of Busoni, and *Doktor Faust* was given its premiere in Dresden the following year. Productions in Frankfurt and Berlin followed two years later, and a concert performance was given in London in 1937. In 1974 Busoni's sketches for the final scenes, which Jarnach had used, came to light, and a new completion of the opera by Antony Beaumont, based on this material, was staged for the first time in Bologna in 1985.

The opera begins with an orchestral introduction towards the end of which an unseen chorus sings the word 'Pax' (Peace). An actor steps before the curtain to explain how the opera came to be written.

First prologue. Faust's study in Wittenberg. Three students from Cracow present Faust with a book from which he will be able to acquire magic powers.

Second prologue. Faust's study, at midnight. With the aid of the book, Faust summons six of Lucifer's attendant spirits, the last of whom, Mephistopheles, claims to be 'swifter than the thoughts of mankind'. Faust signs with his own blood a pact with Mephistopheles. He will be given the fulfillment of every wish until his death, after which he will serve Mephistopheles for all eternity.

Interlude. A Romanesque chapel in a great cathedral. When the brother of

Gretchen, the young woman whom Faust has seduced and abandoned, vows to be avenged, Mephistopheles tricks soldiers into killing him.

Scene i. The park of the Duke's palace in Parma. Preceded by his reputation as a celebrated magician, Faust arrives during the Duke of Parma's wedding celebrations and makes the Duchess fall in love with him. The Duke tries to poison Faust but, warned by Mephistopheles, Faust escapes, followed by the Duchess.

Scene ii. A tavern in Wittenberg. As Faust discusses philosophy with quarrelsome students, Mephistopheles brings news of the Duchess of Parma's death, and throws the corpse of a newborn child on the floor to illustrate Faust's guilt. Mephistopheles then sets the corpse alight, and from the flames there arises the figure of Helen of Troy. The students from Cracow return to tell Faust that he is soon to die.

Scene iii. A street in Wittenberg. Faust, wandering in the snow-covered street, gives money to a beggar who is the Duchess of Parma clutching her dead child. Faust covers the child with his cloak, and with the aid of magic words projects his soul into the lifeless body. As Faust dies, the child stands up and walks away.

As can be seen from the above synopsis, Busoni's libretto is hardly a unified whole, nor does it possess much in the way of inner logic or dramatic coherence. His score, too, is an untidy assemblage of pieces taken from various other compositions, among them songs, piano music and unfinished orchestral sketches. However, the opera can succeed in the theatre when given clever and imaginative production.

Recommended recording: Dietrich Fischer-Dieskau (Faust), William Cochran (Mephistopheles), with the Bavarian Radio Chorus and Orchestra conducted by Ferdinand Leitner. DGG 427 413–2

This is, in fact, the only recording, but it is unlikely to be bettered. Fischer-Dieskau is a convincing Faust, and William Cochran a brilliantly charismatic Mephistopheles. The smaller roles are all splendidly performed, and Leitner conducts with great ardour.

EMMANUEL CHABRIER
(b. Ambert, Puy-de-Dôme, 1841 – d. Paris, 1894)

L'Étoile
(The Star)

opéra bouffe in three acts (approximate length: 1 hour, 30 minutes)

King Ouf I   *tenor*
Siroco, court astronomer   *bass*
Hérisson de Porc Épic   *tenor*
Tapioca, his secretary   *baritone*
Chief of Police   *spoken role*
Mayor   *spoken role*
Lazuli, a pedlar   *mezzo-soprano*
Princess Laoula   *soprano*
Aloès, wife of Herisson   *soprano*

LIBRETTO BY EUGÈNE LETERRIER AND ALBERT VANLOO; TIME AND PLACE: LEGEND-
ARY; FIRST PERFORMED AT THE BOUFFES-PARISIENS, PARIS, 28 NOVEMBER 1877

When Chabrier was sixteen his family moved from the country to Paris, where he studied for four years, obtaining a law degree and entering the Ministry of the Interior as a junior clerk. He remained a civil servant for eighteen years and devoted much of his spare time to studying music. He was past thirty when his first composition was published, and almost forty before he gave up his civil service job to devote himself entirely to music. His first musical success, while he was still a civil servant, was with *L'Étoile*, which was followed two years later by a one-act operetta, *Une education manquée* (An Unsuccessful Education). After he had the experience of hearing a performance of *Tristan und Isolde* in Munich, he wrote *Gwendoline*, which is Wagnerian in its use of the leitmotif, followed by *Le Roi malgré lui* (King in Spite of Himself), in which he reverted to the vein of elegant comedy that appears to have been his real *métier*. In his last years Chabrier lapsed into a state of acute melancholia verging on insanity.

Act I. A public square. King Ouf is wandering about the city in disguise looking for a suitable person to execute on his forthcoming birthday, for the King's birthdays are always marked by a public execution. He encounters a foreign ambassador named Hérisson, with his wife Aloès, his secretary Tapioca, and Laoula, the daughter of the neighbouring monarch. They are also disguised, and without Laoula's knowledge Hérisson's intention is to marry her to Ouf. The pedlar Lazuli, who is in love with Laoula, insults Ouf, and thus becomes the candidate for execution. However, when Ouf's astronomer Siroco reveals that Ouf and Lazuli are destined to die on the same day, Lazuli is reprieved and escorted into the palace.

Act II. The throne room in the King's palace. Aloès and Laoula are still disguised (as each other). King Ouf has Hérisson imprisoned, but he escapes. Lazuli and Laoula depart happily together, but Hérisson orders Lazuli to be shot. The sound of gunfire from the lake outside is heard, and Laoula is brought in. Lazuli is thought to have escaped.

Act III. Another room in the palace. Lazuli, who has swum safely ashore, returns. The women enter, and Laoula and Lazuli plan to elope again. Complications ensue when King Ouf arrives, but all ends happily with Ouf pardoning Lazuli, declaring him his heir and allowing him to marry Laoula.

The plot is confused, confusing and ridiculous, and there is far too much dialogue, but Chabrier's music, though hardly memorable, is light and pleasant, its style distinctly Offenbachian.

GUSTAVE CHARPENTIER
(b. Dieuze, 1860 – d. Paris, 1956)

Louise
opera in four acts (approximate length: 2 hours, 15 minutes)

Louise, a young dressmaker   *soprano*
Louise's Mother   *contralto*
Julien, a young artist   *tenor*
Louise's Father   *bass*
39 small roles – street sellers, workmen, dressmakers, beggars, etc.

LIBRETTO BY THE COMPOSER; TIME: 1900; PLACE: PARIS; FIRST PERFORMED AT THE OPÉRA-COMIQUE, PARIS, 2 FEBRUARY 1900

Charpentier studied composition in Paris with Massenet and in 1887 he was awarded the Prix de Rome for his dramatic cantata *Didon*. It was in Rome that he began the composition of his opera *Louise*, for which he wrote his own libretto based to some extent on a Paris adventure of his student days. It was to take him ten years to achieve a production of *Louise*, and when it was eventually staged at the Paris Opéra-Comique in 1900 it was a triumphant success. The work was acclaimed as a masterpiece of social realism which offered a new direction to French opera. In 1902 Charpentier founded a conservatoire to give free musical instruction to working-girls like his heroine, Louise; it functioned until the outbreak of war in 1914. Charpentier was unable to follow up the success of *Louise*. He produced a sequel, *Julien*, in 1913, but it failed to hold the stage. And although he lived on until the age of ninety-six, Charpentier never managed to complete any of his other operatic projects.

Act I. A room in a working-class tenement. This is where a young dressmaker, Louise, and her parents live. Through a window the studio where the young artist Julien lives and works can be seen. Julien serenades Louise, to the displeasure of her Mother. Her Father comes home and reads the letter that Julien has sent, asking for permission to marry Louise.

Act II. A street in Montmartre, with the house where Louise and other dressmakers work. Julien persuades Louise to abandon her parents and run away with him.

Act III. A little garden in Montmartre. Revellers enter the garden, and Louise is crowned Muse of Montmartre. Her Mother arrives and persuades Louise to return home to see her Father, who is dangerously ill and anxious to see her again.

Act IV. The room in the working-class tenement, as in Act I. Louise's Father recovers, and both parents try to persuade Louise to remain at home. When she refuses, her Father loses his temper and orders her out of the house. She flees to Julien, and her Father curses the city of Paris, which has taken her away from home and parents.

Charpentier's score is tuneful, its style revealing the influence of other composers such as Gounod and Massenet. Well known outside the context of the opera is Louise's lyrical aria in Act III, 'Depuis le jour' (Ever since the day), in which she sings of the happiness that has entered her life since she came to live with Julien.

FRANCESCO CILEA
(b. Palmi, 1866 – d. Varazze, 1950)

Adriana Lecouvreur
opera in four acts
(approximate length: 2 hours, 15 minutes)

Adriana Lecouvreur   *soprano*
Maurizio, Count of Saxony   *tenor*
Michonnet   *baritone*
Prince of Bouillon   *bass*
Princess of Bouillon   *mezzo-soprano*
The Abbé de Chazeuil   *tenor*
Quinault   *bass*
Poisson   *tenor*   ⎤ members
Mlle Jouvenot   *soprano* | of the
Mlle Dangeville   *mezzo-soprano* ⎦ Comédie-Française

LIBRETTO BY ARTURO COLAUTTI, BASED ON THE PLAY *ADRIENNE LECOUVREUR*,
BY EUGÈNE SCRIBE AND ERNEST LEGOUVÉ; TIME: 1730; PLACE: PARIS; FIRST
PERFORMED AT THE TEATRO LIRICO, MILAN, 6 NOVEMBER 1902

Cilea's first opera, *Gina*, staged at the Naples Conservatorium in 1889 while he was a student there, created a sufficiently favourable impression for the young composer to be taken up by an important publishing firm. His next opera, *La Tilda*, staged in Florence in 1892, was generally considered disappointing, but *L'Arlesiana* (The Woman from Arles) five years later did somewhat better at the Teatro Lirico, Milan, due mainly to the fact that its leading tenor role was sung by Enrico Caruso. Cilea's only real success came with *Adriana Lecouvreur*, staged in Milan in 1902 with Angelica Pandolfini in the title role and, again, Enrico Caruso in the leading tenor role.

The opera's libretto is based on a play, *Adrienne Lecouvreur*, by Eugène Scribe and Ernest Legouvé that was first performed in Paris in 1849. Adrienne Lecouvreur (1692–1730) was a French actress who was considered the greatest tragedienne of her day. She was famous not only for her roles in the plays of Corneille and Racine but also for her friendship with Voltaire, who wrote an elegy on her death after the church had refused to bury her in consecrated soil. Despite the denouement of both play and opera, it is not necessarily true that the actress was poisoned by a love rival.

Adriana Lecouvreur is still performed in Italy, but it has never achieved great popularity abroad. *Gloria* was a failure in 1907, withdrawn after two performances, and Cilea's sixth opera, *Il matrimonio selvaggio* (The Violent Marriage), composed in 1909, was never performed. Although he lived for another forty years Cilea ceased to compose. He became instead a distinguished teacher of harmony and composition.

Act I. The green room of the Comédie-Française. As the curtain is about to rise on a performance of Racine's *Bajazet*, the stage director, Michonnet, and members of the company make last-minute preparations. The Prince of Bouillon, the lover of La Duclos, one of the actresses, arrives with his friend the Abbé de Chazeuil and compliments the performers. Adriana Lecouvreur enters, rehearsing her lines, and modestly informs those present that she is merely the handmaid of the dramatist ('Io son l'umile ancella'). Michonnet, who has been secretly in love with Adriana for years, is about to propose to her when she confides in him that she is in love with an officer in the service of Maurizio, Count of Saxony. This officer, although she does not know it, is actually the Count himself, who now enters and confesses his love for her ('La dolcissima effigie sorridente'). She presents him with a small bouquet of violets for his buttonhole and goes on stage, promising to meet him after the performance.

The Prince of Bouillon intercepts a note, which he assumes to have been written by his mistress, La Duclos, inviting Maurizio to a rendezvous at her villa. As it is a villa in which he has installed La Duclos, he decides, out of spite, to invite the entire company there after the theatre. The note, however, was not from the Prince's lover but from his wife, who had in the past been Maurizio's lover. Maurizio decides for political reasons, namely his claim to the throne of Poland, to keep the rendezvous with the Princess, and sends a message to Adriana, breaking their appointment. Adriana accepts the Prince's invitation to the villa.

Act II. A room in the villa. The Princess awaits Maurizio, with whom she is still in love. He arrives, and as they talk she suspects he is in love with another woman. He gallantly offers her the violets that he is still wearing. Hearing other people arriving, the Princess takes refuge in an adjoining room. Adriana enters and now discovers the real identity of her lover. Michonnet arrives with a message for La Duclos. Adriana fears that La Duclos must be the lover of Maurizio but he assures her that the woman hiding in the next room is someone with whom his relationship is purely one of politics, and asks her to help the woman escape from the villa under cover of darkness. This Adriana does, but not before the two women have had time to suspect that they are rivals for the love of the same man.

Act III. A reception at the Prince of Bouillon's palace. The Princess, recognizing Adriana's voice as that of the woman she had encountered previously in a darkened room, tests Adriana by saying that Maurizio has been fatally wounded in a duel. Adriana swoons, but revives when Maurizio enters. Various complications ensue, and at the conclusion of a ballet entertainment Adriana and the Princess indulge in some verbal fencing. Adriana insults her rival by pointedly reciting a speech from Racine's *Phèdre* in which the heroine denounces promiscuous women.

Act IV. Adriana's house. It is her birthday. Michonnet and four of Adriana's fellow artists from the Comédie-Française come to offer their congratulations. When a box containing violets arrives, ostensibly from Maurizio, Adriana assumes he has sent the now withered flowers to signify the ending of their love. She gives way to her grief ('Poveri fiori'). But the flowers were sent by the Princess, who has sprinkled them with poison. When Adriana smells them she becomes ill. Maurizio arrives, swearing his devotion and asking her to marry him. She accepts joyously, but becomes delirious, collapses, and dies in his arms.

Cilea spreads his melodic gift thinly. Adriana's music is effective, though nothing else in the score is as memorable as her entrance aria, 'Io son l'umile ancella', the theme of which follows her through the opera.

Recommended recording: Renata Scotto (Adriana), Placido Domingo (Maurizio), Sherrill Milnes (Michonnet), with the Ambrosian Opera Chorus and the Philharmonia Orchestra, conducted by James Levine. Sony M2K79310. Renata Scotto is an exciting and moving Adriana, Domingo an ardent Maurizio, and James Levine conducts stylishly.

DOMENICO CIMAROSA
(b. Aversa, 1749 – d. Venice, 1801)

Il matrimonio segreto
(The Secret Marriage)
opera buffa in two acts (approximate length: 3 hours)

Geronimo, a rich merchant   *bass*
Carolina   *soprano* ⎤
Elisetta   *soprano* ⎦ his daughters
Paolino, Geronimo's clerk   *tenor*
Fidalma, Geronimo's sister   *contralto*
Count Robinson, an English nobleman   *bass*

LIBRETTO BY GIOVANNI BERTATI, BASED ON THE PLAY *THE CLANDESTINE MARRIAGE*, BY DAVID GARRICK AND GEORGE COLEMAN THE ELDER; TIME: THE EIGHTEENTH CENTURY; PLACE: BOLOGNA; FIRST PERFORMED AT THE BURGTHEATER, VIENNA, 7 FEBRUARY 1792

Cimarosa was one of the two most popular Italian composers in the second half of the eighteenth century. (The other was Paisiello.) He wrote nearly sixty operas, most of them comic, the most successful of which, *Il matrimonio segreto*, is the only one to be performed occasionally today. After making his name as the leading Neapolitan opera composer of his generation, Cimarosa in 1787 accepted an invitation to become composer to the court of Catherine II (Catherine the Great) in St Petersburg, where he spent the next four years. He subsequently moved to Vienna and succeeded Salieri as Emperor Leopold II's court Kapellmeister. The first performance of *Il matrimonio segreto* in Vienna in 1792 was so huge a success that the Emperor commanded a second performance to be given on the same evening, after dinner. The opera soon became famous throughout Europe.

Giovanni Bertati's libretto is based on the play *The Clandestine Marriage* (1766), which the famous English actor David Garrick wrote in collaboration with the playwright and theatre manager George Coleman the Elder. The idea for the play had come from William Hogarth's series of etchings, *Marriage à la mode*.

Act I. A room in Geronimo's house. Carolina, the younger daughter of the wealthy but deaf merchant Geronimo, has for some months been secretly married to Paolino, her father's young clerk. She and Paolino hope that the imminent arrival of Count Robinson, an impecunious Englishman, to marry Carolina's elder sister Elisetta, will enable them to confess to Geronimo that they are married, and to ask his blessing ('Cara, non dubitar'). Geronimo is delighted at the prospect of his elder daughter marrying into the aristocracy ('Udite tutti, udite'), but Count Robinson, when he arrives, clearly prefers Carolina ('Sento in petto un freddo gelo'). Geronimo's deafness prevents him from understanding the situation.

Act II. The same. Geronimo agrees to Count Robinson's marriage to Carolina ('Se fiato in corpo avete'). Paolino seeks the help of Geronimo's sister Fidalma, but she confesses that she is in love with him ('Pria che spunti in ciel aurora'). Paolino and Carolina plan to run away together, but are prevented by Elisetta, who arouses the household. The young lovers are forced to admit that they are married, Count Robinson resigns himself to Elisetta, Geronimo accepts the situation, and Fidalma contemplates spinsterhood.

The immediate success of *Il matrimonio segreto* in Vienna and throughout Europe is not difficult to understand, for it is an engaging and tuneful work, warmly and wittily scored, with attractive arias, duets and ensembles. Cimarosa's graceful score is almost Mozartian in style, though his musical characterization hardly matches that of Mozart in complexity.

Recommended recording: Arleen Auger (Carolina), Julia Varady (Elisetta), Dietrich Fischer-Dieskau (Geronimo), Julia Hamari (Fidalma), Ryland Davies (Paolino), Alberto Rinaldi (Count Robinson), with the English Chamber Orchestra conducted by Daniel Barenboim. DG 437 696–2GX3. Sparklingly conducted, and splendidly sung by all.

LUIGI DALLAPICCOLA
(b. Pisino d'Istria, 1904 – d. Florence, 1975)

Il prigioniero
(The Prisoner)
opera in a prologue and one act (approximate length: 1 hour)

The Mother   *soprano*
The Prisoner   *baritone*
The Gaoler   *tenor*
Two Priests   *tenor; baritone*
The Grand Inquisitor   *tenor*

LIBRETTO BY THE COMPOSER; TIME: THE SIXTEENTH CENTURY; PLACE: SPAIN; FIRST PERFORMED AT THE TEATRO COMMUNALE, FLORENCE, 20 MAY 1950

Dallapiccola studied in Graz and Florence, and began his musical career in 1926 as a pianist. He later began to compose, earning his living by teaching, and became one of the leading composers of his time, writing in a style which evolved from his enthusiasm for Mahler, Schoenberg and Berg. His first opera, *Volo di notte* (Night Flight), an imaginative work though rather mixed in style, was composed in the late 1930s and first performed in 1940. *Il prigioniero* (1950) subordinates the composer's musical prowess to his concern for modern man and his predicament. Dallapiccola wrote his own libretto, basing it mainly on a story, 'La Torture par l'esperance', from a volume of stories, *Nouveaux Contes cruels*, by Villiers de l'Isle-Adam, published in 1888. He also used other sources, among them the novel *La Legende d'Ulenspiegel* by Charles de Coster (1868). Dallapiccola's next opera, *Job* (1950), its text derived from the Bible, reveals the strong influence of Webern, whom he had met in Austria in 1942. His final opera, performed in Berlin in 1968, was *Ulisse*, a long, slow-moving work based on Homer.

Il prigioniero is set in a prison, which turns into a nocturnal garden.

Prologue. A Flemish freedom-fighter in a Spanish prison is treated in kindly fashion by his Gaoler.

Act I. Finding his cell-door open, the Prisoner escapes into the open air, only to find that he is in an enclosed garden where he is awaited by the Grand Inquisitor. He has been tortured by having been allowed to hope.

Dallapiccola's complex score, based on three twelve-note rows symbolizing prayer, hope and freedom, strongly supports what is happening on stage.

CLAUDE DEBUSSY
(b. Saint-Germain-en-Laye, 1862 – d. Paris, 1918)

Pelléas et Mélisande
opera in five acts (approximate length: 3 hours, 15 minutes)

Arkel, King of Allemonde   *bass*
Genevieve, mother of Pelléas and Golaud   *contralto*
Pelléas   *high baritone* ⎤
⎟ grandsons of King Arkel
Golaud   *baritone* ⎦

Mélisande   *soprano*
Yniold, Golaud's son from a former marriage   *treble or soprano*
A Shepherd   *baritone*
A Doctor   *bass*

LIBRETTO ADAPTED BY DEBUSSY FROM THE PLAY *PELLÉAS ET MÉLISANDE*, BY MAURICE MAETERLINCK; TIME: THE MIDDLE AGES; PLACE: THE IMAGINARY KINGDOM OF ALLEMONDE; FIRST PERFORMED AT THE OPÉRA-COMIQUE, PARIS, 30 APRIL 1902

Although he planned and began to write other works for the stage, among them a version of Edgar Allan Poe's *The Fall of the House of Usher*, the only opera that Debussy completed was *Pelléas et Mélisande*. He read Maeterlinck's play shortly after its publication in 1892, subsequently attended its premiere in Paris in May 1893, and then immediately sought and obtained Maeterlinck's permission to turn the play into an opera, adapting the playwright's text simply by omitting four of the scenes and making a number of other cuts in the dialogue. Debussy began to compose the opera in September 1893 and had completed a vocal score by August 1895. The orchestration, which he did not begin until the work had been accepted by the Opéra-Comique in 1898, took him a further three years to complete.

At the premiere of *Pelléas et Mélisande* critical opinion was divided. However, the opera was popular enough with audiences to be revived at the Opéra-Comique almost every season until the outbreak of World War I, and it has retained its place in the international repertoire.

The Belgian poet and playwright Maurice Maeterlinck was born in the same year as Debussy (1862) but lived on until 1949. He achieved international fame with his early symbolist plays, among them *Pelléas et Mélisande*, which compensate in atmosphere for what they lack in action or conflict. Later, Maeterlinck turned away from mystical examination of the inner life to a style that he himself described as more human and more truthful. His fairy-tale play *L'Oiseau bleu*, first produced by Stanislavsky in Moscow in 1908, was filmed many times.

Act I, scene i. A forest. Golaud, who has been out hunting and has lost his way in the forest, discovers a young woman weeping by a stream. She shrinks from him with a cry of 'Ne me touchez pas!' (Don't touch me), and answers his questions evasively. She has been hurt by someone, has run away long ago from somewhere, and is lost and frightened. She has dropped her golden crown into the stream, but she will not allow Golaud to retrieve it for her. She tells him her name, Mélisande, and agrees reluctantly to go with him, though he seems not to know where, for he tells her that he too is lost.

Act I, scene ii. A room in Arkel's castle. Golaud's mother, Genevieve, the daughter of Arkel, reads to the almost blind old King a letter sent by Golaud to his half-brother Pelléas, describing how he met Mélisande to whom he has now been married for six months, and about whom he still knows as little as when he first encountered her. In his letter, Golaud requests Pelléas to prepare Arkel for his arrival at the castle with Mélisande. Pelléas now enters. He has received another letter informing him that a friend is seriously ill and longing to see him before he dies. Pelléas wants to visit his friend, but Arkel insists that he await the return of his half-brother.

Act I, scene iii. Outside the castle. Genevieve and Mélisande are walking in the grounds, their conversation about darkness and light both wispily inconsequential and heavily symbolic. When Pelléas joins them, they observe down below in the harbour a ship putting out to sea. Mélisande recognizes it as the ship that brought her to Arkel's domain, and she fears that it may get wrecked in the storm which is threatening. Genevieve leaves, and Pelléas guides Mélisande down a steep path. He tells her he may be leaving the next day, and she asks him why.

Act II, scene i. A shady spot in the castle park. Pelléas and Mélisande are sitting by the well whose waters, he informs her, once had the power to restore the sight of the blind. Mélisande leans over the water, her long hair dangling into it. As she plays with the wedding ring given to her by Golaud, it slips from her hand and falls into the well on the stroke of noon. When Mélisande asks Pelléas what they should say to Golaud, he replies 'The truth'.

Act II, scene ii. A room in the castle. Golaud is lying on his bed, being nursed by Mélisande. He had been wounded, on the stroke of noon that day, when his horse suddenly fell, landing on top of him. Mélisande bursts into tears and Golaud tries sympathetically to discover why, but she is unable to tell him. He notices that she is not wearing her ring, and she says that it slipped from her finger when she was gathering shells for Golaud's son Yniold in a cave by the sea. In great agitation, Golaud tells her that she must find it immediately before the tide carries it away. If she is afraid of the darkness in the cave, she should take Pelléas with her. Mélisande leaves, weeping.

Act II, scene iii. The entrance to a cave. Mélisande enters the cave with Pelléas, pretending to look for her ring. She is afraid of the darkness. When a shaft of moonlight reveals three old beggars sleeping in the cave, she and Pelléas flee.

Act III, scene i. A tower of the castle. Mélisande sits at a window in the tower, combing her hair. Pelléas appears on a path below, tells Mélisande that he finds her beautiful, and asks to kiss her hand, for he must leave the next day. As she leans out of the window trying to reach him, her long hair falls down upon him. Pelléas winds it about himself, and the two of them confess their love for each other. They are interrupted by the arrival of Golaud, who chides them for their childish behaviour.

Act III, scene ii. The castle vaults. Golaud leads Pelléas down into the vaults where a stench of death arises from the stagnant water.

Act III, scene iii. Outside the vaults. As they emerge into the fresh air, Golaud tells Pelléas to avoid Mélisande as much as possible, for she is a delicate creature and is also pregnant.

Act III, scene iv. Outside the castle. Golaud roughly questions his son Yniold about the way Pelléas and Mélisande behave when they are alone together, and is frustrated by his son's innocently elusive answers. Finally he lifts Yniold onto his shoulders so that the child can see into a room where Pelléas and Mélisande are sitting silently, gazing fixedly at the light of a lamp.

Act IV, scene i. A room in the castle. Pelléas has been told by his father (who has been ill, and who never actually appears in the opera) that he must travel. Pelléas asks Mélisande to meet him by the well in the park that evening, for it will be the last time that they see each other.

Act IV, scene ii. The same. Arkel tells Mélisande that Pelléas's father is out of danger and that he hopes she will be able to bring sunshine and joy back to the castle. He pities her, for she seems so unhappy. Golaud enters and speaks brutally to Mélisande. He calls Arkel's attention to her wide-open eyes, to which the King replies that he sees in them only a great innocence. Golaud seizes Mélisande by the hair, forcing her to her knees, but then regains his composure, informing her coldly that she may do as she pleases for he will not spy upon her. After he has left, Mélisande bursts into tears, crying that she is not happy ('Je ne suis pas heureuse').

Act IV, scene iii. Near the well in the park. Yniold tries to retrieve his ball, which has rolled under a large stone. A Shepherd passes with his flock, and the boy has an enigmatic exchange with him concerning the bleating of the sheep.

Act IV, scene iv. The same. Pelléas says farewell to Mélisande, and they declare their love for each other. They hear in the distance the sound of the castle gates being shut and, as they embrace passionately, Mélisande tries to warn Pelléas that she can see Golaud crouching behind a nearby tree. Golaud rushes from his hiding place, sword in hand, and kills Pelléas. Mélisande flees, pursued by Golaud.

Act V. A bedroom in the castle. Mélisande, who has given birth to a daughter, lies dying. The Doctor assures Golaud that it is not the small wound he inflicted upon her that is causing her death. Golaud reproaches himself, asking Mélisande to tell him if her love for Pelléas was a guilty passion, but he does not know whether to believe her when she answers that it was not. The serving women fall to their knees as a sign that Mélisande has died.

The dramatic aspect of *Pelléas et Mélisande* is heavily, and in places impenetrably, symbolic. However, if one can surrender to its strange, shadowy world, the opera can prove rewarding. Debussy sets Maeterlinck's words in a declamatory style that stays close to the contours of spoken French. The great strength of the opera lies in Debussy's writing for the orchestra, which is where such dramatic tension as the work possesses is to be found. His harmonies owe much to Wagner and something to Mussorgsky's *Boris Godunov*, and his gently restrained orchestration has a translucent quality that is almost hypnotically effective.

Recommended recording: Maria Ewing (Mélisande), François Le Roux (Pelléas), José van Dam (Golaud), with the Vienna State Opera Chorus and the Vienna Philharmonic Orchestra, conducted by Claudio Abbado. DG 435 344–2. Made in conjunction with a staged performance at the Vienna State Opera, this is an exemplary account of the work.

LÉO DELIBES
(b. Saint-Germain-du-Val, 1836 – d. Paris, 1891)

Lakmé
opera in three acts (approximate length: 2 hours, 15 minutes)

Lakmé   *soprano*
Mallika, her servant   *mezzo-soprano*
Ellen   *soprano*
Rose   *soprano*
Mistress Bentson, a governess   *mezzo-soprano*
Gérald, an English officer   *tenor*
Frederic, an English officer   *baritone*
Nilakantha, a Brahmin priest   *bass-baritone*
Hadji, his servant   *tenor*

LIBRETTO BY EDMOND GONDINET AND PHILIPPE GILLE; TIME: THE NINETEENTH CENTURY; PLACE: INDIA; FIRST PERFORMED AT THE OPÉRA-COMIQUE, PARIS, 14 APRIL 1883

Best known for his ballet scores, of which the most famous is *Coppélia*, Delibes also wrote a number of operettas before turning to the composition of operas for the Opéra-Comique in Paris. *Le Roi l'a dit* (The King Says So, 1873) and *Jean de Nivelle* (1880) were followed by his masterpiece, *Lakmé*. Delibes began another opera, *Kassya*, which was completed after his death by Massenet and performed in Paris in 1893 to no great success.

It was the librettist Edmond Gondinet who suggested to Delibes the idea for *Lakmé*. Orientalism was very much in vogue in France at the time, and Gondinet recommended the novels of Pierre Loti, then at the height of his popularity, as a possible source for an opera to be set in the mysterious East. Loti (1850–1923) was a French novelist whose career as a naval officer took him to a number of distant places which he used as backgrounds for his romantic novels. It is usually stated by commentators that *Lakmé* is based on Loti's *Le Mariage de Loti* (1880), but the plot of this novel, set in Tahiti, bears only a general resemblance to that of *Lakmé*. Gondinet and his co-librettist, Philippe Gille, concocted a plot the ingredients of which were those of a typical Loti novel: an exotic locale, a European hero, an oriental heroine and an unhappy ending. (Puccini's *Madama Butterfly*, twenty-one years later, was to have its provenance in Loti's *Madame Chrysanthème*.)

Delibes wrote *Lakmé* between July 1881 and June 1882, and its premiere the following year at the Opéra-Comique in Paris was an immense success. The opera has retained its popularity in France and is occasionally to be encountered elsewhere.

Act I. A secluded garden, at dawn. In the background can be seen the house that Nilakantha, a Brahmin priest forbidden by the British rulers of India to practise his religion, has converted into a Brahmin temple. While Nilakantha broods on the day when the gods will bring him deliverance from the British, the voice of his daughter Lakmé can be heard within the house singing an invocation to the gods Dourga, Siva and Ganesa, with Hindu worshippers adding their voices to hers. Dismissing the worshippers, Nilakantha tells his daughter, whom he loves dearly, that he must leave her for a time, as he is to attend a religious festival to be held the next day in a nearby town.

Left alone, Lakmé and her servant Mallika prepare to bathe in the sacred stream that flows through the garden ('Dôme épais'). Lakmé removes her jewellery, which she places on a stone bench, and the two women step into a small boat and float downstream. After they have gone, a group of five English people break through the fence and enter the garden, exclaiming at its beauty and charm. They are Gérald and Frederic, officers in the British occupying army, accompanied by three women. Ellen is the daughter of the governor of the province and is engaged to be married to Gérald. Rose is Ellen's cousin, and the third woman, older than the others, is Mistress Bentson, Rose's governess. Although Frederic warns his companions not only that some of the flowers in the garden are poisonous but also that the house belongs to a dangerous Brahmin, the girls insist on exploring the garden. Frederic describes Nilakantha and his beautiful daughter to the others, and they discuss the differences between women's lives in India and women's lives in Europe.

When Frederic prevents the girls from examining the jewels left behind by Lakmé, pointing out to them that these foreigners and their religion are easily offended, Gérald suggests that the others return to town while he stays to sketch the jewels, whose design Ellen has said she would like copied. His companions leave, and Gérald handles the jewels, musing on their beautiful owner ('Fantaisie aux divins mensonges'). Hearing Lakmé and her servant returning, he hides. The young women arrive and pray to Ganesa to protect them, after which Mallika enters the house while Lakmé asks herself why, surrounded by the beauties of nature, she should feel simultaneously happy and troubled ('Pourquoi dans les grands bois').

Suddenly catching sight of Gérald, Lakmé gives a cry of alarm, which brings Mallika and Hadji, her father's servant, running to her aid. Realizing, however, that she is in no danger, she dismisses them and warns Gérald that a word from her would have brought about his death. She is aware that he is attracted to her, but urges him to leave the garden, which is a sacred place, and to forget her, a hand-maiden of the gods. Gérald refuses to leave. When she wonders what gives him the courage to face a terrible death, he replies that it is the god of youth and spring ('C'est le dieu de la jeunesse, c'est le dieu du printemps'). Lakmé's voice joins his in an ardent love duet, interrupted by the return of her father, whom Hadji had gone to fetch. Gérald makes his escape through the fence, as Nilakantha and other Hindus cry for vengeance on whoever has dared to enter their sacred ground.

Act II. A bazaar in the city. Soldiers, sailors, tourists and natives promenade through the crowded market-place, examining the wares on offer. Mistress Bentson, who has been separated from her party, is accosted by beggars, fortune-tellers and merchants, and has her watch stolen. Frederic comes to her aid as the market closes for the day and the festival begins. Girls perform exotic dances, at the conclusion of which Nilakantha enters in disguise, accompanied by Lakmé, whom he has brought with him to sing, hoping that her voice will attract the unknown intruder on whom he can then be avenged. Gérald, in answer to a query from his fiancée about the daughter of the Brahmin priest whom he had encountered in the garden, replies only that she was strange. Frederic tells Gérald that their regiment is to go into action early next morning against a group of native rebels.

Lakmé begins her song, which tells of an Indian maiden who charms wild beasts with her little bells, thus saving the life of someone who turns out to be the god Vishnu ('Où va la jeune hindoue?'). At first, no one appears in response to Lakmé's song, but she is forced to resume it just as Gérald and Frederic reappear among the crowd. When Lakmé, in mid-song, sees Gérald, she collapses in his arms, but then recovers herself and tries to continue singing. All this, however, has been observed by Nilakantha.

English troops march through the square, which empties as the crowd follows them. Nilakantha and his associates plan their revenge upon Gérald, and then leave. Gérald and Lakmé sing a love duet. Lakmé envisages a new life for them, in a little hut hidden in the forest where she can visit him every day, but Gérald protests that he could not leave his regiment. A religious procession of Brahmins comes into view, under cover of which Nilakantha creeps up on Gérald, stabs him and escapes in the crowd. Lakmé rushes to Gérald's side. Relieved to discover that he is only slightly wounded, she hopes now that he will be hers for ever and summons Hadji to help her remove him to her hut in the forest.

Act III. The hut in the forest. Gérald lies on a couch while Lakmé sings to him ('Sous le ciel tout étoilé'). When he awakens in a state of confusion she reminds him of what has happened and explains that Hadji carried him to the hut. Gérald expresses his happiness at being alone with her, far from the world ('Ah, viens, dans la forêt profonde'). In the distance they hear a chorus of lovers who have come to drink the waters of the sacred spring nearby in order to be blessed with eternal love. When Lakmé leaves to fetch water from the spring for Gérald and herself to drink, Frederic, who has followed Gérald's bloodstained trail through the forest, enters and appeals to Gérald, on his honour as a soldier, not to continue his unsuitable liaison, for their regiment is about to leave. Although he had apparently been willing to abandon Ellen, the woman to whom he is engaged, Gérald now cannot forget his duty.

Frederic leaves. Lakmé returns with a cup of the sacred water and notices a change in Gérald, who appears distracted as he listens to the distant sound of his regimental march. When she holds out the cup Gérald hesitates, and Lakmé realizes that all is over between them. While his attention is absorbed by the march, she tears a leaf from the deadly datura tree and chews it, unnoticed by Gérald. Observing her agitation, he agrees to stay with her, and together they drink the sacred water, which will make their love eternal. Lakmé then tells Gérald that she has taken poison. When Nilakantha rushes in, Lakmé confesses to him that she and the English officer have drunk the sacred water. Gérald utters a cry of despair as Lakmé dies, but the fanatical Nilakantha is content in the knowledge that his daughter has been received by the gods.

Although it can hardly be described as dramatically powerful, *Lakmé* is a charming piece, full of tuneful numbers of which the most popular, a favourite with coloratura sopranos, is the famous Bell Song ('Où va la jeune hindoue?'), sung by Lakmé in Act II. The Act I duet for Lakmé and Mallika ('Dôme épais') is especially attractive, as is much of Gérald's music, in which elegance triumphs over passion.

Recommended recording: Joan Sutherland (Lakmé), Alain Vanzo (Gérald), Gabriel Bacquier (Nilakantha), with the Monte Carlo Opera Chorus and Orchestra, conducted by Richard Bonynge. Decca 425 485–2. Richard Bonynge conducts the sweetly scented score impeccably, and Joan Sutherland tosses off the fiendish coloratura of Lakmé's Bell Song with careless ease. Her French colleagues give fine performances, Alain Vanzo ideal as Gérald and Gabriel Bacquier a vivid Nilakantha.

GAETANO DONIZETTI
(b. Bergamo, 1797 – d. Bergamo, 1848)

Anna Bolena
(Anne Boleyn)
opera seria in two acts (approximate length: 3 hours, 15 minutes)

Anna Bolena (Anne Boleyn)   *soprano*
Giovanna Seymour (Jane Seymour)   *mezzo-soprano*
Smeton   *mezzo-soprano*
Lord Riccardo Percy (Richard Percy)   *tenor*
Enrico VIII (Henry VIII)   *bass*
Lord Rochefort   *bass*
Hervey   *tenor*

LIBRETTO BY FELICE ROMANI; TIME: 1536; PLACE: WINDSOR AND LONDON; FIRST
PERFORMED AT THE TEATRO CARCANO, MILAN, 26 DECEMBER 1830

Donizetti's gift for opera was discovered while he was still a student in Bologna. His first success, *Enrico di Borgogna*, staged in Venice in 1818, led to commissions from other Italian theatres, and he quickly embarked upon a career of writing sub-Rossinian comic operas, though he was also capable of setting serious dramatic texts. Among his early serious operas are *L'esule di Roma* (The Roman Exile; 1828) and *Il paria* (The Outcast; 1829). It was with *Anna Bolena* in 1830 that he arrived at both his mature style and the beginnings of his international success.

The libretto of *Anna Bolena*, provided by Felice Romani, the leading Italian librettist of his day, was based on two plays, *Anna Bolena* by Alessandro Pepoli, performed in Venice in 1788, and *Enrico VIII*, an Italian translation by Ippolito Pindemonte of Marie-Joseph de Chénier's *Henri VIII*, which was first staged in Paris in 1791. At its premiere in Milan in 1830 Donizetti's opera was a resounding success, and it was soon being performed throughout Europe. At the end of the nineteenth century, however, it suffered from the change of taste brought about by the advent of the *verismo* style in opera. The work was to resurface in the middle of the twentieth century.

Act I, scene i. A hall of Windsor Castle. The assembled courtiers wonder why Enrico pays so little attention to his Queen, Anna. Giovanna, one of Anna's ladies-in-waiting, expresses her remorse at having aroused the King's passion, and Smeton, a page who is secretly in love with the Queen, sings consolingly to her ('Come, innocente giovane'). Giovanna wants to break off her relationship with the King ('Ah! Qual sia cercar non oso'), but Enrico tells her that soon she will have no rival.

Act I, scene ii. The park of Windsor Castle. Riccardo, a former lover of Anna, has been summoned back from exile by Enrico, as part of his plan to accuse Anna of infidelity. As arranged by Enrico, Anna unexpectedly encounters Riccardo when the royal hunting party passes through the park.

Act I, scene iii. The antechamber of the Queen's apartment in Windsor Castle. Smeton enters, carrying a locket containing the Queen's portrait. Hearing someone coming, he hides. Anna tells Riccardo that the King now hates her, at which Riccardo declares his love for her ('S'ei t'aborre, io t'amo ancora'), and when she repulses him he draws a sword to kill himself. This brings Smeton out of hiding, for he fears that the Queen is being attacked. Enrico arrives, Smeton inadvertently drops the locket, and the King has Anna, Smeton and Riccardo placed under arrest.

Act II, scene i. Anna's room in the Tower of London. Giovanna informs Anna that if she confesses her guilt and renounces her royal title the King has agreed to spare her life. Although she now realizes that Giovanna is her rival for the King's love, Anna blames Enrico and promises to pray for Giovanna, who expresses her remorse ('Dal mio cor punita io sono').

Act II, scene ii. Outside the council chamber. Courtiers are informed that, having been told that this was the only way to save her life, Smeton has confessed to a guilty relationship with the Queen. Enrico enters, encountering Anna and Riccardo as they are led in by guards. Accusations and counter-accusations of infidelity are made, before Anna and Riccardo are led away to their trial. Giovanna attempts unsuccessfully to soften Enrico's heart towards Anna, but it is suddenly announced that the Queen and her accomplices have been sentenced to death.

Act II, scene iii. A cell in the Tower of London. Anna's mind wanders as she faces death ('Al dolce guidami'). She is taken off to the executioner's block as the sounds of the populace acclaiming their new Queen are heard ('Coppia iniqua').

Anna Bolena is a splendid example of bel canto Romantic tragedy, with tuneful and affecting arias, a dramatic duet of confrontation for Anna and Giovanna in Act II, scene i, and a number of effective ensembles. The final scene, a masterpiece of dramatic construction and melodic inspiration, contains a moving aria for Anna (its opening theme indebted to Sir Henry Bishop's 'Home, Sweet Home'), with an impassioned cabaletta. Since its re-emergence on the stage in the middle of the twentieth century the opera has acted as a vehicle for sopranos such as Maria Callas, Leyla Gencer, Beverly Sills and Joan Sutherland.

Recommended recording: Edita Gruberova (Anna), Delores Ziegler (Giovanna), Stefano Palatchi (Enrico), José Bros (Percy), with the Hungarian Radio Chorus and Orchestra, conducted by Elio Boncompagni. Nightingale NC 070565–2. Edita Gruberova offers a persuasive interpretation of the title-role throughout the opera, culminating in her brilliant solo finale. The male roles are particularly well handled, with Palatchi dominating as Enrico and José Bros bringing an attractive timbre to the tenor role of Lord Riccardo Percy. Boncompagni conducts authoritatively, keeping the action flowing with brisk tempi.

L'elisir d'amore
(The Love Potion)
comic opera in two acts (approximate length: 2 hours)

Adina, a wealthy landowner   *soprano*
Nemorino, a young peasant   *tenor*
Belcore, a sergeant   *baritone*
Doctor Dulcamara, a travelling medicine man   *bass*
Giannetta, a peasant girl   *soprano*

LIBRETTO BY FELICE ROMANI; TIME: THE EARLY NINETEENTH CENTURY; PLACE: AN
ITALIAN VILLAGE; FIRST PERFORMED AT THE TEATRO DELLA CANOBBIANA, MILAN,
12 MAY 1832

After *Anna Bolena* in 1830, Donizetti's next four operas, three of them written for Naples and one for Milan, included nothing that enabled them to equal the success of that work. But in 1832 he composed a brilliant comic opera for the Teatro della Canobbiana in Milan – *L'elisir d'amore*. The text, by Felice Romani, was based on a libretto written by the French playwright Eugène Scribe for an opera, *Le Philtre* by Daniel Auber, staged the previous year in Paris. Scribe's plot, in turn, had been taken from an Italian play, *Il filtro*, by Silvio Malaperta. Although Romani followed Scribe's plot closely, he made a number of modifications, including the addition of scenes that reduce the element of coquettishness in the French work and introduce instead a note of charming pathos. Donizetti had no more than two months in which to compose his opera, which was for him more than sufficient time. At its premiere *L'elisir d'amore* was a huge and immediate success, and one which proved to be enduring. The critic of the *Gazzetta privilegiata di Milano* wrote:

> The composer was applauded for every piece, and when the curtain fell at the end of the acts he was acclaimed time and time again on the stage with the singers, collecting his honourable and merited reward. The musical style of this score is lively, brilliant, truly of the comic genre. The shading from comic to serious can be observed taking place with surprising gradations, and the emotional aspects are treated with that musical passion for which the composer of *Anna Bolena* is famous. Instrumentation that is always rational and brilliant, constantly adapted to the situations, an instrumentation that discloses the work of a great master, accompanies a vocal line now lively, now brilliant, now passionate.

Act I, scene i. Outside Adina's farmhouse. Nemorino, a young peasant who is hopelessly in love with Adina, a rich landowner, watches as Adina sits under a tree reading a book, surrounded by a group of her farm workers ('Quanto è bella'). Adina laughs derisively at the story she is reading of Tristan and Isolde, who fall in love after swallowing a magic potion. A drumroll announces the arrival of a regiment of soldiers, headed by the swaggeringly self-confident Sergeant Belcore, who immediately begins to declare his passion for Adina ('Come Paride vezzoso').

When he is at last left alone with Adina, the shy Nemorino tries to make his feelings known to her, but she replies that, although she considers him a kind and agreeable youth, she is not in love with him, and in any case she is capricious by nature ('Chiedi all'aura lusinghiera').

Act I, scene ii. The village square. Doctor Dulcamara, an itinerant medicine-man, arrives, and begins to sell to the gullible villagers his medicines to cure all ills ('Udite, udite, o rustici'). Nemorino asks Dulcamara if he has any of the potion used by Queen Isolde, and he is sold an elixir (actually a bottle of cheap red wine) which the doctor assures him he has only to drink in order to have his passion reciprocated. The elixir, Dulcamara explains, will take a day to have its effect. (By then, the doctor will have moved on to the next village.)

Nemorino begins immediately to sample the elixir and is quite merry by the time Adina appears. Puzzled by Nemorino's apparent indifference to her, Adina accepts a proposal of marriage from Sergeant Belcore. Even the announcement that they will marry six days hence fails to shake Nemorino's composure, for he is certain that by the next day Adina will have begun to love him. He is upset, however, when Belcore, whose regiment has suddenly been ordered to leave the next morning, brings the wedding date forward to that evening ('Adina, credimi'). While everyone else joyously anticipates the wedding celebration, Nemorino anxiously speeds up his consumption of the elixir.

Act II, scene i. Inside Adina's farmhouse. To the villagers assembled for her imminent wedding to Sergeant Belcore, Adina sings a comic duet with Doctor Dulcamara ('Io son ricco e tu sei bella'). Disturbed by the non-appearance of Nemorino, Adina postpones signing the marriage contract. When Nemorino does arrive, he tells Dulcamara that he is in urgent need of another bottle of the elixir. The doctor duly provides another bottle, and agrees to wait an hour to be paid for it. Nemorino earns the money for the elixir by agreeing to join Belcore's regiment in return for a cash payment ('Venti scudi').

Act II, scene ii. The village square. The girls of the village have discovered that, although he does not yet know it, Nemorino's wealthy uncle has just died, leaving him a fortune. When Nemorino appears, the girls all crowd around him affectionately, which he of course attributes to the magic qualities of the elixir. Seeing Nemorino surrounded by all the village maidens, Adina becomes jealous. Dulcamara boasts to her of the efficiency of his elixir, and when Adina discovers that Nemorino has enlisted in order to pay for a magic potion to win her love she begins to realize that she cares for him as deeply as he does for her. She goes off to buy back Nemorino's enlistment papers from Belcore.

Nemorino recalls the furtive tear he noticed in Adina's eye when she discovered him with the village girls. He is sure this means that she really loves him ('Una furtiva lagrima'). Adina returns and hands Nemorino his enlistment papers, telling him that she has set him free ('Prendi, per me sei libero'); but when it seems that she has nothing further to say to him, he rejects the papers, telling her that if she does not love him he may as well die in battle. This at last brings a confession of love from Adina. Belcore greets the changed situation philosophically, and all join in praising a surprised but self-congratulatory Doctor Dulcamara and his magic elixir.

L'elisir d'amore and the later *Don Pasquale* are Donizetti's masterpieces of comic opera, not only by virtue of their expert construction, attractive and believable characters and sparkling music, but also, especially in the case of *L'elisir d'amore*, because of their composer's ability to inject sentiment and feeling into the texture of the comedy. *L'elisir d'amore* differs in this respect from the most famous of all Italian comic operas, Rossini's *Il barbiere di Siviglia*, whose characters are presented externally as creatures of farce. Donizetti's characters inhabit a world not of farce but of romantic comedy, and the superiority of *L'elisir d'amore* over the composer's earlier comic operas lies predominantly in its musical characterization. Adina's tenderness, which lies below her high-handed flirtatiousness, Belcore's pompous virility, Dulcamara's engaging shiftiness, Nemorino's simplicity and deep feeling – all these qualities are conveyed in the changing moods of Donizetti's score. *L'elisir d'amore* and *Don Pasquale* are both immensely entertaining comic operas, but if *L'elisir* is even more enjoyable than *Pasquale*, this is surely because of its greater human warmth, both in libretto and in score.

From the first high-spirited bars of its prelude to the end of its equally joyous finale, there is not a dull moment in this delightful score. Donizetti's melodic gift is profusely deployed throughout the opera, even in the comic patter of Dulcamara's music. The opera's great moment of pure sentiment arrives with the tenor's beautiful Act II aria 'Una furtiva lagrima', Nemorino's great outpouring of love for Adina. A *locus classicus* of the bel canto style, it was inserted at Donizetti's insistence, his librettist Romani having complained that an aria at this point would hold up the action.

Nemorino is really the star role in this opera, and it has attracted some of the greatest tenors, in the last half century one of the most superb of whom was the great Swedish tenor Nicolai Gedda. Of one of his Covent Garden performances a critic observed that he came out on stage to sing 'Una furtiva lagrima' with the air of a man who knew that, at its conclusion, he would receive an ovation. And he always did. Other notable singers in this role include Roberto Alagna, Luciano Pavarotti and José Carreras.

Recommended recording: Mariella Devia (Adina), Roberto Alagna (Nemorino), Pietro Spagnoli (Belcore), Bruno Pratico (Dulcamara), with the Tallis Chamber Choir and English Chamber Orchestra conducted by Marcello Viotti. Erato 4509–91701–2. This engaging comedy does not lack recommendable recordings, among them a Decca version conducted by Richard Bonynge, with Joan Sutherland sailing impressively through the role of Adina, and Luciano Pavarotti an appealing Nemorino. There is also a fine Philips recording with Katia Ricciarelli a sympathetic Adina and José Carreras a touching Nemorino. But first place must go to Erato's account of the opera, with Mariella Devia an adorable Adina, and opera's current tenor heart-throb, Roberto Alagna, not only singing the role of Nemorino beautifully but also presenting a vivid characterization as the love-sick peasant. The conductor, Marcello Viotti, brings out all the charm and vivacity of Donizetti's irresistible score.

Lucrezia Borgia
opera seria in a prologue and two acts (approximate length: 2 hours, 15 minutes)

Lucrezia Borgia, Duchess of Ferrara   *soprano*
Maffio Orsini, a young nobleman   *mezzo-soprano*
Gennaro, a young soldier   *tenor*
Don Alfonso, Duke of Ferrara   *bass*

LIBRETTO BY FELICE ROMANI, BASED ON VICTOR HUGO'S PLAY *LUCRÈCE BORGIA*; TIME: THE EARLY SIXTEENTH CENTURY; PLACE: VENICE AND FERRARA; FIRST PERFORMED AT THE TEATRO ALLA SCALA, MILAN, 26 DECEMBER 1833

Four operas, all of them written very quickly, separate Donizetti's 1832 *L'elisir d'amore* from his 1833 *Lucrezia Borgia*. They are *Sancia di Castiglia, Il furioso all' isola di San Domingo* (The Madman on the Island of San Domingo), *Parisina* and *Torquato Tasso*. Although they were successful enough at their premieres in Naples, Rome and Florence, by the end of the nineteenth century all had ceased to be performed. They have been revived in recent years, but none is likely to become popular. After *L'elisir d'amore*, Donizetti's next opera for Milan was *Lucrezia Borgia*, this time commissioned by La Scala (then, as now, the leading Italian theatre). Felice Romani was again the librettist, his text based on *Lucrèce Borgia*, a new play by Victor Hugo which had just been staged in Paris. Donizetti received Romani's libretto towards the end of November 1833, and composed the opera at his usual manic speed, finishing it in time for a premiere at La Scala less than a month later.

The critic of the leading Milan newspaper described *Lucrezia Borgia* as 'little better than mediocre'. Nevertheless, it proved popular with audiences, was performed at La Scala thirty-three times during that first season and was soon being produced throughout Italy and abroad. Performances in the first half of the twentieth century were rare outside Italy, but in the last half-century the opera has been staged elsewhere several times.

Prologue. The terrace of a palace in Venice. Gennaro, Orsini and their friends have been enjoying the carnival. Orsini describes how he and Gennaro were once warned by a mysterious figure dressed in black to keep away from the Borgias ('Nella fatal di Rimini'). A masked woman sings tenderly to Gennaro as he sleeps ('Com' è bello'), but when she is unmasked by Orsini as the infamous Lucrezia Borgia who has poisoned many of their relatives, Gennaro and the others turn from her in loathing.

Act I. A square in Ferrara. The interest shown by Lucrezia in Gennaro is misunderstood by her husband, Don Alfonso, Duke of Ferrara, who suspects that she is having an affair with him ('Vieni, la mia vendetta'). But Gennaro is actually Lucrezia's son by a previous marriage. When he is arrested on Alfonso's orders for having insulted the Borgia family, Lucrezia arranges Gennaro's escape.

Act II. The Negroni palace in Ferrara. At a banquet, Orsini sings a lively drinking song ('Il segreto per esser felice'). When Lucrezia appears, announcing that she has poisoned them all, she is shocked to discover Gennaro among them. He refuses the antidote she offers him and is horrified when she confesses that she is his mother. He dies in her arms, and Lucrezia also collapses and dies.

To a much greater extent than in any earlier serious opera by Donizetti, the drama in *Lucrezia Borgia* is impelled by the music. Orsini's romanza 'Nella fatal di

Rimini', in the Prologue, is a highly dramatic narrative, and in Act I Alfonso's aria, 'Vieni, la mia vendetta', and its cabaletta, 'Qualunque sia l'evento', possess an energy that is positively Verdian. Lucrezia's aria 'Com' è bello', sung over the sleeping form of her son, is exquisite and a gift to any soprano able to draw a firm, pure legato line. Famous sopranos who have played the part of the eponymous heroine include Montserrat Caballé, Leyla Gencer, Beverly Sills and Joan Sutherland. The opera's best-known number is Orsini's drinking song in Act II. Although its score is uneven, *Lucrezia Borgia* is an opera that can prove highly effective when performed by first-rate singers with a proper appreciation of its style.

Recommended recording: Joan Sutherland (Lucrezia), Giacomo Aragall (Gennaro), Marilyn Horne (Orsini), Ingvar Wixell (Alfonso), with the London Opera Voices and the National Philharmonic Orchestra, conducted by Richard Bonynge.

  Decca 421 497–2. Joan Sutherland is magnificent, Aragall sings stylishly, and thanks to Richard Bonynge's research the recording includes extra material for the role of Gennaro, including a newly discovered aria.

Maria Stuarda
(Mary, Queen of Scots)
opera seria in three acts (approximate length: 2 hours, 30 minutes)

Maria Stuarda (Mary, Queen of Scots)   *soprano*
Elisabetta (Queen Elizabeth I)   *soprano*
Anna, a lady-in-waiting   *mezzo-soprano*
Leicester   *tenor*
Talbot   *bass*
Cecil   *bass*

LIBRETTO BY GIUSEPPE BARDARI, BASED ON FRIEDRICH VON SCHILLER'S PLAY *MARIA STUART*; TIME: 1587; PLACE: LONDON AND FOTHERINGHAY CASTLE IN NORTHAMPTONSHIRE; FIRST PERFORMED (AS *BUONDELMONTE*) AT THE TEATRO SAN CARLO, NAPLES, 18 OCTOBER 1834

After *Lucrezia Borgia*, Donizetti composed *Rosmonda d'Inghilterra*, an opera about the English King Henry II and his mistress Rosamund Clifford. Not one of his stronger scores, it was followed by another operatic lesson in English history, *Maria Stuarda*, a much finer work, whose libretto by Giuseppe Bardari, a seventeen-year-old law student, was based on the play *Maria Stuart* by the German poet and playwright Friedrich von Schiller (1759–1805).

The opera had been commissioned by the Teatro San Carlo, Naples. However, after it had been given a successful final rehearsal *Maria Stuarda* was banned by order of the King of Naples, presumably because his Queen, Maria Cristina, was a direct descendant of Maria Stuarda (Mary, Queen of Scots). Donizetti had no option but to adapt his music to a revised text, with the names of the characters changed and the action moved to thirteenth-century Florence.

As *Buondelmonte*, the opera was given its first performance in Naples in October 1834. It was received coolly, and Donizetti withdrew his score, determined to have the work staged elsewhere in its original form. *Maria Stuarda* finally reached the stage at La Scala, Milan, on 30 December 1835. After only six performances, some of which were incomplete due mainly to the leading soprano's illness, the Milan authorities banned the opera. The emergence in the second half of the twentieth century of such fine dramatic coloratura sopranos as Joan Sutherland, Montserrat Caballé, Leyla Gencer and Beverly Sills led to the successful revival of *Maria Stuarda*, which is now one of the more popular of Donizetti's serious operas.

Act I. A gallery in the Palace of Westminster. Courtiers and ladies await the return of Queen Elisabetta from a tournament given in honour of the French ambassador. Elisabetta enters, wondering whether to accept an offer of marriage from the French King. Her heart, she reveals in an aside, is engaged elsewhere ('Ah, quando all' ara scorgemi'). Talbot urges her to show mercy to her cousin Maria Stuarda, whom Elisabetta has imprisoned at Fotheringhay Castle, but Cecil's advice is that she should have Maria put to death. Leicester, the man whom Elisabetta secretly loves, arrives, and the Queen asks him to deliver to the King of France her acceptance of his proposal. When Leicester appears not to be upset by this, Elisabetta begins to suspect that he may be in love with Maria.

After the Queen and courtiers have left, Leicester and Talbot discuss Maria. Talbot, who has visited her at Fotheringhay, gives Leicester a letter from her, and a miniature portrait of her ('Questa imago, questo foglio'). Elisabetta returns, and Leicester is obliged to show her the letter, in which Maria requests a meeting with her. Leicester asks the Queen to grant Maria's request, and she agrees to do so, although she is now almost certain that Leicester is in love with Maria ('Sul crin la rivale').

Act II. The grounds of Fotheringhay Castle. Maria Stuarda, accompanied by her lady-in-waiting Anna, rejoices in the beauty of her surroundings, but envies the clouds that are free to waft towards her native France ('O nube che lieve per l'aria ti aggiri'). The sounds of a hunting party are heard, and Maria, realizing that Elisabetta must be hunting in the grounds, becomes apprehensive at the prospect of encountering her. She is about to retreat indoors when Leicester appears and advises her to humble herself before Elisabetta in order to soften the Queen's heart. Maria is at first reluctant to agree, but Leicester swears he will take action himself if Elisabetta remains obdurate.

When the two queens meet, Maria kneels at Elisabetta's feet, asking for her for-giveness ('Morta al mondo'), but Elisabetta, envious of Maria's beauty and dignity, replies contemptuously, until finally Maria is stung into addressing Elisabetta as the 'figlia impura di Bolena' (the unchaste daughter of Anne Boleyn), and calling her a 'vil bastarda' (vile bastard) by whose presence the English throne is pro-faned. Elisabetta's immediate response is to condemn Maria to death.

Act III, scene i. A gallery in the Palace of Westminster. The Queen is seated at a table with Maria's death warrant before her. She hesitates to sign it, not because she feels any compassion for Maria but because she wishes to avoid the recrimination which she fears will follow. Cecil urges her to sign, and when Leicester enters she quickly signs the warrant, telling him that she has done so. Leicester begs for clemency, but Elisabetta orders him to witness Maria's execution ('Vanne, indegno').

Act III, scene ii. Maria Stuarda's room in Fotheringhay Castle. Cecil and Talbot deliver the death warrant to Maria, who receives it without flinching. When Cecil has left, Talbot, who wears a cassock beneath his cloak, reveals that he has come as a Catholic priest to hear Maria's confession. He does so, and absolves her ('Lascia contenta al carcere').

Act III, scene iii. A room next to the execution chamber. Maria prepares her-self for death, asking Cecil to tell Elisabetta that she forgives her. Leicester enters to utter his grief-stricken farewell, and Maria goes calmly to her death ('Ah! Se un giorno').

Although Bardari's libretto is a travesty of Schiller's *Maria Stuart*, eliminating almost all of the playwright's political and religious references, it retains the play's chief emotional situations, around which Donizetti was able to construct an impressive opera. Not all of its numbers reach the same high level of achieve-ment, but the confrontation of Elisabetta and Maria in Act II and the opera's final scenes with Maria's confession and preparation for death are highly affecting. Her confession duet with Talbot has a scale, intensity and inexorable forward move-ment that puts one in mind of Verdi.

Recommended recording: Joan Sutherland (Elisabetta), Huguette Tourangeau (Maria Stuart), Luciano Pavarotti (Leicester), with the Chorus and Orchestra of the Teatro Comunale, Bologna, conducted by Richard Bonynge. Decca 425 410–2.

Sutherland is a dramatic Elisabetta, Tourangeau a powerful Maria, and Pavarotti a passionate Leicester, though perhaps too Italianate for an English aristocrat. Bonynge conducts an exciting account of the score.

Lucia di Lammermoor
opera seria in three acts (approximate length: 2 hours, 30 minutes)

Lucia　*soprano*
Edgardo　*tenor*
Enrico, Lucia's brother　*baritone*
Raimondo Bidebent, a chaplain　*bass*
Arturo　*tenor*
Alisa, Lucia's companion　*mezzo-soprano*
Normanno, a retainer of Enrico　*tenor*

LIBRETTO BY SALVATORE CAMMARANO, BASED ON SIR WALTER SCOTT'S NOVEL *THE BRIDE OF LAMMERMOOR*; TIME: THE LATE SEVENTEENTH CENTURY; PLACE: SCOTLAND; FIRST PERFORMED AT THE TEATRO SAN CARLO, NAPLES, 26 SEPTEMBER 1835

After seeing *Maria Stuarda* onto the stage in October 1834, albeit in its initial bowdlerized version as *Buondelmonte*, Donizetti began work almost simultaneously on his next two operas, promised to Milan and to Paris. He began to compose *Marino Faliero* for Paris, abandoning it temporarily in November to write *Gemma di Vergy* for Milan. Although both operas were successful at their premieres, neither has survived in the international repertoire.

While Donizetti was in Paris for the premiere of *Marino Faliero* in March 1835, he was made a Chevalier of the Legion of Honour. Back in Naples by the end of May, he turned his attention to his next opera, to be composed for the Teatro San Carlo in that city. The subject he chose was Sir Walter Scott's novel *The Bride of Lammermoor*, and his new librettist was Salvatore Cammarano, who would provide the composer with libretti for a further seven operas before going on to write four for Verdi. *Lucia di Lammermoor* was given its premiere in September 1835 at the Teatro San Carlo, where it was an immense success with, as the delighted composer wrote to his publisher, 'every piece . . . listened to in religious silence and honoured with spontaneous *vivas*. To this day it remains Donizetti's most popular work and, unlike so many bel canto operas, it did not completely disappear from the world's stages in the earlier years of the twentieth century.

Sir Walter Scott's novel *The Bride of Lammermoor*, published in 1819, was inspired by a real-life incident that occurred in Scotland in the seventeenth century, involving Jane Dalrymple, the daughter of a noble family, who was forced to marry a man she did not love while she was already secretly betrothed to her true love. On her wedding night the bride was discovered cowering insane in a corner while her husband lay dead, stretched out on the bed and covered in blood. It was around this tragedy that Scott wove his complex plot, a plot which Donizetti and Cammarano reduced to its bare bones, making a few changes and eliminating two characters who provide the novel with a certain degree of comic relief.

Act I, scene i. The grounds of Ravenswood Castle. In the hours before dawn, Normanno and a band of Enrico's huntsmen are searching the area for a mysterious stranger whose presence has been reported and whom Enrico suspects may be Edgardo, the rightful heir to Ravenswood, whose title and estates Enrico has usurped. Normanno learns from Enrico that the family's fortunes are not prospering, a situation exacerbated by the refusal of Enrico's sister Lucia to marry the wealthy man whom Enrico has selected for her. The chaplain, Raimondo, suggests that Lucia may still be grieving over the recent death of her mother, but Normanno reports that she has been having clandestine meetings with a stranger who saved her from an attack by a wild bull. Enrico is certain that this must be Edgardo, and he launches into a diatribe against Lucia for what he considers to be her treachery to the family ('Cruda, funesta smania'). When the huntsmen return to tell of having seen a man on horseback whom they were able to recognize as Edgardo, Enrico swears to destroy his hated enemy ('La pietade in suo favore').

Act I, scene ii. By the ruins of a fountain in the park of Ravenswood Castle, at night. While she awaits Edgardo, Lucia recounts to her companion Alisa the legend of the fountain, where a Ravenswood once killed his mistress, whose body still lies in the depths of the water but whose ghost Lucia has seen ('Regnava nel silenzio'). When Alisa, who considers this story an ill omen, begs Lucia to renounce a love fraught with danger, Lucia makes it clear that she will never forsake Edgardo, the light of her life ('Quando rapito in estasi'). Edgardo arrives and tells Lucia that he must leave for France the next morning on business of the Stuart cause, but that, before he goes, he intends to make his peace with Enrico and ask for Lucia's hand in marriage. With difficulty Lucia, who fears her brother's temper, persuades Edgardo not to attempt this. Edgardo flies into a rage, reminding her that he has sworn an oath of vengeance against her family. She calms him, and they exchange rings as a token that they are now married in the sight of heaven. The lovers part tearfully, with Lucia begging Edgardo to write to her and assuring him that her sighs will reach him even in France ('Verrano a te sull' aure').

Act II, scene i. Enrico's apartment in Ravenswood Castle. Enrico is planning with Normanno how to destroy Lucia's love for Edgardo. They have been intercepting the lovers' correspondence, and they now intend to show Lucia a letter they have forged, purporting to be from Edgardo to another woman. Meanwhile, guests are already beginning to arrive for the wedding of Lucia and the wealthy Arturo, which has been arranged by Enrico. Normanno is despached to greet the bridegroom as Lucia enters. When Enrico comments on her pale cheeks, she replies that he knows well the cause of her distress ('Il pallor funesto orrendo'). Enrico speaks of the husband he has procured for her, and when Lucia protests that she is already betrothed he hands her the forged letter. After perusing it, Lucia almost swoons with shock and grief. Sounds of the bridegroom being welcomed can be heard as Enrico tells his sister that she must, for his sake, marry Arturo. The political situation, with William dead and Mary about to ascend the throne, is such that only an alliance with Arturo's family can ensure Enrico's safety.

As Enrico rushes out to greet Arturo, Raimondo enters. He has delivered a letter from Lucia to Edgardo but, believing that it was never replied to, he now advises Lucia that she should marry Arturo for her brother's sake and that of their dead mother ('Ah, cedi, cedi'). Lucia finally submits, and Raimondo assures the unhappy young woman that she will receive her reward in heaven.

Act II, scene ii. The great hall of Ravenswood Castle. The guests who have assembled to witness the signing of the marriage contract sing a chorus of welcome to Arturo ('Per te d'immenso giubilo'), who replies, promising to restore the prosperity of the family into which he is about to marry ('Per poco fra le tenebre'). As Enrico attempts to explain Lucia's late arrival to the bridegroom and to dismiss the rumours Arturo has heard concerning her and Edgardo, the reluctant bride enters. She involuntarily draws back when she sees Arturo but, at the urgent *sotto voce* command of her brother, signs the marriage contract. Immediately, a commotion is heard outside and Edgardo angrily bursts in. The various characters express their differing emotions in the celebrated sextet 'Chi mi frena in tal momento?': Edgardo's fury is softened by the sight of Lucia's distress, Enrico is torn between pity for his sister and hatred of Edgardo, the others express their horror and Lucia longs for death. At the conclusion of the sextet Enrico and Arturo draw their swords and fling themselves upon Edgardo, but Raimondo separates them. Edgardo takes back the ring he gave Lucia and departs in a blind fury.

Act III, scene i. A room in the half-ruined tower of the Castle of Wolf's Crag. It is night, and a storm is in progress. Edgardo is visited in his present family residence by Enrico who takes delight in telling him that Lucia has gone to the altar with Arturo, and that the couple have now retired to the bridal bed. He challenges Edgardo to a duel the following morning, a challenge which Edgardo readily accepts.

Act III, scene ii. The great hall of Ravenswood Castle. The wedding of Lucia and Arturo is being joyously celebrated by the assembled guests when Raimondo rushes in to announce that on hearing a cry from the bridal chamber he entered it to find Arturo dead and Lucia standing over him, clutching the murdered man's own dagger. Lucia smiled witlessly at Raimondo and asked him, 'Where is my husband?' ('Dalle stanze ove Lucia'). The stunned guests have hardly had time to react when Lucia herself enters, her bridal gown splattered with blood. She has lost her senses, and in her delirium she imagines she is being married to Edgardo ('Ardon gl'incensi'). Enrico returns from his visit to Edgardo in time to hear Lucia assuring an imaginary Edgardo that although she is about to die they will be reunited in heaven ('Spargi d'amaro pianto'). Enrico asks Alisa to take Lucia away and begs Raimondo to look after her. Raimondo accuses Normanno of having been responsible for all that has occurred. (This last brief exchange involving Enrico, Raimondo and Normanno is usually omitted, with the scene ending as Lucia swoons at the conclusion of her mad scene.)

Act III, scene iii. Edgardo's family graveyard, shortly before dawn. Edgardo, who has arrived for his duel with Enrico, wanders among the family tombs, determined to let himself be killed since life has nothing now to offer him ('Fra poco a me ricovero'). Some Lammermoor family retainers enter, grieving for Lucia. They inform Edgardo that she is dying and that she is asking for him. A funeral bell begins to toll, indicating that Lucia has died. Edgardo attempts to console himself with the thought that he and Lucia will be reunited in heaven ('Tu che a Dio spiegasti l'ali') and then, despite Raimondo's attempt to restrain him, stabs himself and dies.

Lucia di Lammermoor, by far the finest and most successful of Donizetti's serious operas, is the epitome of the bel canto style and is unlikely to go out of favour with audiences as long as there are dramatic coloratura sopranos with the technique, agility and range necessary to surmount the difficulties of Lucia's celebrated mad scene. Famous interpreters of the title role around the beginning of the twentieth century included the great Australian Nellie Melba, the Viennese Selma Kurz and the Italian Luisa Tetrazzini. The French soprano Lily Pons was a popular Lucia at the Metropolitan Opera, New York, in the thirties, and a Covent Garden production by Franco Zeffirelli in 1959 launched the international career of another great Australian soprano, Joan Sutherland. The opera is tautly constructed, its music consistently serves the drama, and the composer's melodic invention is prodigious. The sextet 'Chi mi frena in tal momento?' vies with the quartet in Verdi's *Rigoletto* as the most famous ensemble in all opera.

Recommended recording: Joan Sutherland (Lucia), Luciano Pavarotti (Edgardo), Sherrill Milnes (Enrico), Nicolai Ghiaurov (Raimondo), with the Chorus and Orchestra of the Royal Opera House, Covent Garden, conducted by Richard Bonynge. Decca 410 193–2. Maria Callas and Joan Sutherland were both famous for their portrayals of Lucia in the theatre. Callas recorded the role twice in the studio, but she is to be found at her most exciting in a live EMI recording of a Berlin performance conducted by Herbert von Karajan. Fans of Callas will want to have this, but my own preference is for Joan Sutherland, who realises the drama of the role as forcibly as Callas, though by vastly different means, and who sings it more beautifully and with greater vocal security and style. Sutherland too recorded Lucia twice, and it is her second recording that is to be preferred. Her range and agility, and again the sheer beauty of her tone, made her Lucia not only viscerally exciting but also intensely moving. Her duet with the excellent Enrico of Sherrill Milnes, sung a tone higher than usual – as it is found in Donizetti's autograph score – makes a thrilling effect, as does her Mad Scene. Pavarotti is likewise eloquent as Edgardo, and Richard Bonynge conducts a fast-moving account of the score with great panache.

La Fille du régiment
(The Daughter of the Regiment)
opéra comique in two acts (approximate length: 1 hour, 30 minutes)

Marie *soprano*
Tonio *tenor*
Sergeant Sulpice *bass*
The Marquise de Birkenfeld *mezzo-soprano*

LIBRETTO BY JULES-HENRI VERNOY DE SAINT-GEORGES AND JEAN-FRANÇOIS-ALFRED BAYARD; TIME: THE EARLY NINETEENTH CENTURY; PLACE: THE SWISS TYROL; FIRST PERFORMED AT THE OPÉRA-COMIQUE, PARIS, 11 FEBRUARY 1840

The year 1839 was a busy one for Donizetti. He had agreed to compose two operas to French texts for the Paris Opéra, the first of which was to be *Les Martyrs*, a French adaptation of *Poliuto*, an opera he had written the previous year to an Italian libretto for the Teatro San Carlo, Naples, but which had been suppressed by command of the King of Naples, its offence being that it dealt with Christian martyrdom in Roman times. By May, Donizetti had completed *Les Martyrs*, which was not performed until the following year, and had begun to compose *Le Duc d'Albe*, an opera which, due to a number of complicated legal wrangles, was not ever performed during its composer's lifetime. When it became clear that the production of *Les Martyrs* at the Paris Opéra would be delayed, Donizetti employed the time until its rehearsals were due to begin by composing an opera for another Paris theatre, the Opéra-Comique.

This new opera was *La Fille du régiment*, a comedy in two acts with a libretto by Jules-Henri Vernoy de Saint-Georges and Jean-François-Alfred Bayard, a partnership of prolific French dramatists. (Bayard, on his own, is said to have written more than two hundred comedies over a period of twenty years.) *La Fille du régiment* was rehearsed throughout January 1840 and on 11 February was given its premiere at the Opéra-Comique. The first night appears not to have been a particularly happy one, not only because the tenor sang noticeably below pitch throughout the performance, but also because of a hostile demonstration organized by some of Donizetti's envious French rivals. Nor were matters improved by an unfavourable and distinctly unfair review by the composer and critic Hector Berlioz in the *Journal des débats*, in which he falsely accused Donizetti of having used, for the most part, music from one of Berlioz's early Italian operas.

However, it took only a few months for Paris to warm to *La Fille du régiment*, which was given fifty-five performances in the following year. In due course the opera became a great popular favourite and until comparatively recent times was regularly staged at the Opéra-Comique on Bastille Day, 14 July, as a manifestation of light-hearted but sincerely felt French patriotism. Marie's exhilarating 'Salut à la France' took on the status of a national song.

Some months after its Paris premiere Donizetti staged the opera at La Scala, Milan, in an Italian translation, as *La figlia del reggimento*, for which he made some alterations to his score, as well as replacing the spoken dialogue of the French version with sung recitative. It was in this Italian translation that the opera was popular in Italy in the 1930s with Toti dal Monte as Maria. The original French version was revived at the Metropolitan Opera, New York, in 1940 with Lily Pons, and at the Royal Opera House, Covent Garden, in 1966 with Joan Sutherland.

Act I. A valley in the mountains of the Tyrol. The Marquise de Birkenfeld, accompanied by her steward, has strayed too near a battlefield. While she rests, the local peasants watch from high ground a battle which is being fought in a neighbouring valley, and the women of the community pray to the Virgin Mary. The French regiment is victorious, and soon their Sergeant Sulpice enters, followed shortly afterwards by the vivacious Marie, a young woman who was found as a small child, adopted by Sulpice's regiment and brought up by them ('Au bruit de la guerre').

Marie confides to Sulpice that she has fallen in love with a young Tyrolean, Tonio, who saved her life when she almost fell from a precipice. Some of Sulpice's soldiers now enter with Tonio, whom they are about to shoot as a spy, having found him lurking in the vicinity. Tonio had, of course, merely been looking for a chance to approach Marie, and they now sing of their love for each other ('De cet aveu si tendre'). Learning that the man whom Marie marries must be a member of the regiment, Tonio promptly enlists, and Marie celebrates by singing the regimental song ('Chacun le sait, chacun le dit').

Required to give safe conduct to the Marquise de Birkenfeld, Sulpice realizes that Birkenfeld was the name to which certain papers found on Marie as a child were addressed. On being questioned by Sulpice, the Marquise informs him that she is the aunt of the young woman, who was lost when she was little more than a baby. She insists on taking Marie away with her to her chateau. Tonio returns, now in uniform, to claim his bride ('À mes amis'), but Marie, about to depart with her newly found aunt, sings a sad farewell to him and to her beloved regiment ('Il faut partir').

Act II. The chateau of the Marquise. Marie is bored by the elegant life she is being made to live, with lessons in dancing and singing, and she is dismayed by the prospect of marriage to a nobleman selected by her aunt. She and Sulpice, who is a guest at the chateau while recovering from a wound, shock the Marquise by bursting into a lively rendition of their regimental song.

Tonio, now promoted to the rank of captain, enters with the regiment and asks the Marquise for permission to marry her niece ('Pour me rapprocher de Marie'), but she refuses. Marie and Tonio plan to elope, but when Marie discovers that the Marquise is really not her aunt but her mother, who gave birth to her out of wedlock, she feels that she cannot go against her mother's wishes. However, at the reception to announce Marie's engagement, the Marquise realizes what suffering she is about to inflict on her daughter, and gives her consent to Marie's marriage to Tonio. The opera ends in general rejoicing and a patriotic ensemble led by Marie ('Salut à la France').

More so than any other non-French composer, Donizetti was able to adapt his style easily and naturally to the requirements of French *opéra comique*. In *La Fille du régiment* he deployed his genius for elegant and soulful cantilena as well as his aptitude for musical parody, and the result is a vastly entertaining comic opera, one which in many respects fascinatingly anticipates the operettas of Offenbach. Marie's 'Il faut partir' and Tonio's 'Pour me rapprocher de Marie' are superb examples of the opera's pathos, while her 'Chacun le sait, chacun le dit' and his Act I aria with, in its second section ('Pour mon âme'), a succession of high Cs, are but two of the work's exhilarating display pieces. The scene at the beginning of Act II in which the Marquise attempts to wean Marie away from her cheerful coloratura to a more respectable but duller style of singing is sheer delight. It was of this opera that Mendelssohn remarked, 'It's so pretty that I wish I had written it myself'.

Recommended recording: Joan Sutherland (Marie), Luciano Pavarotti (Tonio), Monica Sinclair (The Marquise), Spiro Malas (Sulpice), with the Chorus and Orchestra of the Royal Opera House, Covent Garden, conducted by Richard Bonynge. Decca 414 520–2. This is the cast of a greatly admired 1966 Covent Garden staging, and all are superb, with Joan Sutherland in sparkling form as Marie, the young Pavarotti flinging off his top notes with ease as Tonio, and Monica Sinclair a formidable Marquise. Magnificent.

Don Pasquale

opera buffa in three acts (approximate length: 2 hours)

Don Pasquale   *bass*
Ernesto, his nephew   *tenor*
Dr Malatesta   *baritone*
Norina, alias Sofronia   *soprano*

LIBRETTO BY GIOVANNI RUFFINI; TIME: THE EARLY NINETEENTH CENTURY; PLACE: ROME; FIRST PERFORMED AT THE THÉÂTRE ITALIEN, PARIS, 3 JANUARY 1843

In the three years between *La Fille du régiment* and *Don Pasquale*, Donizetti composed five operas, two of which (*La Favorite* and *Linda di Chamounix*) are occasionally to be encountered in opera houses today, while another (*Maria Padilla*) is seen much more rarely. *Rita*, a one-act comic opera, is sometimes performed in Italian theatres as part of a double bill, but *Adelia*, a three-act *opera seria*, still awaits modern revival.

After the successful 1842 premiere of *Linda di Chamounix* in Vienna, Donizetti found himself at first working on an opera for Paris, *Ne m'oubliez pas* (Don't Forget Me), which he abandoned to begin composing *Caterina Cornaro* for Vienna. This, too, he put aside temporarily, in order to write an opera for the Théâtre Italien in Paris. The subject he chose was one that had already been used by the librettist Angelo Anelli for an opera by Stefano Pavesi, *Ser Marcantonio*, first performed in Milan in 1810. (The ultimate source of the plot, however, is Ben Jonson's 1609 play *Epicoene, or The Silent Woman*.) A new libretto based on Anelli's text was produced by Giovanni Ruffini, an Italian political exile living in Paris, and Donizetti began to compose the opera, *Don Pasquale*, which he claimed took him no more than eleven days to complete.

At its premiere at the Théâtre Italien on 3 January 1843, *Don Pasquale* was received with great acclaim, and within months it was staged in Milan, Vienna, London and Brussels. It remains to this day one of the three most popular of all Italian comic operas, outclassed only by Donizetti's own *L'elisir d'amore* and Rossini's *Il barbiere di Siviglia*.

Act I, scene i. A living-room in Don Pasquale's house in Rome. Displeased with his nephew Ernesto, who has fallen in love with a young widow, Norina, the elderly Pasquale is determined to disinherit Ernesto, who lives in the house with him. Pasquale intends to marry, in order to produce a more direct heir, and is impatiently awaiting the arrival of his friend and medical adviser Dr Malatesta, whom he has asked to find him a bride. Malatesta, however, is also a friend of both Ernesto and Norina. Having failed to dissuade Pasquale from his intention to marry, Malatesta when he arrives assures the old man that he has found the perfect bride for him. She is Sofronia, his sister, whom he describes to Pasquale ('Bella siccome un angelo') as a shy, beautiful girl brought up in a convent. (Sofronia is, in fact, Ernesto's beloved Norina, unrelated to Malatesta but happy to join him in a plot to outwit Ernesto's uncle.) After Malatesta has left, Ernesto arrives and is disconcerted when his uncle, announcing his intention to marry, orders him to leave the house ('Sogno soave e casto'). Ernesto begs his uncle to consult Dr Malatesta before embarking upon such a hazardous enterprise and is astonished to be told that Malatesta is aiding and abetting him.

Act I, scene ii. A room in Norina's house. Norina reads a romantic novel ('Quel guardo il cavaliere') and laughs dismissively at its style and content ('So anch'io la virtù magica'). Malatesta arrives, and they work out the details of their plot to make a fool of Pasquale ('Pronta io son').

Act II. A living-room in Pasquale's house. Ernesto, as he leaves, laments his situation, deprived of home, future prospects and bride ('Cercherò lontana terra'). After his departure Pasquale enters, impatiently awaiting his bride. Malatesta arrives, accompanied by 'Sofronia', a shy young woman wearing a veil, who gives demure answers to Pasquale's questions, assuring him that she wants to lead a quiet domestic life and deal with all the household chores. The old man is over-joyed, and when a notary arrives (who is no notary but a relative of Malatesta) a marriage contract is quickly drawn up, by the terms of which Pasquale endows his young bride with half of his worldly goods.

At this point Ernesto enters tempestuously, to say farewell to Pasquale. Not having been apprised of the plot, he is considerably dismayed to discover his fiancée apparently in the act of marrying his uncle. Malatesta manages to explain the situation to him without arousing Pasquale's suspicions, and Ernesto then cheerfully consents to act as a second witness ('Figliuol, non farmi scene'). As soon as the marriage contract is signed, Sofronia undergoes a startling change of char-acter, speaking sharply to Pasquale, appointing Ernesto as her walking companion and insisting on more servants being employed. Pasquale is almost apoplectic with rage and frustration ('E rimasto la impietrato').

Act III, scene i. A living room in Pasquale's house. The room is now littered with expensive items of feminine attire, and a number of servants rush about – performing various tasks for their mistress, delivering flowers to her adjacent room and ushering in her milliner, who is laden with boxes – while Pasquale sits at a table which is piled high with bills. When Sofronia emerges from her room extravagantly dressed, Pasquale asks where she is going and is told that she is going to the theatre without him. He forbids her to go, they quarrel and she smacks his face, addressing him scornfully and telling him to go to bed. She is contrite when she sees the old man's distress but is determined to keep to the plan agreed with Malatesta.

As she rushes off, Sofronia is careful to drop a note on the floor. Pasquale, dis-illusioned and sad, picks it up and reads it. Addressed to Sofronia, it is from a lover making an assignation with her in the garden later that evening. In need of advice, Pasquale sends a servant to fetch Dr Malatesta. While their master is out of the room, the other servants comment on the strange goings-on in the house, and on the unhappy marriage of Pasquale and Sofronia ('Che interminabile andi-riviene'). Malatesta arrives, and he and Pasquale make plans to catch Sofronia with her lover ('Cheti, cheti immantinente').

Act III, scene ii. The shrubbery in Don Pasquale's garden. Beyond the garden wall, Ernesto serenades his beloved ('Come' è gentil') with a choral accompani-ment. Norina emerges from the house onto the terrace and goes to the garden gate to admit Ernesto, with whom she sings a tender love duet ('Tornami a dir'). The lovers are surprised by Pasquale and Malatesta, but in the darkness Ernesto manages to make his escape. Pasquale is in the process of ordering Sofronia from the house when Malatesta makes a suggestion. Calling to Ernesto, who now re-enters, he tells the young man that his uncle has decided to allow him to marry Norina, and that he will give him a liberal annual allowance as well. Pasquale agrees to this, since his own marriage is clearly over, and tells his nephew to fetch Norina and marry her immediately. Sofronia is then revealed to be Norina, and Pasquale, realizing that he has been tricked, decides to make the best of the situation. He is, after all, relieved to be rid of 'Sofronia'.

Don Pasquale is not only one of the most popular of comic operas, but also one of the most charming – full of beautifully tender, almost Mozartian, melody, as well as typically Donizettian gaiety and good humour. The overture is effervescent; Ernesto's two solos and his duet with Norina are especially graceful and attractive numbers; and the comic duet for Pasquale and Malatesta ('Cheti, cheti immantinente') at the end of Act II is invariably, indeed traditionally, encored. The characters, stock figures though they may be, are humanized by the sympathy in which Donizetti's music has clothed them.

Recommended recording: Renato Bruson (Pasquale), Eva Mei (Norina), Frank Lopardo (Ernesto), Thomas Allen (Malatesta), with the Bavarian Radio Chorus and Munich Radio Orchestra conducted by Roberto Abbado. RCA Victor 09026 61924 2. Renato Bruson and Thomas Allen vividly characterize Pasquale and Malatesta, Frank Lopardo is a charming Ernesto and Eva Mei a lively and engaging Norina.

ANTONIN DVOŘÁK
(b. Nelahozeves, 1841 – d. Prague, 1904)

Rusalka
opera in three acts (approximate length: 3 hours)

Rusalka, a water nymph   *soprano*
The Prince   *tenor*
The Foreign Princess   *soprano*

The Water Goblin   *bass*
Ježibaba, a witch   *mezzo-soprano*
Three Wood Nymphs   *2 sopranos; 1 contralto*

LIBRETTO BY JAROSLAV KVAPL, BASED ON THE FAIRY TALE *UNDINE*, BY FRIEDRICH

DE LA MOTTE FOUQUÉ; TIME AND PLACE: THOSE OF FAIRY TALE; FIRST PERFORMED

AT THE NATIONAL THEATRE, PRAGUE, 31 MARCH 1901

One of the two leaders (the other being Smetana) of the nineteenth-century nationalist movement in music in what was then Bohemia and later became Czechoslovakia, Dvořák composed thirteen operas, few of which have found wide acceptance abroad. Only *Rusalka* (1901) is to be encountered with reasonable frequency in foreign opera houses, though both *The Jacobin* (1889) and *The Devil and Kate* (1899) are occasionally performed. His final opera, the dully conventional *Armida*, was a failure.

Dvořák, whose musical stature is revealed most clearly in his symphonies and chamber music, was not naturally drawn to the stage, though he was involved in opera from quite early in his career when, shortly after graduating from the Prague Organ School, he played the viola in an opera house orchestra for several years. His first opera, *Alfred* (written in 1870), a setting in German of Körner's *Alfred der Grosse*, was not performed until more than thirty years after the composer's death. His second, a comic opera composed to a Czech libretto, was *King and Charcoal Burner*, rejected in its first version and rewritten before being successfully staged in Prague in 1874. *The Cunning Peasant*, staged in 1878, and *The Jacobin* (1889) were Dvořák's most popular operas during his lifetime. In 1899 he composed another successful comic opera, *The Devil and Kate*, and then turned his attention to *Rusalka*, its libretto by Jaroslav Kvapl already in existence.

Kvapl (1868–1950), a Czech poet and dramatist who became the dramaturg of the Prague National Theatre in 1900, had been finding it difficult to persuade any composer of his own generation to set his *Rusalka* libretto, which was an adaptation of *Undine*, a fairy tale by the German author Friedrich de la Motte Fouqué (1777–1843), about the love of a water nymph and a knight. (Fouqué himself made his tale into a libretto which was set to music by E.T.A. Hoffmann and first performed in Berlin in 1816.) The story was later used by the French playwright Jean Giraudoux for his *Ondine* in 1939.

Dvořák responded warmly to Kvapl's libretto, and he worked enthusiastically on the composition of *Rusalka* between April and November 1900. The opera's premiere at the Prague National Theatre in March 1901 was a huge success, and it was soon being performed on other Czech stages and in due course abroad, translated into Slovenian, Serbo-Croat, Polish, German and Lithuanian.

Act I. A meadow by the shore of a lake. In the moonlight, three Wood Nymphs sing banteringly to the Water Goblin, who rises from the bottom of the lake to respond to them. When they have gone, the Water Goblin's favourite daughter, the water nymph Rusalka, asks her father for advice. She tells him that she has fallen in love with a human, a handsome young Prince who comes to swim in the lake ('Often he comes here'), and that she wants to become human so that she can be with him. Distressed at this, the Water Goblin advises Rusalka to consult Ježibaba, the witch who lives nearby. He returns to the depths of the lake, and Rusalka invokes the moon, asking it to tell her beloved Prince that she is waiting for him ('O silver moon'). She then calls to the witch Ježibaba, who listens to her plea and agrees to give her the attributes of humans, except for the power of speech. Rusalka will be able to walk on land, but will not be able to speak. If she should be betrayed by the Prince, both will be accursed for ever. Rusalka agrees to her terms and is transformed into a human as the voice of the Water Goblin is raised in warning from the lake.

Dawn approaches, and the sound of hunting horns is heard, signalling the approach of the Prince and his companions. Feeling a mysterious attraction when he is by the lake shore, the Prince orders the hunters to return to his castle so that he can commune alone with whatever spirit resides in the vicinity. When Rusalka appears, the Prince is immediately enchanted by her beauty. She clings to him without uttering a word and, as the anguished voices of her father and her sister nymphs call from the lake, the Prince takes Rusalka home to his castle.

Act II. The grounds of the Prince's castle. Guests have been invited to a ball to celebrate the forthcoming wedding of the Prince and Rusalka. A Forester and a Kitchen Boy discuss the mysterious bride-to-be, whom the forester thinks must be a witch. The Prince and Rusalka approach. He is perturbed by her silence and her apparent coldness and begins to fear that he has made a mistake. When one of the guests, a Foreign Princess, chides the Prince for having neglected her, the Prince sends Rusalka indoors to dress for the ball and strolls away with the Princess.

As evening falls the dancing begins, momentarily interrupted by the voice of the Water Goblin lamenting the fate of his daughter, while the guests sing a bridal chorus ('White flowers are blooming by the way'). Rusalka emerges from the castle and rushes to her father in the lake, begging him to help her ('Oh, useless it is'). The Prince and the Foreign Princess sing a passionate love duet, and when a desperate Rusalka attempts to intervene, the Prince pushes her aside. As the Water Goblin warns him that he will never be free of Rusalka, the Prince turns to the Foreign Princess for help, only to be scornfully rejected.

Act III. The meadow by the lake shore. It is evening. Lamenting her fate, Rusalka longs for death, but Ježibaba tells her that the curse can be removed from her if she kills her lover. Rusalka refuses to contemplate this and sinks resignedly into the waters of the lake. The Forester and the Kitchen Boy arrive to ask Ježibaba to release the Prince from his enchantment, but she puts them to flight, aided by the Water Goblin. The Wood Nymphs sing and dance until the Water Goblin reminds them of Rusalka's fate.

The Prince, delirious, arrives at the lake shore, calling to Rusalka to return to him. She arises from the waters and responds to his plea for forgiveness by regretting that she was not able to be all that he desired. But a kiss from her now, she warns the Prince, would kill him. Ecstatically, he begs her to kiss him. She does so, and he dies in her arms. They are at last united in eternal love.

A brief orchestral prelude admirably sets the poetic mood of the opera. Dvořák's music throughout is both beautiful and sensuous, and his use of leitmotifs for the various characters emphasizes his debt to Wagner, while still sounding unmistakably like mature Dvořák. Rusalka's Act I aria 'O silver moon' has become widely known out of context, but it is only one of many expressive and affecting episodes in an opera that deserves to be staged more frequently.

Recommended recording: Milada Subrtova (Rusalka), Ivo Zidek (Prince), Eduard Haken (Water Goblin), with the Prague National Theatre Chorus and Orchestra, conducted by Zdenek Chalabala. Supraphon SU 0013–2. A gloriously authentic performance by Czech artists, thrillingly conducted by Chalabala, with Subrtova a most believable and moving Rusalka, and Zidek a Prince of youthful ardour.

FRIEDRICH VON FLOTOW
(b. Tutendorf, 1812 – d. Darmstadt, 1883)

Martha, oder der Markt von Richmond
(Martha, or Richmond Market)
opera in four acts (approximate length: 2 hours)

Lady Harriet Durham, alias Martha   *soprano*
Nancy, her companion, alias Julia   *contralto*
Lionel   *tenor*
Plunkett   *bass*
Sir Tristram Mickleford   *bass*
Sheriff   *bass*

LIBRETTO BY W. FRIEDRICH (PSEUDONYM OF FRIEDRICH WILHELM RIESE); TIME: AROUND 1710; PLACE: IN AND NEAR RICHMOND; FIRST PERFORMED AT THE KÄRNTNERTORTHEATER, VIENNA, 25 NOVEMBER 1847

Although Flotow composed more than thirty operas and a number of ballet scores, he is known today primarily for *Martha, oder der Markt von Richmond.* Born in Germany, he received his musical education in Paris and composed his first opera, *Pierre et Catherine,* before he was twenty-one, to a libretto that had been offered to him by Jules-Henri Vernoy de Saint-Georges (1799–1875), a young French librettist who was to write plays, ballet scenarios and opera libretti for nearly half a century. (He is best remembered now as the co-author, with Théophile Gautier, of the scenario for the ballet *Giselle* by Adolphe Adam.)

Flotow's first operas to be staged – in a private amateur theatre in Paris in 1836 – were *Rob-Roy* and *Serafine.* His earliest opera to be staged at a major opera house was *L'Esclave de Camoëns* (The Slave of Camoëns), a one-act piece with a libretto by Saint-Georges, produced in 1843 at the Paris Opéra-Comique. In the following year, Flotow composed the music for Act III of a three-act ballet-pantomime, *Lady Harriette, ou La Servante de Greenwich,* whose scenario was by Saint-Georges and whose music for Acts I and II was contributed by composers named Burgmüller and Deldevez.

Staged at the Paris Opéra in 1844, *Lady Harriette* was, two years later, to provide the plot of *Martha.* By this time Flotow had achieved his first huge success with *Alessandro Stradella,* a three-act romantic opera which, after its premiere in Hamburg in 1844, was staged in Berlin, Vienna, Budapest and Prague. Invited to compose a new German-language opera for Vienna, Flotow suggested Saint-Georges' *Lady Harriette* plot to Friedrich Wilhelm Riese who, under his pseudonym of W. Friedrich, had written the libretto of *Alessandro Stradella.* Flotow and Riese set to work on the opera which, as *Martha, oder der Markt von Richmond,* was performed in Vienna with great success. Within the next ten years *Martha* was staged throughout Germany and in Budapest, Prague, Riga, London, Helsinki, Warsaw, Basle, Stockholm, New York, Copenhagen, San Francisco, Antwerp,

Sydney, Zagreb, St Petersburg and Paris. An engagingly tuneful and light-hearted opera, *Martha* continued to be popular for the remainder of the century. Although it was then neglected for a time (except for its popular tenor aria 'Ach, so fromm', taken up by Italian tenors as 'M'appari tutt' amor'), *Martha* has begun to creep back into fashion, and in recent years has been performed in Chicago, Vienna, London, Detroit, Cologne, Budapest, Sarasota and Dublin.

Act I, scene i. Lady Harriet Durham's boudoir. The young Lady Harriet, a maid of honour to Queen Anne, is bored with life at court and unresponsive to the attempts of her companion, Nancy, to raise her spirits. Lady Harriet's elderly cousin and boringly persistent suitor, Sir Tristram, arrives to invite her to the donkey races, and when she hears through the open window the singing of happy young peasant girls on their way to the annual fair at Richmond, where they will put themselves up for hire by the local farmers, she decides that she, Nancy, and a reluctant Sir Tristram should dress as peasants, go to the fair and mingle with the crowd.

Act I, scene ii. The market square in Richmond. Plunkett, a young farmer, and Lionel, his foster-brother, arrive at the fair hoping to be able to hire two servant girls. The two men reminisce over the fact that Lionel was brought up by the Plunkett family after being left in their care by a dying father who did not reveal his real identity but left his son a ring to be shown to the Queen if ever he were to find himself in serious trouble ('Wie das schnattert, wie das plappert').

The Sheriff of Richmond opens the market by reading the Queen's proclamation that all hiring contracts are to be binding for a year, once an agreement has been reached. Lady Harriet and Nancy arrive with Sir Tristram and soon attract the attention of Lionel and Plunkett. Giving their names as Martha and Julia, the young women allow themselves, as a joke, to be hired as servants by the two farmers. When they attempt to call off the agreement, the Sheriff rules that they must honour their contracts, and they are taken away by Lionel and Plunkett to Plunkett's farm.

Act II. A room in Plunkett's farmhouse. The young women are horrified to discover that they are expected to perform household tasks of which they have had no experience. When the men attempt to instruct their new servants in the operation of a spinning wheel, Julia (Nancy) overturns the wheel and rushes out of the room, pursued by Plunkett. Left alone with Martha (Lady Harriet), Lionel confesses that he loves her and asks her to marry him. She declines, but agrees to sing for him ('Letzte Rose'). Plunkett returns with Julia, who has wrecked the kitchen in her temper. As it is by now midnight, the girls are locked in their room and the men retire. Shortly afterwards, Sir Tristram arrives with a carriage to rescue the two young women, who escape through a window before Lionel and Plunkett, awakened by the noise, can stop them.

Act III. The exterior of an inn in the country near Richmond. Plunkett is sitting with friends outside the inn, and he leads them in a drinking song ('Lass mich euch fragen'). The sound of hunting horns is heard, and the Royal Hunt approaches. Plunkett recognizes one of the riders, Nancy, as his servant Julia, and attempts to drag her away. However, he is forced to retreat, pursued by the huntsmen. Lionel now appears. He laments the loss of his maid, Martha, and expresses his love for her in the opera's most famous aria ('Ach, so fromm'), failing to notice Lady Harriet when she appears with Sir Tristram, who is still attempting to propose to her. Lady Harriet sends Sir Tristram away, and Lionel, now hearing his beloved Martha's voice, declares his love for her. Pretending not to know him, she calls for help, and when Lionel insists that she is his servant she has him arrested as a madman. Lionel realizes now that Martha is a noblewoman who has played a trick on him ('Mag der Himmel euch vergeben'). As he is led away he gives Plunkett the ring he received from his father, begging his foster-brother to take it to the Queen.

Act IV, scene i. A room in Plunkett's farmhouse. Lionel has been set free, his ring having established him as the son of the unjustly banished late Earl of Derby, and Lady Harriet arrives with Nancy to ask his forgiveness and to offer her hand in marriage. However, Lionel, in the throes of depression and anger, rejects her. Harriet enlists the aid of Nancy and Plunkett in winnng Lionel's affections again.

Act IV, scene ii. Outside Plunkett's farmhouse. Under Lady Harriet's supervision, peasants and servants set up a replica of Richmond Fair ('Hier die Boden, dort die Schenke'), with a farmer dressed as the Sheriff. Harriet and Nancy dress in their peasant costumes as Martha and Julia, and offer themselves again as servants to Lionel and Plunkett. Lionel now realizes that his love for Martha has endured. Both couples embrace, to the delight of the crowd, and the opera ends happily with a choral reprise of Martha's 'Letzte Rose'.

Martha is a work of considerable period charm, with agreeable and fluent melody and a sufficient amount of dramatic flair to make its slight and improbable plot convincing in the theatre. Flotow's score is decidedly eclectic, incorporating the Italian bel canto operatic style of the Act III quintet with chorus, 'Mag der Himmel euch vergeben', the French elegance of the popular tenor aria 'Ach, so fromm', and the folk-song simplicity of 'Letzte Rose', which is, in fact, the old Irish folk tune to which the poet Thomas Moore fitted his poem 'The Last Rose of Summer'. All these elements combine to form a stylistic unity in this delightful example of mid-nineteenth-century homely German *Volksoper.*

Recommended recording: Anneliese Rothenberger (Martha), Brigitte Fassbaender (Nancy), Nicolai Gedda (Lionel), Hermann Prey (Plunkett), with the Bavarian State Opera Chorus and Orchestra, conducted by Robert Heger. EMI CMS7 69339–2.

JOHN GAY
(b. Barnstaple, 1685 – d. London, 1732)

The Beggar's Opera
ballad opera in a prologue and three acts (approximate length: 3 hours)

Captain Macheath, a highwayman   *tenor*
Peachum, a seller of stolen goods   *bass*
Mrs Peachum, his wife   *soprano*
Polly Peachum, their daughter   *soprano*
Filch, a thief employed by Peachum   *tenor*
Lockit, a gaoler   *baritone*
Lucy Lockit, his daughter   *soprano*
The Beggar   *spoken role*

LIBRETTO BY JOHN GAY; TIME: THE EARLY EIGHTEENTH CENTURY; PLACE: LONDON; FIRST PERFORMED AT LINCOLN'S INN FIELDS THEATRE, LONDON, 29 JANUARY 1728

John Gay, who wrote the words and compiled the music of *The Beggar's Opera*, was not a composer but an eighteenth-century English minor playwright and poet who, with *The Beggar's Opera*, invented a new form: the ballad opera. He subsequently went on to create two more ballad operas: *Polly*, a sequel to *The Beggar's Opera*, and *Achilles*. The first of these, however, was banned by the Lord Chamberlain, and the second, staged posthumously in 1733, was initially admired but has not retained its popularity.

In *The Beggar's Opera* Gay, who in 1718 had provided Handel with the libretto for *Acis and Galatea*, produced a popular and vernacular alternative, with dialogue, to the Italian-language operas of the day. The dialogue of the piece, which Gay himself wrote, is interspersed with sixty-nine songs, fifty-one of which are adaptations of existing English, Scottish, Irish and even French popular or folk tunes. The remaining eighteen songs make use of melodies by composers such as Purcell, Handel, Henry Carey, Buononcini, John Eccles, Jeremiah Clarke, John Barrett, Geminiani, Frescobaldi and others, among them Johann Christoph Pepusch.

Pepusch (1667–1752), a German composer and musician who became the music director of more than one London theatre, is usually credited with having arranged the music of the composers used in *The Beggar's Opera*, but there is no firm evidence of this. He was probably in charge of the orchestra on the opening night at Lincoln's Inn Fields Theatre in 1728, and he may have composed the overture, which is based on 'One evening, having lost my way', a tune used in Act III.

The character of the highwayman Macheath was considered to be a thinly disguised caricature of the Prime Minister, Sir Robert Walpole, which is no doubt why Gay's ballad opera was rejected by the Theatre Royal, Drury Lane. When it was staged at a rival theatre in Lincoln's Inn Fields it was an immediate and riotous success. It went on to be performed in London every year for the rest of the century and was produced throughout the English-speaking world, creating a craze for such merchandise as *Beggar's Opera* fans, playing cards and porcelain figures.

By the very nature of the piece, there is no definitive edition of *The Beggar's Opera*. In 1920 an arrangement of the score by the baritone and composer Frederic Austin, staged in London at the Lyric Theatre, Hammersmith, with Austin himself as Peachum, achieved a run of 1,463 performances and gave the work a new lease of life. There have since been other versions, two of the most notable being an adaptation by Benjamin Britten, first performed by the English Opera Group at the Aldeburgh Festival in 1948, and another by Arthur Bliss, made for a film of *The Beggar's Opera* (1953), directed by Peter Brook, with Laurence Olivier as Macheath. Gay's ballad opera was written for and first performed by actors who were able to sing rather than singers able to act, and it is still best and most suitably performed by singing actors.

Prologue. The author, a Beggar, recommends his work to the audience.

Act I. Peachum's house. Mrs Peachum, whose husband is a receiver of stolen goods, suspects that their daughter Polly may be romantically involved with the dashing highwayman Captain Macheath. Polly admits this to be the case, but her mother further discovers that Polly has actually married Macheath. Peachum is uncomfortable at having as a son-in-law someone who knows so much about his professional activities, so he resolves to denounce Macheath to the police and have him hanged. When Macheath arrives, Polly tells him that he must flee to escape arrest.

Act II. A tavern near Newgate, and Newgate prison. The carousing of Macheath's gang is interrupted by the arrival of their leader, who explains to them that he will have to go into hiding for a time. When they leave to hold up and rob a few coaches, Macheath remains behind to cavort with the ladies of the town. These ladies, however, have been bribed by Peachum. While two of them manage to steal Macheath's pistols, a third gives a signal to Peachum, who enters with police constables and has Macheath arrested.

Macheath is taken to Newgate prison, where the gaoler, Lockit, makes it clear to him that any favours, such as less heavy fetters, must be paid for in cash. Lockit's daughter Lucy, who has apparently been made pregnant by Macheath, gloats over his situation, but Macheath convinces her that he is not married to Polly Peachum, and he agrees to marry Lucy. Meanwhile, Lockit and Peachum discuss their business arrangements, at first amicably but soon acrimoniously. Lucy now tries to persuade her father to be merciful to her lover, but the arrival of Polly, who throws herself at Macheath addressing him as 'my dear husband', sends Lucy into a fury. 'How happy could I be with either, were t'other dear charmer away', sings Macheath philosophically. Peachum arrives and eventually succeeds in dragging his daughter away, while Lucy helps Macheath to escape from the prison.

Act III. Newgate prison, a gaming house and Peachum's house. In the prison, Lockit admonishes Lucy, not so much for having helped Macheath to escape as for not getting paid for it. At a nearby gaming house, Macheath confers with two of his colleagues of the road. In Peachum's house, Peachum and Lockit plan Macheath's recapture. A woman who has arrived to purchase stolen materials tells the two men where they can find the highwayman. At Newgate prison, Lucy has prepared ratsbane poison for Polly, but Polly is not foolish enough to accept a drink from the hands of her rival. Macheath is brought in, in chains, and taken off to the Old Bailey. About to be hanged, he is visited in his cell not only by Polly and Lucy but also by several of his other wives. At this point, the Beggar is appealed to, and asked to prevent a tragic ending. He allows Macheath to be reprieved, and the opera ends happily, 'to comply with the taste of the town', with Macheath and Polly leading the final dance and chorus.

Whatever its shortcomings as a satirical comment on the evils of its age, *The Beggar's Opera* is hugely successful as a light-hearted, cynical romp, with a number of agreeable tunes.

Recommended recording: Philip Langridge (Macheath), Ann Murray (Polly), Yvonne Kenny (Lucy), John Rawnsley (Lockit), Robert Lloyd (Peachum), with the Aldeburgh Festival Choir and Orchestra, conducted by Steuart Bedford. Argo 436 850–ZHO2. The work is performed in the arrangement by Benjamin Britten.

GEORGE GERSHWIN
(b. New York, 1898 – d. Hollywood, 1937)

Porgy and Bess
opera in three acts (approximate length: 3 hours)

Porgy, a crippled beggar   *bass-baritone*
Bess   *soprano*
Crown, a stevedore   *baritone*
Serena   *soprano*
Clara   *soprano*
Maria, keeper of the cook-shop   *contralto*
Jake, a fisherman   *baritone*
Sportin' Life, a dope peddler   *tenor*
Mingo   *tenor*
Robbins   *tenor*
Peter, the honey man   *tenor*
Frazier, a 'lawyer'   *baritone*
Annie   *mezzo-soprano*
Lily, Peter's wife   *mezzo-soprano*
Strawberry Woman   *mezzo-soprano*
Crab Man   *tenor*

LIBRETTO BY DUBOSE HEYWARD AND IRA GERSHWIN, BASED ON DUBOSE HEYWARD'S NOVEL *PORGY*; TIME: THE 1920S; PLACE: CHARLESTON, SOUTH CAROLINA; FIRST PERFORMED AT THE ALVIN THEATER, NEW YORK, 10 OCTOBER 1935

One of the most gifted twentieth-century American composers of musical comedy, songs and light orchestral music, George Gershwin wrote a number of popular Broadway musicals, including *Lady, Be Good* (1924), *Strike Up the Band* (1927), *Rosalie* (1928), *Girl Crazy* (1930) and *Of Thee I Sing* (1931). He composed only two operas, the earlier of which, *Blue Monday*, a one-act chamber opera in a jazz idiom which Gershwin and his librettist Buddy De Silva wrote in about five days, was first performed as one of the items in a Broadway revue, *George White's Scandals of 1922*. Gershwin's masterpiece, *Porgy and Bess*, was given its premiere in 1935.

In 1929 Gershwin had signed a contract with the Metropolitan Opera to compose what was described as a 'Jewish opera'. This was *The Dybbuk*, based on Solomon Ansky's play of that title, a study of demoniac possession. However, Gershwin failed to fulfil the commission. He had already read and become intrigued by *Porgy*, the first novel of DuBose Heyward, an American novelist, poet and dramatist, which had been published in 1925. With his wife Dorothy, Heyward adapted his novel as a play, and it was successfully produced in New York by the Theater Guild in 1927. In 1933, Heyward and the Gershwin brothers, George and Ira, signed a contract with the Theater Guild to create an opera based on *Porgy*. As Heyward's novel and play deal with the lives of the black inhabitants of Catfish Row in Charleston, South Carolina, Gershwin spent much of the summer of 1934 in South Carolina, absorbing atmosphere and working on the opera, hoping, as he told a journalist, that it would turn out to be 'a combination of the drama and romance of *Carmen* and the beauty of *Die Meistersinger*'.

By mid-1935 Gershwin had completed and orchestrated his score, and *Porgy and Bess* opened at the Alvin Theater, New York, on 10 October 1935, after a try-out in Boston ten days earlier, just as though it were not 'an American folk opera', which is how it was billed, but a Broadway musical. For an opera, which is what it was, *Porgy and Bess* did well, running for 124 performances. However, viewed as a commercial theatrical venture it was not an immediate success, failing to earn enough to recoup its initial investment. The popularity of *Porgy and Bess* and its general acceptance as a great twentieth-century opera date from its Broadway revival in 1942, when it ran for twice as long as the 1935 production, and then toured the United States for eighteen months. In 1952, *Porgy and Bess* went on an international tour, playing in Vienna, Berlin, London and Paris, and later in the 1950s it toured throughout Europe, the Middle East, the USSR and Latin America. It is now encountered in opera houses all over the world.

Act I, scene i. Catfish Row, Charleston, formerly an elegant courtyard but now a tenement inhabited by blacks. It is a summer night, someone is playing a honky-tonk piano, and Clara sings a lullaby to her baby ('Summertime'). Elsewhere in the courtyard a crap game is in progress. Clara's husband, Jake, takes his turn to quieten their baby ('A woman is a sometime thing'). Porgy, a crippled beggar whose legs are paralysed and who has to haul himself about in a little goatcart, arrives and is greeted by his friends and neighbours. Crown, a stevedore, enters with his woman, Bess, and joins the crap game. A fight develops, in which Crown kills Robbins, one of the players. Bess gives Crown some money to enable him to flee before the police arrive, and Crown leaves, promising to return in due course for Bess. Meanwhile Sportin' Life, a dope peddler, offers to take Bess to New York with him. When she rejects Sportin' Life, Porgy takes her into his humble shack, just as police whistles are heard outside.

Act I, scene ii. Serena's room in Catfish Row. The body of Robbins, her husband, lies on the bed, a saucer on its chest to receive money to cover the funeral expenses. Porgy, Bess and other inhabitants of Catfish Row arrive and place money in the saucer. A policeman enters to investigate Robbins's murder and, although he is told that Crown was responsible, he takes the inoffensive Peter, the honey man, off for questioning. The wake continues, with Serena lamenting her loss ('My man's gone now') and Bess leading the others in a spiritual ('We're leavin' for the promised land').

Act II, scene i. Catfish Row. It is several weeks later, and Jake and the other fishermen are repairing the nets ('It take a long pull to get there'). Happy in his relationship with Bess, Porgy sings a cheerful song ('I got plenty o' nuttin'). Sportin' Life's attempts to peddle dope are frustrated by Maria, the keeper of the cook-shop; and a self-styled lawyer, Frazier, succeeds in selling Porgy an expensive document divorcing Bess from Crown (although she was never legally married to him). A white man arrives to inform Porgy that he will put up the bail money for Porgy's friend Peter, who is now in gaol. Porgy sees a buzzard, which he considers an omen of ill luck ('Buzzard, stay 'way from my door'). He has occasion to warn Sportin' Life to keep away from Bess. As the other inhabitants of Catfish Row prepare to go for a picnic on Kittiwah Island, Bess tells Porgy she prefers to stay at home with him. They sing a tender love duet ('Bess, you is my woman now'), and Porgy persuades Bess to go off and enjoy herself at the picnic.

Act II, scene ii. Kittiwah Island, the evening of the same day. The picnic has been a huge success. Sportin' Life entertains everyone with a light-hearted, cynical sermon on the advantages of scepticism ('It ain't necessarily so'), and Serena reminds them all that it is time to get on board the boat to go home. The others leave, but as Bess is about to follow them she is suddenly confronted by Crown, who has been hiding on the island. He tells her that he will soon be back for her. She pleads to be allowed to stay with Porgy ('What you want wid Bess?'), but she finds Crown hard to resist, and when he takes her in his arms she succumbs. The boat leaves for the mainland without her.

Act II, scene iii. Catfish Row. Jake and his colleagues prepare to go off on a fishing trip, Peter has been released from prison, and Bess, who has been lost for two days on Kittiwah Island, has returned home in a state of delirium. The cries of the streetsellers – the Strawberry Woman, the Honey Man and the Crab Man – are heard, and Bess, now restored to health, tells Porgy she wants to stay with him but is afraid of Crown ('I loves you, Porgy'). Porgy assures her that he will deal with Crown, should he return. The hurricane bell is heard, heralding the approach of a violent storm.

Act II, scene iv. Clara's room. As the hurricane rages outside, everyone has gathered to pray for the safety of themselves and their loved ones. When Clara sees her husband Jake's empty boat floating upside-down in the river, she rushes out into the storm. Crown, who has arrived back from the island, goes after her, stopping only to promise that he will be back to get Bess. The others resume their prayers for deliverance.

Act III, scene i. Catfish Row. As night falls, all are praying for Clara, Jake and Crown, whom they believe lost in the hurricane, although Sportin' Life is convinced that Crown is safe, and wonders what will happen when he returns to claim Bess, whose voice can be heard comforting Clara's baby with a lullaby. After the inhabitants of Catfish Row have drifted off to bed, Crown appears, making his way stealthily to Porgy's door. Porgy, however, has been expecting Crown, whom he kills by plunging a knife into him.

Act III, scene ii. Catfish Row. Policemen investigating the murder of Crown receive no help from the inhabitants of Catfish Row, but they arrest Porgy. Sportin' Life takes the opportunity to offer some of his 'happy dust' to Bess, promising to take her away to a better life up north ('There's a boat dat's leavin' soon for New York'). Bess at first resists him, but she finally accepts the dope he has left behind and decides to go with him.

Act III, scene iii. Catfish Row, a week later. Porgy returns, having been released for lack of evidence. He distributes presents to his friends, having done well at a crap game in prison, but becomes desperate when he fails to find Bess ('Oh Bess, oh where's my Bess?'). When he is told that she has gone to New York with Sportin' Life he resolves to make his way there and bring her back, setting off immediately in his goatcart ('Oh, Lord, I'm on my way').

The most successful American contribution to twentieth-century opera, *Porgy and Bess* contains a wealth of melody, revealing in many of its songs the strong influence of traditional jazz and the Negro spiritual. Stage productions since the mid-1970s have tended to restore some of the music cut out by Gershwin before the New York opening night, confirming the stature of this vital, exhilarating and moving work. Among the score's many highlights are Porgy's carefree 'I got plenty o' nuttin', Sportin' Life's cynical 'It ain't necessarily so' and Clara's gentle lullaby, 'Summertime'.

Recommended recording: Willard White (Porgy), Cynthia Haymon (Bess), Damon Evans (Sportin' Life), with the Glyndebourne Chorus and the London Symphony Orchestra, conducted by Simon Rattle. EMI CDS 7 49568 2. A powerful performance, based on the greatly acclaimed Glyndebourne stage production of 1986.

UMBERTO GIORDANO
(b. Foggia, 1867 – d. Milan, 1948)

Andrea Chénier
opera in four acts (approximate length: 2 hours, 15 minutes)

Andrea Chénier   *tenor*
Carlo Gérard   *baritone*
Maddalena de Coigny   *soprano*
The Countess de Coigny, her mother   *mezzo-soprano*
Bersi, Maddalena's mulatto maid   *mezzo-soprano*
Madelon, an old woman   *mezzo-soprano*
Roucher   *bass*
Pietro Fleville   *baritone*
Fouquier Tinville, public prosecutor   *baritone*
Mathieu, a waiter   *baritone*
An 'Incroyable'   *tenor*
The Abbé   *tenor*
Schmidt, a gaoler   *baritone*

LIBRETTO BY LUIGI ILLICA; TIME: BETWEEN 1789 AND 1794; PLACE: PARIS; FIRST PERFORMED AT THE TEATRO ALLA SCALA, MILAN, 28 MARCH 1896

After studying at the Naples Conservatorium, Umberto Giordano composed his first successful operas in the early days of Italian enthusiasm for *verismo* (realism), immediately after the success of Mascagni's *Cavalleria rusticana*. (Giordano's very first opera, *Marina*, written while he was still a student, came sixth in a competition in 1889 which was won by *Cavalleria rusticana*.) *Mala vita* (Evil Life; 1892), a crude work about a labourer who offers to reform a prostitute if the Virgin Mary will cure his tuberculosis, was quite popular when first performed, but it has failed to survive. Giordano reverted to an old-fashioned Romantic style for *Regina Diaz*, staged in Naples in 1894, but the failure of this opera, which was withdrawn after its second performance, caused him to compose his next work, *Andrea Chénier*, in the popular realistic style of the day. At its premiere in Milan in 1896 it was a resounding success, and the work has remained highly popular in Italy. *Fedora* (Milan, 1898) is still occasionally to be encountered, but *Siberia* (1903) has proved less enduring, and Giordano's later operas, among them *Madame Sans-Gêne* (New York, 1915), *La cena delle beffe* (The Feast of the Jesters; Milan, 1924) and *Il rè* (The King; Milan, 1929), are stronger dramatically than musically.

The hero of Giordano's most popular opera is a real historical character. André Chénier (1762–94), widely considered to be one of the finest of eighteenth-century French poets, was at first in sympathy with the ideals of the French Revolution but later became horrified at the excesses of the most violent radicals, the Jacobins, against whom he wrote denunciatory pamphlets. Arrested by order of Robespierre, whom he had attacked, Chénier was imprisoned, summarily tried, and guillotined. Luigi Illica's libretto, which weaves a fictional plot around the character of Chénier, was written for another composer, Alberto Franchetti, who generously ceded it to Giordano.

Act I. The ballroom of the Château Coigny. The room is being prepared for a reception, and one of the servants, Gérard, provoked by the sight of his aged father having to carry heavy furniture, inveighs against his employers, against the aristocracy in general and against a system of society that allows such great disparity in the distribution of wealth ('Son sessant' anni'). The Countess de Coigny enters with her daughter Maddalena, giving orders to the servants, while Maddalena discusses with her maid, Bersi, what she should wear to the reception. Gérard is secretly in love with Maddalena and comments on her beauty.

The guests begin to arrive, among them Fleville, a novelist, who presents to the Countess two of his friends, an Italian pianist and a French poet. The poet is Chénier. Another guest, the Abbé, brings the latest news about political unrest in Paris where a statue of Henri IV has been defaced by a rioting mob, but Fleville takes the guests' minds off such unpleasant topics by introducing the performance of a madrigal, the words of which he has written ('O pastorelle, addio'). After the madrigal, Maddalena and her friends ask Chénier to recite one of his poems. He replies that, like love, poetry cannot be compelled, but launches into an improvisaton ('Un dì, all' azzurro spazio') in which he contrasts the beauty of France with the misery caused to its poor by the greed of its powerful clergy, politicians and aristocrats. The Countess's guests are offended, but she deals with the situation graciously and commands the musicians to play a gavotte. The dancing is interrupted by the arrival of a crowd of beggars, led in by Gérard. When they are ordered out of the house by the Countess, Gérard angrily strips off his livery and departs with them. The Countess declares in some bewilderment that she has always been generous to the poor, and she bids the dancing continue.

Act II. The Café Hottot. It is three years later, and the Revolution is well under way. Chénier sits alone at a table. Maddalena's maid Bersi, fearing that she is being spied upon, announces to all that she is a true daughter of the Revolution, and joins in the cheering when a tumbril carrying condemned prisoners passes by. Meanwhile, an 'Incroyable' (a beau of the French Directoire period) who is a spy makes notes not only about Bersi but also about Chénier. Roucher arrives with a passport that he has managed to procure for his friend Chénier, whom he advises to flee at once for he has influential enemies. Chénier rejects his friend's advice, as he is confident about his own future ('Credo a una possanza arcana') and is intrigued by the anonymous letters he has been receiving, written in a female hand and signed 'Hope'.

As Chénier is about to leave the cafe, Robespierre and several other leaders of the Revolution arrive, among them Gérard, who describes Maddalena to the 'Incroyable' and is told she will be brought to him that evening. Bersi approaches Roucher with a message for Chénier. He must wait for 'Hope' that evening close to the nearby bust of Marat. In due course 'Hope', who is in fact Maddalena, arrives at the meeting place and is soon joined by Chénier. She asks for his help, and he declares his love for her ('Ecco l'altare'). Summoned by the 'Incroyable', Gérard appears, and he and Chénier draw swords and fight. As Gérard falls wounded, he whispers to Chénier that he must be on his guard, for he is considered to be a counter-revolutionary. Chénier escapes, and when the 'Incroyable' returns with police who ask for the name of Gérard's assailant, Gérard says he did not recognize him.

Act III. The hall of the revolutionary tribunal. Mathieu, a waiter, addresses the crowd, declaring that the country is threatened not only by invasion but also by danger from within. However, the crowd's response is listless until Gérard arrives and makes an impassioned appeal for support for the cause, at which an old woman, Madelon, announces that she has already lost a son fighting for his country but is now ready to offer her fifteen-year-old grandson to replace him. The crowd disperses, singing a revolutionary song.

Newspaper vendors proclaim the arrest of Chénier, and the 'Incroyable' assures Gérard that this will bring Maddalena in search of him. As he draws up the indictment against Chénier, Gérard wonders whether he can, in good faith, describe Chénier as an enemy of his country when he, Gérard, is no longer inflamed by brotherly love but by jealousy ('Nemico della patria'). However, he impulsively signs the indictment and hands it to the 'Incroyable'.

Maddalena is brought before Gérard, who explains that her beloved Chénier has been arrested because he, Gérard, also loves her. Maddalena describes her mother's death and the destruction of their chateau by the mob ('La mamma morta'), but offers to give herself to Gérard if he will save Chénier's life. The court assembles and the accused, Chénier among them, are brought in. When the charges against him are read, Chénier defends himself ('Si, fui soldato'). But although Gérard insists that the accusations against him are false, Chénier is condemned to death.

Act IV. The courtyard of the prison of St Lazare. Chénier sits writing his last poem. When Roucher arrives, Chénier reads it to him ('Come un bel dì di Maggio'). Roucher leaves, and Gérard enters with Maddalena. He has agreed to let her change places with a female prisoner, so that she can die on the scaffold with Chénier. She and Chénier sing an impassioned duet in which they rejoice that death will unite them for ever ('Vicino a te'), and then they are led to the guillotine.

Giordano's music possesses emotive power and theatrical effectiveness, even if the quality of his melody is often commonplace. In *Andrea Chénier* he successfully contrasts the elegant eighteenth-century aristocratic style of Act I with the strident popular emotionalism of the revolutionaries in the later acts. The arias are made to arise naturally from their surroundings, and the short final act with Chénier's aria 'Come un bel dì di Maggio' and the heroic love duet brings the opera to an exciting conclusion. Chénier's 'Sì, fui soldato' and Gérard's 'Nemico della patria' in Act III are among the opera's finest numbers.

Recommended recording: Renata Scotto (Maddalena), Placido Domingo (Chénier), Sherrill Milnes (Gerard), with the John Alldis Choir and the National Philharmonic Orchestra, conducted by James Levine. RCA Victor GD 82046. A 1941 EMI recording with Beniamino Gigli in the title-role is worth seeking out, but the opera has also been well served in more recent recordings. Renata Tebaldi and Mario del Monaco

(Decca) are exciting, while Montserrat Caballé and Luciano Pavarotti, on a later Decca set, are perhaps the more mellifluous pair. The best of modern versions, however, is that conducted with dramatic urgency by James Levine, with Renata Scotto an eloquent Maddalena, Placido Domingo probably the best Chénier since Gigli, and Sherrill Milnes a strongly characterized Gerard.

Fedora

opera in three acts (approximate length: 1 hour, 45 minutes)

Princess Fedora Romazov   *soprano*
Count Loris Ipanov   *tenor*
De Siriex, a diplomat   *baritone*
Countess Olga Sukarev   *soprano*
Grech, a police officer   *bass*
Cirillo, a coachman   *baritone*
Dmitri, a groom   *contralto*
Desire, a valet   *tenor*
Boleslao Lazinski, a pianist   *mime*
Borov, a doctor   *baritone*

LIBRETTO BY ARTURO COLAUTTI, BASED ON VICTORIEN SARDOU'S PLAY *FÉDORA*; TIME: THE LATE NINETEENTH CENTURY; PLACE: ST PETERSBURG, PARIS AND SWITZERLAND; FIRST PERFORMED AT THE TEATRO LIRICO, MILAN, 17 NOVEMBER 1898

After the success of *Andrea Chénier* at La Scala, Milan, in 1896, Giordano found himself firmly established as one of the leading young composers of Italy. At the invitation of the publisher and impresario Edoardo Sonzogno, he set to work immediately on his next opera, based on Sardou's play *Fédora*, which he had seen with Sarah Bernhardt in the title role while he was still a student in Naples. Victorien Sardou (1831–1908) was at that time the most popular living French dramatist, whose plays, designed as vehicles for stars such as Bernhardt (for whom Sardou also wrote *La Tosca*), were performed all over Europe. *Fédora*, first staged in Paris in 1882, was one of his greatest successes.

Act I. Count Vladimir's house in St Petersburg. The Count's servants are playing dominoes while they await their master's return to the house. They discuss his dissolute way of life which, they say, will no doubt have to change, now that he is about to be married to the wealthy Princess Fedora Romazov. Fedora arrives to await her fiancé ('O grandi occhi lucenti'), but when Vladimir returns home he is carried in seriously wounded, accompanied by Grech, a police oficer, and De Siriex, a diplomat. Vladimir is taken to his bedroom, while Grech begins to interrogate the servants as the doctor arrives. Cirillo, Vladimir's coachman, tells of having heard two shots fired, and De Siriex recounts how he arrived on the scene and followed a trail of blood to a house rented by an old woman, where he and Cirillo discovered Count Vladimir lying wounded. The valet Desire recalls that an old woman had visited Count Vladimir that morning, bringing him a letter, which now cannot be found. Dmitri, a groom, says that a young man had also called earlier, but had left without giving his name. When another servant remembers that the young man was Count Loris Ipanov, Fedora immediately concludes that it must have been Ipanov who shot her fiancé. She swears to have vengeance ('Dite coraggio'). Grech leaves in search of Ipanov, who lives nearby, but returns to say that the Count has escaped. The doctor summons Fedora to Count Vladimir's side, just as Vladimir dies.

Act II. Princess Fedora's house in Paris, some months later. Fedora has found Count Loris Ipanov in Paris, whither he had fled, and has invited him to a reception at her house. Among her other guests are the Countess Olga Sukarev, De Siriex and Boleslao Lazinski, a pianist. Fedora tells De Siriex that she followed Ipanov to Paris and succeeded in making him fall in love with her. De Siriex flirts with Olga, singing her a song about Russian women ('La donna russa è femmina due volte'), to which Olga responds with a song about Parisian men ('Il parigino è come il vino'). Ipanov is warned by his friend Borov to beware of Fedora, but when he finds himself alone with her he declares his love, and claims that, despite herself, she loves him in return ('Amor ti vieta').

Borov tells Fedora that he is about to return to Russia, to which she replies that she, too, is returning. Ipanov is clearly upset by this, but has to admit that he cannot go back to Russia. When the pianist Lazinski begins to play for the guests, Ipanov confesses to Fedora that he was forced to leave Russia because he had killed a man. He promises to explain in detail and to justify his deed, after the guests have left. The party breaks up precipitately when news is received of an attempt by nihilists on the Tsar's life.

Left alone, Fedora writes a letter to the chief of police in St Petersburg, denouncing Ipanov. When Grech arrives, she arranges with him that his men will kidnap Ipanov as he leaves her house. Ipanov now returns. He informs Fedora that he killed Vladimir. Having discovered that Vladimir was having an affair with his wife, he burst in on them and fired a shot at Vladimir, but only after Vladimir had already fired at him. Ipanov gives Fedora proof of this, in the form of letters whose contents make it clear that Vladimir had planned to marry Fedora only for her money. Ashamed that she had thought him an assassin, Fedora persuades Ipanov not to leave and encounter his pursuers, but to stay with her. They declare their love for each other ('Lascia che pianga io solo').

Act III. Fedora's villa in Switzerland. Fedora and Ipanov are living together happily, with Olga as their house guest. De Siriex arrives to visit them, and he informs Olga that her friend in Paris, the pianist Lazinski, was really a Polish spy. Left alone with Fedora – Ipanov having gone off to collect the post – De Siriex tells her that Ipanov's brother was arrested as an accomplice in the killing of Count Vladimir, and imprisoned. He drowned in prison when the River Neva flooded his dungeon cell, and the news of his death caused his mother to collapse and die. When De Siriex leaves, Fedora prays that Ipanov be saved from danger ('Dio di giustizia').

Ipanov returns and opens a telegram from his friend Borov informing him that he has been pardoned by the Tsar. But a letter, sent before the telegram, indicates that Ipanov has been denounced by a Russian woman living in Paris and that this has led to the deaths of his brother and his mother. When Fedora tries to suggest that the woman may have acted in the belief that he was a murderer, Ipanov realizes that the woman in question must have been Fedora herself. As he seizes her violently, she swallows poison from the Byzantine crucifix she is wearing. Borov arrives to find her dying in the arms of a remorseful Ipanov.

Though saddled with an overbusy, melodramatic and none too credible plot, and trivial music which often fails to impose itself upon the dramatic situation, *Fedora* remains alive by virtue of its impassioned love duet and Loris Ipanov's aria, 'Amor ti vieta', which seems to be in the repertoire of virtually every Italian tenor, even when the remainder of the role is not.

Recommended recording: Magda Oliviero (Fedora), Mario del Monaco (Ipanov), Tito Gobbi (De Siriex), with the Monte Carlo Opera Chorus and Orchestra, conducted by Lamberto Gardelli. Decca 433 033–2DM2. Oliviero and Del Monaco bring their superb vocal and dramatic resources to the leading roles, and Tito Gobbi as De Sireux is de luxe casting. In this 1969 recording, a young Kiri Te Kanawa sings the small role of Dmitri.

MIKHAIL GLINKA

(b. Novopasskoye, 1804 – d. Berlin, 1857)

A Life for the Tsar

(Zhizn 'za tsarya)

opera in four acts and an epilogue (approximate length: 3 hours)

Ivan Susanin, a peasant   *bass*
Antonida, his daughter   *soprano*
Sobinin, her fiancé   *tenor*
Vanya, an orphan adopted by Susanin   *contralto*
A Polish Commander   *baritone*

LIBRETTO BY BARON GEORGY FYODOROVICH ROZEN; TIME: 1613; PLACE: RUSSIA AND POLAND; FIRST PERFORMED AT THE BOLSHOI THEATRE, ST PETERSBURG, 9 DECEMBER 1836

The father of the nineteenth-century Russian nationalist school of composers, and a pioneer in Russian opera, Glinka completed only two operas, though he made sketches for three more. While in his twenties he attended performances in St Petersburg of a number of operas by Rossini given by a touring Italian company, so it is hardly surprising that his first completed opera, *A Life for the Tsar*, in effect the first real Russian opera, should be cast in the Rossinian bel canto mould. It was, in fact, on his return in 1833 from a three-year residence in Italy, where he met Bellini, that Glinka began the composition of *A Life for the Tsar*.

The opera's story, drawn from Russian history, is that of Ivan Susanin, a peasant who in 1613 saved the life of the first of the Romanov tsars. Glinka composed *Ivan Susanin* quickly, sometimes producing music for particular scenes or incidents before his librettist, Georgy Fyodorovich Rozen, secretary to the Tsarevich, had written the words. During rehearsals the opera's title was changed, with the approval of the Tsar, to the more patriotically stirring *A Life for the Tsar*. A tremendous success at its premiere in St Petersburg in 1836, it became the most frequently performed native opera in Russia until the Revolution. During the Marxist regime in the Soviet Union, it was provided with a new libretto and reverted to its original title.

Act I. The village of Domnino. The peasants rejoice at a Russian victory against the invading Poles. Antonida awaits her fiancé, Sobinin, who is returning from the front line ('I gaze over the broad field'), but her father, Ivan Susanin, expresses his fears for their country's future while they are without a tsar, and he refuses to allow the marriage of Antonida to Sobinin while Russia is in danger. When Sobinin announces that their landlord, Mikhail Romanov, is to be crowned Tsar in Moscow, Susanin agrees to the wedding.

Act II. The Polish camp. A ball is in progress, when news arrives of the election of a new Russian tsar. Soldiers leave to kidnap the Tsar at his country estate of Kostroma before he can be crowned in Moscow.

Act III. Susanin's cottage. Vanya, an orphan adopted by Susanin, laments that he is too young to fight against the Poles. When Polish soldiers arrive and demand that Susanin lead them to the Tsar, Susanin takes them off on a false trail, after telling Vanya to warn the Tsar and advising Antonida not to delay her wedding. Sobinin and his friends leave to rescue Susanin.

Act IV, scene i. A forest glade. Sobinin and his followers arrive, having lost their way ('Brothers, into the storm').

Act IV, scene ii. The gates of the Kostroma monastery. Vanya rouses the inhabitants and warns them of the danger to the Tsar ('My poor horse has fallen in the field').

Act IV, scene iii. A forest glade. Susanin and the Polish soldiers set up camp for the night, and Susanin broods on his fate ('You will come, my dawn?'). The Poles, suspecting that they are being led on a false trail, question Susanin closely. At dawn, knowing that by now the Tsar will be safe, Susanin confesses his deception and is killed. Sobinin and his friends arrive and attack the Poles.

Epilogue. The Kremlin square in Moscow. An exultant crowd acclaims the new Tsar, while Antonida, Sobinin and Vanya lament the death of Susanin.

Full of broad, Italianate melodies, *A Life for the Tsar* can prove dramatically much more effective in performance than a synopsis of its plot might suggest. It is also sufficiently Russian in colouring for its subtitle in 1836, 'patriotic heroic-tragic opera in five acts', to be perfectly feasible.

Recommended recording: Alexandrina Pendachanska (Antonida), Stefania Toczyska (Vanya), Chris Merritt (Sobinin), Boris Martinovich (Ivan Susanin), with the Sofia National Opera Chorus and Sofia Festival Orchestra, conducted by Emil Tchakarov. Sony CD 46487. Well cast and strongly conducted.

Ruslan i Lyudmila
(Ruslan and Lyudmila)
opera in five acts (approximate length: 3 hours, 15 minutes)

Svetozar, Grand Prince of Kiev   *bass*
Lyudmila, his daughter   *soprano*
Ruslan, a knight   *baritone*
Ratmir, an oriental prince   *contralto*
Farlaf, a warrior   *bass*
Gorislava, Ratmir's slave   *soprano*
Finn, a good sorcerer   *tenor*
Naina, a bad sorceress   *mezzo-soprano*
Bayan, a bard   *tenor*
Chernomor, an evil dwarf   *mime*

LIBRETTO BY VALERIAN FYODOROVICH SHIRKOV AND OTHERS, BASED PARTLY ON ALEXANDER PUSHKIN'S POEM *RUSLAN AND LYUDMILA*; TIME: THE LEGENDARY PAST; PLACE: RUSSIA; FIRST PERFORMED AT THE BOLSHOI THEATRE, ST PETERSBURG, 9 DECEMBER 1842

It was shortly after the immensely successful premiere of *A Life for the Tsar* in 1836 that Glinka was invited by Alexander Shakovskoy, the Intendant of the Imperial Theatres, to embark upon a second opera. Shakovskoy had written a dramatic trilogy based partly on Alexander Pushkin's *Ruslan and Lyudmila*, a long poem which had appeared in 1820 and had established Pushkin's reputation as one of Russia's most outstanding younger poets. It was at Shakovskoy's suggestion that Glinka turned to Pushkin's poem for his subject. In fact, Glinka attempted to turn to Pushkin himself, hoping that the poet, whose reputation by this time had been consolidated by the appearance of his major works, *Boris Godunov* (1825), *Eugene Onegin* (1831) and *The Queen of Spades* (1833), would collaborate with him and provide a libretto for *Ruslan and Lyudmila*. Unfortunately, jealousy over his wife's attachment to a guards officer had led Pushkin to challenge the officer to a duel in which, on 29 January 1837, Pushkin was fatally wounded. Undaunted, Glinka began to compose his opera before a libretto had been written. Early the following year, an acquaintance of Glinka told another composer, Alexei Verstovsky, that Glinka's opera 'is almost finished, but as yet there is no text. A strange way of writing!'

In 1838, still at work on the opera, Glinka asked Valerian Fyodorovich Shirkov, a landowner and amateur poet, to fit words to some of the numbers he had composed. Other pieces used Pushkin's own words, in one instance adapted by Nikolai Markevich. When Shirkov left St Petersburg to return to his estate, two other poets, Mikhail Gedeonov and Nestor Kukolnik, contributed the words for two or three scenes. Glinka himself wrote the words of a scene in Act II, and by the beginning of 1842 the opera was complete. Although it was a success at its premiere in St Petersburg at the end of that year, *Ruslan and Lyudmila* soon found itself unable to compete with the fashionable Italian operas that Russian audiences now seemed to prefer. After 1848, Glinka's opera was not performed again during its composer's lifetime.

Act I. The court of Svetozar, Grand Prince of Kiev. Svetozar's daughter Lyudmila is about to marry Ruslan. The guests at the banquet include Lyudmila's rejected suitors, Ratmir and Farlaf. Having been blessed by Svetozar, the happy couple are about to proceed ceremonially to their nuptial bed, when the hall is plunged into darkness and Lyudmila is abducted by an evil dwarf, Chernomor. Svetozar promises his daughter's hand in marriage to whoever rescues her, so Ruslan, Ratmir and Farlaf all rush off to find Lyudmila.

   Act II, scene i. Finn's cave in the mountains. Ruslan arrives to consult Finn, a benevolent sorcerer, who reveals to him the name of Lyudmila's abductor and then recounts the story of his own unhappy courtship of Naina, an evil sorceress.

   Act II, scene ii. A desert place. Farlaf encounters Naina, who promises to help him find Lyudmila.

   Act II, scene iii. A deserted battlefield. Ruslan confronts an enormous head, whose breath produces a tremendous wind, attempting to blow him down. When Ruslan angrily runs the Head through with his lance, the head yields up a sword with which, it assures him, he will be able to defeat the dwarf Chernomor, the brother of the head.

   Act III. Naina's enchanted castle. Gorislava, a maiden who is in love with Ratmir, is Naina's prisoner in the castle. Ratmir arrives, and the dancing of Naina's slave girls hypnotizes him into forgetting his quest. Ruslan, too, when he arrives, is made to forget Lyudmila. The sorcerer Finn appears and frees everyone from Naina's spell. Ratmir and Gorislava embrace, while Ruslan continues his search for Lyudmila.

   Act IV. The garden of Chernomor's magic castle. Lyudmila rejects the advances of her captor, Chernomor. When Ruslan arrives, Chernomor casts Lyudmila into a deep slumber before going off to do battle with him. Ruslan defeats Chernomor by cutting off his beard, the source of the dwarf's magic power. Then, unable to awaken Lyudmila, he departs with her towards home.

Act V, scene i. On the road to Kiev, at night. Farlaf, with the aid of Naina, has abducted Lyudmila, and Ruslan has gone in pursuit of them.

Act V, scene ii. The court of Svetozar. Farlaf has brought Lyudmila back to her father's palace, hoping to be able to claim her as his bride. However, he is unable to awaken her. When Ruslan, Ratmir and Gorislava rush in, Farlaf flees. Ruslan awakens his bride, their wedding feast is resumed and the opera ends in general rejoicing.

Ruslan and Lyudmila is musically full of riches, even more so than Glinka's earlier opera, *A Life for the Tsar*. A seminal work, it profoundly influenced later Russian composers such as Balakirev and Tchaikovsky, and the vivid oriental colouring of much of its orchestration was to be copied by, among others, Borodin and Rimsky-Korsakov. Glinka's score, less Italian in its orientation than that of *A Life for the Tsar*, borrows from the folk music of Russia, Persia, Turkey and Finland. Perhaps because of its cumbersome dramatic structure, *Ruslan and Lyudmila* has never achieved wide popularity outside Russia.

Recommended recording: Vladimir Ognovienko (Ruslan), Anna Netrebko (Lyudmila), Mikhail Kit (Svetozar), with the Chorus and Orchestra of the Kirov Theatre, conducted by Valery Gergiev. Philips 446 746–2PH3. No other conductor today can equal Gergiev, the most authentic and exciting interpreter of Russian opera. His Kirov company, too, is unequalled in the music of their country.

CHRISTOPH WILLIBALD GLUCK
(b. Erasbach, 1714 – d. Vienna, 1787)

Orfeo ed Euridice
(Orpheus and Eurydice)
opera in three acts (approximate length: 1 hour, 45 minutes)

Orfeo (Orpheus)   *mezzo-soprano; originally alto castrato*
Euridice (Eurydice)   *soprano*
Amore (Cupid)   *soprano*

LIBRETTO BY RANIERI DE' CALZABIGI; TIME: THE LEGENDARY PAST; PLACE: CLASSI-
CAL GREECE, AND HADES; FIRST PERFORMED AT THE BURGTHEATER, VIENNA, 5
OCTOBER 1762; FRENCH VERSION, WITH CALZABIGI'S LIBRETTO ADAPTED BY
PIERRE LOUIS MOLINE, FIRST PERFORMED AT THE PARIS OPÉRA, 2 AUGUST 1774

Gluck's importance lies in the fact that, although he began as a composer of
the old *opera seria*, he effected a reform in his later works by rebelling against
the formal conventions of Italian opera and by striking a new balance between
music and drama. Although few of his forty-three operas (which today can seem
as stiffly formal as those against which Gluck rebelled) are now regularly performed, his greatest works have remained in the repertoire. Gluck's first opera,
Artaserse, was performed in Milan in 1741. He composed a further seven operas
for Italy before visiting London in 1746 and writing two operas, *La caduta de'
giganti* (The Fall of the Giants) and *Artamene*, which were staged in that year at
the King's Theatre in the Haymarket to little acclaim. In 1752 he settled in Vienna,
where he composed to both Italian and French texts. The first of his great 'reform'
operas was *Orfeo ed Euridice*, performed in Vienna in 1762.

   Gluck had already composed ballet music and several *opéras comiques* for
Viennese theatres when, in 1761, he met Ranieri de' Calzabigi, an Italian librettist
newly arrived in Vienna, who despised the traditional Baroque operas. It was
Calzabigi who suggested to Gluck the subject of *Orfeo ed Euridice*, the first of the
three operas they were to create together in reaction against the stylization of
Baroque *opera seria*. *Orfeo ed Euridice* was a huge success at its premiere in Vienna
and has remained by far the most popular of Gluck's operas. Its initial acclaim in
Vienna was due, as Calzabigi admitted, not only to the opera's intrinsic merit but
also to the performance of Gaetano Guadagni, the famous alto castrato for whom
Gluck wrote the role of Orfeo.

Act I, scene i. The tomb of Euridice. Orfeo and a chorus of nymphs and shepherds mourn the death of Orfeo's beloved wife, Euridice ('Ah, se intorno a
quest'una funesta'). Orfeo sings of his grief ('Chiamo il mio ben cosi') and then
resolves to bring Euridice back from the land of the dead.

   Act I, scene ii. The same. Amore appears. The god of love tells Orfeo that Zeus
has taken pity on him and will allow him to descend into Hades, charm the Furies
with his singing and rescue Euridice. But if he looks at her on the journey back he
will lose her for ever ('Gli sguardi rattieni').

   Act II, scene i. A hideous grotto near the banks of the River Cocytus. After a violent orchestral introduction, the music of Orfeo's lyre is heard as he approaches.

The Furies sing and dance in a frenzy, and Orfeo tries to calm them. Eventually he succeeds, and they allow him to pass through Hades into Elysium.

Act II, scene ii. The Elysian Fields. The inhabitants sing of their joy in being in such blissful surroundings. Orfeo enters, exclaiming at the beauty of the place ('Che puro ciel'), and the Blessed Spirits tell him that Euridice will soon be restored to him ('Vieni a regni del riposo'). Euridice is brought in, and Orfeo leads her away without looking at her.

Act III, scene i. A dark grotto in an ugly landscape, leading away from Hades. Orfeo leads Euridice by the hand without looking back at her. Euridice cannot understand his strange behaviour, and wants him to explain ('Vieni, appaga il tuo consorte'). When he is unable to do so, she becomes suspicious ('Che fiero momento'). Unable to contemplate her suffering, Orfeo turns to her and she immediately sinks to the ground and dies. Orfeo laments her death ('Che faro senza Euridice?').

Act III, scene ii. The same. Orfeo is about to kill himself when Amore appears, tells him that his constancy has been sufficiently tested and restores Euridice to life.

Act III, scene iii. The temple of Amore. Orfeo and Euridice, with nymphs and shepherds, give thanks to the god of love.

Twelve years after its premiere in Vienna, Gluck revised *Orfeo ed Euridice* for performance in Paris. Calzabigi's libretto was translated and added to by a young French poet, Pierre Louis Moline, and *Orphée et Eurydice* was staged at the Paris Opéra on 2 August 1774. As the castrato voice was virtually unheard of in French music, Gluck recast the role of Orpheus for a high tenor voice, included more ballet music to suit Parisian taste and added other numbers to make the opera longer and grander. One of these additions, a lengthy bravura aria for Orpheus ('L'espoir renait dans mon âme'), makes an exciting conclusion to Act I. The Dance of the Furies, which ends the first scene of Act II in this Paris version, uses music from Gluck's 1761 ballet *Don Juan*.

The French version of the opera is rarely performed today, there being very few tenors who can cope with Orpheus's extremely high tessitura – although Nicolai Gedda undertook the role successfully in Aix-en-Provence (1955) and Paris (1973). Most productions now are of Gluck's original Italian version, with the alto castrato role of Orpheus sung by a female mezzo-soprano or a male falsettist (or, in Germany, by a baritone). In either version, Gluck's classically poised yet deeply expressive score brings the legend of Orpheus and Eurydice most movingly to life. Orpheus's lament, 'Che faro senza Euridice?' (or 'J'ai perdu mon Eurydice') is well known outside the context of the opera.

Recommended recording: Janet Baker (Orfeo), Elisabeth Gale (Euridice), Elisabeth Speiser (Amore), with the Glyndebourne Chorus and London Philharmonic Orchestra, conducted by Raymond Leppard. Erato Libretto 2292–45864–2. Janet Baker's beautiful and deeply expressive voice is ideal for Orpheus, and Elisabeth Gale is a sweet Eurydice. Raymond Leppard conducts an urgent and vivid performance, and includes the final ballet which is usually omitted.

Alceste
opera in three acts (approximate length: 2 hours, 15 minutes)

Alceste   *soprano*
Admetus   *tenor*
Evander   *tenor*
Ismene   *soprano*
Herald   *bass*
High Priest of Apollo   *baritone*
Apollo   *baritone*
Hercules   *bass*
Oracle   *bass*
Thanatos, an infernal deity   *bass*

LIBRETTO BY RANIERI DE' CALZABIGI, BASED ON EURIPIDES' *ALCESTIS*; TIME: CLASSICAL ANTIQUITY; PLACE: CLASSICAL PHERAE, THESSALY; FIRST PERFORMED AT THE BURGTHEATER, VIENNA, 26 DECEMBER 1767; FRENCH VERSION, WITH CALZABIGI'S LIBRETTO ADAPTED BY MARIE FRANÇOIS LOUIS GAND LEBLANC DU ROULLET, FIRST PERFORMED AT THE PARIS OPÉRA, 23 APRIL 1776.

After the success of *Orfeo ed Euridice* in Vienna in 1762, Gluck composed several operas to librettos by other poets before collaborating again with Ranieri de' Calzabigi on *Alceste*, which was given its first performance in Vienna in 1767. When he revised *Alceste* for performance in Paris in 1776, Gluck made extensive alterations to the work, and his French librettist, Leblanc du Roullet, not only translated Calzabigi's Italian text but also substantially altered and added to it. The French version of the opera is now the more frequently performed.

Act I, scene i. Outside the palace of Admetus. The citizens call on the gods to restore their King, Admetus, to health, but a herald announces that the King is close to death. The Queen, Alceste, appears with her two children and asks the gods to show pity ('Grands Dieux! Du destin qui m'accable').

Act I, scene ii. The temple of Apollo. The High Priest invokes the god Apollo, and the voice of the Oracle declares that Admetus will die unless someone is sacrificed in his place. Alceste offers to give her life for Admetus, and the High Priest tells her that her sacrifice is accepted. She must, that day, descend to Hades ('Divinités du Styx').

Act II. A room in the royal palace. Led by Evander, the citizens rejoice at Admetus's recovery. The King is saddened to learn that his survival depends upon the sacrifice of another's life, and when he subsequently discovers that Alceste is the victim he refuses to accept her sacrifice. The citizens beg Alceste not to die, but she is determined to submit to the will of the gods.

Act III, scene i. Outside the palace. The people mourn the deaths of both Alceste and Admetus, who has followed his wife to Hades ('Pleure, o patrie'). Hercules arrives from having completed his labours. When the citizens tell him of the fate of Alceste, he resolves to rescue her.

Act III, scene ii. The entrance to Hades. Alceste pleads with the gods to be admitted at once to Hades. She is joined by Admetus who refuses to be separated from her ('Alceste, au nom des dieux'). When Thanatos, an infernal deity, decrees that only one of them shall enter Hades, each wants the other to live. Hercules arrives and defies the gods. The god Apollo appears, announcing that Hercules by his action has won a place among the gods for himself, and that Admetus and Alceste, having proved themselves a perfect example of conjugal love, shall both live.

Act III, scene iii. Outside the palace of Admetus. Apollo restores Admetus and Alceste to their people, and bids the citizens rejoice.

Especially in its French version, *Alceste* is a work of grave beauty and classical simplicity. It is also by no means lacking in drama, as exemplified by Alceste's magnificent aria 'Divinités du Styx', which concludes Act I, and by the central scene of Act III. *Alceste*'s influence can be discerned in Mozart's *Idomeneo* and *Don Giovanni* as well as in a number of French operas of the late eighteenth century.

Recommended recording: Jessye Norman (Alceste), Nicolai Gedda (Admetus), with the Bavarian Radio Chorus and Orchestra, conducted by Serge Baudo. Orfeo C 02782.

Iphigénie en Aulide
(Iphigenia in Aulis)
opera in three acts (approximate length: 2 hours, 30 minutes)

Agamemnon, King of Mycenae *baritone*
Clitemnestra (Clytemnestra), his wife *soprano*
Iphigénie (Iphigenia), their daughter *soprano*
Achille (Achilles), a Greek hero *tenor*
Patrocle (Patroclus), friend of Achilles *bass*
Calchas, high priest *bass*
Arcas, captain of Agamemnon's guards *bass*

LIBRETTO BY MARIE FRANÇOIS LOUIS GAND LEBLANC DU ROULLET, AFTER THE
PLAY *IPHIGÉNIE EN AULIDE*, BY JEAN BAPTISTE RACINE (1674); TIME: CLASSICAL
ANTIQUITY; PLACE: AULIS, A PORT ON THE ISLAND OF EUBOEA; FIRST PERFORMED
AT THE PARIS OPÉRA, 19 APRIL 1774

In 1772 Marie François Louis Gand Leblanc du Roullet, an attaché at the French embassy in Vienna, showed Gluck a libretto that he had written, based on Racine's tragedy *Iphigénie en Aulide*, which in turn had been derived from the *Iphigenia in Aulis* of Euripides. Gluck, who had not yet written an opera for Paris, was sufficiently impressed by the libretto to begin setting it to music immediately. When the opera was completed it was offered to the Paris Opéra, whose directors accepted it on condition that the composer agreed to write five more operas for Paris. *Iphigénie en Aulide* in fact became the first of seven operas Gluck was to compose for Paris. It was an immediate success at its premiere, and for the next five years Gluck continued to compose his operas in Vienna, for performance in Paris.

Act I. The Greek camp at Aulis. The Greek army has been becalmed on its voyage to Troy, and the Oracle has declared that the anger of the goddess Diana will be appeased and the fleet allowed to continue on its way to Troy only if the Greek King, Agamemnon, who has incurred the goddess's wrath by killing her favourite stag, sacrifices his daughter, Iphigénie. Agamemnon has reluctantly sent to Greece for his wife, Clytemnestra, and their daughter Iphigénie, on the pretext that Iphigénie is to be married to Achilles, a Greek hero who is in love with her. But Agamemnon has had a change of heart ('Brillant auteur de la lumière') and has sent Arcas, captain of his guards, to turn his wife and daughter back to Greece. The message is not delivered, and Iphigénie and Clytemnestra arrive. They are welcomed by the Greeks, and Clytemnestra replies ('Que j'aime à voir ces hommages flatteurs').

In an attempt to remove his daughter from Aulis and save her from being sacrificed, Agamemnon tells Clytemnestra that Achilles has been unfaithful to Iphigénie and that there will be no marriage. Clytemnestra, in a fury, passes this information on to her daughter and urges her to leave. Iphigénie laments that she ever loved Achilles ('Hélas, mon coeur sensible et tendre'), but when that hero arrives he is able to assure her that he has not been unfaithful. They sing of their love and of their imminent marriage ('Ne doutez jamais de ma flamme').

Act II. The Greek camp. Iphigénie expresses her changing emotions concerning her imminent marriage and the bad feeling that now exists between her father and Achilles ('Par la crainte et par l'esperance'). The marriage celebrations begin, but are interrupted by Arcas, who announces that, far from giving his daughter in marriage, Agamemnon intends to kill her as she approaches the altar. Clytemnestra begs Achilles to save Iphigénie ('Par un père cruel à la mort condamnée'). When Achilles and Agamemnon meet, Achilles warns the King that he will not allow his bride to be sacrificed ('De votre audace téméraire'). Left alone, Agamemnon resolves to send Clytemnestra and Iphigénie away, and asks the goddess Diana to take his life rather than his daughter's.

Act III, scene i. The Greek camp. The assembled Greeks, anxious to proceed to Troy, demand that a sacrifice be made. Achilles asks Iphigénie to leave with him, but she insists on submitting herself to the will of the gods ('Il faut de mon destin'). She bids farewell to Achilles who, however, still hopes to save her ('Calchas, d'un trait mortel percé'). After Clytemnestra too has said farewell to Iphigénie, she has a vision of her daughter's sacrifice and calls on Jupiter to intervene ('Jupiter, lance la foudre!').

Act III, scene ii. An altar by the seashore. As Iphigénie kneels on the steps of the altar, the ceremony of sacrifice is interrupted by Achilles and his followers, who are determined to save her. Calchas intervenes to announce that Diana's pity has been aroused and that the sacrifice is no longer required. Amid general rejoicing, Iphigénie is restored to her lover and her parents, and the Greeks prepare to voyage onward to Troy.

Gluck's score has immense dramatic power. From its overture to its final chorus, *Iphigénie en Aulide* holds one's attention throughout, due as much to the way in which the leading characters of Iphigénie, Agamemnon and Clytemnestra come alive as to the opera's profusion of arias and choruses that are not only melodically memorable but also dramatically meaningful.

Recommended recording: Lynne Dawson (Iphigenia), José van Dam (Agamemnon), Anne Sofie von Otter (Clytemnestra), John Aler (Achilles), with the Monteverdi Choir and the Lyon Opera Orchestra, conducted by John Eliot Gardiner. Erato 2292–45003–2. A strong cast, and Gardiner conducts with urgency and power.

Iphigénie en Tauride
(Iphigenia in Tauris)
opera in four acts (approximate length: 2 hours)

Iphigénie (Iphigenia), high priestess of Diana   *soprano*
Oreste (Orestes), her brother   *baritone*
Pylade (Pylades), his friend   *tenor*
Thoas, King of the Scythians   *bass*
The Goddess Diane (Diana)   *soprano*

LIBRETTO BY NICOLAS-FRANÇOIS GUILLARD, BASED ON THE PLAY *IPHIGÉNIE EN TAURIDE* (1757), BY CLAUDE GUYMOND DE LA TOUCHE; TIME: CLASSICAL ANTIQUITY; PLACE: TAURIS (NOW THE CRIMEA); FIRST PERFORMED AT THE PARIS OPÉRA, 18 MAY 1779

Gluck's penultimate opera, and his last great success in Paris, *Iphigénie en Tauride* is one of his finest and most dramatically effective works for the stage, even though in composing it he made lavish use of material from some of his earlier works. Having, in *Iphigénie en Aulide* (1774), taken his subject from a play that ultimately derived from Euripides, he now did so again, for the comparatively recent French play on which Nicolas-François Guillard, a young Parisian playwright and poet, based his libretto was itself based on the *Iphigenia in Tauris* of Euripides. The enthusiasm with which Gluck's opera was received at its premiere signalled the composer's ultimate victory over his great rival, Niccolò Piccinni. Gluck also made a German-language version of the opera, *Iphigenie auf Tauris*, which was performed in Vienna in 1781, but it is the original French opera that has held the stage and had several important modern revivals. Famous twentieth-century sopranos (and mezzo-sopranos, for the role's tessitura is not high) who have sung Iphigénie include Maria Callas, Regine Crespin, Rita Gorr, Shirley Verrett and Sena Jurinac.

Act I. The sacred wood of Diana. The opera begins not with a formal overture but with an orchestral depiction of calm, followed by a storm at the height of which the voices of Iphigénie, now a high priestess of Diana, and her priestesses are heard, imploring the gods to protect them. When the storm has died away, Iphigénie broods on the torment in her heart. She has had a dream in which her mother, Clytemnestra, murdered her father, Agamemnon, and in which she, Iphigénie, was forced to kill her brother Orestes in sacrifice. She begs the goddess Diana to have pity on her ('O toi, qui prolongeas mes jours').

Thoas, King of Tauris, arrives, demanding that Iphigénie sacrifice a stranger in order to appease the gods. After Thoas has sent Iphigénie off to prepare for the ceremony, two Greeks who have landed on the coast are brought in. They are Iphigénie's brother Orestes and his friend Pylades, and it is Pylades who is chosen to be the sacrificial victim.

Act II. A sacrificial chamber in the temple of Diana. Orestes and Pylades are in chains. Orestes, consumed with guilt at having killed his mother, calls on the gods to punish him, and laments that he is the cause of his friend Pylades' imminent death ('Dieux qui me poursuivez'). Before he is taken away, Pylades assures Orestes that their friendship remains undisturbed ('Unis des la plus tendre enfance'). Thinking that Pylades has gone to his death, Orestes calls out in anguish to the gods to kill him as well, and then he tries to assure himself that he feels calmer ('Le calme rentre dans mon coeur'), although his words are contradicted by an anxious ostinato rhythm in the orchestra.

Orestes falls asleep, only to dream that the Furies are tormenting him, and he awakens to find himself confronted by Iphigénie. Brother and sister, who have not met for several years, fail to recognize each other. Iphigénie asks for news of their homeland, and Orestes describes Clytemnestra's murder of her husband Agamemnon and her subsequent death at the hand of her son. He adds that Orestes is now dead. Iphigénie expresses her grief ('O malheureuse Iphigénie'), and together with her priestesses performs funeral rites for Orestes ('Contemplez ces tristes apprets').

Act III. Iphigenia's room. Iphigénie decides to send one of the two prisoners back to Greece with a message for her sister Elektra. Struck by his resemblance to the brother she thinks dead, she chooses Orestes, who swears to end his own life if Pylades is sacrificed. Although each of the two friends wants to die for the other, Iphigénie finally sends Pylades away with a letter to be given to Elektra. Pylades sings a bravura aria before departing ('Divinités des grand âmes').

Act IV. The sacrificial altar of the temple. Iphigénie prays to Diana for strength to perform the sacrifice ('Je t'implore et je tremble'). Orestes is led to the altar, and Iphigénie is about to strike the fatal blow when he addresses his last words to his beloved sister, Iphigénie, whom he imagines has perished in Aulis. Brother and sister now recognize each other, but their joy is cut short by the arrival of a furious Thoas who has discovered that one of the prisoners has been allowed to leave Tauris. Thoas is about to slaughter both Orestes and Iphigénie when Pylades returns with an army of Greeks and kills the King. Fighting breaks out between the Greeks and the Scythians, but the goddess Diana herself intervenes. She orders the Scythians to return her statues to the Greeks, and she pardons Orestes, allowing him to return to Greece with Iphigénie.

For the music of the Furies, Gluck used part of his 1765 ballet *Semiramis*. Arias for Iphigénie and Orestes make use of music he originally composed for *La clemenza di Tito* (1752) and *Antigono* (1756). Nevertheless, the dramatic and fast-moving score of *Iphigénie en Tauride* forms a structural unity, exhibiting remarkable flexibility in its transitions from recitative to aria and chorus. The opera deserves to be considered Gluck's crowning achievement.

Recommended recording: Diana Montague (Iphigenia), John Aler (Pylades), Thomas Allen (Orestes), René Massis (Thoas), with the Monteverdi Choir and the Lyon Opera Orchestra, conducted by John Eliot Gardiner. Philips 416 148–2. Diana Montague is a dignified and compelling Iphigenia, Thomas Allen's Orestes is passionate, and John Aler as Pylades has no difficulties with the demanding tessitura of the role.

CHARLES FRANÇOIS GOUNOD
(b. Paris, 1818 – d. Saint-Cloud, 1893)

Faust
opera in five acts (approximate length: 3 hours, 30 minutes)

Faust, a philosopher   *tenor*
Méphistophélès   *bass*
Marguérite   *soprano*
Valentin, her brother   *baritone*
Siebel, a village youth   *mezzo-soprano*
Wagner, a student   *baritone*
Marthe, Marguérite's guardian   *mezzo-soprano*

LIBRETTO BY JULES BARBIER AND MICHEL CARRÉ, BASED INDIRECTLY ON GOETHE'S
FAUST; TIME: THE SIXTEENTH CENTURY; PLACE: GERMANY; FIRST PERFORMED AT
THE THÉÂTRE LYRIQUE, PARIS, 19 MARCH 1859

Gounod's earliest ambition was to succeed as a composer of sacred music. After winning the Prix de Rome at the age of twenty-one, he became music director of a church in Paris for four years, and then he enrolled at the seminary of Saint-Sulpice; but he abandoned his religious vocation after only a few months to take up the career of opera composer. Through the influence of the famous mezzo-soprano Pauline Viardot, he received a commission from the Paris Opéra to compose *Sapho*. Although the opera met with little success, Gounod received a second commission to set *La Nonne sanglante* (The Bleeding Nun), a libretto by Eugène Scribe, which had already been rejected by several other composers, among them Verdi and Berlioz. Gounod composed the opera, but it was taken off after only eleven performances at the Paris Opéra.

Faust, which Gounod began to compose in 1856, was accepted by the Théâtre-Lyrique, but its production was postponed indefinitely when a rival theatre, the Porte-St-Martin, announced its intention of staging a theatrical version of the Faust legend. While still at work on his *Faust*, Gounod offered it to the Paris Opéra, whose management also declined to compete with the Porte-St-Martin production but instead offered to stage another work by Gounod. The composer set *Faust* aside and composed *Le Médecin malgré lui* (The Reluctant Doctor) in six months. The opera was quite well received at its premiere in January 1858, after which Gounod returned to *Faust*, which the Théâtre-Lyrique was now willing to stage. At its first performance in March 1859 *Faust* was well liked and was soon being staged elsewhere in France and abroad.

Faust was initially an *opéra comique* with spoken dialogue between its musical numbers, but for a production in Strasbourg in 1860 it was given recitatives, and when, nine years later, it finally reached the stage of the Paris Opéra, Gounod added a ballet, which was customary in performances at the Opéra. Although its libretto (based on Michel Carré's play *Faust et Marguérite* (1850), which derived from Goethe's *Faust*) is a sentimental trivialization of Part One of Goethe's masterpiece, Gounod's opera has survived several generations of changing tastes to remain popular, thanks mainly to its composer's dramatic flair and his ability to write immediately attractive and affecting melodies.

Act I. Faust's study. The aged philosopher Faust, depressed at having failed to penetrate the mysteries of the universe, resolves to kill himself. He is about to swallow poison when the sound of a joyful pastoral chorus outside his window causes him to hesitate. He decides instead to resort to alchemy and invokes Satan. The result of this is that Méphistophélès suddenly materializes at his side. The devil's disciple makes a pact with Faust. He will restore the philosopher to youth and serve him in this world in return for Faust's service in the next world. It is only after Méphistophélès has conjured up a vision of a beautiful young woman, Marguérite, that the instantly enamoured Faust signs his soul away. He is transformed into a dashing young nobleman and sets off with Méphistophélès to find the real Marguérite ('À moi les plaisirs').

Act II. The fairgrounds. Townspeople at the fair sing a convivial chorus ('Vin ou bière'). Valentin, a soldier, appears, contemplating a medallion given to him by his sister, Marguérite. He is about to go off to war and asks his friends to look after his sister ('Avant de quitter ces lieux'). Méphistophélès arrives, shocks everyone with a blasphemous song ('Le veau d'or') and picks a fight with Valentin by making a slighting reference to his sister. When Valentin's sword breaks in mid-air, he and his friends realize they are dealing with an evil supernatural being and hold up their swords before them in the sign of the Cross. Méphistophélès temporarily retreats but is soon joined by Faust and a group of dancing townspeople. They encounter Marguérite, to whom Faust gallantly offers his arm, only to be rejected.

Act III. The garden of Marguérite's house. Siebel, a youth in love with Marguérite, enters carrying a bouquet which he leaves for her ('Faites-lui mes aveux'). When he has gone, Faust and Méphistophélès arrive, and Faust lovingly apostrophizes Marguérite's dwelling ('Salut, demeure chaste et pure') while Méphistophélès leaves a box of jewels for Marguérite, close to Siebel's flowers. Faust and Méphistophélès retreat as Marguérite emerges from her house. Sitting at her spinning wheel she sings a ballad ('Il était un roi de Thule') and then notices both the flowers and the box of jewels. More impressed by the jewels than by Siebel's humble gift, she sings an ecstatic aria ('Ah, je ris de me voir').

Faust and Méphistophélès join Marguérite and her guardian Marthe. While his companion engages the attention of the elderly guardian, Faust begins his seduction of Marguérite ('Laisse-moi, laisse-moi contempler ton visage'). In a tender duet, Marguérite confesses to Faust that she loves him ('O nuit d'amour'). She enters her house, and Faust is about to leave when Méphistophélès reappears, urging him to complete his conquest. Faust rushes to an open casement window at which Marguérite has appeared. The lovers embrace passionately as Méphistophélès, at the garden gate, bursts into mocking laughter.

Act IV, scene i. Marguérite's room. Having given birth to Faust's child, Marguérite is ostracized by her neighbours. Faust has abandoned her, and she sits at her spinning wheel singing an unhappy song ('Il ne revient pas') while Siebel attempts to comfort her.

Act IV, scene ii. A public square, on one side of which is Marguérite's house. Soldiers return from the war singing a rousing chorus ('Gloire immortelle de nos aïeux'). Among them is Valentin who, when he receives evasive replies from Siebel to his enquiries about his sister, rushes into their house. Entering the square with Faust, Méphistophélès sings a satirical serenade beneath Marguérite's window ('Vous qui faites l'endormie'). Valentin emerges from the house, demanding to know who is responsible for his sister's condition. Faust and Valentin fight, and Valentin, mortally wounded, curses his sister as he dies.

Act IV, scene iii. The interior of a cathedral. Taunted by a chorus of invisible demons, Marguérite attempts to pray, while Méphistophélès interrupts her with various imprecations, finally causing Marguérite to faint when he declares that the abyss lies in wait for her.

Act V, scene i. The Harz Mountains. It is Walpurgis Night, when witches are abroad. Faust and Méphistophélès encounter will-o'-the-wisps, witches, and great courtesans of antiquity such as Cleopatra and Helen of Troy. (It is in this scene that the obligatory ballet was inserted when *Faust* reached the Paris Opéra, the dances consisting of 'The Nubian Women', 'Cleopatra and the Goblet of Gold', 'The Trojan Women', 'Variation', and 'Phryne's Dance'.) Faust has a vision of the suffering Marguérite and commands Méphistophélès to take him to her.

Act V, scene ii. The interior of a prison. Marguérite has been imprisoned for having killed her child. With the aid of Méphistophélès, Faust gains entrance to her cell, and he and Marguérite sing an ardent love duet ('Oui, c'est toi, je t'aime'). Faust begs Marguérite, whose mind is now wandering, to escape with him, but she takes fright when she sees Méphistophélès, and she calls upon heaven for protection as Faust and Méphistophélès continue to exhort her to flee ('Anges purs, anges radieux'). As Marguérite falls dead, her soul ascends to heaven.

To its early audiences Gounod's *Faust* seemed an innovatory work, with its avoidance of such conventions as the introductory chorus and the concerted finale. It is now admired for its musical virtues and for its sheer theatrical effectiveness, although it leaves much to be desired as an operatic equivalent of Goethe's transcendental poetic drama. Among its highlights are the popular Soldiers' Chorus (lifted from *Ivan le Terrible*, an abandoned earlier opera by Gounod), Marguérite's glittering Jewel Song ('Ah, je ris de me voir'), Faust's passionate 'Salut, demeure chaste et pure' and the opera's final trio.

*Recommended recording: Jerry Hadley (Faust), Cecilia Gasdia (Marguérite),
Samuel Ramey (Mephistopheles), Alexandru Agache (Valentin), with the Welsh
National Opera Chorus and Orchestra, conducted by Carlo Rizzi. Teldec 4509–
90872–2. Persuasively and elegantly sung, and conducted lovingly by Rizzi, this
recording restores some passages cut before the opera's premiere.*

Roméo et Juliette
(Romeo and Juliet)
opera in a prologue and five acts (approximate length: 3 hours, 15 minutes)

Roméo   *tenor*

Juliette   *soprano*

Mercutio   *baritone*

Frère Laurent (Friar Laurence)   *bass*

Stephano, a page   *soprano*

Capulet   *bass*

Tybalt   *tenor*

Gertrude, Juliette's nurse   *mezzo-soprano*

The Duke of Verona   *bass*

Paris   *baritone*

Gregorio, Capulet's servant   *baritone*

Benvolio   *tenor*

LIBRETTO BY JULES BARBIER AND MICHEL CARRÉ, BASED ON SHAKESPEARE'S
ROMEO AND JULIET; TIME: THE FOURTEENTH CENTURY; PLACE: VERONA; FIRST
PERFORMED AT THE THÉÂTRE-LYRIQUE, PARIS, 27 APRIL 1867

After the success of *Faust* in 1859, Gounod began to receive more commissions
to write operas. *Philemon et Baucis,* composed for the summer theatre at
Baden-Baden, was actually first performed in Paris in 1860, and the Baden-Baden
theatre was given *La Colombe* instead. *La Reine de Saba,* staged at the Paris Opéra
in 1862, was a relative failure, nor did *Mireille* fare much better at the Théâtre-
Lyrique in 1864. But with *Roméo et Juliette,* its libretto by Barbier and Carré based
on (and reasonably faithful to) Shakespeare's tragedy, Gounod achieved his
greatest immediate success when the opera was given its premiere in 1867.
Although it is now second in popularity to his *Faust, Roméo et Juliette* is undoubtedly Gounod's finest work for the stage.

Prologue. After an orchestral introduction, a chorus summarizes the action of the opera.

Act I. A masked ball at the Capulet residence. The assembled guests express their delight, and Tybalt assures Paris, a young nobleman, that he will be enthralled by the beauty of Tybalt's cousin, Juliette. Capulet appears, escorting his daughter Juliette, whose beauty is indeed admired by all. After the guests have gone into an adjacent room to dance, Roméo (a member of the rival Montague family) and his friends emerge from hiding. Roméo recounts a dream he has had which fills him with foreboding, but his friend Mercutio airily dismisses the dream as the work of the fairy Queen Mab ('Mab, la reine des mensonges').

When Roméo catches a glimpse of Juliette in the next room, he is instantly smitten. His friends take him aside as Juliette enters with her nurse Gertrude, who attempts to sing the praises of Count Paris. Juliette replies that she is not yet ready for marriage ('Je veux vivre'), but when Roméo steps out of hiding to accost her she immediately realizes that they are meant for each other. The sudden appearance of Tybalt not only interrupts their duet but also makes the young couple aware that they are members of rival families. Roméo and his friends leave hastily, and Capulet restrains Tybalt from giving chase to them.

Act II. The Capulet garden, at night, overlooked by the balcony to Juliette's room. With the help of his page Stephano, Roméo makes his way stealthily into the garden and ardently wills Juliette to appear ('Ah, lève-toi, soleil'). As she comes out onto her balcony, he hides, but he reveals his presence when he hears her confess her feelings for him. The couple declare their love for each other. Temporarily interrupted by Capulet servants running through the garden in search of Stephano, they resume their love duet ('O nuit divine') and agree to marry. Juliette is called indoors by Gertrude, but the young lovers contrive to prolong their meeting for a time ('Ah, ne fuis pas encore').

Act III, scene i. Frère Laurent's cell, at dawn. Frère Laurent sings of the wonders of nature ('Berceau de tous les êtres'). Roméo rushes in to tell him of his love for Juliette, who arrives soon after. The lovers ask Frère Laurent to marry them, and, in the hope that their union might bring an end to the enmity between their two families, he performs the ceremony ('Dieu qui fis l'homme à ton image'). The three of them are joined by Gertrude who shares the young couple's joy.

Act III, scene ii. A street, in front of the Capulet house. Roméo's page Stephano taunts the Capulets in a song, comparing them to a nest of vultures harbouring a white turtle dove ('Que fais-tu, blanche tourterelle'). His song draws Capulet servants, among them Gregorio, from the house, and a fight breaks out between Gregorio and Stephano. Roméo's friends Mercutio and Benvolio appear, followed by Juliette's cousin Tybalt with Paris. Indignant to discover Gregorio duelling with a mere boy, Mercutio arouses the anger of Tybalt. Mercutio and Tybalt begin to fight, and are interrupted by the arrival of Roméo, who begs Tybalt to forget the enmity between their two families. However, Mercutio and Tybalt resume their fight, and Mercutio is killed. In revenge, Roméo attacks Tybalt and mortally wounds him. Capulet arrives in time to hear Tybalt's dying wish that Juliette should marry Paris. The Duke of Verona appears upon the scene and banishes Roméo from the city.

Act IV, scene i. Juliette's room, at dawn. Juliette forgives Roméo for having killed her cousin Tybalt ('Va! Je t'ai pardonné'), and the newly married pair sing a love duet ('Nuit d'hymenée'). When he hears the morning lark Roméo knows it is time for him to leave Juliette, and the lovers bid each other a reluctant farewell ('Il faut partir'). After Roméo has gone, Capulet enters with Frère Laurent to inform his daughter of Tybalt's dying wish. The wedding is to take place immediately. Capulet leaves, and Juliette tells Frère Laurent that she would die rather than go through a ceremony of marriage with Paris. He suggests a plan. Juliette is to take a potion that will, for a time, give her the appearance of death. When she has been laid in the family tomb, Roméo will meet her there. Juliette agrees to do as Frère Laurent suggests.

Act IV, scene ii. A hall in the Capulet house. Juliette is led to the marriage ceremony by her father. As they reach the altar, where Paris is waiting, Juliette falls, apparently lifeless.

Act V. The Capulet family crypt. Juliette lies on a tomb. Frère Laurent, discovering that Roméo has not received the message he sent, leaves to find another messenger. Roméo enters and, grief-stricken at Juliette's death, drinks poison ('O, ma femme! O, ma bien aimée'). As he does so, Juliette awakens, and the couple embrace fervently. Roméo, as life drains from him, tells Juliette what he has done. He dies, and Juliette, unable to contemplate life without him, stabs herself and dies.

Roméo et Juliette captures the spirit rather than the style of Shakespeare's tragedy. Its love duets are highly effective, as are Juliette's exuberant entrance aria 'Je veux vivre', Roméo's ardent 'Ah, lève-toi, soleil' and Mercutio's elegant description of Queen Mab. Except when it is held up by Stephano's song at the beginning of Act III, scene ii, the action moves swiftly, and Gounod's score is attractively melodious throughout. Predominantly lyrical, this fine example of French Romantic opera also contains a superb dramatic ensemble at the end of Act III.

Recommended recording: Placido Domingo (Roméo), Ruth Ann Swenson (Juliette), Kurt Ollmann (Mercutio), with the Bavarian Radio Chorus and Munich Radio Orchestra, conducted by Leonard Slatkin. RCA Victor 0902668440–2. Superbly sung and acted by Ruth Ann Swenson and Placido Domingo, and lovingly conducted by Leonard Slatkin.

FROMENTAL HALÉVY
(b. Paris, 1799 – d. Nice, 1862)

La Juive
(The Jewess)
opera in five acts (approximate length: 3 hours, 30 minutes)

Eléazar, a Jewish goldsmith   *tenor*
Rachel, his daughter   *soprano*
Cardinal Brogni, president of the council   *bass*
Léopold, prince of the empire, alias Samuel   *tenor*
Princess Eudoxie, the Emperor's niece   *soprano*
Ruggiero, provost of the city of Constance   *baritone*
Albert, sergeant in the Emperor's army   *bass*

LIBRETTO BY EUGÈNE SCRIBE; TIME: 1414; PLACE: CONSTANCE, SWITZERLAND; FIRST PERFORMED AT THE PARIS OPÉRA, 23 FEBRUARY 1835

Born in Paris into a Jewish family that changed its name from Levy when he was eight, Halévy became a pupil of Cherubini at the Paris Conservatoire at the age of twelve, and he won the Conservatoire's Prix de Rome when he was twenty. As opera was his chief interest, he held advisory positions at Paris opera houses from 1826 to 1845. Of the thirty-three operas he completed, a few remained unperformed at his death, while others, among them *Clari* (1828), *La Reine de Chypre* (1841) and *Charles VI* (1843), were successful in their day. *La Juive* (1835), which was admired even by the notoriously anti-semitic Wagner, is the only opera by Halévy to have survived in the repertoire, albeit precariously. Gustav Mahler, who conducted *La Juive* in Leipzig in 1886 and Budapest in 1889, declared, 'I am absolutely overwhelmed by this wonderful, majestic work. I regard it as one of the greatest operas ever created.'

Act I. A square in the city of Constance. While Eléazar, a Jewish goldsmith, and his employees, among them a young man known as Samuel, are at work, a *Te Deum* is heard from the nearby church. A holiday is proclaimed to celebrate victory over the dissident Hussites, and when the Jews are harassed by the citizens of Constance for working on a Christian holiday, Cardinal Brogni intervenes on Eléazar's behalf. Eléazar's daughter Rachel, who is in love with Samuel, is puzzled by the influence that the young man appears to have over the Emperor's soldiers. (Samuel is in reality Prince Léopold, the Emperor's son.)

Act II. A room in Eléazar's house. Samuel has joined Eléazar and Rachel for the feast of the Passover, but Rachel is perplexed when Samuel surreptitiously discards the unleavened bread offered to him. The Princess Eudoxie arrives to purchase from Eléazar a gold chain as a gift for her husband, Prince Léopold, to celebrate his victory over the Hussites. Samuel (Léopold), in hiding, is filled with remorse at his deceit, and after Eudoxie has left he admits to Rachel that he is a Christian. Eléazar's wrath at discovering this is subdued only when Rachel says she wants to marry Samuel, who is then forced to confess that he is not free to marry her.

Act III. The gardens of the Emperor's palace. A fete in honour of Léopold is in progress. When Eléazar and Rachel arrive to deliver to Eudoxie the gold chain she has purchased, they discover that Prince Léopold is none other than Samuel. Rachel publicly accuses him of having seduced her, and Cardinal Brogni pronounces an anathema on Rachel, Eléazar and Prince Léopold, who are arrested and led away for trial.

Act IV. The Anteroom to the council chamber. Eudoxie pleads with Rachel to save Léopold's life by declaring his innocence, and Rachel finally agrees. Cardinal Brogni tells Eléazar that he can save Rachel by becoming a Christian, but this Eléazar refuses to do. He reminds Brogni that when the Cardinal's house was destroyed by fire some years previously his daughter was saved by a Jew, and she is still alive. Eléazar knows her whereabouts but will have his revenge by taking the secret with him to his grave.

Act V. A scaffold, in the square. Léopold's sentence has been commuted to one of banishment. As the citizens howl for the death of the two Jews, Eléazar and Rachel are led to the scaffold. Eléazar gives Rachel the opportunity to renounce her faith and become a Christian, but she refuses. Cardinal Brogni begs Eléazar to restore his daughter to him, but it is only when Rachel has been thrown into a boiling cauldron that Eléazar reveals the truth to Brogni: Rachel was a Christian, and the Cardinal's long-lost daughter.

La Juive is a typical example of French *grand opéra*, with its lavish processional scene in Act I, its splendid Act III festival, its boldly colourful orchestration and its strong melodic invention. Eléazar's aria 'Rachel, quand du Seigneur', at the end of Act IV, when he broods on his refusal to reveal Rachel's identity, thus effectively condemning her to death, is a noble expression of his emotion and the only excerpt from the opera to be well known out of context.

Recommended recording: Julia Varady (Rachel), José Carreras (Eléazar), Ferrucio Furlanetto (Cardinal Brogni), June Anderson (Eudoxie), with the Ambrosian Opera Chorus and the Philharmonia Orchestra, conducted by Antonio de Almeida. Philips 420 190–2.

GEORGE FRIDERIC HANDEL
(b. Halle, 1685 – d. London, 1759)

Giulio Cesare in Egitto
(Julius Caesar in Egypt)
opera in three acts (approximate length: 3 hours, 15 minutes)

Giulio Cesare (Julius Caesar)   *originally alto castrato*
Curio, a Roman tribune   *bass*
Cornelia, Pompey's widow   *contralto*
Sesto, Pompey's son   *soprano*
Cleopatra, Queen of Egypt, alias Lydia   *soprano*
Tolomeo, King of Egypt, her brother   *originally alto castrato*
Achilla, an Egyptian general   *bass*
Nireno, Cleopatra's confidant   *originally alto castrato*

LIBRETTO BY NICOLA FRANCESCO HAYM; TIME: 48 BC; PLACE: EGYPT; FIRST PERFORMED AT THE KING'S THEATRE, HAYMARKET, LONDON, 20 FEBRUARY 1724

Handel was born in Germany and produced his first two operas in Hamburg at the age of twenty. He then left for Italy, where he became a composer of Italian operas, and in 1712 took up residence in London, where he remained for the rest of his life. His *Rinaldo* had been staged in 1711 at the Queen's Theatre with such success that it ushered in an era in which Italian opera became the fashion in London. Over the next thirty years Handel composed more than thirty operas for London. *Il pastor fido* (1712), *Teseo* (1713) and *Amadigi di Gaula* (1715) were among his early successes. In 1720 he became a director of the Royal Academy of Music, which presented annual seasons of opera in London until 1728. *Giulio Cesare*, produced at the King's Theatre in 1724, remained during Handel's lifetime one of his most popular operas. Haym's libretto was adapted from an earlier libretto by Giacomo Francesco Bussani, written for Antonio Sartorio's *Giulio Cesare in Egitto*, which had been staged in Venice in 1676.

Act I, scene i. The banks of the Nile. Having defeated the forces of his rival Pompey at Pharsalus, Giulio Cesare crosses the Nile to enter Egypt with his victorious Roman army and the tribune Curio, and is acclaimed by the Egyptians ('Presti omai l'Egizia terra'). Pompey's wife Cornelia and their son Sesto throw themselves on Giulio's mercy, begging for a reconciliation between the two men, but Achilla, an Egyptian general and adviser to Tolomeo, King of Egypt, enters bearing a message of welcome from Tolomeo and a gift which is revealed to be the severed head of Pompey. The Romans are horrified, and Giulio condemns Tolomeo's barbaric cruelty ('Empio, dirò, tu sei, togliti'). Cornelia attempts to kill herself but is prevented by Curio who offers to marry her. Cornelia rejects him, and laments her unhappy state ('Priva son d'ogni conforto'), while her son Sesto vows to avenge his father's murder ('Svegliatevi nel core').

Act I, scene ii. Tolomeo's palace. Cleopatra learns from her confidant Nireno that Pompey was murdered on the orders of her brother Tolomeo. She resolves to seduce Giulio in the hope of becoming the sole ruler of Egypt ('Non disperar'). Achilla informs Tolomeo of Giulio's fury at being presented with the head of Pompey. He offers to kill Giulio and thus stabilize Tolomeo's throne, in return for the hand in marriage of Pompey's widow, Cornelia. Tolomeo agrees and launches into an outburst against Giulio ('L'empio, sleale, indegno').

Act I, scene iii. Giulio Cesare's camp. As he contemplates Pompey's funeral urn, Giulio meditates on human mortality and the transience of fame. Cleopatra arrives, presenting herself as Lydia, a noble Egyptian woman whose fortune has been stolen by Tolomeo. Giulio is enchanted by her beauty ('Non e si vago e bello'). Cleopatra and Nireno observe Cornelia as she kneels before her husband's funeral urn and then seizes his sword and swears vengeance on Tolomeo, a task which her son Sesto determines to take upon himself. In the guise of Lydia, Cleopatra offers her help to Cornelia and Sesto. She exults at the prospect of triumphing over Tolomeo, and sings of her feelings for Giulio ('Tu la mia stella sei').

Act I, scene iv. Tolomeo's palace. Giulio is greeted by Tolomeo, and is royally entertained, though he is in no way deceived by his reception ('Va tacito e nascosto'). When Cornelia and Sesto arrive and challenge Tolomeo to combat, Sesto is imprisoned and Cornelia taken to the royal harem. Mother and son lament their fate in a duet of farewell.

Act II, scene i. Cleopatra's palace. Giulio is brought to the palace, where Cleopatra has planned a lavish entertaiment for him, including a panoramic view of Virtue enthroned on Mount Parnassus. Still in her guise of Lydia, Cleopatra herself plays the role of Virtue and sings a beautifully sensuous aria ('V'adoro pupille'). When Giulio runs towards her, the mountain closes and Virtue disappears, but Nireno assures the Roman Emperor that Lydia will receive him later.

Act II, scene ii. The garden of the harem. Put to work in the harem garden, Cornelia laments her fate ('Deh piangete, o mesti lumi'). She resists the advances of both Achilla and Tolomeo and again considers ending her life, but she is forestalled by Sesto, who has been released from prison by Nireno. Nireno offers to take Sesto secretly to the King, and the youth voices his determination to have his revenge on Tolomeo for the murder of his father ('L'angue offeso mai riposa').

Act II, scene iii. Cleopatra's palace. Giulio arrives to visit Lydia. He and she are on the point of declaring their love for each other when Curio enters to announce that a group of Tolomeo's soldiers are about to make an attempt on Giulio's life. Cleopatra now reveals her identity and leaves to deal with the situation, but she returns almost immediately, advising Giulio to flee. This he refuses to do ('All lampo dell'armi'). Instead he rushes out to face the conspirators.

Act II, scene iv. Tolomeo's harem. Tolomeo is surrounded by the women of his harem, among them Cornelia. Sesto rushes in and attempts to stab Tolomeo but is prevented by Achilla, who informs the King that Giulio has escaped his attackers by jumping from the palace into the harbour. He is presumed to have drowned, and to avenge his death Cleopatra is raising troops against Tolomeo. When Achilla asks for the hand of Cornelia in marriage, as he was promised, Tolomeo refuses. The King rushes out to do battle, and Achilla mutters darkly of a change of alliance. Sesto, in despair at having failed to kill Tolomeo, attempts suicide, but Cornelia again stiffens his resolve to avenge his father's death ('L'aura che spira').

Act III, scene i. A forest outside Alexandria. Achilla and his followers prepare to support Cleopatra against Tolomeo ('Dal fulgor di questa spada'). Battle music describes the conflict, from which Tolomeo's forces emerge victorious, and Cleopatra is taken prisoner ('Piangero la sorte mia').

Act III, scene ii. The harbour at Alexandria. Giulio emerges from the sea, having escaped drowning ('Dall' ondoso periglio'). The mortally wounded Achilla confesses to the murder of Pompey and gives Sesto a signet ring that will gain him command of Achilla's troops. Giulio intervenes, takes the ring and determines to rescue Cleopatra and Cornelia.

Act III, scene iii. Cleopatra's palace. The Queen's sad farewell to her hand-maidens is interrupted by the arrival of Giulio, at which her sorrow turns to joy ('Da tempeste il legno infranto'). Cornelia defends herself with a dagger against an amorous Tolomeo, who is challenged by Sesto to a duel, and killed.

Act III, scene iv. The harbour. Giulio Cesare and Cleopatra appear in triumph, declare their love for each other ('Caro! Bella! Piu amabile belta') and are acclaimed by the populace.

The male castrato voice played a prominent part in opera from the beginnings of the art form until the early nineteenth century. In eighteenth-century Italian opera the leading heroic male role was frequently assigned to a male soprano or alto. The role of Handel's Giulio Cesare was written for Senesino, the famous Italian alto castrato whom the composer engaged for London in 1720 and who sang in all thirty-two operas produced by the Royal Academy of Music between 1720 and 1728, among them thirteen by Handel.

The score of *Giulio Cesare* is one of Handel's most sumptuous. Though its plot may seem risible, the opera can be made by expert stage production to appear dramatically convincing, and the arias for Giulio and Cleopatra are full of character and, especially in the case of Cleopatra's music, melodic beauty. Since its first modern revival at Göttingen in 1922, *Giulio Cesare* has been staged on several occasions, with such notable singers as Lisa della Casa, Irmgard Seefried, Beverly Sills and Joan Sutherland undertaking the role of Cleopatra. When the role of Giulio is not given to a female contralto or mezzo-soprano, it is usually assigned to a bass or baritone.

Recommended recording: Jennifer Larmore (Caesar), Barbara Schlick (Cleopatra), Bernarda Fink (Cornelia), Derek Lee Ragin (Tolomeo), with the Concerto Cologne, conducted by René Jacobs. Harmonia Mundi HMC 901385–87. Jennifer Larmore makes an heroic Caesar, singing with great virtuosity. Barbara Schlick is a seductive Cleopatra, Bernarda Fink a heart-rending Cornelia, and Derek Lee Ragin a suitably vicious Tolomeo.

Ariodante
opera in three acts (approximate length: 3 hours)

Ariodante, a prince   *originally alto castrato*
Ginevra, daughter of the King of Scotland   *soprano*
Dalinda, a lady of the court   *soprano*
Polinesso, Duke of Albany   *originally alto castrato*
Lurcanio, Ariodante's brother   *tenor*
The King of Scotland   *bass*
Odoardo, a courtier   *tenor*

ADAPTATION OF LIBRETTO BY ANTONIO SALVI, DERIVED FROM LUDOVICO ARIOSTO'S POEM *ORLANDO FURIOSO*; TIME: THE MIDDLE AGES; PLACE: EDINBURGH AND SURROUNDINGS; FIRST PERFORMED AT THE COVENT GARDEN THEATRE, LONDON, 8 JANUARY 1735

After the collapse of the Royal Academy of Music in 1728, Handel's new operas continued to be staged at the King's Theatre in the Haymarket. When another company, the Opera of the Nobility, directed at first by his arch-rival Giovanni Bononcini, acquired the use of the King's Theatre, Handel entered into an agreement with John Rich to have his operas performed at Rich's Covent Garden Theatre (on the site of today's Royal Opera House). His first new opera to be staged there was *Ariodante*, its libretto anonymously adapted from Antonio Salvi's text for the opera *Ginevra, principessa di Scozia*, by Giacomo Antonio Perti, staged in Florence in 1708. Despite the Scottish setting and characters of Salvi's libretto, its plot is ultimately derived from *Orlando furioso*, the romantic epic by the Italian poet Ludovico Ariosto (1474–1533), the action of which takes place almost everywhere except Scotland.

Act I, scene i. Ginevra's apartment in the royal palace. Ginevra, daughter of the King of Scotland, confides to her confidante Dalinda that she is in love with the vassal Prince Ariodante, and that her father has given their union his blessing. Polinesso, Duke of Albany, enters and declares his love for Ginevra, but she rebuffs him and leaves, whereupon Dalinda makes it clear to Polinesso that she, Dalinda, is enamoured of him, and reveals to him the name of Ginevra's lover. Polinesso determines to make use of Dalinda's feelings in a plan to take his revenge on Ginevra.

Act I, scene ii. The garden of the palace. Ginevra and Ariodante sing of their love for each other, and the King of Scotland announces that they are to be married the following day. Polinesso, pretending to return Dalinda's affection, persuades her to agree to dress as Ginevra that evening and admit him to the Princess's apartment. Ariodante's brother Lurcanio declares his love for Dalinda, but she rebuffs him. In a pastoral scene, the love of Ariodante and Ginevra is celebrated by shepherds and shepherdesses.

Act II, scene i. The garden of the palace, at night. Ariodante encounters Polinesso, who, pretending to be amazed when he is told of Ariodante's forthcoming marriage to Ginevra, informs the Prince that he, Polinesso, has been enjoying Ginevra's favours. Ariodante swears to kill himself if this proves to be true, and to kill Polinesso if it is not true. Polinesso offers to give him proof. When the door to the royal apartments is opened by Dalinda dressed as Ginevra, and Polinesso is admitted, Ariodante is about to kill himself in his despair ('Scherza infida') when his brother Lurcanio, who has been hiding in the garden and has overheard Ariodante and Polinesso, urges him instead to take revenge upon the faithless woman.

Act II, scene ii. The palace. The courtier Odoardo brings news to the King that Ariodante has thrown himself from a cliff into the sea and is dead. When Ginevra is told this, she swoons with grief. Lurcanio enters, accusing Ginevra of being the cause of his brother's suicide by her unchaste behaviour. He offers a challenge to anyone who will champion her. The King denounces his daughter, at which Ginevra loses her reason ('Il mio crudel martoro'). She collapses, and her dreams are tormented by Furies.

Act III, scene i. A wood. Ariodante, wandering alone and lamenting his fate, hears a cry for help and finds Dalinda being pursued by assassins hired by Polinesso, who requires her death now that she has served her purpose. Ariodante rescues her, and she informs him of the deceitful behaviour of Polinesso, whom she now detests.

Act III, scene ii. The palace. Polinesso presents himself as the champion who will fight to defend Ginevra's honour, and the King orders his daughter, who has been condemned to death for unchastity, to accept his offer ('Al sen ti stringo').

Act III, scene iii. The field of tournament. Lurcanio and Polinesso fight, and Polinesso is mortally wounded. A new champion enters, and reveals himself to be Ariodante. He promises to explain everything if Dalinda is offered a royal pardon. When news arrives that the dying Polinesso has confessed his guilt, the King leaves to give his daughter the welcome news, while Ariodante rejoices ('Dopo notte'), and a chastened Dalinda accepts the love of Lurcanio ('Dite spera, e son contento').

Act III, scene iv. A prison cell. Ginevra awaits her execution. Her despair turns to joy when her father arrives with Ariodante.

Act III, scene v. A hall in the palace. The knights and ladies of the court celebrate the marriage of both couples, and the opera ends in general rejoicing.

With its ravishing arias and duets, spectacular scenes of celebration and excellent libretto, *Ariodante* is one of Handel's most enjoyable operas and a splendid example of Baroque musical drama. Although it has been staged a number of times in the twentieth century, in New York, Berlin, Birmingham, London, Nancy and elsewhere, it deserves to be still more widely known.

Recommended recording: Lorraine Hunt (Ariodante), Juliana Gondek (Ginevra), Lisa Saffer (Dalinda), with the Wilhelmshaven Vocal Ensemble and the Freiburg Baroque Orchestra, conducted by Nicholas McGegan. Harmonia Mundi HMU 907146–48. Lorraine Hunt is a poignant Ariodante, Juliana Gondek a convincing Ginevra, and Lisa Saffer an excellent Dalinda. McGegan conducts briskly, and the orchestral playing is superb.

Alcina
opera in three acts (approximate length: 3 hours, 30 minutes)

Alcina, a sorceress   *soprano*
Ruggiero, a knight   *originally alto castrato*
Morgana, sister of Alcina   *soprano*
Bradamante, betrothed to Ruggiero, alias Ricciardo   *contralto*
Oronte, commander of Alcina's troops   *tenor*
Melisso, Bradamante's governor, alias Atlante   *bass*
Oberto, a noble youth   *soprano*

ADAPTATION OF LIBRETTO BY ANTONIO FANZAGLIA, DERIVED FROM LUDOVICO ARIOSTO'S POEM *ORLANDO FURIOSO*; TIME: THE MYTHICAL PAST; PLACE: ALCINA'S ENCHANTED ISLAND; FIRST PERFORMED AT THE COVENT GARDEN THEATRE, LONDON, 16 APRIL 1735

Three months after the premiere of his *Ariodante* at Covent Garden, Handel had another new opera ready for performance there. *Alcina*'s libretto was adapted from one written by Antonio Fanzaglia for the opera *L'isola d'Alcina* by

Riccardo Broschi, first performed in Rome in 1728. As with *Ariodante* and two other operas by Handel (*Rinaldo* and *Orlando*), the plot was derived from *Orlando furioso*, the romantic epic by Ludovico Ariosto first published in 1516.

Act I, scene i. Alcina's island. The enchantress Alcina has fallen in love with a knight, Ruggiero, and lures him to the magic island where she lives with her sister, Morgana, and her general, Oronte. In an attempt to rescue Ruggiero, his betrothed, Bradamante, arrives on the island disguised as her brother Ricciardo and accompanied by her governor, Melisso. They are discovered by Morgana, who is attracted to 'Ricciardo', and who leads them both to Alcina.

Act I, scene ii. Alcina's palace. When Ricciardo and Melisso arrive at the palace they find Ruggiero in thrall to Alcina, whose magic art has made him fall in love with her and completely forget his former lover, Bradamante ('Di te mi rido, semplice stolto'). Alcina's general, Oronte, declares his love for Morgana, who rejects him, and Ruggiero, worried that he might lose Alcina to Ricciardo, attempts to persuade Alcina to transform the youth, which is what Alcina does to her lovers when she tires of them. Bradamante tries to reveal her true identity to Ruggiero, but he considers this simply one of Alcina's tricks and refuses to believe her. Morgana begs Bradamante to leave the island ('Tornami a vagheggiar').

Act II, scene i. A hall of the palace. In the guise of Ruggiero's old tutor Atlante, Melisso appears to Ruggiero and gives him a magic ring, which releases him from the spell under which Alcina has cast him. Ruggiero immediately recovers from his infatuation with Alcina and remembers his true love, Bradamante. In order to escape from Alcina, he obtains her permission for him to go hunting. Oberto, a youth who has come to the island to search for his lost father, is assured by Alcina that his quest will soon meet with success. Oronte tells Alcina that Ruggiero has fled, and Alcina calls on the gods to witness her distress ('Ah, mio cor!'). Morgana is dismayed to discover the lovers Ruggiero and Bradamante together ('Verdi prati').

Act II, scene ii. A subterranean cave. Alcina attempts to use her magic powers to prevent Ruggiero's departure ('Ombre pallide'), but he is protected by the ring given to him by Melisso.

Act III, scene i. A courtyard of the palace. Morgana confesses her love for Oronte ('Credete al mio dolore'), Alcina fails to persuade Ruggiero to return to her ('Ma quando tornerai'), and Bradamante refuses to leave the island until all of Alcina's enchanted victims have been restored to their proper state ('Mi restano le lagrime').

Act III, scene ii. Outside the palace. When Ruggiero shatters the urn that contains the source of Alcina's magic powers, Alcina and Morgana disappear and all of Alcina's victims are released, among them Oberto's father. The opera ends in rejoicing.

Alcina is regarded as one of the finest of Handel's operas, thanks to the variety and range of its arias and the richness of Handel's writing for the orchestra. Morgana's virtuoso aria 'Tornami a vagheggiar' in Act I is sometimes given to Alcina, and there is historical justification for this – in a 1736 revival of Alcina Handel himself transferred the aria to the singer of the title role. Joan Sutherland, the Alcina of a highly acclaimed Franco Zeffirelli production in Venice, Dallas and London in the early 1960s, certainly appropriated the aria.

Recommended recording: Arleen Auger (Alcina), Eiddwen Harrhy (Morgana), Della Jones (Ruggiero), Kathleen Kuhlmann (Bradamante), John Tomlinson (Melisso), with the Opera Stage Chorus, and the City of London Baroque Sinfonia, conducted by Richard Hickox. CDS 7 49771–2. Arleen Auger is an accomplished Alcina, and Della Jones and Kathleen Kulhmann are both exciting as Ruggiero and Bradamante. Richard Hickox conducts stylishly.

Serse
(Xerxes)
opera in three acts (approximate length: 3 hours)

Serse (Xerxes), King of Persia   *originally alto castrato*
Arsamene, his brother   *originally alto castrato*
Amastre, a foreign princess   *mezzo-soprano*
Ariodate, vassal to Serse   *bass*
Romilda, his daughter   *soprano*
Atalanta, her sister   *soprano*
Elviro, Arsamene's servant   *bass*

ADAPTATION OF LIBRETTO BY SILVIO STAMPIGLIA; TIME: ANTIQUITY; PLACE: PERSIA; FIRST PERFORMED AT THE KING'S THEATRE, HAYMARKET, LONDON, 15 APRIL 1738

After a period of four years in which his operas were performed at the Covent Garden Theatre, Handel returned to the King's Theatre in the Haymarket in

1738 with two operas: *Faramondo*, one of his less successful works for the stage, was given its premiere there in January, and *Serse* followed in April. *Serse*'s libretto was adapted from one written by Silvio Stampiglia for Giovanni Bononcini's opera of the same title, performed in Rome in 1694. Stampiglia's libretto was in turn based on an earlier one written by Nicolo Minato for Francesco Cavalli, whose *Il Xerse* was staged in Venice in 1654.

Act I. A garden. Serse, King of Persia, apostrophizes a beautiful plane tree in the aria 'Ombra mai fu'. (This is the piece popularly known out of context as 'Handel's Largo'. It was performed in Victorian times with an inappropriate religious text and since then has been subjected to countless arrangements for every conceivable instrument or ensemble.) Serse's brother Arsamene enters in search of his beloved Romilda, who is heard singing in the distance, and Serse, enchanted by the sound of her voice, decides that he must marry her. He orders Arsamene to convey his intentions to Romilda, but his brother, understandably reluctant to do this, tells Serse that such a union would be inappropriate, Romilda being the daughter of a vassal prince, Ariodate. However, Arsamene is forced to carry out his brother's instructions. This is of great interest to Romilda's sister Atalanta, who is secretly in love with Arsamene.

When Serse's offer of marriage is rejected by Romilda, the King angrily sends his brother into exile. Amastre, a foreign princess who is officially betrothed to Serse, arrives disguised as a man, and she overhears Serse reflecting on his feelings for Romilda. Romilda warns her sister Atalanta against attempting to steal Arsamene from her.

Act II, scene i. A public square. Arsamene's servant Elviro, disguised as a flower-seller, is questioned by Amastre and informs her of Serse's plan to marry Romilda. Atalanta tells Elviro that Romilda has now transferred her affections to Serse, and she extracts from the servant a letter addressed by Arsamene to Romilda, which Elviro was on his way to deliver. When Serse arrives to find Atalanta reading the letter, she convinces the King that it was addressed not to her sister but to her. Serse is delighted, takes the letter and shows it to Romilda. Romilda gives way to jealousy but still rejects Serse's advances, while Amastre, unable to bear her rejection by Serse, contemplates suicide from which she is dissuaded by Elviro. When Elviro informs his master that Romilda now loves Serse, Arsamene is grief-stricken.

Act II, scene ii. Near Serse's new bridge across the Hellespont. Serse, who has come to inspect his bridge, encounters Arsamene, whom he pardons, telling his brother he is free to marry the woman he loves, namely Atalanta. Arsamene, however, protests that he loves only Romilda. Serse meets Amastre who, still disguised as a man, claims to have been wounded while serving him in the wars. When Serse again asks Romilda to marry him, Amastre calls the King a traitor and draws a sword. She is arrested by Serse's guards but released on the orders of Romilda.

Act III. The temple of the sun. Thinking that he is acting on Serse's instructions, Ariodate gives Romilda in marriage to Arsamene. When Serse arrives to marry her himself, he is furious. A Page brings him a letter purporting to come from Romilda, but it is actually from Amastre, accusing him of infidelity. Serse orders Arsamene to kill Romilda, but Amastre intervenes, revealing her identity. A chastened Serse is reconciled to her and blesses the union of Romilda and Arsamene.

Despite a libretto that is more than usually inane and an eponymous hero whose behaviour is clearly psychopathic, *Serse* is a delightful piece. Musically it is one of the richest of Handel's operas, a work oddly balanced between comedy and tragedy, yet contriving to be stylistically unified, and abounding in arias of great virtuosity, charm and individuality. Its seven main characters, most of them unhappily in love with one another, call for seven first-rate singers, for all are important roles with opportunities for vocal display, and all, however improbably, are brought to life in the glorious music Handel has allotted them.

Recommended recording: Carolyn Watkinson (Serse), Paul Esswood (Arsamene), with the Bridier Vocal Ensemble and La Grand Ecurie et la Chambre du Roy, conducted by Jean-Claude Malgoire. Sony SM3K 326941. A first-rate performance, and currently the only available recording.

Semele
opera in three acts (approximate length: 3 hours)

Jupiter, King of the Gods   *tenor*
Juno, his wife   *contralto*
Iris, Juno's messenger   *soprano*
Cadmus, King of Thebes   *bass*
Semele, his daughter   *soprano*
Ino, Semele's sister   *contralto*
Athamas, Prince of Boeotia   *originally alto castrato*
Somnus, god of sleep   *bass*
Apollo   *tenor*

LIBRETTO BY WILLIAM CONGREVE; TIME: THE MYTHOLOGICAL PAST; PLACE: THEBES; FIRST PERFORMED AT THE COVENT GARDEN THEATRE, LONDON, 10 FEBRUARY 1744

Strictly speaking, *Semele* is not an opera but a secular oratorio, although it lends itself admirably to dramatic performance. Congreve's libretto, its subject matter derived from Ovid's *Metamorphoses*, was in fact written to be set to music as an opera by John Eccles. However, Eccles's opera remained unperformed, and Congreve's text was not used again until Handel caused it to be adapted as the libretto of his *Semele*, which was performed at the Covent Garden Theatre as a concert work. Its first staged performance was given by amateurs in Cambridge in 1925, and it was not professionally produced as an opera until 1959, when it was staged both in Evanston, Illinois, and by the Handel Opera Society at Sadler's Wells Theatre in London.

Act I. The temple of Juno. The marriage of Semele, daughter of Cadmus, King of Thebes, to Athamas, Prince of Boeotia, is about to be solemnized, but Semele seems reluctant to proceed with the ceremony and appeals to Jupiter, King of the Gods, with whom she has been enjoying a liaison, to come to her aid. Her sister Ino, who is herself in love with Athamas, is also unhappy ('Why dost thou thus untimely grieve?'). Suddenly, thunder is heard and the flame on the altar dies down. All rush out of the temple, but Cadmus returns to exclaim that Semele has been borne aloft by an eagle. From a heavenly distance Semele's voice is heard in joyful song ('Endless pleasure, endless love, Semele enjoys above').

Act II, scene i. A pleasant landscape. Jupiter's wife Juno is told by her messenger Iris of the splendid palace that Jupiter has built for Semele. Juno swears vengeance on Semele and invokes the aid of Somnus, god of sleep, to seal in sleep the eyes of the dragons who guard the palace, thus enabling her to gain entry ('Hence, hence, Iris hence away').

Act II, scene ii. Semele's palace. Semele awakens and calls on sleep to return to her ('Oh sleep, why dost thou leave me?'). Jupiter enters in human form, and the pair delight in amorous dalliance. When the god transforms the scene to Arcadia ('Where'er you walk'), Ino arrives, conveyed by zephyrs, and the sisters sing of their pleasure.

Act III, scene i. Somnus's cave. Somnus awakes unwillingly ('Leave me, loathsome light') when Juno arrives to enlist his help. He is persuaded to put Ino and the sentinel dragons to sleep, and to give Jupiter an erotic dream which will induce him to accede to any request Semele may make of him.

Act III, scene ii. Semele's apartment in the palace. Juno, disguised as Ino, arrives with a magic mirror that enhances Semele's beauty ('Myself I shall adore if I persist in gazing'), and she advises Semele to insist that Jupiter appear to her in his own form as 'the mighty Thunderer', knowing that this will cause Semele to be consumed by fire. When Jupiter arrives, he is unable to resist Semele's request. Semele sees him in his god-like form, and dies. Ino returns to Thebes and marries Athamas, while Apollo appears and prophesies that Bacchus, god of wine, will arise from Semele's ashes. The chorus considers this a desirable outcome ('Happy shall we be').

Congreve's English-language libretto is a delight, and Handel's arias and choruses are full of variety and melodic invention, the score containing two of the composer's loveliest songs: Semele's 'Oh sleep, why dost thou leave me?' and Jupiter's 'Where'er you walk'. *Semele* demonstrates how English opera could have developed in the second half of the eighteenth century, had other composers followed Handel's lead.

Recommended recording: Norma Burrowes (Semele), Anthony Rolfe Johnson (Jupiter), with the Monteverdi Choir and English Baroque Soloists, conducted by John Eliot Gardiner. Erato STU 71453

HANS WERNER HENZE
(b. Gütersloh, 1926)

Boulevard Solitude
opera in seven scenes (approximate length: 1 hour, 15 minutes)

Manon Lescaut   *soprano*
Armand des Grieux, a student   *tenor*
Lescaut, Manon's brother   *baritone*
Francis, Armand's friend   *baritone*
Lilaque Senior, a rich old gentleman   *tenor buffo*
Lilaque Junior, his son   *baritone*

LIBRETTO BY GRETE WEIL, BASED ON A PLAY BY WALTER JOKISCH WHICH IS A
MODERN ADAPTATION OF THE NOVEL *MANON LESCAUT* BY THE ABBÉ PRÉVOST;

The son of a schoolmaster, Henze studied at the State Music School in Brunswick, Germany, but he was conscripted at the age of eighteen in 1944, was
taken prisoner by the British army, and was not able to resume his studies until
the end of the war. The most important German composer of his generation, he
has written fourteen operas or works of one kind or another for the theatre. The
earliest, *Das Wundertheater* (The Magic Theatre), a one-act piece described by
the composer as an opera for actors, was first performed in Heidelberg in 1949.
Revised for singers fifteen years later, it was given again in Frankfurt in 1965. *Ein
Landarzt*, an opera for radio based on a story by Kafka, was broadcast from
Hamburg in 1951. Henze revised it for stage performance in 1964, and the following year it was producd in Frankfurt in a triple bill with *Das Wundertheater* and
Das Ende einer Welt, a piece originally written for radio in 1953.

Boulevard Solitude, Henze's first major opera for the stage, is a modern version
of the Manon Lescaut story well known through the operas by Massenet and
Puccini. It was an instant success at its premiere in Hanover in 1952 and is the
Henze opera most likely to be encountered in performance today. *König Hirsch*
(*King Stag*; 1956) and *Der Prinz von Homburg* (The Prince of Homburg; 1960)
advanced Henze's reputation as a composer of opera, but have proved less popu-
lar, and *Elegy for Young Lovers* (1961), its libretto by W.H. Auden and Chester
Kallman, attracted favourable critical attention at the Glyndebourne Festival.
Henze's subsequent operas include *Der junge Lord* (*The Young Lord*; 1965), *The
Bassarids* (1966), *We Come to the River*, a failure at its Covent Garden premiere in
1976, *The English Cat* (1983) and *Das Verratene Meer* (*The Sea Betrayed*; 1990).

Scene i. The crowded waiting-room of a railway station. Manon is being escorted
by her brother to a finishing-school in Lausanne. When he goes off to have a
drink at the bar, she is approached by Armand des Grieux, a young student lonely
in Paris. They go off together.

Scene ii. A small attic in Paris. The self-seeking Manon is persuaded by her
brother to leave Armand and go to live with a rich, elderly admirer, Lilaque
Senior.

Scene iii. An elegant room in the house of Lilaque Senior. Manon is visited by
her brother, who steals money from Lilaque's safe. When Lilaque returns and discovers the theft, he throws Manon and her brother out of the house.

Scene iv. A university library. Armand and his friend Francis are studying the poems of Catullus. When Manon arrives, she and Armand read a love poem together and then reaffirm their love for each other.

Scene v. A cheap bar. Parted from Manon again, Armand has taken to drugs. Lescaut enters with Manon's latest suitor, who is the son of Lilaque. Armand obtains cocaine from Lescaut. Manon arrives but eventually leaves with her brother and Lilaque Junior. Armand sinks into a drug-induced sleep.

Scene vi. A room in the apartment of Lilaque Junior. Manon has spent the night with Armand. Lescaut, who has been keeping watch, warns Armand to leave. Before they leave, Lescaut steals a valuable modern painting from the wall. The elder Lilaque arrives, notices that the painting is missing and sends for the police. Lescaut shoots him, and presses the gun into Manon's hand as he escapes. The young Lilaque enters to find Manon and Armand standing over his father's dead body.

Scene vii. Outside a prison. Armand waits to catch a glimpse of Manon as she is taken to prison. She is led into the prison before they can exchange a word. The opera ends with a symbolical pantomime.

Henze's style is eclectic, with echoes of jazz and popular music as well as of composers such as Kurt Weill and Alban Berg.

PAUL HINDEMITH
(b. Hanau, 1895 – d. Frankfurt, 1963)

Cardillac
opera in three acts (approximate length: 1 hour, 30 minutes)

Cardillac   *baritone*
His Daughter   *soprano*
A Lady   *soprano*
An Officer   *tenor*
A Cavalier   *tenor*
A Gold Merchant   *bass*
A Police Officer   *high bass*

LIBRETTO BY FERDINAND LION, BASED ON A STORY, *DAS FRÄULEIN VON SCUDERI*, BY E.T.A. HOFFMANN; TIME: THE SEVENTEENTH CENTURY; PLACE: PARIS; FIRST PERFORMED AT THE STAATSOPER, DRESDEN, 9 NOVEMBER 1926

The foremost German composer of his generation, Hindemith composed three unsuccessful one-act operas before creating a stir in 1926 with *Cardillac*. The lighter pieces *Hin und Zurück* (There and Back; 1927) and *Neues vom Tage* (News of the Day; 1929) were followed by *Mathis der Maler*, his best-known opera. *Die Harmonie der Welt* (The Harmony of the World), produced in Munich in 1957, deals with the relationship of the artist or scientist to the society of his time, as *Mathis der Maler* had done (Mathis being the painter Mathias Grünewald). Hindemith's only English-language opera was a one-act piece, *The Long Christmas Dinner*, with a libretto by the American playwright Thornton Wilder based on his own play. This work was first produced in Mannheim in 1961, in a German translation made by the composer, as *Das lange Weihnachtsmahl*.

Act I, scene i. A square in Paris. A number of murders have been committed, but the murderer has not been found, and the Parisians are in a state of panic. An officer of the King's guard announces that the murderer, when found, will be burned alive. As the crowd disperses, it makes way reverently for a lone figure. A Lady asks a Cavalier who this mysterious person is, and she is told that it is the goldsmith Cardillac, whose creations are connected with the murders, for each of the victims was known to have purchased an example of the goldsmith's work shortly before death. The Lady promises herself to the Cavalier if he will visit her that night bringing with him the finest piece from Cardillac's workshop.

   Act I, scene ii. The Lady's bedchamber. The Cavalier arrives, bringing with him a beautiful golden belt. They sing a duet, at the climax of which a cloaked intruder appears, stabs the Cavalier to death and escapes with the golden belt.

   Act II. Cardillac's workshop. A Gold Merchant visits Cardillac, whom he suspects of being the murderer. Cardillac consents to his Daughter's marriage to an Officer who buys the golden belt, which has been restored to its place in the goldsmith's collection. Cardillac dons his black robe and mask and goes in pursuit of the Officer.

   Act III. A street in front of a tavern. Cardillac attacks the Officer, but succeeds only in wounding him. Confronted by the crowd, Cardillac confesses and is beaten to death.

The music proceeds mainly in closed forms – arias, duets, fugues, passacaglias and the like – and the action moves swiftly. In 1952 Hindemith produced a revised version in four acts with a new text that he himself wrote, but this version was generally thought to be inferior to the 1926 original and is now rarely performed.

Mathis der Maler

(Mathis the Painter)

opera in seven scenes (approximate length: 3 hours, 15 minutes)

Cardinal Archbishop of Mainz   *tenor*

Mathis (Matthias Grünewald), a painter in his service   *baritone*

Lorenz von Pommersfelden, Dean of Mainz   *bass*

Wolfgang Capito   *tenor*

Riedinger   *bass*

Hans Schwalb   *tenor*

Truchsess von Waldburg   *bass*

Sylvester von Schaumberg   *tenor*

Graf von Helfenstein   *silent role*

Ursula, Riedinger's daughter   *soprano*

Regina, Schwalb's daughter   *soprano*

LIBRETTO BY THE COMPOSER; TIME: THE PEASANTS' WAR, C. 1525; PLACE: IN AND NEAR MAINZ; FIRST PERFORMED AT THE STADTTHEATER, ZURICH, 28 MAY 1938

Mathis der Maler, Hindemith's best-known opera, was composed in 1933–4, but its production was banned by the Nazis and it was not staged until 1938, in Zurich, by which time Hindemith had emigrated to the United States. It deals with the relationship of the sixteenth-century artist Mathias Grünewald to the society of his time.

An instrumental prelude subtitled 'Engelkonzert' (Concert of Angels) is inspired by Grünewald's altarpiece at Isenheim.

Scene i. The courtyard of St Anthony's monastery at Mainz. Mathis is painting a fresco. Schwalb, the leader of the peasants, and his daughter Regina arrive, seeking refuge from the troops pursuing them. Mathis gives them his horse and promises his future support.

Scene ii. A hall in the Archbishop's palace in Mainz. Mathis admits having helped Schwalb escape, and begs his patron the Cardinal to support the cause of the peasants. The Cardinal refuses, and Mathis is obliged to leave his service.

Scene iii. A room in the house of the Lutheran Riedinger. Preparations are being made for the burning of Lutheran books. Mathis and Ursula, Riedinger's daughter, express their love for each other, though Riedinger intends that Ursula shall marry the Cardinal.

Scene iv. A war-ravaged village. Mathis protests against the brutal methods employed by the peasants. Schwalb is killed by soldiers marching through the village, and Mathis takes his daughter Regina away to find shelter.

Scene v. The Cardinal's study in Mainz. The Lutheran Ursula is introduced to the Cardinal as a prospective bride who could help him solve his financial problems. Ursula is willing to submit to this marriage for the sake of her cause, and the Cardinal is so impressed by her faith that he chooses to remain celibate. He gives permission to the Lutherans to declare themselves openly.

Scene vi. The forest of Odenwald. Mathis and Regina pause in their flight, to rest. While Regina sleeps, Mathis endures visionary temptations in which he is finally redeemed by the Cardinal, who appears to him in the guise of St Paul (as in Mathis's Isenheim altarpiece).

Scene vii. Mathis's studio in Mainz. Regina lies dying, comforted by Ursula. The Cardinal takes his last leave of Mathis, who symbolically puts away the tools of his art in preparation for his own death.

Hindemith's contrapuntal style is impressive in its seriousness of purpose, but there is no denying that this is an extremely long and slow-moving opera.

ENGELBERT HUMPERDINCK
(b. Siegburg, 1854 – d. Neustrelitz, 1921)

Hänsel und Gretel
opera in three acts (approximate length: 2 hours)

Hänsel   *mezzo-soprano*
Gretel, his sister   *soprano*
Gertrude, their mother   *mezzo-soprano*
Peter, their father, a broom-maker   *baritone*
Sandman   *soprano*
Dew Fairy   *soprano*
The Witch   *mezzo-soprano*

LIBRETTO BY ADELHEID WETTE, AFTER THE FAIRY TALE BY THE GRIMM BROTHERS; TIME: THE EARLY NINETEENTH CENTURY; PLACE: A GERMAN FOREST; FIRST PERFORMED AT THE HOFTHEATER, WEIMAR, 23 DECEMBER 1893

Humperdinck composed nine works for the stage. The earliest, and the one for which he is remembered today, is the opera *Hänsel und Gretel*, which was composed almost by accident. Humperdinck began by studying architecture at the University of Cologne, but he was persuaded by the composer Ferdinand Hiller to switch to composition, and in his mid-twenties he won a prize which enabled him to visit Italy. There he met Richard Wagner, who invited him to Bayreuth to assist in the preparation of *Parsifal* for the stage and for publication. Humperdinck had begun to write choral and orchestral music, but he had taken up the teaching of music as his profession when his sister, Adelheid Wette, who had written a children's play based on the Hänsel and Gretel story in the famous collection of German fairy tales by the Grimm brothers (1812), asked him to supply four songs for her play.

Humperdinck complied, at first somewhat reluctantly, but he became so fascinated by the story that, with his sister's approval, he expanded the music he had already composed into a full-length operatic score and sent the completed work to Richard Strauss, who wrote back, 'This is truly a masterpiece of the first rank,' and conducted its premiere in Weimar on the evening before Christmas Eve, 1893. *Hänsel und Gretel* was an instant success. It was soon in the repertoire of virtually every German opera house, was performed in London in English the following year on Boxing Day, and in due course became a favourite Christmas entertainment in opera houses all over the world.

The self-contained overture was described by Humperdinck as depicting 'Children's Life'.

Act I. The broom-maker's cottage. The curtain rises on a family kitchen. The broom-maker's two children are at work, Hänsel making brooms and his sister, Gretel, knitting, but their work is interrupted by playing and dancing ('Brüderchen, komm tanz mit mir'). When Gertrude, their mother, arrives, she scolds them, but in doing so she inadvertently knocks over a jug of milk provided by a kindly neighbour. In despair, she sends the children out with a basket to gather strawberries in the forest for supper, while she herself, bewailing the family's poverty, sinks exhausted onto a chair.

Gertrude's attempt at snatching a few minutes' rest is interrupted by the voice of her husband, Peter, singing as he approaches the cottage. She assumes that he is, as usual, drunk, but when Peter enters, singing merrily, he produces sausages, bread, butter and coffee from the basket he is carrying, telling his wife that he has had good luck at the fair. He asks where the children are. Told that they have been sent into the forest, he reminds his wife that there is a wicked witch who lives there, who entices children into her house and bakes them in her oven. Fearful that their children may be in danger, Gertrude and Peter rush off to search for them.

An orchestral entr'acte depicts the terrifying Witch's Ride.

Act II. In the forest. The curtain rises on a peaceful forest scene. The children have filled their basket with strawberries ('Ein Männlein steht in Walde ganz still und stumm'), but – as they enjoy the atmosphere of the forest and the call of a cuckoo – they begin to eat them until, to their dismay, they discover there are none left. By now it has become dark, and Hänsel realizes that they are lost. A Sandman appears and throws sand in the frightened children's eyes ('Der kleine Sandman bin ich'), after which Hänsel and Gretel kneel to say their evening prayers ('Abends wenn ich schlafen geh') and fall asleep in each other's arms under a tree. The clouds in the sky form a staircase, down which fourteen angels descend from heaven to guard the children through the night.

Act III. In the forest, at dawn. A Dew Fairy awakens Hänsel and Gretel by sprinkling dew upon them ('Der kleine Taumann heiss' ich'). The morning mist clears to reveal, nearby, a gingerbread cottage, its fence decorated with gingerbread men, and the delighted children begin to break off pieces of the cottage to eat ('O Himmel, welch Wunder ist hier geschehn'). But the Witch emerges from the cottage, throws a rope around Hänsel's neck and puts both children under a magic spell ('Knusper, knusper knauschen'). Shoving them into the cottage, she thrusts Hänsel into a cage, intending to fatten him up, and forces Gretel to light the oven. Gretel manages to break the spell, free her brother and trick the Witch into looking inside the oven. The children then push the Witch into the oven and slam the door ('Juchhei! Nun ist die Hexe tot'). The oven explodes, and the gingerbread men surrounding the cottage are transformed into real children who had been turned into gingerbread by the Witch. As all the children rejoice at the death of the Witch, Gertrude and Peter arrive. The Witch is removed from the ruined oven as a huge gingerbread cake, and all join in a hymn of thanksgiving.

The familiar story of Hänsel and Gretel is conveyed by Humperdinck with an admirable directness, his more than somewhat heavy, Wagner-like orchestral writing leavened by the catchy children's songs scattered about the score, and by the tenderness of the Evening Prayer, the Dew Fairy's song and the Sandman's song. But whether the opera is really suitable for young children, who have to wait a long time for Act III with its Witch and gingerbread house, is debatable.

Recommended recording: Ann Murray (Hänsel), Edita Gruberova (Gretel), Franz Grundheber (Peter), Gwyneth Jones (Gertrude), Christa Ludwig (Witch), with the Dresden Opera Women's Chorus and Children's Chorus, and the Dresden Staatskapelle, conducted by Colin Davis. Philips 438 013–2. The Dresden orchestra plays Humperdinck's score most lovingly for Davis, and the cast is faultless, with Ann Murray and Edita Gruberova delightful as the children, and Christa Ludwig enjoying herself splendidly as the Witch.

Königskinder
(The King's Children)
opera in three acts (approximate length: 2 hours, 30 minutes)

Goose Girl   *soprano*
King's Son   *tenor*
Fiddler   *baritone*
Witch   *mezzo-soprano*
Woodcutter   *baritone*
Broom-Maker   *tenor*
Innkeeper   *bass*
Innkeeper's Daughter   *mezzo-soprano*
Senior Councillor   *baritone*

LIBRETTO BY ERNST ROSMER (ELSE BERNSTEIN-PORGES); TIME: THE MEDIAEVAL PAST; PLACE: GERMANY; FIRST PERFORMED AT THE METROPOLITAN OPERA, NEW YORK, 28 DECEMBER 1910

Humperdinck's next three operas after *Hänsel und Gretel* were not noticeably successful. Then, in 1894, the writer and editor Heinrich Porges, whom the composer had met at Bayreuth, asked him to provide incidental music for *Königskinder*, a play written, under the pseudonym of Ernst Rosmer, by Porges' daughter, Else Bernstein-Porges (whose life was to end tragically in 1941 in the concentration camp of Terezin). Humperdinck wrote music to be performed under the playwright's dialogue as melodrama, but he also set some of the dialogue in a kind of *Sprechgesang*, or speech-song, anticipating Schoenberg. 'The notes for the spoken word', Humperdinck wrote on the score, 'generally indicate the relative, not the absolute pitch.'

When it was produced at the Royal Court Theatre, Munich, in 1897, the play was successful enough to be taken up by other German theatres and to be translated into English and staged in London later in the year and in New York in 1902, before falling into obscurity. In 1908 Humperdinck decided to refashion the work as an opera, with sung dialogue replacing the *Sprechgesang*. He took nearly three years to complete the task, and the opera was given its premiere at the Metropolitan Opera, New York, in 1910 to great acclaim, with a fifteen-minute ovation at its conclusion. Despite this, and a successful Berlin premiere the following year, *Königskinder* failed to gain the international acclaim that had been accorded to *Hänsel und Gretel*. However, it is still performed occasionally, and was revived at the Wexford Festival in 1986, in London, New York and Cologne in 1992 and in Sarasota in 1997.

The libretto's heavily symbolic text is a bleak one. The Goose Girl, who lives in the house of a Witch, falls in love with the King's Son when he comes to the forest disguised as a beggar. They marry, but die after eating the Witch's poisoned bread.

Much of Humperdinck's score sounds like Wagner with the flavour removed, but it is Ernst Rosmer's allegorical libretto that is largely responsible for the opera's failure to appeal to larger audiences.

Recommended recording: Helen Donath (Goose Girl), Adolph Dallapozza (King's Son), with the Bavarian Radio Chorus and the Munich Radio Orchestra, conducted by Heinz Wallberg. EMI CMS769936–2. A most persuasive performance.

LEOŠ JANÁČEK
(b. Hukvaldy, 1854 – d. Moravska Ostrava, 1928)

Jenůfa
opera in three acts (approximate length: 2 hours)

Grandmother Buryja, owner of the mill   *contralto*
Laca Klemen, her grandson   *tenor*

Števa Buryja, her grandson, Laca's half-brother   *tenor*
Kostelnička Buryja, her daughter-in-law   *soprano*
Jenůfa, the Kostelnička's stepdaughter   *soprano*
The Mill Foreman   *baritone*
The Mayor   *bass*
The Mayor's Wife   *mezzo-soprano*
Karolka, their daughter   *mezzo-soprano*
Barena, a servant at the mill   *soprano*
Jano, a shepherd boy   *soprano*

LIBRETTO BY THE COMPOSER, BASED ON A PLAY, *JEJÍ PASTORKYŇA*, BY GABRIELA
PREISSOVÁ; TIME: THE LATE NINETEENTH CENTURY; PLACE: A VILLAGE IN
MORAVIA; FIRST PERFORMED AT THE NATIONAL THEATRE, BRNO, 21 JANUARY 1904

One of the former Czechoslovakia's greatest three composers (along with Dvořák and Smetana), Janáček produced nine operas, the majority of which have made their way into the international repertoire. His earliest compositions were choral and organ works, reflecting his early musical training at a monastery school in Brno where he later returned to teach. His first opera, *Šárka*, composed in 1887, remained unperformed until 1925. His second, *The Beginning of a Romance*, a one-act piece consisting mainly of folk songs, was withdrawn by the composer after four performances in 1894. It was with his next opera, *Její pastorkyňa* (Her Step-daughter), that Janáček had his first success. He was forty years of age when he began its composition, but he broke off after Act I and did not return to the work until some years later. The opera, known outside the former Czechoslovakia as *Jenůfa*, was first staged in Brno in 1904, its composer's fiftieth year. Although it was a triumphant success in Brno, it took a further twelve years to reach the Prague National Theatre, where its highly favourable reception led quickly to its being accepted by opera houses throughout Europe. At the age of sixty-two, Janáček was now at the outset of his international career as a composer of opera.

Jenůfa's libretto, written by the composer himself, is derived from a play, *Její pastorkyňa* by Gabriela Preissová, first performed in Prague in 1890. (Janáček's second opera, *The Beginning of a Romance*, had been based on a short story by Preissova.) Janáček revised his score slightly in 1906–7, and for the opera's Prague performances he consented to further revisions, which consisted chiefly of cuts required by the conductor Karel Kovařovic. It was only after Charles Mackerras and John Tyrrell reconstructed and recorded Janáček's original score in 1982 that the opera began to be performed again in the fuller version of its Brno premiere.

Act I. The Buryja mill in a remote village in Moravia, towards evening. The family mill, owned by old Grandmother Buryja, is presently managed by her grandson Števa Buryja, whose elder half-brother Laca Klemen works as a labourer in the mill. Both men are in love with their cousin Jenůfa, but she loves Števa, by whom she has been made pregnant. At the rise of the curtain Jenůfa is anxiously awaiting Števa's return, to discover whether he is about to be conscripted into the army. If this happens she will not be able to marry him, and her pregnancy will be discovered. Old Grandmother Buryja sits in front of the mill, peeling potatoes, while Laca stands nearby, shaping a whip-handle with his knife and making sarcastic references to his lowly place in the household. Jano, a shepherd boy, enters to announce joyfully that, thanks to Jenůfa's tuition, he can now read. Laca gives his blunt knife to the Mill Foreman to sharpen and is told by him that Števa has not been conscripted. This news is greeted with delight by Jenůfa and with fury by Laca.

The new recruits are now heard approaching, singing to the accompaniment of the village band. Števa, too, appears, having got drunk to celebrate his escape from conscription. He insists on a reluctant Jenůfa dancing with him, but their dance is interrupted by the entrance of Jenůfa's stepmother, the stern Kostelnička (or Sextoness), who tells Števa that he may marry Jenůfa only after he has remained sober for a year. Grandmother Buryja orders Števa to go and sleep off his drunkenness, and then she attempts to console Jenůfa. When the company has dispersed, and Jenůfa and Števa are left alone, Jenůfa pours out her love for him and her fear that her pregnancy will soon be obvious to all, but Števa's response is petulant and childish. After Števa has left, Laca returns to find Jenůfa alone, and he speaks mockingly to her of Števa. When Jenůfa defends her lover, in a moment of jealous fury Laca slashes her cheek with his knife. She runs into the house screaming, and he is immediately remorseful. Barena, a servant girl at the mill, suggests that it was an accident, but the Mill Foreman accuses Laca of having struck Jenůfa on purpose.

Act II. A room in the Kostelnička's cottage, six months later. It is winter. Jenůfa has given birth to a child secretly, and both she and her child are being kept in hiding by the Kostelnička. Jenůfa's joy in the child is obvious, but her stepmother's pride has been injured by the shame that she feels has been brought upon them. Giving Jenůfa a drugged drink to make her sleep, the Kostelnička sends her stepdaughter into the adjacent room to look after the baby. Her prayers that the baby would die having gone unanswered, she is now prepared to accept a marriage between Jenůfa and Števa. She has sent for Števa, and when he arrives she tells him of the child's birth and implores him to marry Jenůfa. Števa refuses, telling her that he cannot love Jenůfa now that her beauty has been spoiled. All he can offer is money, but it must not be known that he has fathered a child, for he has promised to marry Karolka, the Mayor's daughter. The Kostelnička is horrified.

Števa runs out, and shortly afterwards Laca arrives. He, like the rest of the village, had thought that Jenůfa was away in Vienna and is dismayed when the Kostelnička tells him about the baby. He is still keen to marry Jenůfa, but since he recoils at the thought of accepting her child as well, the Kostelnička pretends that the baby has died. She sends Laca away on an errand and, after wrestling with her conscience awhile, goes into the room where Jenůfa is sleeping, takes the child and runs out to drown it in the icy millstream. When Jenůfa awakens to find her baby gone, she assumes that her stepmother has taken it to show to Števa, and she prays to the Virgin for the child's welfare. The Kostelnička returns, and she convinces Jenůfa that she has been in a fever for two days, during which time the child has died and has already been buried. Jenůfa accepts this information resignedly and, told also of Števa's forthcoming marriage to Karolka, agrees to marry Laca.

Act III. The Kostelnička's cottage, two months later. It is now spring. Jenůfa, who has recovered her strength, is preparing for her wedding to Laca, but the Kostelnička seems haggard and agitated. When the guests have arrived, among them the Mayor, his Wife, his daughter and Števa, old Grandmother Buryja gives Jenůfa and Laca her blessing. Suddenly, shouts are heard from outside, and Jano the shepherd boy rushes in, screaming that the body of a baby has been found in the millstream. Jenůfa is convinced that the body is that of her child, while everyone else suspects that it is she who has murdered it. Laca protects Jenůfa from the villagers, but the Kostelnička makes a full confession of her guilt, and says she is ready to accept the consequences. At first appalled, Jenůfa begins to understand her stepmother's motives and forgives her as she is led off to stand trial. Jenůfa offers Laca his freedom, but he says he still loves her, and she is able to tell him that, through her sufferings, she has come to return his love.

Janáček's passionate, late Romantic score is one of great emotional intensity and expressive power, his method of setting the Czech language making use of, and indeed emphasizing, the contours of that language's speech rhythms. Janáček's strongly delineated characters draw one into their emotional world and, although the vocal lines may sound wayward to non-Czech ears, the dramatically striking music that arises from the orchestra pit is always convincing.

Recommended recording: Elisabeth Söderström (Jenůfa), Eva Randova (Kostelnička), Wieslaw Ochman (Laca), Petr Dvorsky (Steva), with the Vienna State Opera Chorus and the Vienna Philharmonic Orchestra, conducted by Charles Mackerras. Decca 414 483–2. A splendid cast and, in Charles Mackerras, the finest of Janáček conductors.

Katya Kabanova
(Kát'a Kabanová)
opera in three acts (approximate length: 1 hour, 45 minutes)

Marfa Kabanova (Kabanicha), a rich merchant's widow   *contralto*
Tichon Kabanov, her son   *tenor*
Katerina (Katya) Kabanova, Tichon's wife   *soprano*
Varvara, a foster-child of the Kabanov family   *mezzo-soprano*
Savel Dikoy, a rich merchant   *bass*
Boris Grigoryevich, his nephew   *tenor*
Vanya Kudrjash, employed by Dikoy   *tenor*
Glasha, a servant in the Kabanov household   *mezzo-soprano*
Feklusha, a servant   *mezzo-soprano*
Kuligin, friend of Vanya   *baritone*

LIBRETTO BY THE COMPOSER, BASED ON THE PLAY *THE STORM*, BY ALEXANDER NIKOLAYEVICH OSTROVSKY; TIME: THE 1860S; PLACE: KALINOV, A SMALL PROVINCIAL TOWN ON THE BANKS OF THE VOLGA; FIRST PERFORMED AT THE NATIONAL THEATRE, BRNO, 23 NOVEMBER 1921

Janáček's next opera after completing *Jenůfa* was *Fate*, a semi-autobiographical work, which remained unperformed during his lifetime. This was followed by *The Excursions of Mr Broucek*, on which Janáček worked for several years, but which was a failure when it was staged in Prague in 1920. By this time the composer had turned his attention to the work that was to become *Katya Kabanova*. A Czech translation (by Vincenc Cervinka) of the Russian play *The Storm*, by Ostrovsky, was produced in Brno in March 1919. By the beginning of the following year Janáček had received permission to set it as an opera, and this he proceeded to do, adapting Cervinka's text himself. Under the title of *Katya Kabanova* the opera was an immediate success at its premiere in Brno, though it became well known abroad only after a number of years. Among Janáček's works it is now second in popularity only to *Jenůfa*.

Alexander Nikolayevich Ostrovsky (1823–1886) was the author of nearly fifty plays which are said to have laid the foundation for realistic Russian drama. His comedy *The Diary of a Scoundrel* (1868) is still occasionally performed, and his fairy tale in verse *The Snow Maiden* (1873) was made into an opera by Rimsky-Korsakov. *The Storm* (1860), a moving drama about the wife of a merchant in a dreary provincial town who, under the influence of a terrifying thunderstorm, confesses her infidelity to her husband, is generally regarded as Ostrovsky's masterpiece.

Act I, scene i. A public park in the town of Kalinov, overlooking the Volga, with the Kabanov house nearby. Vanya, a clerk in the employ of the rich merchant Dikoy, and Glasha, a servant in the Kabanov household, are sitting on a park bench, idly chatting. They retire discreetly when they see Dikoy approaching with his nephew Boris, whom he is rebuking for his laziness. When Dikoy leaves to look for Kabanicha, Boris confides to Vanya that he is forced to live with his tiresome uncle and obey his every wish, for this is the condition under which he and his sister will inherit money when they come of age, by the terms of their grandmother's will. Boris further reveals to Vanya that he has fallen in love with a married woman.

The Kabanov family are seen returning from church – the elderly widow Kabanova (Kabanicha) accompanied by her son Tichon, his wife Katya and the Kabanovs' foster-child Varvara. It is clear that Katya Kabanova is the object of Boris's love. Kabanicha, an old tyrant, complains that her son now neglects her for his wife, and she orders him to go to the market at Kazan. The weak Tichon obediently complies, although he tries to defend the gentle Katya against his mother's harsh tongue. Varvara, who is devoted to Katya, abuses Tichon for his weakness in dealing with his mother.

Act I, scene ii. A room in the Kabanov house. Katya reminisces to Varvara about her early, carefree life before her marriage, and she contrasts this with her present unhappiness and sense of foreboding. She is tormented by dreams in which a man tempts her to go away with him. When Tichon enters to say goodbye, Katya begs her husband to take her with him. He refuses, and she asks him at least to make her swear not to speak to any other man in his absence. His mother enters, and in her presence Tichon mildly suggests to Katya that she should not see other men while he is away, that she should be industrious, and should obey Kabanicha. Katya embraces her husband as he leaves, only to be rebuked by her mother-in-law for such shameless behaviour.

Act II, scene i. The living-room of the Kabanov house, later the same day.

Kabanicha reprimands Katya for not displaying more grief at her husband's departure. When the old woman has left the room Varvara announces to Katya that she is going for a walk, and that if she should see the man Katya loves, she will tell him that Katya awaits him by the garden gate. She leaves, giving Katya the key to the garden. Katya is left a prey to conflicting emotions, but seems likely to overcome her conscience. She leaves, longing for nightfall, as Kabanicha enters with a somewhat drunken and maudlin Dikoy, who unburdens himself to her and enjoys her scolding.

Act II, scene ii. Outside the garden gate, on a summer evening. Vanya and Boris await Varvara and Katya respectively. Varvara arrives and runs off with Vanya, as Katya enters to meet Boris. The love duets of the two couples intertwine as the light-hearted pair, Vanya and Varvara, return, and the voices of Katya and Boris are heard in the distance. When it is time for them all to part for the night, Vanya calls Boris and Katya to come back.

Act III, scene i. A derelict summer house on a terrace overlooking the Volga. Vanya and his friend Kuligin take shelter from a storm, and they are joined by Dikoy and Boris. Varvara arrives, telling Boris that Tichon has returned and that Katya is distraught. Boris hides as Katya rushes in, followed by Tichon and his mother. Katya interprets the worsening storm as a punishment from God. She confesses her adultery, naming Boris as her lover, and runs out into the storm.

Act III, scene ii. The banks of the Volga, at night. Everyone is searching for Katya, who has fled. Varvara and Vanya decide to elope together to Moscow. A distraught Katya enters, but when Boris appears and attempts to comfort her it is obvious that her mind is wandering. Katya and Boris part, for Boris's uncle is sending him to Siberia. Katya throws herself into the Volga and is already dead when her body is dragged out by Dikoy. When Kabanicha arrives upon the scene, she coldly thanks everyone for their kindness.

With *Katya Kabanova* Janáček entered upon the mature final period of his career. His tender portrait of Katya was inspired by his feeling for Kamila Stosslova, a married woman whom he had met on holiday in a Moravian spa town in 1917, and with whom he remained in love for the rest of his life. The nature of the gentle, tortured Katya is tellingly contrasted with that of the light-hearted lovers Varvara and Vanya and with the harsh, despotic Kabanicha, Janáček's most compelling portrayal of evil.

Recommended recording: Elisabeth Söderström (Katya), Libuse Marova (Varvara), Nadezda Kniplova (Kabanicha), Petr Dvorsky (Boris), Vladimir Krejcik (Tichon),

Dalibor Jedlicka (Dikoy), with the Vienna State Opera Chorus and the Vienna Philharmonic Orchestra, conducted by Charles Mackerras. Decca 421 852–2. This was the first of the superb Janáček opera recordings conducted by Sir Charles Mackerras for Decca. Söderström makes a moving Katya, and Kniplova is a fierce Kabanicha.

The Cunning Little Vixen
(Příhody Lišky Bystroušky)
opera in three acts (approximate length: 1 hour, 30 minutes)

Sharp Ears, the Vixen   *soprano*
The Fox   *soprano*
The Forester   *baritone*
The Forester's Wife   *contralto*
The Schoolmaster   *tenor*
The Priest   *bass*
Pasek, the innkeeper   *tenor*
The innkeeper's Wife   *soprano*
Harasta, the pedlar   *bass*
Lapak, the dog   *mezzo-soprano*
The Cock   *soprano*
Chocholka, the hen   *soprano*
The Badger   *bass*
The Owl   *contralto*
The Woodpecker   *contralto*

LIBRETTO BY THE COMPOSER, BASED ON THE NOVEL *LIŠKA BYSTROUŠKA*, BY RUDOLF TĚSNOHLÍDEK; TIME: AROUND 1920; PLACE: A MORAVIAN FOREST; FIRST PERFORMED AT THE NATIONAL THEATRE, BRNO, 6 NOVEMBER 1924

In 1920 a newspaper in Brno published a series of articles commissioned to accompany a collection of drawings of country life by the artist Stanislav Lolek. The text, by Rudolf Těsnohlídek, was then published as a novel, *Příhody Lišky Bystroušky* (literally: The Adventures of the Vixen Sharp Ears), and it attracted Janáček's attention. (The composer's housekeeper claimed that it was she who had suggested that the subject might make an opera.) In January 1922 Janáček, writing his own libretto based on Těsnohlídek's novel, began work on an opera which, completed in October 1923, was performed in Brno in November 1924. (Těsnohlídek contributed the words of one song in Act II.) Not an easy piece to stage, with its mixed cast of animals and humans, *The Cunning Little Vixen* achieved wide popularity only after a celebrated production by Walter Felsenstein at the Komische Oper, Berlin, in 1956. (The German translation, by Janáček's friend Max Brod, took considerable liberties in tidying up the composer's text.)

Act I, scene i. A forest, on an afternoon in summer. A Badger emerges from his hole, smoking a long pipe, while flies and a dragonfly swirl around him. When the Forester, perspiring and breathless, enters to take a nap, the creatures make themselves scarce, but crickets and a grasshopper dance while he sleeps. A young frog tries to catch a mosquito, but lands instead on the Forester's nose, awakening him. A vixen cub, Sharp Ears, who was watching the frog with interest, is caught by the Forester, who decides to take her home with him.

Act I, scene ii. The Forester's farmyard on an afternoon in autumn. Sharp Ears and the Forester's dog, Lapak, converse, complaining of their lonely and frustrated lives, and the vixen rejects the dog's amorous advances. When the Forester's son and his friend torment Sharp Ears she bites one of the boys and tries to escape, but is recaptured and tied up by the Forester. As night falls, she dreams that she is changed into a human girl.

Act I, scene iii. The farmyard, next morning. The chickens strut about, mocking Sharp Ears, who vainly attempts to arouse them to assert themselves and rebel against domination by humans and cockerels. She then pretends to be dead. When the hens and the Cock approach to investigate, she comes to life and begins biting off their heads. The Forester's wife rushes out, appalled at the carnage and calling her husband, but the vixen manages to bite through her leash and runs off into the forest.

Act II, scene i. The forest, in late afternoon. Sharp Ears peers in at the Badger in his lair, and she tempts him out. She taunts him until he makes a dignified exit, pipe in hand, and then she moves into his lair.

Act II, scene ii. The village inn. The Forester, the Schoolmaster and the Priest drink and play cards. The Forester mocks the Schoolmaster for his backwardness in love, the innkeeper, Pasek, warns the Priest that his drinking is likely to cause a scandal, and the Forester leaves in a bad mood when the innkeeper mentions the escaped vixen, Sharp Ears.

Act II, scene iii. The forest, by moonlight. The Schoolmaster, rather tipsy, is trying to make his way home through the forest. The vixen watches him from behind a sunflower, and the Schoolmaster mistakes her for his distant beloved,

Terynka. The Priest, making his way home separately, mutters about Terynka, whom he too once loved and was accused of seducing. The Forester appears and fires a shot at Sharp Ears, who escapes.

Act II, scene iv. The vixen's lair, on a summer night by moonlight. Sharp Ears is wooed by a handsome Fox who brings her a rabbit he has killed. They fall in love, enter the lair together, and when they emerge the following morning she whispers to him that she is pregnant. They are married by the Woodpecker, and the birds and animals of the forest celebrate their union.

Act III, scene i. The forest at midday, in the autumn. Harasta, a pedlar and poultry dealer, is accosted by the Forester, who suspects him of poaching, and Harasta tells the Forester that he is about to marry Terynka. The Forester lays a trap for Sharp Ears, whose paw prints he has seen nearby. When he has left, Sharp Ears, the Fox and their large family of cubs emerge from their lair. Harasta enters with chickens he has stolen, and Sharp Ears lures him away while the fox cubs delightedly consume the chickens. When Harasta returns in a fury, aiming a gun at the cubs, Sharp Ears protects them with her body, and is killed.

Act III, scene ii. The village inn. The Forester tells the Schoolmaster of his unsuccessful search for Sharp Ears. The Schoolmaster is upset at the news of Terynka's marriage to Harasta. The Forester, now beginning to feel his age, sets out for home.

Act III, scene iii. The forest, in spring. The Forester contemplates the beauty of the scene and remembers the days of his courtship and wedding. He falls asleep, and the creatures of the forest reappear as they did the previous spring. The Forester awakens to see a little vixen among them, looking just like its mother, Sharp Ears. However, he fails to catch it, finding himself grasping a frog instead. The Forester lets his gun fall to the ground.

Janáček's glowing score, with its evocation of nature and its smooth string writing in the lyrical sections alternating with the composer's more familiar jagged, speech-related rhythms, is a delight. The opera's emotional range is impressively wide, and its portrayal of the passing of time and the transience of life, both human and animal, can prove deeply moving in performance.

Recommended recording: Lucia Popp (Vixen), Eva Randova (Fox), Dalibor Jedlicka (Forester), with the Bratislava Children's Chorus, the Vienna State Opera Chorus, the Vienna State Opera Chorus, and the Vienna Philharmonic Orchestra, conducted by Charles Mackerras. Decca 417 129–2. Lucia Popp is a sparkling Vixen, and the rest of the cast, all Czechs, are equally superb. Mackerras's conducting brings out the splendours of the orchestration magnificently, as one would expect from this great Janáček interpreter.

The Makropulos Affair
(Věc Makropulos)
opera in three acts (approximate length: 1 hour, 30 minutes)

Emilia Marty, an opera singer   *soprano*
Albert Gregor   *tenor*
Dr Kolenaty, a lawyer   *bass-baritone*
Vitek, his clerk   *tenor*
Kristina, Vitek's daughter   *soprano*
Baron Jaroslav Prus   *baritone*
Janek, Prus's son   *tenor*
Hauk-Sendorf, an old man-about-town   *tenor*

LIBRETTO BY THE COMPOSER, BASED ON KAREL ČAPEK'S PLAY *THE MAKROPULOS AFFAIR*; TIME: THE EARLY 1920S; PLACE: PRAGUE; FIRST PERFORMED AT THE NATIONAL THEATRE, BRNO, 18 DECEMBER 1926

While he was at work on the composition of *The Cunning Little Vixen* in 1922, Janáček saw a production in Prague of *Věc Makropulos*, a new play dealing with the scientific prolongation of life, by the Czech dramatist Karel Čapek. Janáček immediately contacted Čapek to seek his permission to turn the play into an opera. Čapek raised no objection and, after copyright questions had been settled, Janáček began to work on Čapek's text, even before he had finished composing *The Cunning Little Vixen*. By the end of 1924 he had completed a first draft of *The Makropulos Affair*, and by the end of the following year the opera was ready to be performed. Its premiere in Brno in December 1926 led to performances in Prague some months later, in Frankfurt in 1929 and in Vienna in 1937. The opera has taken longer to establish itself in the wider international repertoire, though it has been staged successfully in recent years in a number of cities, among them London, New York, San Francisco and Los Angeles, and at Glyndebourne.

Act I. Dr Kolenaty's chambers. A celebrated lawsuit involving the Prus and Gregor families has been going on for almost a century. The present contestants are Baron Jaroslav Prus and Albert Gregor, who claims that his ancestor Ferdinand

Gregor should have inherited a large estate when Baron Josef Ferdinand Prus died intestate in 1827. The ruminations of Vitek, Dr Kolenaty's clerk, on the case are interrupted by the arrival of the plaintiff, Albert Gregor, asking for information on the present state of play. Vitek's daughter Kristina, a young opera singer, arrives and tells of her immense admiration for the art and beauty of the famous singer Emilia Marty, whom she has just heard rehearsing. Kristina and her father leave as Emilia Marty herself enters with Dr Kolenaty, who, at Marty's request, gives her all the details of the case, although she already seems to know a great deal about it. The nineteenth-century Baron Prus was thought to have died childless, but Emilia Marty informs the lawyer that there was an illegitimate son, Ferdinand MacGregor, whose mother was Ellian MacGregor, a Scottish singer with the Imperial Opera. Marty is even able to reveal the probable hiding place in the present Baron Prus's house of a document that could furnish proof of the son's existence.

At Gregor's insistence, a sceptical Kolenaty goes off to search for the document, while Marty, left alone with Gregor, intrigues the young man by telling him more about the singer Ellian MacGregor. When Gregor becomes infatuated with Marty, she repels his amorous advances. She asks him to hand over to her a Greek document which she says he will find among the papers he will inherit, and appears perturbed at his apparent lack of knowledge of such a document. Kolenaty returns with Baron Prus, having found the will of Prus's ancestor. Prus asks for further proof that the son mentioned in the will is a direct ancestor of Albert Gregor, and Marty undertakes to provide it.

Act II. The empty stage of a theatre. A stage technician and a cleaning woman discuss the impact that Emilia Marty's performance has had on them. Prus arrives to wait for Marty, and he observes his son Janek in conversation with Kristina, with whom the young man is in love but who is too obsessed with Emilia Marty to pay much attention to Janek. Marty now enters in an irritable mood, behaving impolitely to all who attempt to congratulate her on her performance. She is much pleasanter to her final visitor, Hauk-Sendorf, an elderly man-about-town, who says she reminds him of Eugenia Montez, his lover of fifty years earlier.

Dismissing all except Baron Prus, Marty is questioned by the Baron about her interest in the court case. He has discovered that a parish register refers to the nineteenth-century Baron's illegitimate son not as Ferdinand Gregor but as Ferdinand Makropulos, and he has also noticed that Ellian MacGregor's letters to his ancestor are signed simply 'E.M.', which, he observes, could equally well stand for Emilia Marty, Eugenia Montez or even Elina Makropulos, a sixteenth-century Greek girl who drank an elixir of life concocted by her father. Prus has also discovered among his ancestor's papers a sealed envelope. When Marty offers to buy the envelope from him, he turns away without answering.

Gregor returns, declaring his love for Marty, but she is interested only in attempting to persuade him to retrieve from Kolenaty the document the lawyer found in the Prus archives. Marty falls asleep and Gregor leaves. When she awakes it is to find Janek standing before her in tongue-tied admiration. She asks him to steal the sealed envelope from his father, and he is about to agree when he is shamed by Prus's reappearance. Marty now asks Prus himself for the envelope, and he, as bewitched by her as everyone else has been, agrees to give it to her if she will meet him that evening.

Act III. A hotel room. Baron Prus and Emilia Marty dress, after having spent the night together. Her demeanour is cold as she now asks for and is given the envelope she was promised, and Prus feels cheated, for her love-making was completely unresponsive. Prus receives news that his son Janek has killed himself. He is devastated, but Marty remains unmoved. Hauk-Sendorf enters to propose to Marty that they elope to Spain, to which she consents. However, a doctor removes the demented old man. Kolenaty and the others involved in the case also arrive, and Kolenaty accuses Marty of having forged the signature on the document she gave him. When she goes to change, Kolenaty and his colleagues rifle her trunk, discovering a number of documents relating to Emilia Marty, Montez, Makropulos and others.

Marty returns, somewhat tipsy, and begins to answer Kolenaty's questions. She reveals that her real name is Elina Makropulos, that she was born in Crete in the sixteenth century, and that she is therefore more than three hundred years old. In the nineteenth century she had a son by Baron Prus, and she has changed her name several times, moving from country to country to avoid suspicion but always retaining the initials 'E.M.'. To her son by Baron Prus she left the prescription for the elixir that she drank in 1565 and which has prolonged her life. But unless she now takes more of the elixir, she will rapidly grow old and die. She is beginning to age as she speaks, and has to be carried to her bedroom. A doctor is called to attend to her. Eventually Marty returns, but as a shadow, approaching death. She was determined to acquire the sealed envelope containing the prescription for the elixir, but she now accepts that death will be a welcome release. She gives the envelope to Kristina, telling her it will enable her to live for three hundred years and become a great singer, but Kristina sets fire to it as Emilia Marty, alias Elina Makropulos, dies.

The Makropulos Affair consists for the most part of cleverly composed dialogue above a complex, sophisticated orchestral score. The emotions of the audience are strongly engaged by the powerful finale of Act III, with Marty's moving confession of her realization that, for her, life has become empty and meaningless, and that the death she once feared is something she now welcomes. Given a superb cast of actor–singers the opera can prove highly effective, for it is certainly not overlong.

Recommended recording: Elisabeth Söderström (Emilia Marty), Petr Dvorsky (Albert Gregor), Vaclav Zitek (Jaroslav Prus), with the Vienna State Opera Chorus and the Vienna Philharmonic Orchestra, conducted by Charles Mackerras. Decca 430 372–2. Another in the superlative Decca series of Janáček operas conducted by Mackerras. Elisabeth Söderström gives a superb performance as Emilia Marty.

From the House of the Dead
(Z mrtvého domu)
opera in three acts (approximate length: 1 hour, 30 minutes)

Alexander Petrovich Goryanshikov   *baritone*
Alyeya, a young Tartar   *mezzo-soprano*
Filka Morosov (also known as Luka Kuzmich)   *tenor*
Big Prisoner   *tenor*
Small Prisoner   *baritone*
The Prison Governor   *baritone*
Elderly Prisoner   *tenor*
Skuratov   *tenor*
Chekunov   *bass*
Drunken Prisoner   *tenor*
Cook   *baritone*
Blacksmith   *bass*
Priest   *baritone*
Young Prisoner   *tenor*
Prostitute   *mezzo-soprano*
Prisoner (playing the roles of Don Juan and a Brahmin)   *bass*
Kedril   *tenor*
Shapkin   *tenor*
Shishkov   *baritone*
Cherevin   *tenor*
Guard   *tenor*

LIBRETTO BY THE COMPOSER, AFTER FYODOR DOSTOEVSKY'S NOVEL *MEMOIRS FROM THE HOUSE OF THE DEAD*; TIME: AROUND 1860; PLACE: A PRISON CAMP IN SIBERIA; FIRST PERFORMED AT THE NATIONAL THEATRE, BRNO, 12 APRIL 1930

After he had completed *The Makropulos Affair* in 1925, Janáček turned to orchestral and choral composition with his *Sinfonietta*, his *Capriccio* for piano (left hand) and chamber orchestra and his *Glagolitic Mass*. He also made sketches for a violin concerto, which he intended to call *The Journeying of the Soul*, but he abandoned it and early in 1927 began to write *From the House of the Dead*, a setting of Dostoevsky's novel *Memoirs from the House of the Dead* (1862), an account of life in a Siberian prison based on Dostoevsky's own experiences in a prison in Omsk where he spent four years for having belonged to a study group interested in French Utopian socialism. Janáček created his own libretto as he composed, translating into Czech as much as he needed of the Russian novel as he went along. By the beginning of 1928 he had completed a second draft of the opera. He then worked closely with his two copyists in producing a third version, which incorporated several changes made during the copying process. By the end of July, Janáček had corrected Acts I and II. Act III, though complete in essence, was still on his desk when he died on 12 August 1928.

Before the opera's first performance in 1930, changes were made to Janáček's orchestration by two of his pupils, Bretislav Bakala (who conducted the premiere) and Osvald Chlubna, it being considered that some of the composer's orchestral writing was rather thin. Bakala and Chlubna also altered the ending of the opera to make it less bleak, but in recent years productions have tended to restore Janáček's original ending, thanks in large part to the conductors Rafael Kubelik and Charles Mackerras.

Act I. The yard of a prison camp in Siberia, on the banks of a river. It is early morning, in winter. The inmates are washing, eating, quarrelling and discussing the expected arrival of a new prisoner, reputed to be an aristocrat, or at least a gentleman. The new prisoner, Alexander Petrovich Goryanshikov, duly arrives and is interrogated by the Prison Governor. When Goryanshikov claims that he is a political prisoner, the Governor angrily orders that he be taken away and flogged. Alyeya, a young Tartar, is the only prisoner to react sympathetically to Goryanshikov's cries of pain. The other prisoners play with a captured eagle whose wing is broken. Though they tease the bird cruelly, they admire its defiance.

The Governor returns with guards, and the prisoners are ordered back to work. Some go off, singing a mournful song about their homes, which they fear they will never see again, while others remain, among them Skuratov, who sings a cheerful song which annoys another prisoner, Luka Kuzmich. Kuzmich picks a quarrel with Skuratov, who, after recalling his life in Moscow as a cobbler, dances wildly until he collapses in exhaustion. Luka Kuzmich recalls how, when he was imprisoned elsewhere for vagrancy, he stabbed to death a brutal prison officer, for which he was flogged and tortured until he thought he would die. An Elderly Prisoner naively asks Kuzmich if he did die. Goryanshikov, barely alive after the flogging he has suffered, is brought back by the guards.

Act II. By the riverbank. It is late afternoon in summer, and the steppes can be seen stretching away into the distance. The prisoners are working outdoors, and among them is Goryanshikov, who asks Alyeya about his family and offers to teach the lad to read and write. As the working day ends, the Governor and his guests arrive, along with a Priest who blesses the food the prisoners are about to eat. Skuratov, occasionally interrupted by a Drunken Prisoner, tells the others of the crime for which he was imprisoned: he shot and killed the rich man whom the girl he loved was being forced to marry.

On an improvised stage the prisoners perform two plays. One is about Don Juan and his servant Kedril, and the other is a tale about a miller's wife whose various lovers include Don Juan. After the performance most of the prisoners disperse, while a Young Prisoner goes off with a Prostitute, and Goryanshikov and Alyeya sit drinking tea. A small but belligerent prisoner attacks Alyeya, breaking a jug over his head. Alyeya falls to the ground and guards rush in to restore order.

Act III, scene i. The prison hospital, towards evening. Alyeya, delirious with fever, is watched over by Goryanshikov, while Chekunov waits on them both, to the annoyance of Luka Kuzmich, who lies dying. Shishkov tells the story of a young girl, Akulka, who was generally believed to have lost her virginity to a certain Filka Morosov, who refused to marry her. Shishkov was persuaded to marry the girl, whom he then discovered was a virgin. When he later found out that she had been unfaithful to him with Morosov, whom she had always loved, Shishkov took the girl out into the woods and cut her throat. As Shishkov concludes his story, Luka Kuzmich dies, and only then does Shishkov recognize Kuzmich as Filka Morosov, whose corpse he roundly curses. Guards enter, calling for Goryanshikov, whom they lead out as the young Tartar lad, Alyeya, attempts to cling to him.

Act III, scene ii. The yard of the prison camp, as in Act I. The Prison Governor, who is drunk, apologizes to Goryanshikov for having had him flogged on his arrival. Goryanshikov is to be released and is free to go immediately. He bids a tender farewell to Alyeya, and as he leaves the camp the other prisoners release the eagle, which, its wing now healed, flies off. The guards order the prisoners back to work.

As a prelude to *From the House of the Dead* Janáček used the music he had composed for his violin concerto, which he had abandoned. Throughout the opera, which has virtually no plot and indeed no leading characters, Janáček's music, often sparse in texture, effectively supports the words, rising to great emotional climaxes at the conclusion of each act. His motto for this remarkable work, 'In every creature a spark of God', pervades even its grimmest sequences. This is certainly Janáček's most unusual opera, and some would say his finest.

Recommended recording: Ivo Zidek (Skuratov), Dalibor Jedlicka (Goryanshikov), Vaclav Zitek (Shishkov), with the Vienna State Opera Chorus and the Vienna Philharmonic Orchestra, conducted by Charles Mackerras. Decca 430 375–2. Another completely convincing Janáček recorded performance from Mackerras and his singers.

RUGGERO LEONCAVALLO
(b. Naples, 1857 – d. Montecatini, 1919)

Pagliacci
(Clowns)
opera in a prologue and two acts (approximate length: 1 hour)

Canio, head of a troupe of strolling players   *tenor*
Nedda, his wife   *soprano*
Tonio, a clown   *baritone*
Beppe, a member of the troupe   *tenor*
Silvio, a villager   *baritone*

LIBRETTO BY THE COMPOSER; TIME: BETWEEN 1865 AND 1870, ON THE FEAST OF THE ASSUMPTION; PLACE: MONTALTO, IN CALABRIA; FIRST PERFORMED AT THE TEATRO DAL VERME, MILAN, 21 MAY 1892

After completing his studies in Naples, Leoncavallo composed his first opera, *Chatterton*, while he was still in his teens, although it was not performed until he revised it twenty years later. His earliest success, and easily his greatest, came with *Pagliacci*, which was staged in Milan in 1892, bringing its composer immediate fame. *I Medici*, the first part of a projected trilogy, was a failure the following year, and Leoncavallo did not complete the remaining two parts. His *La Bohème* (1897) suffered by comparison with Puccini's opera based on the same novel by Henry Murger and performed only some months earlier, and with the exception of *Zazà* (1900) Leoncavallo produced nothing further of interest.

It was the success of Mascagni's one-act opera *Cavalleria rusticana* in 1890 that encouraged Leoncavallo himself to attempt a one-act opera in the same realistic style. He wrote his own libretto, based on a newspaper report of a crime of passion committed in the Calabrian village of Montalto. The opera, *Pagliacci*, which turned out to be in two acts, though it lasts no longer than an hour, was successfully launched in Milan in May 1892, conducted by the young Arturo Toscanini. Within two years it had been translated into every European language (even Serbo-Croat), and soon it was being paired on a double bill with Mascagni's *Cavalleria rusticana* (which lasts about an hour and fifteen minutes). *Cav-and-Pag* remains a popular coupling.

Prologue. Tonio, one of a group of strolling players, steps out in front of the curtain, already dressed in his clown costume, to inform the audience that actors are real people like themselves ('Si può?') and that the story about to be enacted is a true one. 'Incominciate' (Let's begin), he exclaims with a flourish, as he retreats and the curtain rises on a rustic scene.

Act I. The outskirts of the village of Montalto, Calabria. It is the feast day of the Assumption, and the villagers have gathered to greet the company of strolling players who have just arrived. Canio, the leader of the troupe, invites the assembled villagers to attend the performance that evening, but when someone in the crowd makes a light-hearted reference to the company's leading actress, Canio's wife, Nedda, Canio answers grimly that anyone who tried to take Nedda from him would be playing a dangerous game ('Un tal gioco').

When the crowd has dispersed and her fellow players have repaired to the village tavern, Nedda wonders to herself whether Canio has begun to suspect her of infidelity. She envies the birds in the sky their freedom ('Stridono lassù'). Tonio returns and attempts clumsily to pay court to Nedda, but she repulses him, striking him with a whip left behind by another member of the company. Tonio retreats, and Nedda's lover, a young villager named Silvio, appears. He and Nedda

make plans to elope that evening after the performance. The jealous Tonio overhears them and fetches Canio, who arrives too late to catch the young villager
whose name he now demands to know. Nedda refuses to tell him, and, left alone to
put on his clown's make-up and costume, Canio reflects bitterly on the situation
of the clown who must make people laugh although his heart may be breaking
('Vesti la giubba').

Act II. An improvised open-air theatre, with the audience assembling. The play
begins. While her husband, Pagliaccio (played by Canio), is absent from home,
Columbine (Nedda) rejects the advances of Taddeo (Tonio) and awaits her lover,
Harlequin (Beppe), who serenades her ('O Columbina, il tenero fido Arlecchin').
Pagliaccio returns home, and he demands to know the name of Columbine's
lover. It soon becomes clear that Canio is having great difficulty remaining in
character. When Nedda, as Columbine, continues to refuse to divulge the name of
her lover, Canio finally shouts, 'No, Pagliaccio non son!' (No, I am not Pagliaccio),
and he stabs Nedda, who, as she falls dying, calls to Silvio to help her. Silvio leaps
onto the stage from the audience, and he too is stabbed by Canio, who then turns
to the audience with the spoken words, 'La commedia è finita' (The comedy is
over). (This, the final line in the opera, was originally uttered by Tonio, but the
tenor Enrico Caruso, playing Canio in an early performance, appropriated it,
since when it has almost invariably been spoken by Canio.)

Together with Mascagni's *Cavalleria rusticana*, *Pagliacci* is one of the masterpieces of the Italian *verismo* school. The operas of *verismo* (realism) deal not with
high-born, romantic personages, but with so-called ordinary people in down-to-
earth, usually violent, situations. Leoncavallo's harmonically expressive score is
imbued with great vitality and dramatic conviction, and Canio's impassioned
outburst of self-pity, 'Vesti la giubba', has become one of the most famous of tenor
arias, beyond the context of the opera. Other highlights of the score include
Nedda's Act I aria, Tonio's Prologue and Canio's intense, desperate ebullition, 'No,
Pagliaccio non son!'.

Recommended recording: see under Mascagni's Cavalleria rusticana.

PIETRO MASCAGNI

(b. Livorno, 1863 – d. Rome, 1945)

Cavalleria rusticana

(Rustic Chivalry)

opera in one act (approximate length: 1 hour, 15 minutes)

Santuzza, a young peasant woman   *soprano*
Turiddu, a young peasant   *tenor*
Alfio, the village carrier   *baritone*
Lola, his wife   *mezzo-soprano*
Mamma Lucia, Turiddu's mother   *contralto*

LIBRETTO BY GIOVANNI TARGIONI-TOZZETTI AND GUIDO MANASCI, BASED ON THE
PLAY CAVALLERIA RUSTICANA, BY GIOVANNI VERGA; TIME: EASTER SUNDAY, 1890;
PLACE: A VILLAGE IN SICILY; FIRST PERFORMED AT THE TEATRO COSTANZI, ROME,
17 MAY 1890

Mascagni was born in Livorno, studied in Milan and then found work as a
conductor of touring operetta companies, one of which performed his first
work for the stage, an operetta, *Il re a Napoli*, staged in Cremona in 1885. In 1888,
deciding to enter a competition for a one-act opera, organized by the publishing
firm of Edoardo Sonzogno, Mascagni chose as his subject the play *Cavalleria rusticana* by Giovanni Verga, which he had seen in Milan four years earlier with the
great Italian actress Eleanora Duse as Santuzza. Verga, the leader of the naturalis-
tic or *verismo* school of Italian writers, had based the play on his own novella of
the same title, published in 1883.

Commissioning a libretto from two fellow citizens of Livorno, Mascagni proceeded to compose his opera. He showed it to Puccini, who was impressed enough
to pass it on to his publisher Giulio Ricordi, who rejected it. Mascagni then entered
the opera in Sonzogno's competition, which it won against seventy-two rival
entries, one of which was by Umberto Giordano. Sonzogno had arranged that the
operas of the three finalists would be included in a season at the Teatro Costanzi
in Rome. When *Cavalleria rusticana* was produced there in May 1890 it was an
immediate and resounding success, and within the following year it was staged to
great acclaim in all the principal cities of Europe and America. It remains hugely
popular today, usually paired in a double bill with Leoncavallo's *Pagliacci*.

After the prelude, which includes a *siciliana* (a song in Sicilian style) sung by Turiddu as a serenade to Lola ('O Lola, ch'ai di latti'), the curtain rises. The entire action of the opera takes place in the square of a Sicilian village, dominated on one side by the village church. Elsewhere in the square is the wine shop and dwelling owned by Mamma Lucia. It is Easter Sunday morning, and the village slowly comes to life as the church bells ring out and people make their way to the service, which is about to begin. Santuzza enters the square and approaches the wine shop, seeking her lover, Mamma Lucia's son Turiddu. Lucia tells Santuzza that Turiddu has not yet returned from a journey the previous day to collect some wine. This puzzles Santuzza, who says that Turiddu was seen in the village during the night. Mamma Lucia invites Santuzza into her house, but Santuzza exclaims that she must not enter, for she has been excommunicated.

Alfio, the village carrier, now enters with his horse and cart, gaily singing of the joys of a teamster's life ('Il cavallo scalpita'). He confirms that Turiddu is in the village, for he saw him earlier that morning not far from his (Alfio's) cottage. Alfio goes on his way, and the church choir begins to intone the *Regina coeli*, to which the villagers in the square contribute alleluias. All kneel and, led by Santuzza, join in the Resurrection hymn ('Ineggiamo, il Signor non è morto'). When everyone else has entered the church, and the square is empty, Santuzza pours out her heart to Mamma Lucia ('Voi lo sapete'). Before he left to become a soldier, she tells Lucia, Turiddu and Lola were lovers. On his return he found Lola married to Alfio, the carter, and turned his attentions to Santuzza, whom he has seduced and betrayed. He has now been taking advantage of Alfio's frequent absences from home to renew his relationship with Lola. Perturbed by what she has heard, Mamma Lucia goes off to church, while Santuzza awaits Turiddu.

When Turiddu arrives, he attempts to ignore Santuzza. Lola enters the square, singing a carefree song ('Fior di giaggiolo') on her way to church, and Turiddu steps forward to meet her but is held back by Santuzza who begs him to remain with her and love her for ever ('No, no Turiddu'). As he no longer cares for her, he pushes her roughly aside and follows Lola into the church. Alfio now returns, and a furious Santuzza tells him that his wife has been unfaithful to him with Turiddu. Alfio vows that he will be avenged, and he and Santuzza leave the square.

While the stage is empty, the orchestra plays the famous intermezzo, at the conclusion of which the villagers begin to emerge from the church, and Turiddu invites everyone to drink with him ('Viva il vino spumeggiante'). Alfio joins the group, but when Turiddu offers him wine he refuses it roughly. Understanding what this means, Turiddu bites Alfio's ear, a Sicilian gesture denoting one's assent to a fight. Alfio leaves, while Turiddu bids Mamma Lucia farewell ('Mamma, quel vino è generoso'), asking her to look after Santuzza if he should not return. As he runs out to fight Alfio, Santuzza and some of the villagers return. Suddenly a voice is heard shouting that Turiddu has been killed. Santuzza collapses, and some of the women rush forward to support Mamma Lucia.

Cavalleria rusticana is a taut, firmly constructed piece of melodrama whose entire action occurs in the course of just over an hour, during which time a rejected lover causes the death of the man who has betrayed her, while the Easter Mass is being celebrated in the village church. The prelude introduces some of the opera's finest melodies, and the introductory crowd scenes are colourfully written (perhaps calling to mind Act IV of *Carmen*). Alfio's entrance song and Turiddu's drinking song provide a welcome lightening of the tension, while the central duet between Turiddu and Santuzza is savage in the fierceness of its passion, and is really the only number in the opera to which the term *verismo* can be wholeheartedly applied. The sweetly sentimental intermezzo, the most famous piece in the opera, serves as a point of repose before the tragedy gathers momentum. Mascagni's finest opera makes an appropriate curtain-raiser to Leoncavallo's equally effect-ive *Pagliacci*.

Recommended recording: Coupled with Leoncavallo's Pagliacci. Maria Callas (Santuzza and Nedda), Giuseppe di Stefano (Turiddu and Canio), Tito Gobbi (Tonio), Rolando Panerai (Alfio), with the Chorus and Orchestra of La Scala, Milan, conducted by Tullio Serafin. EMI CDS 7 47981 8. Maria Callas gives wonderfully dramatic performances in both operas. Di Stefano is on top vocal form, acting and singing with a blazing intensity, and Gobbi is, as always, a vivid interpreter. Tullio Serafin conducts powerfully, and the recording, though more than forty years old, is perfectly acceptable.

L'amico Fritz
(Friend Fritz)
opera in three acts (approximate length: 1 hour, 30 minutes)

Fritz Kobus, a rich landowner   *tenor*
Suzel, a farmer's daughter   *soprano*
Beppe, a gypsy   *mezzo-soprano*
David, a rabbi   *baritone*

Hanezo, friend of Fritz   *bass*
Federico, friend of Fritz   *tenor*
Caterina, Fritz's housekeeper   *soprano*

LIBRETTO BY P. SUARDON (PSEUDONYM OF NICOLA DASPURO), BASED ON THE
NOVEL *L'AMI FRITZ*, BY EMILE ERCKMANN AND ALEXANDRE CHATRIAN; TIME:
THE LATE NINETEENTH CENTURY; PLACE: ALSACE; FIRST PERFORMED AT THE
TEATRO COSTANZI, ROME, 31 OCTOBER 1891

After the spectacular success of *Cavalleria rusticana* it might have been
expected that Mascagni's next opera would be another piece of raw *verismo*.
Instead, it was a sentimental lyrical comedy, *L'amico Fritz*, its libretto by Nicola
Daspuro derived from a novel, *L'Ami Fritz*, published in 1864. When Mascagni's
opera was staged in Rome, seventeen months after the premiere of *Cavalleria
rusticana* in that city, it was received with great enthusiasm and was soon being
performed elsewhere in Italy and abroad. However, *L'amico Fritz* failed to sustain
its initial popularity, although it is still occasionally to be encountered in Italian
opera houses.

Act I. The dining-room of Fritz Kobus's house. Fritz, a wealthy landowner, tells
his friend David, a rabbi, that he cannot understand why young people keep
falling in love and marrying. Hanezo and Federico, friends of Fritz, arrive to have
supper with him on his fortieth birthday. Caterina, Fritz's housekeeper, ushers in
Suzel, the teenage daughter of one of Fritz's tenants, who brings him a bouquet of
flowers ('Son pochi fiori'). Beppe, a gypsy fiddler, entertains the company. After
Suzel has left, the men all comment on her attractiveness. David prophesies that
Fritz will soon succumb to marriage, and Fritz wagers his vineyard that he will
not. A group of orphans whom Fritz has befriended arrive, and the act ends in
general merriment.

   Act II. An orchard. Suzel sings cheerfully as she picks cherries. Fritz arrives,
compliments her on her singing and helps her as she continues to gather cherries
('Suzel, buon dì'). David, Beppe, Hanezo and Federico arrive, and Fritz is invited
to join them for a drive in the country. Rabbi David, pleading fatigue, stays behind
with Suzel. When she offers him water, David tells her that the scene reminds him
of the biblical story of Isaac and Rebecca, and he asks her to read the appropriate
passage, which she does. Fritz and the others return, and David tests Fritz's feelings for Suzel by announcing that he has found a suitable husband for her. Fritz
is horrified at this, and he realizes that he may be falling in love. Determined to

avoid this, he leaves without saying goodbye to Suzel. She is unhappy to see him go, and is comforted by David.

Act III. Fritz's house. Fritz, distraught by the realization that he loves Suzel, is comforted by Beppe, and he broods on the subject of love ('O amore, o bella luce del core'). David arrives to inform him that preparations are in hand for Suzel's wedding, and that his consent, as the landowner, is needed. Fritz refuses to give it and rushes out of the room. Suzel enters and admits to David that she loves Fritz ('Non mi resta che il pianto'). When Fritz returns, he and Suzel finally declare their love for each other. David wins his bet, and he presents Suzel with the vineyard as a wedding gift.

L'amico Fritz is a work of great gentleness and charm, its score mellow yet translucent. Two Alsatian folk songs are introduced to provide local colour, but for the most part Mascagni's music remains on a conversational level, broadening at appropriate moments into lyrical melody. The opera's most memorable numbers are the Cherry Duet ('Suzel, buon dì'), which has become well known outside the context of the opera and which progresses from a casual parlando beginning to a melodically voluptuous conclusion, and the intermezzo preceding Act III.

Recommended recording: Mirella Freni (Suzel), Luciano Pavarotti (Fritz), Vicente Sardinero (David), with the Chorus and Orchestra of the Royal Opera House, Covent Garden, conducted by Gianandrea Gavazzeni. EMI CDS7 47905–8. Freni and Pavarotti are delightful.

JULES MASSENET
(b. Montaud, 1842 – d. Paris, 1912)

Manon
opera in five acts (approximate length: 2 hours, 30 minutes)

Manon Lescaut   *soprano*
Chevalier des Grieux   *tenor*
Count des Grieux, his father   *bass*
Lescaut, Manon's cousin   *baritone*
Guillot de Morfontaine, a nobleman   *tenor*

De Bretigny, a nobleman   *baritone*
Pousette, actress   *soprano*
Javotte, actress   *mezzo-soprano*
Rosette, actress   *mezzo-soprano*

LIBRETTO BY HENRI MEILHAC AND PHILIPPE GILLE, BASED ON THE NOVEL *MANON
LESCAUT*, BY THE ABBÉ PRÉVOST; TIME: EARLY EIGHTEENTH CENTURY; PLACE:
AMIENS, PARIS AND LE HAVRE; FIRST PERFORMED AT THE OPÉRA-COMIQUE, PARIS,
19 JANUARY 1884

Massenet was the most prolific French opera composer of his time, and for a considerable period he was the most important. However, after his death in 1912 his music was regarded for many years by the younger generation of composers and critics as superficial, insignificant and lacking in contemporary relevance. Over the years Massenet's operas have gone in and out of fashion, and even now there are voices to be heard decrying the melodic charm of this most ingratiating of composers. But those who do not object on principle to being entertained in the opera house, rather than hectored, will always find a place in their hearts for Massenet. A serious comment lurks beneath Sir Thomas Beecham's frivolous assertion that he would gladly exchange the whole of Bach for one bar of *Manon*.

Massenet studied at the Paris Conservatoire, won the Prix de Rome at the age of twenty-one and proceeded to write two operas that were not staged before having his third, *La Grand'tante* (The Great Aunt), a one-act *opera comique*, accepted. Produced at the Paris Opéra-Comique in 1867, it was only moderately successful. In his early operas, Massenet tended to concentrate on sacred subjects, and for a time it seemed as though his speciality would lie in injecting a certain eroticism into the treatment of biblical characters such as Eve, Mary Magdalen and even the Virgin Mary. 'I don't believe in all that creeping-Jesus stuff', Massenet wrote to his younger colleague Vincent d'Indy, 'but the public likes it, and we must always agree with the public.'

Of the nine operas that Massenet completed before *Manon*, only *Le Roi de Lahore* (The King of Lahore; 1877) and *Hérodiade* (1881) are occasionally still to be seen. It was with *Manon* in 1884 that Massenet achieved his greatest success, and it remains his most popular work; it is probably the most often performed French opera after Bizet's *Carmen* and Gounod's *Faust*.

The libretto of *Manon*, by Henri Meilhac and Philippe Gille, is based on a novel, *L'Histoire du chevalier des Grieux et de Manon Lescaut*, by Antoine-François Prévost, published in 1731. Prévost (1697–1763) is known as Abbé Prévost, although he was a member of a strict Benedictine order for only a very short time before deciding that he preferred a worldly life. Fearing ecclesiastical reprisals when he left the Benedictines, he fled to Holland and thence to England, returning to France in 1734. His novel, now known simply as *Manon Lescaut*, is actually the final volume of a seven-volume sequence entitled *Mémoires et aventures d'un homme de qualité*, written in London and published in Amsterdam. Prévost's *Manon Lescaut* inspired not only Massenet's *Manon* in 1884 but also, nine years later, Puccini's *Manon Lescaut*.

Act I. The courtyard of an inn in Amiens. Two noblemen, Guillot de Morfontaine, an elderly roué, and his younger companion De Bretigny, are accompanied by three young women, Pousette, Javotte and Rosette, politely and euphemistically described as actresses. Guillot impatiently calls to the Innkeeper to serve their supper. Townspeople awaiting the arrival of the coach from Arras gather in the courtyard, and Lescaut, an officer, arrives to meet his cousin Manon, a teenage girl who will be travelling on the coach on her way to enter a convent. (In Prévost's novel, Manon is Lescaut's sister.) Lescaut dismisses his two fellow officers, telling them to go to a nearby tavern where he will join them later.

The coach arrives, and the townspeople comment on the passengers who bustle about to retrieve their luggage. Manon emerges from the crowd and is greeted by her cousin, to whom she chatters excitedly about her journey ('Je suis encore tout étourdie'). Lescaut goes off to find her luggage, and Manon is approached by Guillot de Morfontaine who, captivated by her beauty, tries to persuade her to travel to Paris with him and become his mistress. Lescaut returns in time to hear the end of their conversation, reproaches Manon for flirting ('Ne bronchez pas') and then goes off to join his companions in the tavern, leaving her to await her coach. Left alone, Manon observes with envy the actresses and their fine clothes, and she speculates on the life she might have been able to lead had her family not insisted on sending her to a convent.

The young Chevalier des Grieux, a student of philosophy, enters to wait for the coach that will take him to Paris to visit his father ('J'ai marqué l'heure du départ'). When he catches sight of Manon, Des Grieux immediately falls in love with her. She responds favourably, and leaves with him in Guillot's private coach ('Nous vivrons à Paris'). Lescaut reappears, now somewhat drunk. Unable to find Manon, he accuses Guillot of having abducted her. When the Innkeeper explains that she was seen to leave with a young man, Guillot swears to be avenged for his wounded pride, Lescaut is determined to pursue Manon and Des Grieux, and the townspeople and travellers are vastly amused.

Act II. The apartment of Des Grieux and Manon in Paris, on the rue Vivienne. Des Grieux writes a letter to his father, asking for his permission to marry Manon. The lovers read the letter together ('On l'appelle Manon'), and Des Grieux is about to leave to post it when he notices flowers on the mantelpiece and asks where they came from. Manon replies that a bouquet was thrown through the window. The maid enters to announce that Manon's cousin Lescaut is outside. She whispers to Manon that a man accompanying Lescaut is De Bretigny in disguise. The two men are admitted, and De Bretigny pretends to restrain Lescaut from being too harsh with Manon. Lescaut is mollified when Des Grieux shows him the letter he is about to send to his father. While Lescaut and Des Grieux are talking, De Bretigny promises Manon great wealth if she will consent to become his mistress. He also warns her that Des Grieux's father plans to have his son abducted from the apartment that very evening.

Lescaut and De Bretigny leave, and Des Grieux goes to post his letter while Manon considers whether to accept De Bretigny's offer. Unable to resist the promise of riches, she decides to leave Des Grieux, although she loves him, and she bids a sentimental farewell to their apartment ('Adieu, notre petite table'). Des Grieux returns and tells her of the blissful life they will share ('En fermant les yeux'). When a knock is heard at the door, Manon begs him not to open it. He does, however, and is forcibly taken away.

Act III, scene i. The promenade of the Cours-la-Reine, by the Seine, where a fête is in progress. Among the crowd of vendors and pleasure-seekers is Lescaut with the three young actresses. Snubbed by the three women, Guillot expresses to De Bretigny his disgust that all three of them have proved unfaithful to him. He teases De Bretigny for having refused to grant Manon's expensive wish to have the dancers from the Opéra perform at their house. Guillot makes plans to secure Manon's favours for himself.

Manon enters, and her resplendent appearance is commented upon by all. She sings ecstatically of the joys of her rich life in Paris society (Gavotte: 'Obéissons quand leur voix appelle'). Des Grieux's father, the Count des Grieux, enters, and Manon overhears him telling De Bretigny that his son has taken holy orders and is now an Abbé at the church of Saint-Sulpice. Manon sends De Bretigny off on an errand and asks the Count how his son has endured their separation. The Count replies that Des Grieux has forgotten her. Guillot returns in triumph with the ballet troupe from the Opéra, whom he has engaged to perform for Manon. However, while their performance is in progress Manon abruptly leaves to go to the church of Saint-Sulpice.

Act III, scene ii. The reception room of the seminary of Saint-Sulpice, in Paris.

Women come from the chapel, enthusiastically praising the eloquence and passion of the new Abbé. The Count des Grieux tries to dissuade his son from completing his holy vows, advising him instead to marry. When he realizes that Des Grieux is adamant, the Count promises to send him his inheritance. After his father has departed, Des Grieux prays for peace of mind, for he is still tormented by his desire for Manon ('Ah, fuyez, douce image'). He leaves to take part in the service, and Manon enters, asking to see him. When he returns, she begs his forgiveness and reminds him of their past love and happiness together ('N'est-ce plus ma main?'). He is unable to resist her, and they once again declare their love for each other.

Act IV. The Hôtel de Transylvanie. Guillot, Lescaut and the actresses are among the gamblers and professional card-sharpers assembled around the gaming tables. Manon enters with Des Grieux. She tries to persuade him to gamble what is left of his inheritance, but he refuses. Eventually he agrees to a game of faro with Guillot, who loses large sums to him. When Des Grieux displays his winnings to an ecstatic Manon, Guillot accuses him of cheating, and he leaves. Manon, afraid of what Guillot may be planning, pleads with Des Grieux to take his winnings and leave immediately with her, but he refuses to do so. Guillot returns with the police and Des Grieux's father. The Count persuades the police to remove his son from the scene and release him later, but Guillot demands that Manon be arrested as a prostitute.

Act V. The road to Le Havre. Des Grieux waits by the roadside where Manon will pass by with other female prisoners to be deported. He and Lescaut have hired a group of men to rescue Manon, but when Lescaut arrives he reports that his men have fled after seeing the guards so heavily armed. The prisoners and guards are heard approaching, and Des Grieux and Lescaut conceal themselves. They overhear two guards talking about a prisoner who is dying. It is Manon. Lescaut bribes a sergeant to let her stay behind until nightfall, and the lovers are left alone together. Manon begs Des Grieux's forgiveness, and she dies in his arms. (In Prévost's novel, and in Puccini's *Manon Lescaut*, Manon is deported to America. Des Grieux exiles himself with her and gravely wounds the son of the governor of Louisiana in a duel. In the desert, Manon dies of exhaustion in Des Grieux's arms.)

As an opera containing spoken dialogue, *Manon* technically belongs to the genre of *opéra comique*. However, it uses unaccompanied dialogue most sparingly, making much greater use of *mélodrame* – dialogue spoken over music. The opera reveals Massenet's mastery of a number of musical styles, the elegant eighteenth-century pastiche of the Cours-la-Reine scene contrasting vividly with the dramatic concerted finale of Act IV and the passionately romantic music of the two lovers, who are skilfully and convincingly characterized. Manon's Gavotte, her seductive 'N'est-ce plus ma main?' and Des Grieux's two arias are the work's highlights.

Recommended recording: Ileana Cotrubas (Manon), Alfredo Kraus (Des Grieux), Gino Quilico (Lescaut), José van Dam (Count des Grieux), with the Toulouse Capitole Chorus and Orchestra, conducted by Michel Plasson. EMI CDS 7 49610 2. Ileana Cotrubas is a most touching, vulnerable Manon, and Alfredo Kraus a stylish, sweet-toned Des Grieux. The other principal roles are well taken, with Gino Quilico a lively Lescaut and José van Dam superb as the elder Des Grieux. Michel Plasson conducts a loving account of this charming work.

Werther
opera in four acts (approximate length: 2 hours, 30 minutes)

Werther, a poet, aged 23   *tenor*
The Bailiff, aged 50   *bass*
Charlotte, his daughter, aged 20   *mezzo-soprano*
Sophie, her sister, aged 15   *soprano*
Albert, Charlotte's fiancé, aged 25   *baritone*
Schmidt   *tenor* ⎤
⎟ friends of the Bailiff
Johann   *bass* ⎦

LIBRETTO BY EDOUARD BLAU, PAUL MILLIET AND GEORGES HARTMANN, BASED ON THE NOVEL *DIE LEIDEN DES JUNGEN WERTHERS*, BY JOHANN WOLFGANG VON GOETHE; TIME: AROUND 1780; PLACE: WETZLAR, A SUBURB OF FRANKFURT; FIRST PERFORMED AT THE HOFOPER, VIENNA, 16 FEBRUARY 1892

In August 1886, Massenet and his publisher Georges Hartmann travelled to Bayreuth, where they attended a performance of Wagner's *Parsifal*. They then undertook a short tour of Germany, visiting Wetzlar and the house in which Goethe had written his novel *Die Leiden des jungen Werthers* (The Sorrows of Young Werther). At this time Massenet was contemplating using his friend Henry Murger's *Scènes de la vie de bohème* as the subject of his next opera (which Puccini was to use a few years later); however, he became enthusiastic about Goethe's novel after his visit to Wetzlar, and Hartmann encouraged him by giving him a copy of the French translation. Massenet quickly decided upon *Werther* for his next opera. Hartmann produced the outline of a libretto, the actual text of which was entrusted to Edouard Blau and Paul Milliet, and Massenet set himself up in a room at Versailles where he wrote the opera.

When it was completed, *Werther* was offered to the Paris Opéra-Comique, where several of Massenet's earlier operas had had their first performances. But the director of the theatre considered the work at best uninteresting and at worst depressing. Whether he would, nevertheless, have agreed to stage the premiere of the opera is uncertain. Matters were taken out of his hands when, in May 1887, the Opéra-Comique was destroyed by fire. In 1890 Massenet's *Manon* proved a huge success at the Vienna Hofoper, and the Viennese approached its composer with the request that he provide a new opera for them. Massenet responded by offering the world premiere of *Werther*. The opera was performed in a German translation of its French text at the Vienna Hofoper on 16 February 1892, and it was staged in Paris in January of the following year by the company of the Opéra-Comique, who were occupying the Théâtre Sarah Bernhardt while their own theatre was being rebuilt. Like Massenet's *Manon*, *Werther* has survived changes of fashion to become a staple of the international opera repertoire.

Die Leiden des jungen Werthers, an early novel by Germany's greatest poet, Johann Wolfgang von Goethe (1749–1832), was published in 1774, when its author was only twenty-five years of age. Goethe himself, who usually referred to his novel simply as *Werther*, described it as the story of an artistically inclined young man, 'gifted with deep, pure sentiment and penetrating intelligence, who loses himself in fantastic dreams and undermines himself with speculative thought until finally, torn by hopeless passions, he shoots himself in the head'. There is a strong autobiographical element in Goethe's novel, for the poet himself, in the summer of 1772, when he was twenty-three, had fallen in love with Charlotte Buff, daughter of the bailiff or mayor of Wetzlar. In the novel the young Werther falls in love with a girl named Charlotte, daughter of the bailiff of Wetzlar. The real Charlotte, who had been engaged for two years to one Johann Kestner when Goethe appeared on the scene, was unable to offer the young poet more than friendship. The Charlotte of the novel confesses her love for Werther but honours her promise to marry her fiancé, Albert. In October 1772 Karl Wilhelm Jerusalem, a young diplomat, borrowed a pair of pistols from Charlotte Buff's fiancé Johann Kestner and shot himself. In the novel, Werther borrows Albert's pistols and shoots himself. Goethe, however, did not shoot himself. Instead, he created art out of his unhappy emotional experience.

The publication of Goethe's *Werther* in 1774 led to an immediate *Werther* epidemic in Germany. Young men began to dress like the hero of the novel, in blue tails and yellow waistcoats, and there was an immediate and huge increase in the number of suicides among Germany's youths. Werther's memory was commemorated at the grave of Karl Wilhelm Jerusalem for several decades. This *Werther* fever was not confined to Germany, but spread throughout those countries into whose languages the novel had been translated. Goethe noted with great satisfaction that even the Chinese had painted Charlotte and Werther on porcelain. There were *Werther* fans, eau de *Werther* perfume and a host of novels and poems written in imitation of the original. Napoleon told Goethe that he had read the book seven times. The novel was dramatized several times, and it was set to music by other composers before Massenet, among them Rodolphe Kreutzer (1766–1831), whose *Charlotte et Werther* was staged in Paris in 1792, and Vincenzo Pucitta (1778–1861), whose *Werter e Carlotta* was performed in Venice in 1802.

Act I: 'The Bailiff's House'. The garden of the Bailiff's house, in July. The Bailiff is teaching his six young children a Christmas carol. He is a widower, looked after by his two elder daughters, Charlotte, aged twenty, and Sophie, aged fifteen. Johann and Schmidt, two friends of the Bailiff, come to take him off to the local inn, but he promises to join them later, and the two men leave as Werther, a young poet and diplomat, arrives to escort Charlotte to a ball, in place of her fiancé Albert, who is absent on business. Overcome by the rustic charm of the surroundings and the singing of the children now inside the house, Werther extols the beauty of nature ('O nature, pleine de grace'). The Bailiff introduces Charlotte to Werther, who is immediately struck by her innocent charm. They leave for the ball, and the Bailiff goes off to join his friends at the inn, leaving Sophie to look after the younger children. Albert then arrives unexpectedly, eager to see his beloved Charlotte. When Sophie tells him she is not at home, he promises to return early next morning.

Time passes. Charlotte and Werther return from the ball, lost in each other. She speaks to him of the shock of her mother's death and of the responsibility it has placed upon her, and he responds with a passionate declaration of his love. The Bailiff returns, announcing as he enters the house that Albert is back. Charlotte tells Werther of her promise to her dying mother that she will marry Albert. Werther says that she must stay true to that promise, although he knows it will mean his death.

Act II: 'The Lime Trees'. The square in Wetzlar, with the church, the parsonage and the inn. It is now September. From the inn, Johann and Schmidt watch people going to church to celebrate the pastor's fiftieth wedding anniversary.

Approaching the church with Charlotte, to whom he is now married, Albert asks her if he has succeeded in making her happy, and he receives her assurances. Contemplating them from a distance, Werther gives way to his jealousy ('Un autre son époux'). Before following Charlotte into the church, Albert tells Werther that he feels almost guilty in his happiness, knowing that Werther must have been attracted to Charlotte, but Werther assures him that he feels only friendship for them both. They are interrupted by Sophie, who arrives with a bouquet for the pastor, and Albert tries to make Werther aware of Sophie's obvious interest in him.

Charlotte emerges from the church, and Werther nostalgically recalls their first meeting. She reminds him of her duties as a wife, and suggests that his pain might be lessened if he were to leave for a time, to return perhaps at Christmas. Alone, Werther contemplates suicide. Then, brusquely informing Sophie that he is leaving for ever, he rushes away. Charlotte and Albert discover Sophie crying, and when she repeats Werther's words to them, Albert realizes that Werther is in love with Charlotte.

Act III: 'Charlotte and Werther'. Albert's house, on Christmas Eve. Charlotte, her heart full of love for Werther, rereads his many letters ('Air des lettres'). Sophie enters, but her attempts to cheer her sister lead to Charlotte bursting into tears. When Sophie has gone, Charlotte prays to God for strength. Werther suddenly appears, and Charlotte tries to confine their conversation to social pleasantries by talking about the house, the children and how nothing has changed. She points out the volume of Ossian that Werther had begun to translate, and he recalls one of the poems ('Pourquoi me réveiller?'). They embrace passionately, but Charlotte, horrified at her momentary weakness, tells Werther they must never meet again, and she rushes from the room. Werther leaves in despair.

Albert arrives home and becomes suspicious of Charlotte's behaviour. His interrogation of her is interrupted by Werther's servant with a message from the poet to say that he is about to go on a long journey and would like to borrow Albert's pistols. Albert orders Charlotte to hand the pistols to the servant, who leaves with them, but as soon as Charlotte is alone she rushes out of the house, hoping to avert a tragedy.

Act IV, scene i: 'Christmas Eve'. A tableau depicts the little town of Wetzlar on Christmas Eve, its trees and rooftops covered in snow, with lights coming on in some of the windows one by one, and snow still falling, while a violent orchestral intermezzo connects the end of Act III to the beginning of the next scene.

Act IV, scene ii: 'The Death of Werther'. Werther's study, on Christmas Eve. Charlotte enters hurriedly, but she is too late. Werther lies stretched out on the floor, mortally wounded. She confesses that she has always loved him. Children's voices are heard singing the Christmas carol from Act I as Werther asks to be buried either under the lime trees at the far end of the churchyard or, if Christian ground is forbidden to him, some unhallowed spot that the priest will avoid but perhaps one woman will come to visit and shed a tear. Werther dies in Charlotte's arms as the sound of the children's carol is heard in the distance.

In *Werther* Massenet skilfully transformed Goethe's essentially Germanic hero into a character more sympathetic to French sensibilities, but without turning him into a travesty of his original self (which is what German music critics had, not surprisingly, accused Gounod of having done in *Faust* thirty years earlier). Paradoxically, however, the Gallic vivacity and lightness of touch that can be found elsewhere in Massenet's oeuvre is here replaced by a romantic melancholy which comes close to the *Weltschmerz* of Goethe's young hero. Max Kalbeck, the Viennese music critic who was responsible for the German translation in which the opera was performed at its premiere, wrote perceptively of *Werther* that it 'inclines more towards the new German school than Massenet's earlier operas, without for a moment affecting the essentially French nature of its composer'.

Massenet's opera is not so much a dramatization in music of Goethe's novel as a musical illustration of it. The dramatic structure of the work is loose, in that its scenes follow one another not as though a plot were being unfolded but as though the pages of an album were being turned. The scenes themselves are described as 'tableaux', each with its own title. The analogy with pictorial illustration survives when one comes to Massenet's orchestration, with its lucid, finely applied colours. Werther's 'Pourquoi me réveiller?' and Charlotte's 'Air des lettres' are among the highlights of a score whose melodic inspiration is almost as rich as that of *Manon. Werther* may be, as an early critic of Massenet remarked, a sugary cake, but it is one baked by a master confectioner.

Recommended recording: Ninon Vallin (Charlotte), Germaine Feraldy (Sophie), Georges Thill (Werther), Emile Rocque (Albert), Armand Narcon (Bailiff), with the Chorus and Orchestra of the Opéra-Comique, Paris, conducted by Elie Cohen. EMI CHS7 63195–2. This famous 1931 award-winning recording is still the best account of the opera on disc. Ninon Vallin's warm tone and vivid characterization make her an ideal Charlotte, and Georges Thill's impassioned Werther is by far the most idiomatic on disc. The recording shows its age, but the conductor balances the score's elegance and passion more successfully than any of his rivals. This is a performance to treasure.

Cendrillon
(Cinderella)
fairy tale in four acts (approximate length: 2 hours)

Cendrillon (Cinderella)   *soprano*
Madame de la Haltière, her stepmother   *mezzo-soprano*
The Prince   *soprano*
The Fairy Godmother   *soprano*
Noémie   *soprano* ⎤
Dorothée   *mezzo-soprano* ⎦ Cendrillon's stepsisters
Pandolfe, Cendrillon's father   *bass*
The King   *baritone*

LIBRETTO BY HENRI CAIN, BASED ON THE STORY *CENDRILLON*, IN *LES CONTES DE MA MÈRE L'OYE*, BY CHARLES PERRAULT; TIME AND PLACE: THOSE OF FAIRY TALE; FIRST PERFORMED AT THE OPÉRA-COMIQUE, PARIS, 24 MAY 1899

The libretto of Massenet's *Cendrillon* is based on the well-known fairy tale of Cinderella. The earliest printed version of the story appeared in Neapolitan dialect in 1634, in a collection of folk tales made by Giambattista Basile called *Lo cunto de li cunti* (The Story of Stories). Towards the end of the nineteenth century a book was published with the title *Cinderella, Three Hundred and Forty-Five Variants*. Since then scholars have unearthed many more versions of the tale: more than five hundred European variants are known, to say nothing of the sea changes the story underwent in being transmitted beyond Europe. The best-known European version is that of the seventeenth-century French poet and critic Charles Perrault, whose book of fairy tales *Les Contes de ma mère l'Oye* (Tales of Mother Goose), published in 1697, contains the story of Cendrillon or Cinderella. It was upon Perrault's story that Henri Cain based his libretto for Massenet. (German children know Cinderella as Aschenbrodel, in the version published by the Grimm brothers early in the nineteenth century. In this, the stepsisters mutilate their feet in a vain attempt to prove that the slipper fits, and as they walk in Aschenbrodel's bridal procession they are punished by having their eyes pecked out by doves!)

The first composer to set the Cinderella story to music was Jean-Louis Laruette, whose one-act *Cendrillon* was performed in Paris in 1759. Nicolas Isouard's *Cendrillon* (1810) was a huge success at its Paris premiere, was immediately produced in other European countries and in 1827 reached New York, although by then it was beginning to be displaced by the Cinderella opera that is today the most often performed of all, Rossini's *La Cenerentola*. Massenet's *Cendrillon* was more than moderately successful at its premiere and, although not as popular as his *Manon* or *Werther*, it is still occasionally revived.

Act I. Madame de la Haltière's house. Madame de la Haltière and her two daughters, Noémie and Dorothée, prepare to go to the royal ball. Her husband, Pandolfe, wonders why he married so overbearing a woman with two daughters ('Ai-je quitté ma ferme et nos grand bois!'), and he regrets having to leave his own daughter, Cendrillon, at home. After the others have departed, Cendrillon goes to sleep by the fire ('Reste au foyer, petit grillon'). Her Fairy Godmother appears, providing her with a magnificent dress as well as a pair of glass slippers, which will prevent her from being recognized by her family ('Pour en faire un tissu'), and she sends her off to the ball, warning her, however, not to stay after midnight.

Act II. The royal palace. The Prince is melancholy. The King, his father, orders him to marry, and eligible princesses are paraded before him. But it is Cendrillon who captures his heart. She, in turn, falls instantly in love with him ('Toi qui m'es apparue'). At midnight Cendrillon leaves hastily.

Act III, scene i. Madame de la Haltière's house. Cendrillon has lost one of her slippers in her haste to leave the ball. Madame and her daughters attempt to persuade Pandolfe that the Prince had not really been attracted to the beautiful stranger at the ball.

Act III, scene ii. A fairy landscape. Cendrillon has retreated to the world of fairy tale, where she and the Prince affirm their love for each other.

Act IV, scene i. The house. Cendrillon has been talking in a delirium about the ball, the Prince and the missing slipper, but her father assures her that she must have dreamt it all ('Printemps revient'). However, when her stepmother announces that princesses from far and wide are assembling to try on a slipper left at the ball, Cendrillon realizes that she has not been dreaming.

Act IV, scene ii. The palace. Cendrillon claims the slipper as hers ('Vous êtes mon Prince Charmant'). She and the Prince embrace, and the opera ends in general rejoicing.

Massenet's fairy-tale opera is a work of great charm, for the most part light and frothy, with passages of witty pastiche of seventeenth-century music. Cendrillon's family are strongly characterized, and the various soprano roles are well differentiated. For example the Prince is given a voice of stronger timbre, while Cendrillon has a purely lyrical role. Although one should not seek in the composer's French sentimentality the sharp comic intelligence of the Latin Rossini, there are never-theless interesting similarities between Rossini's *La Cenerentola* and Massenet's *Cendrillon*. The same feeling of resigned melancholy informs both Cendrillon's song 'Reste au foyer, petit grillon' and Cenerentola's 'Una volta c'era un re', while Massenet's writing for his heroine's awful relatives has much of the vivacity of Rossini. Massenet, however, breaks through the fairy-tale mould to bring a breath of humanity to his characters, while Rossini prefers to stay within a kind of *commedia dell'arte* framework. Massenet's *Cendrillon* is a work both delicate and curiously exotic in texture, whose glitter does not obscure but actually enhances its warmth and humanity.

Recommended recording: Frederica von Stade (Cendrillon), Nicolai Gedda (the Prince), with the Ambrosian Opera Chorus and the Philharmonia Orchestra, conducted by Julius Rudel. CBS CD 79323. Julius Rudel conducts a sparkling per-formance, and Frederica von Stade is a delightful Cinderella. The role of the Prince, intended by Massenet to be sung by a soprano, is here assigned to the tenor Nicolai Gedda, whose splendid voice and high range prove more than acceptable in the role.

Don Quichotte

(Don Quixote)

comédie-héroïque in five acts (approximate length: 2 hours, 15 minutes)

Don Quichotte (Don Quixote)   *bass*
Sancho Panza   *baritone*
La Belle Dulcinée   *mezzo-soprano*
Pedro   *soprano*
Garcias   *soprano*   admirers
Rodriguez   *tenor*   of
Juan   *tenor*   Dulcinée
Tenebrun, the bandit chief   *spoken*

LIBRETTO BY HENRI CAIN, BASED INDIRECTLY ON THE NOVEL *DON QUIXOTE*, BY MIGUEL DE CERVANTES; TIME: THE MIDDLE AGES; PLACE: SPAIN; FIRST PERFORMED AT THE OPÉRA, MONTE CARLO, 19 FEBRUARY 1910

In the last ten years of his life, Massenet established a fruitful professional rela-tionship with Raoul Gunsbourg, a minor composer who was director of the

Monte Carlo Opéra from 1893 to 1951. Seven of Massenet's operas were given their premieres at Monte Carlo (two of them posthumously). The fourth of these was *Don Quichotte*, which Gunsbourg commissioned from Massenet in 1908 and which was successfully staged there in 1910, its title role performed by the great Russian bass Fyodor Chaliapin (who more than twenty years later played Don Quixote again in a French film for which Jacques Ibert composed the score).

In his memoirs Chaliapin gives an amusing account of his first run-through of the role with Massenet at the piano. The singer found his music so affecting that at the end of the fourth act he burst into tears and was sternly ordered by the composer to calm himself, or at least wait until the end of the opera before crying. Massenet, in his own memoirs, had little to say about Chaliapin as Don Quichotte. He clearly preferred the French bass Vanni Marcoux, who sang the role in Paris several months after the Monte Carlo premiere. Massenet did refer to the Monte Carlo Dulcinée, Lucy Arbell, as an 'artiste of genius', but this may have been because he was romantically involved with her.

The novel *Don Quixote*, by Miguel de Cervantes (1547–1616), written at the end of the sixteenth century and published in Madrid a few years later, is generally regarded as a satire on the chivalric romances of the time, though it can also be thought of as an ironic parable on the subject of idealism versus materialism. One of the earliest novels still being read, it offers – with its huge array of minor characters surrounding the idealistic knight Don Quixote and his practical henchman, Sancho Panza – a panoramic view of late sixteenth-century Spanish society.

More than fifty composers have produced works for the stage based on Cervantes's novel, the earliest being John Eccles (c.1668–1735), who provided songs for Thomas D'Urfey's *Comical History of Don Quixote*, staged at the Theatre Royal, Drury Lane, London, in 1694. Other composers of operas based on Cervantes include such little-known names as Louis Clapisson (1808–66), Francesco Feo (1691–1761), Vito Frazzi (1888–1975) and Emile Pessard (1843–1917), as well as a few slightly more familiar ones such as Johann Philipp Fortsch (1652–1732), Giovanni Paisiello (1740–1816) and Wilhelm Kienzl (1857–1941). The Viennese Richard Heuberger (1850–1914) composed an operetta, *Don Quichotte*, which was staged in Vienna only a few months after the Monte Carlo premiere of Massenet's opera.

Henri Cain based his libretto for Massenet not directly on the novel by Cervantes, but on *Le Chevalier de la longue figure*, a verse play about Don Quixote and Sancho Panza by a minor French poet and playwright, Jacques Le Lorrain, which was staged in Paris in 1906, only a few days before the playwright's death. According to Massenet there was a strong autobiographical element in this play by Le Lorrain, who apparently bore a distinct physical resemblance to Don Quixote as described by Cervantes. For some reason Le Lorrain altered the character of the servant girl Aldonza, whom Don Quixote imagined to be the Lady Dulcinea del Toboso. In his play and in Massenet's opera she became simply Dulcinée, a courtesan.

Act I. A square outside Dulcinée's house. A lively fiesta is in progress. Dulcinée emerges on her balcony, to the delight especially of her four current suitors, and sings a flirtatious song about the problems of being loved by all ('Quand la femme a vingt ans'). When the crowd announces the imminent approach of Don Quichotte and Sancho Panza, a suitor of Dulcinée named Juan mocks the eccentric knight and his obsession with Dulcinée. While Sancho goes off in search of refreshment, Quichotte serenades Dulcinée ('Quand apparaissent les étoiles'), but is interrupted by the jealous Juan, who attempts to fight a duel with him, although Quichotte is intent on first finishing his serenade. Dulcinée puts an end to the duel by asking Quichotte to recover a necklace, which she says was stolen from her the previous day by the bandit chief Tenebrun. She leaves with Juan, which disconcerts Quichotte somewhat, although he is convinced that Dulcinée will love him when he returns with her necklace.

Act II. The countryside at dawn. Seated on his mare Rosinante, led by a sweating and puffing Sancho, Don Quichotte is cheerfully composing another song in praise of Dulcinée and busily searching for rhymes. Sancho, convinced that Dulcinée is making fools of them both, launches into an amusing tirade against women in general ('Comment peut-on penser du bien'). The morning mist clears, revealing nearby windmills, which Quichotte imagines to be giants blocking his way. He insists on fighting them, with the result that he becomes caught, by the seat of his trousers, on the arm of one of the windmills. As the curtain falls, he is circling around in the air and Sancho is attempting to rescue him.

A gentle, delicately scored entr'acte, based on Quichotte's Act I serenade, separates Acts II and III.

Act III. The mountains at sunset. On the trail of the bandits, Quichotte enters on all fours, making a careful examination of the tracks on the path, while Sancho watches, holding the bridles of his donkey and the knight's horse. Sancho expresses a strong desire to return home, at which a shocked Quichotte explains to him that a knight who attempts valiant deeds must always be on his guard. However, when Sancho stretches out on the ground, Quichotte himself falls asleep standing up, leaning on his lance.

The bandits suddenly arrive, and Sancho flees. Quichotte is overpowered, and the bandits are about to kill him when their chief is moved by Quichotte's prayer ('Seigneur, reçois mon âme'). Quichotte tells them he is a knight whose task it is to redress wrongs, and he demands the return of Dulcinée's necklace, at which the bandit chief hands it over. Quichotte forgives the bandits and blesses them as he leaves.

Act IV. The garden of Dulcinée's house. Although she is surrounded by her admirers, Dulcinée is melancholy. She sings a sad aria on the transitory nature of love ('Lorsque le temps d'amour a fui'); she then changes her mood to sing in praise of fleeting pleasure ('Ne pensons qu'au plaisir d'aimer'). After her guests have entered the house for supper, Sancho arrives to announce the return of Quichotte. In the presence of the reassembled guests Quichotte triumphantly returns Dulcinée's necklace to her and, to the amusement of all, proceeds to make her a proposal of marriage. Dismissing her guests, Dulcinée gently refuses the knight in a tender duet ('Oui, je souffre votre tendresse'). It is her nature, she tells him, to offer her love to all, and she thinks too kindly of him to deceive him. As she leaves, her guests return to mock Quichotte but are soundly rebuked by the faithful Sancho ('Riez, allez, riez du pauvre idéologue').

A nocturnal entr'acte separates Acts IV and V.

Act V. A mountain path, on a clear, starry night. Quichotte rests against a tree while Sancho prepares a fire and prays that in heaven his master will find that his visions have become real. Quichotte, knowing he has but a short time to live, bids farewell to Sancho, bequeathing him the only gift he has to offer – an island of dreams ('Prends cette île'). In a brightly shining star the knight imagines he sees the divine Dulcinée, and he dies peacefully in the arms of the weeping Sancho.

The opera begins rather slowly and aimlessly, and there is perhaps too much pastiche Spanish colouring in Massenet's score, but as the piece progresses its charm begins to take effect. Although *Don Quichotte* is the work of a composer who has already used up his best ideas, it is oddly attractive in its blend of sentiment and comedy. In a fine production it can emerge as a sensitive and moving portrayal of the foolish, sympathetic old knight of Cervantes's novel.

Recommended recording: Nicolai Ghiaurov (Don Quichotte), Régine Crespin (Dulcinée), Gabriel Bacquier (Sancho Panza), with the Suisse Romande Chorus and Orchestra, conducted by Kazimierz Kord. Decca 430 636–2DM2. Nicolai Ghiaurov brings the knight vividly to life, Régine Crespin is a splendid Dulcinée, and Gabriel Bacquier gives a rounded portrayal of Sancho Panza.

GIAN CARLO MENOTTI
(b. Cadegliano, 1911)

The Medium
opera in two acts (approximate length: 1 hour)

Madame Flora, a medium   *contralto*
Monica, her daughter   *soprano*
Toby, a mute   *dancer*
Mr Gobineau   *baritone*
Mrs Gobineau   *soprano*
Mrs Nolan   *mezzo-soprano*

LIBRETTO BY THE COMPOSER; TIME: THE MID-1940S; PLACE: THE UNITED STATES
OF AMERICA; FIRST PERFORMED AT THE BRANDER MATTHEWS THEATER, COLUM-
BIA UNIVERSITY, NEW YORK, 8 MAY 1946

Menotti was born in Italy and began his musical studies in Milan. After his family moved to America he attended the Curtis Institute of Music in Philadelphia. Primarily a composer of operas, for all of which he provided his own libretti, he had his first success with the one-act *Amelia al ballo*, which was given its premiere in Philadelphia in 1937 in an English translation as *Amelia Goes to the Ball*. Most of Menotti's subsequent libretti were written in English. An opera for radio, *The Old Maid and the Thief*, was broadcast by NBC in 1939. *The Island God*, staged at the Metropolitan Opera, New York, in 1942, was a failure, but *The Medium* was a success at its premiere in 1946 and, when coupled with a one-act curtain-raiser, *The Telephone*, achieved a run of 211 performances on Broadway in 1947–8, establishing Menotti's reputation as the most popular American composer of his day.

Madame Flora, a medium, practises fraud upon her clients with the aid of her daughter Monica and a mute, Toby. Frightened when the world of the occult appears to intervene during a seance, she gets drunk and shoots at what she thinks to be a ghost, killing Toby.

The Medium, Menotti's most Puccinian score, has been described by its composer as a play of ideas that 'describes the tragedy of a woman caught between two worlds, a world of reality which she cannot wholly comprehend, and a super-natural world in which she cannot believe'.

Recommended recording: None currently available.

The Telephone
opera buffa in one act (approximate length: 20 minutes)

Lucy   *soprano*
Ben   *baritone*

LIBRETTO BY THE COMPOSER; TIME: THE MID-1940S; PLACE: THE UNITED STATES OF AMERICA; FIRST PERFORMED AT THE HECKSCHER THEATER, NEW YORK, 18 FEBRUARY 1947

Ben visits Lucy and attempts to propose marriage to her, but he finds her so intrigued with her newly installed telephone that he cannot engage her attention. In desperation, he leaves and calls her from the nearest public telephone. His proposal is accepted.

Menotti's eclectic, light-hearted score, taking little more than twenty minutes to perform, makes an excellent curtain-raiser. It was as such that it achieved a run of 211 performances on Broadway in 1947–8, accompanying Menotti's *The Medium*.

Recommended recording: The only recording, on CBS, dating from 1947, is no longer available.

The Consul
opera in three acts (approximate length: 1 hour, 45 minutes)

John Sorel   *baritone*
Magda, his wife   *soprano*
The Mother   *contralto*
Secret Police Agent   *bass*
The Secretary   *mezzo-soprano*
Mr Kofner   *bass-baritone*

The Foreign Woman *soprano*
Anna Gomez *soprano*
Vera Boronel *contralto*
The Magician *tenor*

LIBRETTO BY THE COMPOSER; TIME: AFTER WORLD WAR II; PLACE: SOMEWHERE IN EUROPE; FIRST PERFORMED AT THE SHUBERT THEATER, PHILADELPHIA, 1 MARCH 1950

Menotti's greatest successes came with *The Consul* in 1950 and *Amahl and the Night Visitors*, which was written for television and first transmitted in 1951. *The Saint of Bleecker Street* and *Maria Golovin* proved less popular. After *Le Dernier Sauvage* (The Last Savage), first performed in Paris in 1963, Menotti began to repeat himself. His best works, however, are theatrically effective, composed in the Italian *verismo* style of the earlier part of the twentieth century, and falling easily on the ear. *The Consul* ran for eight months in New York in 1950, and it won both the Pulitzer Prize and the Drama Critics' Circle Award.

In a police state somewhere in Europe, Magda Sorel attempts to obtain an exit visa for herself and her husband, John, a revolutionary who is being pursued by the secret police. Her attempts to see the Consul are frustrated by a Secretary. When her husband is arrested, Magda kills herself.

Menotti's Puccinian score is for the most part effective, but this grim story of repression under political dictatorship has failed to retain its initial popularity, perhaps because the music does not really illuminate the text.

Recommended recording: Patricia Neway (Magda Sorel), Cornell MacNeil (John Sorel), with orchestra conducted by Lehman Engel. Brunswick LAT 8012 3. This recording uses the cast of the opera's premiere.

Amahl and the Night Visitors
opera in one act (approximate length: 45 minutes)

Amahl, a crippled boy aged about 12 *treble*
His Mother *soprano*
King Kaspar *tenor*

King Melchior   *baritone*
King Balthazar   *bass*
The Page   *baritone*

LIBRETTO BY THE COMPOSER; TIME: THE BIRTH OF CHRIST; PLACE: BETHLEHEM; FIRST PERFORMED, FOR TELEVISION, IN NBC STUDIOS, NEW YORK, 24 DECEMBER 1951

As Amahl, a crippled child who can walk only with the aid of a crutch, sits outside his hut watching the bright new star in the sky, he encounters the three kings who are travelling in search of the newly born Jesus. Amahl's Mother attempts to steal some of the precious gems the kings are carrying as presents for the Holy Child, but she is caught by their Page. Amahl offers his crutch to the three kings as a gift for the infant Christ, and he is miraculously healed.

Menotti derived the inspiration for this melodious Christmas opera from Hieronymous Bosch's painting *The Adoration of the Magi*. The opera, scored for a small orchestra, has proved popular with amateur groups.

Recommended recording: James Rainbird (Amahl), Lorna Haywood (Mother), with the Chorus and Orchestra of the Royal Opera House, Covent Garden, conducted by David Syrus. That's Entertainment, CD TER 1124. An excellent cast, with Lorna Haywood especially effective as the Mother, in a recording made at the same time as stage performances in London.

GIACOMO MEYERBEER
(b. Berlin, 1791 – d. Paris, 1864)

Les Huguenots
(The Huguenots)
grand opera in five acts (approximate length: 4 hours)

Raoul de Nangis, a Huguenot nobleman   *tenor*
Marcel, his servant   *bass*
Marguerite de Valois, betrothed to Henry of Navarre   *soprano*

Urbain, her page   *soprano or contralto*
Valentine, daughter of the Count de Saint-Bris   *soprano*
Count de Saint-Bris   *bass* ⎤
Count de Nevers   *baritone*   } Catholic noblemen
Maurevert   *bass* ⎦
Cossé   *tenor* ⎤
Méru   *bass*
Thoré   *bass*   } Catholic gentlemen
Tavannes   *tenor*
De Retz   *bass* ⎦
Bois-Rosé, a Huguenot soldier   *tenor*

LIBRETTO BY EUGÈNE SCRIBE, GAETANO ROSSI AND ÉMILE DESCHAMPS; TIME: AUGUST 1572; PLACE: TOURAINE AND PARIS; FIRST PERFORMED AT THE PARIS OPÉRA, 29 FEBRUARY 1836

The son of a wealthy Jewish family, Meyerbeer studied in Berlin and Darmstadt. His first two operas, *Jephtas Gelübde* (1812) and *Wirth und Gast* (1813), composed to German texts, were both failures. Between 1817 and 1824 he composed seven Italian operas which were successfully staged in various Italian cities. When the last of them, *Il crociato in Egitto* (The Crusader in Egypt), was accepted for production in Paris, Meyerbeer took up residence in that city and began to compose large-scale works in the style of French *grand opéra*. The first of these, *Robert le diable* (Robert the Devil; 1831), was hugely successful, and the following year Meyerbeer and Eugène Scribe, the librettist of *Robert le diable*, agreed to collaborate on a new work, initially called *Léonore*, its subject matter the confrontation between French Protestants (Huguenots) and Catholics in the sixteenth century. Meyerbeer began to compose the work that was eventually to be called *Les Huguenots*. When Scribe was reluctant to undertake any revision of his work, Meyerbeer called on his former Italian librettist Gaetano Rossi to make some additions, and he also engaged the poet Émile Deschamps to contribute to the libretto. *Les Huguenots* was an immense success at its premiere, and in due course it became the first work to be performed more than a thousand times at the Paris Opéra. The role of Urbain, the page, was originally written for soprano, but at Covent Garden in 1848 Meyerbeer transposed it for the contralto Marietta Alboni.

Act I. The chateau of the Count de Nevers, in Touraine. De Nevers, a Catholic, is holding a banquet. He tells his friends that, because of the recent peace treaty with the Protestants, he has invited a Huguenot nobleman, Raoul de Nangis, to join them. Raoul arrives, and when the guests are invited to toast the women they love he responds with a song about an unknown beautiful woman whom he recently rescued from harassment by riotous students and whom he hopes to encounter again ('Plus blanche que la blanche hermine'). Raoul's retainer, Marcel, a Huguenot soldier, is horrified to see his master carousing with Catholics, and he attempts to appeal to Raoul's conscience by intoning Martin Luther's chorale 'Ein feste Burg', to the amusement of the Catholics. At their request he sings an old Huguenot song ('Piff, paff').

De Nevers is summoned by a servant to speak to a woman who is waiting in the garden. His guests laughingly peer through a window to observe the meeting, and Raoul recognizes the woman as the one he rescued. De Nevers rejoins his guests and reveals that the woman is his betrothed, Valentine, a lady-in-waiting to Queen Marguerite de Valois. She has just informed him that the Queen has forbidden their marriage. Urbain, the Queen's page, arrives ('Nobles Seigneurs') to conduct Raoul to a secret rendezvous.

Act II. The garden of the chateau of Chenonceaux. The Catholic Queen Marguerite awaits Raoul's arrival ('O beau pays de la Touraine') and informs Valentine that, desiring to put an end to the enmity between Huguenots and Catholics, she has asked her to break off her engagement to De Nevers so that she may marry the Huguenot Raoul. Before Raoul arrives the ladies of the court swim in the nearby river, to the delight of the page, Urbain, who secretly watches them.

Blindfolded, Raoul is led into the garden. When the blindfold is removed, and he sees the Queen, he swears his devotion to her ('Beauté divine') and agrees to her suggestion that he marry the daughter of the Catholic Count de Saint-Bris. However, when he realizes that Saint-Bris's daughter is Valentine, he withdraws his promise, for he assumes her to be the mistress of De Nevers. Valentine is mystified, Saint-Bris and his followers draw their swords, and bloodshed is prevented only by the intervention of the Queen.

Act III. An open space in Paris, with a chapel nearby. Pleasure-seekers mill about ('C'est le jour du dimanche') and Huguenot soldiers sing a martial song ('Rataplan') while a Catholic service takes place in the chapel where De Nevers is shortly to be married to Valentine. As Valentine's father, Count de Saint-Bris, leaves the chapel, he is accosted by Marcel, who delivers a message from Raoul, challenging him to a duel. De Nevers, Saint-Bris and Maurevert make plans to ambush Raoul ('Rentrez habitants de Paris'). Valentine, who has overheard them plotting, alerts Marcel to the danger ('Dans la nuit').

As night falls, Raoul and Saint-Bris arrive to fight their duel. Saint-Bris's soldiers are about to attack Raoul when Marcel summons his followers from a nearby inn. A fight is prevented by the arrival of Queen Marguerite, from whom Raoul learns that he has refused the hand of the woman who loves him. Saint-Bris is shocked to discover that it was his daughter who revealed to Marcel his plan to ambush Raoul.

Act IV. A room in De Nevers' house. Though now married to De Nevers, Valentine sings of her love for Raoul ('Parmi les pleurs'). Raoul arrives, determined to see her for one last time, but when others are heard approaching she hides him in an adjacent room. Saint-Bris, De Nevers and their fellow Catholics enter and, in a scene known as the Consecration of the Swords, they discuss a plan to massacre the Huguenots that night, St. Bartholomew's Eve ('Des troubles renaissants'). When De Nevers refuses to take part, he is led away. After the conspirators have departed, Raoul emerges from hiding, having overheard their plans. Valentine begs him not to leave ('O ciel! Où courez-vous?') and declares that she loves him, to which he responds passionately ('Tu l'as dit'). Hearing the bells signalling the massacre, he rushes off to warn his fellow Huguenots.

Act V, scene i. The ballroom of the Hôtel de Nesle. Huguenots have assembled to celebrate the marriage of Queen Marguerite and Henry IV of Navarre. Raoul bursts in to alert them to the massacre and to summon them to arms ('À la lueur').

Act V, scene ii. A Huguenot churchyard. Raoul and Marcel, who have taken shelter in the churchyard, are joined by Valentine. De Nevers has been killed, and Valentine is now free to marry Raoul. She urges him to save himself by wearing a white scarf, which would signify that he was a Catholic, but this he refuses to do. Valentine decides to die with Raoul as a Huguenot, and their union is blessed by Marcel as Catholic soldiers storm into the churchyard.

Act V, scene iii. A street in Paris. The dying Raoul is supported by Valentine and Marcel. Saint-Bris orders his troops to fire on them, and it is only after all three have fallen to the ground that he realizes he has slaughtered his own daughter. Queen Marguerite arrives, helplessly witnessing the massacre of the Huguenots.

The opera's finest music is to be found in Act IV, with its scene of the Consecration of the Swords and the impassioned love duet for Valentine and Raoul, which follows. Elsewhere, Meyerbeer's musical characterization is impressive, as well as his ability to create massive ensembles. Les Huguenots is a work that can still prove exciting and theatrically effective when it is staged lavishly and cast with first-rate singers in its seven leading roles. For a performance at the Metropolitan Opera, New York, on 26 December 1894, the management raised the top price to an unprecedented seven dollars for what it called 'the night of the seven stars'. The stars were Lillian Nordica (Valentine), Sofia Scalchi (Urbain), Nellie Melba (Queen Marguerite), Jean de Reszke (Raoul), Edouard de Reszke (Marcel), Pol Plançon (Saint-Bris) and Victor Maurel (De Nevers).

Recommended recording: Joan Sutherland (Queen Marguerite), Anastasios Vrenios (Raoul), Gabriel Bacquier (Saint-Bris), Martina Arroyo (Valentine), Huguette Tourangeau (Urbain), Dominic Cossa (De Nevers), Nicolo Ghiuselev (Marcel), with the Ambrosian Opera Chorus and the New Philharmonia Orchestra, conducted by Richard Bonynge. Decca 430 549–2. An impressive array of singers has been assembled here. Joan Sutherland is a forceful Queen Marguerite and Martina Arroyo a passionate Valentine, while the other roles are all more than competently filled. Richard Bonynge holds the performance together most impressively, and this is the only recording to give Meyerbeer's score absolutely complete.

Le Prophète
(The Prophet)
grand opéra in five acts (approximate length: 4 hours)

John of Leyden   *tenor*
Fidès, his mother   *mezzo-soprano*
Bertha, his betrothed   *soprano*
Jonas   *tenor* ⎤
Mathisen   *bass* ⎥ Anabaptists
Zacharie   *bass* ⎦
Count Oberthal   *bass*

LIBRETTO BY EUGÈNE SCRIBE; TIME: THE 1530S; PLACE: HOLLAND AND MÜNSTER; FIRST PERFORMED AT THE PARIS OPÉRA, 16 APRIL 1849

Shortly after the premiere of *Les Huguenots*, Meyerbeer and his librettist Eugène Scribe began to plan two new operas, *Le Prophète* and *L'Africaine*. Meyerbeer began to compose *Le Prophète* in 1836, but in 1842 he was still at work on it, and his appointment that year as Prussian General Music Director delayed the opera's progress even further. It was not until 1849 that *Le Prophète* was finally produced at the Paris Opéra, and it was a great success. It continued to be staged throughout the nineteenth century, but is now less frequently performed.

Act I. Outside Count Oberthal's castle, near Dordrecht, Holland. Bertha arrives to ask for the Count's consent to her marriage to the innkeeper John of Leyden. With her is John's mother, Fidès ('Fidès, ma bonne mère'). Zacharie, Mathisen and Jonas, three members of the religious sect of Anabaptists, who attempt to spread discontent among the peasants gathered outside the castle, are chased away by the Count's men. Bertha's plea to Count Oberthal to be allowed to marry John of Leyden ('Un jour dans les flots de la Meuse') is rejected, for the Count has fallen in love with her. He has Bertha and Fidès seized and taken into his castle.

Act II. John's inn, in Leyden. The three Anabaptists, noticing that he bears a strong resemblance to a painting of King David in the cathedral in Münster, try to persuade John to join their cause. His thoughts, however, are of Bertha ('Pour Berthe, moi je soupire'). Bertha suddenly rushes in, having escaped from Count Oberthal's castle, and she begs John to hide her. She is soon followed by the Count, who orders John to produce her ('Ils partent'). When Oberthal threatens to execute his mother, John has no option but to hand Bertha over to the Count's soldiers. After they have gone, the Anabaptists reappear, and John now agrees to become their leader, even though it means that he must leave his homeland and his mother for ever.

Act III, scene i. The Anabaptists' camp, in the forest near Münster. Zacharie and his Anabaptist forces are carousing ('Aussi nombreux que les étoiles'). Men and women skate across a frozen lake bearing provisions, and the Anabaptists are served food and drink and entertained with a skaters' ballet.

Act III, scene ii. Inside Zacharie's tent in the camp. Count Oberthal is brought in as a prisoner. John, learning from him that Bertha is alive and is in Münster, immediately orders that the Count's life be spared.

Act III, scene iii. The camp. John quells a revolt among the Anabaptist troops. Now revered as a prophet, he tells them of a celestial vision he has had and prepares to lead them into battle as the sun rises.

Act IV, scene i. A square in Münster. The Anabaptists have captured the city. Fidès, begging for food ('Donnez pour une pauvre âme'), encounters Bertha and tells her that John is dead, and that the prophet is to blame. Bertha vows to have vengeance ('Un pauvre pelerin').

Act IV, scene ii. The cathedral in Münster. A crowd has gathered to see the prophet crowned king. Fidès vows to strike him down, but when he appears she recognizes him as John and cries out to him. Now considered divine by the people, John denies that he is her son, and by threatening to give up his life if her claim can be substantiated, he forces his mother to declare that she was mistaken.

Act V, scene i. A cellar in the palace of Münster. The Anabaptists Zacharie, Mathisen and Jonas plot to betray the prophet and deliver him, for a reward, to the imperial army now advancing on the city. Fidès, led in as a prisoner, pardons her son ('O toi qui m'abandonnes'). When he appears, she orders him to renounce the Anabaptists and return home to Leyden. Bertha enters, intending to set fire to the palace in order to destroy the prophet. Astonished to find John alive, she is at first happy, but when she realizes that he is the prophet she kills herself. John determines to have revenge on the Anabaptists.

Act V, scene ii. A hall in the palace of Münster. At an assembly to celebrate the glory of the prophet, John orders that the enemy forces be allowed to enter, and then he announces that he has ignited the powder magazine in the cellar. The palace explodes, killing everyone, including John and Fidès.

The coronation scene is spectacularly grandiose, the skaters' ballet engaging and Meyerbeer's colourful score is for the most part theatrically effective. Although Bertha is something of a cipher, and John the prophet fails to come convincingly to life, the role of Fidès is strikingly characterized.

Recommended recording: Marilyn Horne (Fidès), Renata Scotto (Bertha), James McCracken (John), with the Ambrosian Opera Chorus and the Royal Philharmonic Orchestra, conducted by Henry Lewis. CBS M3K 79400. This is the only available recording, well sung and vigorously conducted.

L'Africaine
(The African Girl)
grand opéra in five acts (approximate length: 4 hours)

Selika, a slave   *soprano*
Vasco da Gama, an officer in the Portuguese navy   *tenor*
Inès, daughter of Don Diego   *soprano*
Nelusko, a slave   *baritone*
Don Pedro, president of the royal council   *bass*
Don Diego, a member of the council   *bass*
Anna, Inès's confidante   *mezzo-soprano*
Don Alvar, a member of the council   *tenor*
Grand Inquisitor   *bass*
High Priest of Brahma   *baritone*

LIBRETTO BY EUGÈNE SCRIBE; TIME: EARLY SIXTEENTH CENTURY; PLACE: LISBON
AND MADAGASCAR; FIRST PERFORMED AT THE PARIS OPÉRA, 28 APRIL 1865

Meyerbeer and his librettist Scribe agreed to collaborate on *L'Africaine* as early as 1837. The point of departure of Scribe's plot was 'Le Mancenillier', a poem by Charles-Hubert Millevoye about a young woman who sits under a tree that emits a poisonous fragrance and is rescued by her lover. The project was set aside while composer and librettist worked on *Le Prophète*, and it was not returned to until 1841, when *Le Prophète* was almost finished. By 1843 a first draft of *L'Africaine* had been completed, but Meyerbeer then became weighed down with responsibilities in Berlin, where he had been appointed General Music Director of Prussia. He conducted the court orchestra, organized concerts and composed occasional pieces, among them a *Singspiel, Ein Feldlager in Schlesien* (A Camp in Silesia), written for the reopening of the court opera in 1844 after a fire.

It was not until 1851 that Meyerbeer returned to *L'Africaine*, altering it substantially and changing its title to *Vasco da Gama* before abandoning it in 1853. He began working on it again in 1857, and by the end of 1863 he had fully orchestrated the work, which was accepted for production at the Paris Opéra. Scribe having died in 1861, other librettists were brought in to make final revisions, among them Camille du Locle. Meyerbeer died in May 1864, and it was not until April of the following year that the opera was staged, its title changed back to *L'Africaine* by the Belgian musicologist François-Joseph Fétis, whom Meyerbeer's widow had engaged to take charge of the rehearsals, and who also made some changes to the libretto.

With so many hands involved in its creation, it is hardly surprising that the libretto should be somewhat incoherent. In its original version, the first two acts of the opera were set in Spain, and the slave girl Selika's home was on the Niger river in Africa. Later, when the tenor hero, a naval officer named Fernand, became the historical character Vasco da Gama, the locale was changed to Portugal. Selika now came from India, and the title *L'Africaine* had to be dropped. In the final version, Selika is African again, probably from Madagascar; however, there are still references in the text to the Indian gods Brahma, Vishnu and Shiva. Although its production is said to have been one of the most magnificent spectacles in the history of the Paris Opéra, the undoubted success of *L'Africaine* did not equal that of *Les Huguenots* or *Le Prophète*.

Act I. The royal council chamber in Lisbon. Inès, daughter of the Admiral Don Diego, longs for news of her beloved Vasco da Gama, whose ship has been missing for two years ('Adieu mon beau rivage'). Assuming him to have been lost with his ship, Inès's father wishes her to marry Don Pedro, the president of the royal council. The council meeting is interrupted by the sudden appearance of Vasco da Gama, with two captives, Selika and Nelusko, natives of a far-off country unknown to Europe. Vasco asks the council to support an expedition to this new land. When he retires to allow the council members to discuss his proposal, the Grand Inquisitor argues that to speak of a land not mentioned in the Bible is heresy, and Don Pedro, knowing that Vasco is his rival in love, persuades the council to reject the plan. Informed of this, Vasco accuses the council of ignorance and envy, and he is condemned to life imprisonment along with his two captives.

Act II. A prison cell in Lisbon. Vasco lies asleep. Selika, who is in love with him ('Sur mes genoux, fils du soleil'), protects him from Nelusko who, in love with Selika, wants to kill Vasco. Selika tells Vasco that she can guide him to her native land. Don Pedro enters with Inès, informing Vasco that he is now free. His freedom has been purchased by Inès's agreement to marry Don Pedro, who has been equipped with a fleet to explore the new land, with Nelusko as his guide.

Act III. Don Pedro's ship, at sea. Nelusko, who intends to guide the vessel onto a reef, tells the sailors a tale about a sea monster ('Adamastor, roi des vagues profondes'). Another Portuguese vessel draws alongside, and Vasco comes aboard to warn Don Pedro that he is off course. Don Pedro accuses Vasco of having followed them in order to see Inès, and he has him seized and bound. A violent storm breaks out, and the ship is driven onto reefs. Indians, summoned by Nelusko, board the ship and begin to massacre the crew, capturing Inès and Vasco, whom they take ashore.

Act IV. Outside a Brahmin temple, in a tropical country (usually assumed to be the island of Madagascar). Nelusko informs Selika, now revealed to be the country's Queen, that all of the male Portuguese, except one, have been executed, and that the women are being led to the lethal manzanilla tree to inhale its poisonous fragrances, which will kill them.

Vasco, the sole male survivor, is enchanted by the sight of the beautiful new country ('O paradis, sorti de l'onde'). He is found by natives, who are about to behead him when they are prevented by Selika, who tells them that she is married to the white man. A reluctant Nelusko officiates at a form of wedding ceremony for them. Selika tells Vasco that he is free to go, but he is overcome with affection for her and accepts her as his wife.

Act V, scene i. The garden of Selika's palace. Inès, who has not died under the poisonous tree, tells Selika that she and Vasco have loved each other for a long time. Selika generously renounces Vasco and instructs Nelusko to escort the lovers to a ship that will carry them back to their own country. She herself resolves to die under the manzanilla tree.

Act V, scene ii. The manzanilla tree, on a promontory overlooking the sea. Selika lies under the tree, watching Vasco's ship sail away as she inhales the tree's poisonous vapours ('D'ici je vois la mer immense'). Nelusko arrives to seek death with her, and Selika dies in his arms as he, too, breathes in the tree's perfume.

The famous tenor aria sung by Vasco, 'O paradis, sorti de l'onde', is the finest number in this uneven work, though Nelusko (a baritone role) is the more interestingly developed character. Dramatically rather flaccid, the opera nevertheless can be enjoyed for the exotic locale of its later acts and for Meyerbeer's always original and colourful orchestration.

Recommended recording: Shirley Verrett (Selika), Ruth Ann Swenson (Inès), Placido Domingo (Vasco da Gama), Justino Diaz (Nelusko), with the San Francisco Opera Chorus and Orchestra, conducted by Maurizio Arena. Virgin Classics VVD673. There is no recommendable CD currently available. This is a video.

CLAUDIO MONTEVERDI
(b. Cremona, 1567 – d. Venice, 1643)

Orfeo
favola in musica in a prologue and five acts
(approximate length: 1 hour, 45 minutes)

Music   *soprano*
Orfeo (Orpheus)   *tenor*
Euridice (Eurydice)   *soprano*
Silvia, the messenger   *soprano*
Hope   *soprano*
Caronte (Charon)   *bass*
Proserpina (Proserpine), Queen of the Underworld   *soprano*
Plutone (Pluto), King of the Underworld   *bass*
Apollo   *tenor*

LIBRETTO BY ALESSANDRO STRIGGIO; TIME: LEGENDARY; PLACE: THE FIELDS OF
THRACE, AND THE UNDERWORLD; FIRST PERFORMED AT THE PALAZZO DUCALE,
MANTUA, 24 FEBRUARY 1607

Monteverdi was born into a musical family in Cremona. By the age of fifteen he had already written a group of short religious pieces, which were published in Venice. He was in his twenty-fourth year when, after having composed a number of madrigals and canzonettas, he obtained a position in Mantua as one of the musicians at the court of Duke Vincenzo Gonzaga, eventually being promoted to the position of *maestro di cappella*. When the Duke died, in 1612, Monteverdi was dismissed by the new Duke but became *maestro di cappella* at the basilica of St Mark in Venice, where he remained for the rest of his life.

Opera as we know it today is an art form that came into existence in Italy towards the end of the sixteenth century, having developed over the centuries from ancient Greek theatre (in which music played a considerable part), through mediaeval music drama to the creations of the Baroque school of composers, poets and musicians that flourished in Florence in the last years of the sixteenth century. The music of the earliest-known opera, *Daphne*, by Jacopo Peri, first performed in Florence in 1597, has survived only in fragments. The classical Greek myth of Orpheus and Eurydice was a popular subject for opera from its very beginnings: Peri's *Euridice* was performed in Florence in 1600, and Giulio Caccini's opera of the same title was given, also in Florence, two years later. It was after he had attended the first performance of Peri's *Euridice* at the Palazzo Pitti in Florence, on the occasion of the marriage of Marie de' Medici to Henri IV of France, that the Duke of Mantua decided to commission his court composer Monteverdi to write an opera on the same subject. Alessandro Striggio produced a libretto, based on that which Ottavio Rinuccini had written for Peri, and Monteverdi's first opera was performed before the Duke of Mantua and his court in 1607. Monteverdi's *Orfeo* is the earliest opera that is still part of the current repertoire.

Orpheus may have been a real person, founder of the ancient Greek religious cult of Orphism, or he may have been purely mythical. He is first mentioned in literature in the work of Ibycus, a lyric poet of the sixth century BC, and later appears in Aeschylus and Euripides. In the best-known version of the story, Orpheus, famed for his playing of the lyre, marries Eurydice, who is killed by a snake while fleeing the advances of a god. Orpheus descends into Hades to find her, and his playing so charms the Furies that he is permitted to take her back with him, provided that he does not look at her until they have arrived back on earth. However, unable to bear Eurydice's pleading, he turns to look at her, at which she falls dead once again. In some versions of the myth, the gods take pity on the lovers, and Eurydice is restored to life. In others, an inconsolable Orpheus rejects all women, as a result of which the females of Thrace, affronted by such behaviour, tear him to pieces. Fragments of his body are buried at the foot of Mount Olympus, but his head is thrown into the sea, to be washed ashore on the island of Lesbos, where it becomes a famous oracle. Striggio's libretto for Monteverdi opts for the happier ending.

Prologue. After a toccata, directed by the composer to be played three times before the curtain is raised, the spirit of Music appears, describes the power of her art to soothe or to inflame and announces the subject matter of the drama about to be enacted.

Act I. The fields of Thrace. Orfeo and Euridice enter, accompanied by nymphs and shepherds. A Shepherd announces that this is the wedding day of Orfeo and Euridice and invites everyone to share in their joy. Orfeo sings of his love for his bride ('Rosa del ciel'), and all proceed to a temple to give thanks to the gods.

Act II. The fields. Orfeo sings of his good fortune. Silvia, the messenger, appears with the news that Euridice, while gathering flowers for her wedding garland, has been bitten by a snake and has died ('In un fiorito prato'). Grief-stricken ('Tu sei morta'), Orfeo at first seems not to hear the lamenting of the shepherds, but suddenly he announces that he will descend to the kingdom of the dead to bring Euridice back to life.

Act III. The Underworld. Orpheus is led by Hope to the banks of the Styx, the river that divides the kingdom of the living from that of the dead. Hope then leaves him, for she can go no further ('Lasciate ogni speranza, voi ch'entrate'). Caronte, the boatman, unmoved by Orfeo's sad song ('Possente spirito'), refuses to let him pass. However, the gods intervene, lulling Caronte to sleep while Orfeo takes the oars of his boat and crosses into Hades.

Act IV. The Underworld. Proserpina, wife of Plutone, the King of the Underworld, pleads with her husband to restore Euridice to Orfeo. Plutone agrees, but only on one condition: should Orfeo look back at Euridice, he will lose her for ever. Orfeo, overjoyed ('Qual onor di te sia degno'), prepares to depart with Euridice. Hearing a sound, and imagining that the Furies are carrying off Euridice, he looks back at her. As his gaze falls upon his bride, she disappears, and Orfeo returns to earth alone.

Act V. The fields of Thrace. Orfeo weeps for his lost bride, while Echo responds. Apollo, the divine father of Orfeo, suddenly descends from the heavens to offer him immortality ('Saliam cantando al cielo'). Orfeo and Apollo ascend together to the heavens, where Orfeo will be able to gaze on his beloved Euridice for all eternity.

Although Monteverdi's *Orfeo* is composed mainly in the recitative style of Peri and Caccini, the recitative is both more dramatic and more lyrical than that of the Florentine composers, moving in the direction of arioso, from which later the aria was to develop. Monteverdi's choruses and duets are lively; his instrumentation plays a more important role in the opera than that of his predecessors in their works for the stage, and his harmonic language is more advanced. Monteverdi's *Orfeo* is the earliest great opera.

Recommended recording: John Mark Ainsley (Orpheus), Catherine Bott (Eurydice), with the New London Consort conducted by Philip Pickett. L'Oiseau-Lyre 433 545–2. A definitive performance.

Il ritorno d'Ulisse in patria
(The Return of Ulysses to his Country)
opera in a prologue and three acts (approximate length: 3 hours)

Human Fragility   *soprano*
Time   *bass*
Fortune   *soprano*
Love   *soprano*
Ulisse (Ulysses)   *tenor*
Penelope, wife of Ulisse   *soprano*
Ericlea, Penelope's nurse   *mezzo-soprano*
Melanto, Penelope's attendant   *soprano*
Eurymachus, Melanto's lover   *tenor*
Neptune   *bass*
Jupiter   *tenor*
Minerva   *soprano*
Juno   *soprano*
Eumete, a swineherd   *tenor*
Iro, a parasite   *tenor*
Telemachus, son of Ulisse   *tenor*

Antinous   *bass* ⎤
Pisandro   *tenor* ⎟ Penelope's suitors
Anfinomo   *alto* ⎦

LIBRETTO BY GIACOMO BADOARO, BASED ON BOOKS 13–23 OF HOMER'S *ODYSSEY*;
TIME: AFTER THE TROJAN WARS; PLACE: THE ISLAND OF ITHACA, IN THE IONIAN
SEA; FIRST PERFORMED AT THE TEATRO SAN CASSIANO, VENICE, FEBRUARY 1640

It was in 1607, the year in which his *Orfeo* was first performed, that Monteverdi's wife died, leaving the composer in a state of depression that lasted for several years. He was required to write an opera, *Arianna*, for the wedding celebrations of Prince Francesco Gonzaga and Margherita of Savoy in 1608, but for the following two years he composed nothing, until he produced his celebrated *Vespers* of 1610. After his dismissal from the Mantuan court in 1612, Monteverdi was supported by his father in Cremona for a year, before becoming *maestro di cappella* at St Mark's in Venice. With the exception of *Il ballo delle ingrate*, a one-act ballet-opera composed for Mantua in 1608, and *Il combattimento di Tancredi e Clorinda*, a work containing elements of opera, ballet and cantata, which was staged in Venice in 1624, he wrote little of consequence until he was in his seventies. The first public opera house having opened in Venice in 1637, Monteverdi was invited to contribute to its repertoire. *Il ritorno d'Ulisse in patria*, its libretto by Giacomo Badoaro based on Books 13–23 of Homer's *Odyssey*, was given ten performances in Venice with great success.

In modern times, several composers have edited Monteverdi's score for performance, among them D'Indy, Dallapiccola, Henze and Malipiero. In 1971 the opera was performed in Vienna in an edition by Nikolaus Harnoncourt, and in 1972 it was staged at Glyndebourne, arranged by Raymond Leppard.

Prologue. Time, Fortune and Love taunt Human Fragility with their claim that it is they who control mankind.

Act I, scene i. The palace of Ulisse and Penelope in Ithaca. Penelope laments the prolonged absence of her husband, Ulisse, and awaits his return from the Trojan wars ('Di misera regina').

Act I, scene ii. The same. Melanto and Eurymachus sing of their love ('Dolce mia vita sei') and plot to persuade Penelope to accept one of three suitors as her husband.

(Act I, scene iii. An Ithacan landscape. The music for this scene with Nereids and Sirens is missing.)

Act I, scene iv. An Ithacan landscape. Phaeacians disembark from their ship with the sleeping Ulisse, whom they leave on the beach.

Act I, scene v. The same. Neptune and Jupiter are furious that the Phaeacians have brought Ulisse back to his homeland.

Act I, scene vi. The same. The Phaeacians boast of their independence from the gods, and Neptune punishes them by turning their ship into a rock.

Act I, scene vii. The same. Ulisse awakens ('Dormo ancora'), believing himself to have been abandoned in a foreign country.

Act I, scene viii. The same. Minerva enters disguised as a shepherd ('Cara e lieta gioventù'), informs Ulisse that he is back in Ithaca, reveals her identity, warns him that his wife is besieged by three suitors and advises him to return to his palace disguised as a beggar to outwit the suitors, Antinous, Pisandro and Anfinomo.

Act I, scene ix. The same. Minerva departs for Sparta to find Ulisse's son Telemachus and bring him home to help his father rid Ithaca of Penelope's suitors. Ulisse expresses his happiness ('O fortunato Ulisse').

Act I, scene x. The palace. Melanto urges Penelope to choose one of the suitors ('Ama dunque'), but Penelope refuses.

Act I, scene xi. A forest grove. The swineherd Eumete, a former servant of Ulisse, delights in his pastoral life.

Act I, scene xii. The same. Iro, a parasite, ridicules the pastoral life, but he is driven away by Eumete.

Act I, scene xiii. The same. Ulisse enters, disguised as a beggar, and assures Eumete that his master is alive and will shortly return ('Ulisse, Ulisse è vivo').

Act II, scene i. Minerva's chariot. Minerva brings Telemachus back to Ithaca, and Telemachus joyously anticipates his reunion with his father ('Lieto cammino').

Act II, scene ii. A forest grove. Eumete welcomes Telemachus ('O gran figlio d'Ulisse') and introduces the beggar who brought the good tidings of the return of Ulisse.

Act II, scene iii. The same. Ulisse throws off his disguise, revealing himself to Telemachus ('O padre sospirato'). He sends his son to the palace to inform Penelope of his imminent arrival.

Act II, scene iv. The palace. Melanto and Eurymachus discuss Penelope's unwillingness to accept one of the suitors.

Act II, scene v. The same. Each of the three suitors argues his case ('Ama, dunque, si, si'), but Penelope continues to reject them all ('Non voglio amar').

(Act II, scene vi. The same. A ballet of Moors, the music of which is missing.)

Act II, scene vii. The palace. Eumete informs Penelope that her son Telemachus will soon arrive, and perhaps also her husband. Penelope, however, cannot bring herself to believe him.

Act II, scene viii. The same. The suitors plot to kill Telemachus, but the sight of Jupiter's eagle flying overhead frightens them into abandoning their plan. They decide instead to renew their wooing of Penelope ('Amor è un' armonia').

Act II, scene ix. A forest grove. Minerva promises to help Ulysses to remove the suitors.

Act II, scene x. The same. Eumete reports to Ulisse on Penelope's continued resistance to the suitors, and Ulisse rejoices ('Godo anch' io') as they set off for the palace.

Act II, scene xi. The palace. Telemachus tells his mother of his travels and his encounter with Helen of Troy.

Act II, scene xii. The palace. The suitors meet Eumete and Ulisse, who has resumed his disguise as a beggar. Mocked by the suitors, Ulisse fights one of them, whom he thrashes soundly. Penelope proclaims that she will marry the man who can string the mighty bow of Ulisse. When the three suitors fail the test, the beggar humbly asks to be allowed to compete. He succeeds and, invoking Jupiter and Minerva, shoots arrows at the suitors, killing all three of them.

Act III, scene i. The palace. Iro grieves for the dead suitors and, realizing that he cannot survive without them, kills himself.

(Act III, scene ii. A desert. Mercury confronts the ghosts of the suitors and informs them that they deserved their fate. No music exists for this scene.)

Act III, scene iii. The palace. Melanto tries unsuccessfully to persuade Penelope to take action against the beggar who killed her suitors.

Act III, scene iv. The same. Penelope refuses to believe Eumete when he tells her that the beggar is, in fact, Ulisse.

Act III, scene v. The same. Telemachus is unable to convince Penelope that the beggar is Ulisse.

Act III, scene vi. The sea. Though Neptune objects, Mercury persuades Juno to plead with Jupiter on behalf of Ulisse ('Ulisse troppo errò').

Act III, scene vii. The same. Jupiter is convinced by Juno's plea, and a chorus of celestial spirits rejoices ('Giove amoroso').

Act III, scene viii. The palace. The old nurse Ericlea wonders whether to reveal that she has recognized Ulisse by a scar on his body.

Act III, scene ix. The same. Penelope still refuses to accept the assurances of Telemachus and Eumete that the beggar is Ulisse ('Troppo incredula').

Act III, scene x. The same. Ulysses enters, having discarded his disguise, but Penelope is not convinced it is he until he describes the covering on their nuptial bed ('Illustratevi, o cieli'). She and Ulisse are reunited in a sensuous love duet ('Sospirato mio sole').

In the years between *Orfeo* (1607) and *Il ritorno d'Ulisse in patria* (1640), both Monteverdi's art and the art of opera itself underwent considerable development. In the latter opera, the bulk of the action is no longer carried on principally in recitative, for arioso, aria and duet are given considerably greater prominence. Monteverdi's score is one of great expressive power, and his characters are firmly delineated.

Recommended recording: Christoph Pregardien (Ulysses), Bernarda Fink (Penelope), with the Concerto Vocale conducted by René Jacobs. Harmonia Mundi HMC 910427/29. Based on a French stage production, this is splendidly sung and energetically conducted.

L'incoronazione di Poppea
(The Coronation of Poppea)
opera in a prologue and three acts (approximate length: 3 hours, 30 minutes)

Fortune   *soprano*
Virtue   *soprano*
Love (Cupid)   *soprano*
Ottone   *alto*
Poppea   *soprano*
Nero, Emperor of Rome   *soprano*
Octavia, Empress of Rome   *soprano*
Drusilla, a lady of the court   *soprano*
Seneca, philosopher, Nero's former tutor   *bass*
Arnalta, Poppea's old nurse   *alto*
Nutrice, Octavia's nurse   *alto*
Lucano, poet, friend of Nero   *tenor*
Valletto, Octavia's page   *soprano*
Damigella, Octavia's lady-in-waiting   *soprano*
Liberto, captain of the guard   *tenor*
Pallas Athene, goddess of wisdom   *soprano*
Mercury   *bass*
Venus   *soprano*

LIBRETTO BY GIOVANNI FRANCESCO BUSENELLO; TIME: AD 65; PLACE: ROME; FIRST PERFORMED AT THE TEATRO SS GIOVANNI E PAOLO, VENICE, EARLY 1643

Monteverdi's final work for the stage is the first known opera by any composer to use an historical subject as its basis. Busenello's libretto, drawn mainly from the Roman historians Tacitus and Suetonius, takes as its leading character Poppea, the mistress and later the wife of the Roman Emperor Nero. It is now generally thought that some sections of the work, which was first staged in Venice in 1643 only a few months before the death of Monteverdi, were written by other composers.

L'incoronazione di Poppea was performed in the twentieth century in editions by several composers or conductors, among them Gian Francesco Malipiero, Ernst Krenek, Giorgio Federico Ghedini, Hans Redlich, Walter Goehr and Raymond Leppard.

Prologue. Fortune, Virtue and Love (Cupid) argue their respective powers, the contest being won by Love, the most powerful force in the world, as the story of Nero and Poppea is expected to demonstrate.

Act I, scene i. Outside Poppea's palace. Ottone, who has been absent from Rome, arrives at daybreak and sings of his love for Poppea ('E pur io torno'). When he observes Nero's soldiers sleeping outside her palace, he realizes that the Emperor must be inside with Poppea.

Act I, scene ii. The same. The soldiers awaken, and they complain about their work and about conditions in Rome.

Act I, scene iii. The same. Poppea and Nero emerge from the palace and bid a passionate farewell to each other ('Signor, sempre mi vedi').

Act I, scene iv. The same. Poppea discusses her ambitions ('Speranza, tu mi vai') with her old nurse and confidante Arnalta, who warns her against placing her trust in Love or Fortune ('Per me guerreggia Amor e la Fortuna').

Act I, scene v. Nero's palace in Rome. The Empress Octavia bewails her situation ('Disprezzata regina') and dismisses the suggestion of her nurse, Nutrice, that she should take a lover.

Act I, scene vi. The same. The philosopher Seneca urges Octavia to retain her dignity, and is ridiculed as a pedant by the Empress's page, Valletto. Octavia goes to the temple to pray.

Act I, scene vii. The same. Seneca muses on the unhappiness associated with royalty, and the sadness of life in general ('Le porpore regali e le grandezze').

Act I, scene viii. The same. The goddess Pallas Athene appears, warning Seneca of his impending death. Seneca expresses his willingness to accept death.

Act I, scene ix. The same. Nero informs Seneca of his plans to send Octavia into exile and to marry Poppea ('Son risoluto al fine'). Seneca urges the Emperor to act rationally.

Act I, scene x. The same. Poppea and Nero discuss their situation, and Nero promises to make Poppea his empress. When she, in turn, suggests that Seneca's influence over him is too great, Nero orders a soldier to deliver a death sentence to Seneca.

Act I, scene xi. Poppea's palace. Ottone accuses Poppea of being unfaithful to him with Nero, but she dismisses him ('Chi nasce sfortunato di se stesso si dolga e non d'altrui').

Act I, scene xii. Outside Poppea's palace. Ottone expresses his despair and rage ('Otton, torna in te stesso'), and he contemplates murdering Poppea.

Act I, scene xiii. The same. Ottone assures Drusilla that henceforth she will be his only love. But after Drusilla has departed he admits to himself that Poppea still reigns supreme in his heart.

Act II, scene i. Seneca's villa. The winged messenger Mercury appears, announcing to Seneca that this is the day of his death. Seneca accepts the news gladly ('O me felice').

Act II, scene ii. The same. Liberto, captain of the guard, informs Seneca that Nero has decreed he must die. The philosopher assures Liberto that he welcomes death.

Act II, scene iii. The same. Gathering the members of his household around him, Seneca tells them he is about to die. Despite their protests ('Non morir, Seneca'), he orders a bath to be prepared in which he will kill himself by opening his veins.

Act II, scene iv. Nero's palace. Valletto, Octavia's page, and Damigella, Octavia's lady-in-waiting, flirt with each other ('O caro, o cara').

Act II, scene v. The same. Nero has been told of Seneca's death, and he celebrates with his friend Lucano ('Bocca, bocca').

Act II, scene vi. The same. Ottone regrets having considered harming Poppea, whom he still loves ('Sprezzami quanto sai').

Act II, scene vii. The same. Octavia commands Ottone to kill Poppea, first disguising himself as a woman to avoid being recognized. When Ottone at first refuses, Octavia threatens him.

Act II, scene viii. The same. Drusilla rejoices in her love for Ottone, which she believes to be reciprocated ('Felice cor mio'). Octavia's nurse Nutrice wishes that she, too, were young and in love ('Il giorno feminil').

Act II, scene ix. The same. Ottone tells Drusilla that Octavia has ordered him to kill Poppea, and he asks for her clothes to wear. Although she is distressed to think him capable of murder, Drusilla agrees to his request.

Act II, scene x. Poppea's garden. Poppea rejoices at the news of Seneca's death ('Hor che Seneca è morto') and prays to Cupid, the god of love, to ensure her marriage to Nero ('Amor, ricorro a te'). Her nurse Arnalta sings Poppea to sleep with a lullaby ('Oblivion soave') while Cupid hovers overhead.

Act II, scene xi. The same. Cupid hides near the sleeping Poppea, to protect her ('O sciocchi, o frali').

Act II, scene xii. The same. Dressed as Drusilla, Ottone enters the garden to kill Poppea, but he is prevented by Cupid. As Ottone flees, Poppea awakens and recognizes, as she thinks, Drusilla. Cupid declares that he has saved Poppea ('Ho difeso Poppea').

Act III, scene i. Nero's palace. Drusilla joyously anticipates the death of her rival, Poppea ('O felice Drusilla').

Act III, scene ii. The same. Drusilla is arrested for the attempted murder of Poppea.

Act III, scene iii. Another room in Nero's palace. Brought before Nero, Drusilla confesses to the crime in order to shield Ottone, and she is sentenced to death.

Act III, scene iv. The same. Unable to allow Drusilla to be punished for his attempt to kill Poppea, Ottone confesses, blaming Octavia for having forced him to do it. Nero banishes his wife, Octavia, as well as Drusilla and Ottone.

Act III, scene v. The same. Nero tells Poppea that he can now marry her. They rejoice ('Non più s'interporrà noia a dimora').

Act III, scene vi. Octavia's apartment in the palace. Octavia bids a sad farewell to Rome ('Addio Roma').

Act III, scene vii. Another part of the palace. Arnalta exults in the good fortune of her mistress, Poppea.

Act III, scene viii. A large hall in the palace. Nero and Poppea express their love for each other, Poppea is crowned Empress ('Ascendi, o mia diletta'), and Cupid descends from the heavens with Venus and other celestial bodies to hail Poppea as goddess of beauty on earth. Nero and Poppea sing a final ecstatic duet ('Pur ti miro, pur ti godo').

L'incoronazione di Poppea is Monteverdi's crowning achievement, a work in which his musical characterization – especially of the hedonistic pair, Nero and Poppea – is stronger and more detailed than ever, and in which he takes the art of opera a stage further in its development with his increasing use of the aria for dramatic and emotional emphasis.

Recommended recording: Danielle Borst (Poppea), Guillemette Laurens (Nero), with the Concerto Vocale, conducted by René Jacobs. Harmonia Mundi HMC 901330/32. A superb cast and a conductor who is both scholarly and lively.

DOUGLAS S. MOORE
(b. Cutchogue, NY, 1893 – d. Greenport, NY, 1969)

The Ballad of Baby Doe
opera in two acts (approximate length: 2 hours, 15 minutes)

Baby Doe, a miner's wife   *soprano*
Horace Tabor, mayor of Leadville   *baritone*
Augusta, Tabor's wife   *mezzo-soprano*

LIBRETTO BY JOHN LATOUCHE; TIME: FROM 1880 TO 1935; PLACE: LEADVILLE, DENVER AND WASHINGTON DC; FIRST PERFORMED AT THE OPERA HOUSE, CENTRAL CITY, COLORADO, 7 JULY 1956

Douglas Moore studied in New York, and later in Paris with D'Indy and Nadia Boulanger, before taking up an academic career in music. He taught at Columbia University from 1926 until his retirement in 1962. Of his ten operas, the first to be successfully staged (in New York in 1939) was *The Devil and Daniel Webster*, which is still occasionally revived by American opera companies. Even more successful was *The Ballad of Baby Doe*, first produced in Central City, Colorado, in 1956. Moore's final opera, *Carrie Nation*, staged at the University of Kansas in 1966, is based on the life of an American proponent of temperance.

The complex story of *The Ballad of Baby Doe* is based on historical events, telling the story of Horace Tabor, a late nineteenth-century Colorado silver magnate who built the Tabor Opera House in Leadville. The wealthy Tabor left his wife, Augusta, to marry the young and beautiful Baby Doe, but some years later he lost his fortune with the collapse of silver.

Act I, scene i. Outside the Tabor Opera House, Leadville, in 1880. During the interval of a performance, Tabor and his friends emerge to mix with the girls from the saloon next door, and Tabor is upbraided by his dour wife, Augusta.

Baby Doe, newly arrived in town from Central City, accosts Tabor and asks for directions to the Clarendon Hotel.

Act I, scene ii. Outside the Clarendon Hotel, later that evening. Tabor flirts with Baby Doe.

Act I, scene iii. The Tabor apartment, several months later. Augusta discovers evidence that Tabor is having an affair with Baby Doe. She confronts her husband and threatens to create a scandal.

Act I, scene iv. The lobby of the Clarendon Hotel, shortly afterwards. Baby Doe is about to leave Tabor and writes to her mother to explain why. She confirms this to Augusta, who has come to confront her, but when Augusta contemptuously ridicules Tabor, Baby Doe tears up the letter she wrote and rushes to embrace Tabor when he arrives.

Act I, scene v. Augusta's parlour in Denver, a year later. Augusta's friends inform her that Tabor is divorcing her.

Act I, scene vi. A suite in the Willard Hotel, Washington DC, in 1883. Tabor has married Baby Doe and now intends to have a formal Catholic wedding. When it is revealed that they are both divorced the Priest is scandalized, and a scene is avoided only by the arrival of the President.

Act II, scene i. The Windsor Hotel, Denver, 1893. At the governor's ball, Baby Doe is warned by Augusta that the silver standard is about to collapse, and that she should sell Tabor's Matchless Mine. Tabor, entering, rejects this advice and makes Baby Doe promise that she will never sell the Matchless Mine.

Act II, scene ii. A gaming saloon in Leadville. During a poker game, Tabor is forced to appeal to his friends for financial help.

Act II, scene iii. The Matchless Mine, summer 1896. At the gate of the mine, William Jennings Bryan, the presidential candidate on a 'free silver' platform, makes a rousing address to the voters.

Act II, scene iv. Augusta's parlour in Denver, November 1896. Augusta is visited by Baby Doe's mother, who asks her to help Tabor. Augusta gently rebuffs her.

Act II, scene v. The stage of the Tabor Opera House, Leadville. Tabor, dying and delirious, stumbles onto the darkened stage of the theatre he built. In his last thoughts, he relives the past and foresees the future, discovering that his beloved little daughter Silver Dollar will end up as a prostitute. He cries out for one thing that has not failed him, and Baby Doe arrives to comfort his dying moments. She is then seen as an old woman, many years later, moving towards the Matchless Mine, which is now visible. She sits by the mineshaft as snow falls gently upon her.

Written in an easily accessible idiom that one might describe as sub-Britten, *The Ballad of Baby Doe* is a highly enjoyable work which could today take its place on Broadway beside the quasi-operas of Stephen Sondheim as a piece of American popular theatre. Moore's score is lyrical and melodic, some of its tunes recalling the popular music of the 1890s, and his orchestration is rich and pungent. John Latouche's libretto is mundane, but it tells the story clearly.

WOLFGANG AMADEUS MOZART
(b. Salzburg, 1756 – d. Vienna, 1791)

Mitridate, rè di Ponto
(Mithridates, King of Pontus)
opera seria in three acts (approximate length: 3 hours, 30 minutes)

Mitridate (Mithridates), King of Pontus   *tenor*
Aspasia, betrothed to Mitridate   *soprano*
Sifare, son of Mitridate   *soprano*
Farnace, his elder brother   *alto*
Ismene, daughter of the King of the Parthians   *soprano*
Marzio, Roman tribune   *tenor*
Arbate, governor of Nymphaea   *soprano*

LIBRETTO BY VITTORIO AMEDEO CIGNA-SANTI, BASED ON THE PLAY *MITHRIDATE*, BY JEAN RACINE; TIME: 88 BC; PLACE: IN AND AROUND NYMPHAEA, THE CRIMEA; FIRST PERFORMED AT THE TEATRO REGIO DUCAL, MILAN, 26 DECEMBER 1770

Leopold Mozart, the composer's father, was a violinist and composer in the service of the Prince Archbishop of Salzburg. Wolfgang at the age of three liked to sit at the keyboard picking out chords, and before his sixth birthday he was being toured through Europe by his father as a child prodigy. At the age of eleven he wrote his first works for the stage, and his first full-length opera, *La finta semplice* (The Pretended Simpleton), he wrote at the age of thirteen. In December 1769 Wolfgang, now nearly fourteen, and his father set out on their travels again. In Milan the young Mozart was commissioned to compose an opera to open the new season on 26 December 1770. He and Leopold stayed in Italy long enough for

Wolfgang to write his opera, *Mitridate, rè di Ponto*, and to conduct its first performance from the cembalo.

The rehearsal period had not been without its difficulties. 'Thank God', Leopold wrote from Milan to his wife in Salzburg, 'we have won the first battle and have routed an enemy who composed new arias for the prima donna, and tried to persuade her not to sing any of Wolfgang's.' The first performance of the opera was a great triumph, with cries of 'Evviva il maestro' and demands for encores. The critic of the *Gazzetta di Milano* wrote that the opera had 'met with public satisfaction both for the good taste of its scenery and for the excellence of the music', and that its young composer 'studies the beauty of nature and represents it adorned with the most rare musical graces'. During the season *Mitridate* was performed twenty times, but it appears not to have been staged again until it was successfully revived in Salzburg more than two hundred years later, in 1971.

The Turin poet Vittorio Amedeo Cigna-Santi (1725–85) originally wrote the libretto for another composer, Quirino Gasparini, whose *Mitridate* was staged in Turin in 1767. The libretto was shortened somewhat for Mozart, and altered in several places, but it remains close to the drama on which it was based, Racine's tragedy *Mithridate* (1673), which Cigna-Santi used in an Italian translation by Giuseppe Parini. The historical Mithridates the Great ruled in Pontus, a kingdom bordering the southern shore of the Black Sea (and today part of Turkey), in the years 124 BC to 88 BC. As a result of defeating several neighbouring rulers in battle, Mithridates became King of Armenia Major. During this period he was known as a great liberator, championing Greek culture against the alien power of Rome, and releasing Asia from Rome's repressive rule. The action of Mozart's opera takes place in the last days of the King's life in and around Nymphaea, a seaport in the Crimea. When the opera begins, Mithridates has suffered an enormous defeat by the Romans and is now a fugitive with a price on his head.

Act I, scene i. A square in Nymphaea. Arbate, the governor of Nymphaea, and Sifare, son of Mitridate, have learned of the death of Mitridate in battle. Sifare considers himself the enemy of his half-brother Farnace, not only because of Farnace's treasonous ties with Rome but also because they are both in love with Aspasia, whom Mitridate took as his fiancée and intended queen. Arbate pledges loyalty to Sifare.

Aspasia, fearing the advances of Farnace now that his father, Mitridate, is dead, asks Sifare for his protection, for it is he whom she really loves ('Al destin che la minaccia'). As Aspasia departs, Sifare reflects on his feelings for her ('Soffre il mio cor con pace una belta tiranna').

Act I, scene ii. A temple of Venus. Farnace declares his love for Aspasia. Sifare and Farnace are about to fight when Arbate enters hurriedly, announcing that Mitridate is not dead, and that his fleet is even now approaching the harbour. He urges the two men to cease quarrelling and greet their father ('L'odio nel cor frenate'). The news that Mitridate is alive is received with mixed feelings by Aspasia ('Nel sen mi palpita dolente il core'), and also by Farnace and Sifare. The two brothers agree to conceal from Mitridate their love for Aspasia. Marzio, the Roman tribune, arrives, and Farnace plots with him ('Venga pur, minacci e frema').

Act I, scene iii. The harbour. Mitridate and Ismene, daughter of the King of Parthia, arrive. Mitridate apologizes for having been defeated in battle but asserts that he is returning without disgrace ('Se di lauri il crine adorno'). He next announces that Farnace is to marry Ismene. Although she loves Farnace, Ismene has a premonition that suffering is in store for her ('In faccia all' oggetto').

Mitridate explains to Arbate that he allowed everyone to think him dead in order to trick his sons into betraying their secret love for Aspasia. Arbate tells him that Farnace has already declared his love, but that Sifare has behaved honourably and given no indication of desiring Aspasia. Highly jealous and suspicious by nature, Mitridate determines to discover the truth from Aspasia. Scornful of Farnace's behaviour, he wishes he could see his son bleed to death ('Quel ribelle e quell'ingrato').

Act II, scene i. The royal apartments. When Farnace informs Ismene that he no longer loves her she threatens to tell Mitridate. Farnace replies that he is already out of favour with his father ('Va, va, l'error mia palesa'). Mitridate enters and attempts to console Ismene, suggesting to her that she might find a worthier husband in Sifare. He then questions Aspasia and satisfies himself that Farnace has designs on both his future wife and his throne.

Calling Sifare to him, Mitridate commands him to take good care of Aspasia while he, Mitridate, deals with the traitorous Farnace. When they are left alone, Aspasia reveals to Sifare that it is he whom she loves, but she says that she must never see him again as she is betrothed to his father. Sifare agrees to leave Nymphaea before their love can bring dishonour to them ('Lungi da te, mio bene'). He departs, and Aspasia laments her unhappy situation, torn between love and duty ('Nel grave tormento').

Act II, scene ii. Mitridate's camp. Mitridate plans to gather his depleted army and attack Rome. Farnace dismisses the idea as futile, suggesting instead that a peace treaty with Rome would be the best solution. Marzio now appears, and the full truth of Farnace's treacherous dealings with Rome is revealed. Mitridate orders his son's imprisonment, and Ismene sides with the King in declaring her contempt for Farnace's behaviour ('So quanto a te dispiace'). Farnace admits his guilt but casts blame on Sifare as well, for pursuing Aspasia ('Son reo, l'error confesso'). Mitridate tricks Aspasia into confessing her love for Sifare by telling her she should not waste herself on an old man. Betrayed, as he thinks, by all those closest to him, he condemns both sons and Aspasia to death ('Già di pietà mi spoglio'). He departs in a fury, while Aspasia and Sifare anticipate death together ('Se viver non degg'io').

Act III, scene i. A garden. Ismene pleads with Mitridate to forgive Aspasia, just as she, despite all the suffering he has brought her, will forgive Farnace, whom she still loves ('Tu sai per chi m'accese'). Arbate enters to announce that the Romans are already at the city gates. Mitridate departs to fight, but not before reminding Aspasia that, although he will die in battle, she will precede him to the grave ('Vado incontro al fato estremo').

Aspasia contemplates suicide ('Pallid' ombre, che scorgete'), and she is about to raise a poisoned goblet to her lips when she is prevented by the arrival of Sifare, who expresses a desire to end his own life, which has become unendurable to him ('Se il rigor d'ingrata sorte').

Act III, scene ii. A prison. Farnace is visited in his cell by the Roman Marzio, who aids his escape and promises to have him declared King of Nymphaea ('Se di regnar sei vago'). But Farnace now regrets having plotted against his father, and he determines to help Mitridate defeat the Romans ('Già da gli occhi il velo e tolto').

Act III, scene iii. The courtyard of the palace, with a distant view of the sea and the Roman navy. Recognizing inevitable defeat, Mitridate has tried to kill himself; but he lives long enough to see Farnace set the entire Roman fleet on fire. He is reconciled to both his sons, giving his blessing to the union of Aspasia and Sifare and pardoning Farnace, who is now reunited with Ismene. The dying King is borne away, while the two pairs of lovers and Arbate resolve to continue their fight against the Romans ('Non si ceda al Campidoglio').

Mozart's youthful opera is written in the conventional *opera seria* form of its time. (Twenty of its twenty-three numbers are solo arias.) Its dramatic element must be sought not in complex ensembles of the kind to be encountered later, in his masterpieces *Don Giovanni* and *Le nozze di Figaro*, but within the individual arias and in the recitatives. In *Mitridate* the *secco* recitatives, or recitatives accompanied only on the keyboard, are lively, sensitive, and responsive to the requirements of the text. They are not, as so often in *opera seria*, mere interludes between arias. It is, nevertheless, in the arias that the precocious talent of the young Mozart reveals itself to most impressive effect.

Three of the male roles in the opera were composed by Mozart for castrati: Sifare (soprano), Arbate (soprano) and Farnace (alto). In modern performances these roles are usually entrusted to female voices, although they can also be performed by virtuoso counter-tenors.

Recommended recording: Giuseppe Sabatini (Mitridate), Natalie Dessay (Aspasia), Sandrine Piau (Ismene), Cecilia Bartoli (Sifare), Helene Le Corre (Arbate), Brian Asawa (Farnace), with Les Talens Lyriques, conducted by Chrisophe Rousset. Decca 460 772–2. The only available modern recording, and a perfectly acceptable one.

Lucio Silla
opera seria in three acts (approximate length: 3 hours, 30 minutes)

Lucio Silla, dictator of Rome   *tenor*
Cecilio, an exiled Roman senator   *soprano*
Lucio Cinna, friend of Cecilio   *soprano*
Celia, sister of Lucio Silla   *soprano*
Giunia, wife of Cecilio   *soprano*
Aufidio, a tribune   *tenor*

LIBRETTO BY GIOVANNI DE GAMERRA, REVISED BY PIETRO METASTASIO; TIME: AROUND 80 BC; PLACE: ROME; FIRST PERFORMED AT THE TEATRO REGIO DUCAL, MILAN, 26 DECEMBER 1772

After the success of *Mitridate* in Milan, Wolfgang and Leopold Mozart returned home to Salzburg in March 1771. Within months, however, they were back in Italy, for Wolfgang had received further commissions. For the Teatro Regio Ducal in Milan, where *Mitridate* had been staged, he composed *Ascanio in Alba*, a pastoral opera in two acts, performed to celebrate the wedding of the Archduke Ferdinand, third son of the Austrian Empress Maria Theresa, to the Princess Maria Beatrice Ricciarda d'Este of Modena. Mozart's opera was an overwhelming success at its premiere in October 1771, causing the elderly composer Johann Adolph Hasse, who had also composed an opera for the occasion, to remark, 'This boy will cause us all to be forgotten.'

For a new prince-archbishop in Salzburg the young Mozart composed a dramatic serenade, *Il sogno di Scipione*, performed at the Archbishop's residence in the spring of 1772, and in the autumn he returned to Milan to fulfil another commission for the Teatro Regio Ducal – a new opera to be staged during the Milan carnival season. This was *Lucio Silla*. Although it was successful enough to be performed twenty-six times during the season, it appears never to have been revived or staged elsewhere until 1929, when it was performed in Prague in a German translation. Since its production at the Salzburg Festival in 1964 in an edition by the Austrian Mozart scholar Bernhard Paumgartner, *Lucio Silla* is now occasionally to be encountered in European and American opera houses. Its first performance in Great Britain was given in London at the 1967 Camden Festival, and it first reached the United States the following year when staged by the Chamber Opera Society of Baltimore.

Lucio Silla was a Roman soldier who distinguished himself in the wars between Rome and other Italian tribes and who in due course became dictator of Rome. The opera's not-very-talented librettist, Giovanni de Gamerra (1743–1803), was a playwright, still in his twenties, who had already been both a priest and a soldier. He submitted his libretto to Pietro Metastasio, the leading librettist of the time, who made a number of changes to it as well as writing a new scene in the second act. Two leading male roles, those of Cinna and Cecilio, were written by Mozart for soprano voices. At the first performances only one of these, Cecilio, was sung by a castrato, the famous Venanzio Rauzzini, for whom, some months later, Mozart composed the motet 'Esultate, jubilate'. The role of Cinna was sung by a female soprano, Felicita Suarti.

Act I, scene i. A landscape of trees and ruins, outside Rome. Cecilio, a senator banished from Rome by Lucio Silla, returns secretly and is told by his friend Cinna, a Roman patrician and secret opponent of Silla, that the dictator has declared him dead and has taken Cecilio's wife Giunia into his household. Cecilio may be able to see her when she visits the graveyard containing the tombs of her ancestors ('Il tenero momento').

Act I, scene ii. Lucio Silla's palace. Silla asks his sister Celia to intercede for him with Giunia. When Giunia appears, she rejects Silla contemptuously ('Dalla sponda tenebrosa'), and the dictator's lust turns to fury ('Il desio di vendetta').

Act I, scene iii. The entrance to an underground burial chamber. Giunia enters with her entourage to pray ('O del padre ombra diletta'). Cecilio emerges from the shadows, and Giunia at first thinks it is his spirit that confronts her. When she realizes he is alive, she and Cecilio declare their love for each other ('D'Eliseo in sen m'attendi').

Act II, scene i. An archway in Silla's palace. Aufidio advises Silla to marry Giunia ('Guerrier, che d'un acciaro'). Cinna and Celia are in love, but have not managed to make this clear to each other, Cinna's hatred of the dictator being even stronger than his love for his enemy's sister. When Giunia tells Cinna that she has been bidden to appear before Silla and the senate, Cinna informs her that Silla intends to force her to marry him. He suggests that she should agree, and then murder Silla in bed. Giunia refuses, and Cinna resolves to kill Silla himself ('Nel fortunato istante').

Act II, scene ii. The Hanging Gardens. Cecilio and Giunia embrace for what they fear may be the last time. Celia, who has been told by her brother that she may marry Cinna, urges Giunia to marry Silla ('Quando sugl' arsi campi'), but Giunia decides she would rather kill herself ('Parto, m'affretto').

Act II, scene iii. The Capitol. Silla asks the senate to award him the hand of Giunia in marriage, thus ending the feud between his followers and those of Giunia's dead father. Giunia rejects him and is about to kill herself when Cecilio enters with his sword drawn. Silla has both Giunia and Cecilio arrested, and he expresses his fury at their devotion to each other ('Quell'orgoglioso sdegno').

Act III, scene i. A prison. Cecilio is visited by Cinna and Celia, who promise to save both him and Giunia, Cinna swearing that if Celia fails to move her brother to clemency he himself will kill Silla ('De' più superbi il core'). Giunia is led in to say a last farewell to Cecilio, who is then taken out by Aufidio to face judgment. Giunia is left to lament ('Fra i pensier più funesti').

Act III, scene ii. The Capitol. Silla decrees that Cecilio and Giunia shall be set free, and the senators and populace sing a chorus in praise of their ruler's clemency.

Lucio Silla, though an uneven work, is a fascinating one, for Mozart composed it when he was on the brink of manhood, and when the romantic impulse that was making itself felt in the arts, especially in music, was awakening in him personally. Formally conventional, this, the last opera that Mozart was to compose for Italy, is nevertheless musically the finest of the youthful composer's contributions to the art of *opera seria*. Several of its eighteen arias contain stretches of more than usually difficult coloratura writing for the voice.

Recommended recording: Peter Schreier (Lucio Silla), Edita Gruberova (Giunia), Dawn Upshaw (Celia), Yvonne Kenny (Cinna), Cecilia Bartoli (Cecilio), with the Arnold Schoenberg Choir and the Concentus Musicus Wien, conducted by Nikolaus Harnoncourt. Teldec 2292–44928–2. This is a radically reduced version of a long opera, but Harnoncourt conducts a dazzling account of the work, with superb singers.

La finta giardiniera
(The Pretended Garden-Maid)
opera buffa in three acts (approximate length: 3 hours, 30 minutes)

Don Anchise, mayor of Lagonero   *tenor*
Marchioness Violante Onesti, alias the garden-maid Sandrina   *soprano*
Count Belfiore   *tenor*
Arminda, the mayor's niece   *soprano*
Ramiro, a knight   *soprano*
Serpetta, the mayor's chambermaid   *soprano*
Roberto, servant to the Marchioness, alias Nardo, a gardener   *bass*

LIBRETTO BY RANIERI DE' CALZABIGI, REVISED BY MARCO COLTELLINI; TIME: THE
MID-EIGHTEENTH CENTURY; PLACE: THE COUNTRY ESTATE OF THE MAYOR, AT
LAGONERO, NEAR MILAN; FIRST PERFORMED AT THE SALVATORTHEATER, MUNICH,
13 JANUARY 1775

After *Lucio Silla*, the young Mozart's next commission to compose an opera came from Maximilian III, Elector of Bavaria. Mozart was engaged to write a comic opera for the 1774–5 carnival season in Munich, and the libretto chosen was one that Ranieri de' Calzabigi had written for another composer, Pasquale Anfossi, whose opera *La finta giardiniera* had been produced the previous year in Milan. Mozart began work on his opera in Salzburg, and then he set out with his father for Munich to meet the singers and complete the work. At its premiere on 13 January 1775, two weeks before its composer's nineteenth birthday, the new opera was well received. Four years later, Mozart allowed a touring company to perform it in German as a *Singspiel*, with dialogue replacing the unaccompanied recitatives. This version survived and is still occasionally performed in Germany and Austria. Until the mid-1970s the Italian recitatives of Act I were lost, and it is only since then that the opera has been performed again in its original Italian version.

Act I. The mayor's garden. Don Anchise, the foolish old mayor of Lagonero, is in love with Sandrina, a gardener's maid, who is really the Marchioness Violante.

She has disguised herself in order to search for her lover, Count Belfiore, who has fled after wounding her in a jealous quarrel. Violante is accompanied by her servant Roberto, who is posing as Nardo, the gardener. The mayor's niece Arminda spurns her admirer Ramiro and announces that she is going to marry Belfiore.

Act II. The mayor's house and, later, the forest. Violante is forced to reveal her identity in order to save Belfiore from being arrested for having killed her. She subsequently denies that she is the Marchioness Violante, which causes Belfiore to lose his reason. Serpetta, the mayor's chambermaid, who is thought to be in love with her master, abandons Sandrina/Violante in the forest, where the others come to search for her. Both Sandrina and Belfiore are now deranged, and imagine themselves shepherds.

Act III. The mayor's house and, later, the garden. Sandrina and Belfiore emerge from their temporary insanity to rediscover their love for each other. Arminda returns to her Ramiro, and Serpetta decides to marry Nardo. In a final chorus, all sing of the joys of true love.

For this nonsensical and incoherent libretto Mozart composed a number of delightful arias. It is in this inconsequential work that one finds the young composer taking his first steps along the path that would eventually lead to *Le nozze di Figaro* and *Così fan tutte*. The extended finale to Act II is especially impressive.

Recommended recording: Edita Gruberova (Sandrina/Marchese), Charlotte Margiono (Arminda), Dawn Upshaw (Serpetta), Monica Bacelli (Ramiro), Thomas Moser (Don Anchise), Uwe Heilmann (Belfiore), with the Concentus Musicus Wien, conducted by Nikolaus Harnoncourt. Teldec 9031–72309–2. A delightful cast and authoritative conductor.

Idomeneo, rè di Creta
(Idomeneo, King of Crete)
opera seria in three acts (approximate length: 3 hours, 30 minutes)

Idomeneo, King of Crete   *tenor*
Idamante, his son   *soprano, later rewritten as tenor*
Arbace, the King's confidant   *tenor*
Ilia, daughter of King Priam of Troy   *soprano*
Elettra, daughter of King Agamemnon of Argos   *soprano*

High Priest of Neptune *tenor*
Voice of Neptune *bass*

LIBRETTO BY GIAMBATTISTA VARESCO; TIME: AT THE END OF THE TROJAN WARS; PLACE: SIDON (NOW KHANIA), IN CRETE; FIRST PERFORMED AT THE CUVILLIÉS-THEATRE, MUNICH, 29 JANUARY 1781

After composing *La finta giardiniera* for Munich, Mozart spent what remained of his teenage years in Salzburg, writing a number of important non-operatic works, among them several violin concertos as well as divertimenti, serenades and masses. But, increasingly discontented with life under Archbishop Colloredo, and encouraged by his father to embark upon another tour, Mozart set out in 1777 for Paris, accompanied this time by his mother, who became ill and died there. His next three years were spent composing and performing music to order in Salzburg, but in November 1780 he secured six weeks' leave of absence from the Archbishop and departed for Munich, having received a commission to compose an *opera seria* for the Munich carnival season at the beginning of 1781. The subject chosen was the story of Idomeneo, King of Crete at the time immediately following the Trojan wars. The Salzburg-based Abbé Varesco produced an Italian libretto, based on an earlier French libretto written by Antoine Danchet for André Campra's opera *Idoménée*, which had been staged at the Paris Opéra in 1712.

During the rehearsal period in Munich, Mozart found that he required a number of changes to be made to the libretto, and to achieve this he communicated with Varesco in Salzburg, not directly, but through his father, Leopold Mozart. Some scenes had to be shortened because both the tenor Anton Raaff, who was to sing Idomeneo, and the castrato Vincenzo dal Prato, who was to be Idomeneo's son Idamante, were, in Mozart's opinion, 'the most wretched actors that ever appeared on any stage'. The sixty-six-year-old Raaff proved difficult at rehearsals, and at one point tried to insist on having an additional aria composed for himself to replace the beautiful quartet that Mozart had written for Idomeneo, Idamante, Ilia and Elettra (Act III, scene i). 'There's no opportunity to display the voice,' Raaff complained. But the young composer stood his ground. According to one of his letters to his father, Mozart told the tenor that 'there is nothing in my opera that I'm more content with than this quartet. When you have sung it through once with the others, you are sure to change your mind.'

Raaff accepted Mozart's defence of the quartet but then insisted on the words of his final aria being changed, on the grounds that the vowel sounds were such as to make the vocalization difficult. Not surprisingly, the first performance of

Idomeneo had to be postponed twice. At last, on 29 January, with Raaff's final aria omitted because the opera was too long, *Idomeneo* was given its first public performance in an elegant little rococo theatre in Munich, which is still in use and now called the Cuvilliéstheater, after its architect. The opera was well received at its premiere, but the review in a Munich newspaper three days later began by praising the decor, and it failed to mention the name of the composer.

Several months later, in Vienna, Mozart considered rewriting the tenor role of Idomeneo for a bass, Ludwig Fischer (who was later to create the role of Osmin in *Die Entführung aus dem Serail*). However, he did not do so, and it was not until five years further on, in 1786, that he made extensive alterations to his score for a single private performance by aristocratic amateurs at Prince Auersperg's town palace in Vienna. It was for this occasion that he recast Idamante as a tenor, and it is in this version that the opera is usually performed today.

Act I, scene i. Ilia's apartment in the royal palace at Sidon on the island of Crete. The Trojan Princess Ilia, who has been taken as a hostage by Idomeneo and sent, along with other Trojans, to Crete, bewails her fate and that of her father and brothers and their city of Troy ('Padre, germani, addio'). She has fallen in love with Idomeneo's son Idamante, who, to celebrate his father's imminent return, orders that the Trojan prisoners be freed, and declares his love for Ilia ('Non ho colpa'). Elettra, who has sought refuge on the island after having instigated the murder of her mother, Clytemnestra, is also in love with Idamante, and she reproaches him for favouring the Trojans. Arbace, Idomeneo's confidant, enters to announce that the King has been drowned in a storm at sea. Fearing that if Idamante is now to become king, he will make Ilia his queen, Elettra expresses her jealousy and her determination to seek vengeance on them both ('Tutte nel cor vi sento').

Act I, scene ii. The seashore. The voices of the sailors can be heard, calling on the gods to save them ('Pietà! Numi, pietà!'). Idomeneo staggers ashore with a few of his followers, whom he asks to leave him so that he may confide his suffering alone to his native skies. He already regrets the cruel vow he has made to Neptune that if he is saved from the tempest, he will sacrifice the first person he encounters ('Vedrommi intorno'). The person who now approaches, offering his assistance, turns out to be Idomeneo's own son, Idamante. The King turns from him in despair, and Idamante wonders sadly what he can have done to offend his father ('Il padre adorato ritrovo'). The people of Crete celebrate their King's return and give thanks to the gods.

Act II, scene i. The royal apartments in the palace. Idomeneo explains his dilemma to Arbace, who advises him to send Idamante abroad and find another victim for Neptune ('Se il tuo duol'). Idomeneo resolves to send Idamante to accompany Elettra back to her father's court at Argos. Ilia enters to congratulate the King on his safe return, and she makes it clear that she loves his son and now regards Idomeneo as a father ('Se il padre perdei'). Idomeneo realizes that in addition to being about to cause the death of an unknown person, he is also going to bring sorrow to Ilia and Idamante by separating them. A far worse tempest than the one at sea is raging in his soul ('Fuor del mar'). Elettra happily antici-pates her journey with Idamante to her homeland ('Idol mio'), and a march is heard summoning the travellers to depart.

Act II, scene ii (which follows without a pause in the music). The harbour of Sidon. The chorus sings of the calm, tranquil sea ('Placido è il mar'). Idomeneo's farewell to Elettra and Idamante ('Pria di partir') is interrupted by a violent thunderstorm sent by the angry god Neptune, who summons up a huge monster from the depths of the sea. Idomeneo begs Neptune to punish him alone, as the people rush away in terror ('Corriamo, fuggiamo').

Act III, scene i. The garden of the royal palace. Ilia sings of her love for Idamante ('Zeffiretti lusinghieri'), who arrives to tell her that he is going to fight the monster that is ravaging the country. They swear their love for each other ('S'io non moro a questi accenti'), but are interrupted by the arrival of Idomeneo and Elettra. Idamante asks his father to reveal why he continually avoids him, but Idomeneo instead commands him to leave the country, and he forbids Ilia to go with him ('Andrò ramingo e solo'). Arbace enters, imploring Idomeneo to address and calm the populace.

Act III, scene ii. A square in front of the palace. The High Priest of Neptune demands the name of the sacrificial victim whose death will appease the god, and Idomeneo is forced to reveal that it is his son, Idamante. The assembled citizens express their horror ('O voto tremendo').

Act III, scene iii. The temple of Neptune. Idomeneo prays to Neptune for mercy ('Accogli, o rè del mar'), but when Arbace rushes in with the news that Idamante has slain the monster, he realizes that nothing will now quell the god's fury. Idamante is led in to be sacrificed, and Idomeneo's sword is already raised to strike when Ilia attempts to offer herself in Idamante's place. Suddenly the sub-terranean Voice of Neptune is heard, announcing that love has triumphed, and that Idomeneo must now abdicate in favour of Idamante and Ilia. All rejoice, except Elettra who expresses her despair and jealous fury ('D'Oreste, d'Ajace ho in seno i tormenti').

Act III, scene iv. The square. Idomeneo addresses his people ('Torna la pace al core') and stands down in favour of Idamante and Ilia. The citizens pledge their homage to the new royal couple ('Scenda Amor'). (At the opera's premiere in Munich it was at this point that a thirty-minute-long ballet, for which Mozart wrote five numbers, was performed.)

It was with *Idomeneo*, a work of great power and originality, that Mozart arrived at his artistic maturity as a composer of opera. It is a work which looks to the future with its sense of drama and its newly found freedom of form, while also saying an affectionate farewell to the past, for it is really the last great *opera seria*. Although Mozart was to return to that particular genre once more with his final opera, *La clemenza di Tito*, his masterpieces *Don Giovanni*, *Le nozze di Figaro* and *Così fan tutte* were to be works of a very different kind.

From its majestic overture to its festive final chorus, there is hardly a dull number in *Idomeneo*. No doubt inspired by the high standard of the Munich orchestra, Mozart wrote for its players with a greater freedom of imagination than in his earlier works for the theatre, and the arias he provided for his singers are for the most part magnificent. The fierce dramatic attack of Elettra's great aria 'Tutte nel cor vi sento' sounds startling even today, while Ilia's gentle expression of love, 'Zeffiretti lusinghieri', is imbued with a tender poetry which is deeply moving. Idomeneo's 'Fuor del mar', which exists in two versions, the second a simplified one to suit the elderly Anton Raaff, is a splendid bravura piece. Perhaps the finest number in the opera is the quartet 'Andrò ramingo e solo', which Raaff had attempted to remove. Mozart referred to it as a quartet in which the characters talk more than they sing, and it is true that, at its conclusion, one feels one has experienced an ensemble of great dramatic intensity as well as of rare musical beauty.

It is no surprise to learn that when, nearly forty years after the composer's death, Mozart's widow was visited by the English organist and composer Vincent Novello, she told him that the happiest time of her husband's life was when he was composing *Idomeneo*.

Recommended recording: Anthony Rolfe Johnson (Idomeneo), Anne Sofie von Otter (Idamante), Sylvia McNair (Ilia), Hillevi Martinpelto (Elettra), with the Monteverdi Choir and the English Baroque Soloists, conducted by John Eliot Gardiner. Archiv 431 674–2. Based on live performances given at the Queen Elizabeth Hall in London, this is a thrilling account of Mozart's great opera seria. The conductor's intention, to approach as closely as possible the kind of performance that might have been given in Mozart's time, is successfully realised with the specialist forces of his chorus and orchestra. Anthony Rolfe Johnson brings a fine technique and a lively dramatic imagination to Idomeneo, with Sylvia McNair singing the role of Ilia beautifully. Hillevi Martinpelto is a suitably ferocious Elettra, and Anne Sofie von Otter is perfectly cast as Idamante.

Die Entführung aus dem Serail
(The Abduction from the Harem)
Singspiel in three acts (approximate length: 2 hours, 15 minutes)

Constanze   *soprano*
Blonde, her maid   *soprano*
Belmonte   *tenor*
Pedrillo, his servant   *tenor*
Pasha Selim   *spoken role*
Osmin, overseer of Pasha Selim's estate   *bass*

LIBRETTO BY GOTTLOB STEPHANIE THE YOUNGER; TIME: THE MID-SIXTEENTH CENTURY; PLACE: PASHA SELIM'S PALACE ON THE COAST OF TURKEY; FIRST PERFORMED AT THE BURGTHEATER, VIENNA, 16 JULY 1782

Immediately after the first performances of *Idomeneo* in Munich early in 1781, Mozart was called to Vienna as part of the entourage of his employer, the Archbishop of Salzburg. The letters he wrote home to his father at this time reveal how frustrated and discontented he had become in the Archbishop's service. Smarting from the indignities heaped upon him as someone little better than a servant in Archbishop Colloredo's employ, he angrily offered his resignation. Determined to make a career for himself in Vienna as composer, performer and teacher, Mozart took lodgings with a family he already knew, the Webers (one of whose daughters, Constanze, he was soon to marry), and began to seek commissions.

By the beginning of August he was already at work on an opera, *Die Entführung aus dem Serail*, whose libretto had been given to him by its author, Gottlob Stephanie (1741–1800), the director of the German Opera in Vienna. Stephanie had based his libretto on one written by Christoph Friedrich Bretzner, which had been set to music by Johann André and performed two months previously in Berlin as *Belmonte und Constanze, oder Die Entführung aus dem Serail*. It was Stephanie's hope that Mozart's new opera could be performed later in the year as part of the celebrations connected with the visit to Vienna of the Grand Duke Paul of Russia (the future Tsar Paul I) and his consort, Maria Feodorovna. However, two operas by Gluck were staged instead, and the premiere of Mozart's opera was postponed until July of the following year.

From the beginning, *Die Entführung aus dem Serail* proved a huge success. After the third performance, a delighted Mozart wrote to his father: 'People are absolutely crazy about this opera. It does one good to hear such applause.' By the end of the month he had arranged a suite of music from *Die Entführung* for wind instruments, 'for if I don't, someone will anticipate me and secure the profits'. When Mozart lunched with Gluck, the elderly composer expressed his admiration for the opera.

Within five years of its Vienna premiere *Die Entführung* had been performed in twenty-five other European cities. Well known is the story of the Austrian Emperor Joseph II's equivocal comment on the work, 'Too beautiful for our ears, and an enormous number of notes, my dear Mozart.' To which, with the superb confidence of youth, Mozart replied, 'Only as many as are needed, Your Majesty.'

Act I. The forecourt of Pasha Selim's palace, on the Turkish coast. Belmonte, a young Spanish nobleman, has come in search of his beloved Constanze, who, together with her English maid Blonde and Belmonte's servant Pedrillo, has been captured by pirates and sold to Pasha Selim ('Hier soll ich dich denn sehen'). When the Pasha's surly overseer Osmin emerges from the palace to pick figs ('Wer ein Liebchen hat gefunden'), Belmonte asks for Pedrillo but is angrily chased away.

Pedrillo appears, exciting an outburst of fury from Osmin, his rival for the affections of Blonde ('Solche hergelauf'ne Laffen'). After Osmin has returned within the palace, Belmonte reappears. He and Pedrillo greet each other warmly, and Belmonte learns that the three captives are being treated with consideration by the Pasha, who is enamoured of Constanze ('O wie ängstlich'). Belmonte explains that he has a ship waiting in the harbour to bear them away, and the two men make plans to rescue the women from the palace that night. Meanwhile, Pedrillo promises to introduce Belmonte to the Pasha as a talented Italian architect, and thus gain him entrance to the palace.

Belmonte and Pedrillo retreat as, preceded by a chorus of janissaries singing his praises ('Singt dem grossen Bassa Lieder'), Pasha Selim arrives home from a journey, accompanied by Constanze. Selim tells Constanze that he could force her to love him, but would prefer her to come to him of her own free will. When Constanze replies that her heart belongs to the lover from whom she has been cruelly separated ('Ach, ich liebte!'), Selim gives her one more day to change her mind. Constanze enters the palace sadly, and Pedrillo takes the opportunity to present Belmonte to the Pasha, who agrees to test his ability the following day. After Selim has gone, Osmin, still suspicious of Belmonte, attempts to deny him entrance to the palace, but finally Belmonte and Pedrillo succeed in pushing their way past him.

Act II. The palace garden, on one side of which stands Osmin's kiosk. Osmin and Blonde emerge from the kiosk, quarrelling. He attempts to bully her into submission, whereupon Blonde reminds him that she is an English woman, born to be free ('Durch Zärtlichkeit und Smeicheln'). As Blonde chases Osmin away, Constanze enters the garden, lamenting her separation from Belmonte ('Traurigkeit ward mir zum Lose'). She is soon followed by Selim, who demands to know her decision. When she remains steadfast in her refusal, he reminds her that he could have her tortured, at which she utters her scornful defiance ('Martern aller Arten') and returns indoors.

Pedrillo informs Blonde of Belmonte's arrival and of the plan to rescue her and Constanze later that night. After expressing her delight ('Welche Wonne, welche Lust'), Blonde rushes away to give her mistress the joyful news. Pedrillo summons up his courage ('Frisch zum Kampfe!') and, when Osmin appears, proceeds to ply the overseer with wine until he falls into a drunken stupor ('Vivat Bacchus!').

Belmonte now enters and is joined by Constanze, Blonde and Pedrillo. After his first outburst of joy at seeing his beloved again ('Wenn der Freude Tränen fliessen'), Belmonte expresses his fear that Constanze may have responded to the Pasha's advances, and Pedrillo voices similar doubts about Blonde. The two women take this amiss, and the men are forced to apologize. However, amity is soon restored ('Ach Belmonte, ach mein Leben'), and the two pairs of lovers part, to await midnight and their escape.

Act III, scene i. The palace garden. Pedrillo and a sailor from Belmonte's ship enter stealthily to place two ladders against the palace wall. Belmonte sings of building his hopes on the power of love ('Ich baue ganz auf deine Stärke'), and Pedrillo sings a serenade ('Im Mohrenland') as a signal that all is ready. Constanze and Blonde duly appear at their respective windows and climb down their ladders. However, a black mute servant arouses Osmin, who calls the palace guard, and the four Westerners are captured. Osmin is exultant at the thought of the tortures to which he hopes to be allowed to subject them ('O, wie will ich triumphieren').

Act III, scene ii. A hall in the palace. The four captives are brought before Pasha Selim. Belmonte informs the Pasha that he is not an architect but a wealthy Spanish nobleman whose father will gladly pay any ransom demanded. He reveals his father's name, which unfortunately only increases the Pasha's fury, for Belmonte's father was responsible for driving Selim into exile, robbing him of all that he possessed. Selim withdraws to consider what punishment to inflict upon Belmonte and his companions, while Belmonte and Constanze contemplate their fate, each wishing to die for the other. But when Selim returns, he reveals himself to be a true son of the liberal enlightenment. Not wishing to emulate his despised enemy, Belmonte's father, he pardons the captives and allows them their freedom. The opera ends with the rejoicing of all but Osmin.

Die Entführung aus dem Serail is, after *Idomeneo*, musically the richest of the operas Mozart composed before *Le nozze di Figaro*. The score's ostensibly Turkish colouring is heard as early as the overture, with piccolo, triangle, cymbals, kettle-drums and bass drums very much in evidence in the forte passages, and this Turkish element returns throughout the opera, notably in the choruses and in Osmin's comic outbursts of rage. Belmonte's arias are ardently romantic, while Constanze's, composed for what Mozart described as 'the flexible throat of Mlle Cavalieri', call for a dramatic coloratura soprano of great range and agility.

Since *Die Entführung* is a *Singspiel*, or play with songs, its action is advanced not by unaccompanied recitative but by spoken dialogue. This is sometimes truncated in performance (and Belmonte's aria at the beginning of Act III is more often than not omitted), but it is preferable for this delightful and by no means overlong opera to be presented without cuts.

Recommended recording: Stanford Olsen (Belmonte), Uwe Peper (Pedrillo), Luba Orgonasava (Constanze), Cyndia Sieden (Blonde), Cornelius Hauptmann (Osmin), with the Monteverdi Choir and the English Baroque Soloists, conducted by John Eliot Gardiner. Archiv 435 857–2. A stylish cast, and highly expressive conducting from John Eliot Gardiner.

Le nozze di Figaro
(The Marriage of Figaro)
opera buffa in four acts (approximate length: 3 hours)

Count Almaviva   *baritone*
Countess Almaviva   *soprano*
Figaro, Count Almaviva's servant   *bass*
Susanna, Countess Almaviva's maid   *soprano*

Dr Bartolo   *bass*

Marcellina, his housekeeper   *soprano*

Cherubino, Count Almaviva's page   *mezzo-soprano*

Don Basilio, a music teacher   *tenor*

Don Curzio, a notary   *tenor*

Antonio, Count Almaviva's gardener   *bass*

Barbarina, Antonio's daughter   *soprano*

LIBRETTO BY LORENZO DA PONTE, BASED ON THE PLAY *LE MARIAGE DE FIGARO*, BY PIERRE-AUGUSTIN CARON DE BEAUMARCHAIS; TIME: THE MID-EIGHTEENTH CENTURY; PLACE: COUNT ALMAVIVA'S CASTLE AT AGUAS-FRESCAS, NEAR SEVILLE; FIRST PERFORMED AT THE BURGTHEATER, VIENNA, 1 MAY 1786

Mozart and Constanze Weber were married in St Stephen's Cathedral in Vienna in August 1782, less than three weeks after the premiere of *Die Entführung aus dem Serail*. The favourable reception of his opera, and of several instrumental compositions, led to Mozart's procuring a few pupils. But this source of income soon dried up, and the court appointment that he was always hoping for failed to materialize. It was at about this time that Mozart joined the Society of Freemasons, then a powerful underground organization that was implacably opposed to the Roman Catholic Church.

During the early years of his residence in Vienna, Mozart composed several of the most beautiful and individual of his piano concertos. He also became involved in two abortive projects to compose operas; but in the autumn of 1785 he received a commission to compose a one-act *Singspiel* to be performed at a reception given at the palace of Schoenbrunn by the Emperor Joseph II for distinguished foreign guests. *Der Schauspieldirektor* (The Impresario) was successfully staged at Schoenbrunn and, a few days later, at the Kärntnertortheater in Vienna.

Mozart had already met Lorenzo da Ponte, who had been appointed court poet, and Da Ponte had made it clear that he would be happy to write a libretto for the composer. In his *Memoirs*, written many years later, Da Ponte revealed that the idea to use *Le Mariage de Figaro* by Beaumarchais as the basis of an opera came from Mozart himself. 'I liked the suggestion very much', wrote Da Ponte,

> but a few days previously the Austrian Emperor had forbidden the company at the German-language theatre to perform that same comedy, which he thought was too licentious for a respectable audience. How then to propose

it to him as an opera? . . . I suggested that we write the libretto and the music secretly, and then await a favourable opportunity to show the result to the Directors of the Opera or to the Emperor himself . . . I set to work accordingly, and as fast as I wrote the words Mozart set them to music. In six weeks, everything was in order.

Da Ponte was writing his memoirs twenty years after the event, and his memory was obviously faulty, for the opera took much longer than six weeks to compose. Mozart was already at work on it in November 1785, and he put it aside briefly to write the musical numbers for *Der Schauspieldirektor* in the second half of January 1786. His own catalogue states that he finished *Le nozze di Figaro* on 29 April, which probably means only that he completed the overture at this late date, for the opera was given its premiere at the Burgtheater two days later, on 1 May 1786.

The performance, which Mozart directed from the harpsichord, was received with great enthusiasm, and many numbers had to be encored. On the third night there were seven encores, and one duet had to be sung three times. The day after the third performance the Emperor issued an edict forbidding encores of anything except solo arias, ostensibly to curb the excessive length of opera performances, though it was widely believed that he was persuaded to take this action by persons who were envious of the huge success of Mozart's opera. This success, however, was to be eclipsed later in the year by that of Martín y Soler's opera *Una cosa rara* (A Rare Thing), which upon its production in November 1786 was so widely acclaimed that *Figaro* was immediately forgotten. There were to be no more performances of Mozart's opera in Vienna for the next two years; but it was soon being staged elsewhere, not only in its original Italian version but also in German and in several other languages.

The first play by the French playwright Pierre-Augustin Caron de Beaumarchais (1732–99) to feature the characters encountered in Mozart's opera was *Le Barbier de Séville* (1775), on which Paisiello based his *Il barbiere di Siviglia* of 1782 and Rossini his opera of the same title in 1816. The second play in what one might call Beaumarchais' Almaviva trilogy was *Le Mariage de Figaro*, which followed in 1784, taking up the story of Count Almaviva, Rosina (now his Countess), Figaro and the other characters. The third play, *La Mère coupable* (The Guilty Mother), first performed in 1797, shows the Countess twenty years later on in life.

To read Da Ponte's libretto for Mozart's opera alongside Beaumarchais' play *Le Mariage de Figaro* is to realize that the librettist was forced to emasculate the play in order to reduce it to a manageable length for setting to music. This was to be expected. Nor is it surprising that passages of revolutionary sentiment which would have offended the Austrian Emperor were expunged. Clearly, Da Ponte's *Figaro*, lacking much of Beaumarchais' detail of plot, his social and legal satire, and even some of his characters, is a less complex work than the French play. It is also more tightly knit, and less rambling. The action of the opera is contained, like that of the play, within one day, the 'folle journée' or crazy day of the play's subtitle.

Act I. A partly furnished room in Count Almaviva's castle. It is morning on the wedding day of Figaro, the Count's manservant, and Susanna, the Countess's maid. Figaro is busy taking the measurements of the bedroom that the Count has assigned to them, while Susanna is trying on a new hat ('Cinque, dieci'). Figaro is pleased with their apartment, but Susanna finds it suspicious that the Count should have given them a room so close to his own, for she is aware that he would dearly love to seduce her ('Se a caso madama la notte ti chiama'). Left alone, Figaro voices his determination not to allow his master to outwit him ('Se vuol ballare, signor contino'). He departs, and Dr Bartolo enters with his housekeeper Marcellina. Bartolo is keen to prevent Figaro's marriage ('La vendetta'), for it was Figaro who (in *Le Barbier de Seville*) helped Almaviva to abduct and marry Rosina, Bartolo's ward, thus preventing Bartolo himself from marrying her for her considerable dowry. Marcellina, though she is clearly old enough to be his mother, has designs on Figaro. She loaned him some money, but made him sign a document promising to marry her if he could not repay the loan. She has now come to claim her pound, or more, of flesh.

The Count's adolescent page Cherubino confesses to Susanna that he is in love with all women ('Non so più cosa son, cosa faccio'), but most of all with the Countess. Hearing his master approach, Cherubino hides behind an armchair. The Count enters and begins to flirt with Susanna, but on hearing the voice of the music master Don Basilio outside the room, he hides behind the same chair, as Cherubino stealthily creeps around onto the chair and is covered with a rug by Susanna. Basilio enters and begins to gossip with Susanna about Cherubino, who, he says, is enamoured of both the Countess and Susanna. This brings the Count angrily from his hiding place ('Cosa sento!') to describe how he recently discovered Cherubino with Barbarina, the gardener's daughter. By accident, the Count now discovers his young page again, crouching in the armchair. He is about to send Basilio to fetch Figaro, but thinks better of it when Cherubino reminds his master that he has overheard his conversation with Susanna.

Figaro now returns with a group of the Count's villagers, who sing their master's praises for having abolished the infamous *droit de seigneur* by which a nobleman was entitled to enjoy the favours of any female on his estate before her wedding night. When Figaro asks the Count to perform the wedding ceremony for Susanna and himself, the Count replies that he needs more time to organize a fitting celebration. He gets rid of Cherubino (as he thinks) by making him an officer in his regiment, which he orders the page to join immediately in Seville. Whispering to Cherubino that they must speak before he departs, Figaro proceeds publicly to warn the youth of the rigours of military life ('Non più andrai').

Act II. The Countess's boudoir, that afternoon. The Countess laments that she has lost her husband's love ('Porgi amor'). Figaro reports that the Count, thwarted in his designs on Susanna, is now threatening to marry him off to Marcellina. A plan is concocted by Figaro: he will send the Count a letter supposedly from Susanna, making an assignation in the garden that evening. The assignation will be kept by Cherubino dressed as a woman, and at an appropriate moment the Countess will discover them. Figaro leaves to send Cherubino to the Countess and Susanna for his costume fitting. When the page arrives, he sings to the Countess the new song he has written ('Voi che sapete'), and then he is dressed in women's clothes by Susanna. Noticing that Cherubino has scratched his arm and bandaged it with one of her ribbons, the Countess sends Susanna to fetch sticking plaster. While Susanna is out of the room Cherubino attempts to confess his love for the Countess, but he is interrupted by the voice of the Count outside the door.

The Countess hides Cherubino in her dressing-room before admitting the Count, who, having heard their voices, asks who was with her. The noise of Cherubino upsetting a chair in the dressing-room convinces him that the Countess is hiding a lover. When she refuses to tell him who it is, he compels her to accompany him in a search for tools to break down the door. In their absence, Susanna contrives to take Cherubino's place in the dressing-room while the page, now in his officer's uniform, leaps from the window into the garden and runs off.

The Count, on his return, is about to prise the dressing-room door open when, to his surprise, and indeed that of the Countess, Susanna emerges from the room. The Count asks to be forgiven for his suspicions. He is perplexed, however, by the letter he has received, and the women are obliged to confess that the letter was, in fact, written by Figaro. Figaro enters to announce that all is now ready for his wedding ceremony, and when he is questioned by the Count he denies all knowledge of the letter. The situation is further complicated by the arrival of Antonio the gardener, rather the worse for drink, complaining of the damage done to his garden by the man who jumped from the window. Figaro claims that it was he, and prompted by the Countess and Susanna he is fortunately able to identify the document – Cherubino's army commission – that fell out of the pocket of who-ever jumped, and which was retrieved by Antonio. Marcellina, Bartolo and Basilio now arrive, and the matter of Figaro's indebtedness to Marcellina is raised. The Count agrees to preside over an enquiry later in the day, to the despair of Figaro, Susanna and the Countess.

Act III. A grand hall in the castle, early that evening. Susanna, prompted by the Countess, persuades the Count that she returns his love and that she will meet him later that evening in the garden ('Crudel! Perchè finora'). However, as she is leaving the room, the Count overhears her whisper to Figaro that they have won their case. Realizing that he has been tricked again, he bursts into a jealous rage ('Vedrò mentr'io sospiro').

The opposing parties now assemble for the hearing the Count has promised them, and the notary Don Curzio gives it as his opinion that Figaro is bound by the terms of his agreement either to pay Marcellina immediately or to marry her. Figaro asserts that he cannot marry without the consent of his parents, for he is well-born, and was stolen as a child by gypsies. He displays a birthmark on his arm, at which Marcellina identifies him as her long-lost son, Raffaele, and informs him that Bartolo is his father. When Susanna enters with money to pay off Marcellina, she is disconcerted to find her bridegroom embracing that lady, but the situation is soon made clear to her ('Riconosci in questo amplesso').

When all have left, the Countess enters, again lamenting that she has lost her husband's love, and sadly recalling her earlier happiness ('Dove sono i bei momenti?'). She dictates to Susanna a letter to the Count confirming the assigna-tion that Susanna made with him for later that evening ('Che soave zeffiretto'), and they seal the letter with a pin which is to be returned as a token that the mes-sage has been received. The village maidens now enter, singing a chorus in praise of the Countess, and the wedding celebrations commence, despite the fact that Cherubino, who has joined the girls en travesti, is unmasked by the Count, from whom he was attempting to hide. During the ceremony, Susanna surreptitiously hands the Count the letter that she and the Countess have written.

Act IV. The garden, with various pavilions, later that night. Barbarina searches for the pin that she has been told by the Count to return to Susanna ('L'ho per-duta'). She inadvertently reveals this to Figaro and Marcellina, and Figaro, think-ing that his bride is already about to deceive him, rails against all women ('Aprite un po' quegli occhi'). Susanna, disguised as the Countess, arrives in the garden and sings of her amorous longing ('Deh vieni, non tardar'). Various games of mistaken identity are now played out in the darkness of the garden. Cherubino flirts with the Countess under the impression that she is Susanna; the Count attempts to seduce his own wife, whom he assumes to be Susanna; Figaro mistakes Susanna for the Countess, and so the Count thinks he has discovered Figaro and the Countess together. Imitating the Countess's voice, Susanna asks for forgiveness, which the Count refuses. The Countess now appears in her disguise as Susanna, and reveals her identity. The Count realizes that it is he who must seek forgiveness from her. He kneels before her to ask her pardon, and the Countess generously gives it. The opera ends with all agreeing that the problems thrown up by this day of torments, caprice and folly can be resolved only by the healing power of true love.

Those writers on Mozart who bemoan the loss in *Le nozze di Figaro* of the revolutionary wind which blows through Beaumarchais' play are as misguided as those who proclaim, on the other hand, that Mozart's opera itself is, in a political sense, revolutionary. Not even revolutionary in musical–dramatic terms, it is rather a logical development from earlier eighteenth-century opera. What is more to the point is that it is a work of genius. Da Ponte's elegantly witty libretto inspired the thirty-year-old Mozart to compose an opera which is still today one of the best-loved in the entire operatic repertoire. The characters of the quick-witted Figaro, the wise and loving Susanna, the formidable Count and the unhappy Countess spring to glorious life in their music. Just as the genre of *opera seria* had been raised by Mozart to new heights in *Idomeneo*, so too was the Italian comic opera formula transcended in *Le nozze di Figaro*.

Lacking the customary middle section in a slower tempo, the opera's gaily bustling overture gives the audience a foretaste of the work's lively pace. Some of the solo arias are, of course, intended to express character rather than to advance action, but the many duets and ensembles move the plot along confidently, while contriving to present themselves as highly mellifluous musical entities. In his notes on the characters in his play, Beaumarchais says of the Count's page that 'the basis of his character is an undefined and restless desire. He is entering on adolescence all unheeding and with no understanding of what is happening to him, and throws himself eagerly into everything that comes along.' In the restless and excited movement of the violins in Cherubino's 'Non so più cosa son, cosa faccio', Mozart has caught this characteristic to perfection, and the effervescent sexuality of the page's song underlines its text with wit and tact.

The Countess's two great arias 'Porgi amor' and 'Dove sono i bei momenti?' are full of a tender regret. The twenty-minute-long finale to Act II, the most extended musical number in the opera, is often and rightly pointed to as a perfect example of the marriage of music and drama. So, too, is the magnificent sextet in Act III, in which the differing thoughts and emotions of the characters involved are simultaneously portrayed, their differences being used to motivate the contrasts of rhythm and tempo in the music. At the same time, the action is significantly advanced, but always on the wings of Mozart's seemingly spontaneous melody.

With the exception of two arias that Mozart was obliged to provide for his Basilio and Marcellina at the beginning of Act IV (and which are, in any case, frequently omitted), there is not a dull moment in the entire score of *Le nozze di Figaro*, an opera whose rich humanity, delightful humour and mature wisdom are unlikely ever to appear stale, except when the work is staged by a director who prefers to replace the concept of Mozart and Da Ponte with one of his own.

Recommended recording: Lisa della Casa (Countess), Hilde Gueden (Susanna), Suzanne Danco (Cherubino), Cesare Siepi (Figaro), Alfed Poell (Count), with the Vienna State Opera Chorus and the Vienna Philharmonic Orchestra, conducted by Erich Kleiber. Decca 417 315–2. There are several first-rate recordings, some with period instruments, but this famous Kleiber performance from Vienna in the 1950s is hard to beat, with its stylish singers and the incomparable Vienna Philharmonic Orchestra.

Don Giovanni
(Don Juan)
dramma giocoso in two acts (approximate length: 2 hours, 45 minutes)

Don Giovanni (Don Juan), an extremely licentious young nobleman   *baritone*
Il Commendatore   *bass*
Donna Anna, his daughter   *soprano*
Don Ottavio, her betrothed   *tenor*
Donna Elvira, a noblewoman from Burgos   *soprano*
Leporello, Don Giovanni's servant   *bass*
Masetto, a peasant   *bass*
Zerlina, a peasant girl betrothed to Masetto   *soprano*

LIBRETTO BY LORENZO DA PONTE; TIME: THE MID-SEVENTEENTH CENTURY; PLACE: SEVILLE; FIRST PERFORMED AT THE NATIONAL THEATRE, PRAGUE, 29 OCTOBER 1787

*L*e nozze di Figaro, the first of the three operas Mozart was to complete in collaboration with Lorenzo da Ponte, had been given its premiere in Vienna in

May 1786. In December it was staged in Prague. Told of its great success there, Mozart travelled to Prague in January 1787 and attended one performance of his opera and conducted another. He also gave a pianoforte recital in the National Theatre, where both his music and his playing roused the audience to a frenzy of enthusiasm. When, shortly before his return to Vienna in the middle of February, he was asked to compose an opera for Prague, he immediately agreed. Back in Vienna he consulted Da Ponte and they agreed upon Don Juan as a subject.

Mozart's father died in Salzburg in May. An illness of his own prevented Wolfgang from being with his father at the end, and poverty forced him and his wife, Constanze, to move lodgings from the centre of Vienna to the suburb of Landstrasse. A few days after his father's death, Mozart's pet starling died. Throughout these emotional upsets he worked steadily on his Don Juan opera, *Don Giovanni*, completing it by the end of the summer. At the beginning of October, he and Constanze journeyed to Prague to prepare for rehearsals of the new opera.

The premiere of *Don Giovanni* had originally been planned for 14 October, to celebrate the marriage of the Archduchess Maria Theresia, the Emperor's niece, to Prince Anton Clemens of Saxony. However, the opera was not ready for public performance by that date, so the royal couple were entertained instead with *Le nozze di Figaro*. The first performance of *Il dissoluto punito, o sia Il Don Giovanni* (The Rake Punished, or Don Juan), to give the work its formal title, was conducted by its composer on 29 October at Prague's National Theatre, which is still in use today as the Tyl Theatre. There are several stories told of Mozart's last-minute composition of the opera's overture, the least improbable of which is Constanze's. According to her, Mozart wrote the overture the night before the first performance while she plied him with punch, which made him drowsy, and stories, which woke him up again. By seven the next morning the overture was finished just as the copyist arrived to collect it.

Don Giovanni was received by its first audiences with wild enthusiasm. Five days after the premiere a Prague newspaper published an inadequate and somewhat eccentric notice of the event:

> On Monday October the 29th, the Italian opera company gave the ardently awaited opera by Maestro Mozard [sic], *Don Giovanni* or *The Stone Guest*. Connoisseurs and musicians say that Prague has never yet heard the like. Herr Mozard conducted in person. When he entered the orchestra pit, he was received with threefold cheers, which again happened when he left it. The opera is, moreover, extremely difficult to perform, and everyone admired the fine performance given in spite of this, after such a short period of rehearsal.

Everybody on the stage and in the orchestra strained each nerve to thank Mozard by rewarding him with a good performance. There were also heavy additional costs, caused by several choruses and changes of scenery, all of which Herr Guardasoni [the stage manager] had brilliantly attended to. The unusually large attendance testifies to a unanimous approbation.

Mozart and Constanze remained in Prague for two weeks after the premiere, returning home in mid-November. It was several months before *Don Giovanni* was staged in Vienna, with certain changes and additions (detailed below). The opera did not at first repeat its Prague success, and the Emperor told Da Ponte, 'It is not meat for the teeth of my Viennese.' When his librettist repeated the Emperor's comment to Mozart, the composer replied quietly, 'Give them time to chew on it.' He was right, for in due course the Viennese came to appreciate *Don Giovanni* as greatly as the citizens of Prague had done, and the rest of the civilized world followed suit.

The Don Juan story had been used by dramatists for more than a century and a half before Mozart's librettist came to it. The old legend of the compulsive seducer who is finally dragged down to hell seems to have first made its way onto the stage with *El burlador de Seville*, a comedy by the Spanish monk Gabriel Tellez (1571–1648), who wrote under the pseudonym of Tirso de Molina. His play, which had already become popular in performance by the time of its publication in Barcelona in 1630, served as the basis of other Don Juan plays by Molière (*Don Juan*, 1665), Thomas Shadwell (*The Libertine*, 1676) and Carlo Goldoni (*Don Giovanni tenorio*, 1736), as well as by several lesser-known Italian, French and German playwrights. From the spoken theatre the story found its way into ballet and opera. Mozart was aware of Gluck's ballet *Don Juan*, based on Molière and first staged at the Kärntnertortheater in Vienna in 1761; and Da Ponte certainly knew the one-act opera *Don Giovanni, o sia Il convitato di pietra* (Don Juan, or The Stone Guest), by Giuseppe Gazzaniga, performed in Venice on 5 February 1787, for he drew upon its libretto by Giovanni Bertati in writing his own libretto for Mozart.

The Don Juan legend continued to be used in drama and literature after Mozart and Da Ponte. Byron's unfinished *Don Juan* (1819–1824), written in order to 'strip the tinsel off sentiment', is one of the greatest poems in the English language, and there are Don Juan stories and plays by Prosper Merimée, Alexandre Dumas *père*, Alfred de Musset, Honoré de Balzac, Gustave Flaubert and Alexander Pushkin. There is a 'Don Juan in Hell' scene in George Bernard Shaw's *Man and Superman*, and a musical tone poem, *Don Juan*, by Richard Strauss.

Act I, scene i. The garden of the Commendatore's house in Seville, just before dawn. Leporello waits, grumbling ('Notte e giorno faticar'), outside the house that his master, Don Giovanni, has entered in order to seduce the Commendatore's daughter, Donna Anna. Suddenly Giovanni, his identity concealed by a mask, rushes out of the house pursued by a furious Donna Anna, who calls for help. The Commendatore arrives and is killed by Giovanni, who escapes with Leporello. Anna summons her betrothed, Don Ottavio, and demands vengeance ('Fuggi, crudele, fuggi').

Act I, scene ii. A street, early next morning. Giovanni accosts a woman who turns out to be Donna Elvira, one of his past conquests, whom he had abandoned in another town and who has come in search of him ('Ah, chi mi dice mai'). Giovanni leaves Leporello to tell her of the many other women he has seduced ('Madamina, il catalogo è questo'): 640 in Italy, 231 in Germany, 100 in France, a mere 91 in Turkey, but 1003 in Spain, amounting to a grand total of 2065.

Act I, scene iii. The open country, near Don Giovanni's house. Encountering a peasant wedding party, Giovanni instructs Leporello to invite everyone, including the bridegroom, Masetto, to a banquet at his house. He himself stays behind to seduce the bride, Zerlina ('Là ci darem la mano'). She is about to succumb when Elvira intervenes to rescue her ('Ah, fuggi il traditor'). Elvira also attempts to warn Anna and Ottavio of Giovanni's true character ('Non ti fidar, o misera'), while Giovanni tries to persuade them that Elvira is mad. As Giovanni takes his leave, Anna suddenly realizes that it was he who had attempted to rape her the previous night ('Or sai chi l'onore'). She implores Ottavio to avenge her father's death. (At this point in the Vienna version of the score, Ottavio sings 'Dalla sua pace', an expression of his love for Anna.) Giovanni returns when the others have departed, and he gives Leporello instructions for the banquet ('Finch'han dal vino').

Act I, scene iv. The garden of Don Giovanni's country house. Zerlina mollifies Masetto when he reproaches her for having allowed a nobleman to flirt with her ('Batti, batti, o bel Masetto'). She becomes confused when Giovanni appears, but she and Masetto accept his invitation to attend the banquet. As they enter the house, Anna, Ottavio and Elvira arrive, masked. They, too, are invited to join the party.

Act I, scene v. The ballroom of Giovanni's house. While the peasants are dancing, eating and drinking, Giovanni entices Zerlina into another room. When she screams for help, Giovanni tries to blame Leporello, but the three masked guests identify themselves and tell Giovanni that the world will now learn of his villainy.

Act II, scene i. A street near an inn, late in the afternoon. Leporello is tired of the life he is leading with Don Giovanni ('Eh via, buffone'), but a bribe persuades him to continue in his master's service, and even to exchange clothes with him and entice Elvira away from the inn in which she is staying, so that Giovanni, dressed as Leporello, can seduce Elvira's maid. Giovanni serenades the maid ('Deh, vieni alla finestra') but is interrupted by the arrival of a gang of peasants headed by Masetto, bent on finding and killing him. Giovanni, still disguised as Leporello, separates Masetto from the others and gives him a severe thrashing. Zerlina finds Masetto and comforts him ('Vedrai, carino').

Act II, scene ii. A courtyard in front of Donna Anna's house. The disguised Leporello attempts to flee from Elvira, but is cornered by Anna, Ottavio, Zerlina and Masetto. Revealing his identity, he manages to escape from them. Ottavio asks the others to look after Donna Anna while he alerts the police ('Il mio tesoro'). (In the Vienna version, Zerlina returns, dragging Leporello with her. She ties him up and threatens him in a duet scene, 'Per queste tue manine', and Elvira expresses her mixed emotions concerning Giovanni in an aria, 'Mi tradi quell'alma ingrata'.)

Act II, scene iii. A cemetery, at night. Giovanni has climbed the cemetery wall to escape his pursuers. As he boasts to Leporello of having attempted to seduce his servant's fiancée, a mysterious voice declares that his laughter will have ceased by dawn. The voice seems to have come from a statue of the Commendatore, which bears an inscription to the effect that he awaits vengeance. Giovanni orders a terrified Leporello to invite the statue to supper ('O statua gentilissima').

Act II, scene iv. A room in Donna Anna's house. Anna and Ottavio declare their love for each other, but she asks him to delay their marriage for a year, to enable her to recover from the death of her father ('Non mi dir').

Act II, scene v. The banquet hall in Giovanni's villa. The table is laid for supper, and musicians are playing. Giovanni is eating alone, served by Leporello, when Elvira rushes in, begging Giovanni to change his ways. He answers her scornfully, and as she runs out she is heard to scream. Leporello goes to investigate, and he too screams, for the statue of the Commendatore has accepted Giovanni's invitation and has arrived for supper. The statue calls on Giovanni to repent. When he refuses, the statue disappears, flames appear on all sides, and a chorus of demons drags the still defiant sinner down to hell. After Giovanni's disappearance, everything returns to normal, and the other characters enter, accompanied by a minister of justice, to inform the audience that in this life scoundrels eventually receive their just desserts.

Even more so than with his other two operas composed to libretti by Da Ponte, Mozart is primarily responsible for the stature of the completed work. Da Ponte's

Le nozze di Figaro and *Così fan tutte* are amusing and well planned, but his libretto for *Don Giovanni* is more primitively structured and less successful in bringing the characters to life on the printed page. This latter failing is obscured by Mozart's glorious music, which most emphatically does give life to Da Ponte's characters, even the colourless Don Ottavio. It may be that Da Ponte would have done better to cast himself adrift more boldly from Bertati's libretto for Gazzaniga's opera, for in the process of expanding a one-act libretto into two acts he seems merely to have duplicated in Act II the sequence of events, or at least the sequence of emotions, of Act I. When studied carefully, Da Ponte's libretto is revealed to be full of padding. Fortunately, some of his padding inspired Mozart to his greatest heights.

For the first Vienna performances of the opera, some months after its premiere in Prague, some changes were made. Ottavio's Act II aria, the virile 'Il mio tesoro', proved too difficult for the Viennese tenor, and so Mozart deleted it and inserted a new aria in Act I for Ottavio, 'Dalla sua pace', a tender expression of love. In Act II, 'Il mio tesoro' was replaced by a comic duet for Zerlina and Leporello, 'Per queste tue manine', while, at the insistence of the Viennese soprano who was singing the role, Donna Elvira was given a second aria, 'Mi tradì quell'alma ingrata'. Most stagings today add to the Prague score the new arias, but omit the Zerlina–Leporello duet.

The opera's score is rich both in musical beauty and in characterization. The Act I quartet, 'Non ti fidar, o misera', is a splendid example of this, but indeed Mozart's genius for musical characterization is seen at its finest throughout *Don Giovanni*. To have distinguished between the musical styles of soubrette (Zerlina) and leading lady (Donna Anna) may not have been difficult, but to create two characters (Anna and Elvira) totally different from each other while using the same style of utterance is another matter. Mozart achieves this with apparent ease. Underlying the Commendatore's *post mortem* utterance in the cemetery scene of Act II one hears the deeply solemn timbre of three trombones, an instrument not heard earlier in the opera. When the statue accepts Giovanni's invitation, the orchestral accompaniment to the latter's observation about the strangeness of the scene ('bizarra e inver la scena') sounds like a curious anticipation of nineteenth-century Romanticism.

Some commentators have attempted to prove that despite his categorizing *Don Giovanni* as a humorous work (*dramma giocoso*) Mozart's intention was to write a tragic opera. Others have tried to explain away the more sombre aspects of the work, such as Giovanni being dragged screaming to hell, and to prove that it is a delightful comedy. But *Don Giovanni* deals with the whole of life. It is not only a highly enjoyable, dramatic and prodigiously tuneful opera but also one of the world's great music dramas.

Recommended recording: Joan Sutherland (Donna Anna), Elisabeth Schwarz-kopf (Donna Elvira), Graziella Sciutti (Zerlina), Luigi Alva (Don Ottavio), Eberhard Waechter (Don Giovanni), Giuseppe Taddei (Leporello), Piero Cappuccilli (Masetto), Gottlob Frick (Commendatore), with the Philharmonia Chorus and Orchestra conducted by Carlo Maria Giulini. EMI CDS7 47260–8. This recording is about forty years old, but the cast is virtually ideal both vocally and dramatically, with Waechter an exciting Giovanni. Giulini never lets the pace sag, and secures styl-ish playing from the orchestra.

Così fan tutte
(All Women Are Like This)
opera buffa in two acts (approximate length: 3 hours)

Fiordiligi   *soprano* ⎤ sisters from Ferrara
Dorabella   *soprano* ⎦ living in Naples
Ferrando, Dorabella's betrothed   *tenor*
Guglielmo, Fiordiligi's betrothed   *baritone*
Despina, the sisters' servant   *soprano*
Don Alfonso, an elderly philosopher   *bass*

LIBRETTO BY LORENZO DA PONTE; TIME: THE LATE EIGHTEENTH CENTURY; PLACE: NAPLES; FIRST PERFORMED AT THE BURGTHEATER, VIENNA, 26 JANUARY 1790

The last of the three operas that Mozart wrote with Lorenzo da Ponte as his librettist, *Così fan tutte* for many years trailed in popularity behind the other two, *Le nozze di Figaro* and *Don Giovanni*. However, in the second half of the twen-tieth century it began to be recognized as the wise and witty comedy that it is.

The successful revival of *Le nozze di Figaro* at the Vienna Burgtheater in the summer of 1789 was probably what led the Emperor Joseph II to commission a new opera from Mozart. Da Ponte was again called upon to provide a libretto, and this time instead of adapting someone else's play he produced an original work, which may well have been based upon a real incident that is said to have amused Viennese society not long before Da Ponte and Mozart embarked upon their opera. Perhaps there is a clue offered in the fact that Da Ponte's libretto concerns two sisters from Ferrara who are seduced into infidelity by their disguised lovers, and that the roles of the women were performed at the opera's premiere by singers who were widely, though erroneously, thought to be sisters from Ferrara, one of whom, Adriana Ferrarese del Bene, was known to be Da Ponte's mistress.

Mozart must have given his agreement for 'La Ferrarese' to sing the role of Fiordiligi, although he did not think highly of her as a singer: 'The leading woman here, Madame Allegranti,' he had written to his wife, Constanze, from Dresden earlier in the year, 'is far better than Madame Ferrarese, which, I admit, is not saying much.' The singer of Fiordiligi's sister Dorabella at the premiere was Louise Villeneuve, who was apparently not the real-life sister of La Ferrarese.

Mozart worked on *Così fan tutte* throughout the autumn and early winter of 1789, during which time Constanze gave birth to a girl, their fifth child, who died only an hour after her birth. On New Year's Eve the opera was sufficiently advanced for Mozart to hold a brief rehearsal at home, to which he invited one of his Masonic friends, Michael Puchberg, and the composer Haydn. The first rehearsal with orchestra took place on 21 January 1790 at the Burgtheater. Again Haydn and Puchberg were invited, and Mozart seized the opportunity to borrow money from Puchberg, not for the first time.

Così fan tutte was given its premiere in Vienna at the Burgtheater on 26 January, with the composer conducting from the keyboard. The theatre's poster described the new work as a comic *Singspiel* in two acts, and gave it a subtitle, *La scuola degli amanti* (The School for Lovers). 'The poetry', it announced, 'is by Herr Abbé da Ponte, Poet to the Italian Singspiel at the Imperial and Royal Court Theatre. The music is by Herr Wolfgang Mozart, Kapellmeister in the actual service of His Majesty the Emperor.'

The opera was enthusiastically received, even by a certain Count Zinzendorf, an eighteenth-century Viennese equivalent of Samuel Pepys, whose diary entries on the subject of Mozart's works are usually not very complimentary. This time, however, Zinzendorf wrote: 'The music by Mozart is charming, and the subject rather amusing.' According to a letter that Mozart wrote to Michael Puchberg, he received for his opera the sum of 200 ducats, twice the fee that he was usually given. (To try to estimate the current equivalent of this sum would only be confusing. Two hundred ducats was also the approximate amount of Mozart's annual salary as imperial Kapellmeister.)

Ten performances of *Così fan tutte* were given between January and August 1790, and no doubt there would have been more had the court not gone into mourning for the Emperor, who died a month after the premiere, to be succeeded by his brother Leopold. The opera vanished from the stage for the remainder of Mozart's short lifetime and, following its initial performances, which were in Da Ponte's Italian, was heard in Vienna after its composer's death only in German translation, as *So machen sie's*, until 1850, when it was given again in Italian at the Kärntnertortheater.

That the subject of the piece is 'rather amusing' was by no means universally agreed. Friedrich Ludwig Schröder, a famous German actor of the time, after reading its libretto referred to the new *Singspiel* as 'a wretched thing, which demeans all women, cannot possibly please female spectators, and will therefore not make its fortune'. When he attended a performance of the work in Frankfurt, Schröder exclaimed, 'Miserable! Even of Mozart's music only the second act pleases me.'

Wagner not only thought *Così fan tutte* a poor work but also wrote that he considered its libretto shamefully immoral. Most nineteenth-century performances of the opera were adaptations that bowdlerized Da Ponte's witty libretto. In fact, the general view of *Così fan tutte* in the nineteenth century seems to have been that it was a disappointingly frivolous, if not downright improper, work. This is an opinion that can still be encountered today, though only rarely. Lorenzo da Ponte makes virtually no mention of the opera in his *Memoirs*. In one half-sentence he refers to it by its subtitle as 'an opera that holds third place among the three sisters born of that most celebrated father of harmony'. He mentions the work only because he had written one of its leading roles for his mistress, though he curiously omits to mention her name.

The libretto is theoretically an original work, but it has recently been discovered that, just as he did for *Don Giovanni*, Da Ponte may have plundered the Spanish playwright Tirso de Molina, for at least one or two details of the plot of *Così fan tutte* owe something to incidents in two plays by him: *El amor medico* and *La celosa de si misma*. The similarity of Da Ponte's plot to a story in Ariosto's *Orlando furioso* has also been commented upon, and it has further been suggested that an earlier derivation may have been the tale of Cephalus and Procris in Ovid's *Metamorphoses*. Perhaps it is true that there is nothing new under the sun. In any case, before the nineteenth century no one expected plots to be entirely new. Whether completely original or not, Da Ponte's libretto is neat and highly amusing. Only those who approach it expecting a profound dissertation on the nature of love and fidelity are likely to find it disappointing.

Act I, scene i. A cafe in Naples. Two young officers, Ferrando and Guglielmo, boast to their friend Don Alfonso, an elderly philosopher, of the beauty and fidelity of Dorabella and Fiordiligi, the two sisters to whom they are betrothed. The cynical Alfonso offers to make a wager with them that given the opportunity the sisters will behave like any other women and take new lovers. Confident that they will win, the romantic young officers accept his wager and agree to follow his instructions.

Act I, scene ii. The garden of the sisters' villa, by the sea. Gazing fondly at miniature portraits of their lovers, the two sisters pour out their feelings ('Ah, guarda, sorella'). Alfonso enters, announcing that the two young men are coming to say farewell, having been called to rejoin their regiment. He is followed by Ferrando and Guglielmo, who solemnly take their leave of the sisters ('Sento, o Dio'). When the men have departed, Alfonso finds himself joining the two women in a prayer for their lovers' safety ('Soave sia il vento').

Act I, scene iii. A room in the villa. Despina, their maid, tries to console Fiordiligi and Dorabella ('In uomini, in soldati'), and Alfonso enlists her aid in the plot about to be enacted. Despina agrees to help him introduce two strangers, friends of his, into the house. The two young officers now reappear disguised as Albanians, and they proceed to make ardent declarations of love to the sisters, Ferrando choosing his friend Guglielmo's fiancée Fiordiligi, and Guglielmo addressing himself to Dorabella. The sisters consider themselves insulted, Fiordiligi sings of her rock-like constancy ('Come scoglio') and they both flounce out of the room, to the delight of the officers, who are nevertheless obliged to continue the masquerade for the full twenty-four hours stipulated by Alfonso. Guglielmo now begins to look forward to his lunch, but Ferrando sings of the greater refreshment offered by the aura of love that surrounds their two dear treasures ('Un' aura amorosa').

Act I, scene iv. The garden. As the sisters are lamenting the absence of their lovers, the two Albanians come rushing into the garden, apparently desperate with love, each holding a small bottle whose contents they proceed to swallow. They collapse, and Alfonso explains that they have taken poison and in a few minutes will be dead. Despina is sent to fetch a doctor, and the sisters are moved by feelings of tenderness for the poor misguided Albanians. When Despina returns disguised as a doctor, reviving the two men with the aid of a magnet, the Albanians immediately resume their ardent declarations of love, to the consternation of the sisters.

Act II, scene i. A room in the villa. Encouraged by Despina ('Una donna a quindici anni'), the sisters are persuaded that there can be no harm in light flirtation. They agree to meet the Albanians that evening in the garden, Dorabella admitting that she finds the little dark one quite amusing, and Fiordiligi expressing her willingness to accept the compliments of the fair one ('Prenderò quel brunettino').

Act II, scene ii. The garden. When the couples are paired off, Guglielmo finds it not too difficult to win the heart of Dorabella ('Il core vi dono'), but Fiordiligi refuses to give in to Ferrando ('Per pietà, ben mio, perdona'). The men compare notes: a smug Guglielmo is delighted to learn that Fiordiligi has not yielded to his friend, but Ferrando is dismayed and enraged at Dorabella's betrayal. Guglielmo tries to console him with a cynical appraisal of all women ('Donne mie la fate a tanti').

Act II, scene iii. A room in the villa. In order to avoid further temptation Fiordiligi is about to dress herself as a soldier and go off to join her fiancé, but the disguised Ferrando enters, renewing his protestations of love ('Fra gli amplessi'). This time, she succumbs to him. Don Alfonso claims his victory and the two men prepare to be married to the wrong women.

Act II, scene iv. A room in the villa, with several doors leading from it. Before a notary, who is actually Despina in disguise, the two couples sign marriage contracts, but the ceremony is interrupted by the sound of a march signalling the return of the officers' regiment. The two Albanians are bundled into an adjoining room and very soon reappear through another door as their real selves. Pouncing on the marriage contracts, which have been dropped on the floor, they castigate the two sisters and rush into the next room to assassinate the Albanians, returning half-dressed in their Albanian disguises to the mortified astonishment of Fiordiligi and Dorabella, who attempt to place the blame on Don Alfonso. Ferrando and Guglielmo condescend to forgive the women, Alfonso advises all four of them to have a good laugh and consider themselves fortunate to be reunited, and the lovers now return to their original couplings. (Or at least they do in the opera as created by Mozart and Da Ponte. There have been modern productions in which they do not.)

Nowadays, although most people's favourite Mozart opera may still be *Don Giovanni* or *Le nozze di Figaro*, few would deny the stature of *Così fan tutte*. The English literary critic and editor Cyril Connolly once told me that, although he could admit its musical perfection, *Così fan tutte* was the one Mozart opera he could not endure, because it condoned the corruption of innocence. But it condones nothing of the kind, nor are Fiordiligi and Dorabella necessarily innocent. Although the earlier Mozart–Da Ponte operas may range more widely, Mozart's final collaboration with Da Ponte deals with human relationships sympathetically, though totally without sentimentality, and has a formal shapeliness denied to

Don Giovanni and *Le nozze di Figaro*. Is *Così fan tutte* as serious a comedy as *Figaro*? It certainly contains some of Mozart's most deeply moving music – for example the trio 'Soave sia il vento', its accompaniment of muted violins and soft wind chords suggesting the murmur of wind and waves. But much of the sisters' music in Act I satirizes the high passions of *opera seria*.

Perhaps this is an opera for the lover of music in general rather than of opera in particular, for the characters in the other Da Ponte operas are in many respects more interesting, and the action more complex. But the score of *Così fan tutte* is the equal of that of the earlier two operas, and in some moods it is difficult not to think it superior. Fiordiligi's two arias are among Mozart's finest creations, and the duets for the two sisters, as they contemplate being unfaithful to their lovers, are possessed of an irrepressible *joie de vivre*.

Recommended recording: Elisabeth Schwarzkopf (Fiordiligi), Christa Ludwig (Dorabella), Hanny Steffek (Despina), Alfredo Kraus (Ferrando), Giuseppe Taddei (Guglielmo), Walter Berry (Don Alfonso), with the Philharmonia Chorus and Orchestra conducted by Karl Böhm. EMI CMS 7 69330 2. Several excellent recordings are available, but none outclasses this version of over forty years ago. The sopranos Elisabeth Schwarzkopf and Christa Ludwig, who often sang Fiordiligi and Dorabella together on the stage in Vienna and Salzburg in the mid-twentieth century, made a delightful pair of sisters, singing beautifully and bringing their characters vividly to life. Steffek is a perfect Despina, and the three male roles are equally strongly cast. Kraus's silken tones make the most of Ferrando's music, Taddei is an ebullient, Italianate Guglielmo, and Berry is in his element as the cynical and manipulative Alfonso. Karl Böhm, one of the finest Mozart conductors of his day, chooses the right tempi and keeps the action moving naturally and spontaneously.

La clemenza di Tito
(The Clemency of Titus)
opera seria in two acts (approximate length: 2 hours, 15 minutes)

Tito (Titus) Vespasiano, Emperor of Rome   *tenor*
Vitellia, daughter of the deposed Emperor Vitellio   *soprano*
Sesto (Sextus), friend of Tito   *soprano*
Servilia, Sesto's sister   *soprano*
Annio, friend of Sesto   *soprano*
Publio, commander of the Praetorian Guard   *bass*

LIBRETTO BY PIETRO METASTASIO, REVISED BY CATERINO MAZZOLÀ; TIME: AD 80; PLACE: ROME; FIRST PERFORMED AT THE NATIONAL THEATRE, PRAGUE, 6 SEPTEMBER 1791

The story of Mozart's last years is one of increasing poverty and distress. When, some months after the premiere of *Così fan tutte* in 1790, an opportunity arose for him to go to England and compose two operas in London for a fee of £300, Mozart declined the offer. Da Ponte had already established himself in London, and it is fascinating to speculate on what the course of English opera in the nineteenth century might have been had Mozart survived and he and Da Ponte continued their operatic collaboration in London. But Mozart did not leave Vienna, nor did he survive. He composed two more operas in the few months that were left to him. Renewing his friendship with Emanuel Schikaneder, an actor–manager whom he had known in his Salzburg days, he began to write a sublime pantomime-opera, *Die Zauberflöte*, for Schikaneder's theatre in a Viennese suburb, turning aside from it temporarily to accept a commission from Prague to compose an *opera seria* for performance on the occasion of the Austrian Emperor Leopold II's coronation in Prague as King of Bohemia.

For this coronation opera a libretto by the famous Italian poet and dramatist Pietro Metastasio was chosen. Metastasio (1698–1782) had been court poet in Vienna earlier in the century, serving the Emperor Charles VI and later the Empress Maria Theresa. His libretto was originally written for Antonio Caldara's *La clemenza di Tito*, which was produced in Vienna in 1734, and it was subsequently set by Gluck, whose opera was performed in Naples in 1752, and by a number of other composers, among them Leonardo Leo (1735), Francesco Veracini (1737), Georg Wagenseil (1746), Davide Perez (1749), Andrea Adolfati (1753), Niccolo Jommelli (1753), Vincenzo Ciampi (1757), Baldassare Galuppi (1760), Giuseppe Scarlatti, the grandson of Alessandro Scarlatti (1760), Gioacchino Cocchi (1765), Johann Naumann (1769) and Giuseppe Sarti (1771), whose operas were staged in various European cities. Metastasio's libretto had therefore been well worked over, but after Mozart it seems to have been used only once more, by Bernadino Ottani (Turin, 1798). Since Metastasio had died nine years previously, his text was revised for Mozart by Caterino Mazzolà, who reshaped the three-act libretto into two acts, shortened Metastasio's lengthy recitatives and contributed verses of his own for new arias and ensembles.

When Mozart was given the revised libretto in Vienna in mid-July 1791, he put *Die Zauberflöte* aside and began to compose *La clemenza di Tito*. He set out for Prague in mid-August with the opera still incomplete, continuing to work on it during the three-day journey, by day in the carriage and at night at the inns where he, his wife Constanze, and his pupil and assistant Franz Zaver Süssmayr stayed. Mozart began to write the role of Sesto for the tenor voice, but found on his arrival in Prague that Sesto had been assigned to a soprano castrato. Working against time, he completed his score in Prague with the aid of Süssmayr, who composed the recitatives.

On 2 September, Mozart conducted a performance of *Don Giovanni*, which was attended by the Emperor. The coronation took place on 6 September, and on that evening *La clemenza di Tito* was given its premiere, also conducted by the composer. The opera was coolly received. The Empress is said to have described it as 'una porcheria tedesca' (German swinishness), and the egregious Count Zinzendorf, who had travelled from Vienna for the coronation, made a note of it in his diary as 'the most tedious spectacle'. A few performances were given, the last of them on 30 September (the date of the premiere of *Die Zauberflöte* in Vienna), but the Mozart party had left Prague in mid-September, for the composer still had work to do on *Die Zauberflöte*.

Act I, scene i. Vitellia's apartments in Rome. Vitellia, furious that the Emperor Tito has chosen Berenice as his queen, incites Sesto to kill Tito and set fire to the Capitol ('Come ti piace imponi'). Although he is a friend of Tito, Sesto reluctantly agrees, for he is in love with Vitellia. When Sesto's friend Annio announces that Tito has changed his mind about marrying Berenice and has sent her away, Vitellia orders Sesto to postpone carrying out her plan, for she may yet be chosen as Empress. Annio asks Sesto to obtain Tito's permission for him to marry Sesto's sister, Servilia.

Act I, scene ii. The Forum. Tito tells Sesto and Annio that he has decided to marry Servilia. When Servilia enters, Annio has to tell her that she is to be Empress. They sing of their unhappy love ('Ah perdona al primo affetto').

Act I, scene iii. The imperial gardens on the Palatine Hill. Publio warns Tito of a conspiracy. Servilia confesses that she loves Annio, and Tito generously gives her permission to marry him. Vitellia, thinking that she has been passed over in favour of Servilia, orders Sesto to go ahead with their plot. Sesto departs reluctantly to assassinate his friend ('Parto, parto'). Vitellia then learns that Tito has resolved that she shall be his Empress. She attempts to call Sesto back, but is too late.

Act I, scene iv. A square in front of the Capitol. The Capitol is already burning, and Sesto is about to confess his crime when Vitellia silences him.

Act II, scene i. The imperial gardens. Sesto, who thought that he had killed

Tito, discovers that the Emperor is still alive, and confesses his treachery to Annio, who urges him to appeal to Tito for mercy ('Torna di Tito a lato'). Vitellia urges Sesto to leave Rome before their complicity can be discovered, but Publio enters to announce that the man stabbed by Sesto was not Tito but Lentulus, who has survived to name his attacker. Sesto is arrested and taken before the senate.

Act II, scene ii. The great hall of the senate. Sesto has been condemned to die in the arena, but before signing the warrant Tito sends for his friend, hoping to find a way to save him. Sesto, however, can say nothing without implicating Vitellia, and is led away to the arena.

Act II, scene iii. A great arena. Sesto is brought before Tito. Vitellia, who has realized that she cannot allow Sesto to be put to death for a crime to which she incited him, throws herself at Tito's feet and confesses. Although he is understandably exasperated at discovering how many people wished him dead, the magnanimous Tito pardons everyone.

La clemenza di Tito is an opera to command respect rather than love, for with this work Mozart, who had taken *opera seria* to such heights in *Idomeneo*, seems to have returned to the genre only dutifully, if not reluctantly. The opera does contain, in its formal arias, much beautiful music, but it is hardly a dramatic work of any magnitude, and its characters are either deeply unpleasant or highly improbable, or both. It is nevertheless a fine example of the old *opera seria*, with several impressive arias for Tito, Sesto and Vitellia.

Recommended recording: Sylvia McNair (Servilia), Julia Varady (Vitellia), Anne Sofie von Otter (Sesto), Anthony Rolfe Johnson (Tito), with the Monteverdi Choir and the English Baroque Soloists, conducted by John Eliot Gardiner. DG Archiv 4311 806-2. The cast is near ideal, with Anthony Rolfe Johnson a convincing Tito and Anne Sofie von Otter singing Sesto's music with wonderfully fluent technique. The orchestra, using period instruments, is splendidly conducted by John Eliot Gardiner.

Die Zauberflöte
(The Magic Flute)
Singspiel in two acts (approximate length: 2 hours, 30 minutes)

The Queen of Night   *soprano*
Pamina, her daughter   *soprano*
Papagena   *soprano*

Three Ladies   *2 sopranos; 1 mezzo-soprano*
Three Boys   *soprano; mezzo-soprano; alto*
Tamino, an Eastern prince   *tenor*
Monostatos, a Moor   *tenor*
Sarastro, high priest of Isis and Osiris   *bass*
Papageno   *baritone*
The Speaker of the Temple   *bass*
Two Priests   *tenor; bass*
Two Men in Armour   *tenor; bass*

LIBRETTO BY EMANUEL SCHIKANEDER AND KARL LUDWIG GIESECKE; TIME: THE ANCIENT PAST; PLACE: EGYPT; FIRST PERFORMED AT THE THEATER AUF DER WIEDEN, VIENNA, 30 SEPTEMBER 1791

Mozart first met Emanuel Schikaneder when the actor–manager arrived in Salzburg in September 1780 with his company to perform a wide range of plays from *Le Barbier de Séville* to *Hamlet*. At that time, Mozart wrote, or at least promised to write, a song for Schikaneder to insert into one of the plays. A letter to Mozart, who was in Munich to stage *Idomeneo*, from his father in Salzburg, complains: 'The way you are treating Mr Schikaneder is quite shameful. On my name-day, when we went shooting, I said to him "The aria is sure to be here tomorrow." Knowing what I did, what else could I say to him?'

Nine years later Schikaneder and his wife settled in Vienna to run a theatre in the Wieden district, and Mozart renewed his friendship with them. And when, in May 1791, Schikaneder, a fellow Mason, asked Mozart to compose the music for *Die Zauberflöte*, a magic opera (*Zauberoper*) that he and his stage manager, Karl Ludwig Giesecke, were writing, Mozart agreed. However, his work on the opera was interrupted by two rather more lucrative commissions: a requiem for an anonymous patron, and an *opera seria*, *La clemenza di Tito*, for performance in Prague.

When Mozart returned to Vienna in mid-September after the Prague premiere of *La clemenza di Tito*, he still had several numbers to write for *Die Zauberflöte*. On 28 September he composed the overture and the March of the Priests; on the 29th he noted in his private catalogue that the opera had been completed; and on 30 September he conducted its first performance at Schikaneder's Theater auf der Wieden. Schikaneder himself performed the role of the bird-catcher, Papageno, whose music Mozart had tailored for him by keeping its style simple and its vocal range narrow.

Die Zauberflöte was a great success from its very first performances. It was played almost nightly throughout October, and Mozart, who attended several of the performances, wrote after one of them to his wife, Constanze, who was recuperating from illness in the nearby spa of Baden:

> I have just returned from the opera, which was as full as ever. As usual, the duet 'Mann und Weib' and Papageno's glockenspiel in Act I had to be repeated, and the trio of the boys in Act II. But what always gives me the most pleasure is the <u>silent approval</u>. You can tell that this opera is becoming more and more esteemed.

Act I, scene i. A rocky desert, with trees and hills in the distance and a temple in the foreground. Tamino, a handsome young prince dressed in an exotic Eastern hunting costume, enters pursued by a serpent. Exhausted, he falls unconscious as three veiled women, the Queen of Night's Ladies, appear. They kill the serpent, comment admiringly on the youth's attractiveness, and quarrel over who will stay to guard him while the others report to the Queen. Finally, all depart together. Tamino recovers consciousness as Papageno, a comical creature wearing a garment of feathers and carrying on his back a cage full of birds, arrives playing his pan pipes and enticing more birds into his cage ('Der Vogelfänger bin ich, ja'). Tamino assumes that it is Papageno who has saved him from the serpent, and Papageno does not disillusion him. The bird-catcher is punished for his deceitful boasting by the Three Ladies, who return to place a padlock on his mouth and to give Tamino a portrait of the Queen of Night's daughter, Pamina. Tamino gazes at the portrait, enraptured ('Dies Bildnis ist bezaubernd schoen').

The Queen of Night appears in person, informing Tamino that her daughter has been abducted by a villainous enemy. If Tamino succeeds in rescuing her, he may claim her as his bride ('Zum Leiden bin ich auserkoren'). Her Ladies now present Tamino with a magic flute, and they free Papageno's mouth from its padlock, giving him a set of magic chimes and instructing him to accompany Tamino to the palace of the evil Sarastro, whither they will be guided by genii in the form of Three Boys.

Act I, scene ii. A room in Sarastro's palace. Pamina has attempted to escape but has been recaptured by Monostatos, a Moor who now threatens her with his amorous advances, but who flees in terror at the sudden appearance of the strange-looking Papageno, whom he assumes must be the Devil. Papageno tells Pamina that he has been sent by her mother, the Queen of Night, and that a prince who loves Pamina will shortly arrive to rescue her. They leave to meet

Tamino, but not before Pamina has consoled Papageno when he complains that he has no mate ('Bei Männern, welche Liebe fühlen').

Act I, scene iii. A grove, in front of a temple with three doors. Led by the Three Boys, Tamino enters. Two of the temple doors, those of Reason and Nature, remain closed to him, but the third door, that of Wisdom, opens at his approach, and a priest (described in the libretto as a *Sprecher*, a Speaker or Orator) emerges to explain to Tamino that Sarastro is not evil and that Pamina has been removed from her mother's influence for very good reasons. When mysterious voices assure him that Pamina is still alive, Tamino plays his flute joyously, and wild animals come out of the forest to listen, entranced.

Hearing Papageno's chimes, Tamino rushes off to find him. However, Pamina and Papageno are captured by Monostatos and his assistants. Papageno's magic chimes bewitch their captors, but Sarastro and his priests now enter. Pamina kneels before Sarastro to confess that she attempted to escape, but only because she was being molested by the Moor. Sarastro explains that he cannot allow her to return to her mother, for women need the guidance of men. At this point, Tamino is dragged in by Monostatos. Tamino and Pamina fall into each other's arms, while Sarastro orders a sound whipping for Monostatos and instructs his priests to lead Tamino and Papageno, with their heads veiled, into the temple for initiation into the Brotherhood.

Act II, scene i. A porch of the temple. Sarastro instructs his Priests to take charge of the two initiates, and then he leads the Priests in a prayer to the gods Isis and Osiris ('O Isis und Osiris').

Act II, scene ii. The crypt of the temple, at night. The two men prepare themselves for their first ordeal, Tamino resolutely, and Papageno with extreme reluctance. Warned to respond to women with complete silence, they succeed in rebuffing the Three Ladies and are led away to their next ordeal.

Act II, scene iii. A garden. Monostatos creeps up on the sleeping Pamina and is about to attempt rape ('Alles fühlt der Liebe Freuden') when a thunderbolt brings the Queen of Night onto the scene to protect her daughter. Learning from Pamina that Tamino appears to have defected to the Priests, the Queen explains that her power came to an end when Pamina's father, shortly before his death, voluntarily surrendered to Sarastro's Priests the circle of the sun with its seven compartments, and that this circle is now worn by Sarastro. Giving Pamina a dagger, she urges her to kill Sarastro and retrieve for her the sacred circle ('Der Hölle Rache'). When the Queen of Night has departed, Monostatos, who has overheard everything, threatens to reveal the Queen's plan unless Pamina gives herself to him. She is saved this time by the arrival of Sarastro, who contemptuously dismisses Monostatos and explains to Pamina that the sacred Brotherhood knows nothing of vengeance, being activated solely by love ('In diesen heil'gen Hallen').

Act II, scene iv. A hall of the temple. Tamino and Papageno continue their trials. An ugly old woman who claims to be Papageno's lover vanishes before telling him her name, and the Three Boys bring food and wine, which Papageno is greedily consuming as Pamina enters, distressed when Tamino refuses to speak to her ('Ach, ich fühl's'). Trumpets summon Tamino and Papageno on to their next ordeal.

Act II, scene v. The interior of a pyramid. Sarastro brings Pamina to Tamino and tells the young couple that they must now bid each other a last farewell ('Soll ich dich, Teurer, nicht mehr sehn?'). After using his magic chimes to conjure up a mate for himself ('Ein Mädchen oder Weibchen'), Papageno encounters his ugly old woman again. When she has frightened him into agreeing to marry her, she is instantly transformed into a beautiful young female version of Papageno, but is borne away by a Priest who remarks that Papageno is not yet worthy of her.

Act II, scene vi. A garden. The Three Boys prevent Pamina from killing herself and offer to lead her to the place where Tamino is about to go through his final ordeals of fire and water.

Act II, scene vii. A rocky landscape with two caves, one glowing with fire and the other gushing forth water. Pamina joins Tamino and, protected by his magic flute, they enter and emerge from both caves unscathed.

Act II, scene viii. The garden. Thinking that he has lost his Papagena, Papageno is about to hang himself when the Three Boys enter with her. The two bird-like creatures sing of the joys of love, and they happily anticipate parenthood.

Act II, scene ix. The entrance to the temple. The Queen of Night and her Three Ladies, together with Monostatos, who has joined their cause, are plotting to overthrow Sarastro, when a sudden clap of thunder causes them to be swallowed up by eternal darkness. The temple doors open, and a blazing light reveals Sarastro and his followers with Tamino and Pamina. Sarastro hails the victory of light over darkness, and all give thanks to Isis and Osiris.

It is clear that Sarastro and his followers have something in common with the members of the Masonic lodge in Vienna to which Mozart and Schikaneder belonged. It is likely, therefore, that the opera's plot, for which Schikaneder found several ideas in an oriental anthology, *Dschinnistan*, by Christoph Martin Wieland, is riddled with Masonic symbolism, and that Sarastro himself is modelled upon Baron Ignaz von Born, the Grand Secretary of the Viennese lodge. The work of which Schikaneder and Giesecke made most use in concocting their libretto was a lengthy French novel, *Sethos* (1731), by the Abbé Jean Terrasson.

The Viennese genre of *Zauberoper*, or magic opera, existed well before Mozart's sublime pantomime, and it continued to appear into the nineteenth century, when it dwindled into the magic plays of Raimund and Nestroy. Mozart's opera, with its heartfelt arias for Tamino and Pamina, its fierce coloratura outbursts for the Queen of Night, its down-to-earth songs for Papageno and its two sublime arias for Sarastro, transcends the genre. It is an opera both serious and comic, and its most successful productions are those that do justice to both elements without attempting to force the work into a mould of, on the one hand, Germanic religio-philosophical moral purpose, or, on the other, mindless Viennese farce.

Recommended recording: Gundula Janowitz (Pamina), Nicolai Gedda (Tamino), Lucia Popp (Queen of Night), Walter Berry (Papageno), Gottlob Frick (Sarastro), with the Philharmonia Chorus and Orchestra conducted by Otto Klemperer. EMI CDS 5 55173 2. Otto Klemperer gauges the conflicting moods of Mozart's pantomime-opera perfectly, giving the quasi-Masonic ritual aspects their due solemnity and investing the Papageno scenes with, for Klemperer, an unexpected lightness. Gundula Janowitz is a forthright Pamina, Nicolai Gedda an absolutely exemplary Tamino, surely the finest on disc, and the young Lucia Popp copes brilliantly with the Queen of Night's fierce coloratura. Walter Berry is a lovable Viennese Papageno, Gottlob Frick the weightiest of Sarastros, and Elisabeth Schwarzkopf, Christa Ludwig and Marga Höffgen are lavishly cast as the Queen of Night's Ladies.

MODEST MUSSORGSKY
(b. Karevo, 1839 – d. St Petersburg, 1881)

Boris Godunov
opera in a prologue and four acts (approximate length: 3 hours, 15 minutes)

Boris Godunov   *bass*
Fyodor, his son   *mezzo-soprano*
Xenia, his daughter   *soprano*
Grigory (alias Dmitry, the Pretender)   *tenor*
Pimen, monk and chronicler   *bass*

Prince Shuisky   *tenor*

Andrey Tchelkalov, clerk to the boyars' council   *baritone*

Varlaam   *bass* ⎤
                 ⎥ vagabonds
Missail   *tenor* ⎦

Marina Mnishek, a Polish princess   *soprano*

Rangoni, a Jesuit   *bass*

Innkeeper   *mezzo-soprano*

Yurodivy (Holy Fool)   *tenor*

Xenia's Old Nurse   *contralto*

LIBRETTO BY THE COMPOSER, ADAPTED FROM ALEXANDER PUSHKIN'S PLAY *BORIS GODUNOV*; TIME: 1598–1605; PLACE: RUSSIA AND POLAND; FIRST PERFORMED AT THE MARYINSKY THEATRE, ST PETERSBURG, 8 FEBRUARY 1874

The youngest son of a well-to-do Russian landowner, Mussorgsky began to compose or at least to improvise music as a child, even before he began to have piano lessons. At the age of seventeen he attempted to write an opera, although he had not been taught the rudiments of composition. The following year he met Dargomïzhsky, who was already an established composer, and through him became acquainted with Balakirev, who gave Mussorgsky his first lessons in musical form, and Rimsky-Korsakov. In his mid-twenties Mussorgsky worked for two or three years on an opera based on Flaubert's historical novel *Salammbô*, but eventually he abandoned it. A setting of Gogol's *The Marriage* was also left unfinished.

In 1868, at the age of twenty-nine, Mussorgsky began to compose *Boris Godunov*, an opera based on Alexander Pushkin's famous historical drama of the same title which had first appeared in 1825. At the beginning of 1869 Mussorgsky began work in St Petersburg as a clerk in the Forestry Department of the Ministry of State Property. By the end of July he had managed to complete *Boris Godunov* in vocal score, and in the following year, after he had orchestrated it, he began negotiations with the Maryinsky Theatre, St Petersburg, for a production of his opera. When, in July 1871, *Boris Godunov* was rejected by the Maryinsky management, Mussorgsky, who by this time was sharing lodgings with Rimsky-Korsakov, made a number of drastic changes to the work.

This second version, completed by July 1872, was also rejected, but three scenes from it were performed as part of a benefit evening at the Maryinsky in February 1873 and were favourably received. A vocal score of *Boris Godunov* in its second version with further modifications was published in January 1874, and in February the opera at last reached the stage of the Maryinsky Theatre. Ten performances were given during the course of the season. By now Mussorgsky had begun the heavy drinking that was to lead to alcoholism and to his early death at the age of forty-two.

After the composer's death in 1881, Rimsky-Korsakov, convinced that Mussorgsky's 'clumsiness and illiteracy' had prevented his genius from finding full expression, proceeded to rewrite most of his friend's works, correcting what he referred to as Mussorgsky's 'absurd, disconnected harmony, ugly part-writing, [and] sometimes strikingly illogical modulation'. In 1896 Rimsky-Korsakov produced a new version of *Boris Godunov*, drastically cutting it, rewriting much of it, completely rescoring what survived and inserting some new music composed by himself. He also transposed the order of the opera's final two scenes.

Ten years later Rimsky-Korsakov prepared a fresh version, restoring the cuts but leaving his own additions in the score, and for a Paris production in 1908, the opera's first appearance in western Europe, he composed two further passages for the coronation scene. For many years *Boris Godunov* continued to be staged in Rimsky-Korsakov's version, which is still occasionally to be encountered, but most performances of the opera now use editions such as those of Pavel Lamm (1928) or Dmitri Shostakovich (1963), which attempt to be as faithful as possible to Mussorgsky's intentions.

Prologue, scene i. Outside the Novodivichy monastery. The boyar Boris Godunov is in retreat in the monastery. (After the death of Ivan the Terrible in 1584, Boris Godunov was appointed Regent to Ivan's successor, his son Fyodor. It was widely rumoured that Boris was at that time responsible for the murder of Fyodor's brother Dmitry.) The Tsar, Fyodor, has now died, and the peasants who have assembled outside the monastery are exhorted by Tchelkalov, the clerk to the council of boyars, and by police to beg Boris to assume the throne.

Prologue, scene ii. A courtyard in the Kremlin. The people acclaim Boris as he emerges from his coronation in the cathedral, but the new Tsar's mood is contemplative as he prays for guidance.

Act I, scene i. A cell in the monastery of Chudov, six years later. The old monk Pimen has just finished writing his chronicle of Russian history ('Still one more tale'). His novice Grigory awakes from sleep to describe a dream which Pimen interprets as signifying great worldly ambition. He urges Grigory to remain in the monastery; but when Pimen tells him of the murder of the Tsarevich, Grigory ponders on the fact that he and Dmitry, had he lived, would have been the same age.

Act I, scene ii. An inn on the Lithuanian border. Missail and Varlaam, two renegade friars who are now vagabonds, arrive with Grigory, who has fled from the monastery and who hopes to cross the border in disguise. Police arrive, searching for Grigory, but he manages to escape.

Act II. The Tsar's apartments in the Kremlin. Xenia, Boris's daughter, mourns the death of her fiancé, while her young brother Fyodor and Xenia's Old Nurse try to comfort her. Boris enters, brooding on the crime that has brought him to power ('I have attained the highest power'). Prince Shuisky arrives with news that a pretender to the throne, calling himself Tsarevich Dmitry, has started an uprising. Boris fears that Dmitry may, after all, have survived, and Shuisky graphically recalls how the murdered boy's corpse was left in a church for five days without showing any signs of decomposition. When a mechanical clock begins to chime, Boris imagines the rotating figures on the clock to be visions of the murdered Dmitry. He collapses, sobbing with remorse.

Act III, scene i. The castle of Sandomir in Poland. Princess Marina wishes to seduce the pretender Dmitry (Grigory) in the hope of one day becoming the Tsarina of Russia. Rangoni, a Jesuit, makes her promise to try to convert the heretic Russians back to the true Catholic faith.

Act III, scene ii. The garden of the castle, by moonlight. Rangoni ingratiates himself with Dmitry. After a polonaise has been danced by guests at a reception in the castle, Marina appears in the garden. Her cynicism at first angers Dmitry, but he is soon won over by her beauty. They embrace while Rangoni, concealed from them, exults.

Act IV, scene i. A council chamber in the Kremlin. At a meeting of the council of boyars, the rebellion led by the false Dmitry is being discussed. While Shuisky is informing his colleagues of Boris's overwrought condition, the Tsar himself enters, clearly distraught. He recovers sufficiently to agree to Shuisky's suggestion that a holy man who is waiting for an audience with the Tsar should be admitted. The monk Pimen is brought in, and he reports a miraculous cure at the tomb of the Tsarevich Dmitry. When Dmitry is mentioned, Boris collapses. Realizing that he is close to death, he summons his son Fyodor. Left alone with him, Boris tells Fyodor that he is the lawful heir to the throne ('Farewell, my son, I am dying'). The chanting of monks can be heard as Boris prays for forgiveness, and the boyars return to the council chamber as the Tsar dies.

Act IV, scene ii. A forest near Kromy. The rebels taunt and torture a boyar whom they have captured. A Yurodivy or Holy Fool (the Russian synonym for a simpleton) is robbed by urchins, and the crowd greets the arrival of Dmitry, whom they follow to Moscow to acclaim as their new Tsar. The simpleton is left alone to bewail the sad fate of Russia.

There are two main characters in Mussorgsky's opera: the Tsar Boris and the chorus who represent the Russian people. The Tsar's powerful declamatory utterances and the dramatic use of the chorus combine to make *Boris Godunov* a work of unique power and originality. The composer's own often harsh and primitive scoring is to be preferred to Rimsky-Korsakov's more colourful orchestration, and although its assemblage of disconnected scenes can hardly be said to possess an integrity of structure, Mussorgsky's masterpiece is extremely effective in the theatre. Surely, no opera of greater stature has emerged from nineteenth-century Russia.

Recommended recording: Alexander Vedernikov (Godunov), Vladislav Piavko (Dmitri), Irina Arkhipova (Marina), Vladimir Matorin (Pimen), Artur Eizen (Varlaam), with the USSR TV Large Radio Chorus and Symphony Orchestra conducted by Vladimir Fedoseyev. Philips 412 281–2. This is a thoroughly idiomatic account of the opera in a splendidly conducted performance, with Vedernikov, a great Russian bass, in the title-role.

Khovanshchina
(The Khovansky Affair)
opera in five acts (approximate length: 3 hours)

Prince Ivan Khovansky, leader of the Streltsy   *bass*
Prince Andrey Khovansky, his son   *tenor*
Prince Vassily Golitsin   *tenor*
The boyar Shaklovity   *baritone*
Dosifey, leader of the Old Believers   *bass*
Marfa, a young widow, an Old Believer   *mezzo-soprano*
Susanna, an Old Believer   *soprano*
A Scribe   *tenor*
Emma, a girl from the German quarter   *soprano*
A Lutheran Pastor   *bass*
Varsonofiev, Golitsin's attendant   *baritone*
Kuzka, a musketeer   *baritone*
Streshniev, a young boyar   *tenor*

LIBRETTO BY THE COMPOSER AND VLADIMIR STASSOV; TIME: THE 1680S; PLACE: IN AND NEAR MOSCOW; FIRST PERFORMED AT THE KONONOV HALL, ST PETERSBURG, 21 FEBRUARY 1886

After he had finished revising *Boris Godunov* in 1872, Mussorgsky spent what was left of his short life attempting to complete two more operas, working on them in a most disorganized manner. For *Khovanshchina* he collected a vast amount of information about life in Russia between 1682 and 1689, a period of violent change and of conflict between various groups, prominent among whom were the Streltsy or Musketeers, a band of ill-disciplined troops, and the religious sect of Old Believers – both opponents of the Romanov tsars. Mussorgsky's researches into Russian history were aided by his friend the critic Vladimir Stassov, but there was never a completed libretto, as such, to be set to music. Mussorgsky appears to have made it up as he went along. He did not live to complete the work, and it was left to Rimsky-Korsakov to produce a performing edition of *Khovanshchina* after its composer's death. This was the version performed at the opera's premiere in 1886, given by amateurs, and at its first professional production, at the Maryinsky Theatre, St Petersburg, in 1911. A version orchestrated by Shostakovich and published in 1963 is the one that is now usually preferred.

To understand fully the implications of the stage action in the collection of scenes that make up the opera, one would need a detailed knowledge of Russian history. *Khovanshchina* deals with the struggle for power between groups representing the old Russia and the new. On the death of Tsar Fyodor in 1682, the Streltsy or Musketeers led by Prince Ivan Khovansky staged a rebellion which resulted in Ivan and his younger half-brother Peter being named as heirs, with Ivan's sister Sophia acting as Regent. The opera's three principal characters embody the ideological conflicts of the struggle. Ivan Khovansky, leader of the Streltsy, represents the powerful boyars. (The title of the opera can be translated as The Khovansky Affair – or Plot.) Prince Golitsin represents the new Russia with its Western influences, and Dosifey, leader of the sect of Old Believers, represents the old Russia with its mystical beliefs.

Act I. A square in Moscow, at dawn. A Scribe is approached by the boyar Shaklovity, who dictates a letter to be addressed anonymously to the Tsarevna Sophia, warning her and the nobility that, aided by the Old Believers, Prince Ivan Khovansky and the Streltsy are plotting against the state. Khovansky, however, arrives and announces to the crowd that he is determined to crush the enemies of the state. Khovansky's son Andrey pursues a Lutheran girl, Emma, but is thwarted by Marfa, an Old Believer. Ivan Khovansky, charmed by Emma, orders his soldiers to take her to his palace. Father and son begin to quarrel over Emma but are interrupted by the arrival of Dosifey, leader of the Old Believers, who urges them to forget their differences and unite to protect the old Orthodox religion.

Act II. Prince Golitsin's residence. Golitsin reads a letter from his former lover the Tsarevna Sophia, whom he no longer trusts. Marfa arrives to tell Golitsin's horoscope, and in her divination scene she predicts disgrace and exile for him. Ivan Khovansky enters to complain of Golitsin's interference in the government, and Dosifey arrives, urging them to make peace for the sake of the old Russia. Shaklovity interrupts to announce that the Khovanskys have been declared traitors.

Act III. The Streltsy quarter. The Old Believers march, Marfa laments her past love for Andrey, the Streltsy and their women drink and quarrel, and the Scribe reports that the Tsar's forces are carrying out massacres close to the Streltsy quarter. Khovansky refuses to attack the Tsar's army.

Act IV, scene i. Khovansky's residence. Khovansky is being entertained by his serving girls and slaves when Varsonofiev arrives to warn him of danger. Khovansky ignores the warning. Shaklovity enters, ostensibly to summon him to a meeting of the Tsarevna's council, but he stabs Khovansky in the back as they are leaving.

Act IV, scene ii. The square in front of St Basil's Church in Moscow. Golitsin sets off on the road to exile, and Marfa tells Dosifey that the council has ordered the extermination of the Old Believers. Andrey and Marfa quarrel, and Marfa dares him to summon his Streltsy. The Streltsy now approach, but in slow procession, each carrying an axe and a block for his own execution. Guards arrive to announce that the Streltsy have been pardoned by Tsar Peter.

Act V. A forest near Moscow. Dosifey and the Old Believers prepare to sacrifice themselves on a pyre rather than yield to the Tsar's soldiers. Marfa reminds Andrey of their past love as she sets the pyre alight and they advance towards the flames. The soldiers arrive in time to witness the mass immolation.

Khovanshchina is a lesser work than Mussorgsky's masterpiece *Boris Godunov*. Yet it is capable of being effective in performance as a kind of historical pageant, and at times it is even extremely moving. Shostakovich's version of the opera is more faithful to Mussorgsky's vocal score than is Rimsky-Korsakov's, but the earlier composer's colourful orchestration gives the piece a greater richness of texture, which is welcome.

Recommended recording: Aage Haugland (Khovansky), Vladimir Atlantov (Andrei), Vladimir Popov (Golitsin), Anatoli Kotscherga (Shaklovity), Paata Burchuladze (Dosifey), Marjana Lipovsek (Marfa), with the Vienna State Opera Chorus and Orchestra conducted by Claudio Abbado. DG 429 758–2GH3. A strong cast is supported by a richly sonorous orchestra conducted with authority by Abbado.

Sorochintsy Fair
(Sorochinskaya Yarmaka)
comic opera in three acts (approximate length: 1 hour, 45 minutes)

Tcherevik   *bass*
Khivria, his wife   *mezzo-soprano*
Parassia, his daughter   *soprano*
Gritzko, a young peasant   *tenor*
Kum, Tcherevik's crony   *bass*
Afanasy Ivanovich, son of the village priest   *tenor*
A Gypsy   *bass*

LIBRETTO BY THE COMPOSER, BASED ON NICOLAI GOGOL'S STORY *SOROCHINTSY FAIR*; TIME: THE EARLY NINETEENTH CENTURY; PLACE: SOROCHINTSY, IN THE UKRAINE; FIRST PERFORMED AT THE FREE THEATRE, MOSCOW, 21 OCTOBER 1913

Written concurrently with *Khovanshchina* and, like that work, left unfinished, *Sorochintsy Fair* was based by Mussorgsky on a story of the same title by Nikolai Gogol, set in Gogol's birthplace in the Ukraine. At his death, Mussorgsky had completed no more than six numbers and a few fragments, none of them orchestrated. There can be no question, therefore, of a definitive edition of the opera; the work exists in several different stage versions. At its first performance in Moscow in 1913, the version used was based on editions by Anatoly Lyadov (1904) and Vyacheslav Karatygin (1912). Other versions subsequently staged include those by Cui (St Petersburg, 1917), Tcherepnin (Monte Carlo, 1923) and Shebalin (St Petersburg, then called Leningrad, 1931). A version by Pavel Lamm (1933) is the one now usually performed.

Tcherevik takes his daughter Parassia to the fair, where she encounters her lover Gritzko, who asks Tcherevik for Parassia's hand in marriage. The old man gives his consent. Although Parassia's mother, Khivria, disapproves, her authority is weakened when it is discovered that she has been having an affair with the son of the local priest. All ends happily for the young lovers.

Mussorgsky's gift for musical characterization is much in evidence in this light-hearted piece with its simple, folk-like score; and the composer's relative unfamiliarity with the Ukrainian dialect of the text seems not to have unduly hampered him. For a sequence in which Gritzko has a dream, Mussorgsky was able to make use of the orchestral piece *St John's Night on the Bare Mountain* (better known today as *A Night on Bald Mountain*), which he had composed in 1867, a good five years before embarking upon *Sorochintsy Fair*.

Recommended recording: None currently available.

JACQUES OFFENBACH
(b. Cologne, 1819 – d. Paris, 1880)

Les Contes d'Hoffmann
(The Tales of Hoffmann)
opéra fantastique in five acts (approximate length: 4 hours)

Hoffmann, a poet   *tenor*
Nicklausse, his companion/The Muse   *mezzo-soprano*
Olympia, a doll   *soprano*
Antonia, a singer   *soprano*
Giulietta, a courtesan   *soprano*
Stella, an opera singer   *soprano*
Lindorf, a councillor   *soprano*
Coppelius, a scientist   *bass* or *baritone*
Dr Miracle   *bass* or *baritone*
Dapertutto, a sorcerer   *bass* or *baritone*
Spalanzani, an inventor   *tenor*
Crespel, Antonia's father   *bass*
Cochenille, Spalanzani's servant   *tenor*
Frantz, Crespel's servant   *tenor*
Pitichinaccio, Giulietta's servant   *tenor*
Schlemil, Giulietta's lover   *baritone*
The Voice of Antonia's Mother   *mezzo-soprano*

LIBRETTO BY JULES BARBIER, BASED ON THE PLAY *LES CONTES D'HOFFMANN*, BY JULES BARBIER AND MICHEL CARRÉ; TIME: THE EARLY NINETEENTH CENTURY; PLACE: NUREMBERG, PARIS, MUNICH AND VENICE; FIRST PERFORMED AT THE OPÉRA-COMIQUE, PARIS, 10 FEBRUARY 1881

Jacques Offenbach, the son of a synagogue cantor, studied in his native city of Cologne and in Paris and became a cellist in the orchestra of the Paris Opéra-Comique. The most famous composer of French operetta of his day, he achieved his first huge international success with *Orphée aux enfers* in 1858. This was followed by *La Belle Hélène* (Beautiful Helen; 1864), *La Vie parisienne* (Parisian Life; 1866), *La Grande-Duchesse de Gérolstein* (The Grand Duchess of Gerolstein; 1867) and *La Périchole* (1868).

The last few years of Offenbach's life were devoted to the composition of what he hoped would prove to be his masterpiece, a serious opera based on *Les Contes d'Hoffmann*, a play by Jules Barbier and Michel Carré which had first been staged in 1851. It was Barbier who fashioned a libretto for the composer, who set to work on his opera with the intention of having it produced at the Théâtre de la Gaité-Lyrique during the season of 1877–8. When that theatre became bankrupt Offenbach refashioned his score for the Opéra-Comique, making his baritone hero Hoffmann a tenor and replacing the sung recitatives with spoken dialogue. Although its orchestration was incomplete, and its fourth and fifth acts still needed attention, the opera was in rehearsal at the Opéra-Comique when Offenbach suddenly died. At the request of his family, another composer, Ernest Guiraud (1837–92), was brought in to produce a finished version of the work. Guiraud restored the recitatives, composing them afresh, and reversed the order of Acts III and IV, placing the Giulietta scene before the Antonia scene. The Giulietta scene was, in fact, not performed at the opera's premiere on 10 February 1881, as it still needed work done on it.

Over the years *Les Contes d'Hoffmann* has undergone a number of changes. For a production in Monte Carlo in 1904 an aria from an earlier work by Offenbach was inserted into the score for Maurice Renaud, the baritone who was singing the role of Dapertutto. The aria, 'Scintille, diamant', has remained firmly in the score ever since. It was also for the Monte Carlo production that a septet, put together by André Bloch and based on the theme of the celebrated Act IV barcarolle, was added. Offenbach's intention to have all the leading soprano roles – representing different aspects of the same idealized woman loved by Hoffmann – sung by the one singer is not always adhered to, though the opera gains in dramatic effect when it is.

As missing material continues to come to light, there have been new editions of the opera in recent years by Fritz Oeser (first performed in Vienna in 1976) and Michael Kaye (Los Angeles, 1988). The Oeser edition that includes additional music subsequently discovered by the conductor and Offenbach scholar Antonio de Almeida, first performed in Miami in 1980, conducted by Almeida with Nicolai Gedda as Hoffmann, would seem most closely to represent Offenbach's intentions.

E.T.A. Hoffmann (1776–1822), a central figure in the development of German Romanticism, was noted for his fantastic and often humorous tales. (He also composed a number of operas, which have not survived, the most successful in his lifetime being *Undine*, performed in Berlin in 1816.) In their play, *Les Contes d'Hoffmann*, Barbier and Carré used Hoffmann as a character, a dissolute poet who recounts the stories of the three great loves of his life.

Act I (Prologue). Luther's tavern, adjoining the opera house in Nuremberg. Hoffmann's Muse, in an attempt to lead the poet away from his life of drunkenness and dissolution, assumes the form of his friend and companion Nicklausse. Councillor Lindorf, the first of four incarnations of evil in the poet's imagination, is Hoffmann's rival for the love of the opera singer Stella, who is appearing in *Don Giovanni* at the opera house next door. In the interval of the opera, students drinking in the tavern prevail upon Hoffmann to tell his story of the dwarf Kleinzach. He does so, but wanders off in mid-narrative to describe not the dwarf but a beautiful woman ('Il était une fois à la cour d'Eisenach'). Noticing Lindorf, Hoffmann recognizes him as the man who has thwarted him in all his romantic adventures. The students encourage Hoffmann to tell them about his three loves, and he begins to do so. The next three acts of the opera recount Hoffmann's three great love affairs.

Act II. The laboratory of the inventor Spalanzani, in Paris. Spalanzani is about to present to the public his latest invention, Olympia, a life-sized singing doll, but is afraid that his former partner Coppelius, responsible for making the doll's eyes, may want to share the rewards. Coppelius arrives ('Je me nomme Coppelius'), and Spalanzani offers to buy him out. When the doll, Olympia, is made to perform for Spalanzani's guests ('Les oiseaux dans la charmille'), Hoffmann, wearing a pair of Coppelius's magic spectacles that make everything seem beautiful, falls in love with her ('Ah! Vivre deux'), despite the warnings from Nicklausse. Coppelius returns, having discovered that Spalanzani has given him a worthless cheque, and takes his revenge by furiously dismantling Olympia, to the dismay of Hoffmann, who now realizes he has been tricked. His foolishness is mocked by the assembled guests.

Act III. A room in the house of Crespel, an instrument maker, in Munich. Although her father has forbidden her to sing, for he is anxious about her health, Crespel's daughter Antonia, seated at the piano, sings a nostalgic song ('Elle a fui, la tourterelle') and then collapses exhausted, for she has inherited the weakness that killed her mother. Hoffmann, in love with Antonia, arrives with Nicklausse, and the poet and Antonia sing of their love ('C'est une chanson d'amour'). When

Hoffmann has left, the evil Dr Miracle, who attended her mother in her illness, examines Antonia, forcing her to sing ever more frantically as he conjures up the Voice of her dead mother to sing with her ('Chère enfant'). Antonia collapses, and a distraught Hoffmann returns in time to hear Dr Miracle declare her dead.

Act IV. A palace on the Grand Canal in Venice. To the strains of a barcarolle ('Belle nuit, o nuit d'amour'), Hoffmann and Nicklausse arrive by gondola at the palace, where a party is in progress. Dapertutto, a sorcerer, promises to give the courtesan Giulietta a diamond ring if she succeeds in procuring for him Hoffmann's soul ('Scintille, diamant'). Hoffmann is easily ensnared, falling in love again at first sight ('O Dieu! De quelle ivresse'), and he and Giulietta sing a rapturous duet ('Si ta présence m'est ravie'), at the conclusion of which she has no difficulty in capturing his soul, making his reflection disappear from the mirror. Giulietta's present lover, Schlemil, finding Hoffmann with his beloved, challenges the poet to a duel. Hoffmann kills him and takes the key to Giulietta's boudoir from Schlemil's body, only to see Giulietta leaving in a gondola in the arms of her servant, Pitichinaccio. A despairing Hoffmann is dragged away by Nicklausse.

Act V. Luther's tavern in Nuremberg. Having concluded his tales, Hoffmann seeks solace in wine. When Stella arrives, fresh from her triumph in *Don Giovanni*, he sees in her merely an amalgam of his three former hopeless loves and allows her to leave with Lindorf. Reassuming the identity of Hoffmann's Muse, Nicklausse exhorts the poet to turn from hopeless love to poetry, the art for which his genius is intended.

Les Contes d'Hoffmann remains a popular favourite, for its wealth of melody and the fascination of its romantic fantasy. It provides splendid opportunities for its singers, notably the soprano, who is required to range from the coloratura virtuosity of Olympia, through the lyrical style of Antonia's music, to the more dramatic requirements of Giulietta. And, of course, she should also undertake the less demanding role of Stella. The four incarnations of the evil genius who frustrates Hoffmann – Lindorf, Coppelius, Dr Miracle and Dapertutto – are also portrayed by one singer, and the three servants of Spalanzani, Crespel and Giulietta are gifts to an experienced character tenor. The role of Hoffmann is especially demanding, calling for a dramatic tenor with plenty of stamina. Hoffmann's 'Legend of Kleinzach' in Act I and the barcarolle at the beginning of Act IV are the best-known numbers in the opera.

Recommended recording: Placido Domingo (Hoffmann), Joan Sutherland (all the heroines), Gabriel Bacquier (all the villains), Hugues Cuénod (all the servants), with the Suisse Romande Chorus and Orchestra, conducted by Richard Bonynge. Decca 417 363–2. Domingo is a splendidly ardent Hoffmann, and Joan Sutherland, in superb voice, is fully equal to the vocal demands of all three heroines and of the opera singer, Stella, as well. Bacquier sings and characterizes all the villains superbly, while the veteran Hugues Cuénod demonstrates his versatility in the four roles for character tenor. Richard Bonynge conducts with aplomb an excellent edition of the opera which he has himself put together from the various choices available.

HANS PFITZNER
(b. Moscow, 1869 – d. Salzburg, 1949)

Palestrina
musical legend in three acts (approximate length: 3 hours, 30 minutes)

Pope Pius IV   *bass*
Giovanni Moronie, papal legate   *baritone*
Bernardo Novagerio, papal legate   *tenor*
Cardinal Christoph Madruscht   *bass*
Carlo Borromeo, Roman cardinal   *baritone*
Cardinal of Lorraine   *bass*
Abdisu, Patriarch of Assyria   *tenor*
Anton Brus von Müglitz, Archbishop of Prague   *bass*
Count Luna, ambassador of the King of Spain   *baritone*
Bishop of Budoja, Italian bishop   *tenor*
Theophilus of Imola, Italian bishop   *tenor*
Avosmediano, Bishop of Cadiz   *bass-baritone*
Giovanni Pierluigi Palestrina   *tenor*
Ighino, his son, aged 15   *soprano*
Silla, his pupil, aged 17   *mezzo-soprano*
Bishop Ercole Severolus, Master of Ceremonies at the Council of Trent
   bass-baritone

LIBRETTO BY THE COMPOSER; TIME: NOVEMBER AND DECEMBER, 1563; PLACE: ROME AND TRENT; FIRST PERFORMED AT THE PRINZREGENTENTHEATER, MUNICH, 12 JUNE 1917

O ne of the last representatives of the German late Romantic school of com- posers, Pfitzner began his career with two operas that were heavily indebted to Wagner: *Der arme Heinrich* (Poor Heinrich), staged in Mainz in 1895, and *Die Rose vom Liebesgarten* (The Rose from the Garden of Love), staged in Elberfeld in 1901. He scored his greatest success with a more individual work, *Palestrina*, first performed in Munich in 1917. Composed to a libretto written by Pfitzner himself, *Palestrina* is a work of homage to the Italian composer whose *Missa Papae Marcelli* (Mass for Pope Marcellus) was thought to have saved the art of counter- point in sixteenth-century church music. A later opera by Pfitzner, *Das Herz*, produced simultaneously in Berlin and Munich in 1931, was generally thought to reveal a sad falling-off in its composer's talent.

Act I. A room in Palestrina's house in Rome. The composer's young pupil Silla has written a piece in a new musical style – that of the Florentine composers with whom he wishes to study. Silla's friend, Palestrina's son Ighino, joins him, and they discuss Palestrina's current mood of sad resignation. Cardinal Borromeo enters with Palestrina and is highly critical of Silla's composition. When the two youths have been sent to bed, Borromeo informs the composer that the Council of Trent (which was first set up eighteen years earlier by Pope Paul III to undertake the reform of the Catholic Church under Jesuit guidance) is about to conclude its deliberations. This, Borromeo explains, poses a threat to polyphonic music, for the Council has it in mind to rule that the Mass must in future be sung to plain- song, and that all polyphonic compositions should be destroyed. However, the present Pope, Pius IV, has decreed that the question should be decided by the composition of a Mass that might persuade the purists that polyphony could be properly devout. Borromeo commissions Palestrina to compose such a Mass.

Palestrina, old and tired, declines, and Borromeo departs angrily. As the weary composer sits at his desk, he is visited by the spirits of great composers of the past, urging him to continue his work. They are followed by angels who sing what will become the opening of the Kyrie in Palestrina's *Missa Papae Marcelli*. As the com- poser begins to write down the music he hears, an apparition of his dead wife joins the angelic choir. When Silla and Ighino enter the room next morning, they find Palestrina asleep at his desk, surrounded by sheets of paper on which he has composed his great Mass.

Act II. A great hall in Trent. After some bickering between the various nation- alities, the Council goes into session. The news has spread that Cardinal Borromeo has had Palestrina imprisoned for refusing to compose the Mass as ordered. The Council's discussion on the subject of music and the Mass degenerates into factional quarrelling, which is continued on a physical level by their servants after the representatives have left. A violent brawl is brought to an end only by the return of Cardinal Madruscht with soldiers whom he orders to fire on the brawlers.

Act III. A room in Palestrina's house. The composer, older and weaker, sits with five young members of his choir and his son Ighino. His Mass, which was taken from the house when he was imprisoned, is now being performed before the Pope. Shouts of rejoicing are heard from the street, and the singers from the papal chapel enter to report that the Mass was favourably received. The Pope arrives to congratulate the composer, inviting him into his service, and a contrite Borromeo begs Palestrina's forgiveness. When the others have departed, Palestrina plays the organ to give thanks to God.

In Germany, Pfitzner's *Palestrina* is revered almost as greatly as Wagner's *Die Meistersinger*, but elsewhere it has not been accorded the same veneration. A lengthy, musically austere and ponderously discursive work, it is, in a sense, autobiographical, for just as Palestrina was the last great master of polyphony, so Pfitzner regarded himself as the last great composer to defend tonality against the atonalists Schoenberg, Berg and Webern. His opera reveals the artist in his spiritual isolation in the slow-moving Acts I and III, in contrast to the worldly intrigue of Act II.

Recommended recording: Nicolai Gedda (Palestrina), Dietrich Fischer-Dieskau (Borromeo), with the Bavarian Radio Chorus and Symphony Orchestra conducted by Rafael Kubelik. DG 427 417–2GC3. A sumptuously cast recording, with Gedda and Fischer-Dieskau at their finest. Kubelik's conducting has a visionary quality.

AMILCARE PONCHIELLI
(b. Paderno Fasolaro, 1834 – d. Milan, 1886)

La Gioconda
(The Ballad Singer)
opera in four acts (approximate length: 2 hours, 30 minutes)

La Gioconda, a ballad singer   *soprano*
La Cieca, her mother   *contralto*
Alvise Badoero, a chief of the State Inquisition   *bass*

LA GIOCONDA 307

Laura, his wife *mezzo-soprano*
Enzo Grimaldo, a Genoese nobleman *tenor*
Barnaba, a spy of the Inquisition *baritone*
Zuane, a boatman *bass*
Isepo, a public scribe *tenor*
A Pilot *bass*

LIBRETTO BY TOBIA GORRIO (AN ANAGRAM OF ARRIGO BOITO), BASED ON THE PLAY *ANGELO, TYRAN DE PADOUE*, BY VICTOR HUGO; TIME: THE SEVENTEENTH CENTURY; PLACE: VENICE; FIRST PERFORMED AT THE TEATRO ALLA SCALA, MILAN, 8 APRIL 1876

Ponchielli, who is regarded as the leading Italian composer of the generation between Verdi and Puccini, was taught the rudiments of music by his father, a church organist in a village near Cremona. He later studied at the Milan Conservatorium, and after graduating he settled in Cremona as a music teacher and organist at a local church. The only one of his ten operas still performed today is *La Gioconda*, first staged at La Scala, Milan, in 1876. None of his earlier operas achieved any success, with the exception of *I promessi sposi*, based on the novel by Alessandro Manzoni, which was enthusiastically received at its 1856 premiere in Cremona, and also when it was staged at La Scala in 1872 in a revised version. Ponchielli composed two operas after *La Gioconda* (The Ballad Singer) – *Il figliuol prodigo* (The Prodigal Son; 1880) and *Marion Delorme* (1885) – but they lacked sufficient individuality to survive in the new period of *verismo* (realism) in Italian opera. In 1881 Ponchielli joined the teaching staff of the Milan Conservatorium, where his pupils included Puccini and Mascagni.

The libretto of *La Gioconda* was written by the distinguished composer and poet Arrigo Boito, who had already begun his collaboration with Italy's greatest living composer, Giuseppe Verdi, and who preferred his text for Ponchielli's opera to appear as the work of Tobia Gorrio, an anagram of his own name, which fooled nobody. Boito based his libretto on the play *Angelo, tyran de Padoue*, by Victor Hugo (1835), which he altered substantially, moving the action from Padua to the more visually spectacular Venice, altering the names of characters and generally reducing the play's stature and, indeed, its intelligibility.

After the successful premiere of *La Gioconda* in Milan, Ponchielli added some numbers for its production some months later in Venice, made further changes for its Rome performances in 1877 and finally produced a definitive version for Genoa in 1879.

Act I: 'The Lion's Mouth'. The grand courtyard of the doge's palace. The Venetians are in festive mood, singing and dancing ('Feste e pane'), observed by Barnaba, who leans against a column. The regatta is announced by bells and trumpets, and the citizens rush away to watch it as La Gioconda, the ballad singer, enters, leading her blind mother, La Cieca. Barnaba is in love with La Gioconda, but his advances to her are scornfully repulsed, and in revenge Barnaba convinces the loser of the regatta that his craft was bewitched by La Cieca. The crowd turns on the blind woman, who is about to be dragged away as a witch when La Gioconda's betrothed, Enzo, a Genoese nobleman in exile in Venice disguised as a fisherman, arrives and attempts to rescue La Cieca. Alvise, a chief of the State Inquisition, emerges from the palace with his wife, Laura, who intercedes for La Cieca, and the blind woman thanks her by presenting her with her rosary ('Voce di donna o d'angelo').

Enzo and Laura, who were lovers before she married, recognize each other, and Barnaba, who is aware of Enzo's real identity, offers to arrange a rendezvous with Laura for him ('Enzo Grimaldo, principe di Santafior'), hoping thus to ingratiate himself with La Gioconda by revealing her lover's treachery to her. Barnaba next dictates to a scribe a letter denouncing Enzo as an enemy of the state, and revealing his plan to elope with the wife of Alvise ('O monumento'). He deposits the letter in the mouth of the great statue of the lion, and departs as the courtyard fills again with masked revellers. His dictation of the letter has been overheard by La Gioconda, who laments that Enzo has forsaken her. Her mother attempts to console her.

Act II: 'The Rosary'. Enzo's ship, a brigantine, at night. The crew are making ready to sail when Barnaba, disguised as a fisherman, arrives to watch the proceedings ('Pescator, affonda l'esca'). After Barnaba has left to fetch Laura, Enzo appears on deck to await her ('Cielo e mar'). When Laura arrives, she and Enzo sing a rapturous love duet ('Deh, non turbare'). Enzo goes below to give orders for their departure, while Laura offers a prayer to the Virgin ('Stella del marinar'). La Gioconda suddenly appears to confront Laura ('L'amo come il fulgor del creato'), and she is about to stab her when she notices her mother's rosary and realizes that it must have been Laura who saved La Cieca's life. She allows Laura to escape in the small boat in which she herself arrived. When Enzo reappears on deck, he finds not Laura but La Gioconda, who points out an approaching craft bearing Laura's husband, Alvise, who has been alerted by Barnaba. Enzo sets fire to his ship and dives into the lagoon.

Act III: 'The Ca' d'oro'. The House of Gold, Alvise's palace. A magnificent reception is being held in the great hall of the palace, while in Laura's room Alvise accuses his wife of adultery and commands her to swallow poison ('Morir! E troppo orribile'). La Gioconda substitutes a sleeping-draught, persuading Laura to drink it and pretend to be dead. After his guests have been entertained by the Dance of the Hours, Alvise shows them the body of the apparently dead Laura. Enzo, masked, is among the guests. Horrified by the sight of Laura's body, he attempts to stab Alvise. He is arrested, and La Gioconda realizes that the only way she can save the man she loves is to offer herself to Barnaba in exchange for his promise that he will rescue Enzo. Barnaba agrees, but in the general confusion he manages to drag La Cieca away as a hostage.

Act IV: 'The Orfano Canal'. The courtyard of a ruined palace on the Isola della Giudecca. Laura, still sleeping, is brought to the palace by friends of La Gioconda, who begs them now to help her find her mother. When they have gone, she contemplates suicide ('Suicidio!'). Enzo arrives, having escaped from prison with the help of Barnaba. He is about to kill La Gioconda when Laura's voice is heard. La Gioconda helps the lovers to escape in a boat, and when Barnaba arrives to claim his reward she stabs herself rather than submit to him. A furious Barnaba shouts at her that he has drowned her mother in a canal, but La Gioconda can no longer hear him.

The plot of *La Gioconda* is preposterous, and most of its characters distinctly unpleasant. The behaviour of the tenor hero, Enzo, is extremely repugnant, and even La Gioconda seems ready to stab people at the drop of a rosary. But Ponchielli's opera is redeemed by the warmth of its passionate melodies and by its effective orchestration. It is an opera that can be made highly enjoyable by really spectacular production. Enzo's 'Cielo e mar' is one of the most popular arias in the tenor repertory, and 'Suicidio!' is a gift to any dramatic soprano; but the music best known outside the context of the opera is that of the ballet, the Dance of the Hours.

Recommended recording: Maria Callas (Gioconda), Pier Miranda Ferraro (Enzo), Fiorenza Cossotto (Laura), Piero Cappuccilli (Barnaba), with the chorus and orchestra of la La Scala, Milan, conducted by Antonino Votto. EMI CDS 7 49518 2. La Gioconda was the role of Callas's Italian debut, and her full-blooded performance here is one of her finest on disc. The rest of the cast are worthy of her.

FRANCIS POULENC
(b. Paris, 1899 – d. Paris, 1963)

Dialogues des Carmélites
(Dialogues of the Carmelites)
opera in three acts (approximate length: 2 hours, 45 minutes)

The Marquis de la Force   *baritone*
Blanche de la Force, his daughter   *soprano*
The Chevalier de la Force, his son   *tenor*
Madame de Croissy, the prioress   *contralto*
Madame Lidoine, the new prioress   *soprano*
Mother Marie of the Incarnation, assistant prioress   *mezzo-soprano*
Sister Constance of St Denis, a young novice   *soprano*
Mother Jeanne of the Child Jesus   *contralto*
Sister Mathilde   *mezzo-soprano*
Father Confessor of the convent   *tenor*
Thierry, a footman   *baritone*
M. Javelinot, a doctor   *baritone*

LIBRETTO BY THE COMPOSER, AFTER THE PLAY *DIALOGUES DES CARMÉLITES*, BY
GEORGES BERNANOS; TIME: BETWEEN 1789 AND 1794; PLACE: PARIS AND COMPIÈGNE;
FIRST PERFORMED AT THE TEATRO ALLA SCALA, MILAN, 26 JANUARY 1957

Though Poulenc was a deeply religious being who described his Catholic faith as 'that of a country priest', there was also a strong element of worldly sophistication in his nature, which led a friend to describe the composer's personality as half monk, half guttersnipe. Poulenc's musical training was for the most part informal, and his earliest works, mostly songs and piano pieces, are in the determinedly avant-garde style of the 1920s. In 1921 he wrote incidental music for a nonsense play, *Le Gendarme incompris*, by Jean Cocteau and Raymond Radiguet, but he withdrew his score soon afterwards, and did not compose his first opera until 1944, when he set Guillaume Apollinaire's play *Les Mamelles de Tirésias* (The Breasts of Tiresias) to music. A comical piece with moments of lyrical beauty, it was a success at its premiere in Paris in 1947.

Poulenc's second opera, *Dialogues des Carmélites*, is a serious study of character and emotion among a group of Carmelite nuns who were guillotined during the

French Revolution. First produced in Milan in 1957, it has been frequently revived in France and abroad. Poulenc's final work for the stage, *La Voix humaine* (The Human Voice), is a forty-minute-long solo for soprano with orchestra, one side of a telephone conversation between a woman and her lover who is breaking off their relationship.

The play by the fervently Catholic French novelist Georges Bernanos (1888–1948) on which Poulenc based his *Dialogues des Carmélites* was in turn derived from a novel by a German Catholic, Gertrude von Le Fort, which told in fictional form the essentially true story of the sixteen Carmelite nuns from Compiègne who went to the guillotine in Paris on 17 July 1794. In 1947 Bernanos was engaged to write the dialogue for a film version of the novel. His script was considered unsatisfactory and was not used, so the author turned it into a play for the stage, in which form it was produced in Paris in 1949. Poulenc saw the play, but it was the firm of Ricordi, his publishers, who suggested it to him as a subject for opera. Poulenc's *Dialogues des Carmélites* was composed between 1953 and 1956 and first staged in Milan, on 26 January 1957, in an Italian translation. The first perform-ance in the opera's original French was given in Paris a few months later, with Poulenc's preferred cast headed by Denise Duval (Blanche de la Force), Régine Crespin (Madame Lidoine), Rita Gorr (Mother Marie) and Liliane Berton (Sister Constance).

Act I, scene i. The library in the Paris house of the Marquis de la Force. The Chevalier de la Force and his father, the Marquis, are concerned about the Marquis's daughter Blanche, a young woman of nervous disposition, for she is out riding in her carriage, which may have been held up by a protesting mob. When Blanche arrives home she appears composed, but she takes fright at the shadow cast by a lamp carried by a servant. Blanche formally requests her father's permission to enter a Carmelite convent, where she hopes to find peace.

Act I, scene ii. The parlour of the Carmelite convent at Compiègne, a few weeks later. Blanche is interviewed by Madame de Croissy, the prioress, who explains to her that the Carmelites cannot guarantee protection to anyone. Blanche is reduced to tears, but the prioress softens towards her and gives the young woman her blessing.

Act I, scene iii. In the convent. Sister Constance, a happy-go-lucky peasant girl, annoys Blanche by chattering away while the prioress lies gravely ill. Constance tells Blanche of a dream she has had, foretelling that she and Blanche will die together, and soon.

Act I, scene iv. The cell of the prioress. The prioress lies dying, in fear and agony. She entrusts to Mother Marie the care of Blanche then lapses into profanity. Her death, harrowing and undignified, is witnessed by Blanche.

Act II, scene i. The chapel of the convent. A requiem is sung for the prioress. Her body is watched over by Blanche, who rushes away in panic but is met by Mother Marie, who admonishes and then forgives her. Constance voices her theory that the old prioress may have been given the wrong death, just as a cloakroom attendant might give one the wrong coat, and that some poor sinner may, in exchange, have been allowed a better death.

Act II, scene ii. The hall of the chapter house. Madame Lidoine, the new prioress, addresses the nuns, reminding them of their duty, which is to pray. An *Ave Maria* is sung, and a bell at the door announces the Chevalier de la Force, who has come to visit his sister.

Act II, scene iii. The parlour. The Chevalier tries to persuade Blanche to leave with him, in order to escape the approaching terror of the Revolution, but Blanche is determined to stay, even if it means martyrdom.

Act II, scene iv. The sacristy. The Father Confessor leads the nuns in prayer, and the prioress warns them against the temptation of martyrdom. An angry crowd is heard outside, as officers arrive to expel the nuns from the convent. Blanche, carrying a statue of the infant Jesus in her arms, drops it in terror at a sudden noise from the street.

Act III, scene i. The chapel, in ruins. Mother Marie proposes that the sisters take a vow of martyrdom. When a secret ballot is held, the only dissenting vote is Blanche's, but Constance claims that it is hers and that she has reconsidered. Afraid to speak out, Blanche runs away.

Act III, scene ii. The library in the Paris house of the Marquis. Blanche's father has been guillotined, and she is living in the house alone, disguised in peasant costume. Mother Marie arrives, telling Blanche that, although she may have saved her life, her soul is in danger. In a street near the Bastille, Blanche learns that all the Carmelites from the convent at Compiègne have been arrested.

Act III, scene iii. The prison of the Conciergerie. The prioress tries to comfort the nuns, and a Gaoler enters to announce that they have all been sentenced to death. In an interlude set in a dark street, Mother Marie hears of the death sentence from the Father Confessor. She is in anguish at not being with her fellow nuns, but the Father Confessor suggests that God may have another purpose for her.

Act III, scene iv. The Place de la Révolution. Watched by a crowd, the prioress and fourteen nuns mount the scaffold singing a *Salve regina*. Every time the drop of the guillotine is heard, there is one voice fewer in the chant. When only Sister Constance is left, she sees Blanche in the crowd and goes to her death with serenity.

The crowd looks on in amazement as Blanche moves forward, takes up the chant of the *Salve regina* and mounts the scaffold to die.

'You must forgive my Carmelites,' Poulenc wrote. 'It seems they can only sing tonal music.' And indeed the music they sing owes debts to the opera's dedicatees, Monteverdi, Verdi, Debussy and Mussorgsky. The inexorable dramatic movement of the work is impressive and, in the final scene in which the nuns walk in procession to the guillotine chanting the *Salve regina*, extremely moving. Poulenc also found an easy and effective style in which to carry forward without monotony the scenes of convent life.

Recommended recording: Catherine Dubosc (Blanche), Rita Gorr (Madame de Croissy), Rachel Yakar (Madame Lidoine), José van Dam (Marquis de la Force), Brigitte Fournier (Constance), with the Lyon Opera Chorus and Orchestra, conducted by Kent Nagano. Virgin VCD 7 59227 2. The old EMI recording, featuring some of the singers whom Poulenc chose for the first production of the opera, is no longer available, but this is equally fine, with a superb cast and conductor, and impeccably balanced modern recording.

SERGEI PROKOFIEV
(b. Sontzovka, 1891 – d. Moscow, 1953)

The Love for Three Oranges
(Lyubov k tryom apel'sinam)
opera in a prologue and four acts (approximate length: 1 hour, 45 minutes)

The King of Clubs, ruler of an imaginary kingdom whose inhabitants are
    dressed as playing cards *bass*
The Prince, his son *tenor*
Princess Clarissa, the King's niece *contralto*
Leandro, Prime Minister, dressed as the King of Spades *baritone*
Truffaldino, jester *tenor*
Pantaloon, adviser to the King *baritone*
Tchelio, a sorcerer, protector of the King *bass*
Fata Morgana, a witch, protector of Leandro *soprano*

Linetta   *contralto*
Nicoletta   *mezzo-soprano* ⎤ princesses in the oranges
Ninetta   *soprano*   ⎦
The Cook   *bass*
Farfarello, a devil   *bass*
Smeraldina, Fata Morgana's black servant   *mezzo-soprano*
Master of Ceremonies   *tenor*
Herald   *bass*

LIBRETTO BY THE COMPOSER, BASED ON CARLO GOZZI'S FAIRY TALE *L'AMORE DELLE TRE MELARANCIE*; TIME: THAT OF FAIRY TALE; PLACE: A LAND OF MAKE-BELIEVE; FIRST PERFORMED AT THE AUDITORIUM, CHICAGO, 30 DECEMBER 1921

Before he graduated from the St Petersburg Conservatorium in 1914, Prokofiev had already composed five operas. The first of these, *The Giant*, was written when he was nine, but only the last of the five, *Maddalena*, was performed, and then not until more than twenty-five years after its composer's death, when it was broadcast by the BBC, and staged in Austria (Graz, 1981) and America (St Louis, Missouri, 1982). Prokofiev's sixth opera, *The Gambler*, composed between 1915 and 1917, was eventually performed in 1929 in Brussels, by which time *The Love for Three Oranges*, commissioned by the Chicago Opera in 1919 and composed in that year, had been given its premiere in Chicago on 30 December 1921.

Choosing a fairy tale by the Italian playwright Carlo Gozzi (1720–1806), Prokofiev wrote his own libretto and composed the opera quickly. Gozzi's *L'amore delle tre melarancie* (The Love for Three Oranges; 1761) was in turn derived from a story in *Lo cunto de li cunti* (The Story of Stories), a collection of fifty tales in Neapolitan dialect by Giambattista Basile (c.1575–1632). Prokofiev wrote his libretto in Russian, but he allowed the opera's premiere in Chicago, which he conducted, to be given in a French translation by himself and Vera Janacopoulos. The first performances in the opera's original Russian were given in St Petersburg (at that time called Leningrad) on 18 February 1926.

Prologue. A grand proscenium, with stage boxes on either side. Various groups of people, among them Tragedians, Comedians and Lyricists, are arguing over the merits of different kinds of entertainment. They are driven off by the Ridiculous People, and a herald announces the beginning of the play.

Act I, scene i. The royal palace. The King of Clubs' physicians tell him that the only cure for the Prince's melancholy is laughter. Pantaloon suggests theatrical entertainments, and the jester Truffaldino agrees to make the necessary arrangements.

Act I, scene ii. In front of a curtain covered with cabbalistic signs. The sorcerer Tchelio, protector of the King, and Fata Morgana, a witch and protector of the King's disloyal minister Leandro, play three rounds of cards, all of which Tchelio loses, to the dismay of the Ridiculous People, who watch and comment upon the performance.

Act I, scene iii. The royal palace. Leandro discusses with his accomplice Clarissa, the King's niece, his plan to hasten the fatal course of the Prince's melancholy by subjecting him daily to very boring poetry readings. Fata Morgana's black servant Smeraldina advises them that her mistress's presence at any entertainments will ensure the success of their scheme, for no one ever laughs in her presence.

Act II, scene i. The Prince's bedroom. The Prince is unamused by Truffaldino's antics, but the jester succeeds in forcing him out of bed to attend the entertainments (to the strains of the famous March).

Act II, scene ii. The great court of the royal palace. The Prince remains unamused by the mock battle of monsters arranged by Truffaldino. Fata Morgana is present, disguised as an old woman, and when she collides with Truffaldino, falling to the ground with her legs waving in the air, the Prince bursts into uncontrollable laughter. A furious Fata Morgana places a curse upon the Prince. He must set off in search of three oranges, with which he will fall in love. The Prince and Truffaldino leave, propelled on their way by the magic bellows of the devil Farfarello.

Act III, scene i. A desert. The Prince and Truffaldino are on their way to the castle of the witch Creonte, in whose kitchen the oranges are kept, guarded by a gigantic Cook. Tchelio gives Truffaldino a magic ribbon to distract the cook, and he warns that the oranges must be cut open only near water.

Act III, scene ii. The courtyard of Creonte's castle. While the gigantic Cook is distracted by the magic ribbon, the Prince sneaks into the kitchen and steals the oranges. He and Truffaldino are magically transported back to the desert, taking the oranges with them.

Act III, scene iii. The desert. The oranges have grown very large. While the Prince is asleep, the thirsty Truffaldino cuts into one of the oranges, hoping for some juice. Instead, a beautiful princess (Linetta) emerges from the orange, calling for water. Truffaldino cuts open a second orange, and another princess (Nicoletta) emerges, also calling for water. Both princesses die of thirst, and Truffaldino runs away in panic. When the Prince awakens and sees the two bodies, he orders four conveniently passing soldiers to bury them. He then opens the third orange, from which steps the beautiful Princess Ninetta, who is saved from death by the Ridiculous People, who lower a pail of water from one of the boxes. The Prince and Princess fall in love, and he rushes off to fetch suitable clothes for her to wear to the palace for their wedding. While he is away, Fata Morgana and her servant Smeraldina appear. The Princess is turned into a rat, and Smeraldina takes her place. When he arrives with the Prince, the King is dismayed to discover that the Princess is none other than Smeraldina, but he nevertheless insists that his son proceed with the wedding.

Act IV, scene i. In front of the cabbalistic curtain. A quarrel between Tchelio and Fata Morgana is interrupted by the Ridiculous People, who abduct Fata Morgana.

Act IV, scene ii. The throne room of the royal palace. The King, the Prince and Smeraldina arrive to find a giant rat occupying the throne, and Tchelio succeeds in turning the rat back into Ninetta. The conspirators are condemned to death but manage to escape, and the Ridiculous People acclaim the happy bride and bridegroom.

The Love for Three Oranges is a highly entertaining comical fairy-tale opera, written in Prokofiev's familiar, spikily declamatory style, with lyrical episodes provided because, as he stated in his autobiography, Prokofiev thought he should take American tastes into account. The action moves quickly, with the good characters being given pleasant, essentially diatonic music, and the evil witches and sorcerers associated with more chromatic, brittle and awkward themes. Prokofiev concocted from its score an orchestral suite of six movements, including the famous March, which soon became more popular than the opera itself.

Recommended recording: Catherine Dubosc (Ninetta), Michele Lagrange (Fata Morgana), Jean-Luc Viala (Prince), Georges Gautier (Truffaldino), with the Chorus and Orchestra of Lyons Opera conducted by Kent Nagano. Virgin VCD 7 59566 2. Vividly characterized performances by a largely French cast, and briskly conducted.

The Fiery Angel
(Ognennyi angel)
opera in five acts (approximate length: 2 hours)

Ruprecht, a knight   *baritone*
Hostess of the Inn   *contralto*
Renata   *soprano*

Servant at the Inn   *baritone*

Sorceress   *mezzo-soprano*

Jakob Glock   *tenor*

Agrippa von Nettesheim, a philosopher   *tenor*

Count Heinrich   *mute*

Mathias   *baritone*

Doctor   *tenor*

Mephistopheles   *tenor*

Faust   *baritone*

Innkeeper at Cologne   *baritone*

Mother Superior   *mezzo-soprano*

Inquisitor   *bass*

LIBRETTO BY THE COMPOSER, BASED ON THE NOVEL *THE FIERY ANGEL*, BY VALERY BRYUSOV; TIME: THE SIXTEENTH CENTURY; PLACE: GERMANY; FIRST PERFORMED IN CONCERT FORM AT THE THÉÂTRE DES CHAMPS-ELYSÉES, PARIS, 25 NOVEMBER 1954 (THOUGH THERE HAD BEEN A BROADCAST PERFORMANCE ON PARIS RADIO, 15 JANUARY 1954); FIRST STAGE PERFORMANCE AT THE TEATRO LA FENICE, VENICE, 14 SEPTEMBER 1955

It was in America in 1919, soon after he had completed *The Love for Three Oranges*, that Prokofiev discovered a novel, *The Fiery Angel*, by Valery Bryusov, which he decided would make ideal operatic material. He immediately began to draft a scenario. Bryusov (1873–1924), a Russian symbolist poet, published his novel in 1907 in the form of a sixteenth-century manuscript, with an unwieldy subtitle that virtually reveals the novel's entire plot:

> A True Story which tells of the Devil not once but often appearing in the image of a Spirit of Light to a Maiden and seducing her to Various and Many Sinful Deeds, of Ungodly Practices of Magic, Alchemy, Astrology, the Cabbalistic Sciences and Necromancy, of the Trial of the said Maiden under the Presidency of His Eminence the Archbishop of Trier, as well as of Encounters and Discourses with the Knight and thrice Doctor Agrippa of Nettesheim, and with Doctor Faustus, composed by an Eyewitness.

After working on the opera between concert engagements over a period of two years, Prokofiev retreated to Ettal in the Bavarian Alps where, late in 1923, he completed *The Fiery Angel* in piano score. With the aid of an assistant, he orchestrated the work after it had been accepted by Bruno Walter for performance at the Berlin

Staatsoper. When the Berlin production failed to materialize, Prokofiev salvaged some of the music for use in his Third Symphony. He returned to the opera in the early 1930s, revising its score when the Metropolitan Opera, New York, expressed interest in it, but in fact *The Fiery Angel* remained unperformed throughout its composer's lifetime.

Act I. A room in a lowly inn. Ruprecht, a knight, hears a woman screaming in the next room. When he opens the door, Renata throws herself into his arms, seeking protection from an imaginary assailant. After Ruprecht has calmed her, Renata tells him that as a child she was protected by an angel, Madiel. When she grew up and offered the angel her love, he disappeared, promising to return in mortal form. For a year she lived with Count Heinrich, imagining him to be Madiel, but since Heinrich abandoned her she has been tormented by dreadful visions. Ruprecht, who has fallen in love with Renata, decides to help her find Heinrich.

Act II. Cologne. Renata and Ruprecht have turned to witchcraft in their search for Heinrich. Jakob Glock, who has provided Renata with occult writings, arranges for Ruprecht to consult the philosopher and magician Agrippa von Nettesheim. Agrippa refuses to help.

Act III. Outside Heinrich's house. Renata has succeded in finding Heinrich, but he has again rejected her, and she now wishes Ruprecht to kill him. The knight challenges Heinrich to a duel, but when Heinrich appears shining like an angel Renata changes her mind and forbids Ruprecht to harm him. However, the duel is fought, depicted by an orchestral interlude, at the end of which Ruprecht is found lying wounded by the banks of the Rhine. Renata sings of her love for Ruprecht and vows to nurse him back to health.

Act IV. A square in Cologne. Renata tells Ruprecht that her love for him is sinful, and that she will enter a convent. Faust and Mephistopheles accost Ruprecht, and he agrees to show them the sights of Cologne.

Act V. A convent. Since the arrival of Renata there has been no peace in the convent. Renata is interrogated by the Mother Superior and the Inquisitor, and the nuns become diabolically possessed as she describes her visions. The Inquisitor sentences Renata to be burned alive as a witch.

The Fiery Angel is not often performed, thanks in large part to its episodic, confused and confusing libretto. Prokofiev's score is an impressive blend of expressionistic and lyrical elements, though its avant-garde style often seems artificially induced, and the music accompanying Renata's hysterical outbursts can sound excessively garish.

Recommended recording: Galina Gorchakova (Renata), Sergei Leiferkus (Ruprecht), with the Kirov Opera Chorus and Orchestra, conducted by Valery Gergiev. Philips 446 078 2. Gergiev penetrates to the essence of this highly individual opera.

War and Peace
(Voina i mir)
opera in a choral epigraph and thirteen scenes (approximate length: 4 hours)

Prince Andrei Bolkonsky   *baritone*
Natasha Rostova   *soprano*
Sonya, Natasha's cousin   *mezzo-soprano*
Maria Dmitrievna Akhrosimova   *mezzo-soprano*
Count Ilya Rostov, Natasha's father   *bass*
Pierre Bezukhov   *tenor*
Helene Bezukhova, his wife   *contralto*
Anatol Kuragin, her brother   *tenor*
Dolokhov, an officer   *baritone*
Colonel Vasska Denisov   *baritone*
Field-Marshal Mikhail Kutuzov   *bass*
Napoleon Bonaparte   *baritone*
Platon Karatayev, an old soldier   *tenor*

LIBRETTO BY THE COMPOSER AND MIRA MENDELSON, AFTER THE NOVEL *WAR AND PEACE*, BY LEO TOLSTOY; TIME: 1805–12; PLACE: RUSSIA; FIRST PERFORMED AT THE MALY THEATRE, LENINGRAD, 1 APRIL 1955 (BUT SEE BELOW)

The gestation period of the work generally regarded as Prokofiev's operatic masterpiece is an extraordinarily complex one. The first theme of the overture was jotted down in the composer's notebook as early as 1933, but it was not until 1941, when he was living with Mira Mendelson, who read the novel aloud to him, that Prokofiev drew up a list of scenes from Tolstoy's *War and Peace* and began to work on the opera, which he composed very quickly between August 1941 and April of the following year.

His score was submitted to the Committee on Art Affairs in Moscow, as a consequence of which he was asked to revise it, strengthening the patriotic element and emphasizing the parallels between Napoleon's invasion of Russia in the nineteenth century and the war then being waged against the Soviet Union by

Hitler. The composer complied, and in this second version *War and Peace* was given concert performances in Moscow in 1944 and 1945. Two more scenes were added for a stage production in Leningrad in 1946, making the work so long that it was decided to perform it over two evenings. Part One was enormously successful at its premiere at the Maly Theatre on 12 June 1946, and it was performed 105 times during the 1946 and 1947 seasons. However, Part Two was suppressed by the authorities after its dress rehearsal, on the grounds that its historical conception was incorrect. Prokofiev then condensed the opera, deleting those scenes that had most upset the Soviet censors, and it was in the resultant truncated version that the opera first became known outside Russia, when it was staged in 1953 at the Maggio Musicale in Florence. The full thirteen-scene version (or, to be exact, eleven scenes of it) reached the stage in Leningrad on 1 April 1955, after Prokofiev's death, but it was not until 15 December 1959 that *War and Peace*, in a choral epigraph and thirteen scenes, was given a relatively complete performance, at the Bolshoi Theatre, Moscow.

Count Leo Tolstoy (1828–1910) began to write his masterpiece, *War and Peace*, in 1860, setting it in the years between 1805 and 1820, covering the invasion of Russia by Napoleon's army in 1812, and Russian resistance to the invader. There are more than five hundred characters in the novel, representing every social level from Napoleon himself to the peasant Karatayev. Several plots are interwoven with the story of the Napoleonic war, involving such characters as Prince Andrei Bolkonsky and Pierre Bezukhov, both of whom are romantically attached to Natasha Rostova, one of Tolstoy's finest creations. Its vast scope and its variety of disparate themes make *War and Peace* the definitive nineteenth-century Russian novel, presenting a portrait of the entire Russian nation. Prokofiev's opera is not unworthy of it.

Part One: 'Peace'

Epigraph. A chorus asserts the invincibility of the Russian people.

Scene i. The house and garden of the Rostov estate. The melancholy thoughts of the young Prince Andrei Bolkonsky in the moonlit garden are dispelled by the sound of Natasha singing of her joy at the coming of spring.

Scene ii. A ball in a country house, New Year's Eve 1810. Natasha arrives at her first ball, with her father Count Rostov. Pierre Bezukhov persuades Prince Andrei to dance with her, and the two fall in love. Count Rostov invites Prince Andrei to visit them.

Scene iii. A room in the town house of Andrei's father, Prince Bolkonsky. February 1812. Following Natasha's engagement to Prince Andrei, she and Count

Rostov pay a call on Andrei's father, who at first refuses to receive them and then insults Natasha, who muses on her love for Andrei.

Scene iv. A room in the house of Pierre Bezukhov and his wife, Helene. May 1812. In congratulating Natasha on her engagement to Prince Andrei, Helene hints that her brother Anatol is also in love with Natasha. When Anatol arrives, he confesses his love to Natasha, who is fascinated by him even though she realizes that her love for Andrei may be placed at risk.

Scene v. A study in Dolokhov's house. 12 June 1812. Dolokhov tries, but fails, to dissuade his friend Anatol from his intention of eloping with Natasha.

Scene vi. The same night. A room in the town house of Maria Dmitrievna Akhrosimova, where the Rostovs are staying. Anatol arrives, but the elopement is foiled by the servants, who have been forewarned, and Anatol is forced to flee the house alone. Pierre Bezukhov arrives to inform Natasha that Anatol is already married. He assures the disgraced girl that were he free he would marry her himself.

Scene vii. The same night. Pierre's study. Pierre arrives home to find his wife entertaining friends, among whom is her brother Anatol. When he demands that Anatol give up Natasha and return her letters, Anatol agrees and leaves. News is received that Napoleon and his army have invaded Russia.

Part Two: 'War'

Scene viii. Before the Battle of Borodino, 25 August 1812. Pierre, who has arrived to observe the battle, bids farewell to Andrei, who has joined the volunteer army in the hope of forgetting Natasha, whom he still loves. Andrei rejects Field-Marshal Kutuzov's offer of a position at headquarters and leaves with his men as the first shots are heard.

Scene ix. A hill overlooking the battlefield, later that day. Napoleon is given news of the battle, which is not going well for the French. Reluctantly, he sends in reinforcements.

Scene x. A hut in Fili, near Smolensk. Kutuzov, having lost the Battle of Borodino, has retreated to Fili. Against the advice of his generals, he decides to abandon Moscow, though he is confident that the city will eventually save itself.

Scene xi. A street in French-occupied Moscow. The city is virtually deserted. Pierre learns that Natasha's family has fled. Napoleon enters Moscow to find that its citizens have set fire to the city.

Scene xii. A hut, behind the Russian lines. Andrei, mortally wounded and delirious, recalls his love for Natasha. She arrives to beg his forgiveness, and before he dies they relive happier times in memory.

Scene xiii. The Smolensk road, in a savage blizzard. November 1812. The French army is retreating with its prisoners, among whom is Pierre. Partisans attack, freeing the prisoners, and Field-Marshal Kutuzov arrives to riotous acclaim, congratulating everyone on a great victory.

Despite its length and its loose, episodic structure, *War and Peace* is an immensely effective work with lyrical melodies, dances and stirring patriotic choruses. Although much of the opera's music was pillaged from earlier scores by Prokofiev, it is cleverly adapted and made utterly convincing in its new context. A selection of scenes from Tolstoy rather than an attempt to adapt the entire novel, the opera justifies itself in performance by its conviction, its power and its lyrical charm.

Recommended recording: Galina Vishnevskaya (Natasha), Katherine Ciesinski (Sonia), Nicolai Gedda (Anatol), Lajos Miller (Andrei), Wieslaw Ochman (Pierre), Nicola Ghiuselev (Kutuzov), Edward Tumagian (Napoleon), with the Chorus of Radio France and the French National Orchestra conducted by Mstislav Rostropovich. Erato 2292–45331–2. Vishnevskaya, who had sung Natasha in 1958, returns to the role many years later in less youthful voice, but is still impressive, and the male roles are all superbly performed, with Rostropovich a passionately committed conductor.

GIACOMO PUCCINI
(b. Lucca, 1858 – d. Brussels, 1924)

Manon Lescaut
opera in four acts (approximate length: 2 hours)

Manon Lescaut   *soprano*
Lescaut, sergeant of the King's guard   *baritone*
The Chevalier Renato des Grieux, student   *tenor*
Geronte de Ravoir, treasurer-general   *bass*
Edmondo, a student   *tenor*
Innkeeper   *bass*
A Dancing Master   *tenor*
A Musician   *mezzo-soprano*

A Lamplighter   *tenor*
A Naval Commander   *bass*
A Sergeant of Archers   *bass*
A Wigmaker   *mime*

LIBRETTO BY RUGGERO LEONCAVALLO, MARCO PRAGA, DOMENICO OLIVA, LUIGI
ILLICA AND GIUSEPPE GIACOSA, BASED ON THE NOVEL *MANON LESCAUT*, BY THE
ABBÉ PRÉVOST; TIME: THE SECOND HALF OF THE EIGHTEENTH CENTURY; PLACE:
AMIENS, PARIS, LE HAVRE AND LOUISIANA; FIRST PERFORMED AT THE TEATRO
REGIO, TURIN, 1 FEBRUARY 1893

Giacomo Puccini, the greatest Italian composer of the generation after Verdi, came of a long line of composers of church music in Lucca. He began his own studies there, before entering Milan Conservatorium. His first opera, *Le villi* (The Willis; 1884), set in mediaeval Germany, tells the story of a deserted village maiden who dies of grief, returning to haunt her faithless lover from beyond the tomb. When it was staged at the Teatro dal Verme in Milan, *Le villi* was successful enough to win its composer a contract with Ricordi, the leading Italian music publisher. However, Puccini's second opera, *Edgar* (1889), based on a play by Alfred de Musset, met with a disappointing reception at La Scala, Milan. It was with his third opera, *Manon Lescaut*, that Puccini's international reputation was made.

The poor reception accorded to *Edgar* had led Puccini to contemplate emigrating to South America, where his brother Michele was already living. 'The theatres here are mean', he wrote to Michele, 'and, because of the critics, the public becomes more and more difficult . . . I shall come, and we will manage somehow. But I shall need money for the voyage, I warn you!' But when his brother, struggling against poverty and illness in Argentina, proved unable to help him, Puccini turned his thoughts towards his next opera. Rejecting two proposals made by Ricordi, he himself suggested that he write an opera based on an eighteenth-century French novel he had been reading: *L'Histoire du chevalier des Grieux et de Manon Lescaut* (The Story of the Chevalier des Grieux and of Manon Lescaut) by the Abbé Prévost. 'Manon is a heroine I believe in, and therefore she cannot fail to win the hearts of the public,' he wrote confidently to Giulio Ricordi.

Remembered today principally as the author of the novel whose title is usually abbreviated to *Manon Lescaut*, Antoine-François Prévost (1697–1763), known as the Abbé Prévost, took holy orders, but his taste for worldly pleasures led him into difficulties and at the age of thirty-one he was forced to flee to London to escape ecclesiastical reprisals and even arrest. His *Manon Lescaut* is actually only the last part of a vast novel, *Mémoires et aventures d'un homme de qualité*, which Prévost published in seven volumes between 1728 and 1731.

Puccini was decidedly competitive in temperament. Although he may not have said so to Ricordi, he was determined to compose an opera about Manon Lescaut, not only because he had been reading the novel but also because he was well aware that Massenet's *Manon*, based on the same source, had been very successfully staged in Paris five years previously. He had even examined a vocal score of *Manon*. 'Massenet', he told Marco Praga, one of the five collaborators on the libretto, 'feels it as a Frenchman, with the powder and the minuets. I shall feel it as an Italian, with desperate passion.'

At first Puccini wanted to write his own libretto, but he accepted Ricordi's view that a professional librettist should be engaged. The choice fell upon Ruggero Leoncavallo, who had not yet composed *Pagliacci* but had proved his worth as a librettist. However, Puccini was dissatisfied with Leoncavallo's ideas regarding the treatment of the subject, so Leoncavallo was removed and replaced by Marco Praga, a well-known playwright. Praga recruited Domenico Oliva, a poet, to write the verses, but Puccini was not happy with the libretto produced by Praga and Oliva. Praga dropped out, and soon afterwards Oliva withdrew as well. At this point, two young playwrights, Giuseppe Giacosa and Luigi Illica, began to work on the libretto, which, in due course, they completed to the composer's satisfaction. (Giacosa and Illica were later to be the librettists of Puccini's three most popular operas, *La Bohème*, *Tosca* and *Madama Butterfly*.)

Acting on the composer's instructions, Puccini's librettists worked directly from Prévost's novel, bypassing the libretto produced for Massenet by Henri Meilhac and Philippe Gille. Although, inevitably, they were able to transfer to the operatic stage no more than selected scenes from the novel, they at least allowed Manon to die in Louisiana, as in the novel, instead of, as in Massenet's opera, on the road to Le Havre.

Act I. The courtyard of an inn in Amiens. The Chevalier des Grieux is lightly flirting with a group of young women ('Tra voi belle, brune o bionde') when the stagecoach from Arras arrives. A teenage Manon steps out of the coach, followed by her brother, Lescaut, and Geronte de Revoir, a wealthy old adventurer. Manon and Des Grieux fall in love immediately. She tells him she is on her way to a convent, but she agrees to meet him before the coach leaves again. Left alone, Des Grieux pours out his feelings for her ('Donna non vidi mai'). When he discovers that Geronte has summoned a carriage in which he plans to abduct Manon, Des Grieux sings a love duet with Manon ('Vedete? Io son fedele'), and they use

Geronte's carriage to make their escape together. Lescaut attempts to console Geronte by assuring him that Manon can easily be persuaded to leave Des Grieux for Geronte's wealth and position.

Act II. An elegant salon in Geronte's house in Paris. Manon has left Des Grieux to become Geronte's mistress. When her brother enters, she recalls nostalgically the joys of the humbler life she and Des Grieux led together ('In quelle trine morbide'), while Lescaut tells her that, under his tutelage, Des Grieux has become a gambler, hoping to win enough money to entice Manon back to him. After Manon has had a dancing lesson, Des Grieux arrives, having discovered her whereabouts. They are reconciled in a passionate love duet ('Tu, tu, amore') that is interrupted by Geronte, who immediately leaves again, threatening to have his revenge. Lescaut urges the lovers to flee, but Manon hesitates, reluctant to leave her luxurious surroundings, to the despair of Des Grieux ('Ah, Manon, mi tradisce il tuo folle pensier'). Having left, Lescaut now comes back to warn them that Geronte is about to return with the police, but Manon wastes precious moments attempting to gather up all the jewellery Geronte has given her. Geronte bursts in with the police, and Manon is arrested on charges of theft and prostitution.

Act III. The harbour at Le Havre. Manon is about to be deported to New Orleans. Des Grieux and Lescaut plan to rescue her by bribing a guard, but their plot misfires, and Manon is taken on board the vessel with the other prisoners. Unable to bear being parted from her, Des Grieux pleads with the captain of the ship to be allowed to accompany them ('Guardate, pazzo son, guardate'). The captain takes pity on Des Grieux and allows him on board as the ship prepares to sail.

Act IV. A bare landscape on the outskirts of New Orleans. Manon and Des Grieux, destitute and dressed in rags, are fleeing from New Orleans. Pale and exhausted, Manon can go no further, and she rests while Des Grieux wanders off in search of water and shelter. Manon gives way to her despair ('Sola, perduta, abbandonata'), and Des Grieux returns to find her close to death. She dies in his arms and, crazed with grief, he falls senseless over her body.

Manon may well be one of the most unadmirable of operatic heroines, but Puccini manages to make her foolish and grasping character seem almost likeable. In *Manon Lescaut* the composer's mature style is already fully formed, and his Romantic melodies and strokes of theatrical effectiveness are present in abundance. Although Massenet's *Manon* stays closer to the manner, if not the matter, of Prévost's novel, Puccini's more full-blooded, Italianate version – with its careful shaping of at least the first three of its four acts, the heartfelt arias for Manon and Des Grieux, and Puccini's fecundity – makes for an immensely enjoyable opera in its own right.

Recommended recording: Mirella Freni (Manon), Luciano Pavarotti (Des Grieux), Dwayne Croft (Lescaut), Giuseppe Taddei (Geronte), with the Metropolitan Opera Chorus and Orchestra, conducted by James Levine. Decca 440 200–2. Mirella Freni brings such passion and sensuality to Manon that she contrives to be more convincing than any of her rivals on disc. Pavarotti is equally impressive, singing with forward tone, clear Italian diction, beautiful legato phrasing and dramatic intelligence. The veteran Giuseppe Taddei makes a welcome appearance as the elderly Geronte, and James Levine offers an account of the score that combines vitality and romantic ardour.

La Bohème
(Bohemian Life)
opera in four acts (approximate length: 1 hour, 50 minutes)

Rodolfo, a poet   *tenor*
Marcello, a painter   *baritone*
Colline, a philosopher   *bass*
Schaunard, a musician   *baritone*
Benoit, landlord   *bass*
Mimi, a seamstress   *soprano*
Parpignol, a toy-seller   *tenor*
Alcindoro, a councillor of state   *bass*
Musetta, a grisette   *soprano*
Customs Officer   *bass*
Sergeant   *bass*

LIBRETTO BY GIUSEPPE GIACOSA AND LUIGI ILLICA, BASED ON HENRY MÜRGER'S NOVEL *SCÈNES DE LA VIE DE BOHÈME*; TIME: AROUND 1830; PLACE: THE LATIN QUARTER OF PARIS; FIRST PERFORMED AT THE TEATRO REGIO, TURIN, 1 FEBRUARY 1896

Puccini's fellow composer Ruggero Leoncavallo, who in 1892 had achieved fame with his opera *Pagliacci*, told Puccini later that year that he was now at work on his next opera, *La Bohème*, based on Henry Mürger's *Scènes de la vie de Bohème*, and he showed Puccini the libretto he himself had fashioned from the novel. Leoncavallo was, understandably, furious when, in March of the following year, Puccini casually mentioned to him, when they encountered each other in a cafe in Milan, that he too was working on an opera based on Mürger's novel. Puccini's *La Bohème* reached the stage first, in February 1896, and Leoncavallo's opera of the same title was performed in Venice in May 1897.

Puccini's opera took a good two years to complete, partly because the composer spent much of the time travelling abroad to supervise productions of his *Manon Lescaut* in various European cities, and partly because the libretto of *La Bohème*, drafted in prose by Giacosa and put into verse by Illica, had to undergo much revision before Puccini finally approved it. Most of the opera was composed between the middle of 1894 and the end of 1895. One night in December 1895, Puccini finished scoring the last act, with the scene of Mimi's death. He later told his biographer, 'I had to get up and, standing in the middle of my study, alone in the silence of the night, I began to weep like a child. It was as though I had seen my own child die.'

An excellent cast was chosen for the premiere of *La Bohème* at the Teatro Regio, Turin, with Mimi sung by Cesira Ferrani, the soprano who three years previously had been Puccini's first Manon, and the opera was conducted by the new music director of the Teatro Regio, the twenty-eight-year-old Arturo Toscanini. The first-night audience seemed to enjoy the opera, but the press reviews were distinctly cool. One critic prophesied that the work would 'leave no great trace upon the history of our lyric theatre, even as it leaves little impression on the minds of the audience', while another wondered 'what has pushed Puccini along this deplorable road'. The critics had perhaps been expecting Puccini's new opera to be in the Romantic vein of his *Manon Lescaut*, and may well have been disconcerted by its light, conversational style. However, audiences became increasingly enthusiastic about the opera they had been told not to enjoy, and *La Bohème* was soon being performed all over the world. It is now one of the most popular of all operas.

Act I. A shabbily furnished and poorly heated garret in the Latin Quarter of Paris. The garret is shared by Rodolfo, a poet, and his friend Marcello, a painter. It is Christmas Eve, and the two young men are attempting to work despite the cold. They are joined by their philosopher friend Colline, who has been unable to find a pawnshop open to take the bundle of books he has been trying to sell. Another friend, Schaunard, a musician, fortunately arrives with food and drink, purchased with money he has earned from an eccentric English aristocrat. After getting rid of the landlord, Benoit, who has come to demand his overdue rent, the four young bohemians decide to spend the evening at the nearby Café Momus. Three of them go off, leaving Rodolfo to finish writing an article before joining them.

Rodolfo's work is interrupted by a young woman who has a room elsewhere in the building, and who needs a light for her candle, which has gone out. Charmed by her, Rodolfo invites her in. She coughs as she enters, and he asks if she is ill. A glass of wine revives her, and Rodolfo prolongs their encounter by telling her about himself ('Che gelida manina'). She in turn tells him her name, Mimì, and describes her lonely life as a seamstress ('Sì, mi chiamano Mimì'). Declaring their love for each other ('O soave fanciulla'), they go off together to join Rodolfo's friends at the Café Momus.

Act II. Outside the Café Momus, a few minutes later. People are sitting at tables on the pavement, under the awnings of the cafe. A crowd is milling about in the street, vendors ply their wares, children cluster around a toy-seller, and the atmosphere is one of a festive Christmas Eve. Mimì and Rodolfo enter a milliner's shop adjacent to the cafe, and Rodolfo buys her a bonnet. They join Rodolfo's friends, to whom Mimì is introduced. Marcello's former lover Musetta arrives on the arm of Alcindoro, an elderly admirer. She begins to flirt covertly with Marcello ('Quando me'n vo"), who at first feigns indifference but soon capitulates. Musetta finds an excuse to send Alcindoro on an errand, from which he returns to find that she has departed with the bohemians, leaving their bill for him to pay.

Act III. The Barrière d'Enfer, the gate leading out of Paris in the direction of Orléans. It is several weeks later, at dawn on a bleak, cold morning, the ground covered with snow. Street-sweepers are being admitted into the city by a Customs Officer. Near the toll gate is a tavern where Marcello is working, painting murals, while Musetta gives singing lessons. Mimì, coughing badly, arrives and asks for Marcello. She tells him that she and Rodolfo have quarrelled because of his uncalled-for jealousy, and asks for Marcello's advice. She hides as Rodolfo emerges from the tavern, and she overhears Rodolfo telling Marcello that it is not his jealousy that is the cause of their unhappiness, but his dismay at her constant fits of coughing, which have made him realize that she is suffering from consumption and cannot have long to live. Mimì's sobs now reveal her presence. Rodolfo attempts to comfort her, but finally he and Mimì agree to part in the spring ('Donde lieta uscì'). In a quartet, Marcello and Musetta bicker with each other while Mimì and Rodolfo part with regret.

Act IV. The garret, several months later. Rodolfo and Marcello are trying to work, but both are thinking of their ex-loves ('O Mimì, tu più non torni'). When Colline and Schaunard arrive with food and drink, they all attempt to behave light-heartedly with their usual horseplay. This is interrupted by the arrival of Musetta with the news that Mimì is outside, dangerously ill and wanting to spend her last hours with Rodolfo. Mimì is brought in, and the others leave to raise money to buy medicine, Colline by pawning his old overcoat ('Vecchia zimarra'), while Rodolfo stays with her. As they reminisce ('Sono andati?'), Mimì gradually drifts off into unconsciousness. The others return, and it is Schaunard who first notices that Mimì has died. Rodolfo utters a cry of anguish as he collapses in tears over her body.

La Bohème is an opera that is easy to criticize, but also an opera that is easy to love. It may be too cloyingly sentimental for some tastes, but its story of love among the penurious young artists of early nineteenth-century Paris is succinctly told in a series of gloriously tuneful arias and duets, the work's joyous and tragic elements perfectly juxtaposed. As Debussy is reputed to have said to Manuel de Falla, 'If one did not keep a grip on oneself, one would be swept away by the sheer verve of the music. I know of no one who has described the Paris of that time as well as Puccini in La Bohème.'

The structure of the work is clear, with each of its four acts short and to the point. Although Puccini does not always appear to care which tune he will reprise in the orchestra at which moment, his style throughout the opera is admirably suited to his subject matter, and his theatrical effects are always cleverly managed. In the opinion of many, this is Puccini's finest opera. The latter part of Act I is a marvellous sequence of three greatly loved numbers: two tuneful arias (Rodolfo's 'Che gelida manina' with its climactic high C, and Mimì's 'Sì, mi chiamano Mimì') and a love duet ('O soave fanciulla'). Act II contains Musetta's popular waltz song, 'Quando m'en vo', Act III is bleaker in atmosphere, and the mood of Act IV, after its initial horseplay, is that of happier times remembered as tragedy encroaches upon the young bohemians.

Recommended recording: Renata Tebaldi (Mimì), Gianna D'Angelo (Musetta), Carlo Bergonzi (Rodolfo), Ettore Bastianini (Marcello), Renato Cesari (Schaunard), Cesare Siepi (Colline), with the Chorus and Orchestra of the Academy of Santa Cecilia, conducted by Tullio Serafin. Decca 425 534–2. Though made in a Rome studio, this forty-year-old recording marvellously captures the atmophere of a stage performance, and there can rarely have been a more beautiful-sounding Mimì than Renata Tebaldi. That great stylist Carlo Bergonzi is an exemplary Rodolfo, and

Ettore Bastianini, a baritone who died young and is still sorely missed, makes a strong Marcello. Tullio Serafin conducts a relaxed and loving account of the opera.

Tosca
opera in three acts (approximate length: 2 hours)

Floria Tosca, a celebrated singer   *soprano*
Mario Cavaradossi, a painter   *tenor*
Baron Scarpia, chief of police   *baritone*
Cesare Angelotti, an escaped political prisoner   *bass*
A Sacristan   *bass*
Spoletta, a police agent   *tenor*
Sciarrone, a gendarme   *bass*
A Gaoler   *bass*
A Shepherd Boy   *alto*

LIBRETTO BY GIUSEPPE GIACOSA AND LUIGI ILLICA, BASED ON THE PLAY *LA TOSCA*, BY VICTORIEN SARDOU; TIME: JUNE 1800; PLACE: ROME; FIRST PERFORMED AT THE TEATRO COSTANZI, ROME, 14 JANUARY 1900

As early as May 1889, shortly after the premiere of his second opera, *Edgar*, Puccini expressed great interest in *La Tosca*, a play written by the popular French playwright Victorien Sardou (1831–1908) for Sarah Bernhardt, the greatest actress of the day. Puccini even asked his publisher, Giulio Ricordi, to take the necessary steps to obtain Sardou's permission for the play to be used as the basis of an opera. 'In this *Tosca*', he told Ricordi, 'I see the opera which exactly suits me, one without excessive proportions, one which is a decorative spectacle, and one which gives opportunity for an abundance of music.'

The suggestion was taken no further at that time, and Puccini composed *Manon Lescaut* instead. Nevertheless, Ricordi commissioned Illica to produce a libretto based on *La Tosca*, and then he offered it not to Puccini but to Alberto Franchetti, another composer whose works he published. When Puccini learned that Franchetti had signed a contract with Ricordi to compose an opera based on Sardou's play, his possessiveness asserted itself and he demanded that Ricordi retrieve the libretto from Franchetti. Ricordi and Illica succeeded in convincing Franchetti that, having given more thought to the matter, they had come to the conclusion that the subject of Sardou's play was far too violent for an opera.

Franchetti relinquished his rights to the subject, which were acquired the following day by Puccini, who was by that time at work on *La Bohème*.

Puccini did not begin to compose *Tosca* until a year or more after the February 1896 premiere of *La Bohème*, for he was first involved in supervising the Milan production of *La Bohème* at La Scala, after which he travelled to England for the British premiere of that opera. He worked on *Tosca* for much of 1898, though he made two visits to Paris during the early part of the year in connection with the first French performances of *La Bohème*. On the second of these visits, he and Illica called on the playwright Sardou in order to discuss their handling of the final act of *Tosca*. The opera was finally completed at the end of September 1899 and sent to Giulio Ricordi, who to Puccini's dismay wrote him a very long letter to say that he was disappointed with the final act, which in his view was 'a grave error of both conception and craftsmanship'. Puccini hastened to reply:

> My dear Signor Giulio,
>
> Your letter was an extraordinary surprise to me!! I am still suffering from the impact of it. Nevertheless I am quite convinced that if you read the act through again you will change your opinion! This is not vanity on my part. No, it is the conviction of having, to the best of my ability, given life to the drama which was before me . . .
>
> I really cannot understand your unfavourable impression. Before I set to work to do it again (and would there be time?) I shall take a run up to Milan and we shall discuss it together, just we two alone, at the piano and with the music in front of us, and if your unfavourable impression persists we shall try, like good friends, to find, as Scarpia [a character in the opera] says, a way to save ourselves . . .

No changes were made to Act III. Giulio Ricordi's son Tito was in charge of the production when *Tosca* was given its premiere at the Teatro Costanzi in Rome on 14 January 1900 before an international audience, with Italian royalty represented by Queen Margherita. The evening began nervously when fifteen minutes before the curtain was due to rise a police officer told the conductor Leopoldo Mugnone that a bomb threat had been received. In the event, however, the performance was disturbed by nothing more dangerous than a number of latecomers. During the evening several numbers were encored, and Puccini was called onto the stage five or six times after the Act III tenor aria 'E lucevan le stelle'. However, the applause at the end of the opera was respectful rather than enthusiastic, and when the newspaper reviews appeared over the next few days they were for the most part unfavourable. The score's lyrical passages were praised, but the composer's apparent fascination with sadism in the torture scene of Act II was considered distasteful. The critic of the *Corriere d'Italia* took a dim view of the entire opera, regretting that Puccini 'should have attempted something the futility of which ought not to have escaped him'.

Slowly but surely, *Tosca* made its way across the world. Six months after its Rome premiere it reached Covent Garden, where it was enthusiastically received, although some of the London critics found the torture scene objectionable. At the Metropolitan Opera, New York, in February 1901, *Tosca* proved more popular with the public than with the press, and within the next few years it was being performed in more than twenty languages. Today it is one of the most popular works in the operatic repertoire.

The entire action of the opera takes place in Rome, in June 1800, within a period of twenty-four hours.

Act I. The church of Sant' Andrea della Valle. It is morning. Cesare Angelotti, a consul of the fallen Roman Republic, enters the church furtively. He has escaped from the prison of the Castel Sant' Angelo and knows that at the base of a statue of the Madonna his sister has hidden the key to a chapel in which he can conceal himself. Finding the key, he enters the chapel. The Sacristan arrives, followed soon afterwards by Mario Cavaradossi, a painter who is working in the church on an image of the Madonna. Cavaradossi prepares to start work, pausing to reflect on the various types of beauty. The Madonna of his painting is a blue-eyed blonde, whereas his lover, the singer Floria Tosca, is dark with black eyes ('Recondita armonia').

After the Sacristan has left, Angelotti emerges from the chapel and recognizes Cavaradossi as an old friend and republican sympathizer. Hearing the voice of Tosca calling him, Cavaradossi pushes Angelotti back into his hiding place, giving him a basket of food and wine. Tosca enters, suspicious of the voices she heard as she approached, and convinced that Cavaradossi has been entertaining another woman. He reasssures her, and they make plans to meet that evening after her performance and go to his villa in the country ('Non lo sospiri la nostra casetta?'). As Tosca is leaving, her jealousy momentarily flares up again when she recognizes the face of the painter's Madonna as that of the Marchesa Attavanti. Again Cavaradossi calms her. She leaves, but not before advising him to change the eyes of the Madonna from blue to black.

Angelotti reappears, and Cavaradossi gives him a key to his villa, telling him that in an emergency he can hide in a concealed chamber in a well in the garden. When a cannon shot rings out, indicating that a prisoner has escaped from the Castel

Sant' Angelo, Angelotti and Cavaradossi leave hurriedly together. The Sacristan returns with news of Napoleon's defeat in a battle, and a crowd begins to gather in the church for a celebratory *Te Deum*. Scarpia, the dreaded chief of police, enters with his henchman Spoletta in search of the escaped prisoner. The discovery in the chapel of a fan belonging to the Marchesa Attavanti (who is Angelotti's sister) persuades Scarpia that Cavaradossi, whom he knows to be Tosca's lover, is implicated in the escape. When Tosca returns, Scarpia deliberately incites her jealousy by suggesting that the appearance in the chapel of the Marchesa's fan may explain Cavaradossi's absence. Tosca immediately leaves, expecting to surprise Cavaradossi at his villa with the Marchesa. On Scarpia's orders she is followed by Spoletta. As the congregation intones the *Te Deum*, Scarpia vows to send Cavaradossi to the gallows and to become Tosca's lover ('Va, Tosca! Nel tuo cuor s'annida Scarpia').

Act II. Scarpia's apartment in the Palazzo Farnese, that evening. Scarpia is enjoying his supper, while through an open window the sound of music is heard from a reception being held in another part of the palace, at which Tosca is expected to perform. Spoletta enters to announce that he could not find Angelotti at the villa but that he has arrested Cavaradossi. The painter is brought in and questioned, but he denies all knowledge of Angelotti's escape. Having been summoned by Scarpia, Tosca arrives just as Cavaradossi is taken into an adjacent room to be tortured. Unable to bear his screams of pain, she tells Scarpia where to find Angelotti. Cavaradossi is dragged back into Scarpia's room just as news arrives of Napoleon's victory at Marengo. The painter's exultant response to this leads to his being immediately dragged away to prison, while Spoletta goes off to apprehend Angelotti. Tosca is given a choice. She can save Cavaradossi's life by becoming Scarpia's mistress, or ensure his execution by rejecting Scarpia. After uttering a despairing prayer ('Vissi d'arte'), Tosca agrees to submit to the chief of police.

In the presence of Spoletta who has returned to report that Angelotti has killed himself, Scarpia pretends to order a mock execution of Cavaradossi. Spoletta leaves to carry out his instructions, and Scarpia writes a safe-conduct for Cavaradossi and Tosca to leave Rome, but when he turns to embrace Tosca she stabs him with a knife from the supper table. She taunts Scarpia as he dies, then takes the safe-conduct from his lifeless hand and quietly leaves after placing candles on either side of his body and a crucifix on his chest.

Act III. The battlements of the Castel Sant' Angelo, at dawn. As a Shepherd Boy is heard singing in the distance, Cavaradossi is brought from his cell to await execution. His thoughts are of his approaching death and his love for Tosca ('E lucevan le stelle'). Tosca arrives, telling him that it will be only a mock execution, after which they can leave Rome together. She instructs him in how to fall convincingly. The firing squad arrives, shots are fired, and Cavaradossi falls to the ground. When Cavaradossi fails to rise after the firing squad has departed, Tosca discovers that he is dead. Soldiers are heard approaching to arrest her for the murder of Scarpia, but Tosca leaps onto the parapet and flings herself over with the defiant cry that she and Scarpia will meet in the presence of God.

Tosca's brutal opening chords, characterizing the evil Scarpia, set the mood of an opera whose melodramatic plot is tautly constructed and clothed in music that impressively alternates dramatic and lyrical elements. Motifs are used to depict characters and situations in an almost Wagnerian manner. The roles of Tosca and Scarpia are gifts to really first-rate singing actors, and although the tenor hero Cavaradossi is less fully developed as a character, he is at least given two most attractive arias, 'Recondita armonia' and 'E lucevan le stelle'. Tosca's moving prayer, 'Vissi d'arte', is one of the musical highlights of the opera. *Tosca* is a work which, though it may not be Puccini's finest creation, does not deserve the scorn heaped upon it by some of the more high-minded critics. A certain American professor's often-quoted description of the opera as a 'shabby little shocker' has failed to lessen the immense popularity of this highly effective example of Italian *verismo*.

Recommended recording: Maria Callas (Tosca), Giuseppe di Stefano (Cavaradossi), Tito Gobbi (Scarpia), with the Chorus and Orchestra of La Scala, Milan, conducted by Victor de Sabata. EMI CMS 7 69974 2. The two chief glories of this version are the totally convincing Tosca of Maria Callas who, in a role not as demanding as many others she undertook, is able to involve herself completely in the dramatic situations, and the Scarpia of the incomparable Tito Gobbi whose vocal inflections bring the character of the evil police chief to life with extraordinary vividness. Giuseppe di Stefano is an exciting Cavaradossi, and the comprimario roles are strongly cast. Victor de Sabata projects the drama of the work with great force and conviction.

Madama Butterfly
a Japanese tragedy in two acts (approximate length: 2 hours)

Madama Butterfly (Cio-Cio-San)   *soprano*
F.B. Pinkerton, lieutenant in the US navy   *tenor*

Suzuki, Butterfly's servant   *mezzo-soprano*
Sharpless, US consul at Nagasaki   *baritone*
Goro, a marriage broker   *tenor*
The Bonze, Butterfly's uncle   *bass*
Kate Pinkerton   *mezzo-soprano*
Prince Yamadori   *baritone*
Imperial Commissioner   *bass*
Yakuside   *baritone*
The Official Registrar   *baritone*
Butterfly's Mother   *mezzo-soprano*
Butterfly's Aunt   *mezzo-soprano*
Butterfly's Cousin   *soprano*

LIBRETTO BY GIUSEPPE GIACOSA AND LUIGI ILLICA, BASED ON THE PLAY *MADAME BUTTERFLY*, BY DAVID BELASCO; TIME: 1904; PLACE: NAGASAKI, JAPAN; FIRST PERFORMED AT THE TEATRO ALLA SCALA, MILAN, 17 FEBRUARY 1904

When Puccini visited London in the summer of 1900 in connection with the first English performances of his *Tosca*, his attention was drawn by a London-based Italian friend to a play at the Duke of York's Theatre, *Madame Butterfly*, which had been adapted by the American playwright David Belasco from a story by John Luther Long, which in turn owes much to *Madame Chrysan-thème* by the French novelist Pierre Loti (1850–1923). Loti's novel was published in 1887, several years before Long's story appeared.

Puccini attended a performance of Belasco's play in London. Although his English was too poor for him to understand much of the dialogue, he was impressed by what he saw and immediately began to negotiate with Belasco for permission to turn the play into an opera. It was not until April of the following year, after Puccini had also considered such subjects as Marie Antoinette, Maeterlinck's *Pelléas et Mélisande* and Zola's *La Faute de l'Abbé Mouret*, that negotiations with Belasco were completed, and Puccini's preferred collaborators, Giacosa and Illica, were engaged to produce a libretto. John Luther Long's story, which differs from Belasco's play in several particulars, was consulted in the writing of the libretto. It was Belasco who introduced Butterfly's suicide and brought Pinkerton back at the moment of her death.

When *Madama Butterfly* reached the stage in February 1904, it was a two-act opera. Its premiere at La Scala, Milan, turned out to be a fiasco. The love duet at the end of Act I was greeted with hisses and catcalls, Butterfly's aria 'Un bel dì' was heard in apathetic silence, and when Butterfly's kimono accidentally billowed up in front of her a cry of 'Butterfly is pregnant' from a member of the audience amused everyone considerably. Puccini immediately withdrew his opera, and four days later he wrote to a friend:

> I am still shocked by all that happened – not so much for what they did to my poor Butterfly, but for all the poison they spat on me as an artist and as a man . . . I shall make a few cuts, and divide the second act into two parts – something which I had already thought of doing during the rehearsals, but it was then too near the first performance.

Puccini made his revisions, and three months later in Brescia the opera, now in three acts, was a triumphant success. The composer continued to make occasional changes: vocal scores published in 1906 and 1907 differ from the Brescia version of 1904. Although the division of Act II into two parts effectively turned *Madama Butterfly* into a three-act opera, Puccini preferred to describe it still as a two-act work, with Act II divided into two parts. The opera is now usually performed in two acts, with no interval between the two parts of Act II.

Act I. The terrace of a Japanese-style house, overlooking the harbour at Nagasaki. The marriage broker Goro has found a house for Lieutenant Pinkerton of the United States navy to lease and has arranged for Pinkerton to marry Cio-Cio-San, a teenage geisha called Butterfly by her friends. Goro is showing the house to Pinkerton and introducing the servants, among them Suzuki, when Sharpless, the American consul, arrives and tries to convince Pinkerton that, although he may treat the forthcoming marriage lightly, the young bride-to-be takes it much more seriously, for she has already secretly renounced her religion in order to become a Christian. Pinkerton, however, remains carefree ('Dovunque al mondo').

Butterfly arrives with her relatives and friends, and a marriage contract is signed. The celebrations are interrupted by the arrival of Butterfly's uncle, the Bonze (a Buddhist priest), who denounces her for having abandoned the faith of her ancestors. Butterfly's relatives and friends reject her, but Pinkerton angrily dismisses all the guests, and he consoles his bride. They sing a love duet ('Viene la sera') and enter the house together.

Act II, part i. The same house, three years later. Although Pinkerton and his ship were sent back to America after he and Butterfly had been married only a few months, Butterfly still patiently awaits his return, for he promised that he would be back 'when the robins nest'. Suzuki prays for Pinkerton's return, and Butterfly sings confidently of the day when she will see his ship arriving in the harbour ('Un bel dì'). Goro enters with Sharpless, who has received a letter from Pinkerton, announcing his imminent return to Nagasaki, but with an American wife. Sharpless attempts to break the news to Butterfly of Pinkerton's American marriage, but she is too excited at the prospect of his return to listen. When Prince Yamadori, a rich Japanese suitor, asks Butterfly to marry him, she scornfully dismisses him. Sharpless makes a final attempt to prepare Butterfly for the shock that awaits her but, not heeding his words, she shows him the child she has borne Pinkerton, whom she has named Dolore (Trouble).

After Sharpless has left, a cannon shot is heard fom the harbour, signalling the arrival of Pinkerton's ship. Butterfly and Suzuki excitedly strew petals over the floor of the house to welcome Pinkerton (Flower Duet: 'Gettiamo a mani piene'), and they settle down to await his arrival. Night falls, and a humming chorus is heard in the distance as Butterfly keeps her vigil while Suzuki and Trouble sleep.

Act II, part ii. As dawn breaks, and there is still no sign of Pinkerton, Suzuki persuades Butterfly to rest in an adjacent room. Sharpless arrives with Pinkerton and asks Suzuki to go into the garden and talk to Mrs Pinkerton. As he gazes around the house, where for a time he was happy, Pinkerton is overcome with remorse and guilt ('Addio fiorito asil'), and he rushes out. Having heard voices, Butterfly enters, hoping to find her husband. Instead she encounters Kate Pinkerton and learns the truth. Pinkerton and his wife have come only to take the lieutenant's child away with them. A heartbroken Butterfly agrees to give up the child if Pinkerton himself will come to collect him. Left alone, she takes up the ceremonial dagger with which, at the Emperor's behest, her father took his own life. Blindfolding her child, she goes behind a screen with the dagger and kills herself just as Pinkerton rushes in calling her name.

Madama Butterfly was Puccini's own favourite among his operas. Authentic Japanese melodies are woven into its score, which is one of his most assured, and the occasionally exotic instrumentation is immensely effective. The action centres closely on Butterfly herself, whose character is strongly delineated, developing from the innocent child-bride of the opera's beginning to the distraught tragic heroine of the final scene. Pinkerton's brief solo utterances are colourless, but the fifteen-minute-long love duet, though it is somewhat rambling in structure, reaches a passionate climax. Butterfly's 'Un bel dì' (One fine day) is an aria known to countless thousands who have never attended a performance of the opera, its vocal line progressing from calm certainty to hysterical frenzy as Butterfly fights to persuade herself that Pinkerton will return.

Recommended recording: Leontyne Price (Butterfly), Richard Tucker (Pinkerton), Rosalind Elias (Suzuki), with the RCA Italiana Opera Chorus and Orchestra, conducted by Erich Leinsdorf. RCA Victor RD86160. Leontyne Price is a sympathetic and moving Butterfly, Richard Tucker is appropriately cast as Pinkerton, and there is a very strong, predominantly Italian supporting cast. Erich Leinsdorf conducts briskly.

La fanciulla del West
(The Girl of the Golden West)
opera in three acts (approximate length: 2 hours)

Minnie   *soprano*
Jack Rance, sheriff   *baritone*
Ramerrez, alias Dick Johnson   *tenor*
Nick, bartender at the Polka Saloon   *tenor*
Ashby, Wells Fargo agent   *bass*
Sonora   *baritone* ⎤
Trin   *tenor*
Sid   *baritone*
Bello   *baritone*   ⎬ miners
Harry   *tenor*
Joe   *tenor*
Happy   *baritone*
Larkens   *bass* ⎦
Billy Jackrabbit, a Red Indian   *bass*
Wowkle, his squaw   *mezzo-soprano*
Jake Wallace, a minstrel   *baritone*
José Castro, a member of Ramerrez's gang   *bass*
Pony Express rider   *tenor*

LIBRETTO BY GUELFO CIVININI AND CARLO ZANGARINI, BASED ON THE PLAY *THE GIRL OF THE GOLDEN WEST*, BY DAVID BELASCO; TIME: THE GOLD RUSH OF 1849–50; PLACE: A MINING CAMP AT CLOUDY MOUNTAIN, CALIFORNIA; FIRST PERFORMED AT THE METROPOLITAN OPERA HOUSE, NEW YORK, 10 DECEMBER 1910

After *Madama Butterfly* in 1904, six years were to pass before Puccini's next opera reached the stage, the first three of those years being spent by the composer in search of an appropriate subject. He considered Victor Hugo's play *Notre Dame de Paris* (known in English as *The Hunchback of Notre Dame*), some stories by Gorky and two synopses prepared for him by the playwright Gabriele d'Annunzio. Deciding against all of these, he discussed with Luigi Illica, the co-librettist of his previous four operas, the possibility of creating an opera about the trial and execution of Marie Antoinette. But when Illica's collaborator Giuseppe Giacosa died in 1906 the composer made it clear that he did not consider Illica capable of producing a satisfactory libretto alone.

Puccini considered a number of other possible subjects while he travelled around the world attending performances of his operas. At the beginning of 1907 he was in New York for the American premiere of *Madama Butterfly* with Gerald-ine Farrar (Butterfly) and Enrico Caruso (Pinkerton), two singers by whom he was not greatly impressed. Farrar, he wrote to a friend, was 'not what she ought to have been', and Caruso 'won't learn anything, is lazy and too pleased with himself'. He admitted, however, that Caruso's voice was magnificent.

In New York, Puccini saw a number of plays, including three by David Belasco, whose *Madame Butterfly* he had already used. Intrigued by Belasco's *The Girl of the Golden West*, he had the play translated into Italian so that he could read it, for his English was still not good enough for him to form a knowledgable opinion from having seen it performed on the stage. Back in Italy, he decided after reading the play that *The Girl of the Golden West* would be his next opera. After agreement had been reached with Belasco, Carlo Zangarini, an Italian dramatist whose mother was American, was engaged to write the libretto. In April 1908, not having received the libretto from Zangarini, Puccini insisted on a second librettist being involved. Guelfo Civinini rewrote the two acts that Zangarini had already com-pleted, and he wrote the third act alone.

Puccini began to compose *La fanciulla del West* in May 1908 at his villa in Torre del Lago, but his work on it was interrupted by a domestic tragedy – his house-maid Doria Manfredi committed suicide after Puccini's neurotically jealous wife, Elvira, had accused her of having an affair with the composer and had vilified her throughout the village. The girl's family brought legal action against Elvira Puccini, and eventually Puccini found himself having to pay the Manfredi family a substantial sum of money.

It was not until September 1909 that he was able to return to his opera. By the following July it had been completed and orchestrated, and Puccini, accom-panied by his son Tonio, travelled to New York, where the work was to have its premiere at the Metropolitan Opera on 10 December 1910. Arturo Toscanini con-ducted, Emmy Destinn sang the title role and Enrico Caruso, despite Puccini's reservations about his performance in *Madama Butterfly*, was the bandit hero. The first-night audience applauded vociferously, fifty-five curtain calls were taken and Puccini was presented with a laurel wreath. The Metropolitan Opera revived *La Fanciulla del West* for the next three seasons, after which the work was not seen again in New York until 1929. For a time, it remained one of Puccini's less frequently performed operas, but in recent years it has become more popular.

Act I. The Polka Saloon. It is sunset. Customers begin to arrive, and soon the bar is full of miners drinking, gambling and quarrelling. A nostalgic song about home ('Che faranno i vecchi miei'), sung by the travelling minstrel Jake Wallace, causes one of the miners, Larkens, to burst into tears, and a collection is taken up to enable him to return to his distant home. Another miner, who has cheated at cards, is saved from being lynched by the intervention of the sheriff, Jack Rance. Ashby, the Wells Fargo agent, arrives and tells Rance that the notorious bandit Ramerrez has been seen in the vicinity. Rance and Sonora, a miner, quarrel over Minnie, the owner of the saloon, whom they both want to marry. Minnie enters, separates the two men and proceeds to read to the miners from the Bible. When the Pony Express rider arrives with the mail, Ashby questions him about Nina, an ex-mistress of Ramerrez whom Ashby believes will lead him to the bandit's hiding place. Ashby leaves to meet Nina, while Rance declares his love for Minnie ('Minnie, dalla mia casa son partito'), who rejects him, telling him that she hopes to find a man she can love as completely as her poor but worthy father and mother loved each other ('Laggiù nel Soledad').

A stranger, who gives his name as Dick Johnson, enters the saloon and is recognized by Minnie as a man she once met while travelling and always hoped to meet again. The sheriff, jealous of Minnie's interest in the stranger, tries unsuccessfully to turn the miners against him. While Minnie and Dick Johnson are waltzing in the adjoining dance hall, Ashby returns with Castro, a member of Ramerrez's gang whom he has captured. Castro gives him false information, offering to lead a posse to the bandit's hideout, but manages to whisper to Dick Johnson (who is really the bandit Ramerrez) that the gang is nearby, awaiting his signal to steal the miners' gold from the saloon where Minnie holds it in safekeeping. A posse is formed and sets out, leaving Minnie and Ramerrez alone in the saloon. They are clearly attracted to each other, and Ramerrez accepts Minnie's invitation to visit her later that evening in her cabin, halfway up the mountainside.

Act II. Minnie's log cabin, an hour later. Billy Jackrabbit, a Red Indian, is talking to his squaw Wowkle (Minnie's housekeeper) and their papoose. Minnie enters, dismisses Billy and orders Wowkle to clean up the cabin in preparation for her visitor. When Ramerrez arrives, Minnie tells him about her life as a saloon-keeper in the miners' camp, and her love of the mountains ('Oh, se sapeste'). They kiss and declare their passion for each other. Ramerrez thinks he ought to leave, but as it is snowing heavily, he accepts Minnie's invitation to stay and retires to her bed while she curls up by the fire. When Rance arrives with Nick the barman, Ashby and Sonora, Minnie hides her visitor behind the bed curtains. By showing her a photograph of Ramerrez, the sheriff is able to convince Minnie that the man she knows as Dick Johnson is in fact the bandit. After Rance and the others have departed, Minnie listens to Ramerrez's justification of his way of life ('Una parola sola'), but then she orders him to leave.

Shortly after Ramerrez has gone, shots ring out, and he is heard to fall against the door. Minnie drags him inside and hides him in the loft as Rance returns. The sheriff searches the cabin and is about to leave again when a drop of blood falling on his hand from above reveals that the bandit is in the loft. Ramerrez is brought down into the cabin, where he faints. To save his life, Minnie proposes a game of poker to the sheriff. If Rance wins, he marries Minnie and takes Ramerrez as his prisoner. If he loses, Ramerrez will go free. Rance agrees, and Minnie wins the game by cheating.

Act III. A clearing in the forest, not far from the mining camp, at dawn, a few days later. The miners have been searching for Ramerrez. News is brought to Rance that he has been caught, and shortly afterwards Ramerrez is dragged in. The miners gleefully anticipate a lynching, but Nick the barman surreptitiously slips away to find Minnie. Ramerrez admits to being a thief but swears that he has never killed anyone. He is then accused by the miners of having stolen not only gold but also the affections of Minnie. Ramerrez asks them to kill him quickly but to allow Minnie to think that he has escaped ('Ch'ella mi creda libero e lontano'). He is about to be hanged when Minnie arrives on horseback, brandishing a pistol. She reminds the miners of all she has done for them, and pleads with them to spare the life of the man she loves. Despite the sheriff's protests, Ramerrez is freed and leaves with Minnie to begin a new life far from California, while the miners express their sorrow at losing their beloved Minnie.

Puccini's opera captures remarkably well the atmosphere of the Californian goldfields. Indeed his score, though written in 1909–10, would not sound out of place accompanying a Hollywood Western of the 1930s. What it in fact accom-panies is a flexible vocal line and some authentic-sounding Californian melodies, wispily strung throughout Act I in particular. La fanciulla del West may lack the fresh melodic prodigality of La Bohème, but it grows on one with repeated hearings – for the subtlety of its orchestration and the modernity of its har-monies, as well as for Puccini's genius for musical characterization. Its arias are shorter, fewer and more closely integrated into the fabric of the composition than those of some of Puccini's earlier operas, but they are no less appealing, especially Jack Rance's 'Minnie, dalla mia casa son partito', with its gloomy beginning and its bitter climax, Minnie's lightly scored 'Laggiù nel Soledad', and the opera's best-known number, Ramerrez's grave and restrained lament, 'Ch'ella mi creda libero e lontano'.

Recommended recording: Carol Neblett (Minnie), Placido Domingo (Ramerrez), Sherrill Milnes (Jack Rance), with the Chorus and Orchestra of the Royal Opera House, Covent Garden, conducted by Zubin Mehta. DG 419 640–2. This recording, lovingly and excitingly conducted by Mehta, benefits from being based on a Covent Garden stage production with the same conductor and many of the same cast. As she did in the opera house, Carol Neblett brings her rich, eloquent timbre to Minnie, and Placido Domingo in sturdy voice is convincing as Ramerrez. Sherrill Milnes is well cast as the sheriff, and a large company of Covent Garden regulars is, without excep-tion, superb.

Il trittico
(The Triptych)
three one-act operas

For some years Puccini had been thinking of composing two or three one-act operas for performance together on the same evening, but it was not until 1912, when he saw a play in Paris, *La Houppelande* (The Cloak) by Didier Gold, that he decided he had found the first of his possible subjects. Giovacchino Forzano, a twenty-nine-year-old playwright and stage director, recommended Ferdinando Martini, an elderly writer and politician, as librettist, but Martini worked very slowly, and when Puccini attempted to speed him up, he relin-quished the task. Giuseppe Adami (who was also to write the text of *La rondine* [The Swallow] for Puccini) completed the libretto of *Il tabarro* within two weeks towards the end of 1913. Puccini composed the opera and then put it aside to work on *La rondine*, a light opera commissioned by the Carltheater in Vienna. By the time he had completed *La rondine* Austria and Italy were fighting on opposite sides in World War I, and so the work was given its first performance not in Vienna but in Monte Carlo, on 27 March 1917.

Two months before the premiere of *La rondine* Forzano showed Puccini a one-act play with an all-female cast, set in a convent, which he had written for a touring theatrical company. The composer thought it would make an ideal companion piece to *Il tabarro* and encouraged Forzano to turn it into the libretto for an opera, which became *Suor Angelica*. While Puccini was composing that, Forzano had another idea, based on a few lines in Dante's *Inferno* about a Florentine rogue called Gianni Schicchi. Puccini was delighted with it, Forzano wrote a libretto and the composer began work on *Gianni Schicchi* even before he had finished what he called his 'nun opera'.

When the three one-act operas, under the joint title of *Il trittico*, were first performed at the Metropolitan Opera House, New York, on 14 December 1918, *Gianni Schicchi* was the only one to be enthusiastically received, and it is this work that has continued to prove the most popular of the three, performed usually with only one other short opera, either *Il tabarro* or a work by some other composer. *Suor Angelica* is the least often performed segment of *Il trittico*. Puccini himself came to accept that the three operas, with intervals separating them, made too long an evening. 'At Bologna', he told Giuseppe Adami, 'they seemed to me as long as a transatlantic cable'.

Il tabarro
(The Cloak)
opera in one act (approximate length: 55 minutes)

Michele, a barge owner, aged 50   *baritone*
Luigi, aged 20   *tenor* ⎤
Tinca, aged 35   *tenor* ⎥ stevedores
Talpa, aged 55   *bass* ⎦
Giorgetta, Michele's wife, aged 25   *soprano*
La Frugola, Talpa's wife, aged 50   *mezzo-soprano*

LIBRETTO BY GIUSEPPE ADAMI, BASED ON THE PLAY *LA HOUPPELANDE*, BY DIDIER GOLD; TIME: THE BEGINNING OF THE TWENTIETH CENTURY; PLACE: PARIS; FIRST PERFORMED AT THE METROPOLITAN OPERA HOUSE, NEW YORK, 14 DECEMBER 1918

The action takes place in Paris, on a barge tied to a landing stage on the Seine. It is twilight. While Michele, the barge owner, stands at the helm watching the sunset, his young wife Giorgetta busies herself with various tasks and the

stevedores finish unloading sacks of cement from the barge onto the quay. When
their work is completed, Michele goes below, Giorgetta produces a jug of wine and
the stevedores drink and dance to the accompaniment of a barrel organ on the
quayside. Giorgetta and Luigi, the youngest stevedore, are dancing together when
Michele comes up on deck again, and the merriment ceases. La Frugola, a rag-
picker, arrives to collect her husband, Talpa, with whom she sets off home as the
sky darkens.

Giorgetta and Luigi, who is her secret lover, make plans to meet later in the
evening. He will come aboard at her usual signal, the lighting of a match. Before
he leaves the barge, Luigi asks Michele to pay him off when they reach Rouen,
for he intends to look for work there. Left alone with his wife, Michele recalls their
past happiness, reminding Giorgetta of the days when he used to shelter her
beneath his cloak as they stood on the deck. He reproaches her for no longer loving him, but she replies that nothing has changed except that they are now both
older, and she goes below to their cabin. Michele, convinced that she has a lover,
wonders which of the stevedores it might be. When Michele lights his pipe, Luigi,
watching from the shadows, mistakes this for Giorgetta's signal and comes on
board. Forcing the youth to confess that he is Giorgetta's lover, Michele strangles
him and hides the body under his cloak. Alarmed by the noise, Giorgetta comes
up on deck. She attempts to make her peace with Michele, and he invites her to
nestle close to him, as she used to do, inside his cloak. As she approaches, he flings
the cloak open, revealing the dead body of Luigi.

Il tabarro's impressionistic score is highly atmospheric. The brooding theme of
the orchestral prelude summons up the weariness of life on the barge, and the
night sounds of Paris and its river permeate the opening scene. There are very few
lyrical moments in the opera, and only one extended aria, Michele's 'Nulla!
Silenzio!', which dramatically portrays the betrayed husband's jealousy and
despair. Though hardly memorable, Puccini's score carries the melodramatic
action along with strength and conviction.

Suor Angelica
(Sister Angelica)
opera in one act (approximate length: 1 hour)

Sister Angelica   *soprano*
The Princess, her aunt   *contralto*

The Abbess   *mezzo-soprano*
The Sister Monitor   *mezzo-soprano*
The Mistress of the Novices   *mezzo-soprano*
Sister Genovieffa   *soprano*
Sister Osmina   *soprano*
Sister Dolcina   *soprano*
The Nursing Sister   *mezzo-soprano*

LIBRETTO BY GIOVACCHINO FORZANO; TIME: THE END OF THE SEVENTEENTH
CENTURY; PLACE: A CONVENT IN ITALY; FIRST PERFORMED AT THE METROPOLITAN
OPERA HOUSE, NEW YORK, 14 DECEMBER 1918

The action takes place in the cloisters of an Italian convent. As the nuns finish singing an *Ave Maria* in the chapel, they emerge to take up their daily tasks. Sister Angelica, who is of noble birth, has been in the convent for seven years, during which time she has received no news of her family, who forced her to enter the convent after she gave birth to an illegitimate child.

Alms collectors arrive, reporting that a splendid carriage has been seen at the convent gate. Angelica questions them about its appearance and its coat of arms, for she hopes it might herald the arrival of one of her relatives. The Abbess enters, asks the other nuns to withdraw and informs Angelica that her aunt, the Princess, has come to visit her.

Angelica's aunt tells her, frigidly, that the estate of Angelica's late parents is to be divided, as her younger sister is about to marry. The Princess has brought with her a document for Angelica to sign, renouncing her inheritance in favour of her sister. When Angelica begs for news of her child, the Princess tells her that the boy became ill and died two years ago. Angelica's sobs of despair elicit no compassion from her aunt, who leaves after Angelica has signed the document.

When night has fallen, Angelica, longing to be united with her child in heaven, takes poison. Immediately remorseful, and fearing that she will die in mortal sin, she prays to the Virgin Mary and is answered by a heavenly choir. The chapel doors swing open and the Virgin appears, leading a small child towards Angelica, who dies in a state of ecstasy.

The sentimental religiosity of Forzano's libretto is matched by a corresponding quality in the music. Angelica's 'Senza mamma' is one of Puccini's finest dramatic arias, but most of his score is distastefully saccharine. Although the work can be effective as part of a complete performance of the triptych, sandwiched between the violence of *Il tabarro* and the humour of *Gianni Schicchi*, the comparative neglect of *Suor Angelica* is not difficult to comprehend.

Gianni Schicchi
opera in one act (approximate length: 55 minutes)

Gianni Schicchi, aged 50 *baritone*
Lauretta, his daughter, aged 21 *soprano*
Zita, cousin of Buoso Donati, aged 60 *contralto*
Rinuccio, Zita's nephew, aged 24 *tenor*
Gherardo, Buoso's nephew, aged 40 *tenor*
Nella, Gherardo's wife, aged 34 *soprano*
Gherardino, their son, aged 7 *contralto*
Betto di Signa, Buoso's brother-in-law, age unguessable *bass*
Simone, Buoso's cousin, aged 70 *bass*
Marco, Simone's son, aged 45 *baritone*
La Ciesca, Marco's wife, aged 38 *mezzo-soprano*

LIBRETTO BY GIOVACCHINO FORZANO; TIME: 1299; PLACE: FLORENCE; FIRST PERFORMED AT THE METROPOLITAN OPERA HOUSE, NEW YORK, 14 DECEMBER 1918

Forzano's idea for *Gianni Schicchi* came from a few lines in Canto XXX of Dante's *Inferno* that refer to 'that hellhound', the Florentine Gianni Schicchi, who, to win himself a mule,

> . . . *lent his own false frame*
> *To Buoso de' Donati, and made a will*
> *In legal form, and forged it in his name.*

The action takes place in a bedchamber in the house of Buoso Donati, a wealthy landowner who has just died. Buoso's relatives have gathered around the bed in which the old man's body still lies. They all feign grief, but when Betto, Buoso's brother-in-law, mentions a rumour that Buoso has left all his wealth to the local monastery, a rapid search is made for the will. The young Rinuccio finds it, but before handing it over he extracts a promise from his aunt Zita that, since they are now all going to be rich, she will allow him to marry Lauretta, the daughter of Gianni Schicchi, an upstart from the country who is looked down upon by the

Donati relatives. Aunt Zita hurriedly agrees, but when Buoso Donati's will is opened it is discovered that he had, indeed, left everything to the monastery.

Rinuccio, who has already sent the child Gherardino to fetch Gianni Schicchi and Lauretta, suggests that they seek the advice of Schicchi, who is renowned for his cunning. When Schicchi and Lauretta arrive, Schicchi at first refuses to help the Donati relatives, but he is finally persuaded by Lauretta, who begs her father to help her marry Rinuccio ('O mio babbino caro'). Schicchi then reveals his scheme. The relatives are to suppress the news of Buoso's death and hide his body until Schicchi, posing as the mortally ill Buoso, has dictated a new will, distributing the old man's wealth equitably among the members of his family. Buoso's body is removed, and Schicchi takes its place in the bed. But when the Notary arrives, Schicchi, posing as Buoso Donati, bequeaths the most valuable parts of the estate to his 'devoted friend, Gianni Schicchi'.

The relatives are aghast but are forced to remain silent, for Schicchi has reminded them graphically that the penalty for falsifying a will entails exile from Florence and the amputation of the right hand. When the Notary has departed, Schicchi drives Buoso's relatives out of the house, with the exception of Rinuccio, who remains on the terrace with Lauretta. Schicchi bids the audience farewell with a brief, self-congratulatory speech.

Puccini's only comic opera is a fast-moving piece that owes something to Verdi's *Falstaff*. Its entire score is melodically inventive and the composer's musical characterization is, as usual, on a high level. Lauretta's sweetly charming aria, 'O mio babbino caro', the opera's only moment of lyrical repose, is well known outside the context of the work.

Recommended recording: Renata Scotto (Giorgetta/Angelica), Ileana Cotrubas (Suor Genovieffa/Lauretta), Placido Domingo (Luigi/Rinuccio), Ingvar Wixell (Michele), Tito Gobbi (Schicchi), with the New Philharmonia Chorus and Orchestra and the London Symphony Orchestra, conducted by Lorin Maazel. CBS/Sony CD79312. Gobbi's Gianni Schicchi is a marvellous piece of vocal acting, Scotto successfully differentiates the voluptuous Giorgetta and the saintly Angelica, and Cotrubas is an appealing Lauretta.

Turandot

opera in three acts (approximate length: 1 hour, 45 minutes)

Princess Turandot   *soprano*
The Emperor Altoum, her father   *tenor*
Timur, the dethroned Tartar King   *bass*
Calaf, his son   *tenor*
Liù, a young slave girl   *soprano*
Ping, grand chancellor   *baritone*
Pang, grand purveyor   *tenor*
Pong, chief cook   *tenor*
A Mandarin   *baritone*

LIBRETTO BY GIUSEPPE ADAMI AND RENATO SIMONI, BASED ON THE PLAY *TURANDOT*, BY CARLO GOZZI; TIME: THE LEGENDARY PAST; PLACE: PEKING; FIRST PERFORMED AT THE TEATRO ALLA SCALA, MILAN, 25 APRIL 1926

After the first performances of *Il trittico*, Puccini lost no time in searching for his next opera libretto. Among the subjects he considered was *Christopher Sly*, based on a character in Shakespeare's *The Taming of the Shrew*, Charles Dickens's *Oliver Twist* and a new play by David Belasco, who had already provided him with two subjects, *Madama Butterfly* and *La fanciulla del West*. Eventually his choice fell upon *Turandot*, a play described by its author, Carlo Gozzi (1720–1806) as a tragicomic Chinese fairy story in five acts. Giuseppe Adami was engaged to write his third Puccini libretto, this time with a collaborator, the Gozzi scholar Renato Simoni. Adami and Simoni adapted the play, tightening up its action considerably, compressing it into three acts, and in the process emphasizing the tragic elements in the plot at the expense of the comic. Puccini played an active role in the preparation of the libretto, corresponding with Adami over a period of four years, and showering instructions and advice upon him. In the spring of 1920 Puccini wrote:

Make Gozzi's *Turandot* your basis, but on that you must rear another figure; I mean – I can't explain! From our imaginations (and we shall need them) there must arise so much that is beautiful and attractive and gracious as to make our story a <u>bouquet</u> of success. Do not make too much use of the stock characters of the Venetian drama – these are to be the clowns and philosophers that here or there throw in a jest or an opinion (well chosen, as also the moment for it), but they must not be the type that thrust themselves forward continually or demand too much attention.

'*Turandot* is groaning and travailing, but pregnant with music,' Puccini reported to Adami in the middle of 1921, but in November 1922 he and Adami were still having trouble with the shape of the opera. 'I am so sad! and discouraged too,' Puccini wrote:

> *Turandot* is there with the first act finished, and there isn't a ray to pierce the gloom which shrouds the rest. Perhaps it is wrapped forever in impenetrable darkness. I have the feeling that I shall have to put this work on one side. We are on the wrong track for the rest of the opera. I think the second and third acts are a great mistake as we have envisaged them. I am coming back, there-fore, to the idea of two acts, and getting to the end now in only one more act.

However, the three-act structure prevailed, and in January 1924 Puccini attempted to orchestrate the first part of Act III while awaiting pieces of text. In September he was still asking for the words of the final duet. He eventually received them in October and thought them 'very beautiful', but he could not begin to set them immediately as he was about to travel to Brussels to consult a famous specialist about a persistent pain in his throat. He was never to return from Brussels. On 24 November he underwent an operation for cancer of the throat. The operation was thought to have been successful, but five days later his heart gave way under the strain of the treatment. He died at four o'clock in the morning on 29 November 1924.

When *Turandot* was given its first performance at La Scala on 25 April 1926, Arturo Toscanini, who conducted, laid down his baton at the end of Liù's funeral procession in Act III and turned to the audience with the words, 'Here ends the opera left incomplete by the maestro, who died at this point.' The love duet and finale, approximately fourteen minutes of music, was completed by Franco Alfano (1875–1954), an experienced composer with, at that time, eight operas to his credit; however, it was only at its second performance that the opera was performed complete with Alfano's ending, which was partly based on sketches left by Puccini. An alternative ending by the Italian composer Luciano Berio was performed for the first time in 2003.

Act I. Outside the imperial palace, at sunset. A Mandarin reads to the assem-bled crowd a proclamation that refers to the decree that the Princess Turandot will marry whichever royal suitor succeeds in answering her three riddles. Those who fail are beheaded, and a sentence of death is now proclaimed upon Turandot's latest unsuccessful suitor, the Prince of Persia, who is to be executed when the moon rises. Among the jostling crowd is a blind old man who is being led by a young girl. When the old man is knocked down, the handsome youth who goes to his aid discovers to his joy that the man is his father, Timur, the deposed King of Tartary. Timur tells his son, Prince Calaf, who, like his father, is travelling incognito, that he was helped to escape by the slave girl Liù, who has led him to Peking.

When the moon rises and the young Prince of Persia is led to the scaffold, the assembled citizens take pity on him and call for mercy. Calaf curses the cruelty of Princess Turandot, but when she appears on a balcony of the palace, gesturing that the execution should proceed, he is struck by her beauty and immediately falls in love with her. Timur and Liù, who is secretly in love with Calaf, try to dissuade him ('Signor, ascolta'), and Calaf, in turn, attempts to comfort them ('Non piangere, Liù'). However, he is about to strike the great gong, to signify his intention of becoming Turandot's next suitor, when his way is blocked by the Emperor of China's three chief ministers, Ping (grand chancellor), Pang (grand purveyor) and Pong (chief cook). The spirits of Turandot's many unsuccessful suitors also appear, proclaiming their love for Turandot from beyond the grave, but Calaf, undeterred, strikes the gong.

Act II, scene i. A pavilion of the imperial palace. Ping, Pang and Pong lament the wretched condition of the country due to Tuandot's cruel law requiring the execution of her unsuccessful suitors. They dream of their homes in the countryside, far from the bloodshed of Peking, and long for a suitor to appear who can answer the riddles and restore happiness to China. Trumpets summon them to the ceremony in which Calaf will be tested.

Act II, scene ii. A large courtyard in the palace. A crowd of citizens watches as the aged Emperor Altoum, seated on his throne at the top of a great marble staircase, attempts without success to dissuade Calaf from his undertaking. Princess Turandot enters. She explains that thousands of years ago her ancestress the Princess Lo-u-Ling was ravished and killed by a barbarian king, and that she, Turandot, is avenging Lo-u-Ling by refusing to be possessed by any man and by killing those who dare to desire her ('In questa reggia'). She poses the first of her three riddles: 'What is the name of the phantom which spreads its wings at night over the black infinity of humankind, which is invoked by all, but which disappears at dawn. What is this thing which is born every night and which dies every day?' Calaf gives the correct answer, which is 'Hope'. Turandot proceeds to her second question: 'It flickers like flame, but is not flame. Sometimes it rages, sometimes it is languorous. When one is defeated, it grows cold. When one is victorious, it is hot.' Again, though this time only after some hesitation, Calaf gives the right answer, 'Blood'. An angry Turandot asks the third question: 'Ice that sets you on fire, but which becomes icier from your fire. One who, setting you free, makes a slave of you. One who, taking you as a slave, makes you a king. What is this frost which gives off fire?' After a long pause, Calaf answers, 'Turandot.' He has solved all three riddles, and the crowd acclaims him. Turandot, humiliated, begs her father not to sacrifice her to a stranger, but the Emperor declares that his oath is sacred. Calaf, however, offers to release Turandot and to die, if she can discover his name before dawn. Turandot signifies her assent, and the Emperor expresses the hope that at dawn he will gain a son.

Act III, scene i. The garden of the palace, shortly before dawn. The voices of heralds can be heard proclaiming Turandot's decree that no one must sleep, for all must help her discover the name of the stranger before dawn. Calaf enters, confident that the dawn will bring him victory and Turandot's love ('Nessun dorma') and scornful of the wealth and beautiful women offered to him by Ping, Pang and Pong in return for his agreeing to leave Peking. Timur and Liù, who have been seen with Calaf, are dragged in by guards who attempt to extract Calaf's name from them. Turandot appears and begins to question Timur, but Liù saves the old man by announcing that only she knows the stranger's name. Liù is tortured, but says she would rather die than reveal the name. When Turandot asks what gives her such strength, Liù replies that it is her love for the man whom she predicts Turandot will also come to love ('Tu che di gel sei cinta'). Fearing, however, that further torture may force her to reveal Calaf's name, Liu seizes a dagger and kills herself.

Liù's body is born away. When Calaf and Turandot are left alone, he reproaches her for her cruelty and then kisses her passionately. Turandot, bewildered, begs him to go and to take the mystery of his name with him. Instead, Calaf confidently gives her his name as trumpets are heard heralding the dawn and summoning all to the palace.

Act III, scene ii. The palace courtyard. An assembled crowd greets the Emperor, Turandot announces that the name of the stranger is Love, and she and Calaf embrace.

Six months before his death, Puccini wrote to Adami: 'Hour by hour and minute by minute I think of *Turandot*, and all the music I have written up to now seems a jest in comparison, and pleases me no more.' Although *La Bohème* is surely Puccini's best-loved opera, *Turandot* is generally regarded as his most accomplished, its musical invention rich, its harmonic language containing features drawn from contemporary music, its orchestral texture highly colourful and its arias always dramatically apt and characterful. Calaf's Act III aria, 'Nessun dorma', has become famous, indeed notorious, out of context, and the cruel Princess's rock-like 'In questa reggia', which begins as an aria, becomes a duet and ends as an ensemble, is the highlight of Act II. *Turandot* is undoubtedly one of the greatest operas written in the twentieth century.

Recommended recording: Eva Marton (Turandot), José Carreras (Calaf), Katia Ricciarelli (Liu), with the Vienna Boys Choir, the Vienna State Opera Chorus and Orchestra, conducted by Lorin Maazel. Sony M2K 39160. On EMI, Birgit Nilsson is a predictably sturdy exponent of the title-role, but this is the best all-round performance, recorded live in Vienna in 1983. Eva Marton is the most exciting Turandot on disc, José Carreras is in fine, youthful voice as Calaf, and Katia Ricciarelli is an affecting Liu. The Vienna chorus and orchestra, under Maazel, are in thrilling form, and the atmosphere in the Vienna Staatsoper, with a highly enthusiastic audience, is well caught.

HENRY PURCELL
(b. London, 1659 – d. London, 1695)

Dido and Aeneas
tragic opera in three acts (approximate length: 1 hour)

Dido, Queen of Carthage *soprano*
Belinda, her confidante *soprano*
Aeneas, a Trojan prince *baritone*
Sorceress *mezzo-soprano or baritone*
Spirit, alias Mercury *soprano*
A Sailor *soprano or tenor*

LIBRETTO BY NAHUM TATE; TIME: CLASSICAL ANTIQUITY; PLACE: CARTHAGE; FIRST KNOWN PERFORMANCE AT JOSIAS PRIEST'S BOARDING SCHOOL FOR GIRLS, CHELSEA, (PROBABLY DECEMBER) 1689

Henry Purcell was born into a musical family and became a chorister in the Chapel Royal at an early age. He was twenty when he was appointed organist of Westminster Abbey and began to compose in virtually every category of music practised in his time. He wrote odes for various royal occasions, songs, and pieces for organ and for harpsichord, but developed a particular interest in music for the theatre. When he was invited by Josias Priest, who ran a girls' boarding school in Chelsea, to produce an entertainment for performance there, Purcell responded with a short opera, lasting no more than one hour. Nahum Tate, the playwright and poet best known for his bowdlerized version of Shakespeare's *King Lear* which gave the play a happy ending, produced a libretto drawn from Book 4 of Virgil's *Aeneid*, and Purcell composed his *Dido and Aeneas*, which was staged at the school some time in 1689, shortly after the accession to the throne of William and Mary. It may be, however, that the opera was originally written for a court performance, and only later adapted for the Chelsea school production, for the earliest surviving score includes a baritone Aeneas, while presumably all the roles at the Chelsea school were sung by 'young gentlewomen'.

After the school performance, *Dido and Aeneas* appears not to have been staged again during Purcell's lifetime. In 1700, when it was inserted into an adaptation of Shakespeare's *Measure for Measure* at the theatre in Lincoln's Inn Fields, the role of the Sorceress was sung by a baritone. The opera disappeared from the stage early in the eighteenth century, to be revived in London by the Royal College of Music in 1895 on the occasion of the bicentenary of Purcell's death. It is now generally recognized as the earliest great English opera.

Act I. The royal palace at Carthage. Dido, Queen of Carthage, is tormented by her growing love for Prince Aeneas ('Ah, Belinda, I am prest with torment'), who having escaped from Troy and set sail for Italy, where he is destined to be the founder of Rome, has been blown off course to Carthage. Belinda, Dido's confidante, assures the Queen that Aeneas returns her love ('Fear no danger'). When Aeneas enters with his followers, he confesses his love to Dido, who after initial hesitation accepts him. The triumph of love is celebrated by Dido's court with music and dancing ('To the hills and the vales').

Act II, scene i. A cave. The Sorceress summons her attendant witches to join her in plotting the downfall of Dido and the destruction of Carthage ('Wayward sisters'). She sends a spirit, disguised as Mercury, to carry a message to Prince Aeneas, ostensibly from Jupiter, to the effect that Aeneas must leave Carthage immediately to fulfil his destiny in Italy.

Act II, scene ii. A grove near Carthage. Dido and Aeneas pause in the middle of a hunt to enjoy their surroundings ('Thanks to these lonesome vales'). A thunderstorm brought about by the Sorceress causes them to leave ('Haste, haste to town'), but Aeneas is met by the Spirit in the guise of Mercury, who instructs him to leave Carthage that same night ('Stay, Prince'). Aeneas curses the gods who condemn him to nights of sorrow before he has enjoyed even one night of joy, but realizes that he must comply with their demand.

Act III, scene i. The quayside. Aeneas's sailors are preparing for departure ('Come away, fellow sailors') when the Sorceress and her witches enter to celebrate the ruin of Dido and the imminent destruction of Aeneas's fleet ('Destruction's our delight').

Act III, scene ii. The palace. Dido confronts Aeneas, who thinks momentarily of defying the gods and remaining in Carthage, but who finally summons up his will-power and departs. Left alone with Belinda, Dido sings a lament ('When I am laid in earth') and dies, mourned by a chorus of cupids ('With drooping wings').

Dido and Aeneas is Purcell's masterpiece and his only full-scale opera, his other works for the stage such as *King Arthur* and *The Fairy Queen* falling into the category of semi-opera (or play with musical episodes, invented by the actor–manager Thomas Betterton in 1673). Aeneas is somewhat sketchily conceived and presented, but the character of the unhappy Queen Dido is given psychological depth, not only in her marvellous lament, 'When I am laid in earth', the best-known number in the opera, but also in her recitatives, composed by Purcell with great rhythmic flexibility. The many choruses and dances are, for the most part, used not simply as divertissements but to advance the action of the work, which moves swiftly and economically to its tragic conclusion.

Recommended recording: Anne Sofie von Otter (Dido), Lynne Dawson (Belinda), Stephen Varcoe (Aeneas), Nigel Rogers (Sorceress, Sailor), with the English Concert Chorus and Orchestra, conducted by Trevor Pinnock. DG Archiv 427 624–2. Von Otter is a Dido both dignified and impassioned, and Varcoe is a sturdy Aeneas. The Sorceress is not the usual mezzo-soprano but a splendid tenor, Nigel Rogers, who also sings the lively Sailor's song delightfully.

MAURICE RAVEL
(b. Ciboure, 1875 – d. Paris, 1937)

L'Heure espagnole
(The Spanish Hour)
comédie musicale in one act (approximate length: 50 minutes)

Torquemada, a clock-maker *tenor*
Concepcion, his wife *soprano*
Gonzalve, a poet *tenor*
Ramiro, a muleteer *baritone*
Don Inigo Gomez, a banker *bass*

LIBRETTO BY FRANC-NOHAIN (PSEUDONYM OF MAURICE ETIENNE LEGRAND), BASED ON HIS PLAY *L'HEURE ESPAGNOLE*; TIME: THE EIGHTEENTH CENTURY; PLACE: TOLEDO; FIRST PERFORMED AT THE OPÉRA-COMIQUE, PARIS, 19 MAY 1911

An innovator in his music for the piano, and an orchestrator of genius, Ravel composed only two operas, both of them one-act works, each lasting less than an hour. His first, *L'Heure espagnole*, was based on a comedy of the same title by Maurice Etienne Legrand (1873–1934) which Ravel had seen in Paris in 1904 at the Théâtre de l'Odéon. Using the pseudonym of Franc-Nohain, Legrand adapted his play as a libretto for the composer, and Ravel completed his opera in vocal score by the autumn of 1907. However, the director of the Opéra-Comique considered its plot somewhat too risqué for his audiences and delayed accepting the work for production until Mme Jean Cruppi, the wife of a cabinet minister, insisted that it be staged. Not surprisingly, Ravel dedicated his opera to Mme Cruppi.

L'Heure espagnole was only moderately successful at its premiere in 1911, when it shared a double bill with Massenet's *Thérèse* at the Opéra-Comique. Two days before the premiere Ravel wrote to a colleague, 'What I've tried to do is fairly ambitious: to breathe new life into the Italian *opera buffa*, following only the principle that the French language, like any other, has its own accents and inflections of pitch.' Critical response was mixed, and even Legrand, the author of the play, thought that the opera was rather too long. It met with real success only after Ravel's death, and is now quite frequently performed, usually in tandem with the composer's only other opera, *L'Enfant et les sortilèges*.

The action takes place in the shop of the clock-maker Torquemada in eighteenth-century Toledo. Ramiro, a muscular muleteer, brings his watch to Torquemada's shop to have it mended. Concepcion, the clock-maker's wife, reminds her husband that it is Thursday, the one day of the week when he must check all the clocks in the town. Torquemada sets out, asking Ramiro to await his return and, in the meantime, allow Concepcion to entertain him. Ramiro is embarrassed because he is shy ('Les muletiers n'ont pas de conversation'), and Concepcion is annoyed because she is expecting her lover, the young poet Gonzalve. To get rid of Ramiro at least temporarily, she asks him to carry upstairs to her bedroom one of two large and heavy grandfather clocks in the shop. Ramiro is delighted to oblige, and staggers upstairs with the clock as Gonzalve arrives.

Gonzalve is still reciting his poems to Concepcion when, to her frustration, Ramiro returns from his task. A clever idea occurs to her. She tells Ramiro that she has changed her mind, and asks him to go back upstairs, return the clock to the shop, and then carry the other clock up to her bedroom. The muleteer goes off, and Concepcion hides her lover Gonzalve in the other clock. She is somewhat put out by the unexpected arrival of Don Inigo Gomez, a banker who is also an admirer of hers, and when Ramiro returns with the first clock and then proceeds to carry the second one upstairs with Gonzalve still inside it, she accompanies muleteer, clock and lover to her bedroom.

Left alone, Don Inigo decides to play a trick on Concepcion and whimsically inserts himself into the first grandfather clock, shutting its door when Ramiro comes back alone. Suddenly, Concepcion returns. Annoyed that Gonzalve has not come up to expectations, she asks Ramiro to go back upstairs and fetch the clock down again, claiming that she finds it too noisy ('Oh! La pitoyable aventure!'). The patient muleteer does as he is told, while Don Inigo takes the opportunity to declare his love for Concepcion. Naturally, he is squeezed back into the clock, and in due course carried up to the bedroom by the unsuspecting Ramiro. Unfortunately, he proves too fat to extricate himself from the clock, which Ramiro carries down again. Eventually, an exasperated Concepcion decides to leave both Gonzalve and Don Inigo to fend for themselves in the shop while she retires to the bedroom with the muleteer.

Gonzalve and Don Inigo manage to get out of their clocks, but they are still in the shop when Torquemada returns. Although he understands the situation perfectly well, the clock-maker pretends to believe their story that they are potential customers, and proceeds to sell them the two clocks. When he tells Concepcion that they now have no clocks, she replies that it does not matter, as Ramiro the muleteer has promised to return every day and tell her the time. The comedy ends with all five characters turning to address the audience in a quintet whose moral, they announce, comes from Boccaccio: 'In the pursuit of love, there comes a moment when the muleteer has his turn.'

From the clock noises of its orchestral introduction to the sparkling quintet with which the opera ends, Ravel's score is a delight, underlining Legrand's witty text with its colourful harmonies and its colloquial writing for the voices. Other than Concepcion's 'Oh! La pitoyable aventure!' there are no formal arias, but Ravel's Spanish dance rhythms, his refined writing for the orchestra and his occasional musical jokes make this elegant comedy immensely enjoyable from start to finish, as long as the singers obey Ravel's injunction to 'speak rather than sing'.

Recommended recording: Jane Berbié (Concepcion), Jean Giraudeau (Torquemada), Gabriel Bacquier (Ramiro), José van Dam (Don Inigo), Michel Sénéchal (Gonzalve), with the French Radio Chorus and Orchestra, conducted by Lorin Maazel. DG 423 718/9–2. (Coupled with Ravel's L'Enfant et les sortilèges.*) A thoroughly French and thoroughly delightful performance.*

L'Enfant et les sortilèges
(The Child and the Spells)
fantaisie lyrique in two parts (approximate length: 45 minutes)

The Child   *mezzo-soprano*
Mother   *contralto*
The Louis XV Chair   *soprano*
The Chinese Cup   *mezzo-contralto*
The Fire/the Fairy Princess/the Nightingale   *soprano*
The Female Cat   *mezzo-soprano*
The Dragonfly   *mezzo-soprano*
The Bat   *soprano*
The Owl   *soprano*
The Squirrel   *mezzo-soprano*
A Shepherdess   *soprano*
A Shepherd   *contralto*
The Armchair   *bass*
The Grandfather Clock   *baritone*
The Teapot   *tenor*
The Little Old Man (Arithmetic)/the Frog   *tenor*

The Tomcat   *baritone*
A Tree   *bass*

LIBRETTO BY COLETTE; TIME: THE EARLY TWENTIETH CENTURY; PLACE: AN OLD
COUNTRY HOUSE AND ITS GARDEN; FIRST PERFORMED AT THE THÉÂTRE DU
CASINO, MONTE CARLO, 21 MARCH 1925

The French novelist, Sidonie Gabrielle Colette (1873–1954), most of whose books were published simply under her surname, wrote *L'Enfant et les sortilèges* during World War I as the scenario for a ballet to be staged at the Paris Opéra with music by Maurice Ravel. When Ravel received her scenario in 1918 he was on active service with the French army, and it was not until 1920 that he was ready to begin the composition of what, by this time, he had decided would be an opera. Colette turned her ballet scenario into an opera libretto by rewriting it in dialogue form, and Ravel, interrupted by poor health and by work on other compositions, proceeded to set Colette's text. The opera was given its premiere not at the Paris Opéra, which had been responsible for initiating the project, but in Monte Carlo, at the opera house in the Casino, on 21 March 1925, Ravel having made the finishing touches only five days previously.

The opera was enthusiastically received, and early the following year it was produced in Paris at the Opéra-Comique, where according to Colette it played 'twice a week before a packed but turbulent house', with one faction in the audience applauding Ravel's distinctly modern, American-influenced score, while another more traditionally minded faction expressed its disapproval. America first heard *L'Enfant et les sortilèges* when it was produced in San Francisco in 1930, but the opera was not professionally staged in Britain until 1965, at Sadler's Wells Theatre, although it had been performed by students of the Oxford University Opera Club in 1958.

Scene i. A room in an old country house, giving on to the garden. A Boy, aged about six or seven, is sitting at a desk, dawdling over his lessons. When his Mother enters to give him his tea, she is annoyed to find that he has not begun his homework, and tells him that as a punishment he will be left alone in the room until supper-time. When she has gone, the naughty Child in a fit of temper rushes about the room attacking everything within reach – smashing a Teapot and Cup, torturing his pet Squirrel who runs away, pulling the tail of the family Tomcat, tearing strips of paper off the wall, swinging on the pendulum of the Grandfather Clock and tearing up his schoolbooks.

Exhausted by his orgy of destruction, the Child sinks into an Armchair, which, to his astonishment, moves away from him and begins a conversation with a Louis XV Chair. One by one, the inanimate objects in the room, which have all suffered abuse from the Child at one time or another, come to life, complaining of the treatment they have received at his hands. The Child approaches the Fire for warmth and consolation, only to find that it spits in his face and pursues him around the room, announcing that while it warms good children, it burns those who are bad. The Fairy Princess in a picture book the Child has torn up, the ending of whose story he will therefore never know, sinks through the floor, and the Child, attempting to find the final pages, uncovers instead the torn pages of an arithmetic book from which there emerges an Old Man (Arithmetic himself) who begins to reel off non-sensical mathematical problems. By the time his tormentors all retire, the Child is exhausted. The moon comes out, the Tomcat sings an amorous duet with his mate, and the walls of the room magically fall away as the scene changes to the garden.

Scene ii. The Child follows the Cats out into the garden, but even here he is not safe, for the Tree whose bark he has cut into, the Dragonfly and the Bat whose mates he has killed, all raise their voices in complaint. Frightened and lonely, the Child calls out to his Mother, at which the animals turn on him menacingly, pursuing him into a corner. In the commotion, the Squirrel is wounded and limps over to the Child, who bandages its paw with a ribbon. The other animals watch this unexpected act of tender sympathy with amazement. Now wanting to help the Child, they try to articulate the word they have heard him call out – 'Maman'. They succeed in imitating the sound of the word and lead the Child back to the house as a light comes on inside. The opera ends with the Child's now confident cry of 'Maman!' as he enters the house.

Ravel's opera is a work of sheer enchantment. His music adopts many styles: American jazz of the 1920s is brilliantly parodied in the foxtrot danced by the Chinese Cup and Teapot, who converse with each other in nonsensical English phrases ('I boxe you, I marm'lad you'); the Fire trills away in lively, bel canto-style coloratura; and the famous duet for the Cats is a veritable apotheosis of those amiable creatures' miaows. Magically orchestrated, the score exudes an innocent, childlike poetry that is as far removed as possible from the work's elegantly artificial companion piece, *L'Heure espagnole*.

Recommended recording: Françoise Ogeas (Child) and a large cast of French singers, with the French Radio Chorus and Orchestra, conducted by Lorin Maazel. DG 423 718/9–2. (Coupled with L'Heure espagnole.*) An ideal performance.*

NIKOLAI RIMSKY-KORSAKOV
(b. Tikhvin, 1844 – d. St Petersburg, 1908)

The Golden Cockerel
(Zolotoi petushok)
opera in three acts with a prologue and an epilogue
(approximate length: 2 hours, 15 minutes)

King Dodon *bass*
Prince Guidon *tenor*
Prince Afron *baritone*
General Polkan *bass*
Amelfa, the royal housekeeper *contralto*
The Astrologer *tenor*
The Queen of Shemakha *soprano*
The Golden Cockerel *soprano*

LIBRETTO BY VLADIMIR IVANOVICH BIELSKY, BASED ON THE VERSE FOLK TALE *THE GOLDEN COCKEREL*, BY ALEXANDER PUSHKIN; TIME: THE LEGENDARY PAST; PLACE: THE IMAGINARY REALM OF KING DODON; FIRST PERFORMED AT THE SOLODOVNIKOV THEATRE, MOSCOW, 7 OCTOBER 1909

Rimsky-Korsakov's fourteen operas are by far the most important part of his oeuvre, although he also composed much orchestral and chamber music and a large number of songs. His first opera, *The Maid of Pskov*, was composed between 1868 and 1872, at the same time that his friend Mussorgsky was beginning work on *Boris Godunov*. During one winter the two composers shared a small room and a piano, Mussorgsky working on his opera in the mornings and Rimsky-Korsakov on his in the afternoons. *The Maid of Pskov* was successfully produced in St Petersburg in 1873, though Rimsky-Korsakov was to make two later revisions of it.

Rimsky-Korsakov's second opera, in a simpler melodic style based on Glinka, was *May Night*, staged in St Petersburg in 1880. Like most of his later operas, it blended fairy tale and legend with supernatural elements, enabling him to indulge his gift for colourful instrumentation. Rimsky-Korsakov wrote his own libretto, basing it on a comical short story from Gogol's *Evenings on a Farm Near Dikanka*. The opera's three acts describe how Levko (tenor), in order to outwit his father, the village Mayor (bass), who will not allow him to marry Hanna (mezzo-soprano), enlists the aid of the water nymph Pannochka (soprano).

Snow Maiden, a four-act opera staged in St Petersburg in 1882, with the composer's own libretto based on a play by Ostrovsky, was followed in 1892 by *Mlada*, an unsuccessful opera-ballet in four acts, and in 1895 by *Christmas Eve*, which is not often revived.

In his autobiography, Rimsky-Korsakov described both *Mlada* and *Christmas Eve* as merely large-scale studies for his next opera, *Sadko* (1897), a work of which he was extremely proud. With a libretto by the composer and Vladimir Ivanovich Bielsky, based on an eleventh-century Russian epic poem, its seven scenes tell the story of a poor minstrel, Sadko (tenor), who is promised by Volkhova the Sea Princess (soprano) that he will be able to catch the golden fish in the sea. He succeeds, but his ships are becalmed because he has failed to pay tribute to the Sea King (bass). Sadko is set adrift on a raft, which sinks to the sea bed, where he is offered the hand of the Sea Princess in marriage. However, the opera ends with the Sea Princess transformed into a river, and Sadko back on shore.

Mozart and Salieri (1898), a short one-act piece that plays with the theory that Mozart was poisoned by his rival Salieri, was followed by *The Tsar's Bride* (1899), a conventional and largely commonplace four-act opera, and in 1901 by *Tsar Sultan*, a four-act opera in which Rimsky-Korsakov returned to the world of fairy tale and fantasy, which he was to continue to explore in *The Legend of the Invisible City of Kitezh* (1907) and *The Golden Cockerel*, which was staged posthumously in 1909.

The Golden Cockerel, Rimsky-Korsakov's final opera, was written over a period of twelve months in 1906–7. Most of it was newly composed, but the score also utilized music that the composer had originally intended for two operas that he had abandoned: *The Barber of Baghdad* (1895) and *Stenka Razin* (1905). Although its libretto is based on an imitation folk tale in verse by Russia's greatest poet, Alexander Pushkin (1799–1837), Rimsky-Korsakov's opera is really a political satire, its King Dodon, a slothful monarch engaged in extremely foolish warfare, being remarkably like the Tsar of Russia, the intelligent but weak-willed Nicholas II. Not surprisingly, in view of the fact that the Russian–Japanese war waged by Nicholas had only recently ended with the humiliating defeat of Russia, the censor forbade the opera's performance unless a number of changes were made to the libretto. These Rimsky-Korsakov refused to accept, with the result that *The Golden Cockerel* was not staged until after his death. At the opera's premiere in Moscow in 1909, King Dodon's stature was reduced to that of a general, and the commander of his forces, General Polkan, became a colonel. The offensive lines sung by the Golden Cockerel to Dodon, 'Rule, and sleep easy in your bed', were cropped to 'Sleep easy in your bed'. *The Golden Cockerel* is the only opera by Rimsky-Korsakov that is performed with reasonable frequency outside Russia.

Prologue. The Astrologer appears before the curtain to inform the audience that the fantastic tale he is about to conjure up has an excellent moral.

Act I. The throne room of King Dodon's palace. An enemy is threatening to attack Dodon's kingdom, and the elderly King, together with his two sons Guidon and Afron, the commander of his forces General Polkan and an assembly of councillors, is considering how to deal with the problem. Unable to agree on a plan of action, they are quarrelling when the Astrologer appears with a Golden Cockerel, which he offers to the King. The magical bird, the Astrologer announces, will crow whenever danger threatens the kingdom and will indicate the direction from which an attack will come. Much reassured, Dodon promises the Astrologer anything he wishes as a reward. The Astrologer replies that he requires nothing immediately, but requests the King to make his offer legal by putting it in writing. Dodon, however, takes offence at this, for he himself is the only law he acknowledges. Dismissing the Astrologer and the entire assembly, King Dodon retires to bed and is sung to sleep by his housekeeper, Amelfa. He is twice awakened by the crowing of the Cockerel. The first time his two sons are sent off at the head of an army, but on the second occasion Dodon himself reluctantly sets off to war.

Act II. A narrow mountain pass, at night. The war has gone badly, and among those killed are the two princes, Guidon and Afron. General Polkan glimpses a tent through the mist and, assuming that it belongs to the enemy, is about to fire upon it when a beautiful young woman emerges from it, causing all but Dodon and Polkan to flee. She sings an aria in praise of the sun (Hymn to the Sun), and tells Dodon that she is the Queen of Shemakha, who has come to conquer him not by force but by her beauty. She has Polkan dismissed and proceeds to seduce Dodon, making him sing and dance for her. Dodon offers her his hand in marriage, and she accepts on condition that General Polkan is whipped. Escorted by the army, Dodon and his Queen start off for Dodon's capital city.

Act III. A square in the capital city. To the cheers of the populace, a great procession arrives in the square, with Dodon and his Queen riding in a glittering chariot. The Astrologer now steps forward to claim his reward, which happens to be the Queen of Shemakha. An enraged Dodon strikes him with his sceptre, and the Astrologer falls dead. The Queen laughs, and when Dodon attempts to embrace her she repulses him. Amid gathering dark clouds, the Cockerel flies down from its perch, crowing loudly, and pecks Dodon on the head. The King falls to the ground, dead. When the clouds clear, both the Queen and the Cockerel have disappeared. The people lament the loss of their King.

Epilogue. The Astrologer begs the audience not to be alarmed by his tale, for he and the Queen were the only real people in it.

Rimsky-Korsakov wove Russian folk tunes into his colourful score with its richly orchestrated dances and choruses and its leading motifs representing the Cockerel, the Queen of Shemakha and the Astrologer. The tenor voice of the Astrologer is given music with an extremely high tessitura that at one point takes him to E above top C, while the Queen's vocal line inclines to coloratura. The sinuous melody of her Hymn to the Sun has become widely popular beyond the confines of the opera.

Recommended recording: No recording available.

GIOACHINO ROSSINI
(b. Pesaro, 1792 – d. Paris, 1868)

Tancredi
melodramma eroico in two acts (approximate length: 2 hours, 45 minutes)

Tancredi   *contralto*
Amenaide   *soprano*
Argirio, her father   *tenor*
Orbazzano   *bass*
Isaura, Amenaide's friend   *soprano*
Roggiero   *soprano*

LIBRETTO BY GAETANO ROSSI, BASED ON THE PLAY *TANCRÈDE*, BY VOLTAIRE; TIME: AD 1005; PLACE: SYRACUSE, SICILY; FIRST PERFORMED AT THE TEATRO LA FENICE, VENICE, 6 FEBRUARY 1813

In November 1812 Rossini was invited by the leading theatre in Venice, La Fenice, to compose an *opera seria* for performance three months later. The subject, Voltaire's five-act tragedy *Tancrède*, had already been chosen, a libretto was written by Gaetano Rossi, who had previously collaborated with Rossini on *La cambiale di matrimonio* (The Marriage by Promissory Note), and Rossini proceeded to compose the opera at what was his usual brisk pace.

At its premiere in Venice in February 1813, *Tancredi* was favourably received. Rossini then made some changes, and when the opera was performed several weeks later in Ferrara, it ended not with Tancredi being united with his beloved Amenaide, but with his death after being wounded in battle, as in Voltaire's play. However, audiences disliked the tragic ending, so the original was used for subsequent performances. *Tancredi* soon began to be staged in other Italian towns, always to great acclaim, and within the next few years it was translated into twelve languages and performed in most of the major European cities as well as in North and South America. Later it disappeared, along with so many other early nineteenth-century Italian operas, but then reappeared with the revival of interest in bel canto opera in the middle of the twentieth century. Giulietta Simionato sang the title role in an important revival of the opera at the Florence Maggio Musicale in 1952, conducted by Tullio Serafin, and in the 1970s and 80s in several European and American cities Marilyn Horne was a greatly admired Tancredi.

Act I. Argirio, lord of the city of Syracuse, has promised his daughter Amenaide in marriage to Orbazzano, the leader of a rival group, in an attempt to unite all factions of the city against their common enemy, the Saracens, who are besieging the city. Amenaide, in despair because she is in love with Tancredi, son of the deposed King of Syracuse, does not tell her beloved of the plans her father has for her marriage. Instead, she warns him that he is suspected of being in league with the Saracens and urges him to flee. When Amenaide refuses to marry him, Orbazzano falsely accuses her of treachery and has her thrown into prison to await sentence by her father.

Act II. Tancredi returns and, in disguise, challenges Orbazzano to a duel to prove Amenaide's innocence, although he himself believes her guilty. Orbazzano is killed in the combat, and Tancredi rushes off to defend the city against an attack by the Saracens. His forces defeat the enemy, the truth regarding Amenaide's supposed treachery is revealed and she and Tancredi are united.

Tancredi is the first of Rossini's great contributions to the genre of *opera seria*. Disconcertingly, its overture is not a newly composed piece, but the overture to an earlier work, the comedy *La pietra del paragone* which, since Venice had not heard that opera, Rossini saw no reason not to use again. Stendhal, in his life of Rossini, described *Tancredi* as 'a genuine thunderbolt out of a clear, blue sky for the Italian lyric theatre', and the opera is indeed one of youthful lyricism and vitality, bolstered by the composer's strong feeling for dramatic movement. 'Di tanti palpiti', the cabaletta of Tancredi's Act I cavatina in which he declares his love for Amenaide, is one of Rossini's most delectable tunes. It quickly became so popular that it was continually being whistled throughout Venice. Other highlights of the score include two love duets for Tancredi and Amenaide in which Rossini tempers the vocal fireworks with tenderness, the Act I finale for sextet and chorus, and Argirio's aria 'Ah! Segnar invano io tento'.

Recommended recording: Ernesto Palacio (Argirio), Marilyn Horne (Tancredi), Lella Cuberli (Amenaide), with the Chorus and Orchestra of the Teatro La Fenice, conducted by Ralf Weikert. Sony S3K 39073. This live recording, made in 1983, does full justice to the work, with Cuberli an expressive and vocally exciting heroine, and Marilyn Horne in splendid form as the eponymous hero. Palacio's agile tenor makes light of the difficult role of Argirio, and Weikert conducts efficiently.

L'italiana in Algeri
(The Italian Girl in Algiers)
dramma giocoso in two acts (approximate length: 2 hours, 15 minutes)

Isabella, a young Italian woman   *contralto*
Mustafa, Bey of Algiers   *bass*
Elvira, his wife   *soprano*
Lindoro, an Italian   *tenor*
Zulma, Elvira's confidante   *mezzo-soprano*
Taddeo, Isabella's companion   *bass*
Haly, in the Bey's service   *bass*

LIBRETTO BY ANGELO ANELLI; TIME: THE PAST; PLACE: ALGIERS; FIRST PERFORMED AT THE TEATRO SAN BENEDETTO, VENICE, 22 MAY 1813

After *Tancredi* at the Teatro La Fenice in February 1813, Rossini had agreed to write an opera for another Venetian theatre, the San Benedetto, for performance in May. By mid-April he had returned to Venice after staging *Tancredi* in Ferrara and was at work on the new opera, *L'italiana in Algeri*. Its libretto by Angelo Anelli had already been used by another composer, Luigi Mosca, whose opera was staged in Milan in 1808. Anelli, a prolific librettist of the day, had based his plot on the legend of Roxelane, the beautiful slave of the sixteenth-century Turkish ruler Suleiman the Magnificent, but he may also have had in mind the story of Antonietta Suini, a young aristocratic Milanese woman whom Algerian pirates abducted from a ship in 1805, and who was returned to Italy a few years later, having been a member of more than one harem in Algiers.

Rossini, proud of his speed in composition, told the Venice correspondent of a German newspaper that it had taken him only eighteen days to write his new opera. At its premiere it was received with noisy enthusiasm, and it soon became immensely popular throughout Italy and abroad. Today it is one of the most frequently performed of Rossini's comedies, after *Il barbiere di Siviglia* and *La Cenerentola*.

Act I, scene i. A small chamber in the palace of Mustafa, the Bey of Algiers. Elvira, the Bey's wife, is unhappy because she has lost the love of her husband. When the Bey enters, he orders her and the harem's eunuchs from the room and then confides to Haly, the captain of his pirates, that he is going to marry Elvira off to Lindoro, a young Italian whom the pirates recently captured and who is now a slave of the Bey. The Bey himself has decided he would like an Italian wife, and gives Haly six days in which to find him one, or face impalement. Haly departs hastily to set about his difficult task, as Lindoro enters lamenting his absence from the woman he loves ('Languir per una bella'). The Bey informs Lindoro, to the youth's dismay, that he is about to be given a beautiful wife.

Act I, scene ii. By the seashore. Haly and his pirates have boarded a storm-wrecked vessel, which is now rapidly subsiding. They have captured its passengers, among whom are Isabella, a beautiful young Italian woman, and Taddeo, her would-be suitor. Questioned by the delighted Haly, Isabella, who has been travelling in search of her beloved Lindoro, pretends that she and Taddeo are uncle and niece. She laments her present situation ('Cruda sorte!') and quarrels with Taddeo ('Ai capricci della sorte') as they are led off to the Bey.

Act I, scene iii. The small chamber in Mustafa's palace. Mustafa is busily arranging for Elvira to be sent to Italy with Lindoro, when Haly enters with the glad tidings that, as ordered, he has found a beautiful Italian woman. The Bey expresses his delight.

Act I, scene iv. A magnificent apartment in the palace. Isabella is brought before the Bey, who is seated upon a luxurious couch. He is enchanted by her beauty, while she finds him an absolutely ridiculous figure and is certain that she can control the situation ('Oh, che muso, che figura!'). When Lindoro and Elvira enter to say farewell to the Bey, Isabella and Lindoro recognize each other and express their joy surreptitiously. Isabella persuades the Bey that if he is to win her love he must give Lindoro to her as her slave, and must not send his wife away. The confused Bey, already hopelessly in love with her, accepts Isabella's conditions.

Act II, scene i. The small chamber. Elvira, her confidante Zulma, the eunuchs and Haly are astonished to observe how docile the ferocious Bey has become, while Lindoro and Isabella confirm their love for each other and plan their escape. In order to impress Isabella, Mustafa bestows the title of Kaimakan, or Lieutenant, upon Taddeo. At first Taddeo attempts to evade the honour, especially as it requires him to be dressed as a Muslim ('Ho un gran peso sulla testa'), but he hastily accepts when the Bey becomes angry.

Act II, scene ii. Isabella's splendid apartment in the palace, with a balcony overlooking the sea. Isabella awaits the arrival of Mustafa to take coffee with her. When she observes the Bey and his Kaimakan Taddeo arriving and watching her from a distance, she pretends to pray to the goddess of love to be made more beautiful so that she will be pleasing to the Bey ('Per lui che adoro'). So that he can be alone with Isabella, Mustafa has instructed Taddeo to send everyone out of the room when he gives the signal by sneezing. However, his sneezes are studiously ignored by all ('Ti presento di mia man').

Act II, scene iii. The small chamber. Lindoro explains to the Bey that the only reason Isabella is reluctant to marry him is that he does not belong to the noble Italian order of 'Pappataci', complaisant husbands who never lose their temper with their wives, and that she intends, in a solemn ceremony, to induct him into the order and make him her personal Pappataci. The Bey agrees.

Act II, scene iv. Isabella's apartment. Mustafa is prepared for the Pappataci ceremony by all the Italian slaves in his household. Isabella intends to take these Italians with her when she and Lindoro escape, and she encourages them with a patriotic aria ('Pensa alla patria'). The Bey's guards are plied with drink, and the ceremony begins. The foolish Bey, now a Pappataci, remains complaisant even when sailors enter to announce to the Italians that their ship is ready to depart. The Italians all leave, and the Bey, realizing too late that he has been tricked, renounces Italian women and begs Elvira's forgiveness.

The earliest of Rossini's great comic operas, *L'italiana in Algeri* is a work in which youthful high spirits and graceful melody alternate. Still widely performed today, it is the kind of sparkling, brittle and unsentimental comic piece most readily associated with the name of Rossini. Its tunes are basically simple, though embellished to give the singers opportunities for display, and its orchestration is attractive and imaginative. Highlights of the score include the hectic, ridiculously onomato-poeic Act I finale, the delightful sneezing quintet ('Ti presento di mia man') in Act II, and Isabella's two arias, the second of which, 'Pensa alla patria' (Think of your country), with its appeal to patriotism, was considered subversive by the censor-ship authorities in several Italian cities. In Rome, the word 'patria' had to be replaced by 'sposa' (wife).

Recommended recording: Teresa Berganza (Isabella), Luigi Alva (Lindoro), Rolando Panerai (Taddeo), Fernando Corena (Mustafa), with the Chorus and Orchestra of the Maggio Musicale, conducted by Silvio Varviso. Decca 417 828–2. This is stylishly conducted by Varviso, with Berganza a most elegant Isabella and three of the finest Italian Rossini singers of the day as the men in her life.

Il turco in Italia
(The Turk in Italy)
dramma buffo in two acts (approximate length: 2 hours)

Selim, a Turkish prince   *bass*
Donna Fiorilla   *soprano*
Don Geronio, her husband   *bass*
Don Narciso, her lover   *tenor*
Prosdocimo, a poet   *baritone*
Zaida, a slave   *mezzo-soprano*
Albazar, Selim's confidant   *tenor*

LIBRETTO BY FELICE ROMANI; TIME: THE EIGHTEENTH CENTURY; PLACE: IN AND AROUND NAPLES; FIRST PERFORMED AT THE TEATRO ALLA SCALA, MILAN, 14 AUGUST 1814

With his *opera buffa L'italiana in Algeri* Rossini suddenly found himself famous throughout Italy. Some months after its premiere in May 1813 he agreed to compose a serious opera, *Aureliano in Palmira*, for La Scala, but when it was performed at the end of the year the opera was unenthusiastically received by its audiences in Milan and described as boring by the local press; it is now seldom performed. However, only a few months after its cool reception at La Scala, the management of that theatre invited Rossini to provide them with another new opera, this time a comedy. The libretto was provided by Felice Romani, who was then at the beginning of his career and who would in time become the most famous librettist of his day. Romani based his libretto on one written by Caterino Mazzola for a minor German composer, Franz Seydelmann, whose *Il turco in Italia* had been staged in Dresden in 1788.

Unfortunately, Rossini's *Il turco in Italia* failed to please the Milanese. Many were misled by the opera's title into assuming that the composer was merely attempting to copy a formula he had perfected in *L'italiana in Algeri*, although in fact the plots of the two operas are vastly different from each other. *Il turco in Italia* was received more favourably in other Italian cities and abroad, but by the middle of the century it had virtually disappeared from the stage, and was not successfully revived until 1950, when Maria Callas sang the leading soprano role of Fiorilla in a production in Rome.

Act I, scene i. A gypsy encampment on the seashore near Naples. Gypsies are singing happily about their carefree life, while Albazar, a Turk, comforts Zaida, a Turkish slave who has run away from her master, Selim. The poet Prosdocimo arrives on the scene in search of inspiration for his next play and decides that a gypsy chorus would make a good beginning. (Prosdocimo continues to comment on the action throughout the opera.) Don Geronio, a Neapolitan, arrives to have his fortune told by the gypsies. Specifically, he wants to know if he will ever be able to control his wife, the flighty Fiorilla ('Vado in traccia d'una zingara'). Told by the gypsies that he was born under the wrong sign of the zodiac and that his wife will always have the upper hand, he flees.

Zaida tells her story to the poet. Her master, Selim, loved her and wanted to marry her, but Zaida's rivals made him believe she had been unfaithful to him, and in a rage he ordered Albazar to kill her. Albazar, however, brought her to Italy instead. Prosdocimo informs Zaida that a Turkish prince is expected to arrive in Naples that very day, to study European customs. Perhaps he can be persuaded to take Zaida back to Turkey with him and arrange her reconciliation with Selim.

Geronio's wife, Fiorilla, now appears, accompanied by several friends, and muses on the folly of restricting one's affections to only one object ('Non si da follia maggiore'). She observes a ship arriving in the harbour, from which a Turkish prince, who turns out to be Zaida's Selim, disembarks with his servants and greets the beautiful country of Italy ('Cara Italia, alfin ti miro'). Fiorilla flirts with Selim ('Un marito – scimunito!') to the fury of her husband Geronio and her young lover Narciso, but to the delight of the poet Prosdocimo.

Act I, scene ii. An elegantly furnished room in Geronio's house. Fiorilla and Selim are taking coffee together when Geronio arrives, followed by Narciso. A quartet ('Siete turchi') develops in which Fiorilla demonstrates her control over husband, lover and amorous Turk.

Act I, scene iii. The seashore, at night. Selim has prepared his ship to sail to Turkey with Fiorilla, but he encounters Zaida on the beach and they are reconciled. Narciso enters, unhappy that his love for Fiorilla is not reciprocated ('Perchè mai se son tradito'), and eventually Fiorilla arrives, spied upon by Geronio. Zaida and Fiorilla quarrel over Selim, and the actions of all are observed with immense satisfaction by Prosdocimo.

Act II, scene i. A room in an inn. Geronio and Prosdocimo are sitting at a table, drinking, when Selim enters, and the poet withdraws to observe him covertly. Selim offers to buy Fiorilla from Geronio, explaining that it is an old Turkish custom for husbands to sell their wives when they tire of them, but Geronio refuses indignantly ('D'un bell'uso di Turchia'). The men leave, and Fiorilla and her friends arrive, followed by Zaida. When Selim returns, Fiorilla and Zaida ask him to choose between them, which he finds difficult. However, when Zaida leaves, Selim and Fiorilla decide that they love each other ('Credete alle femmine').

Prosdocimo tells Geronio that Selim intends to abduct Fiorilla from a masked ball to be held that evening. Having already instructed Zaida to appear at the ball disguised as Fiorilla, he now tells Geronio to attend dressed as Selim. This is overheard by Narciso, who decides that he too will dress as Selim and abduct Fiorilla.

Act II, scene ii. A ballroom. A puzzled Geronio observes two Selims and two Fiorillas dancing, and the two couples themselves are confused about one another's identities ('Oh! Guardate che accidente').

Act II, scene iii. A room in the inn. Albazar, Prosdocimo and Geronio discuss the situation. The poet attempts to manipulate the plot, but Albazar assures the others that Selim and Zaida are reunited and that he has been sent to pack and prepare for their departure for Turkey.

Act II, scene iv. A square outside Geronio's house. Prosdocimo informs Fiorilla that Selim and Zaida are reunited and gives her a letter from her husband, Geronio (which the poet has persuaded him to write), in which he disowns her and forbids her to enter his house. A chastened Fiorilla prepares to return to her parents' humble abode ('Squallida veste'). She leaves, and the poet advises Geronio to follow and pardon her, for she has surely learned her lesson.

Act II, scene v. The seashore. Fiorilla and Geronio are reconciled, Selim and Zaida sail happily away and Narciso promises he will give up philandering. Prosdocimo is delighted at the outcome and expresses the hope that the audience has enjoyed his comedy.

Although there are delightful arias for Fiorilla and Narciso, *Il turco in Italia* is very largely made up of ensembles, some beautiful and others hilarious. The opera is not quite the equal of *L'italiana in Algeri*, and indeed not all of it is by Rossini. As the composer was pressed for time, he had the recitatives, the arias for Geronio and Albazar and the Act II finale composed by Vincenzo Lavigna, a conductor at La Scala (who twenty years later would teach counterpoint to the young Verdi). Nevertheless, *Il turco in Italia* is a highly enjoyable and original *opera buffa*. The trio 'Un marito – scimunito!', in which the poet plans his comedy, is enchanting, and the Act II quintet 'Oh! Guardate che accidente' is both funny and, at one point, touching. This is an opera that deserves to be performed more often.

Recommended recording: Nicola Rossi-Lemeni (Selim), Maria Callas (Fiorilla), Nicolai Gedda (Narciso), Franco Calabrese (Geronio), Mariano Stabile (Prosdocimo), conducted by Gianandrea Gavazzeni. EMI CDS 7 49344–2. Strongly characterized performances from a sparkling cast, and conducted in lively style.

Elisabetta, regina d'Inghilterra
(Elizabeth, Queen of England)
dramma in two acts (approximate length: 2 hours, 15 minutes)

Elisabetta (Elizabeth I, Queen of England)   *soprano*
Leicester, commander of the army   *tenor*
Matilde (Matilda), Leicester's wife   *soprano*
Enrico (Henry), Matilde's brother   *mezzo-soprano*
Norfolk, a lord of the realm   *tenor*

LIBRETTO BY GIOVANNI FEDERICO SCHMIDT, BASED ON THE PLAY *ELISABETTA, REGINA D'INGHILTERRA*, BY CARLO FEDERICI; TIME: THE LATE SIXTEENTH CENTURY; PLACE: LONDON; FIRST PERFORMED AT THE TEATRO SAN CARLO, NAPLES, 4 OCTOBER 1815

After *Il turco in Italia*, Rossini's next work for the stage was an *opera seria*, *Sigismondo*, which was a failure when it was first performed in Venice in December 1814, and which after being staged occasionally in other Italian towns disappeared until 1992, when it was produced in Rovigo, Treviso and Savona, conducted by Richard Bonynge. In the spring of 1815 Rossini signed a contract with the impresario Domenico Barbaia, under the terms of which he was to compose two operas each year for performance in Naples. (In fact, between 1815 and 1822 he composed only ten operas for Naples.) The first was *Elisabetta, regina d'Inghilterra*, the libretto of which was based on a play that had been staged the previous year in Naples, which in turn was derived from an eighteenth-century English novel, *The Recess*, by Sophia Lee.

Elisabetta was an immense success in Naples and several other Italian cities. It reached London in April 1818 but, like so many bel canto operas, fell out of favour for the best part of a century, until it was broadcast by Italian radio in 1953 as a coronation tribute to England's Queen Elizabeth II. There have been occasional stage productions since then, with Elizabeth I portrayed by sopranos of the calibre of Leyla Gencer and Montserrat Caballé.

Act I. At the palace of Whitehall in London, Leicester's military triumph over the Scots is being celebrated. The hero is warmly greeted by the Queen, to the annoyance of his rival, the Duke of Norfolk. Leicester has brought with him the sons of the Scottish nobility as hostages but is surprised to discover among them, dressed as a boy, his wife Matilde, whom he has married secretly, and her brother Enrico. Norfolk discovers from Leicester the story of his marriage and hastens to tell the Queen, who was planning to marry Leicester herself. Elisabetta confronts Leicester and Matilde and offers to make Leicester her consort. When he hesitates, she has Leicester, Matilde and Enrico thrown into prison.

Act II. Elisabetta offers to spare the lives of all three if Matilde will renounce her marriage to Leicester. Matilde reluctantly agrees, but Leicester defies the Queen by tearing up the document his wife has signed, at which Elisabetta has them returned to prison. She also banishes Norfolk, whose duplicity she has begun to recognize. Norfolk visits Leicester in prison and tries to enlist his aid in raising a revolt, but Leicester indignantly refuses. The Queen arrives to see Leicester before his execution. When Norfolk attempts to stab her, he is prevented by Matilde and Enrico. Norfolk is arrested, the Queen pardons Leicester, Matilde and Enrico, and the marriage of Leicester and Matilde is given royal sanction.

For an overture to *Elisabetta, regina d'Inghilterra* Rossini borrowed the one he had composed for *Aureliano in Palmira*. (He was to use it for the third and last time as the overture to *Il barbiere di Siviglia*, as which it is so widely known today.) Also, the concluding section ('Questo cor ben lo comprende') of Elisabetta's attractive Act I entrance aria had already made an appearance in *Aureliano in Palmira*, in Arsace's rondo, 'Non lasciarmi in tal momento', and, hardly changed at all, was to turn up the following year in *Il barbiere di Siviglia* as the cabaletta ('Io sono docile') of Rosina's aria 'Una voce poco fa'.

Elisabetta is a fast-moving work, with a force and energy which at times are almost Verdian, as well as much tuneful and dramatic music in its duets and ensembles. The Act I finale is one of Rossini's most tautly constructed ensembles, culminating in a splendid crescendo section already heard in the overture. A highlight of Act II is the moving duet, 'Pensa che sol per poco', for Elisabetta and Matilde, whose andante section Bellini may well have had in mind when he came to write the duet 'Mira, o Norma' in his opera *Norma* sixteen years later. Elisabetta's beautiful aria 'Bell' alme generose', and its highly decorated cabaletta, 'Fuggi amor da questo seno', in which the Queen renounces love, bring the opera to an exciting conclusion.

Recommended recording: Montserrat Caballe (Elisabetta), José Carreras (Leicester), Valerie Masterson (Matilde), Ugo Benelli (Norfolk), conducted by Gianfranco Masini. Philips 432 453–2.

Il barbiere di Siviglia
(The Barber of Seville)
commedia in two acts (approximate length: 2 hours, 45 minutes)

Count Almaviva   *tenor*
Dr Bartolo   *bass*
Rosina, his ward   *mezzo-soprano*
Don Basilio, a teacher of singing   *bass*
Figaro, a barber   *baritone*
Berta, Rosina's governess   *soprano*

LIBRETTO BY CESARE STERBINI, BASED ON THE PLAY LE BARBIER DE SÉVILLE, BY PIERRE-AUGUSTIN CARON DE BEAUMARCHAIS; TIME: THE EIGHTEENTH CENTURY; PLACE: SEVILLE; FIRST PERFORMED AT THE TEATRO ARGENTINA, ROME, 20 FEBRUARY 1816

Rossini's next opera after *Elisabetta, regina d'Inghilterra* was *Torvaldo e Dorliska*, a melodramatic tale of abduction and rescue, which was no more than moderately successful and which was revived in the twentieth century only twice, in Vienna in 1987 and in Savona in 1989. On the day in December 1815 that

Torvaldo e Dorliska had its premiere at the Teatro Valle in Rome, Rossini signed a contract with another Rome theatre, the Teatro Argentina, to compose a comic opera. The subject eventually chosen was the play *Le Barbier de Séville*, by Beaumarchais, although this had already been made into an opera, *Il barbiere di Siviglia* (1782), by Giovanni Paisiello, one of the most successful and influential Italian opera composers of the second half of the eighteenth century, whose operas are now rarely performed. Paisiello's *Barbiere* was still immensely popular, so it is somewhat surprising that the twenty-four-year-old Rossini should have wanted to challenge the seventy-five-year-old Paisiello so directly. Rossini wrote to Paisiello, explaining that he merely wanted to treat a subject which delighted him and that he hoped to avoid as much as possible using the same situations as those in the libretto of the older composer's opera. According to Rossini, Paisiello replied that he had no objection and that he wished the project well. Cesare Sterbini was engaged by the Teatro Argentina to produce a new libretto, based on what Giuseppe Petrosellini had provided for Paisiello. When he received Sterbini's libretto, Rossini proceeded to compose the music in – again, according to him – thirteen days.

In order to avoid direct comparison with Paisiello's *Barbiere*, Rossini and his librettist decided to call their opera *Almaviva*, after its hero, retaining (in Italian, as *L'inutile precauzione*) the subtitle of Beaumarchais' play, *La Precaution inutile* (The Useless Precaution). This did not prevent Paisiello's supporters in the first-night audience from creating a disturbance. Laughter and catcalls broke out even before the performance began, when Rossini entered the orchestra pit wearing a hazel-coloured Spanish jacket with gold buttons. In Act I the celebrated Spanish tenor Manuel García, singing the role of Almaviva, was tuning his guitar under Rosina's window when a string broke, which produced more laughter and hisses. A few minutes later, when Figaro made his first appearance carrying another guitar, he was greeted by gales of ironic laughter, and hardly a note of his entrance aria 'Largo al factotum' was heard. The evening continued in the same vein.

On the second night Rossini claimed to be ill, stayed at home and went to bed. He was awakened by a deafening uproar and a brilliant glow of torches in the street outside. 'As soon as I got up', he wrote later,

> I saw that they were coming in my direction. Still half asleep, and remember-
> ing the scene of the preceding night, I thought that they were coming to set
> fire to the building, and I saved myself by going to a stable at the back of the
> courtyard. But lo, after a few moments, I heard García calling me at the top
> of his voice. He finally located me. 'Get a move on, you. Come on, now. Listen

to those shouts of "Bravo, bravissimo Figaro". An unprecedented success. The
street is full of people. They want to see you.'

After its initial performances in Rome, *Il barbiere di Siviglia*, as it began to be
called from the time it was staged in Bologna six months later, went on to establish
itself as an enormously successful opera throughout Italy and abroad, sweeping
Paisiello's *Barbiere* from the boards. To this day, it remains not only Rossini's
most popular opera but also one of the best-loved of all comic operas.

Act I, scene i. A small square in Seville, with Dr Bartolo's house, the balcony of
which overlooks the square. It is just before sunrise. As dawn breaks, Count
Almaviva, accompanied by hired musicians, serenades Rosina, who lives in the
house ('Ecco ridente in cielo'). When Rosina fails to appear on the balcony,
Almaviva pays off the musicians, who accept their reward very noisily and depart.
Disappointed at the failure of Rosina to appear, Almaviva is about to leave when
he hears someone approaching, singing ebulliently. It is Figaro the barber, who
exults in his profession as hairdresser and general factotum of the city ('Largo al
factotum'). Figaro and Almaviva recognize each other, and the Count warns
Figaro that he does not want his identity known. He has become enamoured of
Rosina after seeing her in Madrid with an old man whom he assumes is her
father, and he has come to Seville, incognito, to pursue his courtship of her.
Figaro explains that the old man is not Rosina's father, but her guardian, Dr
Bartolo, who intends to marry her himself.

Bartolo emerges from the house and, after locking Rosina in, walks away.
Almaviva begins another serenade, in which he presents himself as Lindoro, a
poor youth who loves Rosina and wants to marry her ('Se il mio nome'). From
the balcony, Rosina begins to respond, but is interrupted from within the house.
Almaviva, determined to gain entry, enlists Figaro's aid, and the barber concocts
a plan whereby Almaviva, disguised as a drunken soldier, will claim to have been
billeted upon Bartolo ('All' idea di quell metallo').

Act I, scene ii. A room in Bartolo's house. Rosina sings of her determination to
outwit her guardian and marry Lindoro ('Una voce poco fa'). Figaro enters, but
hides when he hears Bartolo returning. Don Basilio, Rosina's music master and
Bartolo's friend, brings word to Bartolo that Count Almaviva, attracted by
Rosina's beauty, has arrived in Seville. Bartolo wonders what can be done to thwart
him, and Basilio suggests a campaign of slander against Almaviva ('La calunnia è
un venticello'). When Bartolo and Basilio enter an adjacent room to discuss the
preparation of Bartolo's contract of marriage to Rosina, Figaro emerges from

hiding. He tells Rosina that Lindoro is his young cousin, who is dying of love for her. Will she not write a line or two of encouragement to him? Rosina has already done so, and hands the letter to Figaro ('Dunque io son'), who goes off to deliver it.

Rosina's suspicious guardian accuses her of having written to her lover, and threatens to keep her locked in the house in future ('A un dottor della mia sorte'). Loud knocking is heard at the front door, and Berta, Rosina's governess and Bartolo's housekeeper, goes to open it, admitting Count Almaviva, who, pretending to be very drunk, claims to be the veterinary surgeon of his regiment who has been billeted upon Dr Bartolo. When Rosina appears, he contrives to reveal to her that he is Lindoro. Bartolo produces a paper exempting him from having to accommodate soldiers in his house, but Almaviva noisily thrusts it aside, and in the ensuing commotion he manages surreptitiously to pass a letter to Rosina. Figaro enters to report that the noise from the house can be heard throughout the town, and immediately afterwards the police arrive. When, at Bartolo's instigation, a police officer attempts to arrest Count Almaviva, the Count presents a document at which the officer salutes smartly. All express their stupefaction ('Fredda ed immobile').

Act II. The music room in Dr Bartolo's house. Bartolo ponders the events of the morning, and wonders whether the drunken soldier could perhaps have been an emissary of Count Almaviva. A knock at the door announces a visitor, Almaviva, disguised this time as Don Alonso, a pupil of Don Basilio, who, according to Alonso, is ill and has sent him instead to give Rosina her singing lesson ('Pace e gioia'). Don Alonso gains Bartolo's confidence by giving him Rosina's letter to her lover, which he claims he obtained from the Count, and offering to convince Rosina that Almaviva is merely playing with her affections. Bartolo fetches Rosina, who recognizes Lindoro. She performs for the young music master an aria ('Contro un cor'), in the course of which, while Bartolo dozes, the lovers exchange expressions of endearment.

Figaro arrives to shave Bartolo and finds an opportunity to steal from him the key to the balcony, which will be needed that evening for the elopement of Almaviva and Rosina. When Don Basilio suddenly appears, Almaviva and Figaro try to persuade him that he has scarlet fever and should withdraw. The music lesson is resumed, but Bartolo overhears Almaviva comment on the success of his disguise, and chases him and Figaro out of the house. He sends for Basilio, and when the music master returns he is ordered to fetch the notary, for Bartolo intends to marry Rosina without further delay. By showing Rosina her letter, and pretending he has obtained it from the notorious Almaviva, Bartolo persuades his ward that she has been betrayed. Rosina confesses to Bartolo that she had planned to elope at midnight, and she agrees to marry her guardian immediately.

A storm rages outside. At midnight Figaro and Almaviva enter from the balcony, and when Rosina accuses Lindoro of intending to deliver her to the vile Almaviva, he admits that he himself is Count Almaviva. The lovers fall into each other's arms, while Figaro urges them to hurry from the house ('Ah! Qual colpo inaspettato'). When they attempt to leave through the balcony, they discover that their ladder has been removed. Basilio enters with the notary, and Almaviva bribes Basilio into witnessing his marriage to Rosina. Bartolo arrives too late, Almaviva reveals his identity to all ('Cessa di più resistere') and Bartolo is forced to accept the situation.

Il barbiere di Siviglia, one of the wittiest and most immediately appealing of comic operas, a work bubbling over with gaiety and high spirits, is as fresh to the ear now as when it burst upon its Roman audiences in 1816. Its dramatic energy may falter somewhat towards the end, but its score is full of delightful and apt melodic invention, and many of its arias, among them Almaviva's romantic serenades, Rosina's charming 'Una voce poco fa', Figaro's lustily self-confident 'Largo al factotum' and the comic pieces for Bartolo and Basilio, have become well known beyond the confines of the opera. The Act I finale, 'Fredda ed immobile', is Rossini at his magnificent best. Count Almaviva's lengthy 'Cessa di più resistere' in Act II is nowadays usually omitted, ostensibly because it holds up the action, but more likely because the singer finds it difficult. This is to be regretted, for it is an impressive formal aria with an excitingly florid cabaletta, an even more highly decorated version of which Rossini was to use a year later in *La Cenerentola*. As the eighty-five-year-old Verdi told an interviewer in 1898, 'With its abundance of real musical ideas, its comic verve and its truthful declamation, [*Il barbiere di Siviglia*] is the most beautiful opera buffa in existence.'

Recommended recording: Jennifer Larmore (Rosina), Raul Gimenez (Almaviva), Hakan Hagegard (Figaro), Alessandro Corbelli (Bartolo), Samuel Ramey (Basilio), with the Chorus of the Grand Theatre, Geneva, and the Lausanne Chamber Orchestra, conducted by Jesus Lopez-Cobos. Teldec 9031–74885–2. Hakan Hagegard is a near-ideal Figaro, with plenty of vocal personality and charm, and Jennifer Larmore brings a warm and alluring timbre to Rosina. Raul Gimenez copes easily with Almaviva's music, even 'Cessa di più resistere' with its demanding cabaletta, and the two bass roles are cast from strength. Jesus Lopez-Cobos conducts with elegance and flair.

La Cenerentola
(Cinderella)
dramma giocoso in two acts (approximate length: 2 hours, 30 minutes)

Angiolina (known as Cenerentola – Cinderella), stepdaughter of Don
    Magnifico *contralto*
Don Magnifico, Baron of Monte Fiascone *bass*
Don Ramiro, Prince of Salerno *tenor*
Dandini, his valet *bass*
Clorinda, daughter of Don Magnifico *soprano*
Tisbe, daughter of Don Magnifico *mezzo-soprano*
Alidoro, tutor to Don Ramiro *bass*

LIBRETTO BY JACOPO FERRETTI; TIME AND PLACE: MYTHICAL; FIRST PERFORMED
AT THE TEATRO VALLE, ROME, 25 JANUARY 1817

After the Rome premiere of *Il barbiere di Siviglia* in February 1816, Rossini
returned to Naples to compose his next two operas for that city. The first of
these was *La gazzetta* (The Gazette), a comedy that reached the stage in September only to be withdrawn after a few performances, the general opinion being
that its libretto was clumsy and its music undistinguished. It was followed three
months later by *Otello*, the libretto of which is a ludicrous adaptation of Shakespeare's tragedy, but its music is delightful, though not always dramatically
felicitous.

By mid-December Rossini was back in Rome, having agreed to write another
opera for the Teatro Valle, where his *Torvaldo e Dorliska* had been staged twelve
months previously. Jacopo Ferretti, who had provided several libretti for Rome's
opera houses, suggested the story of Cinderella as a subject, to which Rossini
immediately agreed. Ferretti wrote his libretto very quickly, basing it not directly
on the fairy story in Charles Perrault's 1698 collection *Les Contes de ma mère l'Oye*
(Tales of Mother Goose) but on a libretto derived from Perrault which Charles-
Guillaume Etienne had produced for Nicolas Isouard's *Cendrillon*, performed at
the Paris Opéra-Comique in 1810. Rossini composed *La Cenerentola* at his usual
brisk pace, and the opera was staged at the Teatro Valle on 25 January 1817, surviving a not very successful first performance before a noisy and hostile audience
to become one of Rossini's most popular operas, as well as the most often performed Cinderella opera.

Act I, scene i. The hall of Don Magnifico's ramshackle castle. Angiolina lives with her stepfather, Don Magnifico, and her two stepsisters Clorinda and Tisbe, all of whom call her Cenerentola (Cinderella) and treat her as a servant. When a beggar (Alidoro, the Prince's tutor, in disguise) comes to the door asking for food, her stepsisters attempt to get rid of him, but Cenerentola gives him a crust of bread and some coffee. A group of the Prince's friends arrive to announce that the Prince, Don Ramiro, is to give a ball that evening in his palace, at which he will choose the most beautiful woman present to be his wife. Clorinda and Tisbe immediately begin to order Cenerentola about, to help them dress. When the Prince himself arrives, having exchanged clothes and roles with his valet Dandini, he notices Cenerentola and at once they fall in love with each other ('Un soave non so che'); but he is told by her relatives that she is only a servant. Cenerentola begs to be allowed to go to the ball ('Signor, una parola'), but Don Magnifico orders her to stay at home. Alidoro, now in his proper attire as the Prince's tutor, returns with a list of all the eligible young women in the Prince's domain and asks to see Don Magnifico's third daughter, but is told that she is dead. When everyone else has departed, Alidoro promises Cenerentola a happy future ('Là del ciel') and takes her to the ball.

Act I, scene ii. An apartment in the Prince's palace. Dandini, still posing as the Prince, appoints Don Magnifico as the palace vintner, while Clorinda and Tisbe, thinking Dandini to be the Prince, make advances to him.

Act I, scene iii. Another apartment in the palace. The new vintner, with the aid of the gentlemen of the Prince's entourage, samples the wine liberally and dictates some new drinking laws. The Prince, who has been told by Alidoro that one of Don Magnifico's daughters is a rare beauty, asks his valet's opinion of the two stepsisters and is told by Dandini that they are vain and empty-headed. When Clorinda and Tisbe enter, they treat the Prince with disdain, believing him to be the valet. Alidoro announces the arrival of a mysterious veiled woman. When Cenerentola, magnificently attired, enters and unveils herself, her stepfather and stepsisters are struck by the newcomer's resemblance to the girl they have left at home, while the Prince is again stunned by her beauty.

Act II, scene i. An apartment in the palace. Don Magnifico, convinced that either Clorinda or Tisbe will marry the Prince, begins to imagine his future life as a royal father-in-law ('Sia qualunque delle figlie'). The Prince overhears Cenerentola rejecting the advances of Dandini, whom she thinks is the Prince, because she is in love with his valet. However, when the Prince himself, still posing as Dandini, asks for her hand in marriage, she leaves, but not before giving him a bracelet. He must search for her, and will find her wearing its twin. If he still wishes to marry her, she will accept him. The Prince instructs Dandini to throw Magnifico and his two daughters out of the palace and prepares to hasten after Cenerentola ('Si, ritrovarla, io giuro').

Act II, scene ii. A room in Don Magnifico's castle. Don Magnifico, Clorinda and Tisbe arrive home from the ball to find Cenerentola sitting by the fire in her usual ragged attire; they berate her for resembling the mysterious woman at the ball. The Prince, whose carriage Alidoro has caused to overturn in front of the castle, enters and is delighted to find Cenerentola ('Siete voi'), whom he takes away with him, to the fury and amazement of her relatives ('Questo à un nodo avviluppato').

Act II, scene iii. The throne room of the palace. At the festivities to celebrate her marriage to the Prince, Cenerentola forgives her stepfather and stepsisters and is acclaimed by all ('Nacqui all' affanno').

Though by no means the equal of the previous year's *Il barbiere di Siviglia*, Rossini's version of the familiar fairy tale is a highly entertaining work, with splendid comic opportunities for Don Magnifico and Dandini, and richly expressive music for the Prince and, above all, for Cenerentola, whose aria ('Nacqui all' affanno') and cabaletta ('Non più mesta') make an exhilarating end to the opera. 'Non più mesta' is actually a more highly decorated version of Count Almaviva's cabaletta ('Ah, il più lieto') in *Il barbiere di Siviglia*. The scene and duet ('Un soave non so che') in which the Prince and Cenerentola fall in love with each other at first sight is a charming blend of tenderness and gaiety, and Rossini's ensembles are, as usual, masterly, especially the comic sextet 'Questo è un nodo avviluppato'.

Recommended recording: Jennifer Larmore (Cenerentola), Raul Gimenez (Prince), Gino Quilico (Dandini), Alessandro Corbelli (Don Magnifico), with the Chorus and Orchestra of the Royal Opera House, Covent Garden, conducted by Carlo Rizzi. Teldec 4509–94553–2. Jennifer Larmore's warm and sympathetic timbre is ideally suited to the title-role, which she sings with great elegance and, in her final aria, astonishing agility. Raul Gimenez has no difficulties with the Prince's music, and Alessandro Corbelli as Don Magnifico demonstrates that he is the leading Italian basso buffo of the day. Gino Quilico is an engaging Dandini, and Carlo Rizzi, conducting, proves a superb Rossinian.

La gazza ladra
(The Thieving Magpie)
melodramma in two acts (approximate length: 3 hours, 25 minutes)

Fabrizio Vingradito, a rich farmer   *bass*
Lucia, his wife   *mezzo-soprano*
Giannetto, Fabrizio's son, a soldier   *tenor*
Ninetta, a servant in Fabrizio's house   *soprano*
Fernando Villabella, Ninetta's father, a soldier   *bass*
Gottardo, mayor of the village   *bass*
Pippo, a young peasant in Fabrizio's service   *contralto*
Isacco, a pedlar   *tenor*
Antonio, a gaoler   *tenor*

LIBRETTO BY GIOVANNI GHERARDINI, BASED ON THE PLAY *LA PIE VOLEUSE*, BY T. BADOUIN D'AUBIGNY AND LOUIS-CHARLES CAIGNIEZ; TIME: THE PAST; PLACE: A VILLAGE NEAR PARIS; FIRST PERFORMED AT THE TEATRO ALLA SCALA, MILAN, 31 MAY 1817

It was less than three weeks after the premiere of *La Cenerentola* that Rossini left Rome to compose his next opera for La Scala, Milan, where his *Il turco in Italia* had been so ungraciously received three years previously. The libretto of the new opera was written by Giovanni Gherardini, a Milanese poet and philologist, who based his text on a recent French play, *La Pie voleuse*, which had been staged in Paris in 1815. When he was given Gherardini's libretto, Rossini wrote to his mother that he thought it 'bellissimo'. *La gazza ladra* was a success at its premiere in Milan in 1817 and was soon making its way across Europe. After years of neglect, it has recently begun to be staged again.

Act I, scene i. The courtyard of Fabrizio's house. Fabrizio and Lucia, together with their friends and neighbours, are awaiting the return from military service of their son, Giannetto, who is in love with their maid, Ninetta ('Di piacer mi balza il cor'). Lucia complains that Ninetta is irresponsible and that she has mislaid a valuable silver fork. When Giannetto arrives, he and Ninetta confirm their love for each other ('Vieni fra queste braccia'), and Pippo, a young peasant in Fabrizio's service, leads everyone in a drinking song ('Tocchiamo, beviamo').

The others leave the courtyard, and Ninetta is approached by a man whom at first she does not recognize, but who is in fact her father, Fernando, wanted by the military authorities as a deserter. Fernando gives Ninetta a silver spoon, asking her to sell it for him and hide the proceeds in the hollow of a chestnut tree ('Come frenar il pianto'). When Gottardo, the village mayor, who has amorous designs on Ninetta ('Il mio piano è preparato'), asks her to read to him an urgent message he has received which he cannot decipher without his spectacles, Ninetta realizes it is an order to arrest her father, which she falsifies by changing the description of the wanted man ('M'affretto di mandarvi'). As the mayor departs after his advances to Ninetta have been rebuffed, a pet magpie, which has been sitting by its open cage, snatches one of Lucia's spoons and flies off with it, unnoticed.

Act I, scene ii. A room in Fabrizio's house. Ninetta sells her father's spoon to Isacco, an itinerant pedlar. Lucia counts her spoons, discovers one is missing and accuses Ninetta of having stolen it. When Pippo inadvertently discloses that Ninetta has sold a spoon to Isacco, all assume her to be guilty, and the mayor has her marched off to prison.

Act II, scene i. The prison. Ninetta is visited by Giannetto, to whom she declares her innocence, but without betraying her father ('Forse un dì conoscerete'). The mayor offers her freedom in return for her love, and again she rejects him. When Pippo arrives to visit her, Ninetta gives him the money she has received from Isacco, asking him to take it to the hiding place designated by her father.

Act II, scene ii. A room in Fabrizio's house. Lucia reveals Ninetta's situation to Fernando, who determines to save his daughter even at the cost of his own life ('Accusata di furto').

Act II, scene iii. The courtroom in the town hall. Ninetta is sentenced to death ('Tremate, o popoli'), and the dramatic intervention of Fernando merely leads to his being arrested as well.

Act II, scene iv. The village square. While Pippo is counting his money, the magpie steals a coin and flies off, pursued by the youth. Ninetta, as she is led to the scaffold, pauses to pray for her father ('Deh tu reggi'). Pippo and Antonio, the gaoler, discover the magpie's secret hiding place in the bell tower, containing the spoon and other stolen items. Ninetta is set free, a royal pardon arrives for her father, and all (except the mayor) rejoice at the happy outcome.

Although it is known today mainly for its popular overture, La gazza ladra contains some beautiful music. Ninetta's opening aria, 'Di piacer mi balza il cor', is delightful, her Act I duet with her father has an appealing quality of tenderness, and the chorus, 'Tremate, o popoli', at the beginning of the trial scene, is powerfully affecting. The character of the mayor is ambiguous, veering between the comical and the villainous, and in two acts of about 105 minutes each the opera is somewhat too long, suffering also from its uncertainty of tone, at times tragic, at times comic. However, it is an ambitious work that deserves occasional revival.

Recommended recording: Katia Ricciarelli (Ninetta), William Matteuzzi (Giannetto), Samuel Ramey (Gottardo), Bernadette Manca di Nissa (Pippo), with the Prague Philharmonic Choir and the Turin Radio Symphony Orchestra, conducted by Gianluigi Gelmetti. Sony CD45850. A sparkling performance from a first-rate cast and conductor.

Mosè in Egitto
(Moses in Egypt)
azione tragico-sacra in three acts (approximate length: 1 hour, 30 minutes)

Mosè (Moses), leader of the Israelites   *bass*
Aronne (Aaron), his brother   *tenor*
The Pharaoh, King of Egypt   *baritone*
Osiride, the Pharaoh's son   *tenor*
Mambre, an Egyptian officer   *tenor*
Elcia, a Jewish maiden   *soprano*
Amenosi, Elcia's confidante   *mezzo-soprano*
Amaltea, the Pharaoh's wife   *soprano*

LIBRETTO BY ANDREA LEONE TOTTOLA, BASED ON THE PLAY *L'OSIRIDE*, BY FRANCESCO RINGHIERI; TIME: AROUND 1230 BC; PLACE: EGYPT; FIRST PERFORMED AT THE TEATRO SAN CARLO, NAPLES, 5 MARCH 1818

A few weeks after the premiere of *La gazza ladra* in Milan, Rossini returned to Naples to work on his next opera for that city. *Armida* was moderately well received at its first performance on 11 November 1817, and for a time it was popular outside Italy. However, it soon disappeared from the repertoire, emerging from obscurity only when it was revived in Florence in 1952 with Maria Callas in the title role. Six weeks after the 1817 Naples premiere of *Armida*, Rossini's next opera, *Adelaide di Borgogna*, was staged in Rome. Described by Stendhal as a failure, and by a later Rossini biographer as 'the worst of Rossini's serious operas', it languished until given a concert performance in London in 1979 and a stage production in Italy at the Valle d'Itria Festival in 1984.

Returning to Naples after the unsatisfactory Rome premiere of *Adelaide di*

Borgogna, Rossini composed *Mosè in Egitto* for the Teatro San Carlo. Based on *L'Osiride*, by Padre Francesco Ringhieri, a play that was first staged in Padua in 1760, Andrea Leone Tottola's libretto wove a romantic plot into the Old Testament story, in the Book of Exodus, of the enslavement of the Jews in Egypt, and their deliverance when 'Moses stretched out his hand over the sea; and the Lord caused the sea to go back by a strong east wind all that night, and made the sea dry land, and the waters were divided.'

At its premiere on 5 March 1818, *Mosè in Egitto* was a huge success, even though, according to Stendhal, who was present, the effect of the parting of the Red Sea left much to be desired:

> The stage technician of the San Carlo, desperately intent upon finding a solution to an insoluble problem, had finished up by producing a real masterpiece of absurdity. Seen from the pit, the 'sea' rose up into the air some five or six feet above its retaining 'shores'; whereas the occupants of the boxes, who were favoured with a bird's-eye view of the 'raging billows', also had a bird's-eye view of the little rascals whose job it was to 'divide the waters' at the sound of Moses' voice.

Nine years later, Rossini adapted *Mosè in Egitto* for performance at the Paris Opéra. A French text based on Tottola's libretto was produced by Luigi Balocchi and Victor-Joseph-Etienne de Jouy, and the composer wrote much new music as well as adapting parts of his original score – *Moïse et Pharaon* was a success in Paris in 1827 and soon began to travel abroad. Translated back into Italian, the new version became known in Italy as *Il Mosè nuovo* (The New Moses), and in one version or the other the opera managed to hold the stage. The synopsis that follows is of the original Italian opera, a tauter and more dramatically effective work than the Paris version.

Act I, scene i. The royal palace. Because the Pharaoh has broken his promise to allow the Israelites to depart from Egypt, God has plunged the country into total darkness. The terrified Egyptians beg their ruler to rescue them ('Ah! Chi ne aiuta?'), and Pharaoh sends for Mosè, promising the Israelites their freedom if light can be restored to Egypt. Mosè addresses the Almighty in prayer, and light returns to the land ('Eterno! Immenso! Incomprensibil Dio!'). However, Osiride, the Pharaoh's son, and Elcia, a Jewish girl whom Osiride loves, lament their imminent separation, and Osiride persuades the Pharaoh, through Mambre, to go back on his word once again ('Cade dal ciglio il velo') and keep the Jews in Egypt.

Act I, scene ii. A vast plain. When he is told that any Israelite attempting to flee the country will be put to death, Mosè waves his rod, bringing a new plague of hailstones and fire raining down from heaven.

Act II, scene i. The royal apartments. Once more the Pharaoh agrees to allow the Israelites to go, and he informs Osiride that he is to be married to an Armenian princess ('Parlar, spiegar non posso').

Act II, scene ii. A dark cave. Osiride and Elcia go into hiding but are found by Queen Amaltea, the Pharaoh's wife, who is sympathetic to the Israelites ('Mi manca la voce').

Act II, scene iii. The palace. The young lovers refuse to be parted, and the Pharaoh again revokes his permission for the departure of the Israelites. Mose warns him that his son and all the first-born of Egypt will be struck by lightning, but the Pharaoh has Mosè put into chains and orders Osiride to pronounce sentence of death upon him. Elcia reveals that she is the lover of Osiride and offers her life in return for the freedom of the Israelites ('Porgi la destra amata'). When Osiride raises his sword to kill Mosè, he is immediately struck dead by a bolt of lightning.

Act III. On the shores of the Red Sea. Pursued by the Pharaoh's army, the Israelites can go no further. Mosè prays to God ('Dal tuo stellato soglio'), and the waters part. The Israelites pass through the middle of the divided waters and reach the other shore. When the Egyptians attempt to follow, the waters close over them and they are drowned.

Unusually for Rossini, there is no overture to this fascinating opera. After three C major chords in the orchestra to call the audience to attention, the curtain rises on a dark stage, with the Egyptians lamenting their plight in a gravely beautiful ensemble. Choruses and ensembles dominate the opera, the finest of them being the great prayer in Act III, 'Dal tuo stellato soglio', begun by Mose. This, the most popular number in the score, was not heard at the premiere, but was added by Rossini when the opera was revived in Naples in March of the following year. A quintet in Act I, 'Celeste man placata', is one of the composer's finest and most affecting ensembles. Although some of the most effective numbers in Act II were taken from earlier Rossini operas, Mosè in Egitto has a cohesion and unity that make it one of the composer's liveliest and most attractive serious operas.

Recommended recording: Ruggiero Raimondi (Moses), Siegmund Nimsgern (Pharaoh), Ernesto Palacio (Osiride), June Anderson (Elcia), with the Ambrosian Opera Chorus and the Philharmonia Orchestra, conducted by Claudio Scimone. Philips 420 109–2. This is an exemplary recording and unlikely to be surpassed.

La donna del lago
(The Lady of the Lake)
melodramma in two acts (approximate length: 2 hours, 15 minutes)

Elena   *soprano*
Albina, her confidante   *mezzo-soprano*
Malcolm Graeme   *mezzo-soprano*
Giacomo (James V), King of Scotland, alias Uberto   *tenor*
Douglas d'Angus, Elena's father   *bass*
Serano, Douglas's retainer   *tenor*
Rodrigo di Dhu   *tenor*

LIBRETTO BY ANDREA LEONE TOTTOLA, BASED ON THE POEM *THE LADY OF THE LAKE*, BY SIR WALTER SCOTT; TIME: THE SIXTEENTH CENTURY; PLACE: SCOTLAND; FIRST PERFORMED AT THE TEATRO SAN CARLO, NAPLES, 24 SEPTEMBER 1819

The March 1819 premiere of Rossini's *Ermione* at the Teatro San Carlo in Naples was followed in April by that of his *Eduardo e Cristina* at the Teatro San Benedetto in Venice. This opera about the secret marriage of a Swedish soldier was hardly new, for nineteen of its twenty-six musical numbers were taken from earlier works by Rossini. Nevertheless, it was a huge success, one newspaper describing the premiere as 'a triumph like no other in the history of our musical stage'. *Eduardo e Cristina* remained popular for a few years in Italy and abroad, though there were few performances after 1840, and there were none in the twentieth century until it was exhumed at a Rossini festival in Wildbad, Germany, in 1997.

From Venice, Rossini returned to Naples to compose his next opera for the Teatro San Carlo. *La donna del lago* was based on Sir Walter Scott's long narrative poem *The Lady of the Lake*, which had been published in 1810 and which Rossini had read in a French translation. By the beginning of September he had completed the opera, which at its premiere on the 24th was received with indifference. The second-night audience enjoyed it more, and the opera subsequently became popular, although it disappeared from the stage after 1860 until it surfaced again in Florence in 1958, since when it has been occasionally revived. At Houston in 1981 and Covent Garden in 1985, Frederica von Stade sang Elena and Marilyn Horne was Malcolm, while at La Scala in 1992 (Rossini's bicentennial year), with Riccardo Muti conducting, those roles were taken by June Anderson and Martine Dupuy.

Act I, scene i. The rock of Benledi, covered at the summit by a thick wood, on the shores of Lake Katrine. A hunting party can be heard in the distance, and shepherds begin their daily tasks as Elena crosses the lake in a small boat, hoping to find her lover, Malcolm, among the hunters ('Oh mattutini albori'). As she steps ashore, she encounters a man who introduces himself as Uberto, claiming to have been separated from his fellow huntsmen. Impressed by Elena's beauty, he accepts her offer of shelter, and they sail to her father's cottage in the middle of the lake as the other hunters return, in search of Uberto ('Uberto! Ah, dove t'ascondi?').

Act I, scene ii. Douglas's cottage. Elena tells Uberto that her father is Douglas, a former follower of Giacomo (King James V), and now a rebel. Douglas has agreed to give his daughter to the warrior Rodrigo in marriage, but Elena refers to her love for someone else, and Uberto mistakenly believes himself to be the object of her love ('Le mie barebare vicende').

After Uberto has been escorted back to the shore, Malcolm arrives and sings of his love for Elena ('Elena! Oh tu, che chiamo!'). Told by Serano, Douglas's retainer, that Rodrigo and his followers are gathering in a nearby valley, Malcolm hides when Elena and Douglas return. Douglas leaves after expressing his displeasure at Elena's resistance to her forthcoming marriage ('Taci, lo voglio'), and the lovers, Elena and Malcolm, sing a tender duet ('Vivere io non potrò').

Act I, scene iii. A vast plain surrounded by mountains. Rodrigo is greeted by his warriors ('Qual rapido torrente') and responds in a florid aria ('Eccomi a voi, miei prodi') in which he swears to fight bravely against the King's army. He then turns his thoughts to Elena, who is now led in by her father. When Malcolm and his followers arrive to join the rebels, Rodrigo's reference to Elena as his bride-to-be almost leads to dissension, and it is only news of the approach of the royal forces that unites everyone in a warlike ensemble of defiance ('Già un raggio forier'), led by a chorus of holy bards.

Act II, scene i. A thick wood near the lakeside. Now disguised as a shepherd, Uberto has returned to the shores of the lake to declare his love to Elena ('Oh fiamma soave'). When Elena appears, she informs him that she is in love with someone else and can offer him only friendship. Uberto gives her a ring, which he says was presented to him by the King of Scotland, whose life he saved. Should Elena or any member of her family ever be in danger, she must take the ring to the King, who will grant them his protection ('Alla ragion, deh rieda'). Uberto and Elena have been overheard by Rodrigo, and when Uberto proudly declares himself to be on the side of King Giacomo, the two men challenge each other and rush off to fight.

Act II, scene ii. A cavern. Malcolm, in search of Elena, is lamenting her disappearance ('Ah! Si pera') when rebel warriors enter to announce that their cause is lost, Rodrigo has fallen and the King of Scotland's forces have won the day.

Act II, scene iii. A room in the royal castle of Stirling. In the hope of saving the lives of her father and Malcolm, who have been captured and imprisoned, Elena has come to the castle to show to the King the ring that Uberto gave to her. Uberto appears, revealing that he is, himself, the King. He not only pardons Douglas and Malcolm, but also blesses the union of Elena and Malcolm, at which Elena gives voice to her great joy ('Tanti affetti in tal momento').

La donna del lago, an original and imaginatively scored work of great lyrical charm, contrives miraculously to preserve the spirit of Sir Walter Scott's poem, despite being saddled with a libretto by Tottola which is in places almost a travesty of that spirit. Rossini's music conjures up the atmosphere of the Scottish Highlands just as successfully as he was later to bring the landscape of the Swiss Alps onto the stage in *Guillaume Tell*. The highlights of *La donna del lago* include its many ensembles, especially the chorus of bards, accompanied by harp, violas and pizzicato cellos; the exciting confrontation of Uberto and Rodrigo in Act II, scene i, the two tenors vying with each other in high-lying vocal agility, with Uberto reaching a high D; and Elena's joyous rondo, 'Tanti affetti in tal momento', with which the opera ends.

Recommended recording: Katia Ricciarelli (Elena), Lucia Valentini Terrani (Malcolm), Dalmacio Gonzalez (Uberto/Giacomo); Samuel Ramey (Douglas), with the Prague Philharmonic Chorus and the Chamber Orchestra of Europe, conducted by Maurizio Pollini. CBS CD39311. Splendidly sung and conducted.

Semiramide
melodramma tragico in two acts (approximate length: 3 hours, 45 minutes)

Semiramide, Queen of Babylon   *soprano*
Arsace, commander of Semiramide's forces   *contralto*
Idreno, an Indian king   *tenor*
Azema, a princess   *soprano*
Assur, a prince   *bass*
Oroe, high priest of the magi   *bass*
The Ghost of Nino   *bass*

LIBRETTO BY GAETANO ROSSI, BASED ON THE PLAY *SÉMIRAMIS*, BY VOLTAIRE; TIME:
ANTIQUITY; PLACE: BABYLON; FIRST PERFORMED AT THE TEATRO LA FENICE,
VENICE, 3 FEBRUARY 1823

Rossini's next four operas after *La donna del lago* were not among his most
successful. *Bianca e Falliero*, staged at La Scala in December 1819, did reasonably well there, although outside Italy it was performed only in Lisbon, Vienna,
Barcelona and Cagliari (Sardinia), disappearing after 1846 until its revival in 1986
at the Rossini Festival in Pesaro. *Maometto II*, first performed in Naples in December 1820, was not greatly liked but proved more popular when its composer
adapted it for Paris in 1826 as *Le Siège de Corinthe*. There have been occasional
performances of both versions in recent years. *Matilde di Shabran*, given its
premiere in Rome in February 1821, is an uneven piece which in the twentieth
century had no more than one or two revivals, while *Zelmira*, first staged in
Naples in February 1822, was no more successful.

Zelmira was the last opera Rossini was to compose for Naples. On the day after
its final performance, he and the opera's prima donna, Isabella Colbran, set out
for Vienna, stopping en route to get married. In Vienna *Zelmira* was staged at the
Kärntnertortheater, which was under the management of Colbran's ex-lover,
the impresario Domenico Barbaia.

During his time in their city, Rossini was feted by the Viennese. He succeeded
in meeting the reclusive Beethoven, whom he greatly admired; and although he
did not meet Schubert, Rossini's music certainly made a deep impression on the
young Viennese composer.

In mid-December 1822 Rossini arrived in Venice to stage a slightly revised version of *Maometto II* and to compose (in, according to him, thirty-three days) his
next opera for the Teatro La Fenice. This was *Semiramide*, its libretto based on
Voltaire's 1748 tragedy *Sémiramis*. The opera was favourably received in Venice and
was immediately taken up by other opera houses in Italy and abroad. It remained
popular until the end of the century, after which it was staged only twice, in
Rostock in 1932 and in Florence in 1940, until Joan Sutherland (as Semiramide)
and Giulietta Simionato (as Arsace) triumphed in a highly acclaimed production
at La Scala, Milan, in 1962. Since then, *Semiramide* has been performed in a number of cities in Europe, America and Australia.

Act I, scene i. The temple of Baal. A crowd has gathered to hear Queen Semiramide announce the name of the successor to the throne of her late husband,
Nino, who was assassinated. Among the aspirants to the throne, and to the hand

of the Princess Azema, are Idreno, an Indian king, and Prince Assur, Semiramide's former lover who was her accomplice in the murder of Nino. Semiramide is about to name the new king when she is prevented from speaking by lightning and thunder, which extinguish the altar flame, causing the crowd to flee in terror. Arsace, the young commander of Semiramide's army, who is in love with Azema, arrives from his border post, delivering to the high priest Oroe a casket that belonged to Nino and a letter revealing the truth about his murder.

Act I, scene ii. The Hanging Gardens of Babylon. Overjoyed at Arsace's return, Semiramide sings of her love for the youth, whom she does not know is really her own son ('Bel raggio lusinghier'). When Arsace enters, he tries to tell Semiramide of his love for Azema, but she misunderstands him and is convinced that he returns her love ('Serbami ognor si fido').

Act I, scene iii. The throne room of the palace. When Semiramide announces that the new king, and her consort, is to be Arsace, Prince Assur is furious and Arsace himself is shocked. The Ghost of Nino appears, declaring that Arsace will indeed ascend the throne, but that he must first seek out and punish Nino's murderers ('Qual mesto gemito').

Act II, scene i. A room in the palace. Semiramide and Assur recall their past crimes, each threatening to expose the other ('Se la vita ancor t'è cara').

Act II, scene ii. The palace sanctuary. Arsace learns from the high priest that he is the son of Nino and Semiramide, and that Semiramide and Assur were responsible for Nino's death. Arsace resolves to kill Assur, but hopes that Semiramide can be spared ('In sì barbara sciagura').

Act II, scene iii. Semiramide's apartment. Arsace confronts Semiramide with his knowledge of her crime. She admits her guilt and offers her life to her son, but he cannot bring himself to punish his own mother ('Ebben – a te, ferisci').

Act II, scene iv. The entrance to Nino's tomb. Assur is determined to kill Arsace. Told that his crimes have been revealed to the populace by the high priest Oroe, he begins to lose his reason ('Deh, ti ferma').

Act II, scene v. Inside Nino's tomb. Assur searches for Arsace. Semiramide follows her son, hoping to protect him, but in the darkness Arsace mistakes her for Assur and strikes her down. Assur is arrested, and a horrified Arsace attempts to kill himself, but is prevented from doing so by Oroe. Arsace is acclaimed by the populace as their King.

The last of Rossini's operas to be written in Italian for Italy, *Semiramide* is an ambitious and imposing work, though musically uneven. Classical in form and in spirit, its greatest strengths lie in its choruses, its duets for Semiramide and

Arsace, and Semiramide's dazzling aria 'Bel raggio lusinghier'. The duet for Semiramide and Assur, 'Se la vita ancor t'è cara', is a fascinating adumbration of the duet for the quarrelling guilty couple in Verdi's *Macbeth* of 1847. *Semiramide* is well worth reviving when singers can be found who are able to do justice to its stylistic demands and to its calls for vocal agility. Its majestic overture, constructed on themes from the opera, has become a popular concert item.

Recommended recording: Joan Sutherland (Semiramide), Marilyn Horne (Arsace), Joseph Rouleau (Assur), with the Ambrosian Opera Chorus and the London Symphony Orchestra, conducted by Richard Bonynge. Decca 425 481–2 DM3. Joan Sutherland and Marilyn Horne are in sparkling form, and Richard Bonynge conducts with sensitivity and flair.

Le Comte Ory
(Count Ory)
opéra comique in two acts (approximate length: 2 hours, 15 minutes)

Countess Adèle   *soprano*
Isolier, page to Count Ory   *mezzo-soprano*
Ragonde, companion to Countess Adèle   *contralto*
Count Ory, alias Sister Colette   *tenor*
The Tutor   *bass*
Raimbaud, friend of Count Ory   *baritone*
Alice, a peasant girl   *soprano*

LIBRETTO BY EUGÈNE SCRIBE AND CHARLES GASPARD DELESTRE-POIRSON; TIME: THE CRUSADES; PLACE: TOURAINE; FIRST PERFORMED AT THE PARIS OPÉRA, 20 AUGUST 1828

In August 1824 Rossini arrived in Paris, where he was welcomed as one of the most celebrated of living composers and given the general management of the Théâtre Italien, the Paris theatre in which Italian operas were performed in Italian. But with his sights set on the more prestigious Paris Opéra, Rossini composed only one Italian-language opera for the Théâtre Italien. This was *Il viaggio a Reims* (The Voyage to Rheims), an occasional piece staged in June 1825 as part of the festivities honouring the coronation of Charles X, and it turned out to be his last Italian opera. Rossini then produced *Le Siège de Corinthe*, a French-language adaptation of his *Maometto II* which was given its premiere at the Paris Opéra in October 1826, and *Moïse et Pharaon*, a French version of *Mosè in Egitto*, staged at the Opéra in March 1827. These were followed by Rossini's first original French-language opera, *Le Comte Ory*, whose light-hearted libretto by Eugène Scribe and Charles Gaspard Delestre-Poirson was an adaptation of a one-act comedy they had written ten years previously.

Act I. Outside the gates of the castle of Formoutiers. The Count de Formoutiers is away at the Crusades and has left his sister, the Countess Adele, and her companions to reside in the castle without male protection. In order to gain entrance to the castle and seduce Adèle, the young Count Ory, accompanied by his friend Raimbaud, disguises himself as a hermit and claims to be able to tell fortunes and to give advice ('Que les destins prospères'). Ragonde, Adèle's companion, tells the hermit that the Countess Adèle, having sworn to avoid the society of men while her brother is absent, has become depressed and wishes to seek the hermit's advice.

Count Ory's page, Isolier, enters, accompanied by the Count's Tutor, who is searching for Ory. Failing to recognize his master, Isolier confides to the hermit that he is in love with Adèle and that he plans to gain admission to the castle in the guise of a pilgrim. Ory resolves to adopt this scheme himself ('Une dame de haut parage'). When Adèle comes to consult the hermit ('En proie à la tristesse'), he advises her to avoid Isolier, the page of the notorious philanderer Count Ory, and find a more suitable person to love. At this moment, Ory's Tutor returns and recognizes him, thus foiling his plans. News arrives of the return next day of the Crusaders, at which Ory resolves to put to good use the little time left to him and devise another plan to gain entrance to the castle.

Act II. Inside the castle. The women discuss their narrow escape from Count Ory ('Dans ce séjour calme et tranquille'), while outside a storm is raging, and the voices of women, poor pilgrim nuns, can be heard begging for shelter and protection from Count Ory and his men, who are pursuing them. The nuns (Ory and his men in disguise) are admitted to the castle, and their leader, Sister Colette (Ory himself), thanks Adèle profusely ('Ah! Quel respect, madame'). Left alone, the nuns carouse in a lively drinking song, Raimbaud having discovered the castle's wine cellar ('Buvons, buvons'). Isolier recognizes Count Ory and lays a trap for him, as a result of which, in a darkened bedroom, Ory finds himself making advances to his page instead of to Adèle ('À la faveur de cette nuit obscure'). Suddenly, trumpets announce the imminent return of the Crusaders, and Ory and his men are forced to retreat ('Écoutez ces chants de victoire').

Five of the numbers in *Le Comte Ory* were taken by Rossini from *Il viaggio a Reims*, which he did not expect would be staged anywhere else after its initial three performances in 1825 to celebrate the coronation of Charles X. (Indeed, Rossini withdrew the opera after its third performance.) In Act I of *Le Comte Ory* only one piece is entirely new, with most of the opera's freshly composed music occurring in Act II. Nevertheless, the work was a huge success at its premiere in 1828, and it seems all of a piece, with its own individual mood and atmosphere – quite different in style from Rossini's more ebullient Italian comedies. The graceful trio, 'À la faveur de cette nuit', for Ory, Adele and Isolier in Act II, when Ory finds himself soliciting his page, Isolier, by mistake, is positively Mozartian in its delicacy and wit. This trio, which Berlioz considered to be Rossini's 'absolute masterpiece', is one of the highlights of the score. Another is the Act I finale, 'Ciel! O terreur, o peine extreme', a septet with chorus, adapted from *Il viaggio*'s 'Gran pezzo concertato', which was written for fourteen solo voices. *Le Comte Ory* is an *opéra comique* of great charm.

Recommended recording: John Aler (Ory), Sumi Jo (Adèle), Diana Montague (Isolier),Gino Quilico (Raimbaud), with the Lyon Opera Chorus and Orchestra, conducted by John Eliot Gardiner. Philips 422 406–2. Based on a stage production in Lyon, this recording has great theatrical presence, is conducted stylishly and gloriously sung by its entire cast.

Guillaume Tell
(William Tell)
opera in four acts (approximate length: 3 hours, 45 minutes)

Guillaume Tell (William Tell)   *baritone*
Hedwige, Tell's wife   *soprano*
Jemmy, Tell's son   *soprano*
Mathilde, Habsburg princess   *soprano*
Arnold Melcthal   *tenor*
Melcthal, Arnold's father   *bass*
Gessler, governor of the cantons of Schwyz and Uri   *bass*
Walter Furst, a Swiss conspirator   *bass*
Leuthold, a herdsman   *baritone*

LIBRETTO BY VICTOR-JOSEPH ETIENNE DE JOUY, HIPPOLYTE-LOUIS-FLORENT BIS AND ARMAND MARRAST, BASED ON THE PLAY *WILHELM TELL*, BY FRIEDRICH VON

Rossini's most important and influential opera for Paris, composed immedi-ately after *Le Comte Ory*, was *Guillaume Tell*, which also turned out to be his very last opera. Rossini was only thirty-seven and at the height of his creative powers, but, although he lived on to the age of seventy-six, and in his old age wrote a number of short piano pieces and songs for performance at his weekly soirées, he composed nothing more for the stage.

Schiller's *Wilhelm Tell* (1804) uses the figure of the legendary national hero of Switzerland primarily as a vehicle for his own political and moral idealism. William Tell was supposedly a popular leader in the fourteenth-century Swiss uprising against Austrian rule. Because of his refusal to salute the Austrian gover-nor of the cantons of Schwyz and Uri, Tell was forced to attempt to shoot an apple from the head of his own son with his crossbow, which he succeeded in doing. A libretto derived from Schiller's play was written for Rossini by De Jouy, but was found unsatisfactory and was partly rewritten by Bis. Further changes were made to one scene, at Rossini's request, by Marrast.

At nearly four hours, the opera is rather long, and given its subject it is curi-ously leisurely in pace. At its premiere in August 1829 it was politely received, but soon after the first performance cuts began to be made to reduce the work to a more convenient length. (Some years later when the director of the Paris Opéra mentioned to Rossini that Act II of *Guillaume Tell* was to be performed, the com-poser exclaimed in mock astonishment, 'What, the whole of it?')

Act I. On the shores of Lake Lucerne. As dawn breaks over the mountains, the villagers prepare for a triple wedding to be celebrated that day ('Quel jour serein le ciel présage!'). William Tell is in low spirits, lamenting his country's subjection to tyrannical Austrian rule. Melcthal, a respected patriarch of the village, expresses to his son Arnold his disappointment that he has not yet thought of marriage. Arnold, a patriotic Swiss who has been forced to serve in the Austrian garrison, answers his father evasively, for he is in love with the Austrian Princess Mathilde, whose life he once saved in an avalanche.

Tell extracts from Arnold his promise that when the time is ripe to rise against the Austrians he will play his part ('Où vas-tu?'). The village festivities com-mence, among them an archery contest, which is won by Tell's son Jemmy, but the joyous atmosphere is interrupted when Leuthold, an elderly herdsman, enters in great distress. He has killed an Austrian soldier who was attempting to rape his daughter and is being pursued by Austrian troops. Tell ferries Leuthold across to safety on the opposite shore of the lake just as the soldiers arrive. When the villagers refuse to identify Leuthold's rescuer, old Melcthal is dragged away as a hostage.

Act II. The heights of Rutli, overlooking Lake Lucerne. A hunting party, returning home, pauses to sing of the glories of the chase ('Quelle sauvage harmonie'). After they have left, Princess Mathilde enters, musing on her love for Arnold ('Sombre forêt'). Arnold arrives, and they declare their love for each other ('Oui, vous l'arrachez à mon âme'), but are interrupted by the sound of people approaching, and Mathilde has barely left before William Tell and Walter Furst, a fellow Swiss conspirator, enter to inform Arnold that his father has been killed by Gessler, the Austrian governor. Arnold swears to avenge his father ('Quand l'Helvétie est un champ de supplices'), and almost at once men begin to emerge from the forest, representatives of the cantons who are gathering to plan their uprising ('Des profondeurs de bois immense').

Act III, scene i. An old ruined chapel in the gardens of the Altdorf palace. Arnold breaks the news of his father's death to Mathilde. They both recognize that, at least for the time being, their love must be forgotten, and they bid each other a tender farewell ('Pour notre amour, plus d'espérance').

Act III, scene ii. The main square at Altdorf. Gessler has arranged festivities to celebrate one hundred years of Austrian rule. The reluctant citizens are forced to sing and dance and are ordered to walk past a symbol of Austrian authority, bowing to Gessler's hat. When Tell refuses to obey Gessler's order, he is recognized as the man who helped Leuthold to escape. Knowing of Tell's reputed skill as an archer, Gessler plucks an apple from a tree and has it placed on young Jemmy's head. He orders Tell to transfix the apple with a single bolt if he wishes to save the lives of both himself and his son. Instructing Jemmy to remain still ('Sois immobile'), Tell succeeds in shooting the apple from his son's head. When he inadvertently drops a second arrow which, in the event of failure, he had held in reserve for Gessler, Tell is arrested. Mathilde takes Jemmy under her protection, and Gessler orders that Tell be taken to a castle across the lake and fed to the reptiles.

Act IV, scene i. Melcthal's house. Arnold comes to pay a final visit to his birthplace ('Asile héréditaire'). When his companions arrive with the news that Tell is now a prisoner of the Austrians, Arnold directs them to a cache of arms hidden by his father and Tell, and he leads them away to rescue Tell ('Amis, amis, secondez ma vengeance').

Act IV, scene ii. A rocky shore of Lake Lucerne. Tell's house is visible, high up on a ledge. Jemmy is returned to his grieving mother by Mathilde, who has decided to offer herself as a hostage in return for Tell. Leuthold reports that Tell is being taken across the lake, but that a storm is raging and Tell's captors have had to free his hands, as only he knows how to control the boat. Jemmy, having earlier been instructed by his father, gives the signal for the insurrection to begin. When Tell reaches the shore, he sees Gessler on a rocky precipice and shoots an arrow at the tyrant, who falls, dead, into the lake. Arnold and his followers capture the castle at Altdorf and, as the storm subsides, the Swiss offer up a heartfelt prayer of thanksgiving ('Tout change et grandit en ces lieux').

Verdi admired *Guillaume Tell*, though he felt that it had about it a 'fatal atmosphere of the Paris Opéra'. Taken on its own terms, however, it is an opera one can grow to love. Its famous large-scale overture, with a calm opening section for five cellos, a spirited allegro depicting a storm on the lake, a Swiss pastoral melody introduced on cor anglais and flute, and a final hectic galop, must be known to every orchestra (and brass band) in the world. The opera's many choruses are impressive; the whole of Act II is generally regarded as the work's musical and dramatic peak; and Arnold's music is exciting, though its fearsome tessitura has taken its toll on many tenors over the years. When an Irish tenor, John O'Sullivan, sang the role in Paris in 1929, his admirer the novelist James Joyce commented, 'I have been through the score of *Guillaume Tell*, and I discover that O'Sullivan sings 456 Gs, 93 A flats, 54 B flats, 15 Bs, 19 Cs and 2 C sharps. Nobody else can do it.' In the last half-century, only Nicolai Gedda has been able to encompass all of Arnold's notes, mellifluously and with apparent ease.

The role of Tell is curiously peripheral to the action for much of the time, but his aria 'Sois immobile', sung as he prepares to shoot the apple from his son's head, is moving in its simplicity and sincerity and also impressive in the manner in which its declamatory vocal line is dictated by, and in consequence perfectly suited to, the rhythm of the words. Berlioz thought that the Act II finale, the gathering of the three cantons, was sublime – a word that is not too strong to use in describing the entire opera.

Recommended recording: Gabriel Bacquier (Tell), Montserrat Caballé (Mathilde), Nicolai Gedda (Arnold), with the Ambrosian Opera Chorus and the Royal Philharmonic Orchestra, conducted by Lamberto Gardelli. EMI CMS 7 69951 2. This absolutely complete recording is superb, with Bacquier a convincing Tell, Caballé exquisite, and Nicolai Gedda (see above) incomparable.

CAMILLE SAINT-SAËNS
(b. Paris, 1835 – d. Algiers, 1921)

Samson et Dalila
(Samson and Delilah)
opera in three acts (approximate length: 2 hours)

Samson *tenor*
Dalila (Delilah) *mezzo-soprano*
The High Priest of Dagon *baritone*
Abimelech, satrap of Gaza *bass*
An Aged Hebrew *bass*
A Philistine Messenger *tenor*

LIBRETTO BY FERDINAND LEMAIRE, DERIVED FROM THE BOOK OF JUDGES, CHAPTER 16; TIME: AROUND 1150 BC; PLACE: GAZA; FIRST PERFORMED AT THE GROSSHERZOGLICHES THEATER, WEIMAR, 2 DECEMBER 1877

A fluent and prolific composer, Saint-Saëns wrote thirteen operas, of which the only one to achieve international success was *Samson et Dalila*. Among his other operas are *Etienne Marcel* (1879), *Ascanio* (1890), both of which contain much agreeable music, though they are generally considered deficient in theatrical effect, and *Henry VIII* (1883), whose principal theme is based on a traditional English tune that the composer discovered in the library at Buckingham Palace. His final opera, *Déjanire* (Dejanira), was staged in Monte Carlo in 1911.

Saint-Saëns first intended to use the biblical story of Samson and Delilah as the basis of an oratorio, but he was persuaded by his librettist, Ferdinand Lemaire, to turn it into an opera. A private concert performance of Act II, organized by the singer Pauline Viardot, for whom Saint-Saëns had designed the role of Dalila, was given in Paris with Viardot as Dalila and the composer playing the orchestral part on the piano, but it failed to move its audience, among whom was the director of the Paris Opéra. Unable to persuade any French opera house to take an interest in the project, Saint-Saëns was fortunately encouraged by Liszt to complete the work, which in 1877 was given its premiere at the theatre in Weimar which was under Liszt's control. It was not until 1890 that *Samson et Dalila* was seen in France, at Rouen. In due course it became one of the most popular of French operas.

Act I. A public square in the Palestine town of Gaza. The people of Israel lament their subjugation by the Philistines, but Samson incites them to rise against their oppressors ('Arrêtez, o mes frères'). When Abimelech, the satrap of Gaza, blasphemes against the God of Israel, Samson seizes the satrap's sword and kills him. The High Priest of Dagon emerges from the temple and curses Israel. Young Philistine maidens, among them Dalila, dance to celebrate the coming of spring, and although an Aged Hebrew warns him against her wiles Samson cannot resist Dalila when she invites him to visit her that evening ('Printemps qui commence').

Act II. Outside Dalila's house in the valley of Sorek, at nightfall. Dalila calls on the goddess of love to help her with her seduction of Samson ('Amour! Viens aider ma faiblesse'). When the High Priest comes secretly to see Dalila, she agrees to do all in her power to discover the secret of Samson's great strength. At last Samson arrives, torn between his desire for Dalila and his awareness of his destiny as a leader of the Hebrews. Gradually he succumbs to Dalila's charms ('Mon coeur s'ouvre à ta voix') and enters the house with her. He tells her the secret of his strength, which lies in his hair, and she renders him harmless by cutting off his hair while he sleeps. At a signal from Dalila, Philistine soldiers enter the house and overpower Samson.

Act III, scene i. The prison in Gaza. Samson, his hair shorn and his eyes blinded, is in chains, laboriously turning the millwheel to which he has been tied ('Vois ma misère, hélas'). A chorus of captive Jews is heard, rebuking him for having betrayed their cause, and Samson prays to God for forgiveness.

Act III, scene ii. A hall in the temple of Dagon, with two great marble columns in the centre. The Philistines, in celebratory mood, are holding a bacchanal. Samson, led in by a small boy, is mocked by Dalila and the High Priest. Samson asks the boy to lead him between the two marble columns. Imploring God to restore his former strength to him, he succeeds in pushing the columns apart. The temple collapses, crushing everyone beneath its rubble.

In its time it was considered distinctly Wagnerian, but now *Samson et Dalila* seems a quintessentially French opera. The almost Bach-like choruses in Acts I and III are a reminder that the work was originally intended to be an oratorio, but Dalila's arias are suitably seductive, and the great duet scene in Act II for Dalila and Samson, with the languorous melody of 'Mon coeur s'ouvre à ta voix', is undeniably erotic. The music of the Act III bacchanal soon became, and still remains, highly popular beyond the confines of *Samson et Dalila*. Throughout the opera, Saint-Saëns's orchestration is masterly.

Recommended recording: Placido Domingo (Samson), Waltraud Meier (Dalila), with the Chorus and Orchestra of the Bastille Opera, conducted by Myung-Whun-Chung. EMI CDS 7 54470 2. Domingo is a splendidly heroic Samson and Meier a dramatically convincing Dalila.

ARNOLD SCHOENBERG
(b. Vienna, 1874 – d. Los Angeles, 1951)

Moses und Aron
(Moses and Aaron)
opera in three acts
(approximate length of the completed two acts: 1 hour, 45 minutes)

Moses   *spoken role*
Aron (Aaron), his brother   *tenor*
A Young Girl   *soprano*
An Invalid Woman   *contralto*
A Young Man   *tenor*
A Naked Youth   *tenor*
Another Man   *baritone*
Ephraimite   *baritone*
A Priest   *bass*
Four Naked Virgins   *2 sopranos; 2 contraltos*

LIBRETTO BY THE COMPOSER, DERIVED FROM THE BOOK OF EXODUS; TIME: THE FOURTEENTH CENTURY BC; PLACE: EGYPT; FIRST PERFORMED AT THE STADT-THEATER, ZURICH, 6 JUNE 1957

Arnold Schoenberg is famous as the first composer to develop the atonal method of composition, or music that discards the use of a key system. His serial or twelve-note technique influenced several other composers, though it was not widely adopted and was never accepted other than by small coteries.

His four operas span the greater part of Schoenberg's creative life. *Erwartung*, composed in 1909 but not performed until 1924, when it was staged at a contemporary-music festival in Prague, is a one-act monodrama for soprano and orchestra. *Die glückliche Hand* (The Fateful Hand), another one-act piece, written immediately after *Erwartung* and in a similar musical style that is not easy on the ear, also remained unperformed until 1924. *Von Heute auf Morgen* (From One Day to the Next), staged in Frankfurt in 1930, is a one-act comedy hampered by an atonal score ill-suited to the expression of humour.

In 1930 Schoenberg embarked upon his only full-length opera, *Moses und Aron*, for which he wrote his own libretto based on the Old Testament Book of Exodus. However, he found composition of the opera laborious and abandoned it after completing two of its projected three acts, though to the end of his life nearly twenty years later he continued to speak of his intention to return to the work. In the year of his death, Schoenberg wrote, 'Agreed that the third act may simply be spoken, in case I cannot complete the composition.'

Six years after Schoenberg's death the two completed acts of *Moses und Aron* were staged at the Zurich Stadttheater and were well received. A less successful production in 1959 in Berlin included Act III, using music taken from Act I. There have since been other performances.

Act I, scene i. A rocky place. The Voice of God speaks to Moses from the Burning Bush, naming him leader of the Israelites and giving him the task of leading his people from their bondage in Egypt to the Promised Land. Moses demurs, for he fears that he lacks eloquence, but God assures him that his brother Aron will be his spokesman.

Act I, scene ii. The desert. Moses and Aron meet. The two brothers have widely differing concepts of God. While to Moses God is pure thought, Aron believes God to be a product of man's highest imagination, and cannot understand how the people can be asked to worship an invisible, unknowable God whom they cannot visualize.

Act I, scene iii. A public place in Egypt. The Israelites are becoming agitated. A Young Girl says she has seen Aron going off to the wilderness in a state of exaltation, while a Young Man says he has seen him appear in a cloud of light. Differing views are expressed, as Moses and Aron are seen approaching.

Act I, scene iv. The same. Moses recounts the incomprehensible attributes of God, while Aron more practically arouses the people's pride in being the chosen race, and also their longing for freedom. Aron changes Moses' staff into a writhing snake, a miracle that fills the people with a fearful conviction of the power of God. In a state of exaltation, the Israelites prepare to set out on their journey through the desert to the Promised Land.

Interlude. In the darkness, the people ask in a whisper, 'Where is Moses?'

Act II, scene i. Below Mount Sinai. Moses has been absent on the Mount of Revelation for forty days, and the people are becoming restive.

Act II, scene ii. The same. Aron is forced to allow the people to return to their old form of religion, promising them a visible image to worship.

Act II, scene iii. The same. The mood of the crowd changes to one of rejoicing as they dance around the Golden Calf that Aron has fashioned for them. They offer sacrifices and indulge in orgiastic revels. Four Naked Virgins are embraced by priests and then stabbed, while the Young Man, who expresses his disapproval of the Golden Calf, is killed.

Act II, scene iv. The same. Moses is seen descending from the mountain, bearing the Tablets of the Law, which contain the Ten Commandments. When Moses, with a gesture, dismisses the Golden Calf, it smashes into fragments. The people flee in terror.

Act II, scene v. The same. Moses and Aron face each other. Aron justifies his attitude and his actions, and claims that the Tablets of the Law are themselves graven images, tangible expressions of thought, to be worshipped. In frustration, the inarticulate Moses smashes the Tablets. On the horizon a column of fire can be seen, showing the way to the Promised Land. Aron and the people follow it, leaving Moses alone in an agony of self-doubt and despair.

Act III (not composed). Aron is brought in, in chains, and Moses accuses him of leading the people away from the true God. When the guards ask if Aron should be put to death, Moses orders them to free his brother, since God will choose whether or not he lives. As soon as he is released from his chains, Aron falls dead.

The final despairing words of Moses at the end of Act II, 'O Wort, du Wort das mir fehlt' (O word, you word that I lack), could almost be said to sum up Schoenberg's difficulty in coming to grips with Act III of *Moses und Aaron*, and indeed the impossibility of satisfactorily composing an opera on the philosophic argument around which Schoenberg's libretto is constructed. Is God a concept to be understood, or something utterly unknowable and incomprehensible?

Schoenberg's score is impressively complex, but his device of having the inarticulate Moses utter only in *Sprechgesang*, in which the voice speaks on pitch but does not sustain note values, while the articulate Aron sings in a lyrical tenor voice, is not entirely satisfactory, and indeed even somewhat superficial. The opera's vivid and colourful orchestral music in the scene of the orgiastic revelling around the Golden Calf is immensely effective.

Recommended recording: Gunter Reich (Moses) Richard Cassilly (Aron), with the BBC Singers and BBC Symphony Orchestra, conducted by Pierre Boulez.

DMITRI SHOSTAKOVICH
(b. St Petersburg, 1906 – d. Moscow, 1975)

The Lady Macbeth of Mtsensk
(Ledi Macbet Msenskovo ujyezda)
opera in four acts (approximate length: 2 hours, 30 minutes)

Boris Timofeyevich Ismailov, a merchant   *high bass*
Zinovy Borisvich Ismailov, his son   *tenor*
Katerina Lvovna Ismailova, Zinovy's wife   *soprano*
Sergei, a workman   *tenor*
A Drunken Peasant   *tenor*
Aksinya, a cook   *soprano*
The Priest   *bass*
A Police Sergeant   *baritone*
A Police Constable   *bass*
Sonyetka, a convict   *contralto*
An Old Convict   *bass*

LIBRETTO BY ALEXANDER PREIS AND THE COMPOSER, AFTER A SHORT STORY, *THE LADY MACBETH OF MTSENSK*, BY NIKOLAI SEMIONOVICH LESKOV; TIME: THE MID-NINETEENTH CENTURY; PLACE: RUSSIA; FIRST PERFORMED AT THE MALY THEATRE, LENINGRAD, 22 JANUARY 1934

Shostakovich, the last of the great symphonic composers, wrote only two operas. *The Nose*, a satirical comedy based on a short story by Gogol, was produced in Leningrad in 1930, at a time when the comparatively young Soviet Union was still in a state of artistic experiment. A difficult work to stage, and not sufficiently rewarding, *The Nose* did not find popularity outside Russia. *The Lady Macbeth of Mtsensk*, which Shostakovich composed shortly afterwards, is by contrast a grim melodrama based on a story by the Russian novelist Nikolai Semionovich Leskov (1831–95).

Shostakovich first encountered Leskov's story when his artist friend Boris Kustodiev illustrated a new edition of it in 1930. 'As a Soviet composer', Shostakovich wrote shortly after completing the opera, 'I determined to preserve the strength of Leskov's story, and yet, approaching it critically, to interpret its events from our modern point of view.' If this was his attempt to smooth the way for his opera in Stalin's Russia, it did not succeed. At its premiere in 1934 *The Lady Macbeth of Mtsensk* provoked a mixed reaction, but it continued to be performed in the Soviet Union until December of the following year, when Stalin attended a performance and disapproved of the opera. An article in *Pravda* followed as a matter of course, denouncing the work as a 'deliberately discordant, confused stream of sounds', its acceptance abroad explained by the fact that 'it tickles the perverted bourgeois taste with its fidgety, screaming, neurotic music.'

There had been productions abroad, in Cleveland, New York, Philadelphia, Stockholm and Prague; but following *Pravda*'s criticism, Shostakovich thought it expedient to withdraw from circulation both the opera and his recently completed Fourth Symphony. (His Fifth Symphony, a year or so later, was subtitled 'A Soviet artist's practical reply to justified criticism'.) *The Lady Macbeth of Mtsensk* vanished from the scene until 1962, when, in the marginally more liberal climate of opinion in Soviet Russia which followed the death of Stalin, Shostakovich revised and reissued the opera as *Katerina Ismailova*, purging it of anything that might still have been found offensive by Soviet society at the time. Since the composer's death in 1975, the original unbowdlerized version of *The Lady Macbeth of Mtsensk* has returned to favour.

Act I, scene i. Katerina's bedroom. Katerina, the young and beautiful wife of the wealthy merchant Zinovy Ismailov, is bored by life in the Ismailov household. As she lies in bed, she is berated by her father-in-law, Boris Ismailov, for not having given his son an heir. He orders her to prepare some poison for the rats, to which she murmurs that nothing would please her more than to poison him. Zinovy departs to attend to a burst dam, but first he introduces Sergei, a new and handsome young labourer. Boris makes Katerina swear to be faithful to Zinovy in his absence, and Aksinya, the cook, mentions to Katerina that Sergei lost his last job because he was having an affair with his employer's wife.

Act I, scene ii. In the Ismailovs' yard. Workers, among them Sergei, are playfully molesting Aksinya. When Katerina orders them to stop, she finds herself being forced to wrestle with Sergei, who throws her to the ground just as Boris arrives. Boris threatens to report Katerina's behaviour to her husband.

Act I, scene iii. Katerina's bedroom. When the voice of her father-in-law is heard outside, ordering her to bed, Katerina undresses, but she is interrupted by Sergei, who appears at her door on the pretext of wanting to borrow a book. Soon they are locked in a passionate embrace.

Act II, scene i. The Ismailovs' courtyard, at night. Boris prowls up and down beneath Katerina's window, musing on the sexual prowess of his youth. Seeing a light in his daughter-in-law's window, he is about to pay her a visit when he catches sight of Sergei leaving her room by the drainpipe. Boris calls the workers, has Sergei stripped and tied to a post, and whips him. Katerina slides down the drainpipe and attacks her father-in-law. Sergei is carried off to the storeroom, and Boris orders Katerina to serve him mushrooms for supper. He sends a worker to warn his son Zinovy that there is trouble at home and then proceeds to eat the mushrooms, which Katerina has laced with rat poison. Boris collapses, calls for a Priest and accuses Katerina before he dies.

Act II, scene ii. Katerina's bedroom. Katerina and Sergei are in bed together, but he is worried that when her husband returns their affair will come to an end. He falls asleep, and Katerina is terrified by the appearance of Boris's ghost. When Zinovy stealthily approaches the bedroom door, Sergei hides. Zinovy, suspicious of Katerina, picks up Sergei's belt from the bed and begins to beat her with it. Sergei emerges from his hiding place, and the lovers batter Zinovy to death, hiding his body in the cellar.

Act III, scene i. The Ismailovs' house. On their wedding day, Katerina and Sergei contemplate their crimes. When they have left for the wedding celebration, a Drunken Peasant breaks into the cellar in search of more liquor, finds Zinovy's decomposing corpse and rushes off to inform the police.

Act III, scene ii. The police station. The Sergeant and his men lament both their present unemployment and the fact that they have not been invited to Katerina's wedding. They interrogate a nihilist teacher who is brought in, and are delighted when the Peasant arrives with news of a corpse in the Ismailovs' cellar. They hurry off to the scene of the crime.

Act III, scene iii. The Ismailovs' garden. The wedding celebration is in progress, the guests are well and truly inebriated, and the Priest makes advances to the bride. When Katerina notices that the padlock of the cellar door is broken, she realizes that their crime has been discovered. She alerts Sergei, and they are about to leave with money he has taken from the house when the police arrive. Katerina gives herself up, and Sergei attempts to escape but is caught.

Act IV. By the banks of a river. Shackled convicts, on their way to Siberia, have halted by a bridge. Katerina bribes a guard to let her speak to Sergei, who rejects her, blaming her for his present predicament, and begins to flirt with another female convict, Sonyetka, who demands that he bring her Katerina's stockings. Sergei persuades Katerina to part with the stockings and gives them to Sonyetka, who, together with the other women, taunts Katerina. As the convicts are being made to leave, Katerina seizes Sonyetka and, clinging to her, jumps into the river. The two women drown, and the other convicts resume their journey.

Shostakovich, together with his co-librettist, made numerous changes to Leskov's story, softening Katerina's character and making excuses for her crimes. For Leskov's cruel and greedy murderess he substituted a woman whose murders he described – like the obedient Communist he was at the time – as being 'not so much real crimes as a revolt against her circumstances and against the sordid and sickening atmosphere in which middle-class merchants of the nineteenth century lived'. This line of argument failed to convince the Soviet authorities, who were outraged by the music of the opera as well as by its plot. The score is, of its kind, brilliant, with admittedly some brassily noisy caricature and a certain amount of that neurotic screaming that upset *Pravda*, but also much attractive lyrical writing for the voices. The work does have its longueurs, and the various satirical episodes, especially the operetta-like scene in the police station, tend to disrupt its overall dramatic atmosphere, but the orchestral writing throughout the opera is clearly that of a major symphonist. A highly eclectic work, *The Lady Macbeth of Mtsensk* owes much to Mahler and Berg, as well as to Expressionist ideas that had found their way into Russian theatre in the 1920s only to be severely frowned upon by the authorities.

Recommended recording: Maria Ewing (Katerina), Aage Haugland (Boris), Philip Langridge (Zinovy), with the Chorus and Orchestra of the Bastille Opera, conducted by Myung-Whun-Chung. DG 437 511–2.

BEDŘICH SMETANA
(b. Litomysl, Bohemia, 1824 – d. Prague, 1884)

The Bartered Bride
(Prodaná nevěsta)
comic opera in three acts (approximate length: 2 hours, 15 minutes)

Krušina, a farmer   *baritone*
Ludmila, his wife   *mezzo-soprano*
Mařenka, their daughter   *soprano*
Micha, a landlord   *bass*
Hata, his wife   *mezzo-soprano*
Vašek, their son   *tenor*
Jenik, Micha's son from his first marriage   *tenor*
Kečal, a marriage broker   *bass*
Circus Ringmaster   *tenor*
Esmeralda, a dancer   *soprano*
A Circus Artist (Indian)   *bass*

LIBRETTO BY KAREL SABINA; TIME: THE MID-NINETEENTH CENTURY; PLACE: A VILLAGE IN BOHEMIA; FIRST PERFORMED AT THE PROVISIONAL THEATRE, PRAGUE, 30 MAY 1866

Smetana, the first major Czech nationalist composer, wrote eight operas, which led to his being considered the father of modern Czech music. His first opera, *The Brandenburgers in Bohemia*, performed in Prague in January 1866, won him the chief conductorship of the Provisional Theatre in that city, a post he held for eight years. With his second opera, *The Bartered Bride*, which was given its premiere only four months after that of *The Brandenburgers in Bohemia*, Smetana showed on the operatic stage the very embodiment of his country's character. Although there was a Czech language, there was, of course, no Czechoslovakia in Smetana's day, Bohemia constituting part of the Austro-Hungarian empire, but *The Bartered Bride* played an important role in raising the national consciousness of the Czechs. This did not happen overnight; indeed, the opera was only moderately successful when it was first performed. However, its popularity quickly grew, and by the mid-1870s it had come to be regarded as the quintessential Czech opera. It has ever since remained in the repertoire of Prague's National Theatre, where it has now been performed more than 2,500 times, and it is also staged all over the world.

The libretto of the opera was commissioned by Smetana from Karel Sabina, who had provided the libretto for his first opera. After the initial performances of *The Bartered Bride* in 1866, Smetana made changes to the work on several occasions until September 1870, when the opera's definitive version was performed in Prague.

Act I. The village square, with an inn on one side. The villagers are cheerfully celebrating the consecration festival of their church. Mařenka does not join in the general merriment for, as she confesses to her beloved Jenik, her parents are forcing her to marry the son of Micha, a wealthy landowner from another village. Mařenka is puzzled by Jenik's apparently complacent acceptance of this news, and she is puzzled also by Jenik's past. When she asks him why he left his home, Jenik explains that he comes from a good family but was driven out of his father's house by his stepmother. He asks Mařenka to promise to remain faithful to him, and in a duet they pledge to each other their eternal love ('Like a mother').

Mařenka's parents have agreed that their daughter will marry Micha's son. According to the marriage broker Kečal, Mařenka will have to marry Vašek, Micha's son by his second marriage, since the son of Micha's first marriage has not been heard of for years. Mařenka insists that she will marry nobody but Jenik, and Kečal goes in search of Jenik to attempt to talk sense into him. The act ends with a spirited polka, sung and danced by the villagers.

Act II. The village inn. After an opening chorus in praise of beer by Jenik and the young men of the village, Kečal approaches Jenik, and the two go off together, while the women of the village enter and join with the men in dancing a *furiant* (an exuberant Bohemian folk dance in 3/4 time). Mařenka's suitor Vašek makes his entrance. A shy and nervous youth, given to stammering, he is in a state of great alarm at the prospect of having to marry, and when Mařenka accosts him without revealing her identity, and proceeds to warn him against the flighty young woman his parents have selected for him, she has no difficulty in making Vašek promise to reject his proposed bride.

In a duet ('I know a girl who has ducats') Kečal offers Jenik a large sum of money if he will give up Mařenka. Jenik accepts on condition that Mařenka marry no one but Micha's son. An agreement is drawn up, and Jenik signs it in front of witnesses. The villagers berate him for selling off his fiancée so callously.

Act III. The village green. A circus troupe arrives in the village, and Vašek falls instantly in love with the dancer, Esmeralda. When the Circus Artist who is to play a big American bear is discovered to be hopelessly drunk, Vašek allows himself to be dressed in the bear's costume to replace him.

Mařenka is in despair, having heard that Jenik has been bribed to give her up, but when Vašek realizes that she is the girl he is supposed to marry, he is delighted, and he proposes to her. Mařenka asks for time to make up her mind, and she refuses to listen to Jenik's attempt to explain his actions.

When Micha and his wife arrive they recognize Jenik as Micha's elder son. Since Kečal's contract with Jenik stipulates merely that Mařenka marry 'the son of

Tobias Micha', Mařenka makes her choice without difficulty. Kečal is furious at having been duped. The bear rushes in, to the terror of all, but is soon revealed to be Vašek, whom his mother leads away. The opera ends with general rejoicing, as Micha blesses the marriage of Jeník and Mařenka.

The vivacious overture to *The Bartered Bride*, which gallops along at a sparkling pace, has long been a favourite concert piece. The opera itself – with its lively choruses, its romantic, somewhat sentimental arias for Jeník and Mařenka, its irres-istible comic duet for Jeník and Kečal, and its dances (late additions to the score but now an integral part of it) – is a work of immense charm, full of the most attractive and immediately enjoyable music, a folk opera in the best sense of the term. The folk spirit is never far away, nor are the sounds and rhythms of Bohemian music. Certainly the most popular of Czech operas, Smetana's master-piece is also, without a doubt, one of the finest.

Recommended recording: Gabriela Benackova (Mařenka), Peter Dvorsky (Jeník), Richard Novak (Kečal), Miroslav Kopp (Vašek), with the Czech Philharmonic Chorus and Orchestra, conducted by Zdenek Kosler. Supraphon 10 3511–2. Recorded in Prague in 1981 with some of the finest Czech singers of the time, this is an authen-tic and highly enjoyable account of the opera. Peter Dvorsky is in his element as Jeník, and Marenka is most appealingly sung by Gabriela Benackova. The entire cast sounds thoroughly at home, and the Czech Philharmonic is on top form.

Dalibor
opera in three acts (approximate length: 2 hours, 15 minutes)

Vladislav, King of Bohemia   *baritone*
Dalibor, a knight   *tenor*
Budivoj, captain of the guard   *baritone*
Beneš, a gaoler   *bass*
Vítek, Dalibor's squire   *tenor*
Milada, sister of the burgrave of Ploskovice   *soprano*
Jitka, a country girl   *soprano*

LIBRETTO BY JOSEF WENZIG, BASED ON HIS PLAY *DALIBOR*; TIME: THE FIFTEENTH CENTURY; PLACE: PRAGUE; FIRST PERFORMED AT THE NEW TOWN THEATRE, PRAGUE, 16 MAY 1868

The libretto of Smetana's third opera was drawn by Josef Wenzig (who wrote in German) from his own play *Dalibor*, and its original German was translated into Czech by the playwright's pupil, Ervin Spindler. Smetana began to compose the work in April 1865, even before Wenzig had finished writing the libretto, and he finally completed it in full score at the end of December 1867. It was given its premiere on the day of the ceremonial laying of the foundation stone of the National Theatre in Prague, on 16 May 1868.

Dalibor was at first not popular with audiences. Although Smetana had conceived it as a tribute to a legendary Czech hero who personified every conceivable national virtue, his opera was criticized in the press for being too Wagnerian and not sufficiently Czech. After the first performances the composer made some changes to the work, but it did not begin to achieve popularity until 1886, when it was staged at the Prague National Theatre. After 1919, when the country became independent, *Dalibor* began to be viewed in Czechoslovakia as something of a national institution, but it has never really established itself in the international repertoire.

Act I. The courtyard of Prague castle. The people await the outcome of the trial of Dalibor, accused of attacking and destroying the castle of the burgrave of Ploskovice and of killing the burgrave in revenge for the death of Dalibor's friend, the minstrel Zdeněk, who had been killed in one of Dalibor's feuds with the burgrave. Before sentencing Dalibor, the court invites testimony from Milada, sister of the burgrave. Milada at first calls for vengeance, but after she has heard Dalibor describe his love for his friend, and the emptiness of his life since Zdeněk's death, she relents and begs instead for mercy for him. Dalibor is sentenced to languish in gaol until he dies, but Milada conceives a plan to rescue him.

Act II, scene i. A street in the city, with an inn. Jitka, a country girl on Dalibor's estates, meets her lover, Vítek, and describes how Milada has disguised herself as a boy and entered the castle in search of Dalibor, who is imprisoned there.

Act II, scene ii. A room in the castle. Milada, dressed as a boy, brings food to Beneš the gaolor, who has taken her into his employment. Dalibor has asked for a violin to ease his boredom, so Beneš goes to fetch his own instrument, while Milada expresses her feelings at the thought of seeing Dalibor. Beneš returns with a violin, which he gives to Milada for her to take to Dalibor's cell.

Act II, scene iii. Dalibor's prison cell. Dalibor awakes from a dream about Zdeněk and imagines embracing his friend once more. When Milada enters with the violin, she reveals her real identity to Dalibor, who greets her as his liberator. They sing a love duet.

Act III, scene i. The royal chamber. King Vladislav is warned by Budivoj, the commander of his guard, of a rebellion by Dalibor's followers. At the instigation of his advisers, the King decrees that Dalibor must die immediately.

Act III, scene ii. Dalibor's prison cell. Dalibor sings of his imminent rescue by Milada. He is about to give the prearranged signal on his violin when Budivoj and his soldiers arrive to bear him off to execution.

Act III, scene iii. Outside the castle, at night. Milada and her friends await Dalibor's signal. However, when they hear instead a chorus of monks chanting a death knell, Milada realizes that their plans have gone awry and charges into the castle at the head of her followers. They return with Dalibor, but Milada has been mortally wounded. Before she dies, she and Dalibor bid farewell to each other. Budivoj and his guards emerge from the castle, and Dalibor is killed, his serene dying thought being that he will now be reunited with both Zdeněk and Milada.

The similarities between the plot of *Dalibor* and that of Beethoven's *Fidelio* (q.v.) have surely been noted, though it must be observed that Dalibor and Milada are no Florestan and Leonore. Indeed, Dalibor's love for his dead friend Zdeněk seems to take precedence over his feelings for the living Milada. Smetana's orchestral music is dramatically effective, but his writing for the voices lacks the melodic fluency that he displayed in his comedy *The Bartered Bride*.

Recommended recording: Vilem Pribyl (Dalibor), Eva Depoltova (Milada), with the Brno Janáček Opera Chorus and the Brno State Philharmonic Orchestra, conducted by Vaclav Smetacek. Supraphon 1416 2921–3. An exemplary performance and recording.

JOHANN STRAUSS II
(b. Vienna, 1825 – d. Vienna, 1899)

Die Fledermaus
(The Bat)
operetta in three acts (approximate length: 2 hours, 15 minutes)

Gabriel von Eisenstein, a wealthy Viennese gentleman, alias the
  Marquis Renard   *tenor*
Rosalinde, his wife   *soprano*

Frank, governor of the prison, alias Chevalier Chagrin   *baritone*

Prince Orlovsky, a rich young Russian   *mezzo-soprano*

Alfred, a singer   *tenor*

Dr Falke, Eisenstein's friend   *baritone*

Dr Blind, a lawyer   *tenor*

Adele, the Eisensteins' maid   *soprano*

Frosch, a gaoler   *spoken role*

LIBRETTO BY CARL HAFFNER AND RICHARD GENÉE, BASED ON A FARCE, *LE RÉVEIL-LON*, BY HENRI MEILHAC AND LUDOVIC HALÉVY; TIME: THE 1870S; PLACE: A SPA NEAR VIENNA; FIRST PERFORMED AT THE THEATER AN DER WIEN, VIENNA, 5 APRIL 1874

The most famous member of the celebrated family of composers of Viennese light music, Johann Strauss II, whose waltzes include such perennial favourites as *The Blue Danube* and *Tales from the Vienna Woods*, is the father of nineteenth-century Viennese operetta. It was at the instigation of the French composer Jacques Offenbach that Strauss was persuaded to try his hand at what was to him an unfamiliar genre. Offenbach, a great admirer of Strauss's effervescent waltzes and polkas, was on a visit to Vienna with one of his own highly successful operettas when he encouraged the Viennese composer to write his first operetta.

Strauss composed sixteen operettas in all, most of which were first performed in Vienna at the Theater an der Wien. His first, *Die lustigen Weiber von Windsor* (The Merry Wives of Windsor), was never produced, but his second, *Indigo und die vierzig Räuber* (Indigo and the Forty Thieves), was staged in 1871 to great acclaim and was followed two years later by *Der Karneval in Rom* (The Roman Carnival), which was an even greater success. Neither of these last two works is performed at all frequently today, but Strauss's fourth operetta, *Die Fledermaus*, became immensely popular throughout the world and today can be found not only in theatres specializing in operettas and musicals but also in the world's most prestigious opera houses, among them the Vienna Staatsoper, the New York Metropolitan Opera and London's Royal Opera House.

The plot of *Die Fledermaus* derives from *Le Réveillon*, a French farce by Meilhac and Halévy (the co-authors of a number of libretti for Offenbach). *Le Réveillon* had been a huge success in Paris, and was translated into German by Carl Haffner for production in Vienna. When it was suggested that the play should be turned into an operetta by Strauss, another librettist (Richard Genée) was called in to adapt Haffner's translation. Strauss was enchanted with the result and immediately set to work on his score, which took him forty-three days to compose. When it was staged at the Theater an der Wien in April 1874 *Die Fledermaus* ran for a mere sixteen nights. It was only when it was revived at the same theatre later in the year that it became wildly popular.

Act I. A room in Eisenstein's house. From outside the house, the tenor voice of Alfred, an opera singer, can be heard serenading his former lover Rosalinde, who is now the wife of Gabriel von Eisenstein ('Täubchen, das entflattert ist'). Adele, the Eisensteins' maid, enters reading a letter from her sister Ida, inviting her to a party that evening at the villa of the rich and eccentric Russian Prince Orlovsky. When Rosalinde enters, Adele makes up a story about her aunt being ill, and she asks for the evening off. Rosalinde refuses, for her husband is about to start a five-day prison sentence for a minor offence, and Adele cannot be spared. Alfred, the tenor, enters through a window, and Rosalinde, who cannot resist his top notes, persuades him to leave by promising him that he can return later, after her husband has gone off to gaol.

Eisenstein now enters, quarrelling with his inept, stammering lawyer, Dr Blind, who has somehow managed to get Eisenstein's sentence extended to eight days ('Nein, mit solchen Advokaten'). After Blind has left, Eisenstein's friend Dr Falke arrives, having concocted a plan to take his revenge on Eisenstein, who after a recent masked ball had forced Falke to walk home in broad daylight dressed as a bat, to the jeers of passers-by. Falke gives Eisenstein an invitation to Prince Orlovsky's party that evening, pointing out that he need not turn up at the prison to begin his sentence until the next morning at six. Eisenstein agrees, and goes off merrily, ostensibly to serve his prison sentence.

Rosalinde decides to give Adele the evening off so that she herself can receive her admirer, Alfred, in private. Her intimate supper with Alfred ('Trinke, Liebchen, trinke schnell') is, however, interrupted by the arrival of Herr Frank, the prison governor, who has come in person to escort Eisenstein to gaol. Frank naturally assumes that the man now sitting at his ease in Eisenstein's dressing gown is Rosalinde's husband, and Rosalinde, to avoid being compromised, of course agrees that he is ('Mein Herr, was dächten Sie von mir?'). The hapless Alfred has no option but to allow himself to be taken off to prison.

Act II. Prince Orlovsky's villa. The blasé young Prince Orlovsky exhorts his guests to enjoy themselves ('Ich lade gern mir Gäste ein'). Adele, wearing one of her mistress's gowns, encounters her sister Ida and discovers that it was not Ida who wrote to invite her to the party. The girls decide that someone must have played a trick on them, and Ida introduces Adele to the Prince as an actress. Falke presents his friend Eisenstein to the Prince as a French nobleman, the Marquis Renard, and the prison governor, Frank, arrives using the name of Chevalier Chagrin. Eisenstein recognizes Adele, but she has no difficulty in persuading the assembled company that she is no chambermaid ('Mein Herr Marquis').

Having been summoned to the party by Falke, Rosalinde makes an impressive entrance disguised as a Hungarian countess, and when Eisenstein immediately begins to flirt with her ('Dieser Anstand, so manierlich') she contrives to gain possession of his watch. To prove she is Hungarian, Rosalinde sings a fiery csárdás ('Klange der Heimat'). Orlovsky proposes a toast to King Champagne ('Im Feuerstrom der Reben'), and Dr Falke leads the by-now-not-entirely-sober company in a sentimental hymn to brotherly love ('Brüderlein und Schwesterlein'). A ballet is followed by a waltz, interrupted by a clock striking six, which sends both Frank and Eisenstein rushing off to fulfil their obligations to the gaol as, respectively, governor and prisoner.

Act III. The prison governor's office. Alfred can be heard singing away in his prison cell, as the drunken gaoler Frosch enters and embarks upon a comic monologue. Frank, the prison governor, arrives from Orlovsky's party, thoroughly drunk, and tries to sleep at his desk. Adele and Ida arrive in search of Chevalier Chagrin, who at the party offered to help them in their careers, and Adele boasts of her acting ability ('Spiel' ich die Unschuld vom Lande'). When Eisenstein arrives to serve his sentence, he is astonished to find that Chagrin is Frank, the governor of the prison, and even more astonished when Frank assures him that Eisenstein is already in a cell, having been arrested at his home the previous evening.

When Rosalinde arrives hoping to secure Alfred's release, Eisenstein disguises himself as his lawyer, Dr Blind, and questions Rosalinde and Alfred. Finally, he flings off his disguise and confronts them in a fury, only to be disconcerted when Rosalinde produces his watch as proof of his own attempted infidelity. Falke and the other party-goers now turn up at the prison; Falke explains the elaborate practical joke he played on Eisenstein, and all agree to blame everything on the champagne.

Die Fledermaus is without a doubt the most brilliant and tuneful of Viennese operettas. It is full of delightful numbers, especially in its second act, which contains Adele's high-spirited laughing song ('Mein Herr Marquis'), Rosalinde's spirited czárdás, the elegant duet 'Dieser Anstand, so manierlich', in which Eisenstein unwittingly attempts to seduce his own wife, the exhilarating chorus in praise of champagne ('Im Feuerstrom der Reben') and the magnificent finale to the act, launched with Falke's tipsily sentimental 'Brüderlein und Schwester-lein'. Act I is almost equally rich, with its ironic farewell trio when Rosalinde, Eisenstein and Adele are all secretly looking forward to their evening of delight ('So muss allein ich bleiben'), and the supper duet for Rosalinde and Alfred ('Trinke, Liebchen, trinke schnell'), with its wise and lilting refrain, 'Glücklich ist wer vergisst was nicht mehr zu ändern ist' (Happy is he who ignores what cannot be altered). Only the perfunctory and musically thin Act III disappoints, though it can be enlivened when the gaoler, Frosch, is played by a skilful comedian. Throughout the entire work Strauss's orchestration is subtle, imaginative and always dramatically appropriate. The overture, a potpourri of the operetta's best tunes, has deservedly become a popular concert favourite.

Recommended recording: Julia Varady (Rosalinde), Lucia Popp (Adele), Hermann Prey (Eisenstein), Ivan Rebroff (Orlovsky), Rene Kollo (Alfred), Bernd Weikl (Falke), with the Bavarian State Opera Chorus and Orchestra, conducted by Carlos Kleiber. Deutsche Grammophon DG 415 646–2. Kleiber conducts with real Viennese feeling, and has the benefit of a cast which, with one exception, it would be difficult to improve upon. Eisenstein was written by Strauss for the tenor voice, but its tessitura is not high and the baritone Hermann Prey here sails through the role with stylish aplomb. Varady and Popp are entrancing, Weikl is a delightful Falke and Kollo a convincing Alfred. Orlovsky should be a mezzo-soprano, but the role is here entrusted to a male falsettist who emits the wrong kind of sound.

There are two fine alternative versions, but they both date from the 1950s. Herbert von Karajan on EMI has the exemplary Viennese operetta duo of Elisabeth Schwarzkopf and Nicolai Gedda as Rosalinde and Eisenstein, while on Decca a his-toric performance with Clemens Krauss conducting the Vienna Philharmonic has an echt Wienerisch cast headed by Julius Patzak and Hilde Gueden.

Der Zigeunerbaron
(The Gypsy Baron)
operetta in three acts (approximate length: 2 hours)

Count Peter Homonay   *baritone*
Count Carnero   *baritone*
Sándor Barinkay   *tenor*
Kálmán Zsupán, a pig-farmer   *baritone*
Arsena, his daughter   *soprano*

Czipra, a gypsy   *mezzo-soprano*
Saffi, her foster-daughter   *soprano*
Mirabella, Arsena's governess   *contralto*
Ottokar, her son   *tenor*

LIBRETTO BY IGNAZ SCHNITZER, BASED ON A NOVELLA, *SAFFI*, BY MAURUS JÓKAI;
TIME: THE MID-EIGHTEENTH CENTURY; PLACE: HUNGARY AND VIENNA; FIRST
PERFORMED AT THE THEATER AN DER WIEN, VIENNA, 24 OCTOBER 1885

With *Der Zigeunerbaron*, Strauss succeeded in composing an operetta that is closer in mood to Romantic opera than to the effervescent gaiety of *Die Fledermaus*. The libretto was drawn from a novella, *Saffi*, by the Hungarian novelist Maurus Jókai, whom Strauss had met when he was in Budapest to conduct his operetta *Der lustige Krieg* (The Merry War). At its premiere in Vienna in 1885 *Der Zigeunerbaron* was received with wild enthusiasm, and today it is granted the status of an opera by being performed in opera houses worldwide.

Act I. A swamp by a river on the outskirts of a Hungarian village, with a ruined castle in the background. A general amnesty having been announced, the young Sándor Barinkay returns to his childhood home, from which he and his father were banished twenty-five years earlier, when their family estate was confiscated ('Als flotter Geist'). He finds the castle in ruins, the property derelict and the fields used as a camping-ground by gypsies. Czipra, an old gypsy, recognizes Barinkay as the son of their overlord. She reads his fortune and predicts that he will find a wife and also riches. The wealthy but illiterate pig-breeder Kálmán Zsupán, who has annexed most of the Barinkay property and is reluctant to return it, suggests that Barinkay marry his daughter Arsena. However, Arsena is in love with Ottokar, the son of her governess, Mirabella, and tells Barinkay that she would not marry him unless he had the title of baron. When Czipra's daughter Saffi enters, singing a gypsy song ('So elend und so treu'), Barinkay remembers the song from his childhood. He falls in love wih Saffi, proclaims himself a gypsy baron and announces his intention of marrying Saffi.

Act II. The gypsy camp. Helped by Czipra, Barinkay finds a hoard of treasure that his father buried many years previously ('Ha, seht es winkt'). When Count Carnero, the commissioner for public morals, asks for details of the status of their relationship, Saffi and Barinkay cheerfully inform him that they were married by a bullfinch, and that a nightingale sang at the wedding ceremony ('Wer uns getraut?').

Count Homonay arrives with his hussars, seeking recruits for the war that Hungary is about to wage against Spain ('Her die Hand, es muss ja sein'), and Zsupán and Ottokar are tricked into joining. Czpira produces a document proving that Saffi is of noble blood, the daughter of a Turkish pasha, at which Barinkay, believing that this puts her beyond his reach, hastily joins the army.

Act III. Outside the Kärntnertor, Vienna. The army has returned victorious ('Freuet Euch'), and Barinkay, having distinguished himself in battle, is made a real baron. He now declares his love for Saffi, for there is nothing to prevent him from marrying her. Arsena and Ottokar also celebrate their imminent wedding.

Strauss's score is rich in Hungarian colouring and full of enchanting melodies, among them Barinkay's ebullient entrance song, 'Als flotter Geist', the sensuous duet 'Wer uns getraut?', and the joyous waltz trio that accompanies the finding of the treasure.

Recommended recording: Herbert Lippert (Barinkay). Pamela Coburn (Saffi), with the Arnold Schoenberg Choir and the Vienna Symphony Orchestra, conducted by Nikolaus Harnoncourt. Teldec 4509–94555–2. Harnoncourt restores the music excised from the score before the operetta's premiere in 1885, Lippert brings a real Viennese timbre and style to the title-role, and the American soprano Pamela Coburn is a delightful Saffi. The rest of the mainly Austrian cast give excellent and authentic performances, and Harnoncourt conducts impeccably.

RICHARD STRAUSS
(b. Munich, 1864 – d. Garmisch-Partenkirchen, 1949)

Salome
opera in one act (approximate length: 1 hour, 45 minutes)

Herod, tetrarch of Judaea   *tenor*
Herodias, his wife   *mezzo-soprano*
Salome, daughter of Herodias   *soprano*
Jokanaan (John the Baptist)   *baritone*
Narraboth, captain of the guard   *tenor*
Herodias's Page   *alto*

LIBRETTO DRAWN BY THE COMPOSER FROM HEDWIG LACHMANN'S GERMAN
TRANSLATION OF THE PLAY *SALOME*, BY OSCAR WILDE; TIME: AROUND AD 30;
PLACE: HEROD'S PALACE AT TIBERIAS, ON THE SEA OF GALILEE; FIRST PERFORMED
AT THE KÖNIGLICHES OPERNHAUS, DRESDEN, 9 DECEMBER 1905

The son of Franz Strauss, who was a distinguished horn player and a professor at the Music Academy in Munich, Richard Strauss began his musical studies at the age of four and produced his first composition, a Christmas carol, when he was six. By his early twenties he had composed much chamber music, piano music and a number of songs, had completed a symphony and had become an assistant conductor at the Munich Hofoper, where his father played first horn in the orchestra.

Guntram, the first of Strauss's fifteen operas, was composed mostly in Egypt, where the composer had gone in 1892 to convalesce after having been ill with bronchitis. At its premiere in Weimar in 1894, *Guntram* failed to please, and Strauss did not attempt to write another opera for a good six years, concentrating instead upon the composition of songs, many of which he dedicated to his wife, the soprano Pauline de Ahna, and orchestral tone poems, among them *Till Eulenspiegels lustige Streiche* and *Don Quixote*. His next opera, *Feuersnot* (Fire Famine), staged in Dresden in 1901, was successful at its premiere but has failed to hold the stage, although it is still performed occasionally in Germany.

It was with his third opera, *Salome*, that Strauss's career as a composer of opera really took wing. Oscar Wilde's *Salome* had been written in French for Sarah Bernhardt (who, however, never performed it), and Strauss had first become acquainted with the play in 1902, when an Austrian poet, Anton Lindner, sent him a copy, suggesting that it would make a fine opera. Strauss was interested, but was not impressed by Lindner's verse adaptation of the opening scene, and it was not until some months later, when he saw Wilde's play performed in Berlin in Hedwig Lachmann's German prose translation with Gertrud Eysoldt as Salome, that he finally decided to use it as the basis of his next opera, setting Lachmann's text as it stood, except for making a few cuts.

The biblical story of Salome is found in the New Testament, where it is related by both St Matthew and St Mark, though neither gives her a name. She is merely 'the daughter of Herodias', who on Herod's birthday dances for him to his great delight, whereupon, according to St Matthew,

> he promised with an oath to give her whatsoever she would ask.
> And she, being before instructed of her mother, said, Give me
> here John Baptist's head in a charger.

And the king was sorry; nevertheless for the oath's sake, and them
which sat with him at meat, he commanded it to be given her.
And he sent, and beheaded John in the prison.
And his head was brought in a charger, and given to the damsel:
and she brought it to her mother.

At its premiere in Dresden in December 1905, conducted by the Dresden
Opera's music director, the Austrian Ernst von Schuch, Strauss's *Salome* was a
triumphant success with the audience and was quickly taken up by other German
opera houses, despite generally abusive reviews, and outcries from churchmen
about its immorality. Gustav Mahler, forbidden by the Catholic Archbishop of
Vienna from staging Strauss's opera in that city, wrote to his wife after seeing it in
Berlin: 'It is emphatically a work of genius, very powerful, and decidedly one of
the most important works of our day.'

Salome finally reached Vienna in 1918. It is now in the repertoire of opera houses
all over the world, yet when it was first performed in London in 1910, conducted
by Sir Thomas Beecham, the Lord Chamberlain demanded that all biblical references be deleted. The action was moved from Judaea to Greece, John the Baptist
became a prophet named Mattaniah, and his severed head did not appear on
stage. The New York premiere of *Salome* in 1907 caused such a scandal that the
opera was withdrawn after its first performance and did not reappear until 1934.

The action takes place on a terrace leading out of the banqueting hall of Herod's
palace at Tiberias on the Sea of Galilee. From the terrace, Narraboth, a handsome
young captain of the guard who is hopelessly in love with Herod's stepdaughter
Salome, gazes into the banqueting hall at her, while a young Page, in love with
Narraboth, tries vainly to dissuade him from feasting his eyes upon Salome,
warning him that something terrible may happen. Jews and rival sects at the banquet can be heard quarrelling, while the voice of the prophet Jokanaan (John the
Baptist), who has been imprisoned by Herod, rises from the cistern in the courtyard, announcing the coming of the Messiah.

When Salome comes out onto the terrace to escape the lust in her stepfather's
eyes and the coarse behaviour of his guests, her curiosity is aroused by the voice
of Jokanaan, whom she asks to see. But the guards are afraid to disobey Herod's
order that the prophet be confined to his dungeon. Salome persuades Narraboth
to have Jokanaan brought before her by promising to throw the young captain a
flower when she next passes by him in her carriage.

The pale, emaciated Jokanaan emerges, fulminating against Herod and his wife, Salome's mother, Herodias. To Jokanaan's horror, Salome is fascinated by him. When he commands her to repent of her sins and seek out the Son of Man, she asks if this Son of Man is as beautiful as Jokanaan. She begs Jokanaan to allow her to kiss his mouth, at which a despairing Narraboth kills himself, hardly noticed by Salome. She continues her attempted seduction of the prophet, who curses her and descends into his prison.

Followed by Herodias and their guests, Herod emerges onto the terrace in search of Salome, whom he desires sexually. Stumbling over the body of Narraboth, which he orders to be removed, he tries to persuade Salome to drink and eat with him. When the voice of Jokanaan is heard again Herodias asks Herod to have him silenced, but Herod refuses, for he fears Jokanaan, believing him to be a holy man.

Herod asks Salome to dance for him, but she refuses. He persists, and she finally agrees to dance if he will, in return, grant whatever wish she may express. Herod, now almost insane with lust for Salome, agrees, sealing his promise with an oath.

Salome proceeds to perform her provocative dance of the seven veils, at the conclusion of which she calmly asks for the head of Jokanaan. Herod, appalled, tries to offer alternative rewards, such as the largest emerald in the world, his beautiful white peacocks, or even the veil of the sanctuary in the Jewish temple; but Salome is implacable, and reminds him of the oath he has sworn. Finally, Herod accepts defeat. The executioner is sent to the dungeon, and some minutes later he returns with the head of Jokanaan on a silver dish. Salome seizes it. Nothing can now prevent her from kissing Jokanaan's lips. Sick with disgust, Herod calls to his guards to kill Salome, and the soldiers crush her to death beneath their shields.

The score of *Salome*, a masterpiece of twentieth-century opera, is one of power and originality, from the swift upward arpeggio on clarinet as the curtain rises on Narraboth exclaiming at the beauty of the Princess Salome, to the final perverted *Liebestod* as Salome – 'a sixteen-year-old with the voice of Isolde', as Strauss described her – slobbers over the severed head of Jokanaan, and the various themes associated with her are heard to sound kaleidoscopically as the shields of Herod's soldiers crush her. Strauss's huge orchestra of 105 is used at times with the delicacy of a chamber-music ensemble, while at other times it thunders forth impressively. The roles of the depraved Salome and the neurotic Herod are marvellously characterized, the morbid passion of the teenage Princess described with utter conviction in her two arias of lust for the prophet, the first one sung to him while he is alive, and the second addressed to his severed head. Strauss is less successful in conveying the pious utterances of Jokanaan, but his orchestra brilliantly conjures up the exotic opulence of Herod's court. The grisly sounds produced by four double basses – pinching the string high up between the thumb and fore-finger and striking it sharply with the bow as Jokanaan is being decapitated – were said by Strauss not to represent 'cries of pain uttered by the victim, but sighs of anguish from the heart of an impatiently expectant Salome'. One can more readily interpret the sound as representing a head being sawn off. But, however one interprets the passage, it is as startling today as it must have been to the ears of its first audience in 1905.

Recommended recording: Catherine Malfitano (Salome), Bryn Terfel (Jokanaan), Hanna Schwarz (Herodias), Kenneth Riegel (Herod), with the Vienna Phil-harmonic Orchestra, conducted by Christoph von Dohnanyi. Decca 444 178–2. Malfitano is a convincing Salome, Terfel a dignified Jokanaan, and the Vienna Philharmonic plays magnificently for Dohnanyi.

Elektra

tragedy in one act (approximate length: 1 hour, 45 minutes)

Klytemnestra (Clytemnestra), widow of Agamemnon   *mezzo-soprano*
Elektra (Electra)   *soprano* ⎤
Chrysothemis   *soprano*   ⎦ her daughters
Aegisth (Aegisthus), Klytemnestra's paramour   *tenor*
Orest (Orestes), son of Klytemnestra and Agamemnon   *baritone*
Orest's Tutor   *bass*
Klytemnestra's Confidante   *soprano*
Klytemnestra's Train-Bearer   *soprano*
A Young Servant   *tenor*
An Old Servant   *bass*
The Overseer   *soprano*

LIBRETTO BY HUGO VON HOFMANNSTHAL, BASED ON THE PLAY *ELECTRA*, BY SOPHOCLES; TIME: CLASSICAL ANTIQUITY, AFTER THE TROJAN WAR; PLACE: MYCENAE, GREECE; FIRST PERFORMED AT THE KÖNIGLICHES OPERNHAUS, DRESDEN, 25 JANUARY 1909

A year after he had seen Gertrud Eysoldt in Oscar Wilde's *Salome* in Berlin and had decided to compose his opera based on the play, Strauss saw the same actress at the same Berlin theatre, this time in a new German translation of

Sophocles' *Electra* by the young Austrian poet and playwright Hugo von Hofmannsthal. After the premiere of *Salome* Strauss approached Hofmannsthal, who
agreed to allow his *Elektra* to be used as the basis of an opera.

With *Elektra*, Strauss and Hofmannsthal were to begin a collaboration that
lasted until the poet's death nearly a quarter of a century later. Hofmannsthal,
whose ancestry was Jewish on his mother's side and half-Austrian and half-Italian
on his father's, was a man of wider culture than Strauss, and their published correspondence reveals that, throughout their years of collaboration, on several
occasions the librettist thought the composer's ideas and suggestions deplorable.
When, at the outset, Strauss delayed committing himself completely to *Elektra*
because of its similarities in style and structure to *Salome*, and he asked if Hofmannsthal had 'an entertaining renaissance subject' that they might use instead,
the librettist replied, 'I do not believe there is any epoch in history which I and,
like me, every creative poet among our contemporaries would bar from his work
with feelings of such definite disinclination, indeed such unavoidable distaste, as
this particular one.'

After making one or two other suggestions to the poet which were no more
favourably received, Strauss gradually became immersed in the world of *Elektra*
and began to compose his opera based on Hofmannsthal's text. He worked on the
score intermittently throughout 1907 and the first half of 1908, interrupted frequently by his busy schedule of conducting engagements, and in June 1908 he
found that he needed to ask Hofmannsthal to provide more text for the moment
of repose that arrives immediately after Elektra's recognition of Orest. When he
had received the additional lines from the poet, Strauss wrote, 'Your verses when
Elektra recognizes Orest are marvellous, and I've already set them to music. You
are the born librettist – the greatest compliment, to my mind, since I consider it
much more difficult to write a good operatic text than a fine play.'

Elektra was given its premiere in Dresden in January 1909, conducted by Ernst
von Schuch, with Annie Krull in the title role, Margarethe Siems as Chrysothemis,
and Ernestine Schumann-Heink as Klytemnestra. The composer was dissatisfied
with the performance of Schumann-Heink; it is said that at the dress rehearsal he
called to the orchestra, 'Louder! I can still hear Frau Heink.' Shortly after the premiere the formidable contralto referred to Strauss's music as 'a horrible din',
insisting that she would never sing the role of Klytemnestra again, 'not even for
three thousand dollars a performance'.

The premiere was a success, and in the following months *Elektra* was staged
in Berlin, Vienna and Milan. Nevertheless, a number of jokes were made in the
German press, mainly at the expense of Strauss's huge orchestra. One cartoon

showed the Dresden audience squeezed into the orchestra pit while the orchestra occupied the rest of the theatre. The score's dissonance to the ears of 1909 was also wittily commented upon, with the claim that at one of the Dresden performances half the orchestra played *Salome* while the other half played *Elektra*, with neither musicians nor audience noticing anything amiss. Strauss bore all this in reasonably good humour.

The action takes place in the inner courtyard of the royal palace at Mycenae, where Klytemnestra and her paramour Aegisth now live together, having murdered Klytemnestra's husband, King Agamemnon. Serving maids, drawing water from the well, speak scornfully of Elektra, daughter of Agamemnon and Klytemnestra, who is treated as a slave, frequently beaten, and forced to sleep with the dogs. The only maid who speaks sympathetically of Elektra is set upon by the others. Elektra now emerges from the palace, lamenting her condition and recalling her father's murder ('Allein! Weh, ganz allein'). She works herself into a frenzy as she dreams of avenging her father's death with the help of her sister Chrysothemis and their brother Orest, who is in exile and has not been heard of for many years. Chrysothemis comes into the courtyard, warning Elektra that their mother intends to imprison her in a tower. Chrysothemis, who is younger than Elektra, does not share her sister's obsession with revenge, and she sings of her longing for a normal life ('Ich hab's wie Feuer in der Brust').

Sounds from the palace indicate the imminent arrival of Klytemnestra. Warning her sister once more against their mother, Chrysothemis rushes away in order to avoid encountering her. A retinue of torch-bearing servants and slaves leading animals for a sacrifice precedes the entrance of Klytemnestra, who tells Elektra – whom she believes may have clairvoyant powers – that she is being tormented by hideous dreams and asks how she may find release. Elektra informs her that the gods will be placated only when a sacrificial victim – Klytemnestra herself – falls beneath a kinsman's axe. The Queen's terror at the thought of this solution to her problems gives way to triumphant laughter after her Confidante has arrived and whispered some news to her.

As Klytemnestra and her retinue leave, Chrysothemis comes out from the palace to deliver the same information to Elektra, which is that Orest is dead. Elektra tries to persuade Chrysothemis to help her avenge their father's death, but her sister refuses and rushes out in horror, followed by the curses of Elektra, who realizes that she must now act alone ('Nun denn, allein!'). As she digs frantically for the axe that killed Agamemnon and which she has buried in the courtyard, a stranger appears. It is Orest, who is accompanied by his Tutor. Brother and sister at first do not recognize each other, and he, assuming Elektra to be a servant, says he has come to tell Klytemnestra of her son's death, at which Elektra berates him for being alive when a better man than he is dead. When he realizes her identity he whispers to her that Orest is alive, but it is only when servants who have followed the stranger into the courtyard come forward and kiss his garments that Elektra recognizes him as Orest, and her ferocity gives way to a lyrical tenderness.

Elektra impresses on Orest what has to be done. Klytemnestra's Confidante appears at the palace doors to lead the two men within, and shortly afterwards Klytemnestra's screams are heard. Aegisth returns from a day's hunting. He calls for lights, and Elektra derisively lights his way to the palace door. Soon after he has entered, he appears again at a window shouting for help, only to be struck down. Chrysothemis and attendants rush into the courtyard, calling that those faithful to the memory of Agamemnon are fighting the soldiers of Aegisth. Chrysothemis joins in her sister's joy at the return of Orest, but Elektra, having achieved her revenge, has begun a dance of triumph, whirling about in a frenzy until, at the climax of her ecstasy, she falls dead. Chrysothemis beats on the doors of the palace, calling for Orest, but there is no answer.

The opera's leading motif is a four-note phrase that represents the four-syllable name 'Agamemnon', first heard as the curtain rises, recurring whenever Elektra invokes her father's spirit, and returning again at the very end of the opera, when his death has been avenged. The other main theme, by way of contrast, is a fervent, expansive melody that speaks of the deep emotion binding Agamemnon and his children, heard to most moving effect in the scene in which Elektra recognizes her brother.

By comparison with the colourful, glittering savagery of *Salome*, *Elektra* sounds both more harshly violent and more single-minded in its relentless thrust, battering at its hearers' senses with a vehemence which is surely not unlike that with which classical Greek tragedy assaulted its first audiences. The opera's four climactic dramatic passages are Elektra's first solo scene, her confrontation with Klytemnestra, her great recognition scene with Orest and her final wild dance of triumph. But, although the role of the opera's obsessed heroine provides magnificent, though taxing, opportunities for a dramatic soprano, it is finally Strauss's huge orchestra that is the dominant force in *Elektra*.

It is sometimes said that the score of this opera marks Strauss's most advanced position along the road to atonalism, a road from which he then turned aside to explore nostalgically the atmosphere of old Vienna in his next opera, *Der Rosenkavalier*. However, to take this view is to misunderstand Strauss's pragmatic method of composition, which invariably suited the style to the subject. The predominantly harsh musical language of *Elektra* is entirely apposite to its subject; but, even so, there are occasional lush Romantic harmonies to be heard at appropriate moments.

Recommended recording: Birgit Nilsson (Elektra), Marie Collier (Chrysothemis), Regina Resnik (Clytemnestra), with the Vienna Philharmonic Orchestra, conducted by Georg Solti. Decca 417 345–2. The Vienna Philharmonic is always at its incomparable best in Strauss, and so is the conductor, Solti. Birgit Nilsson's firm and powerful soprano voice makes her an ideal Elektra, Marie Collier is a vivid Chrysothemis, and Regina Resnik a frighteningly convincing Clytemnestra.

Der Rosenkavalier
(The Knight of the Rose)
opera in three acts (approximate length: 3 hours, 15 minutes)

The Princess of Werdenberg (the Marschallin)   *soprano*
Baron Ochs of Lerchenau   *bass*
Octavian, Count Rofrano (called Quinquin), alias Mariandel   *mezzo-soprano*
Herr von Faninal, a rich man, recently ennobled   *baritone*
Sophie, his daughter   *soprano*
Marianne Leitmetzerin, Sophie's duenna   *soprano*
Valzacchi, an intriguer   *tenor*
Annina, his partner   *contralto*
The Police Commissioner   *bass*
The Marschallin's Major-Domo   *tenor*
Faninal's Major-Domo   *tenor*
A Notary   *bass*
An Innkeeper   *tenor*
An Italian Singer   *tenor*

LIBRETTO BY HUGO VON HOFMANNSTHAL; TIME: THE MID-EIGHTEENTH CENTURY, THE FIRST YEARS OF THE EMPRESS MARIA THERESA'S REIGN; PLACE: VIENNA; FIRST PERFORMED AT THE KÖNIGLICHES OPERNHAUS, DRESDEN, 26 JANUARY 1911

Determined that his next opera, after the horrors of *Salome* and *Elektra*, should be an elegant comedy, Strauss suggested to Hofmannsthal that they

should attempt something in the manner of Mozart. Within weeks of the premiere of *Elektra* in January 1909, Hofmannsthal responded with the scenario of
Der Rosenkavalier, containing two major roles, one for baritone or bass and the
other 'for a graceful girl dressed up as a man à la Farrar or Mary Garden' (attractive young American sopranos of the time), and set in the old Vienna of the
Empress Maria Theresa. Strauss liked the idea, Hofmannsthal began to write his
libretto, and after the composer had received the words of the opening scene he
told his librettist, 'You're Da Ponte and Scribe rolled into one.'

Work on *Der Rosenkavalier* continued throughout 1909 and until September of
the following year, when Strauss finally completed his score. As with *Feuersnot* in
1901, *Salome* in 1905 and *Elektra* in 1909, the new opera was given its premiere
in Dresden, conducted by the Dresden Opera's music director, Ernst von Schuch.
The first performance, on 26 January 1911, was a huge success, and within weeks
there were productions of the opera in Nuremberg (the day after the Dresden
premiere), in Munich, and in Hamburg, where a new young soprano, Lotte
Lehmann, understudied the role of Sophie. She was in due course to become the
greatest of Marschallins in by far the most popular of Strauss's operas.

Act I. The Marschallin's bedroom. It is early morning. In the absence of her husband, the Field Marshal, the Marschallin has spent the night with her seventeen-
year-old lover, Count Octavian Rofrano ('Wie du warst, wie du bist'). As they
exchange terms of endearment, lying half in and half out of bed, their talk is
interrupted by the arrival of the Marschallin's little black page with her breakfast
chocolate, and Octavian is made to hide behind a screen. He hides again, in an
alcove, a few minutes later, when a commotion in her antechamber has made the
Marschallin fear that her husband has returned home unexpectedly. It is, however,
only a visitor, the Marschallin's cousin, the coarse and countrified Baron Ochs,
who has come to seek her assistance in the matter of his engagement to Sophie,
the daughter of the newly ennobled Herr von Faninal. Specifically, Ochs wants his
cousin to recommend a young nobleman to act as bearer of the traditional silver
rose to his betrothed. When Octavian returns to the bedroom disguised as a
chambermaid, the Baron immediately begins to flirt with him. The Marschallin
suggests as the bearer of the rose her kinsman the young Count Rofrano, and she
shows the Baron his portrait. Ochs is struck by the portrait's strong resemblance
to the chambermaid and concludes that she must be the young nobleman's
illegitimate sister.

The Marschallin's morning levée now begins. Various tradesmen and petition-
ers arrive, among them the intriguer Valzacchi and his accomplice Annina; an

Italian Singer, who performs an aria ('Di rigori armato'); a noble but impover-
ished widow and her three daughters; as well as the Marschallin's hairdresser, her
chef, and a Notary. Ochs discusses his matrimonial affairs noisily with the Notary,
and before he departs he leaves with the Marschallin a casket containing the silver rose. Left alone, the Marschallin reflects both on the boorishness of her cousin
Ochs and (at thirty-two) on her consciousness of advancing age ('Da geht er hin').

When Octavian returns, properly dressed, he finds the Marschallin in melancholy mood. Despite his protestations, she tells him that the time will come when
he will leave her for a younger woman and expresses her fears about the passing
of time ('Die Zeit, die ist ein sonderbar Ding'). After she has dismissed Octavian,
the Marschallin realizes that she did not kiss him goodbye, and she has her servants attempt to call him back. They are too late, however, so she sends her young
page after Octavian to deliver to him the casket containing the silver rose for
Sophie von Faninal.

Act II. The reception hall of Faninal's town house. Sophie, her father, and her
duenna are excitedly awaiting the arrival by coach of the bearer of the silver rose.
When Octavian makes his ceremonial entrance, and presents the rose to Sophie,
the two young people are immediately attracted to each other ('Mir ist die Ehre
widerfahren'). Sophie's intended bridegroom, Baron Ochs, whom she has not
previously met, is ushered in by Faninal and, to her dismay, begins to fondle her
lecherously. Octavian resolves to prevent their marriage. While Ochs and Faninal
are discussing the marriage contract in an adjoining room, Sophie and Octavian
declare their love for each other ('Mit Ihren Augen voll Tränen'). They are apprehended in an embrace by Valzacchi and Annina, and Ochs is called. Octavian
challenges the Baron to a duel, draws his sword and wounds him very slightly in
the arm. Ochs makes a dreadful fuss and calls for a doctor, Faninal threatens his
daughter with incarceration for life in a nunnery if she refuses to marry Ochs, and
in the confusion Octavian, who has thought of a plan to thwart the Baron, manages to secure for himself the services of the two intriguers, Valzacchi and Annina.
When the Baron's arm has been bandaged and he is left alone to rest, Annina enters
with a note purportedly from the Marschallin's chambermaid 'Mariandel', agreeing to a rendezvous. Delighted, Ochs sings to himself his favourite waltz ('Ohne
mich').

Act III. A private room at a suburban inn. Valzacchi, Annina and others, under
the supervision of Octavian, prepare the room with various trapdoors with
which they intend to frighten and confuse Baron Ochs. Octavian pays his helpers,
and they all leave, Octavian entering again shortly afterwards in his Mariandel
disguise, on the arm of Ochs. They sit down to supper, but Mariandel rejects

Ochs's advances ('Nein, nein, nein, nein, i' trink kein Wein'), and to his consternation strange figures begin to appear at the windows, and trapdoors spring open
to reveal leering faces. Suddenly, a woman dressed in black (Annina in disguise)
rushes in, claiming Ochs as the father of her children, who all begin shouting
'Papa'.

The police arrive, and Ochs attempts to explain to the Commissioner that he is
merely attempting to have an innocent supper with his fiancée, Sophie von
Faninal. But Octavian, who shows the Police Commissioner a bed concealed in
the alcove, which he enters to divest himself of his Mariandel costume, has
arranged for Sophie and her father to be sent for. They now arrive, and refute the
Baron's story. The Marschallin, summoned by Ochs's servant, also arrives, to
Octavian's consternation. She sums up the situation, has no trouble in dismissing
the police, and orders a perplexed and chastened Ochs to leave, which he does,
pursued by children and the staff of the inn. Accepting that she has lost Octavian
to Sophie, the Marschallin gives her blessing to the young lovers ('Hab mir's
gelobt') and leaves with Faninal, inviting them all to return to Vienna in her
coach. Sophie and Octavian reaffirm their love ('Ist ein Traum') and, when they
have left, the Marschallin's page rushes in to search for Sophie's handkerchief,
which she had dropped. Finding it, he waves it above his head and runs out as the
curtain falls.

Dominated by waltz tunes, Strauss's sumptuous score for *Der Rosenkavalier*,
written as usual for an orchestra of well over a hundred, is irresistible. That the
waltz did not become the prevailing dance rhythm of Vienna until several generations after the period of the opera hardly matters at all, for the spirit of *alt Wien*
pervades Strauss's music, linking the centuries. Much of the opera's action is
advanced in a lyrical conversational style more tuneful than recitative but less formal than aria, a style that broadens at climactic moments into quasi-arias such as
those for the Marschallin in Act I and Ochs (his delightful waltz song) in Act II,
as well as duets for the young lovers and the sublime Act III trio in which they sing
of their joy while the Marschallin sadly but wisely accepts the situation.

Hofmannsthal's marvellous libretto clearly inspired Strauss, and despite occasional longueurs in Act I (mainly in the role of Ochs) the opera's essential blend
of those two Viennese moods of high spirits and nostalgic melancholy is masterly. The Marschallin is one of the most impressive of all operatic characters,
dominating the entire action of *Der Rosenkavalier* although she appears only in
Acts I and III. She and Octavian might also be said to appear in the opera's
orchestral prelude, for it clearly represents their night of love, exultant horns

most graphically depicting Octavian's sexual climax, after which the prelude subsides into a mood of wistful detumescence.

Recommended recording: Maria Reining (Marschallin), Sena Jurinac (Octavian), Hilde Gueden (Sophie), Ludwig Weber (Ochs), with the Vienna State Opera Chorus and Vienna Philharmonic Orchestra, conducted by Erich Kleiber. Decca 425 950–2. Kleiber's 1954 performance with the Vienna Philharmonic and a cast of the finest Vienna State Opera-based singers of the day has not yet been surpassed. All lovers of this opera should try to track down the famous Viennese abridged recording of 1933 with Elisabeth Schumann as Sophie, Richard Mayr as Ochs, and the great Lotte Lehmann as the Marschallin.

Ariadne auf Naxos
(Ariadne on Naxos)
opera in one act, with a prologue (approximate length: 2 hours)

Characters in the prologue:
The Major-Domo   *spoken role*
Music Master   *baritone*
The Composer   *soprano*
The Tenor (who plays Bacchus)   *tenor*
An Officer   *tenor*
A Dancing Master   *tenor*
A Wig Maker   *bass*
A Lackey   *bass*
Zerbinetta   *soprano*
The Prima Donna (who plays Ariadne)   *soprano*
Harlequin   *baritone*
Scaramuccio   *tenor*
Truffaldino   *bass*
Brighella   *tenor*
Characters in the opera:
Ariadne   *soprano*
Bacchus   *tenor*
Naiad   *soprano* ⎤
Dryad   *contralto* ⎟   three nymphs
Echo   *soprano* ⎦

Zerbinetta	*soprano*	⎤	
Harlequin	*baritone*		
Scaramuccio	*tenor*	troupe of comedians
Truffaldino	*bass*		
Brighella	*tenor*	⎦	

LIBRETTO BY HUGO VON HOFMANNSTHAL; TIME: PROLOGUE – THE FIRST HALF OF
THE EIGHTEENTH CENTURY; OPERA – THE MYTHICAL PAST; PLACE: PROLOGUE –
VIENNA; OPERA – THE ISLAND OF NAXOS; FIRST PERFORMED AT THE HOFOPER,
VIENNA, 4 OCTOBER 1916 (BUT SEE BELOW)

Strauss's librettist Hugo von Hofmannsthal began to suggest subjects for their next opera while *Der Rosenkavalier* was still being rehearsed. One possibility was an adaptation of *Das steinerne Herz* (The Stony Heart), a fairy story by Wilhelm Hauff; but when Strauss responded positively to this, Hofmannsthal withdrew his suggestion. 'What a confounded fool I was', he wrote, 'to tell you the title and the subject, and thus direct your imagination to Hauff's fairy tale which, except for the central germ, has nothing in common with what exists in my own imagination.' What existed in Hofmannsthal's imagination would surface again, to become in due course the opera *Die Frau ohne Schatten*, but for the present he put forward another suggestion: he would adapt and translate Molière's comedy *Le Bourgeois Gentilhomme*, compressing the play's five acts into two. Strauss would provide incidental music for the play and, instead of the Turkish ceremony with which the original Molière play ends, there would be an opera on the theme of Ariadne, who, in Greek mythology, was the daughter of Minos, King of Crete. Strauss would compose the opera, which would be performed 'after dinner, in the presence of Jourdain, the Count and the dubious Marquise' (characters in the play).

The two men proceeded to work on the project, their collaboration carried forward, as usual, by correspondence. When Hofmannsthal attempted to explain to Strauss the symbolism of the myth of Ariadne, the composer replied that a mere superficial musician could not hope to understand it and, that being the case, might not audiences, too, fail to grasp it? Hofmannsthal's reaction was prickly, as it was also when Strauss suggested that if the librettist needed to learn about the form of the coloratura aria, he should ask the Viennese soprano Selma Kurz to sing him some Bellini or Donizetti. 'I shall make myself acquainted with the formal requirements of coloratura,' Hofmannsthal wrote, 'though not through Mme Kurz with whom I am not on those kind of terms and whom I would definitely not like to bring into anything.'

When it was produced in Stuttgart in October 1912, the Strauss–Hofmannsthal
–Molière melange was received without enthusiasm. Some members of the audience objected to an opera being tacked on to Molière's play, while others were
annoyed at having to sit through a tedious play before the opera began. Over the
following months the work was performed in Zurich, Prague, Berlin and Amsterdam, and in London, where it was staged by Sir Thomas Beecham in May 1913
with Molière's play translated by Somerset Maugham. Beecham conducted it
again with the Glyndebourne Opera Company at the Edinburgh Festival in 1950,
when the Molière–Hofmannsthal play was newly translated by the actor Miles
Malleson, who also played Monsieur Jourdain.

The 1912 coupling of Molière and Strauss is now only rarely performed. In 1916,
while Strauss was completing the composition of their next opera, *Die Frau ohne
Schatten*, he and Hofmannsthal decided to revise *Ariadne auf Naxos*, dropping
Molière's play and replacing it with a prologue to the opera, with text by Hofmannsthal. It took no more than seven weeks for Strauss to compose the Prologue
and make what changes he and Hofmannsthal thought necessary to the opera
itself, and the new version was staged in Vienna at the Hofoper (now the Staatsoper) in October 1916. Franz Schalk conducted, and the leading roles were sung
by Maria Jeritza (Ariadne), Selma Kurz (Zerbinetta) and Béla Környey (Bacchus).
In the Prologue, the role of the Composer was sung by the young Lotte Lehmann,
recently arrived in Vienna from the Hamburg Opera, where she had sung the
small role of Echo in the first version of *Ariadne*. Lehmann's performance made
her overnight the idol of Vienna and marked the beginning of her long associ-
ation with Strauss, of whose operas she was to become one of the greatest interpreters. The new *Ariadne* was enthusiastically received in Vienna, and later in
Berlin, Budapest, Amsterdam, London and elsewhere. It is this second version of
the work which has remained in the international repertoire.

Prologue: The town house of a *nouveau riche* Viennese gentleman. A large room
has been adapted for use as a theatre, where a new opera by a young Composer is
about to be performed that evening. The Composer's Music Master learns with
dismay from the Major-Domo that their patron has decided to follow the performance of the opera with a *commedia dell'arte* farce. The Composer arrives,
hoping to be able to rehearse his opera, but he finds that the musicians are busy
playing for their patron and his guests, who are still at dinner. The soprano who
is to sing the role of Ariadne is in a foul temper, and the Tenor objects to his wig.
The Composer is charmed by Zerbinetta, the leader of a troupe of comedians, but
when the Major-Domo announces that, to allow a grand display of fireworks to

begin promptly at nine, the opera and the farce will have to be performed simultaneously, the young Composer is both outraged and bewildered. The Dancing Master assures him that Zerbinetta is expert in improvisation and will have no difficulty as long as the Composer agrees to delete the more boring passages of his opera. Zerbinetta works her wiles on the Composer, who agrees to everything and expresses his faith in the power of music ('Musik ist eine heilige Kunst'), although at the last moments of backstage chaos he regrets having allowed his opera to be performed in mutilated form.

Opera: A deserted beach on the island of Naxos, with a cave in the background. Ariadne, who has been abandoned on the island by Theseus, lies sleeping, while three nymphs, lamenting her sad fate, watch over her. When she awakes, Ariadne recalls the memory of Theseus, but her one desire now is for death ('Es gibt ein Reich'). Zerbinetta enters with her troupe of four comedians, Harlequin, Scaramuccio, Truffaldino and Brighella, and they attempt to distract Ariadne with their songs and dances, but to no avail. Finally, Zerbinetta dismisses her companions and addresses Ariadne directly, trying to persuade her to take a more light-hearted view of love and lovers ('Grossmächtige Prinzessin'). Ariadne pays no attention to Zerbinetta and retires to her cave, whereupon Harlequin and the other three comedians return to declare their amorous intentions towards Zerbinetta, whose clear preference is for Harlequin.

The nymphs suddenly rush in excitedly, announcing the imminent arrival of Bacchus. The young god has escaped from the enchantress Circe, who attempted to change him into an animal. In the distance, the voice of Bacchus can be heard, still singing of the charms of Circe ('Circe, Circe'). Ariadne emerges from the cave, drawn by the sound of his voice, for she believes that he must be the longed-for messenger of death. When Bacchus approaches Ariadne, he realizes that he has been changed by the power of love. Ariadne and Bacchus embrace, confessing their love for each other in a lengthy duet ('Bin ich ein Gott'). The sky above them is now full of stars, and a canopy descends from above to enclose them. The three nymphs are heard again in the distance, murmuring words of encouragement to the lovers, and Zerbinetta returns with a sly reference to the final words of the aria with which she had earlier failed to impress Ariadne: 'When the new god approached, I surrendered without a word.'

Unlike Strauss's earlier operas, *Ariadne auf Naxos* is scored for a small orchestra of fewer than forty players. Like his earlier and his later operas, however, it is unique in having its own individuality and musical character. The Prologue is written in a conversational, parlando style, broadening into a more melodic arioso only for such moments as, for example, that in which a musical theme, announced hesitatingly by a flute, enters the young Composer's mind, the scene in which Zerbinetta flirts with him, and the Composer's final ecstatic hymn of heartfelt gratitude to the art of music.

The style of the opera proper is a blend of the late Romantic and the neo-Baroque. The trio of nymphs at the beginning calls to mind, perhaps deliberately, the music of the Rhinemaidens in Wagner's *Ring*. Ariadne's music, especially her ecstatic aria 'Es gibt ein Reich', is elevated in style, while the music of the comedians, in contrast, is jauntily attractive, although Harlequin, a lyric baritone, is allowed a romantic note in his solo number, 'Lieben, Hassen, Hoffen, Zagen'. Zerbinetta's aria, 'Grossmächtige Prinzessin', has become a virtuoso showpiece for coloratura sopranos, usually in the slightly modified form in which it appears in the definitive 1916 version of the opera, the original 1912 version having been even more difficult to sing. The 1916 Zerbinetta needs not only an extraordinarily agile voice but also one that can manage a sustained F above high C. The love duet for Bacchus and Ariadne almost outstays its welcome. It is, in its way, a splendid example of impassioned late Romantic writing for the voice, of the kind that Hofmannsthal once referred to as 'erotic screaming', but it can sound, in a less than ideal performance, as though it will never end. The finest passages of *Ariadne auf Naxos* are numerous enough for it to have retained a place in the repertoire.

Recommended recording: Elisabeth Schwarzkopf (Ariadne), Irmgard Seefried (Composer), Rita Streich (Zerbinetta), Rudolf Schock (Bacchus), with the Philharmonia Orchestra, conducted by Herbert von Karajan. EMI CMS7 69296–2. None of the more recent recordings can match this classical performance from 1954. Schwarzkopf is a moving Ariadne, Seefried a warm-hearted Composer, Streich an exciting Zerbinetta, and Schock an ardent Bacchus. Karajan conducts with style and intensity.

Die Frau ohne Schatten
(The Woman without a Shadow)
opera in three acts (approximate length: 3 hours, 30 minutes)

The Emperor   *tenor*
The Empress   *soprano*

The Nurse   *mezzo-soprano*

A Spirit Messenger   *baritone*

A Guardian of the Threshold of the Temple   *soprano or counter-tenor*

Apparition of a Youth   *tenor*

The Voice of the Falcon   *soprano*

A Voice from Above   *contralto*

Barak, the dyer   *bass-baritone*

The Dyer's Wife   *soprano*

The One-Eyed   *high bass* ⎤

The One-Armed   *bass*   ⎬ brothers of Barak

The Hunchback   *tenor*   ⎦

LIBRETTO BY HUGO VON HOFMANNSTHAL; TIME: THE MYTHICAL PAST; PLACE: THE
SOUTH EASTERN ISLANDS, A MYTHICAL REGION; FIRST PERFORMED AT THE STAATS-
OPER, VIENNA, 10 OCTOBER 1919

After the premiere of the first version of *Ariadne auf Naxos* in Stuttgart in 1912,
Strauss and Hofmannsthal collaborated on a ballet, *Josephslegende*, which
was performed in Paris in 1914. They then turned to discussing their next opera,
which derived from the fairy story – *Das steinerne Herz*, by Wilhelm Hauff – that
Hofmannsthal had first mentioned to Strauss while *Der Rosenkavalier* was in
rehearsal. Taking from the story his central idea, that of someone turned to stone,
Hofmannsthal proceeded to write an extremely complex libretto, heavy with
symbolism, which Strauss found difficult to understand. Nevertheless, the composer set to work on the music in August 1914, shortly before the outbreak of
World War I, having received the first two of Hofmannsthal's three acts.

Strauss did not finish the composition of *Die Frau ohne Schatten* until
September 1916. While he was still at work on Act III, he wrote to Hofmannsthal:

> My own inclination is for realistic comedy with really interesting people –
> either like *Der Rosenkavalier* with its splendid Marschallin, or with a bur-
> lesque, satirical content, somewhat in the manner of Offenbach's parodies
> ... Characters [in *Die Frau ohne Schatten*] like the Emperor and Empress,
> and also the Nurse, can't be filled with red corpuscles in the same way as a
> Marschallin, an Octavian, or an Ochs. No matter how I rack my brains – and
> I'm toiling really hard, sifting and sifting – my heart's only half in it. When the
> head has to do the major part of the work, you get a breath of academic chill
> (what my wife very rightly calls 'note-spinnng') which no bellows can ever

kindle into a real fire. Well, I have now sketched out the whole ending of the opera (the quartet and the choruses), and it's got verve and a great upward sweep – but my wife finds it cold and misses the heart-touching, flame-kindling melodic texture of the *Rosenkavalier* trio.

In 1919 the Austrian monarchy collapsed; the Vienna Hofoper (Court Opera) was renamed the Staatsoper (State Opera), and Strauss became its artistic supervisor. He took up his duties in December 1919, but before then, as though to herald his new relationship with the Staatsoper, *Die Frau ohne Schatten* was given its premiere there, conducted by Franz Schalk. Recalling the occasion many years later, Strauss wrote that in Vienna his opera was

> lavishly produced with a grand cast (Karl Oestvig as the Emperor; Maria Jeritza as the Empress; Lucie Weidt as the Nurse; Richard Mayr as Barak; Lotte Lehmann as the Dyer's Wife). After this great success, its way over the German stage was fraught with misfortune. In Vienna itself, owing to the strain imposed by the vocal parts and to the difficulties over the sets, the opera had to be withdrawn more often than it was performed. At the second theatre (Dresden) it came to grief because of the imperfections of the production . . . which forced me to ask Count Seebach after the dress rehearsal to postpone the first performance for several days. Although the orchestra under Fritz Reiner was excellent, the performance suffered from the inadequate Dyer's Wife. It was a mixed pleasure.
>
> It was a serious blunder to entrust this opera, difficult as it was to cast and produce, to medium and even small theatres immediately after the war. When, on another occasion, I saw the Stuttgart production (done on the cheap!) I realized that the opera would never have much success. But it has succeeded nevertheless and has made a deep impression . . . Music lovers in particular consider it to be my most important work.

Act I, scene i. A flat roof overlooking the imperial gardens. To one side, dimly lit, is the entrance to the royal apartments. The Nurse crouches in the shadows, keeping watch outside the bedchamber of the Emperor and Empress. (Twelve months earlier, the Emperor, hunting with his Falcon, had pursued a gazelle. As he aimed his arrow and was about to shoot, the gazelle resumed its real form as the daughter of Keikobad, master of the spirit world. The Emperor took her home and married her.) The Nurse sees a light flying swiftly across the lake towards her. She fears it may be Keikobad, but it is his Messenger, who has come to warn her that if the Empress does not cast a shadow – that is, become pregnant – within three days, she will be returned to the arms of her father, and the Emperor will be turned to stone.

The Emperor now emerges from the bedchamber. He recounts the events of the day on which he first found the Empress, since when he has not seen his Falcon, whom he struck in rage on that day ('Denn meine Seele'). He tells the Nurse he is going hunting and will be away for three days. After he has left, the Empress appears and hears the Voice of the Falcon relating the fate in store for her and the Emperor. In desperation, she asks the Nurse where she can find a shadow, and the Nurse tells her she must descend to the stagnant world of mankind and purchase a shadow from a mortal woman. The Empress and the Nurse fly together down to earth.

Act I, scene ii. The hut of Barak, the dyer. Barak's three brothers, one a Hunchback, another lacking an arm, and the third lacking an eye, are fighting until stopped by the Dyer's Wife, who throws a bucket of water over them. When Barak returns home, he laments that his Wife has not given him children, and goes off again to the market to sell his dyed skins. The Empress and the Nurse enter, dressed as servants, and the Nurse, conjuring up images of great wealth, tricks the Dyer's Wife into believing that such riches can be hers, if she will sell her shadow and renounce motherhood. The Dyer's Wife agrees to this, and her visitors leave, promising to return the next day and enter her service as poor relations. Before she goes, the Nurse makes fish fly through the air and land in the frying-pan for Barak's supper, and she also causes the marital bed to split into two separate halves. The Dyer's Wife is appalled to hear the voices of unborn children which seem to come from the frying-pan, calling out in fear. When Barak returns, his Wife tells him that two cousins of hers will be arriving to be her maids, and that henceforth he will sleep alone.

Act II, scene i. The same. The Nurse and the Empress are now installed as servants. After Barak has left for the market with his brothers, the Nurse conjures up the Apparition of a handsome youth whom the Dyer's Wife had once seen fleetingly and admired. The Dyer's Wife cannot quite bring herself to approach the youth, and he is made to vanish as Barak and his brothers return with food.

Act II, scene ii. Outside the imperial falcon-house. The Emperor has found his Falcon, and the bird has led him to the falcon-house, where the Empress told him she would be staying for three days. Observing her and the Nurse entering the house, the Emperor senses that the Empress has lied to him and has been to earth, to the world of mankind. His first impulse is to kill her, but he cannot bring himself to do so and bids the Falcon lead him away again.

Act II, scene iii. Barak's hut. The Nurse gives Barak a sleeping-draught, and while he sleeps she again produces the Apparition of the handsome youth. The Dyer's Wife is about to succumb to the youth's caresses when, instead, on an impulse she awakens her confused husband. The Nurse makes the Apparition vanish without being seen by Barak, and she and the Dyer's Wife leave the hut together.

Act II, scene iv. The Empress's bedroom in the falcon-house. The Empress murmurs in her sleep that she has sinned against Barak. She dreams of the Falcon's warning and of the Emperor being turned to stone.

Act II, scene v. Barak's hut. A storm is brewing, and Barak's brothers howl in fear. The Dyer's Wife tells her husband that she has sold her shadow and that, in consequence, her womb will never be fruitful for him or any other man. When the fire in the hut is stirred into flame, it reveals that she no longer casts a shadow, and Barak now wants to kill his Wife. She claims that she has not yet sold her shadow, but says that she is willing to die at her husband's hands. A flashing sword flies through the air into Barak's hand, but before he can use it the earth opens, and Barak and his Wife are swallowed up. The Empress and the Nurse leave, as rushing waters pour into the room through the cracked walls.

Act III. An underground vault, divided into two by a thick wall. On one side sits Barak, and on the other his Wife – they are unaware of each other's presence. The Dyer's Wife sings of her regret for her actions, while Barak expresses his love for her, and his horror that he came close to killing her ('Mir anvertraut'). A Voice summons Barak, and he begins to climb a winding staircase that has suddenly been revealed by a shaft of light. The Voice summons the Dyer's Wife too, and she hastens up the staircase. The scene magically changes to a rocky terrace over a river, with steps leading up to a bronze door, where Keikobad's Messenger is waiting. The Empress and the Nurse arrive by boat, and the Empress is summoned to appear before her father, Keikobad. Called upon to drink the water of life, she refuses, even when she is given a glimpse of the Emperor turned completely to stone except for his eyes, for she knows that if she drinks from the fountain the Dyer's Wife will be deprived of her shadow. However, when she cries 'I will not', her husband is brought back to life, and she herself is seen to cast a shadow. The Emperor and the Empress are reunited, as are Barak and his Wife, while the voices of yet-to-be-born children can be heard singing happily.

Despite Strauss's doubts about Hofmannsthal's pretentious but nonetheless fascinating libretto, he seems to have understood it, at least intuitively, for he has matched it with a score that follows the text's changing moods very closely, using a large orchestra, which he deploys skilfully and variously. Although (or perhaps because) he was not aware that Hofmannsthal had based the Dyer's Wife on

Strauss's own wife, the shrewish Pauline, the composer produced a telling musical portrait of the sharp-tongued but warm-hearted character. Indeed, with the exception of the tenor role of the somewhat colourless Emperor, the musical characterization throughout the opera is superb. (Strauss was rarely at his best when writing for the tenor voice.) There is not a great amount of lyrical melody in *Die Frau ohne Schatten*, but its opulent score and astonishingly wide range of instrumental colour make it an exciting work to experience in the theatre.

Recommended recording: Birgit Nilsson (Dyer's Wife), Leonie Rysanek (Empress), James King (Emperor), Walter Berry (Barak), with the Vienna State Opera Chorus and Orchestra conducted by Karl Böhm. Deutsche Grammophon DG 445 325–2. For many years Leonie Rysanek virtually owned the role of the Empress, as did Walter Berry that of Barak, and here they are caught at the peak of their form. Birgit Nilsson gives Wagnerian stature to the Dyer's Wife, and James King is a poetic Emperor. The conductor, Karl Böhm, had no equals in this opera, and the Vienna orchestra plays gloriously for him.

Intermezzo
bourgeois comedy in two acts (approximate length: 2 hours, 15 minutes)

Christine Storch   *soprano*
Robert Storch, her husband, a conductor   *baritone*
Franzl, their eight-year-old son   *spoken role*
Anna, their chambermaid   *soprano*
Baron Lummer   *tenor*
The Notary   *baritone*
His Wife   *soprano*
Stroh, a conductor   *tenor*
A Commercial Counsellor   *baritone*
A Legal Counsellor   *baritone*
An Opera Singer   *bass*

LIBRETTO BY THE COMPOSER; TIME: 1924; PLACE: GRUNDLSEE AND VIENNA; FIRST PERFORMED AT THE SÄCHSISCHE STAATSTHEATER, DRESDEN, 4 NOVEMBER 1924

When Strauss suggested to Hofmannsthal that they should write a light, 'entirely modern, absolutely realistic domestic and character comedy . . . or some amusing piece of love and intrigue', his librettist replied immediately,

'My dear Dr Strauss, I could not help having a good laugh over your letter. The things you propose to me are to my taste truly horrid, and might put one off being a librettist for the rest of one's life.' On an earlier occasion when Strauss had made a similar suggestion, Hofmannsthal had advised him to contact the Viennese critic and dramatist Hermann Bahr. Strauss now approached Bahr with his idea for a modern, domestic opera, to be based on a real incident that had occurred in Berlin thirteen years earlier when a letter intended for one of his colleagues was accidentally delivered to Strauss's house. It was opened by Pauline Strauss, who read, 'Dear Sweetheart, do bring me the ticket, Your faithful Mitzi.' Pauline immediately assumed the worst and consulted a solicitor about a divorce, and Strauss found it extremely difficult to convince her of his innocence.

Hermann Bahr agreed to write a libretto for Strauss, based on this incident, and produced a synopsis, which Strauss found unsatisfactory. In due course, encouraged to do so by Bahr, Strauss wrote the libretto himself, during a week's stay at a sanatorium in Munich in the summer of 1917. He then proceeded to compose his autobiographical opera, *Intermezzo*, a task which, between conducting engagements, occupied him over the next six years, and which he completed in August 1923 during a visit to Buenos Aires.

His relations with the Vienna Staatsoper having become strained, Strauss arranged for *Intermezzo* to have its premiere in Dresden, as part of the celebrations for his sixtieth birthday. At his suggestion, Lotte Lehmann was engaged to sing the role of Christine, the character based on Pauline Strauss. The opera was well received in Dresden and was later staged in Hamburg, Berlin, Graz and, eventually, Vienna. It reached New York in 1963, and Great Britain in 1965, when it was performed at the Edinburgh Festival. *Intermezzo* was not seen in England until 1974, when it was staged at Glyndebourne. In his 1942 reminiscences, Strauss recalled that the premiere of *Intermezzo* in Dresden coincided with his dismissal from his post at the Vienna Staatsoper.

Act I, scene i. The dressing-room of Storch's house in the Austrian ski resort of Grundlsee. Storch is packing for a two-month engagement in Vienna, while his short-tempered wife, Christine, berates the servants. After her husband has left, Christine goes tobogganing with a friend.

Act I, scene ii. The ski slopes. Christine's toboggan collides with a young man on skis. She blames him for the accident, but when she discovers that he is Baron Lummer, and that their parents are acquainted, she invites him to her house.

Act I, scene iii. The inn at Grundlsee. At a ball, Christine and Baron Lummer enjoy themselves dancing.

Act I, scene iv. A furnished room in the house of the Storchs' Notary in Grundlsee. Christine examines the room, which she intends to rent for the Baron, gossiping to the Notary's wife as she does so.

Act I, scene v. The Storchs' dining-room. Christine writes to her husband about her new and penurious young protegé. The Baron arrives for his daily visit, drops hints about a loan, and is promised Storch's patronage on his return.

Act I, scene vi. The Baron's lodgings. When the Baron's girl-friend arrives, he sends her out while he writes to Christine asking for money.

Act I, scene vii. The Storchs' dining-room. Christine is indignant at the Baron's request for money, and when he arrives she rebukes him. The maid enters with a letter for Storch, which Christine opens. She reads with horror a request for opera tickets from a certain Mieze Meier, coupled with the promise of a rendezvous after the performance. Christine immediately sends a telegram to her husband in Vienna, announcing that she is aware of his liaison with Mieze Meier and declaring that she is leaving him for ever.

Act I, scene viii. Franzl Storch's bedroom. Christine explains to their eight-year-old son that his father has betrayed him. The child defends his father.

Act II, scene i. The living-room of the Commercial Counsellor's house. Four friends – the Commercial Counsellor, the Legal Counsellor, an Opera Singer and a conductor named Stroh – are playing skat (incidentally, Strauss's favourite card game), and they are discussing their colleague Storch's daunting wife. When Storch enters he eulogizes Christine, but her telegram then arrives, filling him with consternation, since he has never heard of Mieze Meier. He rushes off, failing to take in a remark by Stroh, who has expressed his astonishment that Storch, too, knows Mieze.

Act II, scene ii. The Notary's office. The Notary is surprised to learn from Christine that she wants a divorce not because of her involvement with the Baron, but because of what he, the Notary, considers her flimsy evidence against her husband.

Act II, scene iii. The Prater in Vienna. A storm is raging. Storch is wandering about, distraught, when Stroh rushes up to confess that Mieze Meier's note was obviously meant for him, and that she must have been confused by their not dissimilar names when she consulted the telephone directory. Storch insists that Stroh explain this to Christine in person.

Act II, scene iv. Christine's dressing-room in the Storchs' house. Christine is packing, having sent Baron Lummer off to Vienna to interview Mieze Meier. A telegram from her husband arrives, announcing that Stroh is on his way to explain all. At that moment, Stroh is announced.

Act II, scene v. The dining-room of the Storchs' house. Storch rushes in expecting a reconciliation, but Christine demands an apology from him, at which he storms out in a fury.

Act II, scene vi. The dining-room, immediately afterwards. Baron Lummer enters to report on his interview with Mieze Meier, but he is dismissed brusquely. Storch reappears and pretends to be jealous of his wife's friendship with the Baron, about which he has heard from the Notary. He magnanimously offers to help the young man. Soon the Storchs are reconciled, as Christine asks her husband's forgiveness and tells him she thinks their marriage perfect.

Throughout much of the opera, the dialogue is carried on in a conversational manner with few opportunities for sustained lyrical flights. It is in the twelve orchestral interludes linking the scenes that the principal musical interest of *Intermezzo* lies. Many of the scenes last no longer than two or three minutes, but the opera is made to cohere by Strauss's fluent writing for the orchestra, which becomes excessively sentimental only in the work's closing moments. Fritz Busch, who conducted the Dresden premiere, wrote in his memoirs nearly thirty years later that as Strauss grew older he 'passed ever more indifferently and unemphatically over passages when conducting, as if he were ashamed at having composed them'.

Recommended recording: Lucia Popp (Christine), Dietrich Fischer-Dieskau (Storch), Adolf Dallapozza (Baron Lummer), with the Bavarian Radio Symphony Orchestra, conducted by Wolfgang Sawallisch. EMI CDS 49337–2. Popp is enchanting as Christine, and Fischer-Dieskau is a forceful Storch. Sawallisch, a Strauss specialist, conducts superbly.

Arabella
lyrical comedy in three acts (approximate length: 2 hours, 30 minutes)

Count Waldner, retired cavalry officer   *bass*
Adelaide, his wife   *mezzo-soprano*
Arabella   *soprano* ⎤
Zdenka   *soprano* ⎦ their daughters
Mandryka, a Croatian landowner   *baritone*
Matteo, an officer   *tenor*
Count Elemer, suitor of Arabella   *tenor*

Count Dominik	*baritone*	⎤
Count Lamoral	*bass*	⎦ suitors of Arabella
Fiakermilli	*soprano*	
A Fortune-teller	*soprano*	

LIBRETTO BY HUGO VON HOFMANNSTHAL; TIME: 1860; PLACE: VIENNA; FIRST PER-
FORMED AT THE SÄCHSISCHE STAATSOPER, DRESDEN, 1 JULY 1933

In 1922, while Strauss was still composing *Intermezzo*, Hofmannsthal suggested Helen of Troy as a subject for an opera. He produced a libretto, which combined a tortuous plot with portentous philosophizing and obscure symbolism, and which included in its cast of characters a singing seashell called 'Die Alleswissende Muschel' (The Omniscient Mussel). Strauss coped remarkably well with all of this and composed the opera *Die ägyptische Helena* (The Egyptian Helen). It was given its premiere in Dresden in June 1928, but did not meet with success, the general opinion being that the work was ponderous and lacking in inspiration.

Some months before the premiere, Strauss had mentioned to Hofmannsthal that now that he had completed *Die ägyptische Helena* he had no work to do. 'So please write some poetry,' he requested. 'It may even be a second *Rosenkavalier* if you can't think of anything better. If the worst comes to the worst, a little stop-gap job – a one-act piece – to keep my hand in. Oil to prevent the imagination from rusting up.' This, of course, was not the kind of language to use with Hofmannsthal. 'I cannot just dash something off for you,' the sensitive librettist replied. 'The day when I could do this would be accursed, and your work would not prosper.' But two days later he wrote again to Strauss, mentioning *Der Fiaker als Graf* (The Cabby as Count), a comedy he had begun to write two years previously and had abandoned. He now combined it with the plot of *Lucidor*, a novella he had written nearly twenty years earlier, and in due course produced the libretto of the opera which became *Arabella*.

Progress was slow, for both composer and librettist were ill in the early part of 1929. On 10 July, Hofmannsthal sent a final draft of Act I to Strauss, and on the evening of 14 July the composer responded by telegram: 'First act excellent. Heartfelt thanks and congratulations.' The telegram was delivered on the morning of 15 July, but Hofmannsthal never read it. It was the day of the funeral of his son Franz, who had killed himself two days earlier. As he was dressing to attend his son's funeral Hofmannsthal suffered a stroke, and he died within minutes.

Strauss proceeded with the composition of *Arabella*, using Hofmannsthal's unrevised drafts of Acts II and III as they stood. It took him more than three years to finish the opera, in between carrying out other tasks and engagements, and *Arabella* was finally given its premiere in Dresden in July 1933, conducted by Clemens Krauss. By this time Hitler's National Socialist Party had come to power in Germany and established a one-party rule. Lotte Lehmann, for whose warm, beautiful voice Strauss had composed the title role, made it clear that she would not sing in Germany while the Nazis were in power, so the role of Arabella was sung in Dresden by Viorica Ursuleac (who later married the conductor Clemens Krauss).

Arabella met with a polite reception; it was not until the Vienna performances three months later, with Lotte Lehmann as Arabella, that the opera was received with enthusiasm. A two-act version was performed for the first time in Munich in 1939, omitting the final waltz and chorus of Act II and using the prelude to Act III to cover the scene change; however, the original three-act version is generally preferred. The opera's international popularity dates from the 1950s when, for many years, Lisa Della Casa was an enchanting Arabella, often partnered by the incomparable Mandryka of Dietrich Fischer-Dieskau.

The entire action of the opera takes place in the course of one day, Shrove Tuesday, in the year 1860.

Act I. The drawing-room of the Waldners' suite in a Viennese hotel. Count Waldner and his wife, Adelaide, have two daughters, the younger of whom, Zdenka, is always dressed as a boy and referred to as Zdenko, for the Count has huge gambling debts, as a result of which he and his wife are unable to afford to have two daughters coming out in society at the same time. Zdenka is in love with an officer, Matteo, who thinks she is a boy, and who is in any case in love with Zdenka's sister, Arabella, who hardly notices him. Arabella has many suitors, but tells her sister that she is still waiting for the right man ('Aber der Richtige'). Learning from Zdenka that Matteo has left roses for her, Arabella is disappointed that they have not come from the handsome stranger whom she has noticed watching her in the street.

Count Waldner has written to an old army colleague, a rich eccentric Croatian named Mandryka, enclosing a photograph of the beautiful Arabella in the hope that Mandryka might come to Vienna and marry her, thus rescuing the Waldner family from genteel poverty. But Waldner's army colleague has died, and the Mandryka who turns up at the door of the hotel suite, having found Arabella's photograph enchanting, is the old man's nephew and namesake, who presents himself now to Count Waldner, offers him money from a bulging wallet and asks for Arabella's hand in marriage. When the delighted Waldner wants to introduce

Mandryka to his wife and to Arabella at once, Mandryka declines. He would rather they met later, more formally, for he considers his first meeting with his future bride too sacred an occasion to be rushed into unceremoniously.

Matteo asks Zdenka if Arabella has left a letter for him, and Zdenka hastily assures him that there will be a letter from Arabella, and he will receive it that evening at the cabbies' ball. Meanwhile, Arabella has agreed to go for a sleigh-ride with another of her suitors, Count Elemer, but insists on taking Zdenka along as well. Sending her sister off to dress for the sleigh-ride, Arabella soliloquizes about her rival suitors ('Mein Elemer'), but finds her thoughts returning to the stranger in the street, whose appearance has fascinated her. She attempts to put him out of her mind by telling herself that he is probably married, and she forces herself to look forward with the expectation of pleasure to that evening's ball.

Act II. A public ballroom, that evening. Three of Arabella's suitors, the counts Elemer, Dominik and Lamoral, invite her to waltz, but are turned away. When her father introduces Mandryka to her, Arabella recognizes him as the stranger who has been watching her in the street. It is clear that they are already in love with each other. Mandryka tells Arabella of his estates in far-off Croatia, with four thousand serfs dependent upon him; he explains that he is a widower and asks Arabella to marry him. She accepts his proposal ('Und du wirst mein Gebieter sein'), and he describes to her a charming custom in his village by which the engagement of lovers is marked: the woman draws a glass of water from the well and offers it to her fiancé as a token that they are betrothed in the eyes of God and man.

Arabella asks to be allowed to say farewell to each of her three suitors. Fiaker-milli, the cabbies' mascot, presents a bouquet of flowers to Arabella, naming her Queen of the Ball, and sings a florid coloratura solo ('Die Wiener Herrn'). Meanwhile, Zdenka, dressed of course in male attire as Zdenko, gives Matteo a letter, which she says is from Arabella. When Matteo opens the envelope he finds no letter but a key, which Zdenka says is the key to Arabella's room at the hotel. Matteo is to go there now and await Arabella. Bewildered but excited, Matteo leaves quickly. Unfortunately, his conversation with Zdenka has been overheard by Mandryka, who is shocked and appalled. He becomes drunk very quickly, flirts with Fiakermilli and speaks brusquely to Arabella's mother, Adelaide, when she asks if he knows where her daughter is. Adelaide calls her husband away from a card game to deal with the situation, and Mandryka leaves with the Waldners to return to the hotel and confront Arabella.

Act III. The lobby of the Waldners' hotel, late at night. Emerging from a room, Matteo is about to descend the staircase to the lobby when a ring at the outer door causes him to conceal himself. He is astonished to see Arabella enter, for he thinks he has just left her in her room. They converse tensely, at cross-purposes. When Mandryka enters the lobby, he recognizes Matteo as the recipient of, as he thinks, Arabella's letter. He assumes the worst and announces his intention of leaving Vienna immediately. Arabella calls on Matteo to clear her name, but his manly silence seems a further accusation. By now a crowd of hotel residents awakened by the noise has assembled on the balcony to observe the goings-on. Count Waldner challenges Matteo to a duel.

Suddenly Zdenka, wearing a negligee, rushes down the stairs and confesses, to the embarrassment of Matteo, that she had taken the role of Arabella in the darkened bedroom. Mandryka attempts to apologize to Arabella and then takes charge of the situation, presenting Matteo to Count Waldner as a suitable husband for Zdenka. Arabella asks Mandryka's servant to bring a glass of water to her room, to which she now retires. Contrite and in despair, Mandryka expresses his remorse to himself, but a few moments later Arabella reappears at the top of the staircase holding the glass of water, which, having remembered the custom of Mandryka's village, she presents to him ('Das war sehr gut, Mandryka'). Mandryka drinks, and then he smashes the glass as a token that they are, at last, truly betrothed.

With the exception of such lyrical passages as the duet for the two sisters in Act I, the intimate scene between Arabella and Mandryka in Act II, and Arabella's solo at the conclusion of Act III, all of which are based on Croatian folk tunes, the score of *Arabella* does not represent Strauss at his most inspired. Much of the music by which the somewhat shapeless plot is advanced is no more than competent, and the structure of Acts II and III leaves much to be desired. However, given two engaging performers as Arabella and Mandryka, the opera can exert great sentimental charm; and Strauss's scoring is as colourful as ever, with the smaller roles boldly characterized.

Recommended recording: Lisa Della Casa (Arabella), Dietrich Fischer-Dieskau (Mandryka), Anneliese Rothenberger (Zdenka), with the Bavarian State Opera Chorus and Orchestra, conducted by Joseph Keilberth. Deutsche Grammophon DG 437 700–2. This was recorded live at the 1963 Munich Opera Festival, when Lisa Della Casa, the most superb Arabella of her time, was at the height of her form, as was Dietrich Fisher-Dieskau, who was surely created by an opera-loving God to portray Mandryka. Anneliese Rothenberger is ideally cast as Zdenka, and the supporting roles are all strongly sung and characterized.

Daphne

bucolic tragedy in one act (approximate length: 1 hour, 45 minutes)

Daphne   *soprano*
Peneios, a fisherman, her father   *bass*
Gaea, his wife, Daphne's mother   *contralto*
Leukippos, a shepherd   *tenor*
Apollo   *tenor*

LIBRETTO BY JOSEPH GREGOR; TIME: MYTHICAL ANTIQUITY; PLACE: GREECE, IN THE VICINITY OF MOUNT OLYMPUS; FIRST PERFORMED AT THE SÄCHSISCHE STAATSOPER, DRESDEN, 15 OCTOBER 1938

Two years after the death of Hofmannsthal, Strauss met the distinguished Austrian novelist and biographer Stefan Zweig, and the two men collaborated on *Die schweigsame Frau* (The Silent Woman), an opera based on the comedy *Epicoene, or The Silent Woman*, by Ben Jonson. A not unattractive work, its Dresden premiere in June 1935 was successful enough, but after four performances it was banned by the Nazis. Further collaboration with Zweig, a Jew, was not possible for Strauss, who chose to remain in Germany throughout the Nazi period, but Zweig recommended several politically acceptable Aryan librettists to the composer, one of whom, Joseph Gregor, a close friend of Zweig, Strauss accepted. Their first collaboration, *Friedenstag* (Peace Day), a one-act opera whose libretto Gregor had based on a synopsis by Zweig, was performed in Munich in 1938.

Strauss and Gregor had intended *Friedenstag* to be one of two operas to be performed on the same evening, the other being *Daphne*, a version of the Greek myth in which the daughter of a river god is transformed into a tree. Although at its Munich premiere in July 1938 *Friedenstag* shared the programme with a ballet, Strauss still conceived of *Daphne* as a companion piece to it. When *Daphne* was given its premiere in Dresden three months later, it was as a curtain-raiser to *Friedenstag*. However, in due course the two operas went their separate ways, *Daphne* proving to be the more popular of the two.

The action takes place outside the hut of Peneios, by the river which bears his name, with Mount Olympus in the background. Shepherds are summoned to attend the feast that is about to be held in honour of Dionysus. Daphne, the daughter of the fisherman Peneios, yearns for the fading day to stay awhile so that she can continue to commune with the trees, the flowers and the river ('O bleib, geliebter Tag!'). The young shepherd Leukippos, Daphne's friend since childhood, declares his love for her, but physical love has no meaning for Daphne. When her mother, Gaea, appears with two servants to dress Daphne for the revels, she runs away. Leukippos is persuaded to dress in Daphne's festive garments. Peneios has invited the gods to the feast of Dionysus, and Apollo arrives, disguised as a herdsman. Entranced by Daphne, the god attempts to embrace her, but she recoils from him.

As the sky darkens, the Dionysiac revels begin. Leukippos, still disguised as a girl, dances with Daphne, but the jealous Apollo brings on a thunderstorm to halt the festivities. When Leukippos accuses the god of wooing Daphne in disguise, he is killed by Apollo. Daphne, horrified to have lost her friend, refuses to go with Apollo, who asks Zeus, father of the gods, to grant Daphne's wish and transform her into one of the laurel trees that she loves. Apollo leaves, and Daphne stands immobile, singing a greeting to her brother and sister trees as she feels the earth rise within her ('Ich komme, ich komme'). As she is slowly transformed into a laurel tree, her wordless voice continues to sound for a time, before trailing off into silence.

Daphne is a lyrical tone poem in the reflective style adopted by Strauss in his later years. The delicate texture of his large orchestra beautifully conjures up the atmosphere of the approaching night in Daphne's first aria, while the quiet ecstasy of her transformation scene at the end of the opera is Strauss at his most magical. Apollo reveals his identity in a gloriously rhapsodic outburst ('Jeden heiligen Morgen'), and Daphne's moving lament over the body of Leukippos is another highlight of this opera's translucent score.

Recommended recording: Hilde Gueden (Daphne), James King (Apollo), Fritz Wunderlich (Leukippos), with the Vienna State Opera Chorus and Vienna Symphony Orchestra, conducted by Karl Böhm. Deutsche Grammophon DG445 322–2. Recorded live on the occasion of the opera's belated first Viennese performance in 1964 at the Theater an der Wien, this is magnificent. Karl Böhm conducts, as he did at the opera's 1938 Dresden premiere, Hilde Gueden's silvery, individual timbre is ideal for the eponymous heroine, and a first-rate cast of popular Viennese regulars of the time presents the work to its best possible advantage.

Capriccio

conversation piece for music in one act
(approximate length: 2 hours, 15 minutes)

The Countess Madeleine, a young widow   *soprano*
The Count, her brother   *baritone*
Flamand, a musician   *tenor*
Olivier, a poet   *baritone*
La Roche, a theatre director   *bass*
Clairon, an actress   *contralto*
Monsieur Taupe, a prompter   *tenor*
A Male Italian Singer   *tenor*
A Female Italian Singer   *soprano*
The Major-Domo   *bass*

LIBRETTO BY CLEMENS KRAUSS; TIME: AROUND 1775; PLACE: A CHATEAU NEAR PARIS;
FIRST PERFORMED AT THE BAYERISCHE STAATSOPER, MUNICH, 28 OCTOBER 1942

Shortly after the premiere of *Daphne* in October 1938, Strauss, now in his
seventy-fifth year, began to compose his next opera, *Die Liebe der Danae* (The
Love of Danae), its plot a combination of two classical Greek legends. The opera
was completed in June 1940, but by this time World War II had begun, and Strauss
decided that he did not want the work staged until 'at least two years after the
conclusion of an armistice'. (It was eventually to have its premiere at the 1952
Salzburg Festival.) In July 1941 Strauss began work on the composition of an
opera which he and his librettist, the conductor Clemens Krauss, decided to call
Capriccio, having considered and rejected *Wort oder Ton* (Word or Note) and several other possible titles.

The idea that led to the composition of *Capriccio* had first occurred to Strauss
and Stefan Zweig in 1934, when they had just completed *Die schweigsame Frau*.
Zweig had it in mind at the time to adapt a libretto by Giambattista Casti (1724–
1803), an Italian poet and librettist, who during the years he spent in Vienna was
Lorenzo da Ponte's great rival. Casti's libretto *Prima la musica e poi le parole* had
been set to music by Antonio Salieri and first performed in Vienna in 1786 on the
same evening as Mozart's *Der Schauspieldirektor*.

The political situation in Germany in 1934 put an end to the collaboration of
Strauss and Zweig, who was Jewish, but Strauss hoped to be able to work on the
opera with Zweig's friend Joseph Gregor (his librettist for *Friedenstag, Daphne*

and *Die Liebe der Danae*). It was while Strauss was composing *Die Liebe der Danae* in 1939 that he and Gregor began seriously to discuss the project, but Gregor appeared not to understand exactly what kind of libretto Strauss wanted, and the composer found it difficult to express his ideas in words. The conductor Clemens Krauss was brought into their discussions, and at one stage all three men seem to have been busy producing their own versions of Casti's libretto. Eventually Krauss took over the actual writing of it, and Strauss began to compose the opera, the orchestration of which he completed on 3 August 1941.

At its premiere in Munich in October 1942, when it was conducted by Clemens Krauss, *Capriccio* was received enthusiastically. It was given a number of performances in Munich until October 1943, when the opera house was destroyed in an air raid. Though not among Strauss's two or three most often performed operas, *Capriccio* is now quite frequently to be encountered, especially in German and Austrian theatres. It proved to be Strauss's last opera. The composer died in 1949 at the age of eighty-five.

The action takes place in the drawing-room of the Countess Madeleine's chateau, not far from Paris, on an evening in the year 1775. The overture to the opera is provided by a string sextet. When the curtain rises, the andante of the sextet is drawing to a conclusion. Flamand, its composer, and Olivier, a poet, stand near the door, listening to the music, which is being rehearsed in an adjoining room. They are also watching their hostess, the beautiful Countess Madeleine, with whom they are both in love. The theatre director La Roche is asleep in an armchair. Flamand's sextet and a play by Olivier, to be directed by La Roche, are to be performed in honour of the Countess's forthcoming birthday. The Count, her brother, is to act in the play mainly because he is in love with the Parisian actress, Clairon, who is expected to arrive shortly to rehearse.

Olivier and Flamand discuss the relative importance of words and music, each defending his own art form. When the Count and Countess enter, they too join in the discussion. Clairon arrives, and she and the Count rehearse. A sonnet by Olivier, actually his declaration of love to the Countess, is declaimed by the Count to Clairon, and Flamand is immediately inspired to set it to music ('Kein Andres, das mir so im Herzen loht'). He sings it to the Countess and asks her to decide whether she prefers his music or Olivier's words. The Countess promises to give Flamand her answer next morning at eleven, in the library.

The company are entertained, first by a dancer and three musicians, and then by two Italian singers. The discussion on the subject of words and music continues, becoming more heated as all express their views (Fugue: 'Tanz und Musik').

When the others mock (in an octet ensemble) his description of the entertainment that he intends to produce for the Countess's birthday, La Roche replies with a lengthy monologue on the subject of the director's art ('Hola, ihr Streiter in Apoll!'). The Countess suggests that Flamand and Olivier should collaborate on an opera for La Roche to direct. After *Ariadne auf Naxos* and *Daphne* have been mentioned as possible subjects, the Countess suggests that their opera should be about themselves and the events of that day. This is agreed, and the guests leave for Paris, the Count accompanying Clairon. The prompter, who has been asleep, wakes up and almost convinces the Countess's Major-Domo that without a prompter there could be no theatrical performance.

The Major-Domo gives the Countess a message from Olivier, who will await her in the library next morning at eleven to learn how the opera should end. In an expansive, lyrical aria, the Countess muses on this ('Morgen mittag um elf!'). How, indeed, should the opera end? Will she choose Olivier and words, or Flamand and music? She asks her image in the mirror to advise her. Is there, she wonders, an ending that is not trivial? With a deep curtsy to her reflection, the Countess goes in to supper in the highest spirits. That she is not singing the words but humming the melody of Flamand's sonnet as she leaves the room is presumably Strauss's hint as to the outcome.

After the first performance of *Capriccio* Strauss said with tears in his eyes, 'I can do no better.' His farewell to the stage could not have been better, for this dissertation on the rival claims of words and music is a work of mellow beauty. Except in the large ensembles, the words are always clearly to be heard above the fairly large orchestra, which was not always the case with certain earlier operas of Strauss. The words might be thought to be winning the argument, for much of Strauss's music in *Capriccio* merely supports the words, allowing them to be heard almost as heightened conversation. In the final twenty minutes of the opera, however, when the Countess considers the problem in her long solo aria, the music becomes lyrically expansive and utterly beautiful. And earlier, in the ensembles of disputation and laughter, music takes precedence over the words. The instrumental sextet with which the opera begins is a fine example of Strauss's late autumnal style, with its air of wistful regret. The answer, surely, is that words and music need each other in the partnership of opera, with music the senior partner.

Recommended recording: Elisabeth Schwarzkopf (Countess), Christa Ludwig (Clairon), Nicolai Gedda (Flamand), Dietrich Fischer-Dieskau (Olivier), Eberhard Waechter (Count), Hans Hotter (La Roche), with the Philharmonia Orchestra, conducted by Wolfgang Sawallisch. EMI CDS 7 49014 8. This 1957 recording is close to ideal. Schwarzkopf, all artifice and style until that final impassioned solo, is in her mannered element as the Countess, Gedda and Fischer-Dieskau are unsurpassable as her ardent suitors, and Hotter vividly characterizes La Roche. Sawallisch conducts with clarity and wit.

IGOR STRAVINSKY

(b. Oranienbaum [now Lomonosov], 1882 – d. New York, 1971)

Oedipus rex
(King Oedipus)
opera-oratorio in two acts (approximate length: 50 minutes)

Oedipus, King of Thebes   *tenor*
Jocasta, his wife   *mezzo-soprano*
Creon, Jocasta's brother   *bass-baritone*
Tiresias, a soothsayer   *bass*
A Shepherd   *tenor*
A Messenger   *bass-baritone*
The Speaker   *spoken role*

LIBRETTO BY JEAN COCTEAU, BASED ON THE PLAY *OEDIPUS TYRANNUS*, BY SOPHOCLES; TIME: THE MYTHICAL PAST; PLACE: THEBES; FIRST PERFORMED AS AN ORATORIO AT THE THÉÂTRE SARAH BERNHARDT, PARIS, 30 MAY 1927; FIRST PERFORMED AS AN OPERA AT THE STAATSOPER, VIENNA, 23 FEBRUARY 1928

Stravinsky, one of the greatest of twentieth-century composers, wrote operas at various stages of his career. He was a pupil of Rimsky-Korsakov, and his earliest opera, *The Nightingale*, reveals something of that composer's influence. In three short acts and lasting less than an hour, it has a libretto by the composer and Stepan Mitusov, based on a story by Hans Andersen. The song of the Nightingale (soprano) in the forest has become so famous that the Chinese imperial court arrives in search of the bird, who agrees to sing for the Emperor (baritone) but disappears when a mechanical nightingale is installed at the Emperor's bedside by envoys from Japan. Death (contralto) promises to grant the Emperor a reprieve if the Nightingale should return and sing. This the bird does, and the Emperor is saved. First seen in Paris in 1914 as *Le Rossignol*, the opera was later produced in Russian, as *Solovey*. It is still occasionally encountered.

Stravinsky's next works for the stage were *The Wedding*, a choral ballet composed between 1914 and 1917 but not performed until 1923, and *L'Histoire du soldat* (1918), which contains dancing and acting but no singing. Stravinsky's unconventional attitude to opera was continued with *Renard* (1922), in which the action is mimed by dancers, the singers being placed in the orchestra. *Mavra*, a one-act comedy staged in Paris in 1922, is more traditionally operatic, but the first of Stravinsky's two major operas is *Oedipus rex*. Described by the composer as an opera-oratorio, it was first performed in Paris in 1927 in concert as an oratorio, apparently because the funds for a stage production at that time could not be found, and then it was staged in 1928 in Vienna as an opera.

Having conceived the idea of creating an opera in Latin, a language 'not dead but turned to stone', on a subject with which his audience would be familiar, Stravinsky decided to use the play *Oedipus tyrannus*, by Sophocles, and asked Jean Cocteau to provide him with a libretto in French. Those parts of the text that were to be sung were translated into Latin by Jean Daniélou. Cocteau's text is spoken by a narrator in modern dress who introduces each of the work's six episodes.

Act I, episode i. A plague is raging throughout Thebes, and the people call upon King Oedipus, who rescued the city from the Sphinx, to save Thebes again. Oedipus promises to do so ('Liberi, vos liberabo').

Act I, episode ii. Creon, the king's brother-in-law, returns from Delphi, where he has learned from the oracle that the murderer of the former King, Laius, is still living in Thebes. Until he is found and driven out, the city will continue to suffer ('Respondit deus'). Oedipus undertakes to find the murderer and avenge the death of Laius ('Non reperias vetus skelus').

Act I, episode iii. Oedipus calls upon the blind soothsayer Tiresias, who refuses to tell what he knows ('Dicere non possum'). When Oedipus accuses him of being the murderer, Tiresias announces that the murderer of the King is a king. Oedipus claims that Tiresias and Creon are plotting against him. The argument that follows is interrupted by the arrival of Queen Jocasta, who is acclaimed by the populace ('Gloria!').

Act II, episode iv. The final chorus of Act I ('Gloria!') is repeated. Jocasta rebukes Oedipus and Creon for quarrelling ('Non erubescite, reges') and declares that oracles are liars ('Mentita sunt oracula'), for did not an oracle predict that her former husband, Laius, would be killed by his son, whereas he was killed by thieves at a crossroads outside the city? Oedipus is seized with a sudden fear, for he recalls that years previously, on his way from Corinth to Thebes, he killed an old man at a crossroads ('Pavesco subito, Jocasta'). He resolves to discover the truth from an old Shepherd who witnessed the crime.

Act II, episode v. A Messenger enters to annouce the death of Polybus, King of Corinth, the supposed father of Oedipus, who on his deathbed admitted that Oedipus was only his adopted child ('Mortuus est Polybus'). The old Shepherd testifies that he rescued Oedipus in the mountains, where he was abandoned as a child ('Oportebat takere'). Guessing the truth, Jocasta hurriedly withdraws. Oedipus now realizes the dreadful truth – that he was the son of Laius and Jocasta, abandoned by them in order to confound the oracle's prophecy that Laius would be killed by his son. But the oracle's prophecy was correct. Oedipus murdered his father and married his mother ('Natus sum quo nefastum est').

Act II, episode vi. The Messenger announces that Jocasta has killed herself ('Divum Jocastae caput mortuum'), and that Oedipus has put out his eyes with her golden pin. The blinded Oedipus now appears, and the people sing him a last farewell before they expel him, gently, from the city.

By the time he came to compose *Oedipus rex*, Stravinsky had abandoned the exotic Russian idiom of his earlier period, and had embarked upon a more broadly based European neo-classical style. There are, however, a number of varied stylistic tendencies to be discerned in the opera. The coloratura of Oedipus's arias in Act I is reminiscent of Handel, while elsewhere there are echoes of Bellini, Verdi, Puccini and, in the Messenger's song, Mussorgsky. The overall impression given by this monumental work is one of epic grandeur, only slightly vitiated by the vernacular narration, whose Brechtian alienation-effect now seems irrelevant.

Recommended recording: George Shirley (Oedipus), Shirley Verrett (Jocasta), John Westbrook (Narrator), with the Washington Opera Society Chorus and Orchestra, conducted by Igor Stravinsky. Sony CD 46290. There is an earlier recording, also conducted by the composer and with Jean Cocteau, who wrote the text, as Narrator, but it is no longer available. This 1962 performance is conducted magisterially by Stravinsky, and sung with fervour and dedication by a young American cast.

The Rake's Progress
opera in three acts and an epilogue (approximate length: 2 hours, 15 minutes)

Trulove *bass*
Anne, his daughter *soprano*
Tom Rakewell *tenor*
Nick Shadow *baritone*
Mother Goose, a brothel-keeper *mezzo-soprano*
Baba the Turk, a bearded lady *mezzo-soprano*
Sellem, an auctioneer *tenor*
Keeper of the Madhouse *bass*

LIBRETTO BY W.H. AUDEN AND CHESTER KALLMAN; TIME: THE EIGHTEENTH
CENTURY; PLACE: ENGLAND; FIRST PERFORMED AT THE TEATRO LA FENICE,
VENICE, 11 SEPTEMBER 1951

Stravinsky, who had settled in the United States of America in 1940, saw *A Rake's Progress*, the series of engravings by the eighteenth-century English artist William Hogarth, at the Chicago Arts Institute in May 1947. Hogarth's engravings depict the career of a wealthy but foolish young man as he makes his way through the pleasure-houses of London to the madhouse. Fascinated by the engravings, and deciding that the story of the rake and his profligate progress into madness would make fine operatic material, Stravinsky consulted Aldous Huxley, his friend and neighbour in Los Angeles, who recommended the poet W.H. Auden as librettist. In October 1947 Stravinsky wrote to Auden, who responded favourably. Composer and poet worked out a plot together, and Auden then proceeded to write the libretto, calling in as co-author his partner Chester Kallman. The Auden–Kallman libretto was handed over to Stravinsky at the end of March 1948, and Stravinsky proceeded to compose the three-act opera, which he completed in April 1951. *The Rake's Progress* was given its premiere in Venice in September 1951, conducted by the composer.

Act I, scene i. The garden of Trulove's house in the country. Tom Rakewell and his fiancée, Anne Trulove, sing of their love and of the joys of spring ('The woods are green'), while Anne's father expresses his doubts about Tom. He offers the young man a position in a counting house, but Tom refuses, for work to him is drudgery ('Since it is not by merit'). When Tom wishes that he had money, Nick Shadow suddenly materializes, with the news that a distant relative of Tom's has died and left him a fortune ('Fair lady, gracious gentlemen'). Tom prepares to depart for London with Shadow, whom he takes into his employ, agreeing to pay him after a year and a day have passed. The lovers take leave of each other ('Farewell for now'), Tom promising to send for Anne and her father as soon as he has established himself in London.

Act I, scene ii. Mother Goose's brothel, London. Roaring-boys and Whores cavort ('With air commanding'), while Shadow and Mother Goose instruct Tom in the ways of loose living. Tom is momentarily disconcerted at the mention of love, but is soon drinking and carousing with the others. Nick formally initiates Tom into the brothel ('Love, too frequently betrayed'), and Mother Goose takes him to her room for the night, serenaded by the company ('The sun is bright, the grass is green').

Act I, scene iii. The garden of Trulove's house. Anne has had no news of Tom since he left for London. She resolves to go in search of him ('I go to him').

Act II, scene i. The morning room of Tom's house in a London square. Tom, already bored with the pleasures of London, longs for the simple life he left behind in the country ('Vary the song'). When he wishes that he were happy, Shadow enters with a newspaper report about Baba the Turk, a bearded lady who is on display at a fair. Shadow suggests that Tom should marry Baba, to demonstrate his freedom from conventional appetites ('In youth the panting slave pursues'). Tom cheerfully agrees ('My tale shall be told both by young and by old').

Act II, scene ii. The street in front of Tom's house. Anne has arrived in London and is waiting outside the house for Tom's return ('O heart be stronger'). When Tom arrives in a sedan chair preceded by servants, he confesses himself unworthy of Anne and tries to persuade her to return home ('Anne! Here!'). Baba impatiently pokes her head out from the sedan chair, and Tom admits to Anne that Baba is his wife ('Could it then have been known'). Anne leaves, and Tom leads Baba into the house, but not before she has been acclaimed by a crowd of passers-by ('Baba the Turk is here!').

Act II, scene iii. The morning room of Tom's house. Baba the Turk has filled the house with possessions that she has collected from all over the world. She chatters away about herself ('As I was saying'), and when Tom expresses his disgust she flies into a rage ('Scorned! Abused!'). He silences her by covering her face with his wig, and then he falls asleep. Shadow enters with a machine that makes bread out of stones, thereby alleviating the sufferings of mankind, and Tom awakes, having been dreaming of just such a machine. Shadow persuades Tom that marketing the machine commercially will make his fortune ('Thanks to this excellent device').

Act III, scene i. The morning room, now covered in cobwebs and dust. Baba still sits in her chair, silent and unmoving, with Tom's wig covering her face. Tom has disappeared, leaving large debts behind him, and the contents of his house are about to be sold by auction. People have gathered to examine the goods, and Anne arrives in search of Tom. The auctioneer Sellem begins the sale ('Who hears me, knows me'). When he arrives at Baba, he removes the wig from her face and she continues her aria of rage from the point at which she had left off. Tom and Nick Shadow can be heard singing in the street outside ('Old wives for sale!'). Baba suggests that Anne should find Tom, who still loves her, and look after him. She (Baba) will return to her career.

Act III, scene ii. A churchyard, at night. Shadow tells Tom that the time has come for him to claim his wages, and that he requires Tom's soul rather than his money. However, if Tom can beat Shadow at a card game, he may save himself from hell. Tom wins the game, but a furious Shadow condemns him to madness and then sinks from sight into a grave.

Act III, scene iii. Bedlam. Tom, surrounded by other madmen, imagines that he is Adonis, about to be visited by Venus ('Prepare yourselves, heroic shades'). Anne enters, and Tom greets her as Venus. They sing a love duet, and Anne rocks him to sleep with a lullaby ('Gently, little boat'). When he awakes to find her gone, Tom dies of grief ('Mourn for Adonis').

Epilogue. Tom, Anne, Trulove, Baba and Nick Shadow appear before the curtain to sing a moralistic quintet ('Good people, just a moment').

The Rake's Progress is Stravinsky's most conventional opera, with its use of formal, harpsichord-accompanied recitatives, its arias and cabalettas, and its ensembles. It is also his most assured, confident and approachable work for the stage, and is generally considered to mark the culmination of its composer's neo-classical period. (Shortly afterwards, Stravinsky was to begin a flirtation with serialism.) Although echoes of Handel, Mozart, various composers of the early nineteenth century, and even Verdi are to be found in the score, the overall effect is a unified one. The highly literary Auden–Kallman libretto is at times too precious for immediate comprehension, but this is a minor blemish on an extremely enjoyable opera.

Recommended recording: Alexander Young (Tom Rakewell), Judith Raskin (Anne), John Reardon (Shadow), Regina Sarfaty (Baba), with the Sadler's Wells Chorus and the Royal Philharmonic Orchestra, conducted by Igor Stravinsky. Sony CD 46290. Conducted by the composer, this is the definitive version. Alexander Young, said to be

Stravinsky's favourite exponent of the role, is a vivid Tom Rakewell, with Judith Raskin a charming Anne, and John Reardon a splendidly saturnine Nick Shadow.

KAROL SZYMANOWSKI

(b. Tymoszowka, Ukraine, 1882 – d. Lausanne, 1937)

King Roger

(Król Roger)
opera in three acts (approximate length: 1 hour, 45 minutes)

Roger II, King of Sicily   *baritone*
Roxana, his wife   *soprano*
Edrisi, an Arab scholar   *tenor*
The Shepherd   *tenor*
The Archbishop   *bass*
An Abbess   *contralto*

LIBRETTO BY JAROSLAW IWASZKIEWICZ; TIME: THE TWELFTH CENTURY; PLACE: SICILY; FIRST PERFORMED AT THE WIELKI THEATRE, WARSAW, 19 JUNE 1926

An important figure in Polish music in the first half of the twentieth century, Szymanowski composed an operetta and two operas, one of which, *Król Roger*, is still quite frequently performed.

Act I. The cathedral in Palermo. Priests ask King Roger to imprison a young Shepherd who has been preaching a philosophy that they consider to be anti-Christian. Urged by his wife, Roxana, to hear the Shepherd before deciding, King Roger commands him to be produced. The Shepherd answers the King's questions, explaining his philosophy ecstatically, and Roxana is clearly impressed by the youth. The King orders him to appear at the palace that very night.

Act II. The inner courtyard of the King's palace. The Shepherd arrives with his disciples, announcing that he comes from Benares on the banks of the Ganges in India, and that he has been sent by God. When he and his followers dance and sing, Roxana and the courtiers are enthralled and join them. The King has the Shepherd put in chains, but he bursts free and leads Roxana and the courtiers away to what he describes as the Kingdom of Light. The King is left alone in his grief.

Act III. The ruins of a Greek temple. King Roger cries out to Roxana, and he is answered by the voice of the Shepherd seeming to come from everywhere around him. Roxana appears, and the Shepherd is revealed to be the Greek god Dionysus. He and his followers dance a bacchanal, in which Roxana joins, and gradually they all disappear, leaving the King alone but now enraptured, greeting the rising sun.

Szymanowski's score has a Romantic intensity of expression, with something of the opulence of his contemporaries Scriabin and Richard Strauss.

PETER ILITSCH TCHAIKOVSKY

(b. Kamsko-Votkinsk, 1840 – d. St Petersburg, 1893)

Yevgeny Onyegin
(Eugene Onegin)
lyrical scenes in three acts (approximate length: 2 hours, 30 minutes)

Madame Larina, an estate owner   *mezzo-soprano*
Tatiana   *soprano* ⎤
                          ⎥ her daughters
Olga   *contralto* ⎦
Filipievna, Tatiana's nurse   *mezzo-soprano*
Lensky, Olga's fiancé   *tenor*
Yevgeny Onyegin (Eugene Onegin), his friend   *baritone*
Prince Gremin   *bass*
Monsieur Triquet, a Frenchman   *tenor*

LIBRETTO BY THE COMPOSER AND KONSTANTIN STEPANOVICH SHILOVSKY, BASED ON THE NOVEL IN VERSE *EUGENE ONEGIN*, BY ALEXANDER PUSHKIN; TIME: THE 1820S; PLACE: RUSSIA — A COUNTRY ESTATE AND ST PETERSBURG; FIRST PERFORMED AT THE MALY THEATRE, MOSCOW CONSERVATORY, 29 MARCH 1879

Tchaikovsky is regarded primarily as a composer for the orchestra, whose three ballets (*Swan Lake, Sleeping Beauty, The Nutcracker*) and at least three of whose symphonies are deservedly popular. Nevertheless, he composed more operas than symphonies, though only two of his operas are regularly performed outside Russia. He destroyed his earliest opera, *Voyevoda* (The Provincial Governor), after its 1869 premiere at the Bolshoi Theatre, Moscow, but the work was later reconstructed from the surviving orchestral parts and other material, and Tchaikovsky used much of its music again in *The Oprichnik*, performed in St Petersburg in 1874. *Vakula the Smith*, first performed in St Petersburg two years later, is somewhat more individual in style than the earlier operas. It was later revised as *The Slippers* and staged at the Bolshoi in 1887.

Tchaikovsky's next opera, *Eugene Onegin*, is his masterpiece. It is also the most personal of his operas, for certain aspects of its plot closely parallel his situation at the time of its composition. The subject was taken from a seminal work of Russian literature, *Eugene Onegin*, a novel in verse by Alexander Pushkin, first published in 1831. Pushkin's novel relates the experiences of its Byronic hero, Onyegin, who, bored with the social life of St Petersburg, meets at a country estate an innocent young girl, Tatiana, who falls in love with him and naively pours out her feelings in a letter to him. The worldly Onyegin is not interested, and he tells her so. The plot develops tragically.

That he should use *Eugene Onegin* as the basis of his next opera was suggested to Tchaikovsky by the contralto Elizaveta Lavrovskaya. Only some weeks previously, an attractive young woman named Antonina Milyukova, a twenty-eight-year-old former music student, had written to Tchaikovsky, confessing that she had been secretly in love with him for some time. When the composer began to work on *Eugene Onegin* at the end of May 1877, having written a libretto with the help of his friend Konstantin Shilovsky, he turned first to the scene in which Tatiana writes to Onyegin, confessing her love. While he was occupied with the composition of this scene, Tchaikovsky received a second letter from Antonina Milyukova. He agreed to meet her and, far from behaving like Onyegin, he actually proposed marriage to her. By the time of their wedding, which took place only a few weeks after their first meeting, he had already composed most of the opera.

A guilt-ridden homosexual, the thirty-seven-year-old Tchaikovsky not surprisingly found his marital situation unbearable. Only a few days after his wedding, he told his brother Anatoly that he found his bride physically repulsive. He left her, attempted to drown himself and was taken abroad by his brother to Switzerland, where he recovered from the disastrous episode sufficiently to work on the orchestration of the music he had already composed for the opera. By the end of January 1878 *Eugene Onegin* was complete. It was given its premiere by students in Moscow in March 1879, and its first professional performances followed at the Bolshoi Theatre, Moscow, in January 1881.

Act I, scene i. The garden of Madame Larina's country house. While her daughters Tatiana and Olga rehearse a duet inside the house ('Have you not heard?'),
Madame Larina sits reminiscing with the old nurse Filipievna. Farm workers
celebrating the end of the harvest present Madame Larina with a harvest wreath
as they sing and dance. The light-hearted Olga takes part in the celebrations, but
her more serious-minded sister Tatiana remains a little apart, absorbed in the fate
of the lovers in a novel she is reading.

Lensky, a neighbourng landowner and Olga's fiancé, arrives with his friend
Onyegin, a sophisticated young man who, a newcomer to the district, seems bored
with the world in general. While Lensky and Olga talk of their love ('I love you,
Olga'), Onyegin and Tatiana take a stroll around the garden together. Onyegin
tells Tatiana of his life, while she, clearly enamoured of him, listens ecstatically.

Act I, scene ii. Tatiana's bedroom, that night. As Filipievna helps her prepare
for bed, Tatiana suddenly confesses to her that she is in love. Then, dismissing her
nurse, she writes a highly emotional letter to Onyegin, declaring her love ('Even if
it means I perish'). When dawn breaks, Filipievna returns to find Tatiana still
awake. She is given the letter, for her grandson to deliver to Onyegin.

Act I, scene iii. The garden. Tatiana waits at the spot where she has asked
Onyegin to meet her. When he arrives he addresses her with a cold formality,
declaring that he cannot reciprocate her love and reproving her for her lack of
self-control. Stunned and humiliated, Tatiana takes the arm he offers and allows
herself to be led back to the house.

Act II, scene i. A reception room in Madame Larina's house. A ball is in
progress, for Tatiana's name day. The company commander and a number of military men are present, and the younger guests dance a waltz while their elders sit
exchanging reminiscences. Lensky has brought Onyegin, who, obviously bored
by such country revels, dances with Olga and flirts with her merely to annoy his
friend Lensky. An elderly French tutor, Monsieur Triquet, sings a song he has
composed in Tatiana's honour ('A cette fête conviée'), after which, when the
dancing begins again, Onyegin continues his flirtation with his friend's fiancée.
The two men quarrel, and Lensky, after challenging Onyegin to a duel, to the shock
and dismay of Madame Larina and her guests ('In your house!'), bids farewell to
Olga and rushes out.

Act II, scene ii. An old deserted millhouse, at dawn on a winter morning. While
he and his second await Onyegin, Lensky sings a sad farewell to Olga ('Whither
did you flee?'). Onyegin arrives, bringing his valet as his second. Lensky and
Onyegin pause momentarily, musing to themselves on their long friendship,
but neither man makes a move towards reconciliation. The duel with pistols

proceeds. Onyegin fires first and is horrified when Lensky falls to the ground, dead.

Act III, scene i. An elegant house in St Petersburg, where a ball is in progress. After years of wandering abroad, Onyegin has returned to Russia, restless, bored and still consumed with guilt at having killed his friend. He watches the guests dancing a polonaise and is astounded to recognize a beautiful, elegant woman, who arrives with the elderly Prince Gremin. It is Tatiana. Onyegin asks Prince Gremin who the woman is, and is told that she is his wife, whom he loves dearly ('To love all ages must submit'). Gremin presents Onyegin to Tatiana, but she receives him coldly. When she has gone Onyegin realizes that he is now in love with her ('Alas, I have no doubts, I am in love').

Act III, scene ii. A room in Prince Gremin's house. Tatiana awaits Onyegin, who has written to her asking for a meeting. When Onyegin enters and throws himself at her feet, she reminds him of his heartless behaviour to her when they first met. His passionate declaration of love convinces Tatiana that Onyegin is sincere, and in a moment of weakness she admits that she still loves him. But she adds that she respects her husband and will never be unfaithful to him. Dismissing Onyegin for ever, she rushes from the room, leaving him shattered.

Tchaikovsky took from Pushkin only what he needed, making no attempt to be completely faithful to the verse novel or to encompass its every mood and incident, which is why he chose to describe his *Eugene Onegin* not as an opera but as 'lyrical scenes'. However, it is a magnificent and coherent work in its own right, romantic and passionate, its melodies fluent and its orchestration rich and sumptuous. The two highlights are Tatiana's letter-writing scene, whose contrasting themes represent emotional abandonment and innocent, childlike trust, and Lensky's deeply moving aria before his duel with Onyegin. The lively, infectiously tuneful waltz danced by Madame Larina's guests has become popular beyond the confines of the opera.

Recommended recording: Evgeny Belov (Onyegin), Galina Vishnevskaya (Tatiana), Sergei Lemeshev (Lensky), with the Bolshoi Theatre Chorus and Orchestra, conducted by Boris Khaikin. BMG Melodiya 74321 17090 2. This 1956 recording represents the Bolshoi at its best, with Vishnevskaya a vulnerable Tatiana, heading a superb cast.

The Queen of Spades

(Pikovaya dama)

opera in three acts (approximate length: 2 hours, 45 minutes)

Herman   *tenor*
Count Tomsky   *baritone*
Prince Yeletzky   *baritone*
Tchekalinsky   *tenor*
Sourin   *bass*
The Countess   *mezzo-soprano*
Lisa, her granddaughter   *soprano*
Pauline, Lisa's confidante   *contralto*
In the pastoral play:
Chloe   *soprano*
Daphnis (Pauline)   *contralto*
Plutus (Tomsky)   *baritone*

LIBRETTO BY MODEST TCHAIKOVSKY, BASED ON THE NOVEL *THE QUEEN OF SPADES*,
BY ALEXANDER PUSHKIN; TIME: THE END OF THE EIGHTEENTH CENTURY; PLACE:
ST PETERSBURG; FIRST PERFORMED AT THE MARYINSKY THEATRE, ST PETERSBURG,
19 DECEMBER 1890

After *Eugene Onegin* Tchaikovsky's next three operas were comparative failures. *The Maid of Orleans*, based on *Die Jungfrau von Orleans*, Schiller's play about Joan of Arc, was staged in St Petersburg in 1881. A dull piece containing one fine aria for Joan, it was rarely performed during its composer's lifetime and is not likely to be successfully revived. *Mazeppa*, based on an epic poem by Pushkin, was given its premiere in Moscow in 1884. Its score is livelier than that of *The Maid of Orleans*, but it too has failed to survive. Nor did *The Sorceress*, derived from a play of the same title by Ippolit Shpashinsky, fare any better at its St Petersburg premiere in 1887. However, with his next opera, *The Queen of Spades*, Tchaikovsky regained something of his earlier form. (It was followed by his final opera, *Iolanta*, which is disappointingly thin, both musically and dramatically.)

It was the composer's brother Modest who, in 1889, drew his attention to Pushkin's novel *The Queen of Spades* (published in 1834) as a subject for opera, and who provided him with a libretto. Tchaikovsky composed the work in the first six months of 1890, and it was staged at the Maryinsky Theatre, St Petersburg, in December of that year. Though critical reaction was at first by no means entirely favourable, the opera eventually achieved some popularity in Russia and abroad, and it is still performed.

Act I, scene i. The Summer Garden, St Petersburg, on a day in spring. While people stroll in the garden, and children play, two officers, Tchekalinsky and Sourin, discuss the odd behaviour of their friend and colleague Herman, who has taken to spending all his evenings at the gaming table, watching others play, but never participating.

Herman arrives with his friend Count Tomsky, to whom he reveals that he has fallen in love with a young woman whose name he does not know. Prince Yeletzky arrives, announcing that he has, that morning, become engaged to be married. He points out his fiancée, Lisa, who has just entered the garden with her grandmother, the Countess, and Herman is distressed to recognize her as the girl with whom he has fallen in love.

Tomsky tells his friends that the old Countess was in her youth a great beauty at the court of Louis XV in Paris, but that she was an obsessive gambler, known as the Queen of Spades. One day she lost her entire fortune at the gaming table and turned for help to the Count St Germain, who in return for an assignation told her the secret of three cards that would always win. As a result the Countess had an amazing run of luck, and she passed on the secret of the three cards to her husband and, years later, to a young lover. In a vision it was revealed to her that should she disclose the secret to a third person she would die.

Tomsky's story makes a great impression on Herman. When a thunderstorm breaks out, and all run for cover, Herman remains alone as if in a trance, vowing that he will discover the secret of the cards, become rich and win Lisa from Prince Yeletzky.

Act I, scene ii. Lisa's room. Lisa and her confidante Pauline are entertaining friends, singing, playing and dancing. When a governess enters to complain of the noise, the visitors depart. Lisa is left alone and her thoughts turn to the unknown young man whom she has frequently observed watching her. Suddenly, Herman appears on her balcony. At first she begs him to leave, but soon begins to respond to his fervent declaration of love. When Lisa's grandmother, the Countess, is heard approaching, Herman hides. The old woman orders Lisa to bed, and then leaves. Herman emerges from his hiding place, muttering about the prophecy of the three cards, and Lisa throws herself into his arms.

Act II, scene i. A reception room in an elegant house, where a masked ball is in progress. Yeletzky sings to Lisa of his love for her ('I love you beyond measure'), but her thoughts are elsewhere, for she has made an assignation with Herman.

After a pastoral play has been performed by some of the guests, Lisa surreptitiously gives Herman a key, telling him how to get to her bedroom by passing through the Countess's apartment. As the guests at the ball line up to meet the Empress Catherine the Great, the curtain falls.

Act II, scene ii. The Countess's bedroom. Herman enters, on his way to Lisa's room, but his attention is arrested by a huge portrait of the Countess as a beautiful young Queen of Spades. He hides behind a curtain as he hears the Countess approaching with her maids, who prepare her for bed. Dismissing them, the Countess sings softly to herself an aria from Grétry's opera *Richard Coeur de Lion* ('Je crains de lui parler la nuit'), and then she is startled by the appearance of Herman. He urges her to tell him the secret of the three cards but, paralyzed with fear, she cannot utter a word. When he threatens her with a pistol, she dies suddenly of shock. Lisa enters and is horrified at what has happened. Herman tries to assure her that he had not intended to harm the Countess, but Lisa, disillusioned, orders him to leave.

Act III, scene i. Herman's room in the barracks, late at night. Herman, haunted by his conscience, hears funereal chanting and sees the body of the Countess on her bier. He has received a letter from Lisa, forgiving him, accepting his explanation and asking him to meet her at midnight by the banks of the River Neva. The Countess's ghost appears to Herman, imparting the secret of the three cards – three, seven, ace.

Act III, scene ii. The banks of the Neva. A distraught Lisa, awaiting Herman, sings of her grief ('Ah, I am worn out by grief'). When Herman arrives they begin to sing of their future together, but he can think only of the fortune he expects to win. Pushing Lisa aside, he rushes off to the gaming house. Realizing that his obsession has driven Herman to madness, Lisa throws herself into the river.

Act III, scene iii. The gaming house. After Tomsky has performed a rousing song for his colleagues ('If pretty girls could fly like birds'), the maniacal Herman arrives, bets the huge sum of forty thousand roubles on three, and wins. He then puts double the sum on seven, and wins again. Only Prince Yeletzky will now bet against him, as Herman plays his last card. The ace wins, but Herman's card turns out to be the Queen of Spades. Cursing the Countess, Herman stabs himself and dies.

A somewhat problematical opera, gripping in its finest moments but difficult to stage because of its formlessness and its stop-go attitude to dramatic narrative, *The Queen of Spades* requires a director of genius and, in the central role of Herman, a tenor who is also a compelling actor. With the exception of Lisa's moving aria in Act III, scene ii, and a few other lyrical passages, the music is less immediately attractive than that of *Eugene Onegin*, though the opera's strongest dramatic moments are impressively conveyed by the orchestra. The sense of doom that pervades the story of Herman's obsession is too often dissipated by scenes unnecessary to the drama, in which Tchaikovsky resorts to Mozartian pastiche. Specifically, these are (a) the scene in which Lisa and Pauline entertain their guests, (b) the irrelevant pastoral play that dominates the ballroom scene, and (c) parts of the opera's opening scene in the Summer Garden. The small but telling role of the Countess is a gift to a soprano of strong personality and mature years, but Lisa is a rather pallid heroine and Herman the most unappealing of anti-heroes.

Recommended recording: Gegam Gregorian (Herman), Maria Guleghina (Lisa), Vladimir Chernov (Yeletzky), Irina Arkhipova (Countess), with the Kirov Opera Chorus and Orchestra, conducted by Valery Gergiev. Phillips 438 141–2. Gergiev keeps the action moving, Grigorian is a magnificently intense Herman, and there are no weak links in the entire cast of Kirov regulars.

MICHAEL TIPPETT
(b. London, 1905 – d. London, 1998)

The Midsummer Marriage
opera in three acts (approximate length: 2 hours, 30 minutes)

Mark, a young man of unknown parentage   *tenor*
Jenifer, his betrothed   *soprano*
King Fisher, Jenifer's father, a businessman   *baritone*
Bella, King Fisher's secretary   *soprano*
Jack, Bella's boyfriend, a mechanic   *tenor*
Sosostris, a clairvoyante   *contralto*
He-Ancient, priest of the temple   *bass*
She-Ancient, priestess of the temple   *mezzo-soprano*
Strephon, one of the dancers

LIBRETTO BY THE COMPOSER; TIME: THE PRESENT; PLACE: A CLEARING IN A WOOD, WITH A RUINED TEMPLE; FIRST PERFORMED AT THE ROYAL OPERA HOUSE, COVENT GARDEN, LONDON, 27 JANUARY 1955

The most successful twentieth-century British composer of opera after Benjamin Britten, Tippett composed in the late 1930s two one-act operas, which he described as plays for children, with words by his friend the playwright Christopher Fry, but he did not write his first major opera until 1946. He had, at the beginning of World War II, sketched out a synopsis for a work that he conceived as a protest against the Nazi persecution of Jews, and was at first undecided whether it should be intended for the stage or the concert platform. When he showed the poet T.S. Eliot his synopsis and asked him to write the libretto, Eliot persuaded Tippett to undertake the task himself, advising him not to 'let the poets loose on your librettos; because they are going to do with the words what your music should do'. Tippett proceeded to compose *A Child of Our Time* as an oratorio, writing the text himself. When, after the war, he came to compose his full-length operas, he remembered Eliot's advice and always wrote his own librettos.

A moment of intense personal vision convinced Tippett that he had become, as he put it, 'the instrument of some collective imaginative experience', and it was in the light of this conviction that he wrote *The Midsummer Marriage*, an opera whose allegorical story is a kind of retelling in modern, Jungian terms of the message of Mozart's *Die Zauberflöte*. Tippett first drafted the libretto of Act I, and then he composed the music, following the same procedure for Acts II and III. It took him seven years to complete the opera, which was given its premiere at the Royal Opera House, Covent Garden, in January 1955. John Pritchard was the conductor, and a first-rate cast had been assembled, headed by Joan Sutherland and Richard Lewis as Jenifer and Mark. Its first audiences found the work obscure, and press reviews were for the most part unfavourable, especially regarding Tippett's libretto, which was generally considered confused and pretentious. It was not until a second Covent Garden production in 1968, after Tippett's next opera, *King Priam*, had been staged there, that *The Midsummer Marriage* began to be widely admired.

Act I. A clearing on a wooded hilltop, with a ruined temple. (This is the setting of the entire opera.) It is morning. Mark and Jenifer plan a runaway wedding, and their friends have assembled to meet them and celebrate the event. The friends greet the rising sun and then hear soft music coming from the temple. They hide, as dancers, led by Strephon and followed by the Ancients, emerge from the temple. Mark arrives, calling for a new dance for his wedding day, but the He-Ancient orders the old dance to be repeated, and he trips Strephon with his stick, warning him that he will learn a new dance before the day is over.

Jenifer arrives and announces that there will be no wedding, for she wants not love but truth. She and Mark quarrel. She notices a spiral staircase by the temple, and climbs it, while Mark chooses another path, downwards into a hillside cave. Jenifer's father, the businessman King Fisher, arrives, accompanied by his secretary, Bella, in search of Jenifer, and attempts to enlist the aid of the Ancients in finding her. When the Ancients refuse to open the gate of the temple, Bella's boyfriend, Jack, a mechanic, is summoned to help. Jack's attempts to open the gate are interrupted by the voice of Sosostris, urging caution.

Jenifer and Mark reappear, and the Ancients announce a contest between them. Jenifer sings of the spiritual purity of her experience, while Mark sings of the earthlier nature of his. Jenifer holds up a mirror to Mark, to show him how animal-like he has become, but his gaze shatters the mirror. She now enters the cave to share his experience, while he mounts the staircase in search of hers. King Fisher rushes out, perplexed and furious, and the chorus of friends proclaim themselves 'the laughing children'.

Act II. Afternoon. Strephon begins to dance, but hides when the chorus is heard off-stage, celebrating Midsummer's Day. Jack and Bella sing a love duet and then disappear into the forest. A sequence of three ritual dances follows, in each of which Strephon plays the role of the pursued. In 'The Earth in Autumn' the hound chases the hare. In 'The Waters in Winter' the otter chases the fish. In 'The Air in Spring' the hawk chases the bird. In this final dance, the bird is about to be killed when Bella, who has been watching, screams. She is comforted by Jack, as the chorus sings again in praise of midsummer.

Act III. Evening and night. The chorus is in festive mood. King Fisher interrupts to announce that he has sent for his private clairvoyante, Sosostris, and the chorus goes off to greet her. The Ancients warn King Fisher of the dangers involved in meddling with powers he does not understand, but he pays no heed. The chorus returns with Sosostris, who turns out to be Jack in disguise. When the real Sosostris appears, a crystal bowl is placed before her, and she sings of the physical and spritual union of Jenifer and Mark. In a fury, King Fisher smashes the crystal bowl and tears at the clairvoyante's veils, only to find that Sosostris has miraculously been replaced by Jenifer and Mark, seen 'in radiant transfiguration'. King Fisher aims a pistol at Mark, but when Mark and Jenifer turn their gaze upon him he falls dead. The chorus and the She-Ancient sing a requiem. King Fisher's body is carried into the temple, and a fourth ritual dance is performed, at the end of which Strephon is consumed by fire, while Mark and Jenifer are reborn to return to the everyday world and marry.

Clearly, one needs to be able to tolerate large doses of high-flown (and clumsily written) Jungian mysticism if one attempts to take the verbal content of Tippett's opera seriously. However, the librettist Tippett has to be taken seriously, for his words have drawn from the composer Tippett music of great richness and transcendent power. What Tippett attempts foolishly and incoherently to say in words, he succeeds in saying magnificently in music that defies verbal description.

The juxtaposition of two pairs of lovers, one pair (Mark and Jenifer) poetic (like Tamino and Pamina) and the other pair (Jack and Bella) earthly (like Papageno and Papagena), has led critics into finding similarities between *The Midsummer Marriage* and Mozart's *Die Zauberflöte*. What the two operas have in common is their celebration of sexual union as an aspect of divine love.

Recommended recording: Alberto Remedios (Mark), Joan Carlyle (Jenifer), Stuart Burrows (Jack), Elizabeth Harwood (Bella), Raimund Herincx (King Fisher), with the Chorus and Orchestra of the Royal Opera House, Covent Garden, conducted by Colin Davis. Lyrita SRCD 2217. Remedios, a lyrical Mark, heads a superb cast, and the opera is conducted stunningly by Colin Davis.

King Priam
opera in three acts (approximate length: 2 hours)

Priam, King of Troy   *bass-baritone*
Hecuba, his wife   *dramatic soprano*
Hector, their eldest son   *baritone*
Andromache, Hector's wife   *lyric dramatic soprano*
Paris, Priam's second son   *tenor; boy soprano in Act I, scene ii*
Helen, wife to King Menelaus of Sparta   *mezzo-soprano*
Achilles, a Greek hero   *heroic tenor*
Patroclus, his friend   *light baritone*
The Nurse   *mezzo-soprano*
The Old Man   *bass*
A Young Guard   *lyric tenor*
Hermes, messenger of the gods   *high light tenor*

LIBRETTO BY THE COMPOSER; TIME: CLASSICAL ANTIQUITY; PLACE: TROY AND SPARTA; FIRST PERFORMED AT THE BELGRADE THEATRE, COVENTRY, 29 MAY 1962

For his second opera, Tippett turned from private to public myth and found his subject in Homer's *Iliad*, choosing a number of scenes featuring King Priam and his sons Hector and Paris. Again, Tippett wrote his own libretto. The opera, composed between 1958 and 1961, was commissioned by the Koussevitsky Music Foundation, and it was first performed by the company of the Royal Opera, Covent Garden, at the Coventry Festival of 1962, held to mark the consecration of the new Coventry Cathedral.

Act I, scene i. Priam's palace at Troy. The child Paris is born to King Priam and Queen Hecuba. Hecuba is troubled by a dream which is interpreted by an Old Man as meaning that the son will cause his father's death. Priam is forced to decide Paris's fate, and he commands that the child be killed.

Interlude. The Nurse, the Old Man and a Young Guard, who constitute a chorus, comment on Priam's decision.

Act I, scene ii. The countryside outside Troy. Priam and his eldest son, Hector, on a bull hunt, meet a young boy who tells them that he wants to be a hero, and that his name is Paris. Priam accepts the lad as his son, who was not killed but given to a shepherd.

Interlude. The chorus tells of Hector's marriage to Andromache, of Paris growing to young manhood, of friction between the brothers, and of Paris's departure for Greece and the court of Menelaus.

Act I, scene iii. Menelaus's palace at Sparta. Paris and Helen, the wife of Menelaus, are in love. Wondering whether to abduct Helen and take her to Troy, Paris prays to Zeus. Hermes, the messenger of the gods, appears and asks Paris to choose between three goddesses, Athene, Hera and Aphrodite. Paris is reminded by Athene and Hera of his mother Hecuba and his sister-in-law Andromache, so he chooses Aphrodite, as representing Helen. The other two goddesses curse him, and he takes Helen away to Troy.

Act II, scene i. Troy. Hector and Paris quarrel. Paris's abduction of Helen has led to war, and the brothers rush off, separately, to fight.

Interlude. The Old Man is taken by Hermes to the Greek camp to gloat over Achilles.

Act II, scene ii. Achilles' tent. Achilles refuses to fight, because of a quarrel with Agamemnon. His friend and lover Patroclus persuades Achilles to allow him to fight in his friend's place, dressed in Achilles' celebrated armour.

Interlude. The Old Man asks Hermes to warn Priam of the danger.

Act II, scene iii. Troy. Patroclus has been killed in combat by Hector. As Priam, Paris and Hector are celebrating over the dead body, the blood-curdling sound of Achilles' war cry is heard.

Act III, scene i. The royal palace at Troy. Andromache has a premonition of the death of her husband, Hector, and berates Helen as the cause of his death. Andromache, Helen and Hecuba pray to their various goddesses.

Interlude. Serving women comment on the impending defeat of Troy.

Act III, scene ii. The royal palace at Troy. Paris tells Priam of Hector's death and goes off to kill Achilles, while Priam reflects bitterly on the vagaries of fate.

Interlude. Purely instrumental.

Act III, scene iii. Achilles' tent. Priam brings the body of Patroclus to Achilles and begs for that of his son Hector. Achilles grants his wish, and the two men drink to their own deaths.

Interlude. Hermes announces the imminent death of Priam and sings a hymn to the divine power of music as an instrument of healing.

Act III, scene iv. Troy. Paris tells Priam that he has killed Achilles, but Priam has withdrawn into a private world and speaks only to Helen before he is killed.

Tippett's musical language in *King Priam* is completely different from that in *The Midsummer Marriage* – less lyrical and more abrasive. His orchestra is split into various units, representing the different characters, and his writing for the voices is largely declamatory. Achilles' war cry at the end of Act II has a tremendous effect in the theatre, and the intimate scenes, such as those between Achilles and Patroclus and between Priam and Achilles, are immensely moving. Some of the opera's music found its way into subsequent works by Tippett, among them the Second Piano Sonata and the Concerto for Orchestra. Achilles' song in Act II became the first of a suite of three *Songs for Achilles*, for tenor voice and guitar.

Recommended recording: Norman Bailey (Priam), Heather Harper (Hecuba), Philip Langridge (Paris), Yvonne Minton (Helen), Robert Tear (Achilles), with the London Sinfonietta Chorus and Orchestra, conducted by David Atherton. Decca 414 241–2. A fine cast and a sympathetic conductor.

GIUSEPPE VERDI
(b. Le Roncole, near Busseto, 1813 – d. Milan, 1901)

Oberto, conte di San Bonifacio
(Oberto, Count of San Bonifacio)
opera in two acts (approximate length: 2 hours, 15 minutes)

Cuniza, sister of Ezzelino of Romano   *mezzo-soprano*
Riccardo, Count of Salinguerra   *tenor*
Oberto, Count of San Bonifacio   *bass*
Leonora, his daughter   *soprano*
Imelda, Cuniza's confidante   *mezzo-soprano*

LIBRETTO BY ANTONIO PIAZZA AND TEMISTOCLE SOLERA; TIME: 1228; PLACE: EZZELINO'S CASTLE NEAR BASSANO; FIRST PERFORMED AT THE TEATRO ALLA SCALA, MILAN, 17 NOVEMBER 1839

Italy's greatest composer, the son of an innkeeper in the village of Le Roncole, near Parma, revealed a talent for music as a child and was taught by the organist of the village church. By the age of ten he had advanced sufficiently to be sent for further tuition to the nearby small town of Busseto, where Antonio Barezzi, a merchant, took the lad into his house and gave him a job. Soon the young Verdi was composing marches for the local Philharmonic Society as well as music for the church. In his nineteenth year, aided by Barezzi and by a grant from a local charitable trust, Verdi left for Milan, hoping to gain admittance to the Conservatorium; but he was refused, being four years over the maximum age for entrance, and instead he studied privately with Vincenzo Lavigna, La Scala's chief conductor.

The libretto of Verdi's first opera, given to the composer by Antonio Piazza, a Milanese journalist, may have begun life as a story about a British aristocrat. Altered and added to by Temistocle Solera, a young poet and composer, it became *Oberto, conte di San Bonifacio*, which Verdi composed in the winter of 1837–8. The opera was accepted for production at La Scala, Milan, where it was warmly received at its premiere in November 1839. Bartolomeo Merelli, the impresario of La Scala, immediately put the twenty-six-year-old composer under contract to write three more operas over a period of two years. *Oberto* was subsequently staged in Turin, Genoa and Naples, after which it was not performed for several years until it was staged at La Scala in 1889, on the fiftieth anniversary of its premiere. In recent years the revival of interest in Verdi's early operas has led to *Oberto* being performed in several Italian towns, as well as in New York, London, San Diego, Edinburgh, and on tour in Great Britain.

Although *Oberto* is in two acts, it is really a three-act piece with Act I missing, for at least a third of the relevant action has taken place before the curtain rises. Riccardo, Count of Salinguerra, has seduced and subsequently abandoned Leonora, daughter of Oberto, Count of San Bonifacio. The opera begins at the point where Riccardo has fled to a neighbouring state and is about to marry Cuniza, sister of the local potentate Ezzelino of Romano. (Ezzelino does not appear in the opera, though its entire action takes place in his castle and its environs.)

Act I. Leonora arrives on the day of the wedding, seeking revenge on the man who has treated her so cruelly. She is followed by her father, Oberto, who at first disowns his daughter but forgives her when she tells him she now hates Riccardo. Father and daughter inform Cuniza of the real nature of the man she is about to marry.

Act II. Cuniza insists that Riccardo marry Leonora. Riccardo expresses his remorse, and Leonora discovers that she still loves him. However, Oberto challenges Riccardo to a duel, in which Oberto is killed. A distraught Riccardo flees the country, and the opera ends with Leonora in despair.

Verdi was able to take Piazza's libretto seriously enough to clothe it in music that combines a Bellinian delicacy with an energy in which the new young composer's individual voice can be clearly discerned. *Oberto* may be no masterpiece, but it contains a wealth of enjoyable melody, some of which would not disgrace the pages of *Il trovatore*. In the overture, the melodic fluency that was never to desert Verdi asserts itself almost immediately in a charming and graceful andante. Among the opera's finest numbers are Leonora's Act I aria, her duet with Oberto, which is the first of Verdi's great father–daughter confrontations, Oberto's Act II aria and cabaletta, Riccardo's beautiful and all too short aria, and a superb quartet ('La vergogna ed il dispetto'), which its composer continued to think well of in later years.

Recommended recording: Rolando Panerai (Oberto), Ghena Dimitrova (Leonora), Carlo Bergonzi (Riccardo), with the Chorus and Orchestra of Bavarian Radio, conducted by Lamberto Gardelli. Orfeo C 105 842 H. A fine cast, with the two veteran male singers in superb form, and a conductor who unerringly chooses the right tempos.

Nabucco

opera in four parts (approximate length: 2 hours, 15 minutes)

Nabucco (Nabucodonosor), King of Babylon   *baritone*
Ismaele, nephew of Sedecia, King of Jerusalem   *tenor*
Zaccaria, high priest of the Hebrews   *bass*
Abigaille, slave, presumed to be the elder daughter of Nabucco   *soprano*
Fenena, daughter of Nabucco   *soprano*

High Priest of Baal   *bass*
Abdallo, an elderly officer in Nabucco's service   *tenor*
Anna, sister of Zaccaria   *soprano*

LIBRETTO BY TEMISTOCLE SOLERA, BASED ON THE PLAY *NABUCODONOSOR*, BY AUGUSTE ANICET-BOURGEOIS AND FRANCIS CORNU; TIME: 586 BC; PLACE: JERUSALEM AND BABYLON; FIRST PERFORMED AT THE TEATRO ALLA SCALA, MILAN, 9 MARCH 1842

Verdi's second opera, *Un giorno di regno* (King for a Day), failed miserably at La Scala in September 1840. The young composer, whose wife and two infant children had died, wanted to give up his attempt at a career in Milan and return to Busseto, but the impresario Merelli persuaded him to undertake a third opera, based on the biblical story of the Babylonian King Nebuchadnezzar. Temistocle Solera originally produced the libretto for an opera that Merelli had commissioned from the German composer Otto Nicolai; however, when Nicolai professed his dissatisfaction with the libretto, Merelli offered it to Verdi. The libretto took its plot from a French play, *Nabucodonosor*, by Anicet-Bourgeois and Cornu.

Verdi found Solera's libretto deeply moving and proceeded to compose the opera. At its first performance at La Scala, Milan, *Nabucodonosor* was received with great enthusiasm. (The use of the diminutive *Nabucco* soon caught on, and the opera is now known by that name.) Recalling the occasion many years later, Verdi wrote, 'With this opera it is fair to say my artistic career began . . . The first scene in the temple, for instance, produced such an effect that the audience applauded for ten minutes.' The first-night audience was sent into a state of delirium by the chorus, 'Va, pensiero', in Act III, in which the captive Jews, toiling by the banks of the Euphrates, sing longingly of their homeland. Suffering under Austrian rule, the nineteenth-century Milanese equated themselves with the Jews of the Old Testament and thus adopted the chorus as their anthem. There is no reason to think that Verdi had any other conscious intention than to set the biblical story in Solera's verses to the best of his ability; but his sympathies were, understandably, with the Italian nationalist liberal cause, and he was by no means displeased to be thought of as the composer of the Risorgimento, the movement towards a united and free Italy.

Otto Nicolai, for whom Solera's libretto had originally been intended, wrote in his diary, 'Verdi is the Italian opera composer of today. He has set the libretto which I rejected, and made his fortune with it. But his operas are absolutely dreadful, and utterly degrading for Italy.'

Nabucco is in four parts, each of which is headed by a subtitle and a brief quotation or paraphrase from the Old Testament Book of Jeremiah.

Part one: 'Gerusalemme' (Jerusalem)
'Thus saith the Lord: Behold I will give this city into the hands of the king of Babylon: he will burn it with fire.'

The temple of Solomon in Jerusalem. The Hebrews bewail their defeat by Nabucco and call upon God to defend their holy temple. Zaccaria, the high priest of the Hebrews, enters with Nabucco's daughter Fenena, whom he has taken hostage. Giving her into the care of Ismaele, a young Hebrew officer, nephew of the King of Jerusalem, Zaccaria leads the crowd in a prayer invoking God's aid against the Babylonians. When they are alone, Fenena and Ismaele, who first met when Ismaele was ambassador to Babylon, confess their love for each other.

Fenena's sister, the warlike Abigaille, suddenly enters, sword in hand, at the head of a band of Babylonian soldiers. She has captured the temple but offers Ismaele his safety in return for his love, an offer which he contemptuously refuses. When Nabucco, the father of Abigaille and Fenena, triumphantly enters the temple on horseback, Zaccaria seizes Fenena, threatening to kill her if Nabucco continues to profane the temple ('Tremin gl' insani'). Fenena is rescued from Zaccaria by Ismaele, and Nabucco orders his soldiers to plunder and burn the temple.

Part Two: 'L'Empio' (The Wicked Man)
'Behold the whirlwind of the Lord goeth forth with fury; it shall fall upon the head of the wicked.'

Scene i. The royal apartments in Nabucco's palace in Babylon. Abigaille enters with a parchment she has found, proving that she is not the daughter of Nabucco but a slave girl whom he adopted. She gives voice to her jealousy of Fenena, whom Nabucco has appointed Regent while he is away fighting, and vows that her fury will descend upon Fenena, Nabucco and the entire kingdom. The Babylonian High Priest, who has spread a rumour that Nabucco has been killed in battle, incites Abigaille to seize the throne ('Anch'io dischiuso un giorno').

Scene ii. A large hall in the palace. Zaccaria prays for guidance ('Tu sul labbro del reggenti'), and departs. A crowd assembles, but when Ismaele attempts to address them he is shunned as a traitor for having assisted Fenena. Zaccaria returns with Fenena, whom he has converted to the Jewish faith. Abdallo, a loyal old retainer of Nabucco, enters, warning Fenena to flee, as Nabucco's death has been announced and the people are calling for Abigaille. Abigaille suddenly enters, demanding the crown, but she is closely followed by Nabucco, who, seizing the crown from Fenena's head, places it upon his own ('S'appressan gl'istanti'). When he declares himself to be God, and orders that all must worship him, he is struck down by a thunderbolt. Muttering of the phantoms that torment him, Nabucco collapses and loses his reason. Abigaille snatches up the fallen crown and reaffirms the glory of Baal.

Part Three: 'La profezia' (The Prophecy)
'The wild beasts of the desert shall dwell in Babylon, together with owls; and
hoopoes shall dwell therein.'

Scene i. The Hanging Gardens of Babylon. The High Priest of Baal is about to persuade Abigaille to sign Fenena's death warrant, when a dishevelled Nabucco appears, still out of his mind. He is tricked by Abigaille into signing the death warrant, but when he realizes what he has done he angrily informs Abigaille that she is not really his daughter. He searches for the proof, but she herself produces the document and tears it into pieces. Nabucco begs for Fenena's life, but Abigaille is unmoved ('Deh perdona, deh perdona').

Scene ii. The banks of the Euphrates. After the Hebrews, in chains, have sung nostalgically of their homeland ('Va, pensiero, sull' ali dorate'), Zaccaria rouses them to a more defiant mood ('Del futuro del buio').

Part Four: 'L'idolo infranto' (The Broken Idol)
'Baal is confounded: his idols are broken in pieces.'

Scene i. An apartment in the palace. Nabucco awakes from a nightmare to hear the sounds of the procession conducting Fenena to her place of execution. Falling to his knees, he prays to the God of the Hebrews, promising to restore the temple of Judah if God will clear his mind of its confusion ('Dio di Giuda'). His reason is suddenly restored to him, and he summons his warriors to save Fenena ('O prodi miei, seguitemi').

Scene ii. The Hanging Gardens. Fenena and the condemned Hebrews are led in, and Zaccaria comforts Fenena. Suddenly Nabucco enters, sword in hand. He orders the idol of Baal to be destroyed, and the statue immediately shatters. Nabucco commands that the Jews be released and that a new temple be built to their God ('Immenso Jehova'). Abigaille, who has taken poison, is carried in, dying and repentant. Before she dies, she asks Nabucco to bless the union of Fenena and Ismaele, and she implores God to forgive her.

Nabucco, the earliest opera by Verdi to hold its place in the repertoire, is a work that combines freshness, vigour and emotional intensity with something of the

gracefulness of Bellini and the melodramatic flair of Donizetti. The opera's greatest strength lies in its choruses, and indeed its composer was soon being called
'papa dei cori' by his Milanese public. But Verdi's gift for individual characterization, too, has already begun to assert itself in *Nabucco*. Abigaille is temperamen-
tally an ancestor of Verdi's Lady Macbeth, just as the more nebulous Nabucco is a
sketch for Macbeth, a character equally dominated by a female relative. The solo
utterances of Nabucco and Abigaille are impressive, and 'Va, pensiero, sull' ali
dorate' is one of Verdi's most affecting and best-loved choruses. The entire score
is pervaded by a sense of exile and loss, with the yearning of the captive Jews of
Jerusalem and the tortured despair of the neurotic Nabucco omnipresent behind
the opera's marches and ceremonial pomp.

*Recommended recording: Tito Gobbi (Nabucco), Elena Suliotis (Abigaille), Bruno
Prevedi (Ismaele), Carlo Cava (Zaccaria), with the Vienna State Opera Chorus and
Orchestra, conducted by Lamberto Gardelli. Decca 417 407–2. Tito Gobbi's vocal
and dramatic gifts make him an ideal Nabucco, and Elena Suliotis, a young soprano
who far too soon wore herself out vocally, is caught near the beginning of her career
as a vivid Abigaille. Gardelli conducts his Viennese forces authoritatively.*

I lombardi alla prima crociata
(The Lombards at the First Crusade)
opera in four acts (approximate length: 2 hours, 15 minutes)

Arvino, son of Folco, governor of Rhodes   *tenor*
Viclinda, his wife   *soprano*
Giselda, their daughter   *soprano*
Pagano, Arvino's brother   *bass*
Pirro, his steward   *bass*
The Prior of Milan   *tenor*
Acciano, tyrant of Antioch   *bass*
Sofia, his wife   *soprano*
Oronte, their son   *tenor*

LIBRETTO BY TEMISTOCLE SOLERA, BASED ON THE EPIC POEM *I LOMBARDI ALLA
PRIMA CROCIATA*, BY TOMMASO GROSSI; TIME: 1099; PLACE: MILAN, ANTIOCH AND
THE COUNTRY NEAR JERUSALEM; FIRST PERFORMED AT THE TEATRO ALLA SCALA,
MILAN, 11 FEBRUARY 1843

After the highly successful premiere of *Nabucco*, Bartolomeo Merelli, the impresario of La Scala, immediately asked Verdi to write another opera, assuring him that he could name his own terms. On the advice of Giuseppina Strepponi, the soprano who had created the role of Abigaille in *Nabucco* (and whom Verdi was eventually to marry), the young composer asked for, and was given, a fee equal to that which Bellini had received eleven years previously for *Norma*. In consultation with Temistocle Solera, the librettist of *Nabucco*, the subject chosen was *I lombardi alla prima crociata*, a long narrative verse epic by Tommaso Grossi, which had been published in 1826. Grossi (1790–1853) was one of a group of Milanese poets and playwrights who were followers of the novelist and patriot Alessandro Manzoni.

Solera wrote a muddled and perfunctory libretto very quickly, and Verdi composed *I lombardi* within a few months. The Archbishop of Milan, having heard that it included a stage representation of the sacrament of baptism, attempted to have the opera banned, but Verdi was defiant, and the work was performed with its baptism scene intact. One slight change was made in an aria: the words 'Ave Maria' had to be altered to 'Salve Maria'.

The premiere of *I lombardi* was a riotously successful event, and a local police edict forbidding encores was ignored again and again. The Milanese, who at the first performances of *Nabucco* eleven months previously had noisily identified with Old Testament Hebrews, this time decided that they were Lombards, that the Holy Land being defended was Italy, and that the Saracens were Austrians. In the opera's final act, when the crusaders were incited to battle with the words 'La Santa Terra oggi nostra sarà' (Today the Holy Land will be ours), people in the audience shouted, 'Sì!', and there was a prolonged outburst of cheering.

In the summer of 1847, four years after the premiere of *I lombardi*, Verdi was invited by the Paris Opéra to compose a work for their autumn season. Reluctant to produce a new opera at such short notice, he agreed instead to adapt *I lombardi*. Solera's libretto was refashioned in French by Gustav Vaëz and Alphonse Royer, the Lombard crusaders became French crusaders, and the opera was renamed *Jérusalem*. Alterations to the plot necessitated the composition of some new music; but much of the score of *I lombardi* had merely to undergo minor revision, occasional change of key and rearrangement of order. *Jérusalem* (later translated into Italian and produced in Milan in 1850 as *Gerusalemme*) failed to repeat the success of *I lombardi* and is now rarely encountered.

Act I: 'La vendetta' (The Revenge). Scene i. The Piazza di Sant' Ambrogio, Milan. The citizens welcome back from exile Pagano, who years previously attempted to kill his brother Arvino, whose wife, Viclinda, he loves ('T'assale un tremito'). As the Prior of Milan announces that Arvino has been chosen to lead the Lombard crusaders, an unrepentant Pagano surreptitiously makes plans to abduct Viclinda that night, and to kill Arvino ('Sciagurata, hai tu creduto').

Act I, scene ii. A gallery in the palace of Folco, the father of Pagano and Arvino. Giselda, the daughter of Arvino and Viclinda, prays to the Virgin Mary ('Salve Maria'). Pagano and his henchman Pirro enter stealthily, and in the darkness Pagano kills his father by mistake. He is overcome with horror and remorse ('Mostro d'averno orribile').

Act II: 'L'uomo della caverna' (The Man in the Cave). Scene i. A hall in the palace of Acciano, the tyrant of Antioch. Giselda has been captured by the Muslims, and Oronte, the son of Acciano, has fallen in love with her ('La mia letizia infondere').

Act II, scene ii. The entrance of a cave in the mountains. Pagano, attempting to expiate his sins, has become a locally renowned holy hermit. He is consulted by his former henchman Pirro, who has become a Muslim, and by Arvino, who has come to seek the hermit's aid in rescuing Giselda from her Muslim captor. Without revealing his identity, the hermit assures his brother that all will be well.

Act II, scene iii. The women's quarters in Acciano's palace. Giselda, taunted by the other members of the harem, calls despairingly upon heaven for help ('Se vano è il pregare'). The crusaders, led by Arvino and the hermit, attack the palace, and Giselda is rescued. Told that Arvino has killed both the tyrant and his son Oronte, Giselda recoils from her father in horror, crying that God cannot have willed such slaughter ('No, giusta causa non è Iddio').

Act III: 'La conversione' (The Conversion). Scene i. The valley of Jehoshaphat. Giselda, distraught and dishevelled, encounters Oronte, who has only been wounded. They declare their love for each other ('Seguirti io voglio').

Act III, scene ii. Arvino's tent. Arvino invokes the wrath of heaven against his daughter. Told that Pagano has been seen in the vicinity of the crusaders' camp, he swears vengeance upon his brother as well ('Più d'uno Pagano').

Act III, scene iii. A grotto, through an aperture of which the banks of the River Jordan can be seen. Giselda and Oronte, who is now dying of his wounds, have taken shelter. Before he dies, Oronte is baptized in the Jordan by the hermit ('Qual volutta trascorrere').

Act IV: 'Il santo sepolcro' (The Holy Sepulchre). Scene i. A cave in the hills outside Jerusalem. The sleeping Giselda experiences a vision in which Oronte tells her that the fountain of Siloam will bring water to the parched crusaders ('In cielo benedetto').

Act IV, scene ii. The Lombard camp near the sepulchre of Rachel. The crusaders and pilgrims lament their fate, without water and surrounded by desert ('O Signore dal tetto natio'). Giselda, Arvino and the hermit arrive to announce that the fountain of Siloam is miraculously flowing. Refreshed, the crusaders are led into battle by Arvino.

Act IV, scene iii. Arvino's tent. The hermit, who has been mortally wounded, reveals to Giselda and Arvino that he is Pagano. Arvino forgives him and opens the door of the tent to reveal to his dying brother a distant view of the Holy City of Jerusalem, from the towers of which the banners of the crusaders' cross can be seen fluttering.

In *I lombardi* Verdi's inspiration is fleeting and rarely sustained, brilliant passages alternating with mechanical contrivance. The finest pages of the score, however, possess that melodic fluency and creative energy that were to become Verdian characteristics. Giselda's exquisite Act I aria, 'Salve Maria', is imaginatively scored, and Oronte's 'La mia letizia infondere' is a graceful aria for which Verdi wrote alternative cabalettas. The March of the Lombards, which recurs throughout the opera, is banal, but the many ensembles are impressive, and the scene in which Oronte is baptized is superb. It opens with a long orchestral introduction containing a part for solo violin whose charming cantabile leads into a brilliant allegro, and it continues with a beautiful, somewhat Bellinian, trio, 'Qual volutta trascorrere'. The predominantly unison C major chorus 'O Signore dal tetto natio', with which Verdi clearly wished to repeat the success of *Nabucco*'s 'Va, pensiero', is by no means unpleasing but is nowhere near as effective as its model.

Recommended recording: Cristina Deutekom (Giselda), Placido Domingo (Oronte), Ruggiero Raimondi (Pagano), with the Ambrosian Singers and the Royal Philharmonic Orchestra conducted by Lamberto Gardelli. Philips 422 420–2. Deutekom's phrasing is impressive, Domingo is in superb voice, and Raimondi's villain is well characterized. Gardelli conducts dramatically.

Ernani
opera in four acts (approximate length: 2 hours, 15 minutes)

Ernani, a bandit   *tenor*
Don Carlo, King of Spain   *baritone*
Don Ruy Gomez de Silva, grandee of Spain   *bass*
Elvira, his ward and his betrothed   *soprano*

Giovanna, her confidante   *soprano*
Don Riccardo, the King's steward   *tenor*
Jago, Silva's steward   *bass*

LIBRETTO BY FRANCESCO MARIA PIAVE, BASED ON THE PLAY *ERNANI*, BY VICTOR HUGO; TIME: 1519; PLACE: SPAIN AND AIX-LA-CHAPELLE; FIRST PERFORMED AT THE TEATRO LA FENICE, VENICE, 9 MARCH 1844

His first four operas having all been staged at La Scala, Milan, Verdi accepted a commission to compose an opera for the Teatro La Fenice in Venice. Francesco Maria Piave, a Venetian poet and friend of one of the theatre's officials, was engaged as librettist, and the subject chosen was Victor Hugo's play *Ernani*, which had first been staged in Paris in 1830. Verdi's opera *Ernani* was a success at its premiere and continued to hold the stage for many years. Though now less frequently performed, it is still to be encountered, especially in Italian opera houses.

Act I: 'Il bandito' (The Bandit). Scene i. The mountains of Aragon. Ernani, an outlawed nobleman turned bandit, has heard that Elvira, whom he loves, is about to be married against her will to her elderly guardian, Silva. Ernani and his followers plan to kidnap Elvira from Silva's castle ('Come rugiarda al cespite').

Act I, scene ii. Elvira's apartment in Silva's castle. Elvira yearns for Ernani ('Ernani, Ernani involami'). She is visited by Don Carlo (King Charles V of Spain), who is attempting to persuade her to elope with him ('Da quel dì che t'ho veduta') when Ernani, Carlo's political rival, enters by a secret door. They are about to fight when Silva suddenly bursts in, shocked to discover his bride-to-be in the company of two young men. He expresses his disillusionment with Elvira, whom he considers to have dishonoured his family ('Infelice! E tu credevi'). When the King's identity is revealed he convinces Silva that he made his visit to the castle incognito because he wished to consult Silva on a secret matter. Pretending that Ernani is one of his retinue, Carlo allows his rival to escape by the simple expedient of ordering him to depart immediately.

Act II: 'L'ospite' (The Guest). A magnificent hall in Silva's castle. It is Silva's wedding day. The celebrations are interrupted by the arrival of Ernani, fleeing from Don Carlo's soldiers disguised as a pilgrim. Discovering that Silva and Elvira are about to be married, Ernani flings off his disguise and suggests that Silva take him prisoner and hand him over to the King. Silva's strict rules of hospitality will not allow him to betray Ernani, a guest in his castle, so when the arrival of Carlo and his troops is announced he hides the bandit in a secret compartment. Carlo orders a search of the castle, but failing to find Ernani, he takes Elvira as a hostage ('Vieni meco, sol di rose').

When Carlo and his troops have left with Elvira, Silva challenges Ernani to a duel, but the bandit refuses to fight an old man. Learning that Elvira has been taken away by Carlo, Ernani surprises Silva with the information that Carlo is, in fact, their rival for the hand of Elvira. Silva agrees to allow Ernani to help him rescue Elvira, after which Ernani must die. The bandit gives Silva his hunting horn and swears that should Silva ever sound the horn, he (Ernani) will take his own life.

Act III: 'La clemenza' (Clemency). A vault in the catacombs of Aix-la-Chapelle, containing the tomb of Charlemagne. Elsewhere, the electors are about to choose a new Holy Roman Emperor. Carlo, who hopes to be chosen, enters the vault, knowing that a group conspiring against him is about to meet there. While he awaits them, he broods on the greatness and moral stature of Charlemagne and resolves to emulate him ('O de' verd' anni miei'). He hides in Charlemagne's tomb as the conspirators assemble, Silva and Ernani among them. Ernani is chosen to assassinate Carlo. Silva offers to release him from his suicide oath in return for the pleasure of killing Carlo, but Ernani refuses to give up this honour. The conspirators sing a hymn to freedom ('Si ridesti il Leon di Castiglia'). When three cannon shots announce his election as Holy Roman Emperor, Carlo emerges from Charlemagne's tomb and denounces the conspirators.

A ceremonial procession, including Elvira, enters with the crown of the Holy Roman Empire, and Carlo is proclaimed Emperor. He calls for the arrest and execution of the conspirators, but Elvira pleads with him to pardon them. He does so, and magnanimously he offers Elvira to Ernani in marriage ('Oh sommo Carlo').

Act IV: 'La maschera' (The Mask). The terrace of Don Giovanni of Aragon's palace in Saragossa, where the wedding festivities of Elvira and Ernani are in progress. The lovers sing of their happiness, but suddenly the sound of a horn is heard. A masked figure presents itself to Ernani. It is Silva, who has come to remind Ernani of his pledge and to offer him the choice of poison or a dagger. Ernani stabs himself and dies, Elvira swoons, and Silva stands gloating ('Ferma, crudele, estinguere').

Ernani marks an advance on Verdi's earlier operas in that the composer's musical characterization is more assured. It is also a work full of gloriously singable tunes. Ernani's aria 'Come rugiarda al cespite' is the first of these to be heard, and Elvira's 'Ernani, Ernani involami' in the second scene is a deservedly popular concert item, the cabaletta of which, 'Tutto sprezzo che d'Ernani', has great character and force. Silva's cavatina, 'Infelice! E tu credevi', is an impressive bass aria with an irresistibly martial cabaletta, and Carlo's splendid 'Oh de' verd' anni miei' in Act III has an orchestral postlude, a mere eight bars, which is one of those moving moments when Verdi allows his orchestra a compassionate comment on a character's situation. The trio with which the opera ends is one of great melodic and harmonic beauty.

Recommended recording: Carlo Bergonzi (Ernani), Leontyne Price (Elvira), Mario Sereni (Don Carlo), Ezio Flagello (Silva), with the RCA Italiana Opera Chorus and Orchestra, conducted by Thomas Schippers. RCA Victor GD 86503. Those great Verdians, Carlo Bergonzi and Leontyne Price, are superb, Sereni is an effective Don Carlo, and Flagello is particularly splendid as the elderly Silva. Thomas Schippers conducts with a fine sense of drama.

Attila
opera in a prologue and three acts (approximate length: 1 hour, 45 minutes)

Attila, King of the Huns　*bass*
Ezio, Roman general　*baritone*
Odabella, daughter of the Lord of Aquileia　*soprano*
Foresto, Aquileian knight　*tenor*
Uldino, Attila's slave　*tenor*
Leone, an old Roman　*bass*

LIBRETTO BY TEMISTOCLE SOLERA, BASED ON THE PLAY *ATTILA, KÖNIG DER HUN-NEN*, BY ZACHARIAS WERNER; TIME: AD 454; PLACE: ITALY; FIRST PERFORMED AT THE TEATRO LA FENICE, VENICE, 17 MARCH 1846

After *Ernani*, Verdi's next operas were *I due Foscari* (The Two Foscari), *Giovanna d'Arco* (Joan of Arc) and *Alzira*, of the last of which he is reported to have said, years later, 'Quella è propria brutta' (That one is really awful). *Alzira* was given its premiere in Naples in August 1845. Back in Milan after its first performances, Verdi found himself committed to several projects and began work first on an opera he had agreed to write for Venice, the subject chosen being *Attila, König der Hunnen*, a play by the minor German playwright Zacharias Werner (1768–1823). Verdi had earlier sketched out a draft synopsis for a libretto which he had sent to Francesco Maria Piave, the Venetian librettist with whom he had already collaborated on *Ernani* and *I due Foscari*, asking Piave to versify it. He now decided that the gentle Piave was not the right man for *Attila* and instead engaged Temistocle Solera, the librettist of *Nabucco*, *I Lombardi* and *Giovanna d'Arco*, to provide the verses.

During the composition of *Attila* Verdi became afflicted with the psychosomatic illnesses – rheumatism, gastric fever and laryngitis – that tended to accompany his creative processes. When he arrived in Venice in December 1845 to produce the opera on New Year's Eve, he had composed hardly any of it. Finally, however, *Attila* was completed, and it was given its premiere, eleven weeks later than intended, at the Teatro La Fenice in March 1846. It was a huge success. Verdi found himself feted as a hero on the first night and escorted to his hotel with flowers, music and a torchlight procession. 'The applause and calls were too much for a poor invalid,' the basically healthy thirty-two-year-old composer wrote to a friend.

Prologue, scene i. The main square of Aquileia. The town has been razed by Attila's hordes of Huns and Ostrogoths. Odabella – daughter of the Lord of Aquileia, who has been killed by Attila – has fought bravely, and she is taken into Attila's entourage, still expressing defiance ('Allor che i forti corono'). Ezio, a Roman general, proposes a pact under the terms of which he and Attila would divide Italy between them ('Tardo per gli anni, e tremulo'). Attila rejects Ezio's offer and prepares to march on Rome.

Prologue, scene ii. The Rio-Alto in the Adriatic lagoons. Foresto, a survivor from Aquileia, arrives with other refugees. He laments that his beloved Odabella is a prisoner of Attila ('Ella in poter del barbaro'), but rouses himself to exhort his followers to build, by the lagoons, a new and wonderful city (which will become Venice).

Act I, scene i. A forest near Attila's camp. Foresto arrives in disguise, but reveals his identity to Odabella and accuses her of having betrayed their cause. Odabella convinces him that she remains by Attila's side only in order to assassinate him ('Si, quello io son, ravvisami').

Act I, scene ii. Attila's tent. Awaking from a dream in which he was stopped at the gates of Rome by an old man who prophesied disaster for him ('Mentre gonfiarsi l'anima'), Attila rouses his troops for an immediate assault on Rome. They are halted by a procession led by Leone, a Roman, whom Attila recognizes as the old man of his dream. When Leone repeats the old man's words, Attila falls to the ground in terror ('No, non è sogno').

Act II, scene i. Ezio's camp outside Rome. Ezio reflects on the contrast between

Rome's present decadence and its former glory ('Dagl'immortali vertici'). He and Foresto make plans to bring about Attila's downfall at a banquet to which Attila has invited Ezio.

Act II, scene ii. The banquet in Attila's camp. Uldino, a slave bribed by Foresto, attempts to poison Attila, but is prevented by Odabella, who is determined that Attila will die by her hand alone. A grateful Attila announces that he will marry Odabella.

Act III. The forest. Ezio and Foresto make plans to ambush the Huns. When Odabella appears, Foresto again accuses her of treachery, and she pleads with him to believe her ('Te sol quest'anima'). They are interrupted by the arrival of Attila, who, surprised to discover his bride-to-be consorting with his enemies, reproaches all three of them. Odabella stabs Attila, who falls dead.

Attila may not be one of the better early Verdi operas, for its characters are morally confused ciphers, its plot is disjointed and its score is uneven. It does, however, contain several felicities, among them Odabella's ferocious aria and cabaletta in the Prologue; the second scene of Act I, in Attila's camp, in which Attila's dream is re-enacted in reality; Ezio's suavely elegant aria in Act II; and the elegiac trio, 'Te sol quest'anima', in the brief final act. This is an opera that is beginning to return to the repertoire. A revival in 2002 at the Royal Opera House, Covent Garden, of a ten-year-old production was highly acclaimed.

Recommended recording: Samuel Ramey (Attila), Cheryl Studer (Odabella), Neil Shicoff (Foresto), Giorgio Zancanaro (Ezio), with the Chorus and Orchestra of La Scala, Milan, conducted by Riccardo Muti. EMI CDS7 499522–2. Ramey is a firm and resolute Attila, Cheryl Studer's Odabella is beautifully sung, with sensitive phrasing, and Zancanaro makes a powerful Ezio. Muti, an ideal Verdi conductor, secures exciting playing from his orchestra.

Macbeth
opera in four acts (approximate length: 2 hours, 30 minutes)

Macbeth, a general in King Duncan's army   *baritone*
Banquo, another general   *bass*
Lady Macbeth   *soprano*
Macduff, a Scottish nobleman   *tenor*
Malcolm, King Duncan's son   *tenor*

Gentlewoman, attendant on Lady Macbeth   *mezzo-soprano*
A Doctor   *bass*

LIBRETTO BY FRANCESCO MARIA PIAVE, BASED ON SHAKESPEARE'S PLAY *MACBETH*;
TIME: 1040; PLACE: SCOTLAND AND JUST OVER THE ENGLISH BORDER; FIRST PER-
FORMED AT THE TEATRO DELLA PERGOLA, FLORENCE, 14 MARCH 1847

After the premiere of *Attila* in March 1846, Verdi succumbed to that nervous
exhaustion to which his temperament rendered him peculiarly vulnerable.
At the insistence of his doctors he took six months' complete rest before directing
his attention once again to his operatic commitments. Having agreed to write
operas for London and Florence, he began work on them both, more or less
simultaneously, abandoning *I masnadieri*, the London opera, when it was half-
finished, to concentrate on the completion of *Macbeth* for Florence.

Piave's libretto for *Macbeth* is based on Count Andrea Maffei's prose translation
of Shakespeare's play. Verdi composed the opera more slowly than had been his
custom, concerning himself in advance with every aspect of the work's eventual
production at the Teatro della Pergola. He even wrote to London to discover how
the appearance of Banquo's ghost was usually staged, and, as he told the Florence
impresario Alessandro Lanari, he also 'consulted prominent scholars as to period
and costumes'. Verdi took pains to ensure that his *Macbeth* would be staged with the
greatest possible dramatic effect. He was as much concerned about his performers'
acting ability as about their singing. A letter he wrote several months after the Florence premiere to Salvatore Cammarano, who was rehearsing a Naples production
of the opera, comments on Cammarano's choice of soprano for Lady Macbeth:

> Madame Tadolini is a handsome woman with a beautiul face, and I want
> Lady Macbeth to be ugly and evil. Madame Tadolini sings to perfection, and
> I don't want Lady Macbeth to sing at all. Madame Tadolini has a wonderful
> voice, clear, flexible and strong, while Lady Macbeth's voice should be hard,
> stifled and dark. Madame Tadolini has the voice of an angel, and Lady
> Macbeth's should be that of a devil . . .

In Florence *Macbeth* was rehearsed assiduously, and its premiere on 14 March
1847 was a huge success, with Verdi taking thirty-eight curtain calls. Soon it was
being staged throughout Italy and the whole of Europe, and eventually as far
afield as Havana, Rio de Janeiro and Sydney. It reached New York in 1850 and
Manchester in 1860, but curiously was not performed at the Royal Opera House,
Covent Garden, until 1960.

Eighteen years after *Macbeth*'s premiere the opera was staged in Paris in a French translation, and Verdi took the opportunity to revise his score, adding the obligatory ballet sequence for Paris. It is this 1865 revision that is most frequently performed today (though usually in Italian and without the ballet).

Act I, scene i. A wood. A coven of witches greets Macbeth and Banquo with the prophecy that Banquo will beget kings, though he himself will not reign, and that Macbeth will become Thane of Cawdor and also King of Scotland. Messengers arrive with the news that the Thane of Cawdor has been arrested on a charge of treason, and that his lands and title have been bestowed by King Duncan upon Macbeth. Macbeth's ambition is stirred ('Due vaticini compiuti or sono'). As he and Banquo leave, the witches reappear ('S'allontanarono').

Act I, scene ii. A room in Macbeth's castle at Inverness. Lady Macbeth reads a letter from her husband in which he tells her of the strange circumstances of his advancement, and she hopes that he will prove ruthless enough to attain his ambitions ('Vieni, t'affretta'). When a messenger announces that King Duncan will be accompanying Macbeth to the castle, she calls on the spirits of darkness to fill her 'from the crown to the toe, top full of direst cruelty' ('Or tutti sorgete, ministri infernali'). Macbeth arrives, and he and Lady Macbeth implicitly agree that Duncan must die.

After King Duncan has been greeted and has retired to his quarters, Macbeth imagines he sees a dagger hovering before his eyes, leading him on ('Mi si affacia un pugnal?'). He goes off to murder Duncan. When he returns, with a bloodstained dagger in his hand, he is already racked with guilt. Lady Macbeth has to seize the dagger from him and return it to Duncan's room to incriminate the guards ('Fatal mia donna, un murmure'). Banquo and Macduff arrive to attend upon the King, and the murder is discovered ('Schiudi, inferno, la bocca ed inghiotti').

Act II, scene i. A room in the castle. Macbeth's conscience troubles him, but Lady Macbeth reminds him that Duncan's son, Malcolm, has fled to England, which is regarded by all as proof of his guilt. However, Banquo and his son Fleance must be killed, in order to frustrate the witches' prophecy regarding Banquo. Macbeth goes off to arrange the assassination of Banquo and his son, while Lady Macbeth exults at having attained the throne ('La luce langue').

Act II, scene ii. The park of the castle. As Banquo and Fleance make their way towards the castle ('Come dal ciel precipita'), they are attacked by assassins hired by Macbeth. Banquo is killed, but Fleance escapes.

Act II, scene iii. The banqueting hall of the castle. Lady Macbeth leads the guests in a drinking song ('Si colmi il calice'), and an assassin surreptitiously reports to

Macbeth. As Macbeth rejoins the banquet, he is appalled to see the ghost of Banquo sitting in his chair. He breaks out in terror, is calmed by Lady Macbeth, but collapses again as the ghost reappears to him. While the guests speculate on his strange outbursts, Macbeth determines to consult the witches.

Act III. The witches' cave. The witches are brewing potions and casting spells ('Tre volte miagola') when Macbeth arrives to ask about his future. They conjure up apparitions which warn him to beware of Macduff, but they assure him that he cannot be harmed by anyone born of woman, and that he will never be conquered until 'Great Birnham Wood to high Dunsinane Hill shall come against him'. When Macbeth asks if Banquo's issue will ever reign, a silent parade of eight kings appears, the last of whom is Banquo carrying a mirror and pointing at the others as though to indicate that they are his heirs. Macbeth swoons. As he regains his senses, Lady Macbeth arrives, and they resolve to exterminate all who stand in their way ('Ora di morte').

Act IV, scene i. A deserted landscape, just over the English border. Scottish exiles lament the condition of their country ('Patria oppressa!'), Macduff reflects bitterly on the murder of his wife and children ('Ah, la paterna mano'), and Malcolm arrives with a troop of English soldiers. Macduff and Malcolm lead their forces against Macbeth's army, Malcolm first ordering his soldiers to cut branches from the trees of nearby Birnham Wood and carry them as camouflage ('La patria tradita').

Act IV, scene ii. A hall in Macbeth's castle. Watched by a Doctor and a Gentlewoman, Lady Macbeth walks and talks in her sleep, recalling the murders she and Macbeth have committed ('Una macchia è qui tuttora').

Act IV, scene iii. A room in the castle. Macbeth broods on the course of events and realizes that he has lost for ever the compassion, love and respect of his fellows ('Pietà, rispetto, amore'). He is told that Lady Macbeth has died, but his feelings by now are dulled. Soldiers enter to announce that Birnham Wood is on the move, and he rouses himself to fight. As he rushes off, the scene changes to a battlefield. The sight of Birnham Wood appearing to move towards Dunsinane is daunting enough, but when Macduff, confronting Macbeth, reveals that he (Macduff) was 'from his mother's womb untimely ripped', Macbeth realizes that his end has come. They fight, and Macbeth is killed. The opera ends with a hymn of victory ('Macbeth, Macbeth ov' è?').

Verdi's *Macbeth* is worthy to stand beside Shakespeare's. It is in this, the earliest of his three great Shakespeare operas, that Verdi's art takes an immense leap, away from the conventional operatic demands of his time, and towards dramatic truth and a musical style combining psychological depth with a continuing abundance of that melodic gift that was never to desert him. Lady Macbeth's Act I aria and cabaletta are close to Shakespeare in mood, but the particular point in the score where one can hear Verdi lifting Italian opera out of its conventions is reached with the duet 'Fatal mia donna, un murmure', in which Lady Macbeth's vocal line abounds in nagging staccato while Macbeth's is confined to a desperately swelling legato. Lady Macbeth's 'La luce langue' and her sleepwalking scene are superb pieces of musical characterization, and Macbeth's 'Pietà, rispetto, amore' is moving in its almost serene acceptance of despair.

Recommended recording: Leonard Warren (Macbeth), Leonie Rysanek (Lady Macbeth), Carlo Bergonzi (Macduff), with the Metropolitan Opera Chorus and Orchestra, conducted by Erich Leinsdorf. RCA Victor GD84516. The great Viennese soprano Leonie Rysanek is a magnificent Lady Macbeth, with the American Leonard Warren fully her equal as Macbeth. Carlo Bergonzi is a stylish Macduff, and Erich Leinsdorf conducts a brisk, strongly dramatic account of Verdi's marvellous score.

I masnadieri
(The Brigands)
opera in four acts (approximate length: 2 hours, 15 minutes)

Massimiliano, Count Moor   *bass*
Carlo   *tenor* ⎤
               ⎬ his sons
Francesco   *baritone* ⎦
Amalia, orphan, and niece of the Count   *soprano*
Arminio, a servant of the Moor family   *tenor*
Moser, a clergyman   *bass*

LIBRETTO BY COUNT ANDREA MAFFEI, BASED ON THE PLAY *DIE RÄUBER*, BY FRIEDRICH VON SCHILLER; TIME: THE BEGINNING OF THE EIGHTEENTH CENTURY; PLACE: GERMANY; FIRST PERFORMED AT HER MAJESTY'S THEATRE, LONDON, 22 JULY 1847

As soon as *Macbeth* had been successfully launched in Florence in March 1847, Verdi resumed work on *I masnadieri*, the opera he had agreed to write for London and which he had abandoned when half-finished in order to concentrate on *Macbeth*. Accompanied by his young pupil and amanuensis Emanuele Muzio, he travelled to London, where he completed the opera after he had met the singers engaged to appear in it. Rehearsals proceeded amicably, and the composer was especially pleased with the famous 'Swedish nightingale' Jenny Lind, who was to sing the leading soprano role. Verdi conducted the first performance, at Her Majesty's Theatre, which was attended by Queen Victoria and Prince Albert and was received with great enthusiasm. According to Muzio, 'the Maestro was cheered, called onto the stage, both alone and with the singers, and pelted with flowers. All you could hear was "Evviva Verdi! Bietifol [beautiful]!"'

Die Räuber, on which *I masnadieri* is based, is Schiller's earliest play, a long, sprawling work written in an extraordinary prose that gathers up such diverse influences as those of Goethe, the Bible and demotic German speech into a new and heady style of its own. The plot of the opera is a simplified version of that of the play.

Carlo, son of Count Moor, from whose house he has been banished through the intrigue of his brother Francesco, has formed a band of brigands. Carlo's betrothed, Amalia, repulses Francesco's advances and is reunited with Carlo, who rescues his father from Francesco, who imprisoned him. Carlo kills his evil brother. When Carlo's followers, the band of brigands whom he leads, refuse to release him from his oath of loyalty to them, Carlo stabs Amalia to death rather than see her dishonoured by a life with him and the bandits. He then rushes off with a cry of 'Ora al patibolo!' (And now to the gallows).

In a return to its composer's pre-*Macbeth* style, *I masnadieri* displays all the energy and creative vitality of the early Verdi. The opera's individuality and distinction lie to a great extent in the tension between its darkly romantic arias, usually at moderate tempos, and its exciting cabalettas. It succeeds by virtue of its combination of tunefulness and vigour. Its orchestration is not uninteresting, particularly in the significant use Verdi makes of his woodwind instruments, but its mood of sombre violence is what really distinguishes *I masnadieri*. It is not frequently performed nowadays, but Joan Sutherland undertook Jenny Lind's role of Amalia with great success in San Diego in 1984, since when there have been occasional performances in other parts of the world.

Recommended recording: Montserrat Caballé (Amalia), Carlo Bergonzi (Carlo), Piero Cappuccilli (Francesco), with the Ambrosian Singers and the New Philharmonia Orchestra, conducted by Lamberto Gardelli. Philips 422 423–2. Splendid principal singers, with Gardelli a sympathetic conductor.

Luisa Miller

opera in three acts (approximate length: 2 hours, 15 minutes)

Luisa Miller   *soprano*
Miller, her father, a retired soldier   *baritone*
Count Walter   *bass*
Rodolfo, his son, alias Carlo   *tenor*
Federica, Duchess of Ostheim, the Count's niece   *mezzo-soprano*
Wurm, in the employ of the Count   *bass*
Laura, a village girl   *mezzo-soprano*
A Peasant   *tenor*

LIBRETTO BY SALVATORE CAMMARANO, BASED ON THE PLAY *KABALE UND LIEBE*, BY
FRIEDRICH VON SCHILLER; TIME: THE EARLY SEVENTEENTH CENTURY; PLACE: A
VILLAGE IN THE TYROL; FIRST PERFORMED AT THE TEATRO SAN CARLO, NAPLES, 8
DECEMBER 1849

After *I masnadieri* Verdi dashed off quickly an opera he had agreed to provide
for the publisher Francesco Lucca. This was *Il corsaro*, its libretto by Piave
based on *The Corsair*, a poem by Byron. Emanuele Muzio was sent by Verdi to
Trieste to produce and conduct the opera, whose premiere in October 1848 the
composer himself did not attend. When Salvatore Cammarano, the librettist of
Verdi's *Alzira*, suggested an idea for a propaganda piece urging Italy to unite and
expel the Austrians, Verdi responded positively. The result was *La battaglia di
Legnano* (January 1849), which roused its first Roman audiences to a frenzy of
enthusiasm. However, there were but few productions in other Italian towns, and
the opera is seldom performed nowadays.

After *La battaglia di Legnano*, Verdi and Cammarano collaborated again some
months later on the composer's next opera, for the Teatro San Carlo, Naples. Cammarano wrote a libretto based on Schiller's play *Kabale und Liebe*, and he and Verdi
decided to call the opera *Luisa Miller*, after Schiller's heroine. By the beginning of
October 1849 the opera was complete in vocal score but had still to be orchestrated. When Verdi arrived in Naples he discovered that the Teatro San Carlo was
experiencing financial difficulties and could not pay him the first instalment of
his fee, which was due. He threatened to dissolve the contract if the management
of the theatre did not immediately deposit with a third party the entire sum due
to him. The San Carlo management then threatened to have the composer
arrested if he attempted to leave Naples without handing over his score. Verdi

responded by declaring that he would take himself and his opera on board one of the French warships in the Bay of Naples and demand that France protect him.

Somehow the situation resolved itself, peace of a kind was restored between Verdi and the Teatro San Carlo, and *Luisa Miller*, by now orchestrated, went into rehearsal. The opera was a huge success at its premiere on 8 December, but Verdi left the city five days later, vowing never again to compose an opera for Naples. (Nor did he, although he entered into negotiations with the theatre again, on more than one occasion.)

Cammarano's well-constructed three-act libretto is even further removed from Schiller's five-act play than an opera libretto usually is from its source. Schiller's title, *Kabale und Liebe* (Intrigue and Love), had been carefully chosen, for his play contrasts idealism and expediency, selfless Romanticism and self-interested practicality. Schiller's proposition is that love does not always triumph over all obstacles, and that the machinery of political intrigue is more than a match for the spirituality of romantic feeling. In reducing the play to a manageable length for opera, Cammarano made most of his cuts in Schiller's scenes of intrigue rather than in those of love. He also dispensed with two of the play's most important characters, transferred the action from a princely court to a Tyrolean village, and substituted a local lord of the manor for Schiller's Prime Minister. Nevertheless, although it is inadequate as an adaptation of Schiller's fascinating play, Cammarano's libretto enabled Verdi to compose an unusual opera – the composer's first attempt to portray on the stage, in the household of Miller and his daughter Luisa, something of the world of bourgeois respectability, and thus a step along the path to *La traviata*.

Act I: 'L'amore' (Love). Scene i. The village square. On her birthday, her friend Laura and the other villagers greet Luisa, the daughter of Miller, a retired and widowed soldier. Luisa sings of her love for Carlo, a young stranger who has recently arrived in the village with the new Count ('Lo vidi, e il primo palpito il cor sentì d'amore'), while her father attempts to warn her against him. Carlo emerges from the crowd, and the young lovers express their happiness ('T'amo d'amor ch'esprimere'). When all have gone off to the church in response to the pealing of its bells, Luisa's father is approached by Wurm, an employee of Count Walter. Wurm is in love with Luisa and has the support of the Count, but Miller insists that he will not coerce his daughter into marriage against her will ('Sacra la scelta è d'un consorte'). The jealous Wurm reveals to Miller that Luisa's beloved Carlo is, in fact, none other than the Count's son Rodolfo ('Ah! Fu giusto il mio sospetto!').

Act I, scene ii. A room in Count Walter's castle. Told by Wurm of his son's involvement with Luisa Miller, Count Walter gives vent to his confused paternal feelings ('Il mio sangue, la vita darei'). He sends for Rodolfo and informs him that he must marry his cousin and childhood friend, the widowed Federica, Duchess of Ostheim. Left alone with Federica, Rodolfo places himself at her mercy, confessing his love for Luisa. Federica, however, loves Rodolfo ('Dall' aule raggianti di vano splendor') and will be pitiless towards any rival ('Deh! La parola amara').

Act I, scene iii. A room in Miller's house. Miller tells Luisa the truth about 'Carlo'. When Rodolfo arrives, he swears that he loves Luisa and wants to marry her. Miller is convinced of the youth's sincerity, but fears the consequences of his defying his father. Count Walter himself enters, insults Luisa and is angrily challenged by her father. The Count has Miller and Luisa arrested, but Rodolfo murmurs privately to his father that unless they are released he will inform the world how his father became Count Walter. Luisa and Miller are set free.

Act II: 'L'intrigo' (Intrigue). Scene i. A room in Miller's house. Villagers tell Luisa that they have seen her father being dragged in chains to the Count's castle. Wurm enters and informs Luisa that her father will be sentenced to death unless she writes Wurm a letter swearing that she loves him and that her only interest in Rodolfo has been to secure an advantageous match ('Tu puniscimi, o Signore'). Luisa has no alternative but to write as directed, and to agree to repeat before the Count and Federica that she loves only Wurm ('A brani, a brani, o perfido').

Act II, scene ii. A room in Count Walter's castle. The Count and Wurm recall how, years previously, they killed the Count's cousin to enable Walter to inherit the title. The Count informs Wurm that Rodolfo knows of this and is threatening to reveal it ('L'alto retaggio non ho bramato'). Federica enters, and Luisa is brought in to confirm that she loves Wurm and cares nothing for Rodolfo.

Act II, scene iii. The gardens of the castle. Rodolfo has been shown Luisa's letter to Wurm, and he recalls sadly his past happiness with her ('Quando le sere al placido'). When Wurm enters, Rodolfo challenges him to a duel, but the frightened Wurm fires his pistol in the air, which brings the Count and servants rushing to the scene. Bitterly, Rodolfo agrees to marry Federica ('L'ara o l'avello apprestami').

Act III: 'Il veleno' (Poison). A room in Miller's house. Luisa resolves to kill herself ('La tomba è un letto'), but then relents and agrees to stay with her father for the rest of his life ('Andrem, raminghi e poveri'). Rodolfo enters, brandishing Luisa's letter to Wurm. He tricks Luisa into drinking poison with him, and when the church bells sound for his imminent wedding he informs her that they are both about to die. In the lovers' last moments Luisa tells Rodolfo the truth, and he is overcome with remorse and despair. Miller returns in time to embrace his dying daughter ('Padre ricevi l'estremo addio'). The Count and Wurm arrive as Luisa dies, and Rodolfo runs his sword through Wurm before also falling lifeless to the ground.

Luisa Miller, a transitional work between the youthful excitement of Verdi's earlier operas and the maturer voice that speaks decisively from *Rigoletto* onwards, could be said to initiate the composer's second or middle-period style. The transition occurs between Acts II and III of *Luisa Miller*, whose first two acts still inhabit, to some extent, the world of Bellini and Donizetti, a world to which Verdi seems to bid a reluctant farewell in Rodolfo's nostalgic 'Quando le sere al placido' before going on to anticipate, in the intimate, domestic tone of Act III, the atmosphere and musical style of *La traviata*. Highlights of *Luisa Miller*, in addition to Rodolfo's aria, include Luisa's entrance aria, which uses coloratura not simply as an embellishment but as a significant form of expression; her affecting 'Tu puniscimi, o Signore' in Act II; and the wonderfully expressive trio finale of Act III ('Padre ricevi l'estremo addio').

Recommended recording: Montserrat Caballé (Luisa), Luciano Pavarotti (Rodolfo), Sherrill Milnes (Miller), with the London Opera Chorus and National Philharmonic Orchestra, conducted by Peter Maag. Decca 417 420–2. Caballe is ideally cast as the gentle Luisa, Pavarotti does full justice to the famous aria 'Quando le sere al placido', Milnes is convincing as Luisa's father, and Peter Maag conducts strongly.

Stiffelio
opera in three acts (approximate length: 1 hour, 45 minutes)

Stiffelio, evangelical minister   *tenor*
Lina, his wife   *soprano*
Stankar, Lina's father   *baritone*
Raffaele, a nobleman   *tenor*
Jorg, an elderly minister   *bass*

LIBRETTO BY FRANCESCO MARIA PIAVE, BASED ON THE PLAY *LE PASTEUR*, BY ÉMILE SOUVESTRE AND EUGÈNE BOURGEOIS; TIME: THE BEGINNING OF THE NINETEENTH CENTURY; PLACE: GERMANY; FIRST PERFORMED AT THE TEATRO GRANDE, TRIESTE, 16 NOVEMBER 1850

Verdi agreed to provide his publisher Ricordi with a new opera for production in the autumn of 1850 in any one of the leading Italian theatres 'except La Scala, Milan', with whose management the composer had been seriously displeased for some years. Piave, his preferred librettist, suggested as a subject a French play, *Le Pasteur*, which Piave had seen in Italian translation as *Stiffelio*. Verdi accepted his suggestion, and their opera was produced in Trieste in November 1850.

Stiffelio met with censorship difficulties because of its plot involving a Protestant clergyman and his adulterous wife. When it was subsequently staged in a few other Italian towns it was retitled *Guglielmo Wellingrode*, its leading character now no longer a clergyman but the fifteenth-century Prime Minister of a German principality. In 1857 the opera had a new lease of life as *Aroldo*, with its leading character, Aroldo, a thirteenth-century English crusader. Minor alterations were made to the music of *Stiffelio*, except for the final scene, which was completely rewritten. Until the mid-twentieth century it was as *Aroldo* rather than as *Stiffelio* that the opera survived. However, a production of *Stiffelio* in Parma in 1968 proved the opera to be perfectly viable, and indeed preferable, in its original form.

Act I. While Stiffelio is abroad, preaching, his wife Lina has an affair with Raffaele. When Stiffelio returns home, Lina's father, Stankar, prevents his daughter from confessing her adultery, which he considers would dishonour the family. Instead, Stankar challenges Raffaele to a duel.

Act II. The duel is interrupted by Stiffelio, who, when he learns the cause of it, is about to fight Raffaele himself when he is stopped by the sound of singing from the nearby church and the appearance of Jorg, an elderly minister, who calls on him to pardon his wife.

Act III. Stiffelio offers Lina a divorce, to enable her to marry Raffaele. However, Stankar kills Raffaele, to avenge the honour of his family. In the church, Stiffelio enters the pulpit, opens his Bible at the story of the woman taken in adultery, and is moved to forgive Lina.

Stiffelio marks another step on the domestic path leading from *Luisa Miller* to *La traviata*. The music of its Act I finale achieves an almost *Otello*-like intensity, and other highlights include Lina's aria, 'Ah! Dagli scanni eterei', at the beginning of Act II; the quartet, 'Ah no, è impossibile', in the same act, prefiguring the famous *Rigoletto* quartet; and Stankar's aria 'Lina, pensai che un angelo', with its imaginative cabaletta, 'Oh gioia inesprimibile', in which Lina's father whispers his anticipation of vengeance, breathlessly overcome with joy, before suddenly producing the final bars *tutta forza*.

Recommended recording: Sylvia Sass (Lina), José Carreras (Stiffelio), Matteo Manuguerra (Stankar), with the Austrian Radio Chorus and Orchestra, conducted by Lamberto Gardelli. Phillips 422 432–2.

Rigoletto
opera in three acts (approximate length: 2 hours)

The Duke of Mantua, alias Gualtier Maldè   *tenor*
Rigoletto, his jester, a hunchback   *baritone*
Sparafucile, a professional assassin   *bass*
Count Monterone   *baritone*
Marullo, a courtier   *baritone*
Borsa, a courtier   *tenor*
Count Ceprano   *bass*
Gilda, Rigoletto's daughter   *soprano*
Giovanna, her nurse   *mezzo-soprano*
Maddalena, Sparafucile's sister   *contralto*
Countess Ceprano   *mezzo-soprano*

LIBRETTO BY FRANCESCO MARIA PIAVE, BASED ON THE PLAY *LE ROI S'AMUSE*, BY VICTOR HUGO; TIME: THE SIXTEENTH CENTURY; PLACE: MANTUA; FIRST PERFORMED AT THE TEATRO LA FENICE, VENICE, 11 MARCH 1851

In March 1850 Verdi accepted a commission to compose an opera for performance in the following year at the Teatro La Fenice in Venice. The subject, suggested by Verdi to the Venice-based librettist Francesco Maria Piave, was Victor Hugo's play *Le Roi s'amuse*, and Verdi told Piave that he thought the character of Triboulet, the court jester, 'one of the greatest creations to be found in the theatre of all countries and all times'. After the first performances of *Stiffelio* in Trieste in November, Verdi made his way to Venice with Piave's draft libretto of their opera in order to obtain formal approval from the censorship authority for *La maledizione* (The Curse), which was at this stage the working title of the opera that was to become *Triboletto* and in due course *Rigoletto* (from the French *rigoler*, to make fun of).

Eventually, after a number of compromises had been agreed, the General Director of Public Order in Venice gave his approval, Piave finished his libretto quickly and Verdi proceeded to compose the opera. He had in fact written much of it some months earlier, but throughout January of the new year he bullied Piave, demanding here some verses in a decasyllabic metre, there 'six fine lines which express the joy of revenge', and calling for a hendecasyllable in a piece of tenor recitative. On 5 February, Verdi was able to inform Piave that the work was now complete. As usual, he planned to orchestrate it during the rehearsal period, estimating that this would take him five or six days. On 19 February he arrived in Venice and began to rehearse *Rigoletto*, whose first performance he conducted at La Fenice on 11 March 1851. It was a huge success in Venice and has remained one of Verdi's most popular operas.

Act I, scene i. A magnificent hall of the ducal palace in Mantua. An elegant assembly of courtiers and ladies moves through the hall and adjacent rooms, from one of which comes the sound of music for dancing. The Duke of Mantua tells Borsa, one of his courtiers, of his lust for a beautiful young woman he has seen in church. Then, admiring Count Ceprano's wife, he sings of his delight in the beauty of women and of the desirability of making love to as many of them as possible ('Questa o quella'). When the Duke's flirtatious dance with Countess Ceprano ends with their wandering off into another room, the hunchbacked court jester Rigoletto mocks the enraged but helpless Ceprano. The other courtiers are amused when one of their number, Marullo, arrives with the latest gossip, which is that Rigoletto is keeping a young mistress at his house. Rigoletto is so free with his gibes, and so sure of the Duke's protection, that Ceprano decides with the aid of his fellow courtiers to punish the jester. When Count Monterone forces his way into the assembly to denounce the Duke for having seduced his daughter, he is ridiculed by Rigoletto. Monterone, as he is placed under arrest, responds by placing a father's curse not only on the Duke but also on the now terrified jester.

Act I, scene ii. The end of a blind alley, revealing both the courtyard of Rigoletto's house and the lane on the other side of its wall. On his way home, Rigoletto broods on Monterone's curse. A man steps out from the shadows, giving his name as Sparafucile and offering his services as a hired assassin. Rigoletto dismisses him, reflecting that his own tongue is as sharp as any murderer's dagger ('Pari siamo!'). He enters his courtyard to be greeted by his daughter Gilda, who comes out of the house and rushes into his arms. When she questions him about her long-dead mother, Rigoletto nostalgically describes his wife as an angel ('Deh, non parlare al misero'), adding that Gilda is now everything to him. But he will not reveal to her his name, nor will he allow her to leave the house except to go to church. He warns Gilda's nurse Giovanna to admit no one into the house ('Veglia, o donna, questo fiore').

Hearing a noise at the gate, Rigoletto runs out to the street to investigate, and then he leaves. At the same moment, the Duke slips into the courtyard, unnoticed by Gilda, just as she is confessing to Giovanna that she is in love with the young man who follows them to church. Waving Giovanna away, the Duke tells Gilda that he returns her love ('E il sol dell'anima'), and that he is a penniless student named Gualtier Maldè. At the sound of footsteps in the lane (where Ceprano and Borsa are now lurking with the rest of the courtiers), Gilda begs him to leave, and they exchange excited farewells ('Addio, addio, speranza ed anima').

Repeating the young man's name to herself, Gilda goes up to bed ('Caro nome'). Meanwhile, the courtiers stop Rigoletto as he is returning to the house and ask him to help them abduct the Countess Ceprano from Ceprano's house on the other side of the lane. The jester is tricked into wearing a blindfold and holding a ladder against his own garden wall. The courtiers break into his house ('Zitti, zitti') and carry off Gilda. Rigoletto discovers the deception only when he hears his daughter's cry for help. Tearing off the blindfold, he rushes into his house, only to discover that Gilda is not there. Distraught, he remembers Monterone's curse.

Act II. A drawing-room in the ducal palace. The Duke is deeply distressed over the kidnapping of Gilda ('Parmi veder le lagrime'). When his courtiers return, telling him that it is they who have taken her and that she is now in his chamber, he rushes off to the conquest ('Possente amor mi chiama'). Rigoletto enters, pretending indifference, but surreptitiously searching for any evidence of Gilda's whereabouts. Though the courtiers are astonished to learn that she is his daughter, they bar his way. He lashes out at their cruelty ('Cortigiani, vil razza dannata'), but when they continue to restrain him he begs, without success, for their pity.

Suddenly Gilda appears, running in shame to her father. Rigoletto drives the courtiers out of the room and, alone with him, Gilda tells her father that she fell in love with the young man she saw at church, that he, the Duke, courted her in the guise of a student, and that she was abducted ('Tutte le feste al tempio'). When Monterone crosses the room under guard on his way to prison, Rigoletto declares that he will avenge both him and the Duke ('Sì, vendetta, tremenda vendetta'), although Gilda begs her father not to harm the Duke.

Act III. The right bank of the River Mincio. On one side is a two-storeyed house, through the frontage of which one can glimpse the inside of a rustic inn.

It is late at night. Rigoletto and Gilda wait outside the inn where Sparafucile lives with Maddalena, his sister and accomplice. When Gilda insists that she still loves the Duke, Rigoletto makes her look through an opening in the wall. She watches in disbelief as the Duke, disguised as a soldier, laughs at the fickleness of women ('La donna è mobile') and makes love to Maddalena.

Rigoletto cautions his broken-hearted daughter, as Maddalena flirts with the amorous Duke ('Bella figlia dell'amore'). Ordering Gilda to leave for Verona, but not before going home and dressing in male attire for the journey, Rigoletto then hires Sparafucile to murder the Duke. As Rigoletto leaves, a storm breaks out. Gilda, now dressed as a young man, returns in time to overhear Maddalena urging her brother to spare the stranger and kill Rigoletto instead. The assassin's professional honour will not allow him to murder his client, but he agrees to substitute the next person who comes to the inn. Gilda, resolved to sacrifice herself for the Duke, knocks at the door and is immediately stabbed.

As the storm subsides, Rigoletto returns to claim his victim, only to hear the Duke's voice singing in the distance. Frantically opening the sack in which Sparafucile has delivered the body to him, he finds his daughter. Gilda dies, asking her father's forgiveness ('Lassù in cielo'), and Rigoletto cries out that Monterone's curse has been fulfilled.

A use of the orchestra as eloquent and skilful as that of Berlioz, brilliant delineation of the minor characters, in particular Sparafucile, Maddalena and Monterone, a prodigality of melodic invention, an advance towards integral structure, and remarkable psychological insight into character motivation: these are a few of the attributes that combine to make *Rigoletto* one of the most popular of operas, as well as one of the finest musically and dramatically. A resilient work, it triumphantly survives non-production, determinedly wrong-headed production, and the vain foibles of musically illiterate singers. Conversely, it offers superb opportunities to the intelligent interpreter of its title role, so memorably 'burnt into music by Verdi', as George Bernard Shaw observed. The role, indeed the entire opera, is infused with a humanity that puts one in mind of Mozart, and Tito Gobbi's mid-twentieth-century interpretation of the role has not yet been surpassed.

In *Rigoletto* Verdi's working unit is no longer the aria, but the scene. The backbone of the opera is the series of magnificent duets between Rigoletto and Gilda, Rigoletto and Sparafucile, and Gilda and the Duke, but it is the scene that is the formal unit. The scene may contain arias, duets, recitatives and choruses, but the length and position of these depend on the structure of the entire scene, whereas in the past the scene had merely been the total of the independent units of aria, recitative, cabaletta and ensemble contained within it. However, to over-emphasize the technical innovation in *Rigoletto* is to do the opera an injustice. What is most remarkable about the work is its sustained level of inspiration.

The opera's highlights are too many to list, among them the rakish rhythm of the Duke's 'Questa o quella', a forerunner of the swing music of the 1920s; the atmospheric scene between Rigoletto and Sparafucile in Act I, scene ii, set as vividly by clarinet, bassoon and lower strings as by any scenic designer; Rigo-letto's 'Pari siamo', equal in stature to one of Hamlet's soliloquies, and an example of Verdi's extraordinary ability to harness his psychological insight to his melodic genius; Gilda's 'Caro nome', not only an enchanting aria but also completely in character, its unique quality of virginal young love underlined by the delicacy of the accompaniment; Rigoletto's 'Cortigiani, vil razza dannata', both highly dra-matic and, in its second section with cello obbligato, intensely moving; and the vulgar, catchy tune of 'La donna è mobile'. The quartet 'Bella figlia dell'amore' is one of the highlights not only of *Rigoletto* but also of all Italian opera. The four characters voice their widely differing feelings in themes which, each individually suitable and distinct, blend into a beautiful and harmonious whole. When Victor Hugo, author of the play on which the opera is based, saw *Rigoletto* in Paris in 1857, he exclaimed of the quartet: 'If I could only make four characters in my plays speak at the same time, and have the audience grasp the words and the senti-ments, I would obtain the very same effect.' During rehearsals, Verdi told his Rigoletto, the baritone Felice Varesi, that he never expected to compose anything better than the quartet. In a sense, he was right. No one could do better; Verdi went on to do differently.

Recommended recording: Tito Gobbi (Rigoletto), Maria Callas (Gilda), Giuseppe di Stefano (Duke of Mantua), with the Chorus and Orchestra of La Scala, Milan, conducted by Tullio Serafin. EMI CDS 7 47469 8. Recorded as long ago as 1955, this performance is conducted lovingly and masterfully by Serafin. Tito Gobbi's Rigoletto is powerful and moving, and although her voice is not ideally suited to the role of Gilda, Maria Callas gives one of her most intelligent dramatic performances. Giuseppe di Stefano is an exciting Duke.

Il trovatore

(The Troubador)

opera in four acts (approximate length: 2 hours, 15 minutes)

Count di Luna, a young nobleman of Aragon   *baritone*
Ferrando, captain in the Count's army   *bass*
Manrico, an officer in the Prince of Vizcaya's forces   *tenor*
Leonora, lady-in-waiting to the Princess of Aragon   *soprano*
Ines, her confidante   *soprano*
Azucena, a Vizcayan gypsy woman   *mezzo-soprano*
Ruiz, a soldier under Manrico's command   *tenor*

LIBRETTO BY SALVATORE CAMMARANO, COMPLETED BY LEONE EMANUELE
BARDARE, BASED ON THE PLAY *EL TROVADOR*, BY ANTONIO GARCÍA GUTIÉRREZ;
TIME: THE FIFTEENTH CENTURY; PLACE: THE PROVINCES OF VIZCAYA AND ARAGON
IN NORTHERN SPAIN; FIRST PERFORMED AT THE TEATRO APOLLO, ROME, 19
JANUARY 1853

Within days of the premiere of *Rigoletto* Verdi was back at home in Busseto giving thought to his next opera. He and Salvatore Cammarano had been in correspondence about the choice of subject, and Verdi had proposed *El trovador*, a play by the Spanish playwright Antonio García Gutiérrez. Cammarano took his time over responding, and then he expressed certain doubts about the play, whose characters he thought implausible. Nevertheless, in due course he produced the outline of a libretto, which the composer found unsatisfactory, telling Cammarano that it would be preferable to abandon the idea of *El trovador* if in their opera they could not retain 'all the novel and bizarre characteristics' of the play. He sent the librettist his own suggestions for a synopsis.

Verdi and Cammarano decided to persevere with *El trovador*, and work proceeded fitfully throughout 1851 on the opera which became *Il trovatore*. Cammarano fell ill, and when he died in July 1852 his libretto was still unfinished, the last words he had written being those of 'Di quella pira', the tenor cabaletta that ends the third of the opera's four acts. Verdi paid Cammarano's widow six hundred ducats instead of the agreed five hundred, and he engaged a young Neapolitan poet, Leone Emanuele Bardare, to complete the libretto and make any necessary revisions. Composition of the opera was finished by mid-December, and its first performance was given in Rome on 19 January 1853 to enthusiastic acclaim.

The day after the premiere, crowds surged through the streets near the theatre shouting, 'Viva Verdi!' The opera was quickly taken up by other Italian theatres, and in due course by theatres all over the world. Some critics complained that Verdi was killing off the art of bel canto by the impossible demands he made on his singers, while others objected to the violence and gloom of the plot of *Il trovatore*. 'People say the opera is too sad, and that there are too many deaths in it,' Verdi wrote to his friend the Countess Maffei. 'But, after all, death is all there is in life. What else is there?'

Act I: 'Il duello' (The duel). Scene i. A hall in the palace of Aliaferia. In order to keep the Count di Luna's soldiers alert, their captain, Ferrando, recounts to them the story of how, many years previously, when the Count was a child, his baby brother was bewitched by a gypsy who claimed she merely wanted to tell the baby's fortune. The baby became ill, and the gypsy was burned as a witch. But the gypsy's daughter exacted a terrible revenge. She kidnapped the baby, and later, on the spot where her mother had been put to death, the half-burned skeleton of a baby was found. The old Count could never bring himself to believe his son dead, and when he himself lay dying, he charged his elder son, the present Count di Luna, with trying to find his brother. Ever since that day the Count has searched for the gypsy's daughter who stole, and probably killed, his brother ('Di due figli vivea padre beato').

Act I, scene ii. The palace gardens, at night. Leonora, a lady-in-waiting of the Princess of Aragon, is strolling in the gardens with her confidante Ines, to whom she confides that in the days before the civil war began she fell in love with an unknown warrior to whom she had presented the prize at a tournament. Recently, she heard him serenading her ('Tacea la notte placida'). Ines advises her to forget her unknown admirer, but Leonora swears her love is so great that she could die for him ('Di tale amor'). As the two women leave, the troubador arrives, again serenading Leonora ('Deserta sulla terra'). At the same time, the Count di Luna, himself in love with Leonora, appears. Leonora returns, and in the darkness she mistakes the Count for the troubador and confesses her love for him. When the nearby voice of the troubador calls her a faithless woman, she realizes her mistake. The troubador lifts his vizor, and Di Luna recognizes his rival as Manrico, a follower of the rebel Prince Urgel. Di Luna challenges Manrico to a duel, and the two men rush away to fight ('Di geloso amor sprezzato').

Act II: 'La gitana' (The gypsy). Scene i. A ruined dwelling on a mountainside in Vizcaya, where a tribe of gypsies have made their camp. The gypsies sing of their work, their wine and their women ('Chi del gitano i giorni abbella?'), and

Azucena, a gypsy woman and Manrico's supposed mother, recalls a woman (her own mother) being burned to death by a mob ('Stride la vampa'). Manrico, who has defeated Di Luna in the duel but spared his life, lies nearby, staring moodily at his sword. Azucena tells him about the death of his grandmother at the stake, adding confusedly that she, Azucena, had taken her revenge by flinging the Count's baby son into the flames, only to discover that she had, by mistake, seized the wrong child and had burned her own son ('Condotta ell'era in ceppi').

Manrico, horrified, interrupts her. If she killed her own son, who, then, is he, Manrico? Azucena persuades him that whenever she recalls those past events her mind becomes confused. Of course he is her son, she assures him. But she cannot understand why recently Manrico should have spared the present Count di Luna when he had had him at his mercy. Manrico himself cannot understand why, except that as he was about to strike he had heard a voice from heaven restraining him ('Mal reggendo'). A Messenger now appears, bringing battle orders for Manrico together with the information that Leonora, believing him dead, is about to enter a convent. Manrico rushes away to prevent her ('Perigliarti ancor languente').

Act II, scene ii. The courtyard of a convent in the neighbourhood of Castellor. The Count di Luna has heard of Leonora's intention to take the veil and plans to abduct her ('Il balen del suo sorriso'). He conceals himself as Leonora arrives with Ines and a procession of nuns, and as Leonora bids farewell to Ines he steps forward to seize her. He is foiled by the sudden appearance of Manrico and his followers, who rescue Leonora and hurry away with her ('E deggio e posso crederlo?').

Act III: 'Il figlio della zingara' (The Gypsy's Son). Scene i. Di Luna's military camp. The Count's troops, preparing to mount an attack on Manrico's stronghold of Castellor, sing a martial chorus ('Squilli, echeggi la tromba guerriera'). The guards bring to Di Luna a gypsy woman they have caught prowling near the camp. It is Azucena. When Ferrando thinks he recognizes her as the daughter of the gypsy they had burned, Azucena calls for Manrico to come and save her ('Giorni poveri vivea'). Realizing that he has Manrico's mother in his power, Di Luna orders her to be dragged away and burned at the stake ('Deh! Rallentate, o barbari').

Act III, scene ii. A hall in the castle of Castellor, adjoining the chapel where Leonora and Manrico are about to be married. Manrico sings of his love and of their future happiness ('Ah! Sì, ben mio'), but when he is told that Azucena has been captured and that a funeral pyre is already being prepared for her, he rushes away to save his mother ('Di quella pira').

Act IV: 'Il supplizio' (The Punishment). Scene i. A courtyard of the palace of Aliaferia, at night. Leonora has arrived to rescue Manrico, who has been captured by Di Luna's forces ('D'amor sull'ali rosee'). Monks chant a 'Miserere' for Manrico, who is to be executed at dawn and whose voice can be heard from within his prison, singing a farewell to Leonora ('Ah, che la morte ognora'). Leonora re-affirms her love for Manrico ('Tu vedrai che amore in terra'), and when the Count appears she offers herself to him if he will allow Manrico to live ('Mira di acerbe lagrime'). Di Luna assents, at which Leonora, unnoticed by him, swallows poison ('Vivrà! Contende il giubilo').

Act IV, scene ii. A prison cell. Manrico comforts Azucena, who, half-crazed with terror, finally sinks into an uneasy sleep ('Ai nostri monti ritorneremo'). Leonora arrives to free Manrico; but, suspecting the nature of the price she may have paid for his freedom, Manrico denounces her. It is only when Leonora collapses, dying, that he understands the sacrifice she has made for him ('Prima che d'altri vivere'). Leonora dies in Manrico's arms as Di Luna enters the cell. In a fury he orders Manrico to be taken out and beheaded, as Azucena awakes. She begs him to stop the execution, but he drags her to a window to watch Manrico die. Azucena then tells the horrified Di Luna that he has killed his own brother. Her mother has been avenged.

Some of Verdi's most familiar and best-loved arias and duets are to be found in the rich score of *Il trovatore*, an opera whose effects are broad and immediate. Its characters, as the nineteenth-century Viennese critic Eduard Hanslick famously observed, arrive on the stage as if shot from a pistol. The great tenor Enrico Caruso said of the work that all it needed for successful performance were the four greatest singers in the world.

Formally, the opera may be a step backwards after *Rigoletto*, but it advances its preposterous plot with a brutal swiftness, clothing it in darkly romantic melody. The work's muscular energy is compelling, its rare lyrical moments irresistible, but, above all, it is for its tuneful spontaneity and its sincerity of purpose that *Il trovatore* continues to be one of Verdi's most popular operas. It is, in a sense, the quintessential mid-nineteenth-century Italian opera, referred to, fancifully but acutely, by the conductor Gianandrea Gavvazeni as 'the Italian St Matthew Passion'. Leonora's arias, the famous choruses for gypsies (Act II) and soldiers (Act III), Di Luna's glowingly romantic love song (Act II) whose passion borders on madness, and, of course, Manrico's warlike cabaletta, 'Di quella pira', its high C not written by Verdi but nowadays expected by audiences – these are but a few of the highlights of this grand old warhorse.

Recommended recording: Placido Domingo (Manrico), Aprile Millo (Leonora), Dolora Zajick (Azucena), Vladimir Chernov (Di Luna), James Morris (Ferrando), with the Metropolitan Opera Chorus and Orchestra conducted by James Levine. Sony S2K 48070. Aprile Millo is a convincing Leonora, Dolora Zajick brings Azucena to fierce and vibrant life, Domingo's Manrico has musicianship, intelligence and attractive vocal quality, and Vladimir Chernov's Di Luna is suavely characterized and sung. The lavish casting of James Morris in the secondary role of Ferrando is a bonus.

La traviata
(The Fallen Woman)
opera in three acts (approximate length: 2 hours)

Violetta Valéry, a courtesan   *soprano*
Flora Bervoix, her friend   *mezzo-soprano*
Annina, Violetta's maid   *soprano*
Alfredo Germont   *tenor*
Giorgio Germont, his father   *baritone*
Gastone, Viscount of Letorierès, friend of Alfredo   *tenor*
Baron Douphol, Violetta's protector   *baritone*
Doctor Grenvil   *bass*
Giuseppe, Violetta's servant   *tenor*

LIBRETTO BY FRANCESCO MARIA PIAVE, BASED ON THE PLAY *LA DAME AUX CAMÉ-LIAS*, BY ALEXANDRE DUMAS *FILS*; TIME: AROUND 1850; PLACE: PARIS AND SUR-ROUNDINGS; FIRST PERFORMED AT THE TEATRO LA FENICE, VENICE, 6 MARCH 1853

At the end of January 1853, after the successful premiere of *Il trovatore* in Rome, Verdi returned to his villa at Sant'Agata near Busseto to complete *La traviata*, much of which had already been composed concurrently with *Il trovatore*. In May 1852 he had agreed to provide a new opera for Venice and had chosen as his subject the play *La Dame aux camélias*, by Alexandre Dumas *fils*, which he and his mistress, Giuseppina Strepponi, had seen in Paris some months previously. The largely autobiographical play was based on Dumas' novel of the same title, which had been published in 1848, only a few months after the death of Marie Duplessis, the famous Paris courtesan on whom the author's 'lady of the camellias', Marguerite Gautier, was based. Marie Duplessis, who was only twenty-three when she died of consumption, had been the mistress of such eminent men as Alfred de Musset, Franz Liszt, and Alexandre Dumas himself. In Dumas' play the courtesan Marguerite attempts to lead a respectable life with Armand, the man she loves, but she leaves him at the request of his father in order to avoid bringing scandal upon the family. This may have seemed to Verdi to have piquant parallels with his own situation; he may well have imagined Giuseppina, the mother of two illegitimate children from an earlier relationship, as Marguerite, himself as Armand, and his father figure, Antonio Barezzi, as Armand's father, for Barezzi (who took the ten-year-old Verdi into his home and employed him) had felt obliged to write to Verdi, rebuking him for not having legalized his union with Giuseppina. Also, the citizens of Busseto considered his relationship with Giuseppina scandalous, which was the major reason why she and Verdi had moved from Busseto to their country villa outside the little hamlet of Sant'Agata.

Piave produced a libretto based on Dumas' play, and Verdi proceeded to compose the opera, *La traviata*, which was given its premiere at the Teatro La Fenice on 6 March 1853. The following day Verdi wrote a terse note to Emanuele Muzio: '*Traviata* last night – a fiasco. Was it my fault or the singers? Time will tell.' Clearly it was the fault of the singers, for when *La traviata* was staged again at a smaller theatre in Venice in the following year, and with a different cast, it was an overwhelming success, and within months it was being produced throughout Italy and elsewhere in Europe. It remains one of the most popular of operas.

Act I. Violetta's house in Paris. A party is in progress. Gastone has brought his friend Alfredo Germont, whom he introduces to their hostess, the beautiful young courtesan Violetta Valéry, as the young man who came every day during her recent illness to enquire after her health. Touched to hear this, Violetta chides her protector Baron Douphol for not having done as much. After Alfredo has proposed a toast, and Violetta has responded ('Libiamo'), the guests go off to an adjacent room to dance. Violetta is prevented from following them by a fit of coughing, and Alfredo stays to confess his love for her ('Un dì felice, eterea'). Violetta says she can offer him only friendship, but gives him a camellia, asking him to return it to her when it has faded. Thus encouraged, Alfredo departs, and Violetta muses on the possibility that he could show her a different way of life ('Ah, fors'è lui'). She decides, however, that given her state of health she had best continue to live for pleasure ('Sempre libera').

Act II, scene i. The drawing-room of a country house outside Paris. Alfredo and Violetta have been living together for some months. Alfredo basks in his happiness ('De' miei bollenti spiriti'), which turns to shame when he discovers from the maid, Annina, that Violetta has been selling her possessions in order to pay for their way of life ('O mio rimorso!'). He hastens to Paris to deal with the situation, and in his absence Violetta receives a visit from his father, Giorgio Germont, who tells her that the marriage prospects of Alfredo's young sister are being threatened by Alfredo's relationship with a courtesan ('Pura siccome un angelo'). Germont extracts from a tearful Violetta a promise that she will leave Alfredo ('Dite alla giovine'). When Alfredo returns, Violetta embraces him passionately ('Amami, Alfredo') and runs out of the room. Just as Alfredo is reading the note she has left, informing him that she is returning to her former protector, his father reappears to offer consolation and to ask him to return home ('Di Provenza il mar, il suol'). But Alfredo notices on the writing desk an invitation from Violetta's friend Flora to a party in Paris that evening and concludes that this is where he will find her. He rushes out, followed by his father.

Act II, scene ii. A salon in Flora's house. Masked revellers, the women dressed as gypsies and the men as matadors and toreadors, entertain Flora's guests. Violetta arrives with her former protector Baron Douphol, who plays cards with Alfredo and loses. When the other guests have gone to supper in an adjoining room, Violetta begs Alfredo to leave before the Baron challenges him to a duel. Alfredo refuses, and in desperation she tells Alfredo that she no longer loves him. Calling the other guests back to witness that he has repaid Violetta all that he owes her, Alfredo flings at her the money he has won from the Baron, and Violetta faints in Flora's arms. Alfredo's father, who has followed his son to Paris, arrives in time to witness this scene and expresses his contempt for Alfredo's behaviour. A distraught Alfredo gives voice to his remorse and accepts the Baron's challenge to a duel.

Act III. Violetta's bedroom in Paris. Violetta lies in bed, seriously ill. When her Doctor arrives he utters encouraging words to her, but quietly he tells Annina that her mistress has only a few hours to live. Violetta rereads a letter she has received from Germont senior, telling her that, having wounded the Baron in a duel, Alfredo has fled abroad but is now hurrying back to Paris. Violetta realizes that it will be too late ('Addio del passato'). Alfredo arrives, and the lovers dream of living together again in the country ('Parigi, o cara, noi lasceremo'). However, when Violetta attempts to dress, she collapses, and they both realize she is dying ('Gran Dio! Morir si giovane'). Annina returns with the Doctor and Alfredo's father, but they can only watch helplessly as Violetta imagines she feels strength returning to her, rises to her feet joyfully and then falls dead.

In *La traviata*, more completely than in *Luisa Miller* and *Stiffelio*, whose plots still retain elements of Romantic melodrama, Verdi brought a new domestic milieu into opera, putting into music the bourgeois world of his own day. (Into music, but not immediately onto the stage, for the conventions of the time forced him to allow the opera's first performances to be staged in early eighteenth-century costumes and settings.) This is an opera in which all of Verdi's finest qualities are to be perceived: his technical mastery, his clarity, his humanity and his psychological penetration.

The dramatic action in this tautly constructed opera is carried on wings of glorious melody, from Violetta's 'Amami, Alfredo' theme, first heard in the prelude to Act I, through the hysterical agility of her 'Sempre libera', to the sombre recollection of Act III's 'Addio del passato'. Violetta's great scene with Giorgio Germont in Act II displays Verdi's dramatic writing at its finest, with her indignation, pride, anxiety, distress and, finally, resignation conveyed as surely as are his initial harshness and his growing sympathy, in tunes of firm character and melodic richness. The ensemble finale of Act II must surely melt the coldest heart, and the prelude to Act III, a poignant andante scored for strings alone, is one of the loveliest orchestral pieces in Verdi's entire oeuvre.

La traviata is not a long opera (four scenes, each of about thirty minutes), so there is no justification for the practice, still occasionally encountered, of omitting both Alfredo's and Germont's cabalettas in Act II, scene i. Their omission leaves awkward musical and dramatic holes.

Recommended recording: Angela Gheorghiu (Violetta), Frank Lopardo (Alfredo), Leo Nucci (Germont), with the Chorus and Orchestra of the Royal Opera House, Covent Garden, conducted by Georg Solti. Decca 448 119–2. The Romanian soprano Angela Gheorghiu portrays a credible and moving Violetta, simply by virtue of singing the role so accurately, with a voice of rich, dark beauty. Lopardo's Alfredo is ardent, tender and vocally elegant, and Nucci succeeds in conveying Germont's concern for his son as well as his harshness towards Violetta. The orchestra plays with delicacy and precision for Solti.

Les Vêpres siciliennes
(The Sicilian Vespers)
opera in five acts (approximate length: 3 hours)

The Duchess Hélène, sister of Duke Frederick of Austria   *soprano*
Henri, a young Sicilian   *tenor*
Guy de Montfort, governor of Sicily   *baritone*

Jean Procida, Sicilian physician   *bass*

Bethune, a French officer   *bass*

Count Vaudemont, a French officer   *bass*

Ninetta, Helene's lady-in-waiting   *contralto*

Danieli, a Sicilian   *tenor*

Thibault, a French soldier   *tenor*

Robert, a French soldier   *bass*

Mainfroid, a Sicilian   *tenor*

LIBRETTO BY EUGÈNE SCRIBE AND CHARLES DUVEYRIER; TIME: 1282; PLACE: PAL-
ERMO AND SURROUNDINGS; FIRST PERFORMED AT THE PARIS OPÉRA, 13 JUNE 1855

Shortly after the premiere of *La traviata* in Venice, Verdi was asked to write a
new work for the Paris Opéra. The subject of the opera was to be the Sicilian
Vespers, the massacre of the French in Palermo in 1282, and the libretto was to be
provided by the French dramatist Eugène Scribe and a collaborator, Charles
Duveyrier. Verdi left for Paris with his mistress, Giuseppina, in October 1853, the
libretto was delivered to him at the end of December, and he spent most of 1854
in Paris slowly composing the opera. When it was produced at the Paris Opéra in
June 1855 it was an enormous success, with the public and also with the critics. It
was performed fifty times during its first season and was immediately translated
into Italian and staged in Italy. The opera has survived, though nowadays it is
more frequently performed in its Italian version as *I vespri siciliani*.

Act I. The main square of Palermo. French soldiers are drinking and carousing,
watched by a mob of discontented Sicilians. The Austrian Duchess Hélène
appears and exhorts the Sicilians to rise against their French oppressors. Fighting
breaks out in the square, but is stopped by the arrival of the Viceroy Guy de
Montfort. Henri, a young Sicilian, arrives and is questioned by Montfort, who
offers him service with the French, which Henri indignantly refuses. Montfort
warns him to stay away from Hélène, but Henri defies him by immediately strid-
ing off towards Hélène's palace.

Act II. A valley outside Palermo, by the sea. Jean Procida, returned from exile
to lead the Sicilian revolutionaries, sings of his love for his native land and his
determination to free it from French dominion. Henri and Hélène arrive, and the
three discuss plans for a rising against the French. Bethune, a French officer, comes
with a message from Montfort inviting Henri to a ball, and when Henri declines
the invitation he is arrested. Young men and girls arrive to dance at a festival of

betrothal, and Procida cleverly inflames anti-French sentiment by encouraging French soldiers to abduct some of the Sicilian girls.

Act III, scene i. Montfort's study in his palace. Montfort reveals to Henri that they are father and son, and Henri reacts in great consternation.

Act III, scene ii. A great ballroom in the palace. After they have been entertained by the ballet of 'The Four Seasons', the guests dance. Procida and Hélène tell Henri, who has changed his mind and turned up, that Montfort will be assassinated during the evening. However, when the conspirators approach Montfort, Henri steps forward and defends him. The conspirators are arrested, Montfort thanks Henri for saving his life, and Hélène, Procida and the Sicilians denounce Henri as a traitor.

Act IV. The courtyard of a fortress where Hélène and Procida are imprisoned. Henri arrives to visit Hélène, and when he explains that Monfort is his father she forgives him and they affirm their love for each other. Montfort arrives to oversee the execution of the prisoners, and it is only when Henri agrees to acknowledge him publicly as his father that Montfort releases them and announces the immediate wedding of Henri and Hélène.

Act V. The garden of Montfort's palace. A crowd has assembled for the wedding celebrations. Hélène is appalled when Procida confides to her that the wedding bells will serve as a signal to the Sicilians to fall upon the French and slaughter them all. Her attempts to stop the marriage are in vain – Montfort orders the bells to be rung, and immediately the Sicilians, armed with swords and daggers, rush into the garden and advance menacingly upon the unsuspecting French.

The more one looks at and listens to *Les Vêpres siciliennes*, the more frustrated one feels at the thought of so much splendid and essentially Italian music married to so unviable a form as that of the five-act French *grand opéra*. It says something for Verdi's taste and sensitivity, and something more for the quality of his musical imagination, that he was able to pour so much fine music into this work. The most enjoyable parts of the opera are those in which Verdi's unabashed sincerity burns through the dead wood of the libretto: the overture, the duet between Henri and Montfort in Act III, the ballet music and much of the fourth act. Hélène's exciting coloratura aria in Act V, often referred to as the Bolero, brilliantly exploits the soprano's range. Part of the Act V trio for the lovers and Procida is interesting and effective, but the massacre at the end of the opera is botched and brutally swift. Incidentally, a comparison of the French and Italian versions of this opera reveals no significant difference in detail. Verdi himself translated the libretto into Italian and made the necessary slight changes to the vocal line. In fact the Italian text declaims more naturally than the French.

Simon Boccanegra

opera in a prologue and three acts (approximate length: 2 hours, 15 minutes)

Simon Boccanegra, a buccaneer in the service of the Genoese republic *baritone*
Jacopo Fiesco, a Genoese nobleman, alias Andrea *bass*
Paolo Albiani, a Genoese goldsmith *baritone*
Pietro, a Genoese citizen *baritone*
Maria, Boccanegra's daughter, alias Amelia Grimaldi *soprano*
Gabriele Adorno, a Genoese nobleman *tenor*

LIBRETTO BY FRANCESCO MARIA PIAVE, REVISED BY ARRIGO BOITO, BASED ON THE PLAY *SIMON BOCCANEGRA*, BY ANTONIO GARCÍA GUTIÉRREZ; TIME: THE FOURTEENTH CENTURY; PLACE: GENOA AND SURROUNDINGS; FIRST PERFORMED AT THE TEATRO LA FENICE, VENICE, 12 MARCH 1857; REVISED VERSION FIRST PERFORMED AT THE TEATRO ALLA SCALA, MILAN, 24 MARCH 1881

After Verdi had written *Les Vêpres siciliennes* for the Paris Opéra in 1855, he busied himself with turning an earlier opera, *Stiffelio*, into *Aroldo*. In March 1856 he travelled to Venice to conduct a revival of *La traviata* at the Teatro La Fenice, and while there he agreed to compose a new opera for production at La Fenice in the following year.

The subject Verdi chose was a play, *Simon Boccanegra*, by the Spanish playwright Antonio García Gutiérrez, on whose *El trovador* his opera *Il trovatore* had been based. *Simon Boccanegra* told the story of the historical character of that name who became doge of Genoa in 1339. Francesco Maria Piave, librettist of several of Verdi's earlier operas, was asked to prepare a libretto under the composer's guidance.

Verdi worked on the opera throughout the remainder of 1856, but by the beginning of 1857 he had not completed it. Dissatisfied with parts of Piave's libretto, he had asked Giuseppe Montanelli, a politician and former professor of law then living in exile in Paris, to rewrite certain scenes. Montanelli complied quickly and competently, but when Verdi arrived in Venice in mid-February 1857 for rehearsals, he still had one act to compose and the entire opera to orchestrate. *Simon Boccanegra* was staged at La Fenice on 12 March 1857 but was not a success with the public, though it interested the critics.

Twenty-three years later, in 1880, the sixty-seven-year-old Verdi, with *Aida* behind him and *Otello* in the process of gestation, was persuaded by his publisher Giulio Ricordi to take another look at *Simon Boccanegra*. The composer was easy to persuade, having retained a fondness for this opera, and he was full of ideas for its revision. 'The score as it stands is impossible,' he told Ricordi. 'It is too sad, too desolate. There is no need to touch anything in the first or last acts, and nothing but a few odd notes in the third. But the whole of the second act must be revised and given more relief, variety and animation.'

The task of improving the libretto was entrusted to Arrigo Boito, who was later to provide Verdi with the libretti for *Otello* and *Falstaff*. For some months the two men worked together. Boito wanted to write a completely new act, but this eventually became the second scene of Act I, the council chamber scene. Verdi revised his original score more extensively than he had at first intended, and also he composed completely new music for the council chamber scene, which is one of the highlights of the opera. At last the revision was complete, and when *Simon Boccanegra* was produced at La Scala, Milan, on 24 March 1881, it was a triumphant success. The role of Boccanegra was sung by the famous French baritone Victor Maurel, whose performance Verdi admired sufficiently to promise that he would write the role of Iago in *Otello* specifically for him.

In Piave's 1857 libretto there are considerable divergences from the play by Gutiérrez, and after Boito's rewriting of 1881 there is, not surprisingly, an even wider gulf between play and opera. The character of Boccanegra is an amalgam of the historical Simon and his brother Egidio, the fictional Simon being saddled with Egidio's seafaring occupation. Piave's Boccanegra is basically the character that the Spanish playwright created: a naval hero, a pirate, perhaps not unlike the Elizabethan sea-adventurers. Boito's additions have the effect of strengthening Boccanegra's personality and of giving him, in the council chamber scene, a greater moral stature. One still, however, has to accept on trust his seafaring and buccaneering qualities, for in the opera he is far from being a man of action.

Prologue. A square in Genoa. A new doge is about to be elected, and Paolo Albiani, leader of the plebeian faction, plots with his colleague Pietro to secure the election of Simon Boccanegra, a buccaneer who has won the gratitude of the Genoese for having rid their coast of African pirates. When Pietro has left to organize the plebeian vote, Simon arrives. He agrees to stand for election only after Paolo has pointed out that as doge he will be able to overcome the opposition of the patrician Jacopo Fiesco to Simon's marriage with Fiesco's daughter Maria, who has already had a child by Simon.

When the square is deserted, Fiesco emerges from his palace, bewailing the death of Maria ('Il lacerato spirito'). Without revealing her death, Fiesco scorns Simon's offer of reconciliation, telling him that he will be forgiven only if he hands over Maria's child. This Simon is unable to do, for the child, whom he entrusted to the care of an old woman, has wandered off and been lost without trace. Simon now enters the Fiesco palace to see his beloved Maria, and Fiesco delights in the thought that he will find there only her cold corpse. When Simon staggers out of the palace, heartbroken, he is acclaimed by a crowd as the newly elected doge of Genoa.

Act I, scene i. The garden of the Grimaldi palace outside Genoa, by the sea. It is twenty-five years later. Amelia Grimaldi awaits the arrival of Gabriele Adorno, a young nobleman with whom she is in love ('Come in quest'ora bruna'). Together with Amelia's guardian, Andrea (who is, in fact, Fiesco living under an assumed name), Gabriele is engaged in plotting against the doge, Boccanegra. Gabriele arrives, and Andrea informs him that Amelia is not really a member of the noble Grimaldi family, but a foundling. When Gabriele reaffirms his love for her, Andrea gives the young man his blessing ('Vieni a me, ti benedico').

The doge is expected, and Amelia fears that he will want to force her into marriage with his favourite, Paolo. However, when Boccanegra arrives and questions her, he discovers from a locket she shows him that she is his long-lost daughter Maria ('Figlia! A tal nome io palpito'). A scene of tearful reunion follows, and when Paolo arrives he is told curtly by the doge to give up all hope of marrying Amelia. Paolo immediately enlists the aid of Pietro in planning to abduct her.

Act I, scene ii. The council chamber in the doge's palace. A meeting of the council is interrupted when a rioting mob arrives, dragging in Andrea and Gabriele. Gabriele announces that Amelia has been abducted, and that he believes it to have been on the doge's orders. He is about to kill Boccanegra when Amelia enters and prevents him. As she tries to denounce Paolo, the patricians and plebeians begin to accuse one another. A fight seems imminent, but the doge intervenes successfully, appealing for peace and amity ('Plebe! Patrizi! Popolo dalla feroce storia'). He then places a curse upon whoever abducted Amelia, and he forces a terrified Paolo to repeat the curse after him.

Act II. A private apartment in the doge's palace. Paolo poisons Boccanegra's drinking water, and in order to make doubly sure of the doge's death, he attempts to bribe the two prisoners, Gabriele and Andrea, to assassinate him in his sleep. Andrea refuses to behave so dishonourably, but Gabriele, when Paolo tells him that Amelia is the doge's mistress, is enraged. Amelia enters and Gabriele accuses her, but she is unwilling to divulge the nature of her relationship to Boccanegra.

Gabriele hides as the doge approaches. At Amelia's urging, her father agrees to consider pardoning Gabriele, whom he knows to have been plotting against him. Left alone, the doge drinks some of the poisoned water. Gabriele enters and is about to stab him when Amelia returns. The doge reveals to Gabriele that Amelia is his daughter ('Perdon, perdon, Amelia') and, when a commotion is heard outside, signalling the beginning of the patrician uprising, Gabriele offers his services to the doge as a messenger of peace. Boccanegra, in return, gives his consent to Gabriele's marriage to Amelia.

Act III. Inside the doge's palace. The plebeians have defeated the patricians, and Andrea is released from prison. Paolo, having fought on the side of the rebels, is being led to execution when he encounters Andrea and boasts to him that he has poisoned Boccanegra. The doge enters, already close to death, to be confronted by Andrea, who reveals his real identity. Overjoyed, Boccanegra can at last give Fiesco his granddaughter. He reveals who Amelia really is, and claims Fiesco's pardon. Gabriele and Amelia enter, and the doge, before he dies, blesses the newly married couple, naming Gabriele as his successor.

That this amalgam-opera of 1857 and 1881 does not strike the listener of today as a patchwork of styles is in some part due to the fact that although Verdi developed continuously and enormously over the years, he never swerved from his ideal of dramatic truth expressed in melodic terms. His most brilliant effects stem from a concern to present his melody in the best possible dramatic light.

Although the score of *Simon Boccanegra* is not laid out on the page in separate numbers, its various arias, duets and ensembles are, for all their fluidity of form, identifiable, just as they would continue to be years later in *Otello* and *Falstaff*. The difference lies in the added interest given to their surroundings. What in Verdi's early operas was recitative is now musically much more significant material.

In *Simon Boccanegra* the musical characterization is superb. The villain of the piece, Paolo, is more than just a rather striking study for Iago – Boito has given him a roundness and a stature which he lacks both in the original play and in Piave's 1857 libretto. It is Paolo's pure hatred of Boccanegra, rather than his desire for wealth and power, that controls his behaviour. Verdi wrote, 'I will see to it that Paolo is no ordinary villain,' and the composer succeeded in conveying as much in the music he wrote for this introverted version of Iago. Curiously, Paolo is viewed by composer and librettist almost more sympathetically than the stoical Fiesco, who nevertheless emerges from the score with something of the dignity and strength of Verdi himself. Perhaps the composer momentarily identified with Fiesco in the scene in which he laments the death of his daughter. It obviously had a real significance for Verdi, who had himself lost two children, and whose deeply felt postlude to Fiesco's aria 'Il lacerato spirito' is a wonderfully compassionate tune.

Amelia's music has a lightness and an innocence which to some extent alleviate the melancholy to be found in much of the score. It is, however, Boccanegra who really bestrides the opera like a colossus. The beauty and eloquence of his music, and the forcefulness and consistency of his characterization, make the doge one of Verdi's most successfully realized roles. He is both statesman and dreamer, and these two aspects are given equal weight in his musical and dramatic utterance. It is by the character of Boccanegra alone that, finally, the opera must stand or fall. And it does not fall. It stands firm.

Recommended recording: Piero Cappuccilli (Boccanegra), Mirella Freni (Amelia), José Carreras (Gabriele), Nicolai Ghiaurov (Fiesco), with the Chorus and Orchestra of La Scala, Milan, conducted by Claudio Abbado. Deutsche Grammophon DG 415 692–2. Cappuccilli is masterly as Boccanegra, Mirella Freni is a youthful-sounding Amelia, and Ghiaurov a dramatically vivid Fiesco. Abbado conducts with intensity.

Un ballo in maschera
(A Masked Ball)
melodramma in three acts (approximate length: 2 hours, 15 minutes)

Riccardo, Count of Warwick, governor of Boston   *tenor*
Renato, a Creole, his secretary   *baritone*
Amelia, Renato's wife   *soprano*
Ulrica, a black fortune-teller   *contralto*
Oscar, a page   *soprano*
Silvano, a sailor   *bass*
Samuel   *bass* ⎤
                    ⎬ enemies of Riccardo
Tom   *bass* ⎦

LIBRETTO BY ANTONIO SOMMA, BASED ON THE LIBRETTO *GUSTAVE III*, BY EUGÈNE SCRIBE; TIME: THE END OF THE SEVENTEENTH CENTURY; PLACE: IN AND AROUND BOSTON; FIRST PERFORMED AT THE TEATRO APOLLO, ROME, 17 FEBRUARY 1859

Despite having sworn, when he left Naples in December 1849 after the premiere of *Luisa Miller*, that he would never again compose an opera for the

Teatro San Carlo, Verdi found himself, some years later, negotiating with that theatre about the opera based on Shakespeare's *King Lear* that he one day hoped to
write. In 1857 he signed a contract with them to compose *King Lear*, but in Verdi's
mind much depended on the availability of the soprano Maria Piccolomini to
sing Cordelia. When it became clear that she would not be available, the composer and his librettist Antonio Somma searched hurriedly for another subject,
and their choice fell upon an existing libretto by the French dramatist Eugène
Scribe. Scribe's libretto, *Gustav III, ou Le Bal masqué*, had been written for an
opera by Auber which was produced in Paris a quarter of a century earlier. It had
also been used subsequently by two other composers, but that did not deter Verdi.
He liked its subject, which was taken from history: the assassination of Gustav III
of Sweden in 1792 at a masked ball in Stockholm.

In October 1857 Verdi asked Somma to translate Scribe's five-act libretto into
Italian, and to recast it in three acts. Somma worked quickly, and by the end of the
month he had finished the first act. Verdi had already submitted a prose synopsis
to the censorship authorities in Naples, anticipating that there might be some
objection to showing on the stage the assassination of a ruling monarch. He was
quite prepared to make the characters fictitious and to alter the locale. Indeed, he
and Somma had already discussed this, and Somma had proposed moving the
action back to the twelfth century. This suggestion was rejected by Verdi:

> I really think the twelfth century a little too remote for our Gustav. It is such
> a raw and brutal period, especially in those northern countries, that it seems a
> serious contradiction to use it as a setting for characters conceived in the
> French style as Gustav and Oscar are, and for such a splendid drama based on
> customs nearer our own time. We shall have to find some great prince or
> duke, whether of the north or not, who has seen something of the world and
> caught something of the atmosphere of the court of Louis XIV.

Eventually, Verdi and Somma decided to move the action from eighteenth-
century Sweden to seventeenth-century Stettin, capital of a Prussian province,
and to alter the title to *La vendetta in domino*. Verdi completed the opera, and it
was not until he arrived in Naples in January 1858 for rehearsals that he discovered the censor had refused to allow the work to be staged, with or without the
changes in time and place. Some weeks previously a bomb had been thrown
under the carriage of Napoleon III on his way to the Paris Opéra, an incident that
increased the nervousness of the Neapolitan monarchy. In the previous year the
King of Naples himself had been attacked with a bayonet by one of his own soldiers, and the censor was not going to allow the theatrical representation of a

monarch, real or fictitious, being shot at a masked ball, which might put ideas into the heads of the citizenry.

The management of the Teatro San Carlo prepared an altered libretto that met the censor's requirements, entitled *Adelia degli Adimari* and set in fourteenth-century Florence. Verdi refused to accept it, at which the theatre threatened legal action. Through his lawyer, Verdi issued a counter-claim. The case was settled out of court, and an agreement was reached in which the contract was dissolved and the composer was allowed to offer *La vendetta in domino* elsewhere, on condition that he return in the autumn to produce *Simon Boccanegra*, his opera of the previous year which had not then been seen in Naples.

While the Neapolitan lawyers were still fighting, Verdi offered *La vendetta in domino* to the Teatro Apollo in Rome, and it had been accepted subject to the approval of the papal censor. The censor now gave his approval to the libretto but insisted on the King being made a lesser mortal, with the action taking place in some other country. After considering several places, Verdi and Somma finally settled on Boston at a time before the American War of Independence, but Somma, annoyed at the indignities to which his work had been subjected, refused to allow his name to appear on the libretto.

Scribe's original subtitle, *Le Bal masqué*, now became in Italian the new title of the opera, *Un ballo in maschera*, which was given its premiere on 17 February 1859. This was the occasion when the cunning acrostic 'Viva Verdi' was first shouted. The cry was taken up all over Italy, painted on walls, displayed on banners and, in northern Italy, uttered in defiance of the Austrians, for 'Verdi' was understood to represent not only the country's most beloved composer but also Vittorio Emanuele, *re d'italia* (Victor Emanuel, King of Italy).

In addition to its popularity as a focal point of patriotic feeling, *Un ballo in maschera* was a huge success in its own right. Audiences responded enthusiastically to it from the beginning, and the critics wrote of it as a step forward in a new direction for Verdi, drawing attention to the warmth and brilliance of the opera's orchestration and to its splendid marriage of theatrical effectiveness and melodic appeal.

Act I, scene i. A reception room in the residence of Riccardo, governor of Boston. Riccardo is giving an audience to his ministers and officials, among whom are Samuel and Tom, the leaders of a group of conspirators plotting to kill him. Oscar, a page, shows Riccardo the proposed invitation list for a masked ball that is being planned, and when the Governor sees on it the name of Amelia, with whom he is in love, he falls into a reverie ('La rivedrà nell'estasi') from which he is awakened by the arrival of his friend and secretary Renato, who is Amelia's husband. Renato tries to warn Riccardo of the plot against his life ('Alla vita che t'arride'), but the governor refuses to listen. A Judge enters with an order for the expulsion of Ulrica, a black fortune-teller accused of witchcraft, but Oscar defends her ('Volta la terrea'), and Riccardo light-heartedly invites everyone to disguise themselves and join him in a visit to the fortune-teller to judge her for themselves ('Ogni cura si doni al diletto').

Act I, scene ii. Ulrica's hut. Seated before a steaming cauldron, Ulrica invokes the lord of the abyss ('Re dell'abisso, affrettati'). Riccardo arrives disguised as a fisherman and conceals himself, as the fortune-teller, watched by a crowd of admiring townsfolk, predicts honour and riches for Silvano, a sailor. Deciding to make her prediction come true, Riccardo thrusts into Silvano's pocket some money and a note offering him a commission. A moment later the astonished sailor discovers these, and Ulrica is acclaimed by all as a great oracle.

The crowd is sent away when a woman, whom Riccardo recognizes as Amelia, arrives to consult Ulrica privately. When she asks to be cured of an illicit love that torments her, the fortune-teller advises Amelia that she can overcome this passion only by gathering a certain magic herb at midnight from beneath the gallows outside the city ('Della città all'occaso'). Overhearing this, Riccardo resolves to join Amelia there.

Oscar and the ministers and officials, Samuel and Tom among them, now arrive, and Riccardo asks to be told his fortune ('Di tu se fedele'). Ulrica warns him that he will be killed by a friend, the next person to shake his hand. Riccardo laughs this off ('È scherzo od è follia'), but no one will shake his hand. Renato arrives and, not having heard the prophecy, spontaneously shakes hands with his friend. Riccardo's identity is revealed, but Ulrica nevertheless repeats her warning as all present join in a song of praise for their governor ('O figlio d'Inghilterra').

Act II. A deserted field outside Boston, used as a place of execution. It is midnight. A terrified Amelia approaches the gallows, attempting to pluck up sufficient courage to gather the magic herb ('Ma dall'arido stelo divulso'). She has been followed by Riccardo, whom she attempts to repulse but to whom, finally, she admits that she returns his love ('Non sai tu che se l'anima mia'). They are interrupted by Renato, who has come to warn Riccardo that an ambush is being prepared for him nearby. Amelia has veiled herself at the sound of her husband's approach, and Riccardo asks Renato to escort the veiled woman back to the city without attempting to discover her identity ('Odi tu come fremono cupi'). Riccardo leaves, and almost immediately the conspirators arrive, led by Samuel and Tom. Disappointed to find Renato instead of Riccardo, they ask who his female companion is. Renato draws his sword, and in the ensuing scuffle Amelia's veil falls, to the delight of the conspirators and the humiliation of Renato, who asks Samuel and Tom to visit him at his house the next day. He then coldly leads his wife home.

Act III, scene i. The library of Renato's house, some hours later. Renato takes up his sword to kill his wife, whose assertion that she has not committed adultery he does not believe. He allows her first, however, to go and bid their son farewell ('Morrò, ma prima in grazia'). Left alone, Renato addresses a portrait of Riccardo and accuses his former friend of having destroyed his happiness and his love for his wife ('Eri tu'). When Samuel and Tom arrive, Renato demands to be allowed to join their conspiracy, and they agree to draw lots for the honour of killing Riccardo. Amelia, who has returned to say that Oscar has arrived, is made to draw the successful name from a vase. The name she draws is her husband's, and from his joyful shout of vengeance she realizes that he plans to kill Riccardo. Oscar now enters to announce that Amelia and Renato are invited to a masked ball to be held that evening. Samuel and Tom murmur that they too will be there, while Amelia wonders how to warn Riccardo ('Di che fulgor').

Act III, scene ii. A study in the governor's residence, adjacent to the ballroom. Riccardo, having decided that his only honourable course of action is to renounce his love for Amelia, signs a document sending her and Renato back to England ('Ma se m'è forza perderti'). He is oppressed by a presentiment of death, but when Oscar enters with an anonymous letter warning him that his life is in danger, he refuses to be intimidated and hastens to the ballroom.

Act III, scene iii. A huge and richly decorated ballroom. Masked guests are dancing and promenading. Renato asks Oscar to describe what Riccardo is wearing. At first, Oscar teasingly refuses to tell him ('Saper vorreste'), but when Renato claims that his business with the governor is urgent the page reveals sufficient details of Riccardo's costume for him to be recognized. Amelia urges Riccardo to flee, but he refuses. He tells her of his plans to send her and Renato away, and is bidding her a last farewell when he is stabbed by Renato. Before he dies, Riccardo swears to Renato that Amelia is innocent, pardons him and the other conspirators and bids farewell to his friends and his country.

Out of all the censorship difficulties, the alterations, reworkings and compromises, one of Verdi's finest operas was born. Neither musically nor dramatically does *Un ballo in maschera* show any of the scars one might, in the circumstances, have expected to find. It is a work whose characters are convincingly drawn, and whose melodies combine the warmth and vigour of the early Verdi with the lightness and elegance that had entered his music with *La traviata*. Its instrumentation reveals the composer continuing to move towards a greater variety of orchestral colour, with more detail in the inner voices and a masterly use of woodwind. Its musico-dramatic form is aesthetically satisfying.

Un ballo in maschera has become increasingly popular in recent years. Somma's libretto, though perhaps somewhat flowery in style and less direct in manner than the work of Verdi's more professional collaborators such as Piave and Cammarano, is tautly constructed and ripe for music. The music that clothes it is not only sumptuous but also perfectly attuned to the style of its subject. In addition to the drama of the events, there is a great deal of laughter in the score, ranging from the quick gaiety of Oscar, through Riccardo's ironic amusement, to the mocking taunts of the conspirators, all depicted with brilliant accuracy. There can no longer be any doubt that this is one of Verdi's middle-period masterpieces.

Although some productions of the opera now revert to the historical characters and the Swedish setting with which the project had begun, there is no real justification for this. Verdi remained quite satisfied with the colonial American setting, and was not especially interested in the historical, homosexual Gustav III of Sweden, who bore no resemblance to the heterosexual lover of Scribe's libretto or of Somma's. The opera's passionate love duet in Act II is after all sung by Riccardo and Amelia, not by Riccardo and Oscar.

Recommended recording: Leontyne Price (Amelia), Carlo Bergonzi (Riccardo), Robert Merrill (Renato), Shirley Verrett (Ulrica), Reri Grist (Oscar), with the RCA Italiana Opera Chorus and Orchestra, conducted by Erich Leinsdorf. RCA Victor GD 86645. Leinsdorf's excitingly conducted performance has two of the finest Verdi singers of the last half-century in the principal roles of Amelia and Riccardo: Leontyne Price in her creamiest, richest voice, and Carlo Bergonzi, as stylish as ever. The rest of the cast is equally strong, with Reri Grist delightful as Oscar, the page.

La forza del destino
(The Force of Destiny)
opera in four acts (approximate length: 3 hours, 15 minutes)

The Marquis of Calatrava   *bass*
Donna Leonora di Vargas, his daughter   *soprano*
Don Carlo di Vargas, his son   *baritone*

Don Alvaro, alias Father Raphael *tenor*

Preziosilla, a gypsy girl *mezzo-soprano*

Father Guardiano *bass* ⎤

⎢ Franciscan monks

Brother Melitone *baritone* ⎦

Curra, Leonora's maid *mezzo-soprano*

Trabuco, a muleteer and pedlar *tenor*

LIBRETTO BY FRANCESCO MARIA PIAVE, REVISED BY ANTONIO GHISLANZONI, BASED ON THE PLAY *DON ALVARO, O LA FUERZA DEL SINO*, BY ANGEL PEREZ DE SAAVEDRA, DUKE OF RIVAS, AND INCORPORATING A SCENE FROM THE PLAY *WALLENSTEINS LAGER*, BY FRIEDRICH VON SCHILLER; TIME: AROUND THE MIDDLE OF THE EIGHTEENTH CENTURY; PLACE: SPAIN AND ITALY; FIRST PERFORMED AT THE IMPERIAL THEATRE, ST PETERSBURG, 10 NOVEMBER 1862; REVISED VERSION FIRST PERFORMED AT THE TEATRO ALLA SCALA, MILAN, 27 FEBRUARY 1869

Nearly four years separate the premieres of *Un ballo in maschera* and Verdi's next opera, *La forza del destino*. Three weeks after the premiere of the former opera in Rome on 17 February 1859, the forty-five-year-old composer spontaneously announced his retirement, at a dinner party that he and Giuseppina gave in their Rome apartment on the eve of their departure from the city. One of their guests, the Rome impresario Vincenzo Jacovacci, had promised to form a really first-rate company for Verdi's next opera, but the composer had replied, 'That would be splendid, but I – no longer compose.'

Verdi's intention was to retire to his country estate at Sant'Agata and live the life of a gentleman farmer; and for a time this is what he did. In the summer of 1859 he and Giuseppina, having lived together for twelve years, were married secretly, and early in 1861 Verdi was elected to represent his district in the first Italian parliament. He began by attending the sessions assiduously, though during the more boring debates he amused himself by scribbling musical jokes on parliamentary paper.

It was when he received a letter from the celebrated tenor Enrico Tamberlick, who was appearing in opera in St Petersburg, that Verdi was tempted to return to composition, and he yielded fairly easily. Tamberlick had contacted the composer at the behest of the Director of Imperial Theatres in St Petersburg, inviting Verdi to provide a new opera for performance in that city. Encouraged by Giuseppina, Verdi accepted the commission. The first subject that he suggested, Victor Hugo's *Ruy Blas*, a play about a valet who becomes the Prime Minister of his country and the lover of the Empress, did not commend itself to the Russian authorities, but

Verdi then remembered a Spanish play he had read, *Don Alvaro, o La fuerza del sino* (Don Alvaro, or The Power of Fate) by Angel Perez de Saavedra, Duke of Rivas. This was acceptable, and in due course was turned by Francesco Maria Piave into the libretto of *La forza del destino*. Verdi signed a contract in June 1861, and in July Piave came to Sant'Agata to work on the opera with the composer.

By mid-November *La forza del destino* was complete, except for the scoring, and on 24 November 1861 Verdi and Giuseppina left Italy for Russia, arriving in St Petersburg on 6 December. They were met with freezing weather, with the illness of the leading soprano, and with a consequent postponement of the opera's premiere. By the end of January it was clear that *La forza del destino* was not going to be staged until the following winter. After visiting Moscow for a few days the Verdis travelled by train to Paris, and on to London, where Verdi composed a cantata, the *Inno delle nazioni* (Hymn of the Nations), for performance at an international exhibition. He spent most of August at home in Italy, orchestrating *La forza del destino*, and towards the end of the month he and Giuseppina set out again for Russia. This time, all went smoothly, and the opera was produced with great success in St Petersburg on 10 November 1862. The critic of the *Journal de St-Pétersbourg* wrote, immediately after the first performance:

> We shall speak again at leisure about this magnificent score and about this evening's performance; but for the moment we wish to report the composer's victorious success and the ovations for the artists who, in order to comply with the insistent demands of the entire audience, had on several occasions to drag the celebrated composer onto the stage, to the sound of wild cheering and prolonged applause.
>
> It is our opinion that *La forza del destino*, of all Verdi's works, is the most complete, both in terms of its inspiration and the rich abundance of its melodic invention, and in those of its musical development and orchestration.

Within a few months of its Russian performances the opera was produced in Rome (as *Don Alvaro*), and in Madrid, where Verdi himself supervised the staging, and the elderly Duke of Rivas, author of the play on which the opera is based, was in the audience.

The original version of *La forza del destino*, as performed in St Petersburg, Rome and Madrid, differs in several respects from the opera as we know it today, for despite its successful reception Verdi was not entirely satisfied with the work. The Spanish play ends, after the death of Leonora, with Alvaro's suicide, and the opera also ended thus in its original version. The gentler ending as we know it today, imbued with the spirit of Christian resignation, stems from the revision to which Verdi subjected the opera for its production at La Scala, Milan, in 1869. In the course of his revision he also deleted some numbers, changed the order of scenes and added the present overture. His librettist, Piave, being by this time immobilized by a stroke, the necessary alterations to the libretto were made by Antonio Ghislanzoni, poet, playwright, erstwhile baritone, and editor of the Milan *Gazzetta musicale*, who some months later was to turn a prose draft of *Aida* into a verse libretto. Ghislanzoni introduced one new scene into *La forza del destino* (the last part of Act III, scene iii) based on material from Schiller's play *Wallensteins Lager* (Wallenstein's Camp).

Act I. The castle of the Marquis of Calatrava, near Seville. Knowing that her father, the Marquis, would never agree to her marrying the Peruvian Don Alvaro, Leonora plans to elope with Alvaro. She bids her father goodnight, and sadly takes leave of the beloved objects surrounding her ('Me pellegrina ed orfana'). When Alvaro arrives, Leonora at first vacillates, but then, realizing the strength of her love, swears to follow him to the ends of the earth. They are about to leave when the Marquis returns with servants, brandishing a sword and denouncing Alvaro as a vile seducer. As a gesture of surrender, Alvaro flings his pistol at the Marquis's feet, but the gun goes off, mortally wounding the Marquis, who dies cursing his daughter. Alvaro leaves, dragging Leonora after him.

Act II, scene i. An inn in the village of Hornachuelos. In their flight, Leonora has become separated from Alvaro. Disguised as a young man, she is on her way to seek refuge in a Franciscan monastery and arrives at the inn as the host and hostess are about to serve supper to an assembled company, among whom Leonora catches sight of her brother, Don Carlo di Vargas, who is travelling in disguise as a student, intent on avenging his father's death. A gypsy girl, Preziosilla, advises all the men present to go and fight in Italy, where war has broken out against the Germans ('Al suon del tamburo'). Don Carlo, claiming to be merely a friend of Leonora's brother, tells the story of the Marquis's death and the flight of the lovers ('Son Pereda, son ricco d'onore').

Act II, scene ii. The courtyard of a monastery on a mountainside near Hornachuelos. Leonora enters, still in her male disguise. Having overheard her brother's narrative, she believes Alvaro must have fled to America, and she calls on the Virgin Mary to forgive her and help her to forget the lover who she thinks has deserted her ('Madre, pietosa Vergine'). When she rings the bell of the monastery door, it is answered by the grumbling Brother Melitone. He fetches Father Guardiano (the Father Superior) who agrees to allow Leonora to live as a hermit, expiating her sins, in a nearby cave ('Più tranquilla l'alma sento'). After a ceremony of dedication ('La Vergine degli angeli'), Leonora sets out for her lonely retreat.

Act III, scene i. A wood near Velletri, in Italy, not far from the camp of the Spanish troops. It is night. Alvaro, now a captain in the army, broods on the misfortunes in his life. His parents, Inca rulers in Peru, were executed. He himself was born in prison and raised in the desert. Thinking Leonora dead, he calls on her soul to look down in pity on him ('O tu che in seno agl'angeli'). A cry for help sends him hurrying off, and when he returns it is with Carlo, whom he has rescued from a gang of thieves. The two men introduce themselves, both using assumed names, and swear eternal friendship.

Act III, scene ii. The Spanish officers' quarters, near the battlefield at Velletri. Alvaro, wounded in the fighting, is carried in on a stretcher. Carlo assures him that for his bravery he will be awarded the Order of Calatrava, and he is astonished by Alvaro's violent reaction to the mention of Calatrava. Before Alvaro receives medical attention he entrusts to Carlo the key of a small casket that he always carries, making Carlo swear to extract from it some papers, which he must burn without reading ('Solenne in quest'ora'). Left alone, Carlo begins to wonder if his friend can be Leonora's seducer and their father's murderer ('Urna fatale del mio destino'). He opens the casket, and although he scrupulously does not examine the papers within it, he discovers a portrait of Leonora. When the surgeon calls from an adjoining room that Alvaro will live, Carlo rejoices at the thought that he will now be able to avenge his father's death ('Egli è salvo').

Act III, scene iii. Another part of the military encampment near Velletri. After satisfying himself that Alvaro is now strong enough to fight a duel, Carlo reveals his own identity and challenges him. Alvaro tries to convince Carlo that the death of the Marquis of Calatrava was an accident, but when Carlo informs him that Leonora is alive but will die when he finds her, Alvaro's anger is aroused and the two men fight. They are separated by the patrol, Carlo is dragged away, and Alvaro in despair decides to enter a monastery.

The sun rises, and reveille is sounded. Preziosilla, who has followed the soldiers to Italy, begins to tell fortunes, peasants beg for food, and Fra Melitone, also temporarily in Italy, attempts to preach a sermon castigating the soldiers for their vices ('Toh, toh! Poffare il mondo!'). Preziosilla restores amity by leading everyone in a military chorus ('Rataplan, rataplan, della gloria').

Act IV, scene i. The courtyard of the monastery near Hornachuelos. Five years have passed. The poor are being fed by Melitone, while the Father Superior paces about, reading his breviary. The recipients of Melitone's charity compare the bad-tempered priest unfavourably with the more charitable Father Raphael. When

Melitone and the Father Superior speak of Father Raphael it is clear that the person they are describing is Alvaro.

Carlo, who has been searching for Alvaro for five years, now arrives, demanding to see Father Raphael. Alvaro is sent for, and again Carlo challenges him, taunting him with cowardice. Alvaro tries not to respond ('Le minaccie, i fieri accenti'), but when Carlo slaps his face Alvaro loses his temper, and the two men rush outside to fight.

Act IV, scene ii. A rocky place in front of Leonora's cave. Leonora longs for peace of mind ('Pace, pace, mio Dio!'). Hearing the sound of fighting, she retreats to her cave, but when Alvaro arrives, calling for someone to come and comfort a dying man, he and Leonora recognize each other. Alvaro tells her to keep away from him, for he has now fatally wounded her brother. Leonora runs off to Carlo and then is heard to utter a cry. The Father Superior arrives supporting Leonora, for her brother has stabbed her before dying. Alvaro begins to blaspheme, but is called on to repent by the Father Superior and by Leonora, who promises him God's pardon. When Alvaro suddenly exclaims that he has been redeemed, Leonora dies serenely, believing that they will meet again in heaven ('Non imprecare, umiliati').

To call La forza del destino flawed, as some commentators have done, simply because it does not observe the Aristotelian unities, is misguided. The opera covers a vast canvas, from the personal to the social, in the manner of Elizabethan drama or the nineteenth-century novel. It is the work of a composer who has read Manzoni's I promessi sposi (The Betrothed). Nor does the opera deserve the epithet 'uneven', which has also been hurled at it. The emotions expressed in the military-camp scenes are simple and banal, and so, frequently, is the music that portrays them. These glimpses of popular life perfectly complement, and indeed make their own explicit comment on, the drama of the Calatrava family and the exiled Inca prince, Alvaro. The opera juxtaposes the contemplative life and the life of action. To audiences today it may appear to consist of a string of glorious arias and duets, but in it Verdi was continuing his move away from strict aria form towards a greater fluidity and an apportioning of even more orchestral and melodic interest to the recitative, or arioso as it was fast becoming.

Much of La forza del destino betrays the fact that it was composed for Russia: the choral writing, the almost Dostoevskian monks with their dark bass voices, the apparent formlessness of the action, and the military scenes. And much of it, especially Melitone's music and the chorus scenes, influenced Mussorgsky when he came to write Boris Godunov six years after La forza del destino's St Petersburg premiere. On paper Verdi's opera may look both messy in shape and old-fashioned in context, but in performance it can come blazingly to life as an exciting and moving work of music drama.

Recommended recording: Leontyne Price (Leonora), Richard Tucker (Alvaro), Robert Merrill (Carlo), with the RCA Italiana Opera Chorus and Orchestra, conducted by Thomas Schippers. RCA Victor GD 87971. Leontyne Price is stylistically superb and in beautiful voice as Leonora, Richard Tucker has one of his best roles as Alvaro, and Robert Merrill is impressive as Carlo.

Don Carlos
grand opéra in five acts (approximate length: 3 hours, 30 minutes)

Don Carlos, Infante of Spain   *tenor*
Elisabeth de Valois   *soprano*
Philip II, King of Spain   *bass*
Rodrigue, Marquis of Posa   *baritone*
Princess Eboli   *mezzo-soprano*
The Grand Inquisitor   *bass*
Thibault, Elisabeth de Valois's page   *soprano*
Count Lerma   *tenor*
A Friar   *bass*
A Royal Herald   *tenor*
A Voice from Heaven   *soprano*

LIBRETTO BY JOSEPH MÉRY AND CAMILLE DU LOCLE, BASED ON THE PLAY *DON CARLOS*, BY FRIEDRICH VON SCHILLER; TIME: 1568; PLACE: FRANCE AND SPAIN; FIRST PERFORMED AT THE PARIS OPÉRA, 11 MARCH 1867

Three years after the premiere of *La forza del destino* Verdi agreed to write a new work for the Paris Opéra. As more than once before, he toyed with the idea of writing his *King Lear*, but he decided against it with the comment that it would hardly be spectacular enough for Paris. The subject he chose was Schiller's *Don Carlos*, and the task of adapting the play was entrusted to Joseph Méry, an elderly librettist who died before his work had been completed. Camille du Locle was called in to finish the libretto, and Verdi began to compose the opera early in 1866, finishing it by September. Rehearsals began, attended by the usual Parisian delays, strikes, postponements, singers' illnesses and other irritations, and finally *Don Carlos* reached the stage of the Paris Opéra on 11 March 1867. The opera was respectfully, even enthusiastically received, and was performed forty-three times during the season, though press reviews were cautious, and some critics claimed to discern the influence of Wagner and Meyerbeer.

Before the premiere, Verdi made a number of cuts in the, for him, unusually lengthy score, and immediately afterwards he authorized further cuts. When the opera was produced at Covent Garden in Italian a few months later, the first act (an addition of the librettists, with no counterpart in Schiller's play) was omitted, and so was the ballet music. Seventeen years later, Verdi was persuaded to revise *Don Carlos* for a production in Vienna. But the Vienna performance was cancelled, and so the revised version in Italian was instead first seen at La Scala in 1884. Verdi had made several changes, had written some new music and had deleted the entire first act, salvaging only Carlos's aria and inserting it (with minor but significant alteration) into Act II, which had now become Act I of a four-act opera.

By this time, the Italian translation had established itself through stagings in Italy as well as in London, St Petersburg, Barcelona, Lisbon, Madrid, Buenos Aires and New York, while the original French text had neither been revived in Paris nor played anywhere else except Brussels. *Don Carlos* had become an Italian opera, *Don Carlo*. In recent years, however, the original French *Don Carlos* has begun to re-establish itself in the international repertoire.

Act I. The forest of Fontainebleau. France and Spain have long been at war, but a peace treaty is about to be signed, and Don Carlos, son of the Spanish King Philip II, has come to France to see Elisabeth de Valois (the daughter of the French King Henri II), to whom he is betrothed ('Je l'ai vu et dans son sourire'). He encounters Elisabeth, whom he has not previously met, and presents her with a portrait of the Infante of Spain (himself). She recognizes him and they fall in love ('De quels transports poignants et doux'). However, when the Spanish ambassador Count Lerma arrives, it is to announce that the French King has given his daughter not to Carlos but to his father, Philip II. For the sake of her country, Elisabeth assents ('L'heure fatale est sonnée').

Act II, scene i. The cloisters of the monastery of San Yuste. A Friar is at prayer before the tomb of Charles V, grandfather of Don Carlos, and Carlos is startled by the sound of the Friar's voice, which resembles that of his late grandfather. Rodrigue, Marquis of Posa, enters, and the two friends greet each other warmly. Rodrigue advises Carlos to try to forget his love for the woman who is now his stepmother and devote his energies to helping the oppressed people of Flanders, suffering under the repressive rule of Carlos's father, Philip II ('Mon compagnon, mon ami'). Carlos agrees, and the two men swear undying friendship ('Dieu, tu semas dans nos âmes').

Act II, scene ii. A garden outside the monastery. Queen Elisabeth's ladies-in-waiting, among them the Princess Eboli and Elisabeth's page Thibault, are passing the time while awaiting the Queen's return. Eboli entertains the others with her Song of the Veil. When the Queen arrives, Rodrigue surreptitiously hands her a note from Carlos, requesting an audience. Elisabeth dismisses her ladies, and Carlos enters. She tells him she will try to persuade his father to send him to Flanders as governor, but when Carlos falls in a swoon and begins to talk deliriously of his love for her she becomes distressed and is forced to remind him that she is now legally his mother.

Carlos rushes out, and King Philip arrives from the monastery. Furious to find his wife unattended, Philip banishes the lady-in-waiting who should have been in attendance. As all are leaving, the King calls Rodrigue back and asks him for his frank advice, but when Rodrigue begs him to adopt a more liberal attitude towards Flanders ('O roi! J'arrive de Flandre'), Philip warns him to beware of the Grand Inquisitor. The King confides his suspicions regarding Elisabeth and Carlos and asks Rodrigue to keep a watch on them, a commission that Rodrigue accepts in the hope that he may in time be able to influence Philip over Flanders.

Act III, scene i. The Queen's gardens in Madrid. It is midnight. Carlos enters, reading an anonymous letter of assignation which he believes to be from Elisabeth. When a veiled woman appears, he embraces her, declaring his love ('C'est vous, c'est vous, ma bien-aimée'), but when she removes her veil he is mortified to discover the woman to be Eboli, and he attempts to dissemble. Eboli soon guesses that it is the Queen whom he loves, and she threatens to reveal this to Philip. Rodrigue arrives and attempts first to cajole and then to frighten Eboli out of this resolve, but she leaves determined upon vengeance ('Malheur sur toi, fils adultère'). Rodrigue asks Carlos to let him have, for safekeeping, any incriminating documents he may be carrying. After a momentary suspicion of his friend, who is now an intimate of the King, Carlos hands Rodrigue a bundle of letters.

Act III, scene ii. The square outside the cathedral of Our Lady of Atocha. A crowd has assembled to watch the burning of the heretics. As the King emerges from the cathedral after his coronation ceremony, a deputation from Flanders led by Carlos appears, begging Philip to show clemency to their country. The King orders them to be removed and rejects Carlos's request for the governorship, at which Carlos draws his sword upon his father. Philip furiously seizes a sword. In order to save Carlos, Rodrigue asks his friend to surrender his weapon. The astonished Carlos does so and is led off under guard as the procession continues. Flames arise from the stake, and a celestial Voice is heard welcoming to heaven the souls of the heretics.

Act IV, scene i. The King's study. Philip soliloquizes about his loveless marriage ('Elle ne m'aime pas!'). The Grand Inquisitor arrives, and the King consults him about the rebellious Carlos. The Inquisitor forces him to agree to the death of Carlos, and goes on to demand that Rodrigue also be handed over to the Inquisition ('Dans ce beau pays'). When the Inquisitor has left, Elisabeth rushes in, claiming that her casket of jewels has been stolen. It is, however, lying on the King's desk, and he forces it open to discover a miniature portrait of Carlos. When he calls the Queen an adulteress, she swoons, and he shouts for aid. Eboli and Rodrigue enter, and when Eboli is left alone with the Queen she confesses not only that it was she who took the casket to Philip but also that she has been the King's mistress. Deeply shocked, Elisabeth orders her to choose between exile and a nunnery. Elisabeth leaves, and Eboli, bitterly repentant, vows to enter a nunnery, but not before she has made an attempt to save Carlos from his imminent death ('O don fatal et détesté').

Act IV, scene ii. A dungeon prison. Carlos is visited by Rodrigue, who has come to sacrifice his life for his friend and for the liberal cause in Flanders. He has arranged for the incriminating letters he took from Carlos to be found on his own person. While the friends are talking, a man in the uniform of the Inquisition steals into the dungeon and shoots Rodrigue, who before he dies manages to tell Carlos that the Queen will be waiting for him at the monastery of San Yuste the next day, to bid him farewell ('Ah, je meurs, l'âme joyeuse').

Philip enters with members of his court. When he attempts to embrace his son, Carlos repulses him. Citizens storm into the prison to demand the release of Carlos, but the Grand Inquisitor suddenly reveals himself and quells them. In the confusion, Eboli helps Carlos to make his escape.

Act V. The cloisters of the monastery of San Yuste. Elisabeth prays before the tomb of Charles V ('Toi qui sus le néant'). When Carlos arrives, she reminds him of his promise to Rodrigue that he would lead Flanders to peace, and Carlos assures her that he has now sublimated his love for her in his determination to liberate Flanders. Their farewells ('Au revoir dans un monde') are interrupted by the sudden arrival of Philip with the Grand Inquisitor and officers of the Inquisition, and Philip orders his son's arrest. Drawing his sword, Carlos retreats towards the tomb of his grandfather. The Friar whom he had earlier heard at prayer suddenly appears from within, dressed in the royal robes of Charles V, and drags

Carlos into the cloister, while the King, the Inquisitor and the guards exclaim that it really is Charles V, King Philip's father.

Schiller's *Don Carlos*, his first play to be written in verse, is no more historically accurate than are Shakespeare's histories. Like Shakespeare, Schiller was concerned with poetic truth, and to achieve it he was willing to sacrifice mundane fact wherever necessary. The historical Don Carlos was not only an epileptic cripple but also a viciously sadistic madman, while Schiller's romantic young prince is merely a trifle overexcitable. But the playwright's characters are superbly realized in dramatic terms, and Philip II's Spain is fully drawn as their background. The libretto that Méry and Du Locle provided for Verdi stays for the most part sufficiently close to the play to be able to offer the composer what he relished: interesting, believable characters, and strong dramatic situations.

Enough of Verdi's old revolutionary ardour remained for him to warm to the Marquis of Posa and his political idealism. Indeed, *Don Carlos* is the one Verdi opera in which political activities are discussed in adult terms. The conflicts between public and private life, between Church and State, between despotism and liberalism, tensions that influence the actions of the main characters – all these were gratefully seized upon by Verdi, whose opera both illuminates and rarefies Schiller's play. The dark orchestral colouring, the rich, complex musical characterization, and the quality of its melody combine to make *Don Carlos* one of the most rewarding of operas to encounter in the theatre.

The charges of Wagnerism and Meyerbeerism need hardly be answered. Verdi was his own Wagner, and although when writing for Paris he had no choice but to cast his opera in the Parisian *grand opéra* mould, there is a world of difference and of quality between his music and that of Meyerbeer. *Don Carlos* is the one opera by Verdi in which the composer can be said to have forsaken his customary sharp conciseness. Nevertheless, the work can hardly be called prolix, and even its one comparatively weak scene, the auto-da-fé or burning of the heretics, adds up to triumphantly more than the sum of its parts. Above all, the opera glows with Verdi's humanity, which he has been able to breathe into characters who on the printed page must have seemed to him at first acquaintance to be frigidly formal.

Recommended recording: Roberto Alagna (Don Carlos), Karita Mattila (Elisabeth), Thomas Hampson (Rodrigue), José Van Dam (Philip II), Waltraud Meier (Eboli), with the Chorus of the Théâtre du Chatelet and the Orchestre de Paris, conducted by Antonio Pappano. EMI 5 56152 2. Alagna's Carlos is beautifully sung, Karita

Mattila is a fine Elisabeth, Hampson an elegant Rodrigue, and Van Dam captures all the complexity of Philip II's character. Pappano conducts with urgency and conviction.

Aida

opera in four acts (approximate length: 2 hours, 15 minutes)

The King of Egypt (Pharaoh)   *bass*
Amneris, his daughter   *mezzo-soprano*
Aida, her Ethiopian slave   *soprano*
Radames, captain of the Guards   *tenor*
Amonasro, King of Ethiopia   *baritone*
Ramfis, high priest of Egypt   *bass*
A Messenger   *tenor*

LIBRETTO BY ANTONIO GHISLANZONI, AFTER A FRENCH PROSE VERSION BY CAMILLE DU LOCLE, IN TURN BASED ON A SCENARIO BY AUGUSTE MARIETTE; TIME: THE EPOCH OF THE PHARAOHS; PLACE: MEMPHIS AND THEBES IN EGYPT; FIRST PERFORMED AT THE OPERA HOUSE, CAIRO, 24 DECEMBER 1871

In the spring of 1870, when he received from the French librettist Camille du Locle the synopsis of an opera plot that was to become *Aida*, Verdi was in his fifty-seventh year. The days when he composed an opera every few months were far behind. The pressures, financial and psychological, had eased, and for some time past he had written operas at intervals of three or four years. Between operas, he was happy to return to the life of a farmer at Sant'Agata. Managements continued to request new operas from him, and librettists suggested subjects, but he could wait. Du Locle, the joint-librettist with Joseph Méry on *Don Carlos*, was keen to collaborate again with Verdi and had put forward various ideas, among them a play by the contemporary Spanish dramatist Lopez de Ayala.

When he sent Verdi the Spanish play Du Locle enclosed the four-page synopsis of an Egyptian subject. His interest aroused, Verdi praised the synopsis and asked who had written it. Du Locle's reply was that he himself had put together the synopsis from a story by his friend the French Egyptologist Auguste Mariette, who had presented his story to the Khedive of Egypt with the suggestion that it could form the subject of an opera. The Khedive had already decided to commission an opera for his new opera house in Cairo which had been constructed to mark the completion of the Suez Canal. The theatre had opened the previous November. The Khedive now entrusted Mariette with the task of finding a composer. Verdi was the Khedive's first choice, followed by Gounod and then Wagner. Had Du Locle been less mysterious in an earlier approach to Verdi, when he asked the composer if he would be willing to compose a new opera for a far-distant country, it might have been possible for the Cairo Opera House to have opened with *Aida*, but at that time Verdi had refused to write a new opera, and the theatre in Cairo had opened with a performance of his *Rigoletto*. (Incidentally, the persistent story that *Aida* was first performed at the opening of the Suez Canal must be disregarded. The Cairo Opera House opened on 1 November 1869 with *Rigoletto*, two weeks before the opening of the canal.)

Verdi now agreed to use Mariette's subject for an opera, and a date for production in Cairo was decided upon that gave the composer only six months to complete the task. Du Locle wrote a libretto in French, based on Mariette's story, but Verdi had decided that the opera should be in Italian. Antonio Ghislanzoni, who some months earlier had worked on the revision of *La forza del destino*, was engaged to translate Du Locle's text into Italian verse. There are traces of both Metastasio's *Nitetti* and Racine's *Bajazet* in the libretto of *Aida*, and the likelihood is that they were introduced by Du Locle in the process of expanding Mariette's idea into a full-length libretto.

Verdi had always played an active part in the shaping and writing of his libretti, and Ghislanzoni found that the composer was concerned to choose not only the right words for each phrase but also the most appropriate form or shape for each scene. On one occasion, Verdi complained that the 'parola scenica' (theatrical word) was lacking. 'I don't know if I can explain what I mean by "theatrical word",' Verdi wrote, 'but I think I mean the word that most clearly and neatly brings the stage situation to life.' He went on to suggest changes in the dialogue, all of them moves in the direction of greater clarity and concision.

His requirements for the opera's final scene were detailed and explicit, but by the time Ghislanzoni's text arrived Verdi had become impatient. The librettist's verses, he admitted, were beautiful – 'But, since you were so late in sending them to me, I have written the music already, in order not to lose time, using the monstrous verses I sent you.' So, as well as composing the music of the ethereal final duet, 'O terra, addio', Verdi was responsible for the words, the 'versi mostruosi', which are, in fact, anything but monstrous. Verdi's words are simple, sincere and, in their context, extremely moving.

Verdi composed the opera in no more than four months. However, due to the Franco-Prussian war, the shipping of the scenery from Paris to Cairo was delayed, and it was not until 24 December 1871 that *Aida* was given its first performance at the Cairo Opera House.

Act I, scene i. A hall of the King's palace at Memphis. Ramfis, the high priest, tells Radames that the Ethiopian forces are reported to be marching on Thebes and the valley of the Nile. In reply to Radames's questions he adds significantly that the goddess Isis has named a certain brave young warrior as leader of the Egyptian army against the invaders. Left alone, Radames dreams of himself as that warrior and of the glory that would be his. His thoughts then turn to the beautiful Aida, whom he loves ('Celeste Aida').

His reverie is interrupted by Amneris, the King's daughter. She does not know – nor does anyone else at court – that her Ethiopian slave Aida is the daughter of Amonasro, the King of Ethiopia. Amneris, in love with Radames, questions him guardedly, secretly hoping that she is the object of his passion. Aida enters, and from the glances that flash between her slave and Radames, Amneris realizes that they love each other. When she asks Aida why she is weeping, Aida replies that she is disturbed by the news of war between Ethiopia and Egypt. Radames, meanwhile, suspects that Amneris has guessed the real state of affairs between Aida and himself ('Quale inchiesta!').

The King enters with his court, guards and priests, and a Messenger arrives with a report that the Ethiopians are approaching the city. The King announces that Radames has been chosen to lead the army, and Amneris presents the young warrior with a banner, urging him to return victorious. The King exhorts the warriors to defend the sacred Nile, and the Egyptian army departs ('Su! Del Nilo al sacro lido'). Aida has joined the others in the call to Radames to return in victory. However, suddenly realizing the significance of her words, she expresses her dismay and calls on the gods to have pity on her suffering ('Ritorna vincitor!').

Act I, scene ii. The interior of the temple of Vulcan. Priests and priestesses led by Ramfis evoke the god Ftha. A stately ritual dance is performed by priestesses, and Radames is given the holy sword ('Nume, custode e vindice').

Act II, scene i. A room in the apartments of Amneris. The Princess reclines on a couch, while slave girls sing the praises of the victorious Radames, and Moorish slave boys dance. When Aida enters, Amneris bids the others depart. She professes sympathy for her slave, whose people have been defeated, and then, watching her closely for her reaction, she leads Aida to believe that Radames has been killed in the fighting ('Fu la sorte dell'armi'). Aida gives a cry of anguish, at which Amneris exclaims that Radames is alive and that she, Amneris, daughter of the Pharaoh, is Aida's rival for his love. Helpless, Aida begs for pity, but Amneris can speak only of hate and vengeance ('Pietà ti prenda del mio dolore'). A fanfare announces the return of the victorious troops, and Amneris sweeps out, instructing her slave to attend her at the triumphal ceremony.

Act II, scene ii. A public square near one of the gates to Thebes. A great throne has been erected at the city gates to welcome the returning army. The King, Amneris, the court, priests and people assemble, and the Egyptian warriers enter ('Gloria all'Egitto'), followed by dancers who perform a colourful ballet. Finally Radames enters, and the victor's crown of laurels is placed on his brow by Amneris. When the King offers him anything he wants, Radames requests that the Ethiopian prisoners be brought in. Aida discovers her father, Amonasro, among them, disguised as an ordinary soldier. Muttering to her not to reveal that he is the Ethiopian King, Amonasro publicly admits that he is her father, and he begs for mercy to be shown to the captives ('Ma tu, re, tu signore possente'). Radames asks the King to grant life and liberty to the prisoners, but the priests demand death for them all. A compromise is reached, and all are freed except Aida's father, who is to remain in Egypt as a hostage. Finally the King announces, without having consulted Radames, that the brave warrior is to be given the hand of Amneris in marriage. All give voice to their reactions in a huge ensemble.

Act III. The banks of the Nile, near a temple of Isis, on a clear, moonlit night. Voices softly chanting a hymn are heard from within the temple. A boat glides up, from which Amneris and the high priest Ramfis alight and proceed to the temple, for it is the eve of her marriage to Radames, and Amneris has come to pray. When they have entered the temple, Aida arrives for a secret tryst with Radames. Apprehensive, she wonders if this is to be their last farewell. Should that be so, the Nile will be her grave. Her thoughts turn to her beloved homeland ('O patria mia').

Amonasro unexpectedly arrives, declaring to Aida that Radames's love for her may yet lead to their escape and finally to victory over the Egyptians. He presses his daughter to extract from Radames the secret of the Egyptians' military plans. When she recoils in horror, he denounces her as a slave of the pharaohs, and she finally agrees, tearfully, to obtain the information he requires ('Rivedrai le foreste imbalsamate'). As Radames approaches, Amonasro hides. Radames embraces Aida, professing his love for her, which she asks him to prove by fleeing from Egypt with her. He resists for a time, but eventually agrees ('Sì, fuggiam da queste mura'), and in answer to her question as to what route they should take to avoid the army, he reveals the whereabouts of the Egyptian forces.

At this, Amonasro steps forward. He exclaims that his warriors will be waiting for the Egyptians and reveals to Radames that he is not only Aida's father but also the King of Ethiopia. Radames realizes that he has dishonoured himself and betrayed his country, and Amonasro and Aida urge him to flee with them ('Tu! Amonasro!'); but at that moment Amneris, Ramfis and guards emerge from the temple. Amonasro and Aida escape, but Radames, filled with remorse, surrenders himself to the high priest.

Act IV, scene i. A Hall in the King's palace. Amneris broods on her love for Radames and is furious that Aida has escaped. She has Radames brought in and urges him to renounce Aida. He refuses, and the jealous Amneris collapses as he is led away to the chamber of judgment ('Già i sacerdoti adunansi'). She overhears Ramfis and the priests denouncing Radames as a traitor and asking him to defend himself. He remains silent and is sentenced to be entombed alive beneath the altar of the god he has offended. As the priests emerge from the chamber of judgment, Amneris alternately pleads with them and curses them.

Act IV, scene ii. Two levels of the temple of Ftha. Above is the interior of the temple, while below is a crypt in which Radames stands while two priests close the stone over him. As Radames thinks of Aida and prays that she may be happy, he is startled to see a form approach through the shadows. It is Aida, who has hidden herself in the tomb to die with him. As the priestesses are heard chanting in the distance, and Amneris prostrates herself on the stone above the tomb to pray for Radames, the lovers utter their farewell to earth and calmly anticipate the bliss of heaven ('O terra, addio').

Aida was a triumph at its premiere and has remained immensely and deservedly popular ever since, though it has perhaps been somewhat misunderstood. It is generally thought of as a spectacular work and staged as such, but despite the spectacle of its triumphal scene (Act II, scene ii), admittedly the grandest scene in the whole of grand opera, *Aida* is intrinsically an intimate work. Much, indeed most, of the music for three of its principal characters – Aida, Radames and Amneris – is scored with the delicacy and clarity of texture of chamber music. It is an opera about individuals and their passions, not about nations and their military exploits. It also has a strong claim to be called Verdi's most original work for the stage, combining as it does the vigour and melodic fecundity of the composer's earlier period with something of the psychological penetration of the two masterpieces, *Otello* and *Falstaff*, that were to follow, without in any way sounding like a transitional work.

From the beginning of the opera to the end, Verdi's level of inspiration remains miraculously and consistently high. His command of the orchestra and his ability to depict character in instrumental terms is complete and daunting, and even more so is the ease with which he contrives to write music that is as beautiful melodically and harmonically as it is dramatically apposite. The score of *Aida* is in no way picturesquely Egyptian. Verdi has created his own Egypt, just as surely as his beloved Shakespeare did in *Antony and Cleopatra*. He has also written four superb roles for his leading singers, and in Amneris he has created the finest of his magnificent series of mezzo-soprano characters.

Recommended recording: Zinka Milanov (Aida), Jussi Bjoerling (Radames), Fedora Barbieri (Amneris), Leonard Warren (Amonasro), with the Rome Opera Chorus and Orchestra, conducted by Jonel Perlea. RCA Victor GD 86652. Zinka Milanov, one of the great Verdi sopranos of the twentieth century, is Aida, Fedora Barbieri is a formidable Amneris, and the incomparable Jussi Bjoerling sings gloriously as Radames. Jonel Perlea conducts impressively.

Otello
opera in four acts (approximate length: 2 hours, 15 minutes)

Otello, a Moor, general in the Venetian army   *tenor*
Iago, his ensign   *baritone*
Cassio, Otello's lieutenant   *tenor*
Roderigo, a Venetian gentleman   *tenor*
Lodovico, ambassador of the Venetian Republic   *bass*
Montano, Otello's predecessor as governor of Cyprus   *bass*
Desdemona, Otello's wife   *soprano*
Emilia, Iago's wife   *mezzo-soprano*

LIBRETTO BY ARRIGO BOITO, BASED ON SHAKESPEARE'S PLAY *OTHELLO*; TIME: THE END OF THE FIFTEENTH CENTURY; PLACE: CYPRUS; FIRST PERFORMED AT THE TEATRO ALLA SCALA, MILAN, 5 FEBRUARY 1887

After the Cairo premiere of *Aida* in December 1871 and its first Italian performances the following year, Verdi considered that his career as a composer of opera had come to an end. He was then only in his late fifties, but he had been a hard-working professional musician for more than thirty years, and his intention now was to pass the remainder of his days on his estate at Sant'Agata. When his idol, the famous poet and novelist Alessandro Manzoni, died in 1873, Verdi composed his great Requiem in memory of him, but he had no plans for further composition. When two years later his old friend the Countess Maffei suggested to him that his conscience would surely oblige him to compose, Verdi's reaction was immediate and firm. 'No, no, you're joking,' he replied, 'because you know better than I do that the score is settled.'

Settled the score might well have been, had not Verdi's publisher Giulio Ricordi in 1879 contrived a meeting in Milan between the composer and Arrigo Boito. This was not their first meeting, for in 1862 Verdi had commissioned the then nineteen-year-old poet and composer to provide the text for a cantata that he, Verdi, had agreed to compose for an international exhibition in London. At that time, however, Boito had a young man's scorn for the middle-aged, and the following year he wrote an ode, *All'arte italiana*, which made reference to the altar of art having been 'stained like a brothel wall'. The implication, at least as inferred by Verdi, was that the work of the older composer was the stain on the wall. Understandably, the relationship between the two men was extremely cool for some years. By 1879, however, Boito was in his mid-thirties, and had become one of Verdi's most enthusiastic admirers.

Three days after their meeting in Milan, Boito gave Verdi his scenario for an opera to be based on Shakespeare's *Othello*, and without committing himself to the project Verdi encouraged Boito to write a complete libretto. Ricordi deviously set in motion another scheme to bring Verdi and Boito together. He suggested revising *Simon Boccanegra*, Verdi's 1857 opera which had been only partially successful. Verdi was interested, and Boito was willing to patch up Piave's libretto, so they set to work and within six months had produced the revised version of *Simon Boccanegra*, which was performed at La Scala, Milan, in 1881. By this time the two men had discussed what they called 'the chocolate idea' on numerous occasions, and gradually it came to be assumed between them that they were actively engaged in planning *Otello*.

Verdi treated his new librettist with somewhat more respect than his earlier collaborators had been wont to receive, but he was nevertheless an active participant in the creation of the final draft of the *Otello* libretto. Work proceeded slowly and with interruptions. Verdi did not begin to compose any of the music until March 1884, but by early October of the following year he was ready to begin scoring, a process that occupied him for a further year. It was not until December 1886 that Verdi was able to inform Boito that the final pages had been sent off to the firm of Ricordi.

The premiere of *Otello* at La Scala followed soon after, on 5 February 1887. For weeks before that date the excited anticipation of the Milanese public had been steadily mounting. Verdi and his wife, Giuseppina, arrived in Milan early in

January, and the seventy-three-year-old composer began coaching the singers, later taking charge of the first orchestral rehearsals. The first-night performance was conducted by Franco Faccio, and it was an absolute triumph. Blanche Roosevelt, an American singer who was present in the audience, described the opera's reception in her book *Verdi: Milan and "Othello"* (1887):

> The ovations to Verdi and Boito reached the climax of enthusiasm. Verdi was presented with a silver album filled with the autographs and cards of every citizen of Milan. He was called out twenty times, and at the last recalls hats and handkerchiefs were waved, and the house rose in a body. The emotion was something indescribable, and many wept. Verdi's carriage was dragged by citizens to his hotel. He was toasted and serenaded, and at five in the morning I had not closed my eyes in sleep for the crowds were still singing and shrieking 'Viva Verdi! Viva Verdi!'.

Act I. Outside the castle, by the harbour. As a tempest rages in the harbour of Cyprus, the citizens await the return of their governor, Otello, a Moorish general in the Venetian army. When his ship is sighted, the Cypriots call on heaven to spare it. Once he is safely in port, Otello proclaims victory over the Turks ('Esultate!'), and enters the castle. His ensign Iago, angered because a rival, Cassio, has been promoted above him, plots his own advancement by encouraging the desire of Roderigo for Otello's wife, Desdemona. Leading a drinking song ('Inaffia l'ugola'), Iago forces the easily intoxicated Cassio to drink a toast to Otello and his wife, and then he provokes Roderigo into fighting with the drunken Cassio. Otello, hearing the brawl, storms out of the castle to demand an explanation, but Iago feigns ignorance. As Desdemona, awakened by the noise, joins her husband, the furious Otello demotes Cassio and instructs Iago to restore order. Otello and Desdemona, left alone in the moonlight, tenderly recall their courtship ('Già nella notte densa').

Act II. A hall on the ground floor of the castle, the next day. Iago advises Cassio to seek Desdemona's aid in regaining Otello's favour. Cassio leaves, and Iago articulates his credo, his belief in a cruel god from whom he derives the ideas for his evil machinations ('Credo in un Dio crudel'). On Otello's arrival, Iago makes innuendos about Desdemona's fidelity as they observe her in the garden with Iago's wife, Emilia, and with Cassio. Iago warns Otello to beware of jealousy.

Women, children and sailors bring flowers to Desdemona, whose beauty softens Otello's growing suspicions, but when she suggests Cassio's reinstatement to him he grows irritable. Fearing he is ill, she tries to soothe his brow with her handkerchief, which he throws to the ground and which is retrieved by Emilia.

Desdemona, confused, pleads her devotion, while Iago surreptitiously wrenches the handkerchief from Emilia ('Dammi la dolce e lieta parola'). When the women leave, Otello bids farewell to his past happiness, which he accuses Iago of having destroyed ('Ora è per sempre addio'), and Iago answers the Moor's demands for proof of Desdemona's infidelity by pretending he has heard Cassio murmur Desdemona's name in his sleep ('Era la notte'). He adds that he has seen in Cassio's hand the decorative handkerchief that Otello gave Desdemona when he first courted her. Urged on by Iago, Otello swears to be avenged ('Sì, pel ciel').

Act III. The great reception hall of the castle. Iago tells Otello that more proof of Desdemona's infidelity is forthcoming, and then he departs as Desdemona greets her husband. Otello hints at his suspicions, but she fails to understand ('Dio ti giocondi, o sposo'). When he demands to see the handkerchief he once gave her, she again pleads for Cassio, driving Otello to call her a courtesan. Although Desdemona, in tears, swears her innocence, Otello sends her away. He pours out his misery ('Dio! Mi potevi scagliar') and then hides at the approach of Cassio and Iago. Iago, flashing the handkerchief he stole, manipulates Cassio's banter about his mistress, Bianca, so that Otello thinks they are referring to Desdemona ('Essa t'avvince coi vaghi rai'). Cassio leaves as trumpets announce dignitaries from Venice. Otello swears to kill his wife.

The court enters to welcome Lodovico, the ambassador, who presents papers recalling Otello to Venice and naming Cassio as his successor. When Cassio steps forward, Otello loses self-control and curses Desdemona, hurling her to the floor. She begs forgiveness for her supposed crime, and the courtiers try to console her, but Otello orders everyone to leave. As he falls unconscious in a fit, Iago mockingly salutes the 'Lion of Venice'.

Act IV. Desdemona's bedroom. As Emilia helps her prepare for bed, Desdemona sings a song about a maiden who was forsaken by her lover (the Willow Song, 'Piangea cantando'). Startled by the wind, she bids Emilia goodnight, says her prayers ('Ave Maria') and retires to bed. Otello steals in and tenderly kisses her, but when she awakes he tells her to prepare for death. Although she protests her innocence, he strangles her. Emilia enters with the news that Cassio has slain Roderigo. Hearing Desdemona's dying sigh, she cries for help, and Iago, Lodovico and Cassio rush in. When Emilia tells of Iago's treachery, the villain rushes out of the room, and Otello, realizing he has been deceived, stabs himself, dying as he makes a last attempt to kiss Desdemona's corpse ('Niun mi tema').

The four acts of the opera follow one another with a relentless dramatic thrust. Boito's ending to *Otello*, or rather Verdi's, for it is the composer who was responsible for condensing the play's final scene, improves upon the play by moving more quickly and clearly after the death of Desdemona. In general, Boito has been faithful to Shakespeare's conception of the characters. In the Credo he has invented a focal point for Iago, who in Shakespeare's play only partially articulates his beliefs. In essentials, however, Boito's Iago is the Elizabethan playwright's embittered nihilist. His Otello is an almost more real and moving character than Shakespeare's when clothed in Verdi's violent and passionate music.

Otello is considered by many to be Verdi's greatest opera, an incredibly fresh and youthfully inspired score for someone in his seventies to have created. How wonderfully the composer sustains the dramatic level from the opera's first shattering chord to its final stillness. What psychological acumen is revealed by the musical characterization. The work's combination of those Elizabethan qualities of tenderness, violence and sensuality never fails to impress and astonish. And Verdi's musical language and style are virtually beyond praise, the melody as glorious as ever, but now freed from the harmonic constrictions of his earlier period and able to range where it will, the numbers merging skilfully and subtly into one another.

Recommended recording: Jon Vickers (Otello), Leonie Rysanek (Desdemona). Tito Gobbi (Iago), with the Rome Opera Chorus and Orchestra, conducted by Tullio Serafin. RCA Victor. GD 81969. In Tullio Serafin's loving approach to the work, Jon Vickers is an affecting Otello and Leonie Rysanek a sympathetic Desdemona. The glory of the performance is Tito Gobbi's incomparable Iago, perhaps the most magnificently acted of all his recorded Verdi roles.

Falstaff
opera in three acts (approximate length: 2 hours)

Sir John Falstaff   *baritone*
Ford, alias Signor Fontana   *baritone*
Fenton   *tenor*
Dr Caius   *tenor*
Bardolph   *tenor* ⎤
Pistol   *bass*   ⎦ followers of Falstaff
Alice Ford   *soprano*
Nannetta, daughter of the Fords   *soprano*

Mistress Quickly   *mezzo-soprano*
Mistress Meg Page   *mezzo-soprano*

LIBRETTO BY ARRIGO BOITO, BASED ON SHAKESPEARE'S *THE MERRY WIVES OF WINDSOR*; TIME: DURING THE REIGN OF HENRY IV; PLACE: WINDSOR; FIRST PERFORMED AT THE TEATRO ALLA SCALA, MILAN, 9 FEBRUARY 1893

In 1889 Verdi was in his mid-seventies. Two years had passed since the triumphant premiere of *Otello*, and he had returned to the life of a gentleman farmer, which he had been trying to lead for some time, and from which he had been lured away by Arrigo Boito and *Otello*. Now, in July 1889, Boito sent Verdi the synopsis of another libretto, based on Shakespeare's *The Merry Wives of Windsor*, and the composer was so delighted by it that he wrote immediately to Boito, criticizing one or two details, but making it clear that he was keen to return to composition. However, on the following day Verdi wrote again, striking a note of caution. 'Have you thought of my enormous weight of years?' he asked the librettist. 'What if I could not stand the strain? What if I could not finish the music?' And since Boito was also a composer and at work on his own opera, *Nerone*, Verdi had scruples about distracting his attention from it. But it was impossible for the aged Verdi to suppress the real delight he felt at the prospect of writing music again. His letter to Boito ends, 'What a joy to be able to say to the public, "Here we are again!! Come and see us!"'

Before composing a note of the opera that he and Boito decided to call *Falstaff*, Verdi reread not only *The Merry Wives of Windsor* but also the other Shakespeare plays in which Sir John Falstaff either appears or is referred to: *Henry IV* (Parts I and II) and *Henry V*. The intention of both composer and librettist from the beginning was not merely to create an opera based on *The Merry Wives of Windsor*, but to put the larger-than-life character of Falstaff onto the operatic stage in all his splendour and vividness. Clearly the plot of *The Merry Wives of Windsor* had to be used, for this was the only play in which Falstaff had the leading role, but Verdi and Boito recognized that a fully developed portrait of the fat knight would have to take into consideration aspects of his character found in the other plays. Boito took a few ideas from the Falstaff episodes in *Henry IV*, Part I, notably some lines that became the basis of the opera's 'honour' monologue, and part of the chatter about Bardolph's nose in Act III, scene iii of the play, which is utilized near the beginning of the opera.

Work on *Falstaff* proceeded at a stately pace, and by September 1892 the opera was complete. Verdi sent off Act III to his publisher, accompanied by a note of affectionate farewell to Sir John Falstaff, scribbled on his manuscript score, paraphrasing a passage in Boito's libretto: 'It's all finished. Go, go, old John. Go on your way for as long as you can. Amusing rogue, forever true beneath the masks you wear in different times and places. Go, go, on your way. Farewell.'

At the beginning of January 1893 Verdi began to rehearse *Falstaff* at La Scala, Milan, sometimes for as long as eight hours a day. His colleagues marvelled at the energy and quick-witted resilience of the composer who, now in his eightieth year, seemed younger and livelier than any of them, and as much a perfectionist as ever. A few days before the premiere Verdi's wife, Giuseppina, wrote to her sister, 'Admirers, bores, friends, enemies, genuine and non-genuine musicians, critics good and bad are swarming in from all over the world. The way people are clamouring for seats, the opera house would need to be as big as a public square.' The occasion itself was a triumphant success. Verdi, leading Boito onto the stage to share the applause, was recalled time and time again. Finally he, Boito and Giuseppina left La Scala by a side exit to avoid the crowds flocking around the stage door. But at the Grand Hotel another cheering crowd awaited Verdi. Alhough he managed to fight his way through them to the entrance, he had to appear on his balcony three times before they eventually dispersed.

Act I, scene i. A room in the Garter Inn. Sir John Falstaff, seated at a table, seals two letters he has written, and then he has to listen to the complaint of Dr Caius that the knight's two followers, Pistol and Bardolph, picked Caius's pockets, having got him drunk, and that Falstaff himself broke into his house, beat his servants and took one of his hordes. Falstaff admits most of this before having Caius thrown out. Examining the landlord's bill and his own purse, he complains that Pistol and Bardolph are costing him too much to maintain. He tells them that he is certain of having attracted the interest of two charming women, the wives of wealthy citizens of Windsor, who hold their husbands' purse strings. He has written love letters to each of them, which he asks Bardolph and Pistol to deliver. Both refuse, Bardolph claiming that his honour forbids him. The inn's young page is given the letters to deliver to Alice Ford and Meg Page, and Falstaff then rounds on his colleagues with a scathing harangue on the subject of honour ('L'onore! Ladri!'), before chasing them out of the room.

Act I, scene ii. The garden of Ford's house. Mistress Alice Ford and her daughter Nannetta meet Mistress Meg Page and a neighbour, Mistress Quickly. Both Alice and Meg have received Falstaff's letters, which they are amused to discover are identical. They resolve to play a trick on their corpulent old admirer. Meanwhile, Bardolph and Pistol have informed Ford of Falstaff's desire to seduce his wife. They go off with Ford to help him plan his revenge, while young Fenton stays behind to steal a kiss from Nannetta ('Labbra di foco').

Act II, scene i. The room in the Garter Inn. Mistress Quickly has been sent to Falstaff to deliver Alice Ford's reply, which is that she will be delighted to see him that afternoon, between two and three when her husband is away from home ('Reverenza!'). After Mistress Quickly has left, a Signor Fontana (Ford in disguise) arrives, offering gold to Falstaff if the knight will win the heart of the prudish Alice Ford and thus pave the way for Fontana, who desires her ('C'è a Windsor una dama'). Falstaff accepts with delight, boasting that he will be seeing the lady that very afternoon, between two and three. Left alone while Falstaff goes to dress for his assignation, Ford gives vent to his jealous fury ('E sogno? O realta?'). When Falstaff returns magnificently attired, the two men leave together.

Act II, scene ii. A room in Ford's house. Mistress Quickly reports to Alice that Falstaff has accepted her invitation. Alice seats herself demurely, strumming on a lute, to await Falstaff. When the knight arrives ('Quand'ero paggio'), she manages to avoid his attempted embraces until Mistress Quickly bursts in, as arranged, to announce that Meg Page is about to arrive. Falstaff hides behind a screen, but when Meg enters it is obvious that she is in earnest when she reports the imminent arrival of Ford. The jealous husband rushes in with Fenton, Caius, Bardolph and Pistol, and they search the room for Falstaff, but failing to find him they rush out again to search the rest of the house, while Falstaff is bundled into a huge laundry basket. When Ford returns he hears the sound of a kiss behind the screen, and to his fury he discovers Fenton kissing Nannetta, whom Ford intends to marry off to Dr Caius. Meanwhile, on the instructions of his wife, the contents of the laundry basket have been emptied from the window into the Thames. Alice Ford leads her husband to the window to see Falstaff splashing about in the water.

Act III, scene i. Outside the Garter Inn. A cold and disgruntled Falstaff sits on a bench, brooding on the world's wickedness ('Mondo ladro'), but he revives somewhat when a glass of mulled wine is brought to him. Mistress Quickly arrives, succeeds in assuring him that the servants were to blame for his soaking in the Thames and tells him that Alice Ford wishes to meet him at midnight under Herne the Hunter's oak tree in Windsor Park. Falstaff is to come to the haunted spot disguised as Herne the Hunter. He agrees, and enters the inn with Mistress Quickly as the other women arrive to plan his further discomfiture. Ford and Dr Caius arrange for Nannetta to be married to Caius that night, but they are overheard by Mistress Quickly as she leaves the inn.

Act III, scene ii. Near Herne's Oak in Windsor Great Park. It is close to midnight. Fenton enters and sings of his love for Nannetta ('Dal labbro il canto estasiato vola'). Having been warned by Mistress Quickly that Nannetta is to be married to Caius, who will be disguised as a monk, the women give Fenton a monk's habit to wear. As midnight sounds, Falstaff arrives, dressed as Herne the Hunter, and attempts to embrace Alice, but she warns him that Meg is not far away. Meg cries out in terror and the two women run away, claiming to be pursued by witches. Nannetta, disguised as Queen of the Fairies, weaves a spell ('Sul fil d'un soffio etesio'). Children dressed as imps and fairies dance around a terrified Falstaff, and with the help of Pistol and Bardolph they begin to torment the knight ('Pizzica, pizzica'). During the horseplay, Bardolph loses his mask and is recognized by Falstaff. At this, the others all reveal themselves, and Falstaff accepts the joke in good humour. Ford now blesses the union of the disguised Nannetta and Caius, and Alice Ford presents a second disguised couple to be blessed. Too late, Ford discovers that he has married Fenton to Nannetta, and Caius to Bardolph. Falstaff proclaims that all the world is a jest, as he leads the company in a brilliant fugue ('Tutto nel mondo è burla').

Sir John Falstaff had for years been one of Verdi's favourite characters in Shakespeare, and the great composer has brought him to unerringly truthful operatic life in this enchanting comedy. It is the very profusion of splendid tunes in *Falstaff* that has occasionally led the casual hearer to suppose that it contains no tunes at all, for in this, his final opera, Verdi rarely repeats his tunes, which he is inclined in any case to discard after a few bars. This is a score whose wit and wisdom are equalled only by the Mozart of *Così fan tutte*, *Don Giovanni* and *Le nozze di Figaro*. Scoring of chamber-music-like delicacy is allied to a wide range of orchestral expression; the evocation of forest and fancy in the final scene is absolutely magical; and the opera's pace is such that it seems to last no longer than one sudden flash of inspiration. In the words of George Bernard Shaw, 'It is not often that a man's strength is so immense that he can remain an athlete after bartering half of it to old age for experience; but the thing happens occasionally, and need not so greatly surprise us in Verdi's case.'

Recommended recording: Rolando Panerai (Falstaff), Marilyn Horne (Mistress Quickly), Sharon Sweet (Alice Ford), Alan Titus (Ford), with the Bavarian Radio Chorus and Orchestra conducted by Colin Davis. RCA Victor 09026 60705 2. Panerai is an engaging Falstaff, Marilyn Horne a formidable Mistress Quickly, Sharon Sweet makes the most of Alice Ford's soaring vocal line in the concerted passages, and Ford is strongly characterized by Alan Titus. Colin Davis conducts with a briskness that does not disguise his evident love of Verdi's golden score.

RICHARD WAGNER
(b. Leipzig, 1813 – d. Venice, 1883)

Rienzi
tragic opera in five acts (approximate length: 4 hours, 45 minutes)

Cola Rienzi, papal notary   *tenor*
Irene, his sister   *soprano*
Steffano Colonna, a Roman patrician   *bass*
Adriano, his son   *mezzo-soprano*
Paolo Orsini, a Roman patrician   *bass*
Raimondo, papal legate   *bass*
Baroncelli, a Roman citizen   *tenor*
Cecco del Vecchio, a Roman citizen   *bass*
A Messenger of Peace   *soprano*

LIBRETTO BY THE COMPOSER, BASED ON THE NOVEL *RIENZI, THE LAST OF THE ROMAN TRIBUNES*, BY EDWARD BULWER-LYTTON; TIME: THE MIDDLE OF THE FOURTEENTH CENTURY; PLACE: ROME; FIRST PERFORMED AT THE HOFTHEATER, DRESDEN, 20 OCTOBER 1842

The greatest German opera-composer of the nineteenth century was as a child interested both in the theatre and in music. He learned to play the piano, and having written a play in his teens he began to take lessons in composition in order to be able to provide incidental music for it. Soon he was involving himself in music to the exclusion of all his other studies. In his eighteenth year he had an orchestral work, an overture, performed in Leipzig. He next produced a piano sonata and a symphony. His main interest, however, lay in combining his literary and musical talents in an opera, and to this end he began work on *Die Hochzeit* (The Wedding), which he left incomplete. Almost immediately he embarked upon the composition of another opera, *Die Feen* (The Fairies), again writing his own libretto, based on the play *La donna serpente* by Carlo Gozzi (1762).

At the age of twenty, Wagner obtained an engagement as chorus master at the theatre in Wurzburg. While there he managed to complete *Die Feen* but, except for its overture, did not succeed in getting the opera performed. (It was first staged in 1888, five years after Wagner's death.) For his next opera, *Das Liebesverbot* (The

Ban on Love), he based his libretto on Shakespeare's *Measure for Measure* (1604). This was staged in 1835 at the Civic Theatre in Magdeburg, where Wagner, now aged twenty-two, had been engaged as music director. Two performances of his opera were announced, the second of which had to be cancelled a few minutes before the curtain was due to rise because a fist-fight had broken out between the husband of the leading soprano and the young, handsome tenor singing the role of Claudio, against whom, according to Wagner's memoirs, 'the soprano's husband had for some time been nursing a secret rancour born of jealousy'. After that single performance in Magdeburg, *Das Liebesverbot* was not staged again until 1923, when it was produced in Munich.

While he was with the Magdeburg company Wagner fell in love with a young actress, Minna Planer, whom he married two years later in Königsberg, where Minna was then performing. His next professional engagement was as music director of the theatre in Riga, where he planned and began to compose his next opera, *Rienzi*, based on the English novelist Edward Bulwer-Lytton's *Rienzi, the Last of the Roman Tribunes*, which had been published in 1834 and which Wagner had read in the German translation that appeared in 1836. When Wagner and Minna had to flee from Riga to escape their creditors, they travelled on a small sailing vessel to London, where the composer tried, without success, to meet Bulwer-Lytton, who was a Member of Parliament. The Wagners then made their way to Paris, where *Rienzi* was completed.

The first performance of *Rienzi*, in Dresden in October 1842, began at six in the evening and did not end until shortly before midnight. When it was revived in the following year, it was performed over two evenings as *Rienzis Grosse* (Rienzi's Greatness) and *Rienzis Fall* (Rienzi's Fall), but audiences complained at having to pay twice for what had the previous year been one opera, so the Dresden management reverted to staging the work on one evening, but with substantial cuts. The shortened *Rienzi* remained Wagner's most popular opera for many years but is now only occasionally revived, and it has never been performed at the Wagner Festspielhaus (Festival Theatre) in Bayreuth.

Act I. A street in Rome. The henchmen of Paolo Orsini try to abduct Rienzi's sister Irene while Rienzi is absent from Rome, but Adriano Colonna, who is in love with Irene, succeeds in rescuing her with the help of his family and the populace. When Rienzi returns, a revolt breaks out, and Adriano, though he is of noble birth, sides with Rienzi, the people's leader.

Act II. A hall in the Capitol. Rienzi now rules Rome, and a plot of the Orsini and Colonna families to kill him is foiled. The conspirators are condemned to death, but Adriano and Irene plead with Rienzi for the life of Adriano's father, Steffano Colonna, and Rienzi pardons the nobles.

Act III. A square in the ancient forum. The nobles have gathered an army together and are now marching against Rienzi. Adriano agonizes over his divided loyalty and begs Rienzi in vain to send him as an ambassador of peace to his father. Rienzi returns from the battle in triumph, and the bodies of Orsini and Colonna are borne in on litters. Adriano throws himself onto his father's body, swearing revenge against Rienzi, who is acclaimed by the people as victor and liberator.

Act IV. The square in front of the Lateran Church. Adriano has called Baroncelli, Cecco and other citizens to a secret meeting to incite them to rebellion. When Rienzi arrives and is about to enter the church, Cardinal Raimondo blocks his way and announces that the Pope has excommunicated him. As everyone else abandons Rienzi, Adriano tries to persuade Irene to desert her brother, but she remains faithful to him.

Act V, scene i. A hall in the Capitol. Rienzi prays to God for aid ('Allmächt'ger Vater'). Irene is ready to stand by her brother to the death, and when Adriano tries to carry her away by force she pushes him aside and rushes out to follow her brother, who has left to arm himself.

Act V, scene ii. The square in front of the Capitol. The people, led by Baroncelli and Cecco, set fire to the Capitol, where Rienzi and Irene stand on the balcony in each other's arms. Adriano attempts to enter the building, but it collapses, burying him, as well as Rienzi and Irene, in its ruins.

It was Wagner's intention that *Rienzi* should be a grand opera to 'outdo all previous examples with sumptuous extravagance'. With its stately pace and its proliferation of marches and processions, it certainly lends itself to spectacular production, but much of its thematic material is banal, and its instrumentation is frequently coarse. Rienzi's dignified prayer in Act V, 'Allmächt'ger Vater', the expressive tune of which is first heard in the opera's overture, is the work's musical highlight. Years later, in a letter to Liszt, Wagner referred accurately to *Rienzi* as a superannuated work of immoderate dimensions.

Recommended recording: René Kollo (Rienzi), Siv Wennberg (Irene), Janis Martin (Adriano), with the Leipzig Radio Chorus, Dresden State Opera Chorus and Orchestra, conducted by Heinrich Hollreiser. EMI CMS 7 63980 2. Fine performances by the principal singers, and a vivid and exciting account of the score by the Dresden State Opera Orchestra.

Der fliegende Holländer
(The Flying Dutchman)
Romantic opera in three acts (approximate length: 2 hours, 15 minutes)

Daland, a Norwegian sea captain   *bass*
Senta, his daughter   *soprano*
Erik, a hunter   *tenor*
Mary, Senta's nurse   *mezzo-soprano*
Daland's Helmsman   *tenor*
The Flying Dutchman   *baritone*

LIBRETTO BY THE COMPOSER; TIME: THE EARLY NINETEENTH CENTURY; PLACE: A
NORWEGIAN FISHING VILLAGE AND NEARBY ROCKY SHORE; FIRST PERFORMED AT
THE HOFTHEATER, DRESDEN, 2 JANUARY 1843

In 1838, while he was engaged as a conductor of opera in Riga, Wagner encountered the legend of the Flying Dutchman in Heinrich Heine's *Memoirs of Herr
von Schnabelewopski*, a crypto-autobiographical work of fiction published in
1834. In one chapter the eponymous hero sees in Hamburg 'a big ship looking like
a sombre giant in a great scarlet cloak' and wonders if it could be the Flying
Dutchman. In the next chapter he describes a play about the Dutchman, which he
saw in Amsterdam. Heine was to tell Wagner, when they met in Paris in 1840, that
the 'Amsterdam play' was his own invention; however, Heine had visited London
in 1827, when Edward Fitz-Ball's *The Flying Dutchman* was playing at the Adelphi
Theatre, and Heine might well have seen it.

The story of the Dutchman is sometimes referred to as 'the English legend'.
Though its origin is obscure, and is most probably not English, the legend certainly
made several appearances in English literature and drama in the early nineteenth
century. In addition to Fitz-Ball's play, an anonymous story on the subject appeared
in *Blackwood's Magazine* in 1821, a play by Douglas Jerrold was staged at the Surrey
Theatre in London in 1829, and *The Phantom Ship*, a novel by Captain Marryat, was
published in 1839. 'This subject', Wagner wrote later, 'attracted me and made an
indelible impression on my mind, yet at the time it did not gather enough force to
compel me into using it creatively.'

When the composer fled from his creditors in Riga, he and his wife, Minna,
made their way to London aboard the *Thetis*, a small vessel of not much more
than one hundred tons. In his memoirs Wagner described the horrors of the voyage. A violent storm had arisen, and the captain was driven to seek refuge on the
Norwegian coast. 'And how relieved I was', wrote Wagner,

to behold that far-reaching rocky coast, towards which we were being driven at such speed! A Norwegian pilot came to meet us in a small boat and, with experienced hand, assumed control of the Thetis, whereupon in a very short time I was to have one of the most marvellous and most beautiful impressions of my life. What I had taken to be a continuous line of cliffs turned out on our approach to be a series of separate rocks projecting from the sea. Having sailed past them, we perceived that we were surrounded not only in front and at the sides but also at our back, by these reefs, which closed in behind us so near together that they seemed to form a single chain of rocks. At the same time the hurricane was so broken by the rocks at our rear that the further we sailed through this ever-changing labyrinth of projecting rocks, the calmer the sea became, until at last the vessel's progress was perfectly smooth and quiet as we entered one of those long sea-roads running through a giant ravine – for such the Norwegian fjords appeared to me. A feeling of indescribable content came over me when the enormous granite walls echoed the hail of the crew as they cast anchor and furled the sails. The sharp rhythm of this call clung to me like an omen of good cheer, and shaped itself presently into the theme of the seaman's song in my Flying Dutchman. The idea of this opera was, even at that time, ever present in my mind, and it now took on a definite poetic and musical colour under the influence of my recent impressions.

Wagner's first intention was to compose a short one-act opera on the subject of the Flying Dutchman, which he hoped might be performed as the curtain-raiser to a ballet at the Paris Opéra, and it was in this form that he wrote the synopsis of a libretto while he was still at work on the composition of *Rienzi*. Giacomo Meyerbeer, a composer then at the height of his fame and influence, introduced Wagner to Leon Pillet, the new director of the Opéra, and Pillet in due course bought Wagner's synopsis – but he handed it over to another composer. Although furious at this, Wagner accepted the sum of five hundred francs for his synopsis and decided to expand his idea into a full-length work for a German opera house. (His original sketch was used for *Le Vaisseau fantome*, an opera by the French composer Pierre Dietsch, which was given eleven performances at the Paris Opéra in 1842.)

Between April and November 1841 Wagner worked first on the libretto and then on the music of *Der fliegende Holländer*; he sent his completed score to the director of the Berlin Hofoper, who accepted it. However, after the not unsuccessful premiere of *Rienzi* in Dresden in October of the following year, when *Der fliegende*

Holländer had still not been staged in Berlin, the Dresden Hoftheater acquired the rights from Berlin, and the opera had its premiere in Dresden on 2 January 1843. Only four performances were given, after which the opera was not revived in that city until 1865. It was for a production in Zurich in 1852 that Wagner revised the orchestration and changed the ending of the overture to the form in which it is known today. He had planned the opera to be performed without intervals, but in Dresden this was found not to be practicable. It was not until *Der fliegende Holländer* reached Bayreuth in 1901, when it was staged by Wagner's widow, Cosima, that the composer's wishes were respected and it was presented in one act. In that form, however, the opera plays for nearly two and a half hours, and most opera houses, not surprisingly, prefer to perform it in three acts, each of manageable length, separated by intervals.

Act I. A rocky shore on the Norwegian coast. The ship captained by Daland, a Norwegian, has been driven by a violent storm to seek shelter in the bay, and Daland has come ashore to reconnoitre. Having satisfied himself that he is not far from home, he returns to his ship and bids his Helmsman keep watch. He goes below, and the young Helmsman soon falls asleep ('Mit Gewitter und Sturm'). As the storm rises again, a strange vessel arrives, its sails blood-red, and casts anchor alongside Daland's ship. The Flying Dutchman, a pale figure dressed in black, steps ashore. He is condemned to travel the seas for ever, but allowed to come ashore once every seven years to seek his salvation in the form of a woman who will be faithful to him ('Die Frist ist um'). When Daland returns on deck he is amazed at the sight of the spectral ship, and he hails its captain. The Dutchman asks if Daland has a daughter, and on being told that he has, he asks permission to court her, offering Daland gold. Daland readily agrees, and as the storm abates, the two vessels set sail together for the nearby fishing village.

Act II. A large room in Daland's house. Senta, her nurse Mary and women from the village sit at their spinning wheels ('Summ und brumm'). While the others spin, Senta dreamily contemplates the portrait of a pale, bearded man, the Flying Dutchman, on the wall above the door. The women tease her about her fascination with the Dutchman, saying that her fiancé, Erik, a hunter, should be jealous of him. However, they listen, absorbed, as she sings the ballad of the Dutchman ('Trafft ihr das Schiff im Meere an'). When she reaches the passage about his salvation being achieved only through the love of a faithful woman, Senta cries, 'I am that woman', to the consternation of her friends.

Erik enters to announce that her father's ship has returned. The others leave to welcome Daland and his crew, while Erik declares his love for Senta, whose attention he fails to hold as she continues to gaze at the Dutchman's portrait ('Mein Herz voll Treue bis zum Sterben'). When Erik tells her of a dream he has had, in which she and the pale stranger embraced and fled into the sea together ('Auf hohem Felsen lag ich traumend'), Senta, enraptured, welcomes this as a good omen, and Erik rushes out in despair. As Senta stands staring at the portrait, the door opens and the Dutchman, an exact replica of the painting, stands before her. Daland introduces him ('Mögst du, mein Kind'), but the Dutchman and Senta ignore him, lost in each other, and Daland discreetly retires. The Dutchman wonders if he has at last found redemption ('Wie aus der Ferne') but warns Senta of the dangers she faces in giving herself to him. She pledges eternal love, and Daland returns to give his blessing.

Act III. The harbour, at night. Daland's ship is brightly lit, and its crew are dancing and singing on board ('Steuermann, lass' die Wacht!'). Close by is the Dutchman's ship, dark and silent. Girls from the village come to the quayside with food and wine, but when they call to the sailors on the Dutchman's ship they receive no answer, and the Norwegian sailors jokingly suggest that the crew of the other ship are either all dead or are staying on board to guard their treasure, like dragons. Suddenly the sea, calm until now, begins to heave around the Dutchman's ship, and a faint, blue flame illuminates the hitherto invisible crew, who sing that they will sail on for all eternity. The Norwegians all flee in terror.

Senta and Erik enter. Horrified that she has agreed to marry the Dutchman, Erik reminds Senta of her pledge of love to him ('Willst jenes Tags du nicht dich mehr entsinnen'). The Dutchman arrives and, overhearing Erik's words, thinks that he has been deceived and betrayed by Senta. Ignoring her protestations, he gives orders for his ship's immediate departure and bids her farewell, telling her of the eternal damnation to which he is now condemned, a fate that she has escaped by not having made her promise before God. He announces that he is the Flying Dutchman and swiftly boards his ship, which puts out to sea. Senta rushes to the top of a cliff, calls to the Dutchman that she will be true to him till death and throws herself into the sea. The Dutchman's ship begins to sink beneath the waves, and in the glow of the rising sun the transfigured forms of the Dutchman and Senta are seen in close embrace, rising from the wreck of the ship and soaring up to heaven.

Seen in the light of the later music dramas of Wagner, *Der fliegende Holländer* is clearly a transitional work, although it is an enormous step forward from *Rienzi*. It is an opera filled with strong passions, its occasionally Italianate tunefulness reminiscent of some of the works Wagner was conducting during its composition, and every page of its score is imbued with the spirit of the storm-tossed ocean. The overture, a tone poem that summarizes the action of the opera, contains all of the work's leading motifs – those of the anguished figure of the Dutchman, his redemption through love, and the vigorous, down-to-earth tune sung by Daland's crew. Highlights of the opera include the Dutchman's Act I monologue, his duet with Senta in Act II, her ballad, and the almost brutally swift finale of Act III.

Recommended recording: Robert Hale (the Dutchman), Hildegard Behrens (Senta), Josef Protschka (Erik), Kurt Rydl (Daland), with the Vienna State Opera Chorus and Vienna Philharmonic Orchestra, conducted by Christoph von Dohnanyi. Decca 436 418-2. Robert Hale's Dutchman is powerful and introspective, Hildegard Behrens is a fervent Senta, Josef Protschka brings the delicacy of a Lieder singer to his aria, and Kurt Rydl is a convincing Daland.

Tannhäuser
Romantic opera in three acts (approximate length: 3 hours, 15 minutes)

Hermann, Landgrave of Thuringia   *bass*
Tannhäuser   *tenor*
Wolfram von Eschenbach   *baritone*
Walter von der Vogelweide   *tenor*
Biterolf   *bass*   minstrel-knights
Heinrich der Schreiber   *tenor*
Reinmar von Zweter   *bass*
Elisabeth, the Landgrave's niece   *soprano*
Venus   *soprano*
A Young Shepherd   *soprano*

LIBRETTO BY THE COMPOSER; TIME: THE EARLY THIRTEENTH CENTURY; PLACE: NEAR EISENACH, THURINGIA; FIRST PERFORMED AT THE HOFTHEATER, DRESDEN, 19 OCTOBER 1845

Early in 1843, some weeks after the Dresden premiere of *Der fliegende Holländer*, Wagner was appointed Kapellmeister to the Saxon court, his duties including the composition of music for official occasions. For the Dresden Choral Society he composed a cantata, *Das Liebesmahl der Apostel* (The Love Feast of the Apostles), which he conducted at a festival of all the Saxon choral societies, when it was performed by a chorus of twelve hundred male voices and an orchestra of one hundred. To celebrate the unveiling of a statue of the late King Friedrich August I he wrote a chorus for male voices. What chiefly occupied his attention, however, was his next opera.

In the previous summer, during a hiking holiday in the mountains of Bohemia, Wagner had begun to plan the libretto of a work that he thought of calling *Der Venusberg* (The Mount of Venus). 'One day', he wrote,

> when climbing the Wostrai [the highest peak in the vicinity], I was aston-
> ished, on rounding a bend and entering a valley, to hear a merry dance tune
> whistled by a goatherd perched up on a crag. I seemed immediately to be
> standing among a chorus of pilgrims filing past the goatherd in the valley.
> However, I could not later recall the goatherd's tune, so I was obliged to help
> myself out in the matter, in my usual fashion.

In due course the opera's title, which had given rise to ribald comments among the composer's friends and acquaintances, was changed to *Tannhäuser und der Sangerkrieg auf dem Wartburg* (Tannhäuser and the Song Contest on the Wart-burg) and soon familiarly shortened to *Tannhäuser*. By May 1843 the libretto had been completed, and Wagner began to compose the music in August. By the end of the following January he had finished Act I. Act II was composed during the summer of 1844, and by April 1845 the opera had been completed and scored. It had been decided that *Tannhäuser* would be given its premiere in Dresden in the autumn, so Wagner travelled with Minna to Marienbad in the summer to take the water cure. Here, he found his thoughts turning to his next opera, *Lohengrin*.

Some preliminary rehearsals of *Tannhäuser* had been held before the Dresden company dispersed for the summer. In September rehearsals were resumed, and the first performance of *Tannhäuser* was given at the Hoftheater on 19 October, conducted by Wagner – with very little decor, for most of the scenery had failed to arrive from Paris in time. The opera's reception was lukewarm, press criticism was unfavourable, and a rumour that the work was Catholic propaganda began to circulate, which of course did nothing to help *Tannhäuser* achieve popularity in a Protestant country. For the second performance the role of Tannhäuser had been shortened, the scenery had arrived, and a far from full house gave the work a warmer reception than the first-night audience had accorded it. At the third performance the theatre was packed.

Wagner continued to make changes to the opera when it was revived in Dres-den in 1847 and produced elsewhere in the 1850s. He revised the score drastically for French-language performances in Paris in 1861 and made further changes for productions he supervised in Munich in 1867 and Vienna in 1875. The opera is now invariably performed in the Vienna version of 1875 (though this is usually referred to as the Paris version).

Act I. A grotto in the interior of the Venusberg (the Horselberg, near Eisenach). Youths, maidens, nymphs and satyrs dance ecstatically. Tannhäuser lies at the feet of Venus, the goddess of love. Satiated with the delights of love-making, he longs for his former life and begs the goddess to allow him to return to the mundane outside world. She commands him to sing of their love, but as he does ('Dir, töne Lob!') he finds his thoughts returning to earth and its joy and pain. He asks Venus again to release him. When she refuses, he calls on the Virgin Mary, at the mention of whose name the goddess and the Venusberg suddenly disappear, and Tannhäuser finds himself in the outside world, in a sunlit valley below the Wartburg. It is spring, a Young Shepherd sings and plays his pipe ('Frau Holda kam aus dem Berg hervor'), and the prayers of pilgrims passing through the valley on their way to seek absolution in Rome are interspersed with the joyous sounds of the Shepherd's pipe. Tannhäuser falls on his knees and prays.

The sound of hunting horns heralds the appearance of the Landgrave and his retinue of five minstrel-knights or minnesingers: Wolfram von Eschenbach, Walter von der Vogelweide, Biterolf, Heinrich der Schreiber and Reinmar von Zweter. They recognize Tannhäuser, who has long been absent from them, and led by Wolfram they welcome him back wholeheartedly. Tannhäuser is reluctant to join them and is about to go on his way, but when Wolfram asks him to stay for Elisabeth's sake he is deeply moved. Wolfram tells Tannhäuser that during his absence the Landgrave's niece Elisabeth, who loves him, has become pale and withdrawn ('Als du in kühnem Sänge uns bestrittest'). Tannhäuser joyously contemplates the prospect of a new life, encouraged and supported by the pure love of Elisabeth, and agrees to return to his former companions, who all express their delight.

Act II. The Hall of Song in the Wartburg. In great excitement, Elisabeth greets the hall in which she is at last to see Tannhäuser again ('Dich, teure Halle, grüss' ich wieder'). Wolfram and Tannhäuser enter, and Tannhäuser throws himself at Elisabeth's feet. To her questions he answers only that he has been travelling in distant lands and that all he can remember is his constant longing for her. Elisabeth confesses her love for him, and they sing a duet in praise of the hour of their reunion and the power that has brought it about ('Gepriesen sei die Stunde'). The Landgrave guesses at the feelings that have led his niece again to grace the song festival with her presence, and then he addresses the company of knights and their ladies who have assembled in a long procession. He informs them that the theme of the song contest is to be 'the true essence of love', and that Elisabeth will give the winner, as his prize, whatever he may demand.

Wolfram begins the contest with a gentle expression of courtly love ('Blick' ich umher'), which is acclaimed by all but Tannhäuser, who pours scorn on it. This almost leads to a fight with Biterolf, averted by the intervention of the Landgrave. Wolfram attempts to save the situation with a prayer to heaven to keep them all free from sin ('O Himmel, lass dich jetzt erflehen'), but this goads Tannhäuser into responding with his song in praise of Venus. Tannhäuser ends by inviting all who have never known the delights of earthly love to join him in a visit to the mountain of Venus. There is general consternation, with the women rushing out of the hall in horror, while the men draw their swords. Elisabeth, however, shields Tannhäuser and asks the Landgrave to pardon him. It is she who has been harmed by him, she insists, yet she now prays for his soul.

Filled with remorse and despair, Tannhäuser sinks to his knees. The Landgrave pronounces sentence of banishment upon him, but adds that a path to deliverance from eternal damnation could open to him if he were to join the pilgrims who are making their way to Rome to seek absolution. As the pilgrims' hymn is heard in the distance, Tannhäuser cries 'Nach Rom!' (To Rome!) and hurries out of the hall to join them.

Act III. The valley of the Wartburg. It is now autumn, and evening is approaching. As the pilgrims return from Rome, Elisabeth looks among them in vain for Tannhäuser, and then she prays to the Virgin to receive her soul in heaven ('Allmächt'ge Jungfrau, hör mein Flehen'). As she leaves, Wolfram, who has followed her unobserved, asks if he may accompany her. Elisabeth gently refuses his offer, and left alone, Wolfram sings a song to the evening star ('O, du mein holder Abendstern'), asking it to salute Elisabeth as her soul soars up to join the angels.

Tannhäuser, his pilgrim's garb torn, now stumbles in and tells Wolfram of his journey to Rome ('Inbrunst im Herzen'). He travelled with the other pilgrims, mortifying his flesh on every possible occasion during the journey, but when he approached the Pope to beg forgiveness and absolution, the Pope replied that Tannhäuser had participated in such wicked practices in the Venusberg that his soul is damned for all eternity. 'Just as this staff in my hand can never blossom,' the Pope declared, 'so deliverance from the flames of hell shall never bloom for you.' With no hope of salvation, Tannhäuser now seeks his way back to the Venusberg. As he mentions Venus, the erotic music of her realm is heard, Tannhäuser's frenzy increases, and dancing shapes, which Wolfram identifies as the forces of hell, can be faintly distinguished in the valley. Venus herself calls seductively to Tannhäuser, who attempts to tear himself from Wolfram's grip and hasten to her. Wolfram cries out in desperation that Elisabeth, the angel who prayed for Tannhäuser on earth, will soon intercede for him in heaven. At the mention of Elisabeth's name, Venus and her followers disappear, and a funeral procession enters the valley bearing the body of Elisabeth. With a cry of 'Holy Elisabeth, pray for me', Tannhäuser falls dead upon her bier. More pilgrims now arrive from Rome, carrying the Pope's staff, which has sprouted leaves as a sign that Tannhäuser's soul has found redemption.

On one level a tale of sacred and profane love, *Tannhäuser* is also a tragic love story, a dissertation on the decline of the Romantic ideal, and even a cry of despair at the standards and tastes of Wagner's materialistic nineteenth century. The two worlds that are contrasted in the opera, the piety of the Middle Ages and the rebellious free thought of post-Renaissance man, both find sympathetic expression in Wagner's music. The eroticism of the Venusberg and the chaste utterance of Elisabeth are equally convincing, and it is at those moments when one is in conflict with the other, or at moments of transition from one to the other, that the composer's creative genius sounds forth most excitingly. The leitmotif technique of the later operas, already adumbrated in *Der fliegende Holländer*, is used consciously and with confidence in *Tannhäuser*, especially in Tannhäuser's Act III narration of his pilgrimage to Rome, a clear forerunner of Wagner's later style with its declamatory vocal line above a symphonic accompaniment of great melodic interest. Elsewhere in the opera, for instance in Wolfram's famous song to the evening star, Wagner retains the old Italianate form of recitative and cavatina with simple accompaniment. The dullest passages in the opera are those for the Landgrave, in whom Wagner apparently could summon up little interest.

Recommended recording: René Kollo (Tannhäuser), Helga Dernesch (Elisabeth), Christa Ludwig (Venus), Victor Braun (Wolfram), with the Vienna State Opera Chorus and Vienna Philharmonic Orchestra, conducted by Georg Solti. Decca 414 581–2. Kollo is an exemplary Tannhäuser, and Helga Dernesch a most affecting Elisabeth. As Venus, Christa Ludwig produces the most gloriously sensuous tone quality, and Victor Braun is a sympathetic Wolfram. The Vienna Philharmonic Orchestra produces playing of superlative quality for Solti.

Lohengrin

Romantic opera in three acts (approximate length: 3 hours, 30 minutes)

Heinrich der Vogler (Henry the Fowler), King of Germany   *bass*
Lohengrin   *tenor*
Elsa von Brabant   *soprano*
Duke Gottfried, her brother   *silent role*
Friedrich von Telramund, Count of Brabant   *baritone*
Ortrud, his wife   *mezzo-soprano*
The King's Herald   *bass*

LIBRETTO BY THE COMPOSER; TIME: THE FIRST HALF OF THE TENTH CENTURY;
PLACE: ANTWERP AND SURROUNDINGS; FIRST PERFORMED AT THE HOFTHEATER,
WEIMAR, 28 AUGUST 1850

Several weeks before the October 1845 premiere of *Tannhäuser*, on his summer visit to the spa of Marienbad (now Marianske Lazne), Wagner had begun to work on his next opera. He had taken with him a copy of the old anonymous German epic *Lohengrin*, which took such a hold of him as soon as he began to read it that he found himself excitedly drafting a libretto on the subject. He later wrote in his memoirs that the opera 'stood suddenly revealed before me, complete in every detail of its dramatic construction'. He tried to put it out of his mind, having been advised by his doctor to rest, and turned instead to *Die Meistersinger*, a cheerful subject, which was less likely to overexcite his nerves:

> I felt I must write it down in spite of the doctor's orders. I therefore proceeded to do this, and hoped that it might free me from the thrall of the idea of *Lohengrin*. I was mistaken, however, for no sooner had I got into my bath at noon than I felt an overpowering desire to write Lohengrin, and this longing so overcame me that I could not wait the prescribed hour of the bath, but when a few minutes had elapsed I jumped out and, barely giving myself time to dress, ran home to write down what I had in my mind. I repeated this for several days until the complete sketch for Lohengrin was on paper.

In November 1845, a month after the Dresden premiere of *Tannhäuser*, Wagner read the text of *Lohengrin* to a group of friends in Dresden, one of whom was the composer Robert Schumann, who failed to understand the musical form implicit in it, since there appeared to be no provision for individual musical numbers. 'I then had some fun', Wagner wrote later, 'in reading different parts to him in the form of arias and cavatinas, after which he laughingly declared himself satisfied.'

The *Lohengrin* libretto assumed its final shape over the following months, and the music was written during the next two years, a hasty outline sketch of the entire score being followed by detailed composition of the three acts, beginning with the third. By March 1848 the opera was complete. However, by the time of its first performance, conducted by Liszt on 28 August 1850 in Weimar, Wagner had fled to Switzerland as a political refugee from Saxony. It was not until 1861 that he witnessed a performance of the work.

Of the Weimar premiere, the critic of the Hamburg *Kleinemusikzeitung* wrote:

> At last Wagner's opera *Lohengrin* has been produced in Weimar. The result, as was expected, was roughly the same as when *Rienzi* was performed in Berlin and Königsberg, in other words a gentle fiasco . . . Wagner reveals himself in this work (not to mention his earlier ones) to be completely unmusical. He has given us not music but noise, and such an ugly noise that only a general cannonade on stage was missing to make it sound like the thunder of hell itself . . . In fact we are amazed that Herr Liszt could dare to present the raw product of a false genius such as Wagner to such a cultivated public. In the town where Goethe, Schiller, Wieland and Herder held sway for so long, only the very finest of present artists should be permitted to have their works staged.

The Weimar premiere, given with a company of inadequate singers and a far too small orchestra, obviously did considerably less than justice to *Lohengrin*. Nevertheless, the opera was staged throughout Germany during the following decade, to be hailed eventually as the apotheosis of German Romantic opera. By then its composer had left German Romantic opera behind him and was immersed in the creation of his new type of music drama.

Lohengrin stands at the crossroads. Romantic in its almost Pre-Raphaelite purity and its static, two-dimensional characterization, it also contrives to anticipate the direction Wagner was to take in his next work, *Tristan und Isolde*, by virtue of its delicate balance, though not yet complete fusion, of music and drama. The music was already being made subservient to the drama whenever the composer felt a tension of interests. In a letter to Liszt only a few weeks before the premiere of *Lohengrin* Wagner wrote:

> Give my opera as it is, without cuts. Just one cut I myself prescribe: I want you to take out the second part of Lohengrin's Narration in the big final scene of the third act. After Lohengrin's words, 'Sein Ritter ich, bin Lohengrin genannt', fifty-six bars are to be omitted, down to 'Wo ihr mit Gott mich alle

Landen saht'. I have many times performed the entire work to myself, and I am now convinced that this second section of the Narration can have only a chilling effect. The passage must also be omitted from the libretto.

The passage was dutifully omitted by Liszt and has only rarely been heard in performances since then.

The figure of Lohengrin makes its earliest appearance in Wolfram von Eschenbach's epic *Parzifal*, which dates from some time near the beginning of the thirteenth century. In the final section of the poem, Parzifal, now the custodian of the Holy Grail, retires to Montsalvat with his son Loherangrin, who in due course ventures forth to marry a princess of Brabant who has rejected all other suitors, declaring that she would consent to wed only a knight sent by God. Loherangrin warns her that he would have to leave if she were ever to ask his name. In this version of the story, Loherangrin and the Princess marry and produce children. It is not until several years have passed that the Princess asks the forbidden question, which leads to her husband's departure.

For the purpose of his opera, Wagner introduced the mythical figure of the knight, whom he called Lohengrin, into a historical situation involving Henry I of Saxony, who reigned from 909 to 936. Known as Henry the Fowler, supposedly because the messengers who came to announce his election as King of Saxony found him hunting with his hawks, Henry I was an early fighter for the cause of German unity, in which cause he contrived to extend his authority westwards over several territories in the Low Countries. In the year 924 he negotiated a nine years' truce with the Hungarians, who had been threatening Saxony. When the truce expired, Henry marched against the Hungarians and defeated them in 933. Shortly before the end of the truce, Henry went to Antwerp, capital of Brabant (a territory now divided between Belgium and Holland), in order to persuade the nobles of Brabant to help him defeat the Magyar hordes, and it is against this historical background that the events in *Lohengrin* take place. The history remains in the background, Wagner's interest lying exclusively in the predicament of the strange outsider, saint or artist, who, in offering salvation, at the same time seeks it for himself.

Act I. A meadow by the banks of the River Scheldt near Antwerp. The King has come to Antwerp to enlist the aid of the Brabantians to fight the Hungarians, but he has found the country leaderless and in a state of discord. Friedrich von Telramund claims the throne of the Duke of Brabant, maintaining that shortly before the Duke's death he was appointed guardian of the Duke's two children,

Elsa and her young brother Gottfried. One day, when she had grown to be a young woman, Elsa went into the forest with Gottfried and returned without him, claiming that the child had wandered away and that she was unable to find him. Telramund now charges Elsa with the murder of her brother and claims the land of Brabant as his own, by virtue of his being a kinsman of the late Duke.

The King summons Elsa to appear, and she passionately invokes as her champion and defender a knight who appeared to her in a dream ('Einsam in trüben Tagen'). The King calls for a trial by combat, but the Herald's summons is sounded twice and no one steps forward to defend Elsa and challenge Telramund. It is only when Elsa falls to her knees in fervent prayer that a boat drawn by a swan is seen approaching, bearing a knight in shining armour. As his boat reaches the bank, the knight bids a tender farewell to the swan ('Nun sei bedankt, mein lieber Schwan') and then declares to the King that he has been sent to defend a woman falsely accused. Elsa greets him as her saviour. When she agrees to marry him if he is victorious in combat, the knight extracts from her a solemn promise that she will never ask or seek to discover his name or his origin. Elsa gives her assurance quickly and unthinkingly, but the knight repeats the promise she must make. Elsa swears to honour this requirement, and Lohengrin declares his love for her. At a signal from the King, the knight and Telramund draw their swords and fight. The knight is the victor, but he spares Telramund's life, suggesting that he devote it to repentance. The knight is hailed by all as a hero, and Telramund falls unconscious at the feet of his wife, Ortrud.

Act II. The citadel of Antwerp. It is shortly before dawn. Telramund and Ortrud, who have been sentenced to banishment, lurk in the shadow of the cathedral. Telramund exhorts Ortrud to flee with him before their presence is discovered. He blames her for his misfortune, for it was under her influence that he slandered Elsa. Ortrud outlines her plan to bring about Elsa's downfall. Telramund is to arouse Elsa's suspicion of her defender by charging him with having resorted to sorcery to win the combat, and Elsa must be induced to ask the knight the forbidden question. Telramund eagerly seizes this chance to redeem his honour, and he leaves as Elsa appears on the balcony of the women's quarters, musing on her newly found happiness ('Euch Lüften, die mein Klagen so traurig oft erfüllt').

Ortrud plaintively calls to Elsa, and by guile succeeds in persuading the innocent girl to take pity on her. When Elsa withdraws after telling Ortrud to wait while she comes down to bring her inside, Ortud calls on her heathen gods, Wotan and Freia, to aid her vengeance ('Entweihte Götter!'). Elsa reappears, and Ortrud abruptly reverts to her former cringing tone. She warns Elsa not to place so blind a trust in her present happiness, suggesting that the knight who arrived so mysteriously might eventually leave her just as mysteriously. Elsa, secure in her faith, merely expresses her pity for Ortrud. As the two women go indoors, Telramund emerges from the shadows with an exultant cry that evil has entered the house.

Day dawns. In the castle courtyard the Herald announces that the King has banished Telramund and has given the dukedom of Brabant to the knight, whose marriage to Elsa will take place that day. The citizens greet this announcement with joy, but as the wedding procession approaches the cathedral its way is suddenly blocked by Ortrud, who orders Elsa to stand back and give precedence to her. Ortrud questions the lineage and the motives of the knight Elsa is about to marry, and the crowd begins to wonder whether there might not be some truth in her words. When Telramund appears and accuses the knight of sorcery, even Elsa's mind begins to be beset with doubt. However, she reaffirms her love to the knight. As they enter the cathedral Elsa looks back to see Ortrud standing with her arm raised as though in triumph.

Act III, scene i. The bridal chamber. The King presents the bride to her husband, and the chorus sings a bridal song ('Treulich geführt'). When the knight is left alone with Elsa he begins a tender love duet ('Das süsse Lied verhallt'); but, as he breathes her name lovingly, Elsa complains that she can never know the sound of his name. Everything he says to calm her only increases her desire to know all. Finally she asks him the forbidden questions. What is his name? Whence has he come? What is his lineage?

As soon as Elsa has asked the questions, Telramund and four of his followers burst into the room, their swords drawn. Shouting a warning to her husband, Elsa hands him his sword and he fells Telramund with a single blow. Telramund's four companions drop their swords in terror and fall to their knees. Elsa swoons, and the knight orders that she be brought before the King. There he will answer his bride's questions.

Act III, scene ii. The meadow on the banks of the Scheldt. The knights of Brabant and their vassals gather in the dawn to join the King and his Saxon forces to do battle against the Hungarians. When the King asks the whereabouts of the new Protector of Brabant, Telramund's four followers enter bearing Telramund's covered body on a bier. They are followed by a sorrowful Elsa and by the knight, who first justifies his killing of Telramund and then accuses Elsa of having broken her pledge, thus forcing him to disclose his name. This he does in a narrative aria ('In fernem Land'). He was sent by the Holy Grail, whose knights travel to distant lands to champion the innocent. When a knight of the Grail is recognized by the profane world, he must leave and return to Montsalvat, the home of the Grail. His father, says the knight, is Parsifal, the keeper of the Grail, and he himself is called Lohengrin.

All respond reverently to his words, with the exception of Elsa, who is filled with horror and remorse. When the swan is seen to approach with the boat to bear him away, Lohengrin addresses the bird sadly and then turns to Elsa in an outburst of grief, telling her that had she but trusted him for a year her brother Gottfried, whom she believed dead, would have been returned to her ('Mein lieber Schwan'). Ortrud triumphantly announces that the swan is none other than Gottfried, whom she, Ortrud, has bewitched. Lohengrin falls to his knees in prayer, and the white dove of the Grail descends, hovering over the boat. The swan sinks into the water, and in its place Lohengrin helps up onto the bank the young Gottfried, whom he proclaims the new Duke of Brabant. At the sight of Gottfried, Ortrud sinks to the ground with a shriek. Lohengrin springs into the boat, which is drawn away by the dove, while Elsa falls lifeless into her brother's arms.

Although *Lohengrin* is the last of Wagner's works for the stage which can be more accurately described as opera than as music drama, it is nevertheless also the first in which he makes quite complex use of the leitmotif or guiding theme, a device on which he was increasingly to rely in his later works. The ethereally beautiful prelude to *Lohengrin* is based entirely on one such motif, that of the Holy Grail. The opera's highlights include Elsa's 'Einsam in trüben Tagen', which begins gently but becomes impassioned as she sings of the knight whom she has seen in her dream; her Act II aria, 'Euch Lüften', in which she tells the evening breeze of her newly found happiness; Ortrud's fierce invocation of her heathen gods, 'Entweihte Götter!'; the Act III love duet and celebrated bridal chorus; Lohengrin's Narration ('In fernem Land'); the great ensembles throughout the opera; and the brilliant (and famous) prelude to Act III, which depicts the wedding festivities of Lohengrin and Elsa.

Although the philosophical meaning and validity of its libretto may be open to question, *Lohengrin* works magnificently in purely dramatic terms. Upon a two-dimensional, mediaeval fear of the unknown world Wagner has superimposed a drama that is modern in its psychology and unerring in its poetic instinct. Thus he retains the best not of two apparent worlds but of three: the spiritual, the psychological and the aesthetic. In a sense they are one, or rather they are three ways of looking at the same world. It is the interplay between these three views of the world, in Wagner's music and his words, which makes *Lohengrin* a great opera.

Tristan und Isolde

opera in three acts (approximate length: 3 hours, 45 minutes)

Tristan, a Cornish knight, nephew of King Marke   *tenor*
King Marke of Cornwall   *bass*
Isolde, an Irish princess   *soprano*
Kurwenal, Tristan's retainer   *baritone*
Melot, a knight at the court of King Marke   *tenor*
Brangäne, Isolde's attendant   *soprano*
A Shepherd   *tenor*
A Helmsman   *baritone*
A Sailor   *tenor*

LIBRETTO BY THE COMPOSER; TIME: THE MIDDLE AGES; PLACE: THE IRISH SEA, CORNWALL AND BRITTANY; FIRST PERFORMED AT THE HOFOPER, MUNICH, 10 JUNE 1865

Fifteen years were to elapse between the premiere of *Lohengrin* in 1850 and that of Wagner's next opera, *Tristan und Isolde*. During this period Wagner not only began to plan a huge work based on the old Nordic myth of the Nibelungs (which was eventually to become his tetralogy, *Der Ring des Nibelungen*), but also worked on a comedy (*Die Meistersinger von Nürnberg*), and wrote lengthy polemical articles, among them the scurrilous anti-Semitic 'Judaism in Music', in which he demanded the elimination of Jews from German society and ended by gleefully prophesying the decline and fall of the entire Jewish race.

One of Wagner's essays, 'Opera and Drama', is important in any consideration of Wagnerian music drama, for in it the composer postulated the new kind of opera that, after *Lohengrin*, he himself was to devote his energies to creating. The drama, presented on a conscious level by the words, would be pursued on a deeper, unconscious level in the orchestra. Musical form, as such, would be irrelevant, and indeed would cease to exist.

In 1857, while Wagner and Minna were living in Zurich, they became friendly with a wealthy silk merchant, Otto Wesendonk, who installed them in a villa close to his own. Wesendonk's wife, Mathilde, fell victim to the Wagner spell, and it was as an expression of his passion for her that Wagner turned aside from the other piece on which he had been working (*The Ring*), to write first the libretto and then the music of *Tristan und Isolde*. During the course of the opera's composition he also wrote five songs to poems by Mathilde Wesendonk, into two of which, 'Träume' (Dreams) and 'Im Treibhaus' (In the Hothouse), he wove themes from the opera. Soon the personal situation of the two families became intolerable. The two wives quarrelled openly, and Wesendonk tactfully took Mathilde on a visit to Italy. Minna was sent to Dresden to intercede with the authorities for a pardon for her husband, while the harassed composer, at a stroke deprived of his benefactor, his muse–mistress and his domestic helpmate, made his way alone to Venice to continue work on *Tristan und Isolde*, finally completing the opera in Lucerne.

In 1859 the Wagners settled again in Paris. A production of *Tannhäuser*, for which Wagner made changes to incorporate the necessary ballet, was interrupted by organized demonstrations. Soon, Minna returned to live permanently in Dresden, while Wagner kept on the move in an attempt to promote his operas, consoling himself with one or two new love affairs. Minna Wagner died in January 1866, by which time Wagner had become emotionally involved not only with Cosima von Bülow, illegitimate daughter of Liszt and wife of the conductor Hans von Bülow, but also with the eighteen-year-old King Ludwig II of Bavaria.

It was in May 1864 in Stuttgart, whither Wagner had fled to avoid creditors and an Austrian warrant for his arrest for debt, that the secretary of King Ludwig brought to the composer the fascinating news that the young King was passionately interested in him and his music and wished to become his protector. Wagner immediately travelled to the Bavarian capital, Munich, and became the close friend of the homosexual monarch, who was already well advanced towards the insanity in which he was to end his days. Wagner received Ludwig's bounty and also his devotion, which was expressed by the King in highly romantic terms:

> The mean cares of everyday life I will banish from you forever. I will procure for you the peace you have longed for, in order that you may be free to spread the mighty wings of your genius in the pure air of rapturous art. O, how I have looked forward to the time when I could do this! I hardly dared indulge myself in the hope of so quickly being able to prove my love to you.

Wagner soon persuaded Ludwig to agree to build him a theatre of his own. However, his relationship with the young King was causing a scandal at the Bavarian court. Ludwig's grandfather, Ludwig I, had been thought disreputable because he had a mistress, the entertainer Lola Montez; now Ludwig II's favourite, Richard Wagner, had the nickname 'Lolette' conferred upon him, and he began to acquire in Munich the reputation of being an active homosexual. Ludwig had given Wagner an opulent apartment, and the composer summoned a Viennese seamstress to Munich to transform it into what one of Wagner's biographers has called 'a whorish fantasy of silks, satins, velvets and laces'.

In April 1865 Cosima von Bülow gave birth to Wagner's child, Isolde, whom Bülow accepted as his own. When *Tristan und Isolde* was given its first performance in Munich on 10 June, Hans von Bülow was the conductor. Many of Wagner's former friends and admirers stayed away from the premiere, preferring not to expose themselves to the monster of vanity they considered the composer had become. Of those who were present, few recognized the stature of one of the great masterpieces of Romanticism, except perhaps King Ludwig, who wrote to Wagner immediately after the performance, quoting the words of Isolde's *Liebestod*:

Only one! Hallowed one!
What rapture! – Perfect. Overwhelmed by delight! . . . to drown . . . to sink – unconscious – highest bliss – Divine work!
Eternally true,
till death and beyond!

Nine years were to pass before *Tristan und Isolde* was staged elsewhere. When the opera reached London in 1882 the critics were divided. One vowed solemnly that, as long as he lived, he 'would never write another word in disparagement of Richard Wagner or his music', while another protested against the composer's musical representation of 'animal passion', but took comfort 'in the fact that Wagner's music, in spite of all its wondrous skill and power, repels a greater number than it fascinates'. Gradually, however, *Tristan und Isolde* came to be recognized as one of the most important musical works of the nineteenth century.

The seeds of *Tristan und Isolde* were sown well before Wagner met Mathilde Wesendonk, his feeling for her merely providing a convenient excuse for turning aside from *Der Ring des Nibelungen* at the moment when the need to compose his great apotheosis of Romanticism welled up in him. The origins of the legend of Tristan and Isolde are lost in antiquity, though it is now generally thought that the story must originally have come from Wales or Cornwall. Wagner approached it through the thirteenth-century epic *Tristan*, by the German minnesinger Gottfried von Strassburg.

Act I. On the deck of Tristan's ship at sea, crossing from Ireland to the northern coast of Cornwall. The Irish Princess Isolde, who is being taken to Cornwall by Tristan against her will to marry his uncle, King Marke, is resolved to die. She orders her attendant Brangäne to summon Tristan to speak to her, but Tristan's friend and loyal retainer Kurwenal answers Brangäne roughly. Told of this, Isolde reacts indignantly, and in a lengthy solo (Isolde's Narration: 'Wie lachend sie mir Lieder singen') she tells Brangäne of the events that have led to her present situation. Tristan killed Isolde's lover Morold in a duel. However, Tristan himself was seriously wounded and asked to be placed in a boat with his weapons and to be cast adrift on the sea to die. When his boat was thrown up on the Irish shore by the tide, Tristan was nursed back to health by Isolde, who was at first unaware of his identity. When she discovered who he was, her first impulse was to kill him, but instead she allowed him to convalesce and in due course to return to Cornwall unharmed. Later, Tristan was sent by King Marke to make peace with Ireland and to demand the hand of Isolde in marriage with Marke by way of sealing the treaty. Isolde was forced to consent. She now curses Tristan and utters an agonized plea for death to come to them both.

Brangäne suggests to Isolde that the magic love-potion Isolde's mother has provided, to be given by Isolde to King Marke on their wedding day, might more usefully be employed now upon Tristan, but Isolde orders her to prepare another potion, a deadly poison. They are interrupted by Kurwenal, who announces that they are nearing land and that Tristan requests Isolde to prepare herself to be received by King Marke. Isolde replies that custom and courtesy require Tristan first to present himself to her, to beg her forgiveness for his treatment of her. While Kurwenal is delivering this message, Isolde instructs Brangäne to prepare the poison that she intends to share with Tristan. Tristan arrives, and although he is aware that he is being offered poison, he drinks it. Isolde snatches the cup from his hand, and she drinks as well. But Brangäne actually substituted the love potion for the poison, and consequently. Tristan and Isolde stand gazing at each other, enraptured, and then fall into each other's arms. Clasped in an embrace, they are oblivious to the voices of the sailors hailing King Marke, and it is only with the greatest difficulty that Brangäne manages to separate them as the King steps on board.

Act II. The garden of King Marke's castle in Cornwall, on a summer night. Horns can be heard in the distance as King Marke's hunting party sets out. Isolde waits impatiently for Brangäne to extinguish the torch burning by the door, as a signal to Tristan that it is safe for him to come to her. However, Brangäne warns her mistress against Tristan's friend Melot, who persuaded Marke to go hunting so that the lovers could meet but whom Brangäne suspects of having set a trap for Tristan. Isolde impulsively extinguishes the torch herself, ordering Brangäne to keep watch in the tower. When Tristan enters, the lovers fall passionately into each other's arms. They sing of the spiteful day that has kept them apart, and bless the night that brings them love ('O sink hernieder, Nacht der Liebe').

Ignoring Brangäne's warning from the tower that dawn and danger approach ('Einsam wachend in der Nacht'), the lovers continue to yearn for night and for death, in whose realm their love will continue for all eternity. Suddenly a scream is heard from Brangäne, and Kurwenal rushes in with his sword drawn, calling to Tristan to save himself. He is closely followed by King Marke, Melot and the hunting party. Marke, bewildered, asks how his nephew could thus betray him ('Mir, dies? Dies, Tristan, mir?'). Tristan cannot give any explanation. Turning to Isolde, he asks her if she is prepared to follow him to the land that he is bound for. She understands his meaning, and answers that she will follow, if he shows her the way. As Tristan kisses her gently on the forehead, Melot starts forward with his sword drawn. Tristan allows Melot to wound him and collapses in Kurwenal's arms.

Act III. The overgrown garden of Tristan's dilapidated castle in Brittany. Kurwenal has brought the wounded Tristan to his hereditary castle in Brittany and laid him, unconscious, in the courtyard. Messengers have been sent to Isolde, and Kurwenal awaits her ship, whose arrival will be signalled by the Shepherd outside the castle walls changing the mournful tune he plays on his horn to a merry one. Tristan recovers consciousness, and Kurwenal describes how he brought his master back to the castle of his ancestors. Tristan, however, in a state of delirium can think only of Isolde and their love.

When the Shepherd sounds his joyful tune, Kurwenal hurries down to the shore to fetch Isolde. Tristan rips the bandage from his wound, struggles to his feet as Isolde rushes in, and dies in her arms. A second ship arrives, bringing King Marke, Melot and their retinue. Kurwenal, in a rage, kills Melot and is himself mortally wounded, dying at the feet of the dead Tristan. Brangäne tells Isolde that she has explained to King Marke about the love potion and that Marke has come to Brittany to forgive Tristan. But Isolde, who has heard nothing around her, fixes her eyes with growing ecstasy on Tristan. In a blissful aura of joy, she sings of his awakening to new life in death and of the radiance of their eternal love, breathing her last as she sinks upon Tristan's body (the *Liebestod*: 'Mild und leise, wie er lächelt').

It had been Wagner's initial intention to create *Tristan und Isolde* in the style of Italian opera, as he expected that this would earn him the most money. He even began negotiations to provide such an opera for performance in Rio de Janeiro. It was not until he fell in love with Mathilde Wesendonk that the opera began to take shape in his mind in the form in which it was finally to emerge. When he actually began to compose *Tristan und Isolde*, all thoughts of deliberately copying the style of contemporary Italian opera were forgotten. The music comes from deep within him and addresses itself to equally deep responses in its hearers. The drama of the work flows smoothly through uninterrupted music that appears to grow, indeed to generate spontaneously, from the seed of the opera's prelude. The score's heavily sensuous chromaticism and the ecstatic richness of its orchestration combine to give the opera a curious psychological strength. It was in *Tristan und Isolde* that Wagner discovered how to reach simultaneously the conscious and subconscious responses of his audience, a discovery he was to put to great use in *Der Ring des Nibelungen*.

Written out of love for Mathilde Wesendonk, *Tristan und Isolde* was also written under the influence of the philosopher Arthur Schopenhauer (1788–1850), whose principal work, *Die Welt als Wille und Vorstellung* (The World as Will and Idea), Wagner had read shortly before he began to compose the opera. From Schopenhauer's assertion that there is, in the world, so great a gap between the ideal and the real that suffering is a natural condition of mankind grew Wagner's theoretical interest in renunciation of the worldly. But he, the most worldly of men, could embrace this belief only by turning from the outside world to the world of feeling, by renouncing day and its falseness in favour of night and love. The juxtaposition of hated day and longed-for night, the idea of day as mundane life and night as death-in-love, which permeates *Tristan und Isolde*, is a specifically Wagnerian element, playing no part in the old Celtic myth or in Gottfried von Strassburg's thirteenth-century epic.

The prelude to the opera, a slow, sensuous, bittersweet evocation of romantic desire, introduces several of the motifs embedded within the score and sets the mood, one of being, as Keats put it in his 'Ode to a Nightingale', 'half in love with easeful death', that persists beneath the work's occasional spurts of action until it finds glorious release in the *Liebestod*. Isolde's Act I Narration, the only passage of plot exposition in the entire opera, gives the performer of Isolde a splendid opportunity to enliven the external aspects of the drama. The love duet in Act II is the very essence of musical Romanticism, and Isolde's *Liebestod* ('Mild und leise, wie er lächelt'), with which the opera ends, surges to a climax of cosmic joy as Isolde sinks upon Tristan's breast, transfigured by death to a higher state of immortal love.

Recommended recording: Siegfried Jerusalem (Tristan), Waltraud Meier (Isolde), with the Berlin State Opera Chorus and Berlin Philharmonic Orchestra, conducted by Daniel Barenboim. Teldec 4509–94568–2. Meier and Jerusalem are near-ideal as the lovers, and Barenboim's interpretation of the score is full of insight.

Die Meistersinger von Nürnberg
(The Mastersingers of Nuremberg)
opera in three acts (approximate length: 4 hours, 15 minutes)

Hans Sachs, cobbler   *bass-baritone*
Veit Pogner, goldsmith   *bass*
Kunz Vogelgesang, furrier   *tenor*
Konrad Nachtigall, tinsmith   *bass*
Sixtus Beckmesser, town clerk   *baritone*
Fritz Kothner, baker   *bass*   mastersingers
Balthasar Zorn, pewterer   *tenor*
Ulrich Eisslinger, grocer   *tenor*
Augustin Moser, tailor   *tenor*
Hermann Ortel, soapmaker   *bass*
Hans Schwarz, weaver   *bass*
Hans Foltz, coppersmith   *bass*

Walther von Stolzing, a young knight from Franconia   *tenor*
David, Hans Sachs's apprentice   *tenor*
Eva, Pogner's daughter   *soprano*
Magdalene, Eva's nurse   *mezzo-soprano*
A Nightwatchman   *bass*

LIBRETTO BY THE COMPOSER; TIME: THE MIDDLE OF THE SIXTEENTH CENTURY; PLACE: NUREMBERG; FIRST PERFORMED AT THE HOFOPER, MUNICH, 21 JUNE 1868

It was in the summer of 1845, while he was taking the cure at Marienbad, that Wagner first became interested in composing an opera on the subject of the mediaeval tradesmen's guilds. As he recalled in his autobiography,

Owing to some comments I had read in Gervinus's <u>History of German Literature</u>, both the Mastersingers of Nuremberg and Hans Sachs had acquired quite a vital charm for me. The Marker alone, and the part he takes in the 'master-singing', were particularly pleasing to me, and on one of my lonely walks, without knowing anything in particular about Hans Sachs and his poetic contemporaries, I thought out an amusing scene, in which the cobbler – as a popular artisan-poet – with the hammer on his last, gives the Marker a practical lesson by making him sing, thereby taking revenge on him for his conventional misdeeds.

To me, the force of the whole scene was concentrated in the two following points: on the one hand the Marker, with his slate covered with chalk-marks, and on the other hand Sachs holding up the soles covered with his chalk-marks, each intimating to the other that the singing had been a failure. To this picture, by way of concluding the second act, I added a scene consisting of a narrow, crooked little street in Nuremberg, with the people all running about in great excitement, and ultimately engaging in a steet brawl. Thus, suddenly, the whole of my comedy about the Mastersingers took shape so vividly before me that, inasmuch as it was a particularly cheerful subject, and not in the least likely to over-excite my nerves, I felt I must write it down in spite of the doctor's orders. I therefore proceeded to do this, and hoped that it might free me from the thrall of the idea of <u>Lohengrin</u>.

It did not, and Wagner turned aside from his comedy to work on *Lohengrin*, not returning to *Die Meistersinger* until sixteen years later, during a train journey from Venice to Vienna:

It was during this journey that the music of <u>Die Meistersinger</u> first dawned on my mind, in which I still retained the outline of the libretto as I had originally conceived it. With the utmost distinctness I at once composed the principal part of the overture in C major . . . I arrived in Vienna in a very cheerful frame of mind. I at once announced my return to Cornelius [the German composer Peter Cornelius, with whom Wagner was on friendly terms] . . . The communication of my plan for the immediate composition of <u>Die Meistersinger</u> made him almost frantic with delight, and until my departure from Vienna he remained in a state of delirious excitement.

In Vienna, Wagner made his second sketch for a libretto on the subject of the mastersingers, consulting Jakob Grimm's *Über den altdeutschen Meistergesang* (On the Old German Mastersong) and Johann Christoph Wagenseil's *Buch von den Meister-Singer Holdseligen Kunst* (Nuremberg Chronicle), a history of Nuremberg published in 1697 which contains an account of the 'Origins, Practice, Utility and Rules of the Gracious Art of the Mastersingers'. From Wagenseil,

Wagner took the names of several Nuremberg mastersingers, though he invented trades for them in his opera. Eisslinger, for example, was not a grocer but a timber merchant. Nor was the historical Beckmesser the talentless pedant that Wagner makes him out to be. (He at first gave the character we now know as Beckmesser the name of 'Veit Hanslich' and maliciously invited the Viennese music critic Eduard Hanslick to hear him read the libretto at the house of a friend. Hanslick attended the reading, but finding himself mocked as a humourless and dishonest pedant, he fled from the room, no doubt to Wagner's amused satisfaction.)

Wagner worked on the score of *Die Meistersinger* over the next few years, finally completing the opera in 1867 in his country house near Lucerne, overlooking the lake, where he was now living with Cosima von Bülow, and where their second child was born and named Eva after the heroine of *Die Meistersinger*. At its premiere in Munich on 21 June 1868 the opera was conducted by Cosima's long-suffering husband, Hans von Bülow. It was a huge success, the only unfortunate incident of the evening occurring when Wagner, who had sat, consort-like, beside his benefactor King Ludwig in the royal box, stepped forward to acknowledge the applause. The Munich bourgeoisie were outraged.

Act I. The interior of St Catherine's Church, Nuremberg. The congregation at the afternoon service on the eve of Midsummer's Day sings a chorale in praise of St John. Eva and her nurse Magdalene sit in one of the back rows, and surreptitious glances pass between Eva and the young Franconian knight Walther von Stolzing, who leans against a pillar. Walther met and fell in love with Eva the previous evening, when he visited her father, the goldsmith Pogner. As the church service ends and the congregation begins to leave, Walther approaches Eva to ask if she is already engaged to be married. Eva explains to him that her father intends to give her in marriage to the winner of the mastersingers' song contest on St John's Day (Midsummer's Day), but that she will marry no one but him. Walther decides to become a member of the mastersingers' guild, in order to be able to compete.

Apprentices, among them Hans Sachs's David, begin to prepare the space in front of the choir for a meeting of the mastersingers. Magdalene asks David, her sweetheart, to teach Walther the rules of the mastersingers, and after Eva and Walther have arranged to meet later that evening the two women depart. David soon discovers that Walther understands nothing of the mastersingers' art, or their complex rules, or the stages one has to go through before one can become a singer.

The mastersingers now begin to arrive, among them Sixtus Beckmesser, the town clerk, who attempts to importune Pogner to intercede on his behalf with Eva, for he hopes to win the contest. He is annoyed to learn from Pogner's formal announcement of the prize ('Das schöne Fest, Johannestag') that the final decision as to whom she will marry is to rest with Eva herself. Walther tells Pogner that he wishes to become a mastersinger, and Eva's father agrees to support the young knight's application, but warns him that he will have to undergo a trial.

When the mastersingers ask who taught him to sing, Walther announces that his teacher was an ancient book by Walther von der Vogelweide and that his school was the depths of the forest ('Am stillen Herd in Winterszeit'). Walther is now required to sing a trial song, whose faults will be noted on a slate by the marker, who is Beckmesser. If more than seven faults are recorded, the candidate is rejected. Walther takes his place in the singing chair and, after Beckmesser's formal invitation to begin ('Fanget an'), improvises a song in praise of spring and young love. Beckmesser finds it full of faults and soon covers his slate with chalk marks. Hans Sachs admires the young knight's originality, but Walther is declared by everyone else to have failed.

Act II. A narrow street in Nuremberg. On one side is Pogner's house, and on the other the simpler dwelling and workshop of Hans Sachs. It is evening. David is engaged in closing the shutters of Sachs's house, while other apprentices can be seen performing similar tasks further down the street, singing and dancing as they work, in joyful anticipation of St John's Day on the morrow. Pogner and Eva return from an evening stroll, and when her father goes into the house Eva learns from Magdalene the bad news concerning Walther. Sachs sits at a bench in his workshop, preparing to work on a pair of shoes he is making for Beckmesser, but he cannot get Walther's trial song out of his mind and muses upon the mysterious nature of art ('Was duftet doch der Flieder so mild, so stark und voll'). Eva approaches Sachs, but cannot bring herself to question him openly about Walther's failure. She wonders if Sachs himself will enter the contest, and when he replies that he is too old for her, she reveals that she has occasionally thought that he might one day take her into his house as both wife and child. Eventually, Sachs admits to Eva that there seems to be no chance of Walther becoming a mastersinger. In order to test the strength of her feeling for the knight, he adds that he wishes the high and mighty young nobleman would leave the honest artisans of Nuremberg to practise their art in peace. From Eva's angry reaction, Sachs realizes that she is in love with Walther and resolves to help the young knight.

Magdalene tells Eva that Beckmesser intends to serenade her later that evening, and the two women decide that Magdalene should dress as Eva and sit in her window to be serenaded, while Eva goes to meet Walther. When Walther arrives, he and Eva begin to plan their elopement, but Sachs, who has been observing them, prevents their flight by placing his lantern so that it sheds a strong beam of light across the street. Beckmesser arrives to serenade Eva but is interrupted by Sachs, who embarks upon a noisy song ('Jerum! Jerum!') ostensibly about Adam and Eve but actually containing a hidden cautionary message to Eva, who, with Walther, has now retreated to a seat under a lime tree.

Beckmesser persuades Sachs to listen to his serenade and advise him, but Sachs imposes a condition. He will mark Beckmesser's faults by tapping on the sole of the shoe he is making for Beckmesser. Sachs taps away at the shoe and manages to complete his work on it well before Beckmesser's song is over. By now the neighbours have been awakened by the noise, and when David thinks he sees his beloved Magdalene being serenaded by a stranger he leaps from his window upon Beckmesser and begins to thrash him. Soon the neighbours and the other apprentices have joined in the fray. In the confusion, Walther and Eva try to make their escape, but Sachs separates them and drags Walther into his house. The Nightwatchman's horn is heard nearby, causing the crowd to disperse. Pogner takes Eva into their house, and Beckmesser limps away down the street. By the time the Nightwatchman has appeared upon the scene, all is tranquil.

Act III, scene i. Sachs's workshop, next morning. David asks his master's forgiveness for his behaviour of the previous evening, and he sings his offering for St John's Day ('Am Jordan Sankt Johannes stand'). Realizing that it is also Hans Sachs's name day, the apprentice attempts to present Sachs with a basket of flowers. Sachs sends the lad off to dress for the festival and, left alone with his thoughts, broods on the state of the world, with people killing and tormenting one another, and madness everywhere ('Wahn! Wahn! Überall Wahn!').

Walther, who has spent the night in Sachs's house, enters from an inner room. He tells the cobbler that he has had a most beautiful dream of love, and Sachs instructs him in the art of interpreting his dream in song. As Walther performs the song, Sachs writes it down. Two of the three stanzas required by the terms of the contest are composed before Walther becomes impatient. Sachs realizes that at the appropriate time the knight will find the inspiration to complete his song, and the two men retire to dress for the festival. While the workshop is empty, Beckmesser enters. Finding Walther's song that Sachs has written out, he assumes it to be a composition by Sachs himself to perform in the contest, and he thrusts it into his pocket. The cobbler enters, now in his festival attire, and Beckmesser accuses him of having the previous evening attempted to rid himself of a dangerous rival by setting ruffians upon him. When Sachs denies this, the town clerk produces the song, and to his astonishment Sachs makes him a present of it. After he has extracted from Sachs a promise that the cobbler will never claim the song as his own, Beckmesser goes off happily.

Eva arrives to consult Sachs, on the pretext that her shoe hurts her. When Walther reappears he is inspired by the sight of his beloved to improvise the final verse of his song, which Sachs acclaims as a *Meisterlied*, a mastersong. Eva, grateful and happy, confesses that Sachs would have been her choice of husband had she not fallen in love with Walther, to which Sachs replies that he knows the story of Tristan and Isolde too well and has no wish to share the fate of King Marke. David and Magdalene now arrive, and Walther's mastersong is christened in a serene quintet ('Selig wie die Sonne meines Glückes lacht').

Act III, scene ii. The Festival Meadow by the banks of the Pegnitz river, with Nuremberg in the background. The guilds march in, the apprentices dance and the townsfolk assemble. Finally the mastersingers enter in solemn procession, and Sachs is acclaimed by the people in a chorale whose words are by the historical Hans Sachs ('Wach' auf, es nahet gen den Tag'). Beckmesser is the first competitor to be called. Having failed to understand Walther's song, he makes a complete mess of it and is rewarded by derisive laughter from the crowd. In a fury, Beckmesser declares that the wretched song was composed not by him but by Hans Sachs, and he makes a hasty exit.

Asked to explain, Sachs says he would never dare to boast of having composed so beautiful a song and calls upon its real creator to come forward and perform it correctly. Walther advances from the crowd, sings his mastersong ('Morgenlich leuchtend im rosigen Schein') and wins unanimous approval from mastersingers and populace alike. Eva delightedly places the victor's laurel-wreath on the brow of her beloved; but when Pogner attempts to adorn him with the gold chain of the guildmasters, Walther rejects it vehemently. At this, Sachs steps forward, advising the knight not to scorn the only guardians of true German art ('Verachtet mir die Meister nicht'). In a jingoistic sermon he warns of the dangers of foreign influence and praises holy German art ('Die heil'ge deutsche Kunst'). The crowd patriotically takes up Sachs's call to 'honour your German masters', Eva removes the wreath from Walther and places it on Sachs's head, while Sachs takes the chain from Pogner and places it around the neck of the now chastened and unresisting Walther. Pogner kneels in homage to Sachs, and all acclaim the cobbler with a cry of 'Heil! Sachs! Nürnbergs teurem Sachs' (Hail! Sachs! Nuremberg's dear Sachs).

Die Meistersinger is an extremely long opera, its third act alone lasting nearly two hours and the entire work taking about four and a quarter hours to perform, and its undoubted warmth and humanity are somewhat vitiated by its appeal to the baser aspects of nationalism. Not only is holy German art upheld as the great ideal, but the means of achieving and maintaining it are spelled out as clearly as Wagner in his polemical writings spelled out how to rid Germany of its Jews. There can be no denying the extraordinary emotive force of Hans Sachs's address to the citizens of Nuremberg, which aroused the opera's first audience in Munich to a frenzy of enthusiasm (and led a Bayreuth audience in the 1930s to rise to its feet and stand with hands raised in the Nazi salute until the end of the opera). The question that Sachs's address presents is whether the nasty taste of the words is redeemed by the beauty and power of the music, or whether those very qualities in the music render more dangerously effective a message that left in Wagner's raw words would surely have less appeal. It is a question that has never been satisfactorily answered, and one that is far removed from the comparatively simple matter of having to accept that artistic genius does not necessarily reside only in the breasts of those of the most impeccable moral purity.

This is a complex and in many respects a genial work containing a great deal of superb music, from the stately C major prelude to that infamous final scene. Hans Sachs is for the most part a highly sympathetic character whose monologues are immensely impressive, and the gentle Eva is one of Wagner's most human and likeable creations. The Act III quintet is music of rare beauty, and Walther's exultant Prize Song is deservedly famous.

Recommended recording: Bernd Weikl (Sachs), Cheryl Studer (Eva), Ben Heppner (Walther), with the Bavarian State Opera Chorus and Orchestra, conducted by Wolfgang Sawallisch. EMI CDS 5 55142–2. Heppner is a thrilling Walther, Cheryl Studer a musically intelligent Eva, and Weikl a down-to-earth Sachs.

Der Ring des Nibelungen
(The Nibelungs' Ring)
a stage festival play for three days and a preliminary evening
(approximate total length: 14 hours, 45 minutes)

1. *DAS RHEINGOLD*, FIRST PERFORMED AT THE HOFOPER, MUNICH, 22 SEPTEMBER 1869. 2. *DIE WALKÜRE*, FIRST PERFORMED AT THE HOFOPER, MUNICH, 26 JUNE 1870. 3. *SIEGFRIED*. 4. *GÖTTERDÄMMERUNG*, FIRST PERFORMED COMPLETE AT THE FESTSPIELHAUS, BAYREUTH, 13, 14, 16, 17 AUGUST 1876

Das Rheingold
(The Rhinegold)
prologue in four scenes (approximate length: 2 hours, 30 minutes)

Wotan *baritone*	
Donner *bass*	
Froh, Donner's brother *tenor*	gods and
Loge *tenor*	godesses
Fricka, Wotan's wife *mezzo-soprano*	
Freia, sister of Donner and Froh *soprano*	
Erda *contralto*	
Alberich *bass-baritone*	Nibelung
Mime *tenor*	brothers
Fasolt *bass-baritone*	giants
Fafner *bass*	(brothers)
Woglinde *soprano*	
Wellgunde *soprano*	Rhinemaidens
Flosshilde *mezzo-soprano*	

LIBRETTO BY THE COMPOSER; TIME: LEGENDARY; PLACE: THE RHINE AND SURROUNDING COUNTRY; FIRST PERFORMED AT THE HOFOPER, MUNICH, 22 SEPTEMBER 1869

The gestation period of *Der Ring des Niblungen*, Wagner's great cycle of four music dramas based on the old mythological stories of the Norse gods and heroes, is lengthy and complex. It was in 1848, when he was in his mid-thirties, that the composer produced his first prose sketch retelling the myth of the Nibelungs, drawing some of his material from the mediaeval German epic *Das Nibelungenlied* and some from the Scandinavian *Edda*, a collection of thirty-five poems in Old Norse which originated as oral poetry around two thousand years ago and was written down at some time during the twelfth century. Wagner's initial intention was to compose an opera about the last days of Siegfried, *Siegfrieds Tod* (The Death of Siegfried), using the earlier parts of the story simply as a preface in the form of a synopsis. He completed a libretto for *Siegfrieds Tod*, but when he began to compose the opera in 1850 he found that he needed to start at an earlier point in the narrative. He therefore discontinued work on the music, to write a libretto on the subject of the young Siegfried. This, in turn, led him to the realization that he would have to begin even earlier, and so he wrote the libretto of *Die Walküre* and finally that of *Das Rheingold*.

Although the four librettos had been written in reverse order, the operas themselves were composed in the correct chronological sequence. *Das Rheingold* occupied Wagner in 1853–4, and *Die Walküre* from 1854 to March 1856. He began *Siegfried* (originally called *Der junge Siegfried*) in 1856, but put it aside to work on *Tristan und Isolde* for two years and *Die Meistersinger* for three, returning to *Siegfried* in 1864 and finally completing it in 1871. The last work of the tetralogy, its title now changed from *Siegfrieds Tod* to *Götterdämmerung* (The Twilight of the Gods), was composed between 1871 and 1874.

It was King Ludwig's desire that the operas of *The Ring* should be given their premieres separately, as soon as each was composed. Although he at first favoured this suggestion, Wagner subsequently turned against the idea. Nevertheless, he was unable to prevent *Das Rheingold* from being given its first performance in Munich in 1869. Refused admission to the rehearsals because he had been making surreptitious attempts to sabotage the production, the composer stayed away from the premiere, sulking in his villa in Switzerland.

The Ring has been subjected to a variety of interpretations, ranging from George Bernard Shaw's analysis of the work as a political allegory, to Robert Donington's description of it in terms of Jungian psychology. It has been viewed both as a history of the world and as a treatise on the corruption of the world. Countless books have been written, discussing it as music drama and relating it to its composer's theoretical writings, but *The Ring* remains larger and more mysterious than the sum of all these attempts to explain it.

Scene i. The depths of the Rhine. The river bed is wrapped in impenetrable gloom. Steep rocks rise from its depths, around which swim the three Rhinemaidens, guarding the magic Rhinegold. The dwarf Alberich, a Nibelung from the dark caves of Nibelheim beneath the river, clambers out of a cleft in the rocks and begins to make advances to the Rhinemaidens, who tease him for his clumsiness and ugliness. When a shaft of sunlight suddenly catches the gold, Alberich asks what it is that gleams so brightly, and the Rhinemaidens foolishly tell him of the treasure and its magic power: he who is willing to renounce love for ever and who succeeds in fashioning a ring from the Rhinegold will become master of the world. Alberich's futile desire now turns to greed. Renouncing love, he snatches the gold from the rock and disappears with it into the depths. As the Rhinemaidens lament the loss of the gold, night falls, and the waters slowly subside. Without a break in the music, the scene changes.

Scene ii. An open space on top of a mountain. As Wotan, the father of the gods, and his wife, Fricka, awake from their sleep their eyes are fixed in astonishment and delight on Valhalla, a superb castle in the clouds, which has been built for them by the giants Fasolt and Fafner ('Vollendet das ewige Werk'). Fricka reminds Wotan that he promised to give Freia, the goddess of eternal youth, to the giants as payment for their work. Wotan, however, has never intended to surrender Freia, for without her daily gift of apples the gods would grow old and tired.

When Fasolt and Fafner arrive to claim their reward, the gods Donner and Froh rush in to protect their sister Freia. The giants are determined to hold Wotan to his word, but when Loge, the cunning god of fire, arrives, Wotan seeks his help. Loge describes the Rhinegold in the possession of Alberich, and the power it bestows, at which the giants agree to accept the gold instead of Freia, whom they nevertheless take with them as a hostage. As Freia is dragged away, the gods suddenly appear aged. Wotan and Loge begin their descent to Nibelheim to obtain Alberich's gold by fair means or foul.

Scene iii. Nibelheim, in the bowels of the earth. Alberich has enslaved his fellow Nibelungs through the power of the magic ring that he has fashioned from the gold, and he has compelled his brother Mime to make him the Tarnhelm, a helmet that enables its wearer to assume any form at will. When Wotan and Loge appear, Alberich boasts of the Tarnhelm's powers, which he demonstrates by transforming himself into a huge serpent. Loge tricks him into turning himself into a toad, and Alberich is quickly captured by the gods, bound and dragged away.

Scene iv. The open space on top of the mountain. Wotan and Loge return from Nibelheim with their captive, Alberich. They force him to part with his hoard of gold, which the Nibelungs carry up from Nibelheim, to the humiliation of the bound Alberich, who is also forced to hand over the Tarnhelm and the ring. When he is released, Alberich places a curse upon the ring. It will now bring destruction upon whoever possesses it ('Wie durch Fluch er mir geriet, verflucht sei dieser Ring').

Fasolt and Fafner arrive with Freia and insist on being given a pile of gold high enough to hide the sight of Freia's body from them. The gold is piled up, and Wotan is obliged to part with the Tarnhelm as well. When the giants insist on having the ring, to close up a remaining chink of light in the pile of gold through which they can still see Freia, Wotan at first refuses to surrender it. However, Erda, the earth goddess, rises from below to warn him of the disasters that will befall the gods if they keep the ring. Wotan relents and hands it over, at which Alberich's curse is seen to be immediately effective, for the giants begin to quarrel over the ring, and Fafner kills his brother Fasolt.

Donner summons up a storm, which soon dies down to reveal a rainbow bridge leading to Valhalla, the gods' new home. As the gods, enthralled, move in stately procession towards Valhalla, the lament of the Rhinemaidens for their lost gold is heard from the depths of the river.

At least a third of the more than ninety motifs that are embedded in the musical texture of *The Ring* are contained within this prologue to the cycle. Many of the most memorable passages in *Das Rheingold* occur in the orchestra, which near the end of the opera paints the serene beauty of the rainbow leading to Valhalla. Wotan's outburst in praise of the beauty and grandeur of the gods' new home, and the orchestral postlude of great splendour accompanying the procession of the gods to Valhalla, end *Das Rheingold* magnificently.

Die Walküre
(The Valkyrie)
music drama in three acts (approximate length: 3 hours, 45 minutes)

Brünnhilde, a goddess *soprano*
Siegmund *tenor*
Sieglinde, Siegmund's sister *soprano*
Wotan, father of the gods *baritone*
Hunding, Sieglinde's husband *bass*
Fricka, Wotan's wife *mezzo-soprano*
Valkyries: Gerhilde, Ortlinde, Waltraute, Schwertleite, *sopranos;*
    Helmwige, Siegrune, Grimgerde, Rossweisse *contraltos*

LIBRETTO BY THE COMPOSER; TIME: LEGENDARY; PLACE: HUNDING'S HUT, A ROCKY HEIGHT AND A ROCK-STREWN MOUNTAIN-TOP; FIRST PERFORMED AT THE HOFOPER, MUNICH, 26 JUNE 1870

After the successful premiere of *Das Rheingold* in Munich, King Ludwig was keen to proceed with the production of *Die Walküre*, the second opera in the *Ring* cycle. Wagner attempted to play for time, for the idea of a special festival theatre in a provincial town, an opera house in which only his works would be performed, had now really taken hold of him. Slowly, the prospect of a theatre in the small Bavarian town of Bayreuth began to take shape. Meanwhile, the composer could not prevent the production of *Die Walküre* in Munich, for the performing rights in the entire cycle had been assigned to King Ludwig. The first performance of *Die Walküre* duly took place in Munich in June 1870, when a distinguished audience, including Brahms, Saint-Saëns, Grieg and the violinist Joseph Joachim, acclaimed the opera effusively. Wagner remained aloof in Switzerland, already planning the first integral production of the tetralogy, two of the operas of which he had yet to complete.

Act I. The interior of Hunding's dwelling, in the middle of which stands a huge ash tree. Siegmund, fleeing from enemies and completely exhausted, stumbles into the house. Sieglinde, Hunding's wife, gives him water to drink, and although they do not recognize each other they feel an immediate bond of sympathy. Hunding arrives and begins to question Siegmund. When the youth tells him that he tried to defend a woman but, being unarmed, was forced to flee, Hunding realizes that his guest is the man he has been pursuing. He tells Siegmund that he is protected by the laws of hospitality and may therefore rest overnight, but that on the following day they must fight. Hunding then orders Sieglinde to prepare his evening drink and follow him to their bedchamber. As she leaves the room, Sieglinde gestures silently to the trunk of the ash tree. Left alone, Siegmund recalls how his father promised him that in his moment of direst need he would find a sword ('Ein Schwert verhiess mir der Vater'). Sieglinde returns and tells Siegmund how her wedding feast was interrupted by a stranger who left a sword embedded in the ash tree, predicting that a hero would one day arrive to pull it from the trunk.

Suddenly, the door of Hunding's house flies open and the bright moonlight of a spring night floods the room. Elated, Siegmund sings rapturously of the passing of winter storms and of the radiant approach of spring ('Winterstürme wichen dem Wonnemond'), and Sieglinde assures him that he is the spring that she longed for in the depths of winter ('Du bist der Lenz'). Excitedly they question each other and discover that they are brother and sister. Siegmund approaches the tree confidently and draws the sword from it ('Siegmund heiss ich und Siegmund bin ich'). He claims Sieglinde as both sister and bride, as they embrace passionately and rush out into the night.

Act II. A wild and rocky place on a mountainside. Wotan instructs Brünnhilde to protect Siegmund in his duel with Hunding, and to make him the victor. Shouting her exultant battle-cry ('Ho-jo-to-ho'), Brünnhilde springs from rock to rock up to the highest peak, warning Wotan that his wife Fricka is hastening furiously towards him in a chariot drawn by two rams. Fricka, the staunch defender of marriage vows, demands that Siegmund's incestuous love for Sieglinde should be punished by his death. Wotan tries to argue that Siegmund is needed to prevent

Alberich gaining possession of the ring, but Fricka points out that, since he is armed with Wotan's sword, Siegmund is no longer a free agent ('Deiner ew'gen Gattin heilige Ehre'). Wotan is forced to concede defeat, and he orders Brünnhilde to follow Fricka's instructions and protect Hunding ('Als junge Liebe Lust mir verblich').

Siegmund and Sieglinde enter, in flight from Hunding. Sieglinde collapses exhausted, and Brünnhilde addresses Siegmund, announcing his imminent death and journey to Valhalla ('Siegmund! Sieh auf mich'). However, Siegmund refuses to be parted from Sieglinde, threatening to kill her and himself, and Brünnhilde is moved by his distress to promise him victory. Hunding arrives and the two men prepare to fight. Brünnhilde intervenes to protect Siegmund, but Wotan suddenly appears, shattering Siegmund's sword with his spear. When Siegmund is killed by Hunding, Brünnhilde seizes the pieces of his shattered sword and flees with Sieglinde. At a contemptuous gesture from Wotan, Hunding falls dead, and Wotan sets off to pursue Brünnhilde and Sieglinde.

Act III. The rocky summit of a mountain. The Valkyries gather on their return from battle (The Ride of the Valkyries). Brünnhilde, the last to arrive, enters with Sieglinde and begs her sisters' help to conceal from Wotan the woman who bears in her womb Siegmund's son, the hero who will one day rebuild the shattered fragments of his father's sword ('O hehrstes Wunder! Herrlichste Maid!'). Sieglinde is sent to a forest in the east, where the giant Fafner guards the ring and the Nibelung treasure, while Brünnhilde stays to face Wotan's rage.

When he arrives, Wotan dismisses the other Valkyries, strips Brünnhilde of her divinity and pronounces sentence upon her. She will fall into a slumber and will be claimed by the first man who awakens her. Appalled, Brünnhilde asks that at least she be awakened only by a hero, and Wotan grants her wish. After a last farewell to her ('Leb' wohl, du kühnes, herrliches Kind!'), he kisses Brünnhilde to sleep, places her on a rock and then summons Loge, the god of fire, to surround the rock with a ring of fire so that only a hero will succeed in reaching Brünnhilde. As flames leap up around the rock, Wotan slowly departs.

Die Walküre is a marvellously rich opera. In *Das Rheingold* most of the excitement was to be found in the orchestra, and *Die Walküre*'s orchestral writing is often thrilling, but by now Wagner had found a way to integrate his voice parts into the overall structure without sacrificing their lyrical independence. Like *Das Rheingold*, *Die Walküre* is still primarily a work for solo voices. It is not until the last act of *Siegfried* that one hears a real duet, and one must wait until *Götterdämmerung* for the introduction of the chorus. There is, however, an impressive ensemble at the beginning of Act III of *Die Walküre* when the eight Valkyries assemble. Although this is a work best experienced as part of a complete performance of *The Ring*, it is also popular enough, and sufficiently self-contained, to be frequently staged on its own.

Siegfried
music drama in three acts (approximate length: 4 hours, 15 minutes)

Siegfried, son of Siegmund and Sieglinde   *tenor*
Mime, a Nibelung   *tenor*
Wotan, father of the gods, alias the Wanderer   *baritone*
Alberich, a Nibelung, Mime's brother   *bass-baritone*
Fafner, a giant (disguised as a dragon)   *bass*
Erda, a goddess   *contralto*
Brünnhilde, a former goddess   *soprano*
A Woodbird   *soprano*

LIBRETTO BY THE COMPOSER; TIME: LEGENDARY; PLACE: VARIOUS PARTS OF A FOREST, THE FOOT OF A MOUNTAIN AND BRÜNNHILDE'S ROCK ON THE MOUNTAIN-TOP; FIRST PERFORMED AS PART OF THE COMPLETE *RING* CYCLE, AT THE FESTSPIELHAUS, BAYREUTH, 16 AUGUST 1876

In May 1871 Wagner formally announced that a theatre would be constructed in Bayreuth to his specifications, and that it would open in the summer of 1873 with a complete performance of *Der Ring des Nibelungen*. The project would be financed through the medium of a society of supporters of Wagner, to be called Patrons of the Stage Festival in Bayreuth. However, people did not rush to donate money to the enterprise as lavishly and enthusiastically as the composer had expected, and the building of the theatre was not completed until early in 1876. King Ludwig, despite Wagner's shabby treatment of him, continued to support the composer with a regular allowance, and he even provided additional funds to enable the construction of a villa in Bayreuth for Wagner and Cosima, who were now legally man and wife.

The Festspielhaus (intended as a temporary structure but still in use today) was given a concealed orchestra pit, for Wagner had always resented the fact that the source of the music of his operas was visible to the audience and thus likely to distract attention from the stage picture. The theatre opened in August 1876 with three complete performances of *The Ring*, the first two parts of which – *Das Rheingold* and *Die Walküre* – had already been staged in Munich in 1869 and 1870. The first *Ring* cycle, spread over four nights between 13 and 17 August, was enthusiastically received, despite some mishaps in stage management and the non-appearance of the dragon, Fafner, in *Siegfried*. (It was discovered later that the English firm that had constructed the dragon had sent it by mistake to Beirut.)

Act I. A rocky cavern in the forest. The Nibelung Mime has brought up the young Siegfried, since Sieglinde died entrusting her child and the fragments of Siegmund's sword to him. Mime is now found at his anvil, attempting without success to forge a sword that he hopes Siegfried will not be able to break, his intention being to make use of Siegfried's great strength and courage to incite him to kill Fafner, who has transformed himself into a dragon and is guarding the Rhinegold, the Tarnhelm and the ring in his lair in the depths of the forest.

Siegfried enters the cavern, dragging a bear after him to frighten Mime. He breaks Mime's latest sword into pieces and, scarcely bothering to conceal his hatred and contempt for the dwarf who has raised him, asks who his parents were. He is told that Sieglinde died, naming him Siegfried and leaving him only the two pieces of a sword, which his father called Nothung. Siegfried charges Mime to forge the two pieces of the sword together, and he rushes out into the forest.

Wotan, in his guise as the Wanderer, arrives and offers to answer any three questions Mime may ask him. To get rid of the stranger, Mime asks who lives under the earth, who on it, and who above it. The Wanderer answers these questions easily, and asks three of his own in return. Mime knows which race was begotten by Wotan, and he knows the name of the only sword that can kill Fafner, but he cannot answer the third question: Who can reforge Nothung? The Wanderer tells Mime that only he who knows no fear can forge Nothung, and he warns the dwarf to beware of such a man.

When Siegfried returns, Mime asks him if he knows fear. On discovering that Siegfried does not, he decides upon a practical lesson. He will lead Siegfried to the dragon's lair and confront the youth with Fafner. Impatient to fight the dragon, Siegfried demands his sword. Mime is forced to admit that only someone who does not know fear can forge Nothung, so Siegfried proceeds to forge the sword himself, singing a joyous song as he does so ('Nothung! Nothung! Neidliches Schwert'). When the weapon is forged, he uses it to split the anvil with one powerful blow.

Act II. A clearing in the forest, close to the entrance of Fafner's cave. It is night. Alberich anxiously keeps watch on the cave in which Fafner, transformed by the

Tarnhelm into a dragon, guards the Rhinegold and the ring. The Wanderer warns Alberich that Mime intends to use Siegfried to get the ring for himself, and then he goes to the mouth of the cave to warn Fafner as well. The dragon, however, is not afraid and asks to be left in peace. The Wanderer departs and, as dawn breaks, Mime arrives with Siegfried and attempts without success to instil into the youth a fear of the fierce dragon. Dismissing Mime, Siegfried rests under a lime tree, taking in the wonders of nature (the Forest Murmurs). Delighted by the singing of a bird, he tries to imitate it on a pipe, which he fashions from a reed, but failing dismally he flings the pipe aside and blows a call on his horn. This awakens Fafner, who emerges threateningly from his cave and challenges Siegfried to fight. Siegfried plunges his sword into the heart of the dragon, who, as he lies dying, warns his slayer against Mime.

As he withdraws his sword from the dragon's body, a little of Fafner's blood splashes onto Siegfried's hand. When he puts his hand to his mouth to suck it away, Siegfried discovers that the blood has given him the ability to understand the song of the Woodbird. The bird tells him that the Tarnhelm and the ring hidden in the dragon's cave could make him ruler of the world. Siegfried enters the cave, and Mime tries to slip in after him but is prevented by his brother Alberich. The two brothers quarrel over the Rhinegold and the ring, but when Mime threatens Alberich with Siegfried, who now emerges from the cave holding both Tarnhelm and ring, Alberich makes himself scarce.

The Woodbird's voice now warns Siegfried not to trust Mime, whose unspoken thoughts Siegfried will, having tasted the dragon's blood, now be able to understand. The hypocritical words of affection uttered by Mime reach Siegfried's ear as threats, to which Siegfried responds by taking his sword and killing Mime, while Alberich's derisive laughter is heard in the distance. Exhausted, Siegfried rests, listening to the Woodbird. When he asks it to find him a faithful friend, the bird offers to lead him to a beautiful woman who sleeps on a high cliff surrounded by a ring of fire, waiting for a hero to overcome the flames and to win her. Siegfried follows the bird, which flutters ahead, showing him the way to Brünnhilde's rock.

Act III, scene i. A wild, rocky place at the foot of a mountain. The Wanderer summons Erda, the omniscient mother of mankind. When she emerges from the depths of the earth he questions her about the future, but is disappointed by her ambiguous replies and tells her that her wisdom as the earth mother is drawing to a close, just as his omnipotence as a god is also ending. As he releases Erda to return to her slumbers, the Wanderer perceives Siegfried approaching. He tries to bar the hero's path to the summit of the mountain, warning Siegfried that Nothung has once before been shattered by his spear. This time, however,

Siegfried's sword breaks Wotan's spear, and the power of the gods comes to an end. The Wanderer steps aside, while Siegfried continues his ascent of the mountain.

Act III, scene ii. Brünnhilde's rock on the peak of the mountain. The light has begun to fade, gradually giving way to a dissolving cloud, which is illuminated as though by the red glow of dawn. The mountain-top now becomes visible, with the sleeping Brünnhilde surrounded by a ring of fire. Siegfried, approaching from below, passes through the flames and draws near to Brünnhilde. At first assuming the figure lying in armour to be a man, he gently removes the helmet and breast-plate and then stands momentarily transfixed in fear, for this is the first woman he has ever seen. However, he soon feels bold enough to kiss her, and as he does so Brünnhilde awakes and greets the radiant sunlight ('Heil dir, Sonne! Heil dir, Licht!'). When Siegfried declares his love for her, she is at first overcome with shame at having lost her status as a god. She finally succumbs to him as passion awakens in her, and they sing an ecstatic love duet ('Ewig war ich, ewig bin ich, ewig in süss sehnender Wonne').

In structure, *Siegfried* is the simplest of the *Ring* operas, a work consisting mainly of nine duologues for various combinations of characters, three in each act. In Act I these three scenes are between Mime and Siegfried; Mime and the Wanderer; and finally Mime and Siegfried again. In Act II they are between the Wanderer and Alberich; Siegfried and Mime; and Siegfried and the Woodbird. Act III has the Wanderer and Erda; the Wanderer and Siegfried; and Siegfried and Brünnhilde.

Fresh in conception, *Siegfried* is full of music that represents Wagner at his most lyrical, its score the most joyous and orchestrally colourful of the entire tetralogy. Siegfried's great forging song at the end of Act I is a fierce celebration of the hero's brute strength; the beautiful sequence in Act II known as the Forest Murmurs is well known out of context; and the final scene of Act III, from Brünnhilde's awakening to the end of the opera, works up to a climax of exuberant ecstasy.

Götterdämmerung
(Twilight of the Gods)
music drama in a prologue and three acts
(approximate length: 4 hours, 15 minutes)

Siegfried *tenor*
Gunther, a Gibichung *baritone*

Alberich, a Nibelung   *bass-baritone*
Hagen, his son, a Gibichung   *bass*
Brünnhilde   *soprano*
Gutrune, Gunther's sister, a Gibichung   *soprano*
Waltraute, a Valkyrie, Brünnhilde's sister   *mezzo-soprano*
First Norn   *contralto*
Second Norn   *mezzo-soprano*
Third Norn   *soprano*
Woglinde   *soprano*
Wellgunde   *soprano*   ⎤ Rhinemaidens
Flosshilde   *mezzo-soprano*   ⎦

LIBRETTO BY THE COMPOSER; TIME: LEGENDARY; PLACE: BRÜNNHILDE'S ROCK ON
THE MOUNTAIN-TOP, GUNTHER'S CASTLE ON THE RHINE AND A WOODED AREA BY
THE RHINE; FIRST PERFORMED AS PART OF THE COMPLETE *RING* CYCLE, AT THE
FESTSPIELHAUS, BAYREUTH, 17 AUGUST 1876

The Norwegian composer Edvard Grieg, who was present at the first performance of the entire *Ring* cycle, wrote, after seeing *Götterdämmerung*:

> Just as in the case of *Die Walküre* with its great use of the forces of nature, so
> in the case of the final work of *The Ring*, it impresses by its tragic power and
> thus becomes equally moving . . . Whatever the shortcomings of detail, one
> thing is certain. Wagner has created a great work, full of audacious original-
> ity and dramatic merit. He has, in his new lively way, brought out old mate-
> rial, little known in Germany, and by means of his clever musical-dramatic
> treatment has breathed new life into it. Many of these profound legends, for
> most people a closed book, will be opened up and made popular by Wagner's
> work. As in a child's picture book, the eye comes to the assistance of the
> mind. It may also be a good tonic for people nowadays, when parties and fac-
> tions rule, to witness these great heroes and personalities with their strong
> passions, selfless actions and complete lives.

Prologue. Brünnhilde's rock, as at the end of *Siegfried*. It is night. The three
Norns, daughters of Erda, sit weaving the rope of fate on which the future of the
world depends and telling of the destiny that binds everything together. They try
to keep the rope taut, but it snaps, and the Norns start up in terror, lamenting the
end of their eternal knowledge as they vanish into the depths to return to the earth
mother. As the sun rises, Brünnhilde and Siegfried emerge from a cave, he fully

armed and she leading Grane, her horse. They reaffirm their love for each other, and Siegfried places on Brünnhilde's finger the fateful ring. In return, she offers him her horse, to bear him away into the world to perform great deeds ('Zu neuen Taten'). Siegfried leads Grane down from the rock, and Brünnhilde watches their descent into the valley, waving rapturously to Siegfried until he is lost from her sight. (The orchestra describes Siegfried's journey down the Rhine before the curtain rises on Act I.)

Act I, scene i. The hall of the tribe of Gibichungs on the Rhine. Gunther and his sister Gutrune, the leaders of the tribe, look to their half-brother Hagen, the son of Alberich, for advice. Hagen observes that Gunther has, as yet, no wife, nor Gutrune a husband, and tells Gunther about Brünnhilde on her rock, and about Siegfried, who alone can pass through the flames to reach her. Hagen's plan is that a magic potion could make Siegfried forget Brünnhilde and desire Gutrune. In exchange for Gunther allowing him to wed Gutrune, Siegfried would be required to help Gunther win Brünnhilde. Brother and sister approve of this plan and, when Gunther asks how they are to find Siegfried, a horn call is suddenly heard from the distance. Hagen goes down to the shore and sees Siegfried and his horse Grane sailing across the Rhine in a boat.

Siegfried is invited ashore. His appearance makes a great impression on Gutrune, who at a sign from Hagen leaves the hall to prepare the magic potion. When Hagen asks about the Rhinegold, Siegfried replies that he took from the dragon's lair only the ring and the Tarnhelm. Hagen then describes the Tarnhelm's powers to him. Gutrune returns with the magic potion, and it takes immediate effect, causing Siegfried to forget Brünnhilde and address Gutrune in passionate terms. It is agreed that Gutrune will become Siegfried's wife, if he will help Gunther to win Brünnhilde. At the mention of Brünnhilde's name, Siegfried seems to be making an intense effort to remember something, but it is clear that he now has no recollection of Brünnhilde. He agrees to use the Tarnhelm to assume Gunther's form, and to deliver Brünnhilde to Gunther. Siegfried and Gunther seal their pact with an oath of blood brotherhood and prepare to depart, leaving Hagen to guard the hall of the Gibichungs ('Hier sitz' ich zur Wacht').

Act I, scene ii. Brünnhilde's rock. Brünnhilde sits at the entrance to the cave, happily contemplating the ring that Siegfried gave her. Thunder and lightning in the distance herald the approach of Waltraute, one of her sister Valkyries, who tells Brünnhilde of the plight of the gods. After his sword was shattered by Siegfried, Wotan returned to Valhalla, where he sits on his throne, speaking to no one and refusing Freia's apples. Waltraute has heard Wotan whisper to himself that the gods and the world could be freed from the weight of the curse placed on the ring if Brünnhilde were to return it to the Rhinemaidens ('Höre mit Sinn, was ich dir sage'). Waltraute implores her sister to do this, but Brünnhilde replies that Siegfried's love means more to her than Valhalla and the glory of the gods, and that she will never part with the ring ('Die Liebe liesse ich nie'). Waltraute rushes away in anger.

Night has now fallen. Brünnhilde observes that the wall of flame around her rock is leaping up furiously, and she thinks that this denotes the return of Siegfried. She shrinks back in fear as a stranger, who is really Siegfried transformed by the Tarnhelm into the form of Gunther, passes through the fire to claim her as his bride, tearing the ring from her finger and driving her before him into the cave. As he enters the cave after her, Siegfried draws his sword, Nothung, which (to himself) he declares he will place between him and Brünnhilde in order to keep faith with Gunther.

Act II. On the shore in front of the hall of the Gibichungs. Alberich appears to his son Hagen in his sleep, reminding him of the ring, which Hagen swears to obtain ('Sei treu, Hagen, mein Sohn!'). Day breaks, and Siegfried arrives, having been magically transported by the Tarnhelm, to announce that Gunther and Brünnhilde are following by boat. He tells a perplexed Gutrune how he won Brünnhilde while yet keeping faith with her and her brother. Preparations for the wedding feast begin, and Hagen issues a jocular invitation to the Gibichung vassals, calling them to take up their weapons, not to pursue an enemy but to slaughter animals on the altars of the gods, so that Gunther's marriage will be blessed.

The boat carrying Gunther and Brünnhilde arrives, and Gunther proudly presents his bride, who keeps her head bowed, raising her eyes only when she hears Siegfried's name. She cannot believe that he has betrayed her and is about to marry Gutrune, but when she sees on Siegfried's hand the ring, which she thought had been taken from her by Gunther, she guesses at his treachery without understanding the circumstances. She accuses Siegfried of having broken his vows to her, but he declares that he is innocent and cheerfully leaves for the wedding feast with Gutrune and her retinue.

Left alone with Gunther and Hagen, Brünnhilde eagerly assents to Hagen's proposal to kill Siegfried. She tells him that Siegfried is vulnerable in his back, the only part of the hero's body she did not protect with her magic, for she knew he would never turn away from an enemy. When Hagen reminds Gunther of the immense power that will be his as possessor of the ring, his half-brother is persuaded to join the conspiracy. Gutrune is to be told that Siegfried has been killed by a boar while hunting. As Hagen, Brünnhilde and Gunther swear to put their plan into action, the wedding procession enters, with Siegfried carried on a shield and Gutrune on a chair. At Hagen's urging, Gunther and Brünnhilde join the procession.

Act III, scene i. A partly wooded, partly rocky valley by the Rhine. The Rhinemaidens rise to the surface of the water to swim, imploring the goddess of the sun to send her rays to illuminate the Rhine, as they once did. Hearing Siegfried's horn in the distance, they beg the goddess to send to them the hero who will restore their gold. Siegfried appears, having lost his way while hunting, and teases the Rhinemaidens, pretending he is about to give them the ring, and then withdrawing it. He is, however, about to return it to them when the Rhinemaidens make the mistake of warning him that a curse is attached to the ring and that evil is in store for him unless he relinquishes it. Siegfried replies that their threats are even less effective than their wheedling, and the Rhinemaidens swim away after prophesying that a proud woman will that day inherit the ring and will give them a better hearing.

Horn calls announce the approach of the hunt, and while they rest Gunther and Hagen ask Siegfried to relate his adventures. He narrates as far as the death of Fafner, and then his memory clouds over. Hagen gives him a drink, which is an antidote to the elixir of oblivion previously given to him, and Siegfried now recalls, with growing emotion, his discovery of Brünnhilde and their exchange of vows. At this moment, Wotan's two ravens of fate circle above Siegfried's head, and as he turns to watch them, Hagen spears him in the back. The vassals, horrified, ask Hagen what he has done, to which he replies that he has avenged perjury. Gunther, whose attempt to restrain Hagen was too late, helps to tend the dying Siegfried, whose last words are of Brünnhilde, with whom he confidently expects to be reunited in death. He dies, and Siegfried's Funeral March sounds forth as his body is solemnly borne towards the hilltop.

Act III, scene ii. The hall of the Gibichungs. It is night, and Gutrune anxiously awaits the return of Siegfried with the hunting party. She hears the grim voice of Hagen calling to her to greet the mighty hero, who has come home, and vassals enter with Gunther, bearing Siegfried's body. Beside herself with sorrow, Gutrune accuses Gunther of having murdered Siegfried, but Gunther places the blame entirely on Hagen, who acknowledges the deed and demands the ring as his reward. When Gunther opposes him, Hagen draws his sword and kills his half-brother. He approaches Siegfried's body to take the ring from his finger, but the hand of the dead hero rises threateningly while all stand transfixed with horror.

Brünnhilde enters the hall. Having learned the truth from the Rhinemaidens, she orders the vassals to prepare a funeral pyre for the hero ('Starke Scheite'). Removing the ring from Siegfried's hand, she places it on her own, then sets fire to the pyre and rides her horse Grane into the flames. The Rhine overflows its banks and the Rhinemaidens take the ring from Brünnhilde. Hagen makes a last, unsuccessful attempt to grasp it from them and is drowned, while the hall of the Gibichungs crashes around him. A rosy glow in the sky reveals that the earthly fire has spread to Valhalla. The twilight of the gods has arrived, Alberich's curse is fulfilled, and Brünnhilde's great sacrifice for love has redeemed the world.

Several writers on Wagner have observed that the ending of the great tetralogy is more than somewhat confusing. As one of his friends asked the composer, 'Why, since the gold is returned to the Rhine, is it still necessary for the gods to perish?' Wagner's reply was unsatisfactory. He had initially planned that Siegfried's death and Brünnhilde's return of the ring to the Rhinemaidens would lead to a new and happier era both for the gods and for mankind, but musically he was drawn to a tragic conclusion, the end of everything, as wished for by the world-weary Wotan in *Die Walküre*. Wagner nevertheless contrived to ensure the amelioration of this pessimistic conclusion, through the consoling power of music. His concept of redemption through love is really redemption through the art of music. Art, he seems to say, consoles as life ends. It is a consummation devoutly to be wished.

It took Wagner more than a quarter of a century to create *Der Ring des Nibelungen*, so it is hardly surprising that the tetralogy is stylistically inconsistent and musically uneven. Its composition is the result of an immense act of the creative imagination, for which the work's occasional longueurs are by no means too high a price to pay. Ideally, *The Ring* should be heard complete and consecutively: the entire work demands a greater degree of concentration from its audiences than any other opera by Wagner or any other composer. This is not because of the system of leitmotifs woven into the immense work, for these are meant to be experienced subliminally, but because of the complex nature of the ideas inherent in it, and the variety of interpretations to which it is susceptible. Considered as an old Norse saga of gods, heroes, dwarfs, dragons and giants, reworked by Wagner into frequently bad and repetitive verse, *The Ring* is obviously a flawed and unsatisfactory affair. However, its power to move an audience lies elsewhere: in the uncanny ability of Wagner's music to bypass its listeners' intellectual and aesthetic responses, communicating directly with the deepest recesses of the psyche. The naive absurdities of its plot and the antiquated trappings of the old saga all fade into insignificance before the emotive force of Wagner's music.

Recommended recording: Teldec 4509–91185–2 (Das Rheingold); 4509–91186–2 (Die Walküre); 4509–94193–2 (Siegfried); 4509–94194–2 (Götterdämmerung). The strong cast of Harry Kupfer's Bayreuth Festival production, staged between 1988 and

1992, with the Bayreuth Festival Chorus and Orchestra, thrillingly conducted by Daniel Barenboim.

Parsifal
Stage dedication play, in three acts (approximate length: 4 hours, 30 minutes)

Amfortas, the King   *baritone*
Titurel, his father   *bass*
Gurnemanz, an elderly knight of the Grail   *bass*
Parsifal   *tenor*
Klingsor, a sorcerer   *bass*
Kundry   *soprano*
First Knight of the Grail   *tenor*
Second Knight of the Grail   *bass*
Four Esquires   *sopranos; tenors*
Klingsor's Six Flowermaidens   *sopranos; altos*

LIBRETTO BY THE COMPOSER; TIME: THE MIDDLE AGES; PLACE: MONTSALVAT, SPAIN, IN AND NEAR THE CASTLE OF THE HOLY GRAIL; FIRST PERFORMED AT THE FESTSPIELHAUS, BAYREUTH, 26 JULY 1882

Although the first performances of *Der Ring des Nibelungen* at Bayreuth in 1876 had been an artistic success, they resulted in a huge deficit, and Wagner was forced to return to the life of a touring conductor in order to raise funds. A Wagner festival of twenty concerts was planned for the Royal Albert Hall in London, but attendance fell well below expectations and only eight concerts were given, increasing the composer's overdraft still further. In 1878 King Ludwig came once again to the aid of the Bayreuth Festspielhaus. Wagner's liabilities were transferred to the state of Bavaria under certain conditions, one of which was that the composer's next opera, whose libretto he had completed the previous year before going to London, should be performed only at Bayreuth, and 'never desecrated by contact with any profane stage'.

Wagner, now in somewhat failing health, devoted himself to the composition of *Parsifal*, whose score was slowly urged into existence, partly at the Villa Wahnfried in Bayreuth and partly in Italy. By January 1882 the opera was complete, and six months later it was given its first performance in Bayreuth. King Ludwig guaranteed the opera's production costs and made available to Wagner the chorus and orchestra of the Munich Opera, whose chief conductor was Hermann Levi, the son of a rabbi. As Wagner regarded official tolerance of Jews to be certain to bring about Germany's ruin, he did his utmost to turn King Ludwig against Levi, whose musical ability he nevertheless admired. The King defied Wagner to the point of insisting that unless Levi were to conduct there would be no performance, at which Wagner resorted to various underhand tactics to get rid of the Jewish conductor, all of which failed. He then wrote to King Ludwig to inform him that Jews were 'the born enemies of pure mankind and all that is noble in it'. It was against this background that Hermann Levi conducted the first performance of Wagner's sacred Christian drama, *Parsifal*, at the Bayreuth Festspielhaus.

After the premiere, at which the music was frequently interrupted by applause, Wagner let it be known that he would prefer the work to be heard to the end without applause, but that the audience could express its appreciation of the performers at the final curtain call. Despite this, the Bayreuth audiences continued to applaud at the end of each act. It was not until after the composer's death in the following year that the custom of applauding only Acts II and III developed in Bayreuth.

Until fairly recently, it was not unknown for entire performances of *Parsifal* to be received in devout silence, which is certainly not what its composer intended. On one occasion in Bayreuth he himself shouted an enthusiastic 'Bravo' at the Flowermaidens in Act II, only to be angrily silenced by the surrounding Wagnerians. Cosima Wagner attempted to restrict productions of *Parsifal* to Bayreuth until thirty years after Wagner's death. However, despite her wishes, the work was soon being staged in New York, Boston, New Orleans, Amsterdam and several other towns. A concert performance of *Parsifal* was given in London in 1884, only one year after its composer's death.

Although it was not until 1877 that he produced a verse libretto for the opera, Wagner had first thought about the knights of the Grail as a possible subject as early as 1857, when he wrote a prose synopsis of *Parsifal*. He had, years previously, read the German mediaeval romance *Parzifal*, by Wolfram von Eschenbach (whom he had included as a character in his opera *Tannhäuser*). Wolfram's work is a lengthy account in verse of the history of the knight who became Lord of the Grail, the Grail being, in Christian mythology, the cup from which Christ drank at the Last Supper, which then came into the possession of Joseph of Arimathea, who caught in it some of the blood that flowed from the wounds of Christ on the Cross. The legend of the Grail is familiar in English literature from the fifteenth-century *Morte d'Arthur* by Sir Thomas Malory and the nineteenth-century *Idylls of the King* by Alfred, Lord Tennyson.

Act I, scene i. A clearing in a shady forest, near the castle of the Grail. Gurnemanz, an elderly but vigorous knight of the Grail, and two youthful Esquires or novices kneel at their morning prayers. The ailing King, Amfortas, is carried to bathe in the holy lake nearby, to refresh him, although nothing can heal his wound or relieve his pain more than temporarily, not even the herbs that Kundry, a strange, unkempt woman whom the knights consider to be a heathen sorceress, brings from distant lands.

Gurnemanz tells the Esquires of the events that led to Amfortas being wounded. Armed with the holy spear with which a Roman centurion had pierced Christ's side, the King went out to fight Klingsor, a knight who had been judged unworthy by the community and driven out by them, and who in his thirst for revenge had turned to sorcery and had built a magic castle where Flowermaidens attempt to corrupt the knights of the Grail by luring them to indulge in forbidden pleasures of the flesh. In Klingsor's castle Amfortas fell victim to the seductive power of an enchantingly beautiful woman, and his holy spear was seized by Klingsor, who used it to inflict a dreadful wound on him. The lost spear, Gurnemanz tells the young Esquires, must be retrieved from Klingsor, for it alone can heal Amfortas's wound. Amfortas has been told in a dream that only a pure fool made wise through pity ('Durch Mitleid wissend, der reine Tor') can achieve this.

As the Esquires repeat the words of the dream's prophecy, shouts are heard from the direction of the lake, and a wild swan, pierced by an arrow, flutters to the ground, dying. Knights bring in a youth who admits to having killed the swan. Gurnemanz rebukes him for having shot at a bird in the precincts of the castle, where all life is considered sacred. Questioned, the youth replies that he does not know his name, but that his mother was called Herzeleide (heart's sorrow). Gurnemanz, acting on an impulse, leads the guileless youth to the castle of the Grail, in the hope that he will prove to be the pure fool of the prophecy. (As they walk, the tolling of bells introduces the orchestral interlude known as the Transformation Music, and the scene begins slowly to change.)

Act I, scene ii. The great hall of the castle of the Grail. Amfortas's father, Titurel, who already lies in his coffin awaiting death, begs for a final glimpse of the Grail. Amfortas, raising himself slowly and painfully from his couch, unveils the chalice while voices from above chant the words of the Communion service. The youth, whom Gurnemanz has brought into the castle, remains standing to one side, motionless. When Gurnemanz, after the service has ended, asks him if he has understood what he has seen, the youth is unable to speak. Annoyed, Gurnemanz calls him a fool and pushes him out by a side door.

Act II. Klingsor's castle. In a magic mirror in his tower, the sorcerer Klingsor discerns the approach of the youth who killed the swan. He summons Kundry, who is in thrall to him. No longer hag-like in appearance, but a young woman of great beauty, it was she who seduced Amfortas. Klingsor now orders her to seduce the young newcomer as well.

Klingsor's tower sinks, and in its place there appears a luxuriant magic garden. Flowermaidens try to detain the youth, who has climbed over a wall into the garden, but he laughingly waves them aside and passes on until he hears Kundry's voice calling him, 'Parsifal', a name he recognizes as that which his mother had once called him in a dream. Kundry attempts to win Parsifal by telling him about his mother and her death ('Ich sah das Kind'), but when she kisses him voluptuously he breaks away from her with a cry of pain. He has in that moment lost his innocence and now recognizes the significance of what he observed in the temple of the Grail ('Amfortas! Die Wunde!').

Kundry confesses that she has been cursed for all eternity because she laughed at Christ on the Cross. She can be saved only by the man who can withstand her charms, and she hopes that Parsifal may be the means of her salvation. When he continues to reject her advances, she curses him. Klingsor suddenly appears and throws the holy spear at Parsifal, but it remains suspended in the air above him. Parsifal seizes the spear and makes with it the sign of the Cross, at which the enchanted garden collapses, Klingsor disappears and the landscape becomes a deserted wilderness.

Act III, scene i. A spring landscape near the castle of the Grail. It is Good Friday. Many years have passed since the day that Parsifal shot the swan and attended the Communion service, but Amfortas has refused to unveil the Grail since then, and the strength of the knights has waned. Gurnemanz, who is now very old and lives as a hermit in the woods, hears a cry and finds Kundry in the undergrowth, numbed and almost lifeless. He succeeds in reviving her. Parsifal enters, carrying the holy spear, having found his way back to the realm of the Grail after countless battles and years of wandering caused by an evil curse. Gurnemanz recognizes the spear and realizes that the day of salvation is at hand. Parsifal is consecrated King of the Grail by Gurnemanz, Kundry washes Parsifal's feet and receives from him the baptism of absolution, and Parsifal and Gurnemanz talk of the beauty and significance of Good Friday (the Good Friday Music). When a distant pealing of bells is heard, Parsifal takes up the spear, and all three make their way slowly to the castle, the scene changing gradually as before.

Act III, scene ii. The hall of the castle. Titurel has died. A procession of knights enters with his coffin, and Amfortas is implored to unveil the Grail. He refuses, springing up in a frenzy and tearing open his garment to reveal his wound, and he begs the knights to plunge their swords into his side to end his torment. Parsifal, who has entered unobserved with Gurnemanz and Kundry, touches Amfortas's wound with the point of the spear, and the wound heals. Parsifal uncovers the Grail, which glows brightly, a dove flutters down to hover above his head, and Kundry sinks lifeless to the ground. Amfortas and Gurnemanz kneel in homage before Parsifal, who waves the Grail in blessing over the worshipping knights.

A study of the libretto in relation to Wagner's various prose writings makes it clear that the composer–dramatist's concern in *Parsifal* was to 'Aryanize' Christianity by divorcing it from its Jewish beginnings. In his essay 'Heldentum und Christentum' (Heroism and Christianity), written in 1881 as a polemical appendage to *Parsifal*, he explains how the Aryans, the Teutonic leaders of mankind, sprang from the gods, only the lesser races being descended from the apes. Christianity's worship of a Jewish tribal god, made flesh in the Jewish Christ, appalled him, and so in *Parsifal* he re-created Christ in his own Wagnerian image. The knight Parsifal is, in fact, an Aryan Christ.

In another essay, 'Religion and Art', Wagner voices his own very strong doubts as to the Jewishness of Jesus. (In the same essay God is taken to task, not only for being Jewish but also for being anti-vegetarian.) Wagner informed his wife, Cosima, that Klingsor in *Parsifal* represented not only the tainted blood of the Jew, but also the Jesuit. The luxurious garden of Jewish art and Jewish voluptuousness is made to disappear by the magical power of the Aryan Cross. In Act III of the opera, the pure blood of the Aryan Jesus glows with desire to rejoin the blood in the sacred chalice. Amfortas, who allowed his blood to mingle with that of the racially inferior Kundry, is redeemed, while Kundry is reduced to menial grovelling, which, in the composer's view, was her proper condition.

The music of *Parsifal* is, at least intermittently, as powerful and compelling as anything Wagner ever composed. To those who cosily and sentimentally equate great art with great morality, the opera stands as an uncomfortable reminder that art and morality are really not on speaking terms. The philosopher Nietzsche, who recognized the power and beauty of much of its music, nevertheless described *Parsifal* as 'a work of malice, of vindictiveness . . . a bad work . . . an outrage on morality'. The opera's finest passages include the sensuously bewitching scene of the Flowermaidens, Kundry's narration in Act II and the fervent Good Friday Music in Act III. The music of the final scene, in which the Grail motif is prominent, can be extremely moving in performance, especially the ethereal harmonies in the closing bars of the opera.

Recommended recording: Siegfried Jerusalem (Parsifal), Waltraud Meier (Kundry), Jose van Dam (Amfortas), Matthias Holle (Gurnemanz), with the Berlin State Opera Chorus and Berlin Philharmonic Orchestra, conducted by Daniel Barenboim. Teldec 9031–74448–2. Barenboim conducts a performance of great conviction, with the musically sensitive and tonally attractive Siegfried Jerusalem an impressive Parsifal, and Waltraud Meier an almost terrifyingly vivid Kundry.

CARL MARIA VON WEBER
(b. Eutin, 1786 – d. London, 1826)

Der Freischütz
(The Free-Shooter)
Romantic opera in three acts (approximate length: 2 hours, 30 minutes)

Max, a forester   *tenor*
Kilian, a wealthy peasant   *tenor*
Cuno, the chief ranger   *bass*
Caspar, a forester   *bass*
Agathe, Cuno's daughter   *soprano*
Aennchen, Agathe's cousin   *soprano*
Ottokar, prince of the region   *baritone*
A Hermit   *bass*
Samiel, the black huntsman   *spoken role*

LIBRETTO BY JOHANN FRIEDRICH KIND; TIME: THE SEVENTEENTH CENTURY, SHORTLY AFTER THE THIRTY YEARS WAR; PLACE: BOHEMIA; FIRST PERFORMED AT THE SCHAUSPIELHAUS, BERLIN, 18 JUNE 1821

Weber was one of the early leaders of the nineteenth-century Romantic movement in German music. He studied in Salzburg with Michael Haydn, brother of the more famous Joseph, composed his first opera, *Die Macht der Liebe und des Weins* (The Force of Love and Wines), at the age of twelve and had his second opera, *Das Waldmädchen* (The Forest Maiden), produced in Freiburg by a travelling company when he was fourteen. In his twenties he composed the operas *Silvana* and *Abu Hassan*, the latter the earliest of his stage works to have survived.

In 1817, at the age of thirty, he took up the position he was to hold for the remaining ten years of his short life – the directorship of the Dresden Hofoper.

It was when, in 1811, he first read the story of the marksman and his magic bullets in the newly published *Gespensterbuch* (Ghost Book) by Johann August Apel and Friedrich Laun that Weber conceived the idea of turning it into an opera. By the time he had become the director of the Dresden Court Opera six years later, the story had been used by at least two other composers, but Weber discussed the idea with Johann Friedrich Kind, who quickly produced a libretto. It took Weber more than three years to compose the opera, which, finally named *Der Freischütz* after two earlier working titles had been discarded, was staged in Berlin in 1821. An enormous success at its premiere, it was soon being staged throughout Europe and was to become the most popular German opera of the first half of the nineteenth century.

Act I. Outside a tavern in the Bohemian forest. Max, a young forester, defeated in a shooting contest by Kilian, a wealthy peasant, is mocked by Kilian and the assembled peasants for having missed all his shots ('Schau der Herr mich an als König'). A fight between Max and Kilian is prevented only by the appearance of Prince Ottokar's chief ranger, Cuno, who warns Max that he will not allow him to marry his daughter Agathe if Max fails to win the shooting trial to be held the following day in the presence of the Prince.

When all have departed, Max gives voice to his despair ('Durch die Wälder, durch die Auen'). Caspar, one of the foresters, joins Max and drinks several toasts with him, enraging him with a coarse drinking song ('Hier im ird'schen Jammerthal'). He gives Max his rifle to shoot an eagle from the sky successfully, and then he explains that the rifle used a type of magic bullet that could enable Max to succeed in the following day's trial. If Max wants some of the magic bullets, he is to go secretly to the Wolf's Glen at midnight. When Max has left, Caspar, who has sold his soul to Samiel, the black huntsman, and can save himself only by providing a new victim, exults in Max's certain damnation ('Schweig, schweig').

Act II, scene i. A room in Cuno's house. Agathe is full of vague foreboding, and her cousin Aennchen tries to cheer her up ('Kommt ein schlanker Bursch gegangen'). Anxiously awaiting Max, Agathe sings of her love for him ('Leise, leise, fromme Weise'), but when Max finally arrives he announces that he must leave again immediately to collect a stag he has shot near the Wolf's Glen. At mention of that haunted spot, the two young women try to dissuade him from going there ('Wie? Was? Entsetzen! Dort in der Schreckensslucht'), but Max insists that a hunter must not seem to be afraid of the forest at night.

Act II, scene ii. The Wolf's Glen. On the stroke of midnight Caspar summons up Samiel, who agrees to allow him three more years of life in return for another victim. Max arrives on the rocks above and, undeterred by visions of his mother and Agathe attempting to discourage him, descends to the glen, where Caspar begins casting the magic bullets with secret incantations. Six of them will hit their mark, but the seventh will be guided by the powers of evil. A devilish uproar becomes more macabre and horrifying until it fills the entire glen. At the casting of the seventh bullet Samiel himself appears to Max, who falls unconscious. In the distance a clock strikes one, and calm returns to the glen.

Act III, scene i. Agathe's room. Agathe, wearing her wedding dress, is deep in prayer ('Und ob die Wolke sie verhulle'). Oppressed by forebodings of evil, she has had a dream in which she saw herself as a white dove, shot at by Max. Aennchen attempts to distract her with a frivolous ghost story ('Einst träumte meiner sel'gen Base'), and Agathe's bridesmaids enter to sing a folk song ('Wir winden dir den Jungfernkranz'). When a box that should contain a bridal garland is opened, a funeral wreath is found instead, but Aennchen makes a new garland from roses given to Agathe by a Hermit, and the bridesmaids' chorus is resumed.

Act III, scene ii. An attractive clearing in the forest. Prince Ottokar and his retinue have assembled for the shooting contest. The men sing of the pleasures of the hunt ('Was gleicht wohl auf Erden'), and Max, who has evidently already shot successfully six times, now aims at a white dove as instructed by the Prince. As he takes aim and fires, Agathe cries out to him not to shoot, for she is the dove. She falls senseless to the ground, as the dove flutters away. When Agathe recovers consciousness, it is discovered that it is Caspar who has been mortally wounded by Max's shot and who lies writhing in his death agonies, uttering maledictions against God and Samiel. The pact between Max and Samiel, the representative of hell, is revealed, and Prince Ottokar is about to banish the young forester when the Hermit intercedes for him, imploring the Prince to grant Max a year's probation, at the end of which, if he proves honest and pious, he should be pardoned and given Agathe's hand in marriage. Prince Ottokar agrees, and all join in a hymn of praise for God's mercy.

The charm of Weber's seminal work of Romantic German opera lies in its immediately appealing melody, its air of romantic enchantment and its brilliant orchestration, especially in the Wolf's Glen scene with its sinister harmonies and its ghostly atmosphere. The overture, constructed from tunes to be found in the opera, is a popular concert item, and the highlights of the work include the great arias for Max and Agathe, the folk song-like choruses and vigorous ensembles, and, most of all, the thrilling Wolf's Glen scene.

Recommended recording: Elisabeth Grummer (Agathe), Rudolf Schock (Max), Lisa Otto (Aennchen), Hermann Prey (Prince Ottokar), Karl Christian Kohn (Caspar), with the Chorus of the Deutsche Oper, Berlin and the Berlin Philharmonic Orchestra, conducted by Joseph Keilberth. EMI CMS 7 69342 2. This 1959 recording is the one that catches the atmosphere of the work most successfully, with Elisabeth Grummer a warm-voiced Agathe, Rudolf Schock a romantic Max, and some of the finest German singers of the day in the other roles. Joseph Keilberth conducts with authority.

Oberon
Romantic opera in three acts (approximate length: 3 hours)

Oberon, king of the elves *tenor*
Puck *mezzo-soprano*
Reiza, daughter of Haroun al Raschid *soprano*
Sir Huon of Bordeaux *tenor*
Sherasmin, Sir Huon's squire *baritone*
Fatima, Reiza's attendant *mezzo-soprano*
Namouna, Fatima's grandmother ⎤
Haroun al Raschid, caliph of Baghdad |
Babekan, a Saracen prince *spoken*
Abdullah, a corsair *roles*
Almanzor, emir of Tunis |
Roshana, his wife ⎦

LIBRETTO BY JAMES ROBINSON PLANCHÉ; TIME: THE MIDDLE AGES; PLACE: FAIRY-LAND, THE BANKS OF THE TIGRIS, AFRICA AND FRANCE; FIRST PERFORMED AT THE THEATRE ROYAL, COVENT GARDEN, LONDON, 1 APRIL 1826

After *Der Freischütz* Weber began to compose a comic opera, *Die drei Pintos* (The Three Pintos), which he eventually abandoned. (More than sixty years later it was completed, on the basis of the composer's sketches, by Gustav Mahler.) As a result of the success of *Der Freischütz* Weber was invited to write an opera for Vienna. *Euryanthe*, given its premiere there in 1823, achieved merely a *succès d'estime* and is now rarely performed. In 1824 the composer was appointed music director of the Theatre Royal, Covent Garden (the forerunner of London's present Royal Opera House), and was commissioned to write an opera to be performed there. His choice fell upon the subject of Oberon, and a libretto in English was commissioned from James Robinson Planché. Drawing upon Christoph Martin Wieland's German epic *Oberon* (1780) and the thirteenth-century French romance *Huon de Bordeaux*, Planché produced a lengthy and complicated libretto with reams of dialogue to be spoken. Weber complained to him that 'the intermixing of so many principal actors who do not sing . . . the omission of music in the most important moments, all these things deprive *Oberon* of the title of an opera, which will make it unfit for all other theatres in Europe, which is very bad for me.' Nevertheless, Weber poured some of his most delightful music into *Oberon*. (His directorship of the London theatre was of short duration, for he was in an advanced stage of consumption when he was appointed, and he died thirteen weeks after conducting the highly successful premiere of *Oberon*.)

Act I, scene i. Oberon's fairy bower. Oberon and Titania have quarrelled, and they have sworn not to be reunited until they have found a faithful pair of lovers. Puck tells Oberon about Sir Huon of Bordeaux, who has been commanded by Charlemagne to travel to Baghdad to surprise the caliph at a banquet, kill the man sitting on the caliph's left, kiss the caliph's daughter and abduct her to France. Oberon resolves to help Huon. He shows the sleeping knight a vision of the caliph's beautiful daughter Reiza and then magically transports Huon and his squire Sherasmin to Baghdad, giving Huon a magic horn that will protect him from danger.

Act I, scene ii. The banks of the Tigris. Huon saves Prince Babekan from a lion. Namouna tells Huon of Reiza's impending marriage to Babekan and of a knight who is to rescue her from it.

Act I, scene iii. The harem in the palace of Haroun al Raschid, caliph of Baghdad. Fatima tells Reiza that the knight she has longed for is now in Baghdad.

Act II, scene i. The banqueting hall in the palace. Babekan sits on the caliph's left. Huon and Sherasmin rush in, Huon stabs Babekan, kisses Reiza and blows his magic horn to paralyze the palace guards. Sherasmin kisses Fatima, and all four make their escape.

Act II, scene ii. The garden of the palace. The fugitives are caught, and in the struggle Huon loses his magic horn, but Oberon appears and conjures up a ship to take them away.

Act II, scene iii. A deserted shore. Puck invokes the spirits of the sea to wreck the ship, casting it up on a deserted shore. Reiza contemplates the awesome sea ('Ocean, thou mighty monster'), and she signals a passing ship, hoping to be rescued. However, the ship is manned by pirates who abduct Reiza, leaving Huon unconscious and bound. Oberon arrives to rescue Huon and instructs Puck to take the knight to the house of the gardener Ibrahim in Tunis.

Act III, scene i. Outside Ibrahim's house in Tunis. Fatima and Sherasmin have been sold as slaves. Puck arrives with Huon, who is told by Fatima that Reiza has been taken to the emir's palace.

Act III, scene ii. The palace of Almanzor, emir of Tunis. The emir's advances are resisted by Reiza, while the emir's wife, Roshana, turns her attentions to Huon, promising to make him emir if he will kill her husband. When Almanzor arrives, Huon is seized and led away.

Act III, scene iii. An open place in front of the palace. Huon is about to be burned alive. When Reiza declares that she is his wife, she is condemned to die with him. Meanwhile, Sherasmin has found the magic horn, and when he blows it their captors begin to dance and sing. Huon and Reiza are freed, and Oberon appears, reconciled with Titania, for the fidelity of Huon and Reiza has released the fairy couple from their oath. Oberon tells the lovers that their trials are at an end, and they are magically transported back to France.

Act III, scene iv. The throne room of Charlemagne. Huon kneels before the Emperor and explains that he has accomplished his mission. He and Reiza are welcomed to Charlemagne's kingdom.

Despite its absolutely dire libretto, Oberon survives, albeit perilously, due to the skilful musical treatment given to Planché's words by Weber, whose Romantic score establishes a supremacy over the lengthy stretches of dialogue that seek to interrupt it. The overture is deservedly popular as a concert item, and Reiza's exhilarating aria 'Ocean, thou mighty monster' is also well known beyond the confines of the opera.

Recommended recording: Inga Nielsen (Reiza), Vesselina Kasarova (Fatima), Peter Seiffert (Huon), Deon van der Walt (Oberon), Bo Skovus (Sherasmin), with the Berlin Radio Choir and the German Symphony Orchestra, conducted by Marek Janowski. RCA 09026 68505 2. A good cast, and a conductor who beautifully evokes the spirit of Weber's score. It is performed in German: there is no available recording in English.

KURT WEILL
(b. Dessau, 1900 – d. New York, 1950)

Die Dreigroschenoper
(The Threepenny Opera)
play with music in a prologue and three acts (approximate length: 3 hours)

The Ballad Singer   *baritone*
Peachum, chief of a band of beggars   *baritone*
Mrs Peachum, his wife   *contralto*
Polly, their daughter   *soprano*
Macheath (Mack the Knife), chief of a band of robbers   *tenor*
Tiger Brown, London's chief of police   *baritone*
Lucy, his daughter   *soprano*
Jenny, a whore   *soprano*

LIBRETTO BY BERTOLT BRECHT; TIME: 1901; PLACE: SOHO, LONDON; FIRST
PERFORMED AT THE THEATER AM SCHIFFBAUERDAMM, BERLIN, 31 AUGUST 1928

For a short time a pupil of Humperdinck, Kurt Weill at the age of 21 settled in
Berlin, where he studied with Busoni for three years. Although his earliest
compositions were instrumental, Weill always thought of himself as a composer
for the theatre. His first operas, one-act pieces written in a contemporary idiom,
were traditional in the sense that they were scored for a normal orchestra and
intended for classically trained singers. But Weill longed for an art that would
decisively mirror his own time and the life of his adopted city of Berlin. (He came
from a Jewish family in Dessau.) It was in this mood that he collaborated with
Bertolt Brecht, who wanted to achieve in poetry the same aims as Weill in music.

The first collaboration of Brecht and Weill occurred in 1927 with *Der kleine
Mahagonny*, a sketch that was later expanded into the full-length *Aufstieg und Fall
der Stadt Mahagonny* (q.v.). After *Der kleine Mahagonny*, Brecht and Weill turned
their attention to *The Beggar's Opera*, an eighteenth-century English ballad opera
that had been revived in London in 1920, when it achieved a remarkable run of
1463 performances. Brecht's collaborator Elisabeth Hauptmann prepared a German working translation of John Gay's English text, which Brecht then adapted,
setting it in early twentieth-century London. Weill composed his score in the
spring and early summer of 1928. When *Die Dreigroschenoper* opened in Berlin in

August 1928 it proved immensely popular. It went on to become the biggest theatrical success of the Weimar Republic and was soon being staged throughout Europe and in the United States. The advent of the Nazis led to its suppression in Germany, but it became popular all over again in 1954, when a translation and adaptation by Marc Blitzstein, entitled *The Threepenny Opera*, ran for 2611 performances in New York, with Weill's widow, Lotte Lenya, making a comeback in the role of Jenny, which she had played in the 1928 Berlin premiere.

Prologue. The Ballad Singer performs a song in praise of Macheath, a robber known as Mack the Knife ('Die Moritat von Mackie Messer' – The Ballad of Mack the Knife).

Act I, scene i. Peachum's shop. Peachum, a receiver of stolen goods, hires out costumes to his beggars guaranteed to arouse the pity of passers-by. He warns his wife that their daughter Polly's beloved is Macheath, a notorious gang-leader ('Anstatt dass-Song' – Instead-of Song).

Act I, scene ii. A stable, fitted out by Macheath's gang with stolen furniture. In the company of his gang, Mack the Knife celebrates his marriage to Polly Peachum ('Hochzeitslied' – Wedding Song), and Polly sings a song about Jenny the pirate ('Seeräuber Jenny' – Pirate Jenny). London's chief of police, known familiarly to the gang as Tiger Brown, arrives to congratulate Mack ('Kanonen-Song' – Cannon Song) and then leaves to make preparations for the following day's coronation celebrations. When all their guests have departed, Mack and Polly sing of their love ('Liebeslied' – Love Song).

Act I, scene iii. Peachum's shop. Polly tells her family that she has married Macheath and that she intends to share the robber's life ('Barbara Song'), but her parents are determined to force Tiger Brown to arrest him. The three Peachums comment on the instability of human existence ('Erstes Dreigroschenfinale' – First Threepenny Finale).

Act II, scene i. The same. Macheath decides to hide out on the moor at Highgate to escape from Peachum, who has persuaded the police chief to arrest him. Mack bids Polly farewell, after telling her how to run the gang in his absence ('Pollys Lied' – Polly's Song). Mrs Peachum bribes Jenny, a whore, to betray Mack to the police ('Die Ballade von der sexuellen Hörigkeit' – The Ballad of Sexual Dependency).

Act II, scene ii. A brothel in Turnbridge. Macheath and Jenny recall the happy hours they have spent together ('Zuhälterballade' – Pimps' Ballad), and Jenny surreptitiously signals to a constable outside to come and arrest Macheath.

Act II, scene iii. The prison. Mack, in his cell, sings The Ballad of the Pleasant

Life ('Die Ballade von angenehmen Leben'). Tiger Brown's daughter Lucy, whom Macheath has pretended to marry, is upset when Polly visits her husband in prison ('Eifersuchtsduett' – Jealousy Duet). After Polly has been dragged away by her mother, Mack succeeds in escaping, with Lucy's help. Peachum arrives to collect his reward for having assisted in the capture of Macheath. When he discovers that his son-in-law has escaped, Peachum blames Tiger Brown and threatens to organize the beggars to disrupt the coronation celebrations ('Zweites Dreigroschenfinale' – Second Threepenny Finale).

Act III, scene i. A street in Soho. Peachum delivers an inflammatory speech to the beggars, but is arrested by Brown. He blackmails the police chief into releasing him ('Das Lied von der Unzulänglichkeit menschlichen Strebens' – The Song of the Insufficiency of Human Endeavour), and again he puts him on the trail of Mack the Knife.

Act III, scene ii. The prison. Macheath, once again betrayed by the whores, has been recaptured and is about to be hanged ('Ruf aus der Gruft' – Call from the Grave). At the last moment a Messenger rides up on a horse to deliver a royal pardon for Macheath. Peachum utters a cynical observation about the difference between real life and opera, and the entire company sings a Bach-like chorale ('Drittes Dreigroschenfinale' – Third Threepenny Finale).

Weill's musical parody of operatic conventions, among them Romantic lyricism and unrealistically happy endings, is in joyous accord with Brecht's cynical view of the world in this engagingly ironic, light-hearted yet serious satire on capitalist economic theory, which cleverly reworks the plot of the eighteenth-century *Beggar's Opera* of John Gay. The orchestra, despite the use of cello and flute, is predominantly a jazz ensemble, and Weill's score makes use of most of the popular musical styles of the day.

Recommended recording: Ute Lemper (Polly), René Kollo (Macheath), Helga Dernesch (Mrs Peachum), Mario Adrorf (Peachum), with the RIAS Chamber Choir and the RIAS Sinfonietta, conducted by John Mauceri. Teldec 9031–72775–2. A Berlin chorus and orchestra and a predominantly German cast perform with aplomb.

Aufstieg und Fall der Stadt Mahagonny
(Rise and Fall of the City of Mahagonny)
opera in three acts (approximate length: 2 hours, 15 minutes)

Jenny   *soprano*
Leokadia Begbick   *contralto*
Fatty, the bookkeeper   *tenor*
Trinity Moses   *baritone*
Pennybank Bill   *baritone*
Jake Schmidt   *tenor*
Toby Higgins   *tenor*
Alaska Wolf Joe   *bass*
Jim Mahoney   *tenor*

LIBRETTO BY BERTOLT BRECHT; TIME: THE 1920S; PLACE: A MYTHICAL AMERICA;
FIRST PERFORMED AT THE NEUES THEATER, LEIPZIG, 9 MARCH 1930

Commissioned by a music festival in Baden-Baden, where it was performed in 1927, *Der kleine Mahagonny* was a *Songspiel* or song-play, consisting of five poems by Brecht about an imaginary American city, set to music by Weill. Its success led the collaborators immediately to plan a full-length opera developed from the *Mahagonny* material. However, they produced *Die Dreigroschenoper* (q.v.) and *Happy End* (a fiasco at its first performance in Berlin in 1929) before completing the opera, which was to be called *Aufstieg und Fall der Stadt Mahagonny*. Having greatly admired *Der kleine Mahagonny*, the conductor Otto Klemperer had undertaken to give the full-scale opera its premiere at the Krolloper in Berlin. But when he was given the completed *Aufstieg und Fall der Stadt Mahagonny* he was perturbed by what he regarded as the depravity of Brecht's libretto, and he rejected the opera. Years later, in conversation with an English music critic, Klemperer described the work as 'a complete failure'. Its first performance in Leipzig in 1930 has been described as one of the greatest scandals in the history of twentieth-century music, with countless protests against the work on moral, political and religious grounds. Subsequently suppressed by the Nazis, *Aufstieg und Fall der Stadt Mahagonny* surfaced again in New York and London in the 1950s and '60s.

Act I. Three fugitives from justice, Leokadia Begbick, Trinity Moses and Fatty, are stranded in a desert landscape when their dilapidated truck breaks down; they decide to build a new city, Mahagonny, on the spot. Soon, Jenny and six other girls arrive to provide relaxation for the citizens who have flocked to Mahagonny in search of an easy life ('Alabama Song').

According to Brecht's captions, which are projected onto a curtain to introduce each scene, 'In the following years the malcontents from all continents descended on Mahagonny, city of gold.' Among these newcomers are Jim Mahoney and his three friends Bill, Jake and Joe, who arrive from Alaska having amassed a fortune there as lumberjacks. When girls for sale are produced by Leokadia Begbick, Jake offers thirty dollars for Jenny, who protests ('Ach, bedenken sie, Herr Jakob Schmidt') and is acquired by Jim.

The citizens of Mahagonny are becoming dissatisfied with a surfeit of peace and harmony, when a hurricane suddenly threatens the city. Jim Mahoney claims that people are just as destructive as hurricanes, and he establishes a new and anarchic law for Mahagonny, by which everything is to be allowed ('Denn wie man sich bettet, so liegt man').

Act II. The hurricane changes direction, bypassing Mahagonny. The city flourishes, and consumption becomes excessive – literally so in the case of Jake, who eats himself to death. Jenny and Jim sing tenderly about two cranes flying in the sky ('Cranes Duet'). A boxing match between Joe and Trinity Moses is announced. Jim bets all his money on Joe, who is knocked out and killed by Trinity Moses. Jim gets drunk, but when Leokadia Begbick presents his bar bill he finds he has no money, so she has him thrown into prison. Jenny leaves him.

Act III. Jim's trial is in progress, his judge being Leokadia Begbick. He is charged with several offences, among them causing Joe's death for financial gain and seducing Jenny. The gravest charge of all is his failure to pay his bar bill, and it is for this that he is sentenced to death. The men dream of another city, Benares, but read in their newspapers that it has been destroyed by an earthquake ('Benares Song'). Jim goes to the electric chair with no regrets; the city of Mahagonny burns; and demonstrators appear, waving placards with various contradictory slogans. The opera's final line, sung at the audience by the chorus, is 'Können uns und euch und niemand helfen'. (We can help neither ourselves nor you nor anyone).

Brecht's crude and confused anti-capitalist harangue is made, if not palatable, at least bearable by the wry lyricism of much of Weill's music, scored for a small orchestra including saxophones, banjo and harmonium. The artistic partnership of the two men did not survive after *Mahagonny*, for Brecht accused Weill of writing 'phony Richard Strauss', while the composer announced that he did not want to spend the rest of his life setting the Communist manifesto to music. Nor did he. By way of Paris and London, Weill arrived in New York in 1935 and turned himself into an impressive composer of Broadway musicals, among them *Knickerbocker Holiday* (1938), *Lady in the Dark* (1941), *One Touch of Venus* (1943) and *Lost in the Stars* (1949), and an opera, *Street Scene* (1947).

Recommended recording: Lotte Lenya (Jenny), Heinz Sauerbaum (Jim Mahoney), Gisela Litz (Leokadia Begbick), Horst Gunther (Trinity Moses), with the North German Radio Chorus and Orchestra, conducted by Wilhelm Bruckner-Ruggeberg. CBS 77341. This recording from the late 1950s boasts Weill's widow Lotte Lenya, a survivor from the Brecht–Weill Berlin days, as Jenny, and a generally superb cast. Bruckner-Ruggeberg conducts powerfully.

BERND ALOIS ZIMMERMANN
(b. Bliesheim, Cologne, 1918 – d. Königsdorf, 1970)

Die Soldaten
(The Soldiers)
opera in four acts (approximate length: 1 hour, 45 minutes)

Wesener, a fancy-goods merchant in Lille   *bass*
Marie   *high soprano*
Charlotte   *mezzo-soprano*   ⎤ his daughters
Wesener's Old Mother   *contralto*
Stolzius, a draper in Armentieres   *high baritone*
Stolzius's Mother   *contralto*
Obrist, Count Spannheim   *bass*
Desportes, a young nobleman in the French army   *high tenor*
Captain Pirzel   *high tenor*
Eisenhardt, an army chaplain   *baritone*
Major Haudy   *baritone*
Major Mary   *baritone*
Countess de la Roche   *mezzo-soprano*
The Young Count, her son   *high lyric tenor*

LIBRETTO BY THE COMPOSER, BASED ON THE PLAY *DIE SOLDATEN*, BY JAKOB MICHAEL REINHOLD LENZ; TIME: YESTERDAY, TODAY AND TOMORROW; PLACE: FLANDERS; FIRST PERFORMED AT THE COLOGNE OPERAHAUS, 15 FEBRUARY 1965

Zimmermann studied in Cologne and Bonn, and after military service during World War II in France he resumed his studies at Darmstadt. His only opera, *Die Soldaten*, was first performed in Cologne in 1965, its libretto by the composer based on Jakob Michael Reinhold Lenz's play of the same title (1775). The opera aroused considerable controversy at its premiere, due mainly to its complex structure. At the time of his death Zimmermann was at work on a second opera, *Medea*.

Act I, scene i. Wesener's house in Lille. Wesener's daughter Marie writes to the Mother of her fiancé Stolzius.

Act I, scene ii. Stolzius's house in Armentieres. The letter is received, and it gives more pleasure to Stolzius than to his Mother.

Act I, scene iii. Wesener's house in Lille. Marie is courted by Baron Desportes, a young officer in the French army, and her father warns her against soldiers.

Act I, scene iv. A public place in Armentieres. French officers discuss morality and the theatre, and the chaplain Eisenhardt expresses his disapproval of the theatre.

Act I, scene v. Wesener's house in Lille. Marie shows her father a love letter she has received from Baron Desportes, and her father advises her to keep her options open with both Desportes and Stolzius.

Act II, scene i. A cafe in Armentieres. Stolzius is teased by the officers about the intentions of Baron Desportes towards Marie.

Act II, scene ii. Three scenes are played simultaneously. In Lille, Desportes seduces Marie; on a darkened stage her grandmother foretells Marie's ruin; in Armentieres, Stolzius is made miserable by Marie's letter breaking off their relationship.

Act III, scene i. A square in Armentieres. Eisenhardt and Captain Pirzel discuss morality.

Act III, scene ii. Major Mary's room in Lille. Stolzius applies to become Mary's batman, and is accepted.

Act III, scene iii. Wesener's house in Lille. Major Mary arrives to take Marie for a drive. He is accompanied by his batman Stolzius, whom Marie only vaguely recognizes.

Act III, scene iv. The house of the Countess de la Roche. The Countess's son has become involved with Marie, and the Countess determines to try to save Marie from ruin.

Act III, scene v. Wesener's house in Lille. The Countess visits Marie and offers to engage her as a companion.

Act IV, scene i. The cafe in Armentieres. The action takes place on several different levels on the stage and on screen, the subject being Marie's downfall. Desportes offers Marie to his Gamekeeper, who rapes her. The scene concludes with a question being asked by all: 'Must those who suffer injustice tremble, and only those who do wrong be happy?'

Act IV, scene ii. Major Mary's room in Lille. Mary is dining with Desportes, and they are waited on by Stolzius. Desportes speaks callously of Marie, and his soup is poisoned by Stolzius. As Desportes dies in agony, Stolzius kills himself.

Act IV, scene iii. A street in Lille. Wesener is accosted by a beggar woman who asks him for money. He fails to recognize that she is his daughter Marie, but gives her a coin. She falls to the ground.

Zimmermann's complicated serial score and angular vocal style do not make for easy listening, but there is no doubt that his opera is an important work of its time, its audiences affected more by the composer's compassion and humanity than by his music.

Index of Titles

General Index

Ponchielli, Amilcare, *La Gioconda* (1876)
306–9
Pons, Lily 115, 117
Ponsard, François 61
Ponselle, Rosa 22
Porges, Heinrich 185
Poulenc, Francis, *Dialogues des carmélites*
(1957) 310–13
Praga, Marco 324; libretto (with Ruggero
Leoncavallo, Domenico Oliva, Luigi
Illica and Giuseppe Giacosa): *Manon
Lescaut* (Puccini) 323, 324
Prague, National Theatre 187, 406, 409; pre-
mieres: *La clemenza di Tito* (Mozart)
(1791) 284; *Don Giovanni* (Mozart)
(1787) 273–4; *Rusalka* (Dvořák) (1901)
123
Prague, New Town Theatre, premieres:
Dalibor (Smetana) (1866) 408
Prague, Provisional Theatre, premieres: *The
Bartered Bride* (Smetana) (1866) 406
Preis, Alexander, and Dmitri Shostakovich,
libretto: *Lady Macbeth of Mtensk*
(Shostakovich) 402
Preissová, Gabriela, *Její pastorkyňa* 187
Prévost, Abbé, *Manon Lescaut* 177, 210–11,
323–4
Priest, Josias 353
Pritchard, John 465
Prokofiev, Sergei, *The Fiery Angel* (1954) 316–
19; *The Love for Three Oranges* (1921)
313–16; *War and Peace* (1955) 319–22
Puccini, Elvira 339
Puccini, Giacomo, 451; Puccini, Giacomo, *La
Bohème* (1896) 326–30; *La fanciulla del
West* (1910) 338–42; *Gianni Schicchi*
(1918) 346–7; *Madama Butterfly* (1904)
97, 334–8; *Manon Lescaut* (1893) 322; *La
Rondine* 342; *Suor Angelica* (1918)
344–6; *Il tabarro* (1918) 343, 343–4; *Il
trittico* (1917) 342–3; *Tosca* (1900) 330–4;
Turandot (1926) 348–52
Puchberg, Michael 280
Pucitta, Vincenzo 216
Purcell, Henry, *Dido and Aeneas* (1689) 353–4
Pushkin, Alexander, *Boris Godunov* 293;
Eugene Onegin 457, 460; *The Golden
Cockerel* 360, 361; *The Queen of Spades*
461; *Ruslan i Lyudmila* 145

Raaff, Anton 259–60, 262
Racine, Jean Baptiste, *Iphigénie en Aulide* 152;
Mithridate 251
Radiguet, Raymond 310
Ravel, Maurice, *L'Enfant et les sortilèges*
(1925) 357–9; *L'Heure espagnole* (1911)
355–7
Redlich, Hans 244
Renaud, Maurice 300
Rich, John 169
Ricordi, Giulio 205, 323, 324, 330, 331, 493,
510, 535
Ricordi, Tito 331
Rimsky-Korsakov, Nikolai 54, 56, 147, 450; as
Mussorgsky's friend and orchestrator
293, 294, 296, 297, 298; *The Golden
Cockerel* (1909) 360–3
Ringhieri, Francesco, *L'Osiride* 383
Rinuccini, Ottavio 238
Romani, Felice, libretti: *Anna Bolena*
(Donizetti) 102; *I Capuleti e i Montecchi*
(Bellini) 11; *L'elisir d'amore* (Donizetti)
104; *Lucrezia Borgia* (Donizetti) 107,
108; *Norma* (Bellini) 19; *La sonnambula*
(Bellini) 14; *Il turco in Italia* (Rossini)
368–9
Rome, Teatro Apollo, premieres: *Un ballo in
maschera* (Verdi) (1859) 513, 515; *Il
trovatore* (Verdi) (1853) 499
Rome, Teatro Argentina, premieres: *Il barbi-
ere di Siviglia* (Rossini) (1816) 373, 374
Rome, Teatro Costanzi, premieres: *L'amico
Fritz* (Mascagni) (1891) 208; *Cavalleria
rusticana* (Mascagni) (1890) 205; *Tosca*
(Puccini) (1900) 330, 331
Rome, Teatro Valle, premieres: *La
Cenerentola* (Rossini) (1817) 378
Roocroft, Amanda 13
Roosevelt, Blanche 536
Rosmer, Ernst [Else Bernstein-Porges],
libretto: *Königskinder* (Humperdinck)
185
Rossi, Gaetano, libretti: *Semiramide*
(Rossini) 389; *Tancredi* (Rossini) 363;
with Eugène Scribe and Émile
Deschamps, *Les Huguenots*
(Meyerbeer) 229
Rossini, Gioachino, 26, 363–96; *Il barbiere di
Siviglia* (1816) 106, 373–7; *La*